The Wiley-Blackwell Handbook of Couples and Family Relationships

Also available from Wiley-Blackwell:

The Wiley-Blackwell Handbook of Family Psychology
Edited by James H. Bray and Mark Stanton

The Wiley-Blackwell Handbook of Adulthood and Aging
Edited by Susan Krauss Whitbourne and Martin Sliwinski

The Wiley-Blackwell Handbook of Infant Development, Second Edition
Edited by J. Gavin Bremner and Theodore D. Wachs

The Wiley-Blackwell Handbook of Childhood Social Development, Second Edition
Edited by Peter K. Smith and Craig H. Hart

The Wiley-Blackwell Handbook of Childhood Cognitive Development, Second Edition
Edited by Usha Goswami

The Wiley-Blackwell Handbook of Individual Differences
Edited by Tomas Chamorro-Premuzic, Sophie von Stumm, and Adrian Furnham

Handbook of Personality and Self-Regulation
Edited by Rick H. Hoyle

Handbook of Jealousy
Edited by Sybil L. Hart and Maria Legerstee

The Wiley-Blackwell Handbook of Couples and Family Relationships

Edited by Patricia Noller and Gery C. Karantzas

WILEY-BLACKWELL

A John Wiley & Sons, Ltd., Publication

This edition first published 2012

Blackwell Publishing was acquired by John Wiley & Sons in February 2007. Blackwell's publishing program has been merged with Wiley's global Scientific, Technical, and Medical business to form Wiley-Blackwell.

Registered Office
John Wiley & Sons Ltd, The Atrium, Southern Gate, Chichester, West Sussex, PO19 8SQ, UK

Editorial Offices
350 Main Street, Malden, MA 02148-5020, USA
9600 Garsington Road, Oxford, OX4 2DQ, UK
The Atrium, Southern Gate, Chichester, West Sussex, PO19 8SQ, UK

For details of our global editorial offices, for customer services, and for information about how to apply for permission to reuse the copyright material in this book please see our website at www.wiley.com/wiley-blackwell.

Library of Congress Cataloging-in-Publication Data

The Wiley-Blackwell handbook of couples and family relationships / edited by Patricia Noller and Gery C. Karantzas.
p. cm.
Includes bibliographical references and index.
ISBN 978-1-4443-3450-0 (hbk. : alk. paper)
1. Families–Psychological aspects. 2. Couples–Psychology. 3. Interpersonal relations. I. Noller, Patricia. II. Karantzas, Gery C.
HQ519.W55 2012
306.87–dc23

2011032986

A catalogue record for this book is available from the British Library.

This book is published in the following electronic formats: ePDF 9781444354089; Wiley Online Library 9781444354119; ePub 9781444354096

Set in 10.5/12.5pt, AGaramond-Regular by Thomson Digital, Noida, India
Printed and bound in Malaysia by Vivar Printing Sdn Bhd

1 2012

To my late husband Charles—for all the ways that you encouraged me throughout my career and to family and friends who supported me through this difficult year of 2011. (P. N.)

To my Mum Mary and Dad Elias—for being shining examples of "secure base" and "safe haven," to my sister Myra—for all your love and support, and finally to my wife Kellie—for helping me chase my dreams (even the seemingly impossible ones) and loving me for all that I am, I stand taller with you beside me. (G. C. K.)

Contents

List of Contributors xi

Introduction 1
Patricia Noller and Gery C. Karantzas

Part I Trends in Couple and Family Relationships 9

1 From Form to Function 11
Ruth Weston, Lixia Qu, and Alan Hayes

2 Social Trends and their Impact on Couple and Family Relationships 25
David de Vaus

3 Changing American Families in the 21st Century 36
Suzanne M. Bianchi, Sara B. Raley, and Lynne M. Casper

Part II Families across the Lifespan 49

4 The Role of the Family across the Lifespan 51
Toni C. Antonucci, Kristin M. Wong, and Sarah Trinh

5 Parents and Adolescents 66
Ross B. Wilkinson

6 Family Caregiving 82
Gery C. Karantzas

7 Late-Life Transitions and Interventions 97
Kathleen Piercy

Part III Communication and Conflict Processes in Couples and Families 113

8 Conflict Avoidance in Families 115
John P. Caughlin, Jennifer L. Hardesty, and Ashley V. Middleton

9 Conflict in Family Relationships 129
Patricia Noller

10 Demand–Withdraw Communication in Couples 144
Kathleen A. Eldridge and Brian Baucom

Part IV Individual Differences Perspectives on Intimacy, Love, and Caregiving 159

11 Adult Attachment and Sexuality 161
Phillip R. Shaver and Mario Mikulincer

12 Sexual Dysfunction in Intimate Heterosexual Relationships 175
Denisa Goldhammer and Marita P. McCabe

13 Regulating Incentives and Threats in Close Relationships 193
Shelly L. Gable

14 Attachment and Caregiving 207
Melanie Canterberry and Omri Gillath

Part V Cognitive and Affective Processes in Couple Relationships 221

15 Attachment Insecurities and Relationship Self-Regulation 223
Zoë J. Hazelwood

16 The Costs and Benefits of Trying to Change Intimate Partners 234
Nickola C. Overall

17 Through the Eyes of Love 248
Garth J. O. Fletcher and Patrick S. G. Kerr

18 Betrayal and Forgiveness in Couple Relationships 259
Julie Fitness

Part VI Education and Intervention in Couple and Family Relationships 271

19 Taking it to the Streets (and Information Super Highways) 273
W. Kim Halford and Samira Hayes

20 Relationship Education 289
Judith A. Feeney and Jennifer Fitzgerald

21 A Common Factors Perspective of Relationship Counseling 305
Ruth Ingrid Sturmey, Patricia Noller, and Gery C. Karantzas

22 The Efficacy of Evidence-Based Couple Therapy 320
Peter Howell

23 Surviving Trauma 333
Susan M. Johnson and Kathryn D. Rheem

24 Children's Adjustment after Parental Separation 345
Susie Sweeper

Part VII Interpersonal Processes, Families, and Mental Health 361

25 Depression and Self-Harming in Adolescence 363
Kerryn Hurd and Patricia Noller

26 Attachment and Depression Across the Transition to Parenthood 377
Jeffry A. Simpson, W. Steven Rholes, and Sandra Shallcross

27 Recent Advances in Research on Social Support in Couples 392
Carolyn E. Cutrona

28 Chronic Illness and Relationships 406
Gery C. Karantzas, Marita P. McCabe, and Sian F. Cole

Part VIII Implications for Policy 421

29 Promoting Positive Pathways for Youth and Young Adults to Healthy Relationships and Marriages 423
Alan J. Hawkins

30 Improving Child and Family Outcomes through a Collaborative Service Model 437
Michael White and Gail Winkworth

31 Are Governments and Marriage Strange Bedfellows? 453
W. Kim Halford and Elizabeth van Acker

Part IX Integration and Conclusion **467**

32 Common Themes in Couple and Family Relationship Research and Practice 469
Gery C. Karantzas and Patricia Noller

Index 481

List of Contributors

Toni C. Antonucci, Institute for Social Research, 426 Thompson Street, Ann Arbor, MI 48106-1248, United States

Brian Baucom, Department of Psychology, University of Southern California, SGM 501, 3620 South McClintock Avenue, Los Angeles, CA, 90089-1061, United States

Suzanne M. Bianchi, Department of Sociology, University of California, Los Angeles, Box 951551, 264 Haines Hall, Los Angeles, CA 90095-1551, United States

Melanie Canterberry, Department of Psychology, University of Kansas, 1415 Jayhawk Blvd. Rm 518, Lawrence, KS 66045-7556, United States

Lynne M. Casper, Department of Psychology, University of Southern California, 3620 South McClintock Avenue, Los Angeles, CA, 90089-1061, United States

John P. Caughlin, Department of Communication, MC-456, University of Illinois at Urbana-Champaign, Urbana, IL 61801, United States

Sian F. Cole, School of Psychology, Deakin University, 221 Burwood Highway, Burwood, Victoria, 3125, Australia

Carolyn E. Cutrona, Department of Psychology, Iowa State University, Ames, IA 50011-3180, United States

David de Vaus, Faculty of Social and Behavioral Sciences, The University of Queensland, Brisbane, Queensland, 4072, Australia

Kathleen A. Eldridge, Pepperdine University, Graduate School of Education and Psychology, 24255 Pacific Coast Highway, Malibu, CA 90263, United States

Judith A. Feeney, School of Psychology, University of Queensland, Queensland, 4072, Australia

Julie Fitness, Psychology Department, Macquarie University, North Ryde, Sydney 2109, Australia

Jennifer Fitzgerald, School of Medicine, Discipline of Psychiatry, K Floor, Mental Health Building, Royal Brisbane and Women's Hospital, Herston, Queensland, 4006, Australia

Garth J. O. Fletcher, Psychology Department, University of Canterbury, Private Bag, 4800, Christchurch, New Zealand

Shelly L. Gable, 3822 Psychology East, Psychology Department, University of California, Santa Barbara, CA 93106-9660, United States

Omri Gillath, Department of Psychology, University of Kansas 1415 Jayhawk Blvd. Rm 518, Lawrence, KS 66045-7556, United States

Denisa Goldhammer, School of Psychology, Deakin University, 221 Burwood Highway, Burwood, Victoria, 3125, Australia

W. Kim Halford, School of Psychology, University of Queensland, Queensland, 4972, Australia

Jennifer L. Hardesty, Department of Communication, MC-456, University of Illinois at Urbana-Champaign, Urbana, IL 61801, United States

Alan J. Hawkins, School of Family Life, Brigham Young University, 2050 JFSB, Provo, Utah, United States

Alan Hayes, Australian Institute of Family Studies, Level 20 South Tower, 485 La Trobe Street, Melbourne, Victoria, 3000, Australia

Samira Hayes, School of Psychology, University of Queensland, Queensland, 4972, Australia

Zoë J. Hazelwood, School of Psychology and Counselling, Queensland University of Technology, Victoria Park Road, Kelvin Grove, Queensland, 4059 Australia

Peter Howell, LDS Family Services, 1st Floor, 1027-1029 High Street, Armadale, Victoria, 3143, Australia

Kerryn Hurd, Brisbane Grammar School, Gregory Terrace, Brisbane, Queensland, 4000, Australia

Susan M. Johnson, C.P.S., University of Ottawa, 11, Marie Curie, Ottawa, Ontario, K1N 6N5, Canada

Gery C. Karantzas, School of Psychology, Deakin University, 221 Burwood Highway, Burwood, Victoria, 3125, Australia

Patrick S. G. Kerr, Psychology Department, University of Canterbury, Private Bag, 4800, Christchurch, New Zealand

Marita P. McCabe, School of Psychology, Deakin University, 221 Burwood Highway, Burwood, Victoria, 3125, Australia

Ashley V. Middleton, Department of Communication, MC-456, University of Illinois at Urbana-Champaign, Urbana, IL 61801, United States

Mario Mikulincer, New School of Psychology, Interdisciplinary Centre, Hezliya, 46150, Israel

Patricia Noller, School of Psychology, University of Queensland, Queensland, 4072, Australia

Nickola C. Overall, Department of Psychology, University of Auckland, Private Bag 92019, Auckland, New Zealand

Kathleen Piercy, Department of Family, Consumer, and Human Development, 2905 Old Main Hill, Utah State University, Logan, UT 84322-2905, United States

Lixia Qu, Australian Institute of Family Studies, Level 20 South Tower, 485 La Trobe Street, Melbourne, Victoria, 3000, Australia

Sara B. Raley, McDaniel College, 2 College Hill, Westminster, MD 21157, United States

Kathryn D. Rheem, The Couple & Family Therapy Center, 5410 McKinley Street, Bethesda, MD 20817, United States

W. Steven Rholes, Department of Psychology, Texas A&M University, College Station, TX 77843-4235, United States

Sandra Shallcross, Department of Psychology, University of Minnesota, Minneapolis, MN, 55455-0344, United States

Phillip R. Shaver, Department of Psychology, University of California, Davis, One Shields Avenue, Davis, CA 95616, United States

Jeffry A. Simpson, Department of Psychology, University of Minnesota, Minneapolis, MN 55455-0344, United States

Ruth Ingrid Sturmey, Relationships Australia, Victoria, PO Box 180, 2 Prospect Hill Road, Camberwell, Victoria, Australia 3124

Susie Sweeper, Department of Psychology, Deakin University, 221 Burwood Highway, Burwood, Victoria, 3125, Australia

Sarah Trinh, Department of Psychology, University of Michigan, 1012 East Hall, 530 Church Street, Ann Arbor, MI 48109-1043, United States

Elizabeth van Acker, Department of Politics and Public Policy, Business 2 (N72), Nathan Campus, Griffith University, 170 Kessels Road, Nathan, Queensland, 4111, Australia

Ruth Weston, Australian Institute of Family Studies, Level 20 South Tower, 485 La Trobe Street, Melbourne, Victoria, 3000, Australia

Michael White, MW Group Consulting, P.O. Box 21228, Little Lonsdale Street, Melbourne, Victoria, 8011, Australia

Ross B. Wilkinson, Department of Psychology, Building 39, The Australian National University ACT, 0200, Australia

Gail Winkworth, Institute of Child Protection Studies, Australian Catholic University, PO Box 256, Dickson, Australian Capital Territory, 2602, Australia

Kristin M. Wong, Department of Psychology, University of Michigan, 1012 East Hall, 530 Church Street, Ann Arbor, MI 48109-1043, United States

Introduction

Patricia Noller and Gery C. Karantzas

There is a growing need to develop an understanding of the positive pathways that strengthen the relationships of couples and families. Couples and families in contemporary Western society are faced with many challenges and pressures that can mitigate against maintaining satisfying and enduring couple and family relationships. For example, increases in the need for dual income families, the working of longer hours, demographic shifts that see older people living longer, and children staying at home longer mean that couples are often required to provide familial care across two generations—frail aging parents and children. These examples highlight just some of the pressures faced by modern-day couples, which can lead to people not taking the time to cultivate their relationships.

The impetus for this book arose out of an international workshop on couple and family relationships supported by the Academy of the Social Sciences in Australia. The aim of the workshop was to deal with many of the issues described above by linking research, policy, and practice in ways that would help families meet such challenges. The workshop brought together leading and emerging Australian and international relationship researchers, practitioners, educators, policy makers, and service-delivery organizations.

Three key themes emerged from the workshop. Firstly, relationships in the 21st century come in all forms, and this means that our past models of relationships (which essentially focused on the roles and responsibilities associated with marriage) have changed. We have increasing numbers of de facto and cohabiting couples living together with and without children, increases in homosexual couples, and adult children staying at home for longer. Yet this diversity is only partly reflected in the way that pop culture, policy, or science often

The Wiley-Blackwell Handbook of Couples and Family Relationships, First Edition.
Edited by Patricia Noller and Gery C. Karantzas.

discuss relationships. Also, pop culture places too much emphasis on the acquisition of financial stability and materialistic possessions as a means of "relationship progress." Having said this, we argue that marriage and the family continue to be highly relevant and important institutions that are fundamental to the social fabric of the nation. Clearly, marriage continues to be the union of choice for many couples, and the evidence suggests that married couples fare better during periods of relationship difficulties than those cohabiting. However, our views of relationships need to broaden if we are to develop policies and practices that are relevant for today's couples.

Secondly, more emphasis needs to be placed on thinking and promoting couple relationships and families as a "public good." The various workshop presentations highlighted that those relationships encompassing positive conflict resolution strategies, forgiveness, and feelings of security and trust in partners lead to better couple functioning and child adjustment. In addition, these "secure" relationships provide good models for young people to follow on how to develop strong and healthy relationships. However, many couples and families are losing sight of how best to foster positive relationships, primarily due to the many stressors and pressures which today's families are faced with. As a result, service providers and policy makers need to rethink ways to educate couples and families to help them maintain good relationships. Relationship education is likely to become more important in the coming years, but at present there are many barriers that preclude couples and families from attending relationship education. Some solutions may be to provide relationship education as part of the pre-existing curriculum in high schools and universities, and programs dealing with life transitions, such as the many existing ante-natal courses.

Thirdly, our capacity to care for others—whether it be our children, our aging parents, or our partners—needs to be understood more clearly, and policy needs to reflect the immense pressure that caring places on people as they juggle the many demands of today's family life. Specific attention needs to be given to policies that best assist adults in the "sandwich generation" as their caregiving responsibilities involve caring for both their children and their parents.

Given the challenges facing contemporary couples and families we believe that this publication will be of great interest and relevance to researchers, policy makers, service-delivery providers, and practitioners. It is hoped that the text will provide insights into how best to integrate research, practice, and policy in improving the well-being of couples and families.

This volume is divided into eight parts as described in the following pages.

Part I: Trends in Couple and Family Relationships

In the first section of the book we examine Western social trends that shape the various forms and functioning of couple and family relationships. The chapters in this section discuss the opportunities and challenges faced by current families that are distinct from those of previous generations. In Chapter 1, Weston, Qu, and Hayes distinguish between family form and family functioning. They provide an Australian perspective on the different family forms that are part of today's society and discuss the social trends that contribute to these changes. These authors note that despite the number of changes in family form, the family still remains as the basic unit of society. In Chapter 2, de Vaus focuses on two related features of social change: risk and choice. He then discusses how these features shape the way we currently form relationships and families. In Chapter 3, Bianchi, Raley, and Casper provide a U.S. perspective on the changes in family formation and functioning. They note that these changes increase instability and inequality and are often detrimental to children.

Part II: Families across the Lifespan

In Part II we explore the ways in which couples and families deal with life transitions and increasing family responsibilities as well as the effects of these demands on couple and family relationships. This section focuses on (i) how contemporary parents maintain positive relationships with their adolescent children who themselves are developing more sophisticated ideas around the importance of relationships, and (ii) the challenges facing the sandwich generation and how familial responsibilities such as caring for elderly parents and adult children can impede the fostering of positive enduring couple and family relationships. In Chapter 4, Antonucci, Wong, and Trinh take a lifespan approach to family form and function recognizing that while attention has focused on the nuclear family, there appears to be an increased awareness that multiple forms of the family can lead to both positive and negative pathways of development. In Chapter 5, Wilkinson argues against the negative and unbalanced view of adolescence and adolescents promoted by both the experts and the media, suggesting that the real problem may lie in their families and communities. He particularly points to problems of poor relationships with parents or poor relationships between parents as creating risks for adolescent well-being.

In Chapter 6, Karantzas examines family caregiving between adult children and older parents. He argues that competing life commitments, gender roles, and family structure can influence the caregiving responsibilities in families. He also points to filial obligation and attachment processes as key motivations that affect caregiving and care receiving currently and in the future. In Chapter 7, Piercy discusses factors that contribute to marital quality and satisfaction in later life. She discusses challenges to couple closeness that are brought on during life transitions including retirement, health problems, dementia care, widowhood, and remarriage.

Part III: Communication and Conflict Processes in Couples and Families

In Part III we critically examine the importance of communication and relationship conflict on couples and families. Contributors discuss the cross-sectional and longitudinal research on communication and conflict and the implications for couple and family relationships before and after separation and divorce. In Chapter 8, Caughlin, Hardesty, and Middleton focus on couples involved in intimate partner violence and divorcing couples. They challenge the traditional view that conflict avoidance is always negative and argue that emphasis on openness and resolving conflict involves risks, particularly for those in abusive relationships. They also suggest that for couples seeking to co-parent, there may be issues that are too heated to discuss constructively and may be better avoided to ensure the safety and well-being of the mother and child(ren). In Chapter 9, Noller also discusses the ongoing conflict that can occur in separated or divorced families and the related risks particularly for the adjustment of the children. She also presents research on conflict in violent and nonviolent couples, and in parent–adolescent and sibling relationships.

In Chapter 10, Eldridge and Baucom review recent developments in research on the demand–withdraw pattern of conflict across various relationship contexts and the immediate and long-term consequences of using this pattern. They also show that culture and gender affect the use of this pattern.

Part IV: Individual Differences Perspectives on Intimacy, Love, and Caregiving

In this section we examine an important but often neglected issue in couple functioning, the need to maintain sexually intimate, caring, and loving relationships. The contributors highlight relationship outcomes of functional and dysfunctional sexual and love relationships. In Chapter 11, Shaver and Mikulincer provide insights from attachment theory to explain individual differences in sexual relationships. These authors review various examples of attachment research, focusing on the effects that attachment anxiety and avoidance have on sexual motives, fantasies, feelings, attitudes, and behavior. In Chapter 12, Goldhammer and McCabe discuss the need for sexual problems to be viewed in a relational context rather than as physiological phenomena. The effect of one partner's sexual dysfunction on the sexual functioning of the other is also considered throughout the chapter, as are the clinical implications of the research findings.

In Chapter 13, Gable discusses individual differences in relationship functioning and outcomes in terms of approach and avoidance motivations. She argues that some people focus on avoiding relationship threats, whereas others focus on gaining relationship rewards. She presents a theoretical model of social motivation of close-relationship processes and the evidence supporting this model.

In Chapter 14, Canterberry and Gillath propose a model of caregiving and provide evidence for the links between attachment and real-world caregiving. They demonstrate that attachment security is associated with the propensity to care for others whereas attachment insecurity is associated with difficulties in providing care. They show that priming security enhances the willingness to care for others and discuss the therapeutic implications of this technique for couple and family relationships.

Part V: Cognitive and Affective Processes in Couple Relationships

In Part V we tackle the ways in which people's thoughts and emotions can shape their actions and interpretations of relationships. Specifically, in this section contributors focus on the circumstances in which people engage in positive and negative attributions about themselves and their partner's actions and the emotional consequences of these attributions. The authors discuss the implications of positive and negative cognitions for the quality of relationships.

In Chapter 15, Hazelwood discusses a program of research that illustrates the mediating role of attachment insecurity in the association between negative partner behavior and relationship self-regulation. For this reason she maintains that targeting attachment insecurity in therapy may not produce long-term changes in relationships unless partners' negative attributions are a focus of therapy. In Chapter 16, Overall emphasizes the difficulties associated with communicating a desire for behavior change in partners through direct and indirect means. She argues for the need to teach couples to express these desires positively and with reassurance of regard. Overall also believes that partners wanting change need also to acknowledge their own contribution to relationship problems and to recognize the efforts their partner makes to resolve relationship issues.

In Chapter 17, Fletcher and Kerr claim that individuals can and often do embrace a charitable and optimistic view of their partners while at the same time keeping a realistic view of their partner's traits and qualities. This positivity bias is likely to be powered by a biologically based need for attachment bonding, which in turn, predisposes individuals to view relationships and relationship partners in a positive light despite their shortcomings. As a result of this need for bonding, Fletcher and Kerr suggest that the positivity bias can be (and often is) rational, can (and does) coexist with reality tracking, and couples may be aware of (and welcome) bias.

In Chapter 18, Fitness discusses research on the features and outcomes of betrayal in couple relationships, and the processes involved in forgiveness of betrayals. She considers the role of punishment as an appropriate response to partner betrayal, and not incompatible with eventual forgiveness and relationship repair. Fitness argues that even the most serious betrayals do not need to destroy couple relationships, and that relationship repair can be facilitated by clinicians and counselors with an understanding of the psychology of punishment and forgiveness.

Part VI: Education and Intervention in Couple and Family Relationships

In Part VI we focus on strengthening couple and family relationships through relationship education, mediation, and counseling. A range of different approaches to assisting families are presented, involving such themes as the challenges to delivering relationship education, helping couples apologize and forgive, the use of technology to strengthen relationships, and surviving trauma and divorce.

In Chapter 19, Halford and Hayes argue the case for flexible delivery of relationship education because of the problems that some couples experience in attending face-to-face sessions. They promote the use of modern technologies such as DVDs, the Internet, and cell phones to assist couples in self-directed learning about developing healthy relationships. In Chapter 20, Feeney and Fitzgerald outline a program of relationship education specifically focused on dealing with hurtful events in couple or family relationships.

They advocate a dyadic approach to dealing with events of hurt and argue that therapists need to balance carefully promoting respect and support for the hurt partner's distress while encouraging the offending spouse's efforts to resolve the issue.

In Chapter 21, Sturmey, Noller, and Karantzas review the common factors that cut across couple and family interventions that bring about relationship change. Common factors include therapist and client characteristics, the therapeutic alliance between the clinician and the client, the client's motivation to change, and the client's expectations regarding the outcome of therapy. In Chapter 22, Howell also argues that there are common factors that contribute to the success of therapeutic interventions over and above the effects of the particular model of therapy being applied. He then reviews and compares in detail two widely used evidence-based therapeutic approaches: Cognitive Behavioral Couple Therapy and Integrative Behavioral Couple Therapy.

In Chapter 23, Johnson and Rheem discuss the attachment-based Emotion-Focused Therapy which focuses on affect regulation and integration and creating a more secure attachment bond between relationship partners. They highlight the importance of couples creating an environment in which they are accessible to each other and responsive to each other's concerns especially in times of trauma and distress.

In Chapter 24, Sweeper argues that professionals in mediation and counseling involving divorcing families should focus their attention on improving relationships between parent and child. She points out the difficulties of trying to improve the conflicted relationship between former partners and the potential for this relationship to expose the children to ongoing conflict.

Part VII: Interpersonal Processes, Families, and Mental Health

In Part VII, we place specific emphasis on the mental health issues of depression and negative affect in close relationships. The factors and situations that increase the risk of depression and negative affect are discussed with applications to counseling interventions.

In Chapter 25, Hurd and Noller describe a program of research involving adolescents in three groups: adolescents with depression; adolescents who have self-harmed; and non-clinical adolescents. They show the importance of parent–adolescent relationships and parenting style to the development of problems with depression and self-harm. In Chapter 26, Simpson, Rholes, and Shallcross also describe a program of research examining depression. They focus on couples undergoing the transition to parenthood, testing the links between attachment insecurity and increases in depressive symptoms in the early stages of this transition. They note that depressive symptoms seem to increase particularly where anxiously attached mothers perceive a decline in partner support following the birth.

In Chapter 27, Cutrona reviews recent research on social support in couples. She welcomes the integration of attachment theory into the conceptualization of social support noting the importance of responsiveness, a key construct borrowed from attachment theory, to effective social support. Cutrona also underscores the influence of the emotional tone of support transactions and the importance of nondefensiveness when trying to elicit social support from one's partner.

In Chapter 28, Karantzas, McCabe, and Cole draw on the sex, attachment, and social support literatures in describing a research program involving chronic illness sufferers' perceptions of their social network support, relationship satisfaction, and mental health outcomes. They show that individuals experiencing high attachment insecurity (i.e., high anxiety and avoidance) who also perceive low social support are most at risk of mental health issues.

Part VIII: Implications for Policy

In this final section, we discuss the implications of research findings for the development and coordination of government policies with regard to couple and family relationships across state and federal levels. The focus of this section is on relationship educational programs, particularly for youth and those in the early stages of marriage. There is also a focus on the coordination of agencies and service delivery involved in meeting the needs of vulnerable families.

In Chapter 29, Hawkins presents a three-phase agenda for relationship education beginning with school-based programs. The second phase involves premarital education for single, dating, and cohabiting young adults; and the third phase involves marital enrichment for those in the early stages of marriage. In Chapter 30, White and Winkworth bemoan the lack of coordination across agencies and jurisdictions that have been set up to help vulnerable families. This lack of coordination they argue means that parents have difficulty accessing these important services and leaves some children at higher risk of harm.

In Chapter 31, Halford and van Acker claim that governments have placed differing priorities on the importance of couple relationship education, which in turn, has affected the resources available for such education. They argue that the focus should be on enhancing the quality of couple relationships so that more people will choose to stay in their relationships thus increasing the stability of families.

In the final chapter, Karantzas and Noller provide a summary of the main themes discussed across the chapters of the book. They highlight eight major themes that are important to consider in increasing our understanding of couple and family relationships. These themes include: family structure versus functioning; attachment theory; divorce and family breakdown; communication and conflict; self-regulation, partner regulation, and behavior change; caregiving and parenting; relationship education; and therapy and policy implications.

PART I

Trends in Couple and Family Relationships

1

From Form to Function

Contemporary Choices, Changes, and Challenges

Ruth Weston, Lixia Qu, and Alan Hayes

Families have undergone profound changes and will continue to do so as their members respond to the pressures, opportunities, and constraints they experience from within and beyond their bounds. Family transitions both reflect societal trends and fuel further changes, including population size and structure, the economy, the physical environment, and social values. Family-level changes include those relating to the prevalence of different family structures or forms (such as single-parent families and couple families with and without children); the paths leading to these various forms; and some of the ways that families operate or function, including the roles that parents have in families.

Nevertheless, some of the fundamental things about families do not change. Most importantly, they remain the basic unit of society—a unit in which much "caring and sharing" occurs—and importantly, the site in which most children are raised. As such, families play a central role in shaping the health and well-being of all immediate family members.

In Western societies, it is the parents who typically have the responsibility for raising their children to become healthy, well-adjusted, and contributing members of society. The extent to which these ends are achieved varies with circumstances, constraints, and opportunity. Parents are also expected to ensure that their family is linked in productive ways to the wider society, and to draw on community resources to help meet their responsibilities.

Given the pivotal role that families play in promoting the well-being of their members, and of society more generally, it is hardly surprising that family trends attract a great deal of

The Wiley-Blackwell Handbook of Couples and Family Relationships, First Edition.
Edited by Patricia Noller and Gery C. Karantzas.

attention. Trends related to families reflect the broad directions in which societies are heading. Governments increasingly monitor these trends closely to adjust policies affecting family life and the well-being of individuals and their communities.

Much of the attention of researchers, policy makers, and practitioners also focuses on trends in family-related transitions, such as couple formation and stability, and on associated family forms, with family functioning often being inferred from these. Yet, by definition, family functioning determines whether a family is a haven, a site of damaging dysfunction, or something in between. As will be shown below, comparisons of family forms tend to amplify, artificially, differences in family functioning between family forms, while ignoring differences in family functioning within the same form. As such, the focus on form risks generating unrealistic stereotypes. These stereotypes can have unfortunate consequences, including the danger that negative stereotypes based on family form can affect the ways members of these families are treated and the ways they see themselves, possibly leading to inappropriately negative, self-fulfilling prophecies.

In this chapter we first examine the prevalence of different family forms that are apparent today. We show the extent to which their prevalence has changed, and discuss factors contributing to these trends. This section is followed by an examination of family functioning, where attention is directed to: (a) the ways some aspects of family functioning have evolved over the generations, reflecting social and demographic changes; (b) the ways in which family functioning can lead to changes in family form; (c) the influences of the evolving context; and (d) the impact of family functioning on child well-being. This section highlights the fact that circumstances relating to family form tend to affect functioning and points to the need to identify the mechanisms underlying such dynamics.

It is worth noting at the outset that the family forms that are identified depend on the dimensions of interest—for instance, attention can be directed to families that vary in terms of: the number of generations present; the number of children present; the age or gender of the children; parents' age or their marital, employment, or socioeconomic status; the families' residential location (e.g., metropolitan, outer urban, rural, and remote); or cultural background. While it is beyond the scope of this chapter to capture all the different ways in which family forms can be categorized, in the following section we focus first on the more "traditional" ways of understanding family forms, then we describe some of the other forms of families. Brief attention is also given to some of the family-related transitions that have contributed to today's most common family forms.

Unpacking Family Form

Definitions of "family" vary, partly because they tend to be developed for different purposes. Defining family frequently involves drawing boundaries that identify the persons who are to be included as "family" and those who are to be excluded. Family boundaries are fluid, and change through partnership formation and separation, as well as births and deaths. This fluidity along with other socio-cultural forces contributes to the diversity that exists in family forms.

"Traditional" family forms

Although the proportion of Australian families that are indigenous is small, there is considerable diversity across indigenous groups. Despite this diversity, indigenous families are "traditional" in the full sense of this term and will therefore be mentioned first. The other "traditional" set of family forms discussed below is based on statistics that define family on the basis of blood and marriage or de facto relationships.

Indigenous families. In indigenous communities a family may include more than 200 widely dispersed people with a common origin, who thereby hold obligations to visit and share with other members. In many cases, the elders play a pivotal role, while the children are seen as the responsibility of the entire family. Children may be raised by family members other than their biological parents, with many moving around their family in the course of their lives (see Bourke, 1993; Butler, 1993; McDonald, 1995).[1]

In fact, Morphy (2006) shows that kinship terminology used in some indigenous communities can vary across communities and differs markedly from that of the "Anglo-Celtic" system. This difference means that the family system as understood in some indigenous cultures cannot be translated into a system understood in the mainstream culture. Indeed, the classification of family forms used by the Australian Bureau of Statistics (ABS) reflects those of the mainstream culture (outlined below).

Household family forms identified by the ABS. For statistical purposes, the ABS (2008) defines families as follows:

> Two or more persons, one of whom is at least 15 years of age, who are related by blood, marriage (registered or de facto), adoption, step or fostering; and who are usually resident in the same household. The basis of a family is formed by identifying the presence of a couple relationship, lone parent–child relationship or other blood relationship. Some households will, therefore, contain more than one family (p. 50).[2]

Under this "household family" definition, families may be composed of: couples with or without co-resident children of any age; single parents with co-resident children of any age; grandparents caring for grandchildren; and other families of related adults, such as brothers or sisters living together, where no couple or parent–child relationship exists—although the boundary excludes relatives beyond first cousins (ABS, 2005a). It is important to acknowledge that the ABS definition differs from that used by individuals. Almost all people will see their family as crossing household boundaries and some will view their family in more or less inclusive ways than others. For example, the point at which a separated parent's new partner is seen as "family" may vary for all concerned, with some children possibly never extending their family boundary to include this person. Some children may eventually see their parent's partner as their stepparent, but exclude the stepparent's own parents. These parents, in turn, may or may not see these children as members of their extended family.

On the basis of the ABS definition of "family," most of today's households in Australia are family households. However, the average household size has declined over the 20th

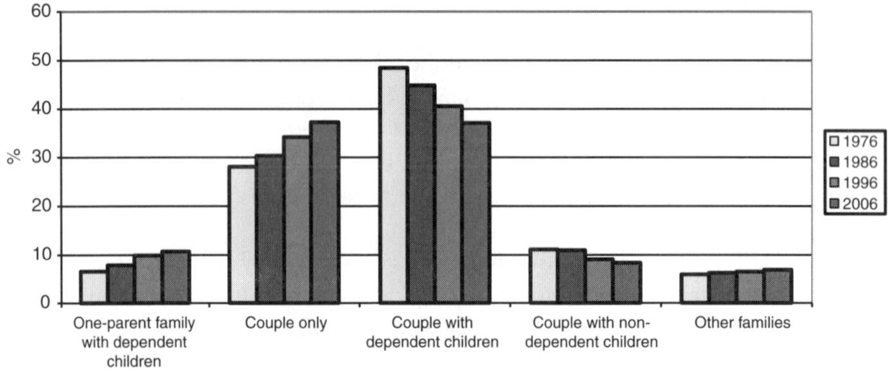

Note: "Other families" includes one-parent families with nondependent children and nonclassifiable families, such as brothers and sisters.

Figure 1.1 "Traditionally-derived" family forms, 1976–2006
Source: Australian Bureau of Statistics (2001, 2002, 2007a)

century and family household has become less "statistically dominant." The average size of households was 2.6 in 2006, falling from 4.5 in 1911. Family households as a percentage of all households declined from 77% in 1986 to 72% in 2006.

Figure 1.1 decomposes family households into five forms derived by the ABS, and shows the proportional representation of each of these forms over four decades, from 1976 to 2006. Although families with dependent children were the most common of all five forms between 1976 and 1996, this was no longer the case by 2006. By this time, couple-only families were just as common as families with dependent children, with each of these forms representing 37% of all family households. The "couple-only" families include couples who have yet to (or may never) have children, those whose children have left home, and couples in which one or both partners have had children of previous relationships who are living elsewhere.

Specifically, the representation of families with dependent children decreased (from 48% to 37% of all household families), while the representation of couple-only families and one-parent families increased (couple-only families: from 28% to 37%; one-parent families: from 7% to 11%). Trends for the other two groups changed to a lesser extent (couples with nondependent children only, and "other families"), but it is perhaps noteworthy that one of these two groups (couples with nondependent children only) became progressively less common (decreasing from 11% to 8%). Very little change was apparent for "other families" (ranging from 6% to 7% of all family households). These families comprised related adults such as siblings, and one-parent families with nondependent children.

It is also worth noting that advances in reproductive technologies have created couples with children whose members come from origins that would have been "inconceivable" in the past—children born to a surrogate mother or via donated sperm or eggs.[3] Gilding (2002) argues that such technological developments will continue, as in the past, to help shape "the scale and scope of family change."

Less common family forms

Other family forms not mentioned above are becoming more visible either because they have become more common, or because their very existence is increasingly being acknowledged. Some of those family forms are listed below.

Extended household families and "grandparent families." The traditional household family approach does not capture the fact that some households contain more than two generations and/or siblings, aunts or uncles of the parents, or cousins of one of the generations.[4] For instance, a grandparent may live with an adult child, or in what in Australia is called a "granny flat" on the property of their adult child, while in other cases a single-parent family may move to live with the children's grandparents. In each of three surveys conducted by the ABS (in 1997, 2003, and 2006–07), multifamily households—covering both extended household families and families whose members are not related to each other—accounted for 3–4% of all family households (ABS, 2008).

"Grandparent families" refers to families in which the grandparents are the guardians or main carers of children aged less than 18 years who are living with them. Such families represented only 0.2% of all families in 2006–07, with the number during this period being lower than that which was apparent in 2003 (14,000 vs. 23,000) (ABS, 2008). However, the often tragic circumstances that lead to such circumstances (e.g., mental health problems or substance abuse of the children's parents) and the multifaceted difficulties that may be experienced within these families (e.g., grandparents' grief, health issues, and financial difficulties; children's traumatization associated with past events), mean that there has been growing attention to the needs of these families (e.g., ABS, 2005b; Dunne & Kettler, 2008; Fitzpatrick & Reeve, 2003; Ochiltree, 2006).

Step- and blended families. Among families with children aged less than 18 years old in 2006–07, 4% were stepfamilies and 3% were blended families. These proportions are the same as those apparent in 1997 and 2003 (ABS, 2008). A stepfamily is formed when a parent re-partners and there is at least one child who is a stepchild to one of the partners, and there are no children born of, or adopted by, the couple. Blended families, on the other hand, include a stepchild and a child who was born of, or adopted by, the couple.

Same-sex couples. Little is known about prevalence of same-sex relationships in Australia. In the 2006 census, 0.6% of individuals were identified as being in a same-sex relationship. However, this statistic may represent a considerable underestimate of the prevalence of same-sex couples, given that some of these couples may be reluctant to disclose the nature of their relationship. The 2001 census showed slightly more same-sex male couples than same-sex female couples (de Vaus, 2004), and this trend is also reflected in the 2006 census data.[5]

Compared to those in heterosexual relationships, individuals in same-sex relationships appear to be younger and better educated, and seem more likely to hold professional occupations and to have no religious affiliation (de Vaus, 2004). However, it is possible that such differences may partly result from some same-sex couples sharing these demographic characteristics compared with others in same-sex relationships who are reluctant to disclose demographic information.

Living apart together. Another form of couple relationship, called *living apart together (LAT)*, has been observed by social scientists in recent decades. Definitions of LAT vary in terms of whether the couple may be married. For instance, Strohm, Seltzer, Cochran, and Mays (2009) define these relationships as unmarried partners living separately but identifying themselves as a couple.

Levin and Trost (1999), on the other hand, also treat married couples that have two households as being in an LAT relationship. And while Strohm et al. refer to married couples who live apart as being in "commuter marriages," Levin and Trost use the term "commuting marriages" to refer to cases in which each partner lives in the same household, while one or both has another apartment where they stay "away from home." Presumably, "commuting marriages," as understood by Levin and Trost, would include cohabiting partners who see themselves as having one home which they share and another apartment where they sometimes stay. Of course each partner may have a different idea about whether they are living in the same home as the other partner, in two homes, or in the home in which the other partner does not live.

Such definitional variations indicate that LAT is a "fuzzy" and difficult to identify family form. Notwithstanding this difficulty, Wave 5 of the Household, Income and Labour Dynamics in Australia HILDA Survey suggests that, in 2005, 1% of married people under 65 years and 19% of unmarried people of this age who were in an intimate, ongoing relationship spent less than half the time living with their spouse or partner.

Reasons for living apart together vary. For example, some couples in an intimate relationship may not yet feel ready emotionally or financially to move in together, and some couples may live in separate households to pursue employment in different locations or to maintain greater autonomy than would otherwise be possible. One partner may move to a new location in order to gain employment, with the other partner following if and when the leaver has become established and is certain that the decision to move is appropriate. The reasons tend to vary according to the age of the partners (e.g., young people who are still living in the parental home, compared with older widowed or divorced individuals who have already established their separate dwellings, Strohm et al., 2009).

Separated families with different patterns of care-time arrangements. Children in general reside with their mothers after the parents separate. Around 85% of single-parent families with children under 18 years old are headed by mothers (ABS, 2008). However, this statistic masks the diverse care-time arrangements that parents make after separation. The closer the equality of time with each parent, the more likely it may be that the children see themselves as having "two homes."

Based on the experience of parents who separated between July 2006 and 2008, Kaspiew et al. (2009) identified nine different care-time arrangements for their children (see Table 1.1), ranging from children who never see their fathers to those who never see their mothers, with some spending equal time with each parent.[6] As evident in Table 1.1, the care-time arrangements vary with children's age. Of course, children's time with each

Table 1.1 Care-Time Arrangements: Proportion of nights per year that children spent with each parent by age of child, 2008

Proportion of nights per year with each parent	*Age of child (years)*					*All children*
	0–2	*3–4*	*5–11*	*12–14*	*15–17*	
			%			
Father never sees child	16.2	8.4	5.3	10.6	13.0	11.1
Father sees in daytime only	34.4	15.5	12.0	14.0	22.6	22.5
87–99% with mother (1–13% father)	13.8	13.9	13.7	14.3	18.3	14.1
66–86% with mother (14–34% father)	25.4	37.1	37.2	31.1	18.7	31.0
53–65% with mother (35–47% father)	5.0	9.3	11.6	7.8	3.3	7.8
48–52% with each parent (i.e., equal care time)	2.1	9.3	11.8	10.7	6.4	7.0
35–47% with mother (53–65% with father)	0.4	1.7	2.3	1.7	1.1	1.3
14–34% with mother (66–86% with father)	0.8	1.9	2.8	3.5	3.7	1.9
1–13% with mother (87–99% with father)	0.5	0.7	1.3	2.3	4.2	1.1
Mother sees child in daytime only	1.0	1.2	1.2	1.7	4.4	1.3
Mother never sees child	0.4	1.0	0.9	2.5	4.3	1.0
Total	*100.0*	*100.0*	*100.0*	*100.0*	*100.0*	*100.0*
Number of observations	2,684	1,309	2,538	627	560	7,718

Source: Kaspiew et al. (2009)

parent may also change according to the changing circumstances of each parent (e.g., one parent's re-partnering, relocation, or changing employment circumstances, or shifts in the quality of the inter-parental relationship).

A number of interacting factors have contributed to the trends outlined in this chapter. These include changes in the dynamics of the labor market, as well as the increased participation of women in education and the labor force (especially including those with children), and the introduction and widespread availability of reliable contraception. Other clearly important and related factors include the rise in cohabitation, increased relationship instability, and delays in achieving those milestones that were once seen as important markers of adulthood: leaving home, marrying, and having children (see de Vaus, 2004; chapter 2 in this volume; Weston & Qu, 2007).

For many young adults, partnership formation and childbearing are now choices to be considered within the range of lifestyle options that are available to them. Thus, societal trends and the choices afforded to contemporary families have significantly added to the diversity of family forms. The various family forms outlined in this chapter differ systematically in ways that can affect the nature and quality of their functioning. However, in discussing such differences, there is always the danger that attention to differences masks the overlap in *quality* of functioning. Such issues are examined in the next section.

Family Functioning

Family functioning has many dimensions and relates not only to internal family dynamics but also to the ways in which family members interact with the outside world. Functioning cannot be understood simply by investigating family members in isolation (Cook, 2010).

Some aspects of family functioning can be measured objectively (e.g., paid work hours of each parent), but many can only be assessed subjectively. It is particularly difficult to infer family functioning on the basis of the latter, for different family members can hold quite different views about how well their family is functioning. It has long been shown that family members differ in their reports concerning issues such as family cohesion, adaptability, sharing of household tasks, and parenting (see Baxter, 1997, 2002; Crouter & Seery, 1994; Olson, McCubbin, Barnes, Larsen, Muxen, & Wilson, 1983). This is not to suggest that subjectively derived information has little use. In fact, the ways family members interpret such dynamics may well influence their behavior and well-being. Thus, an important issue concerns the ways in which form and function influence the well-being of family members. This matter will now be addressed.

Functioning over form?

Stereotypes exist about the quality of functioning of families of different forms, such as single-parent families and stepfamilies. However, family form alone is by no means a reasonable proxy for the nature or quality of family functioning. For example, some couples who live together tend to live quite separate or parallel lives—possibly reflecting a distant, unhappy relationship that may end in separation. These couples could be said to be "living together apart."[7] And as Robinson (2009) points out, single mothers are a diverse group, as evidenced by the different pathways that have led to their status as a single mother, and the fact that some are well-resourced at the outset, and some move successfully from reliance on welfare to reliance on paid work.[8] Furthermore, many sole-parent and couple families that are financially disadvantaged function extremely well, with some clearly doing better than some affluent families, especially those on the brink of separation.

The quality of family functioning is clearly more important than family form to the well-being of family members. While there is evidence supporting the commonsense notion that children are particularly likely to thrive if they live with both biological parents who care deeply for them as well as for each other (see Amato, 2005; Ambert, 1997), children whose parents are locked in acrimonious conflict appear to be better off if their parents separate (Amato & Booth, 2005; see also chapter 8 in this volume).

Comparisons of family forms, however, do suggest differences in the average well-being of family members. For example, children with separated parents have a higher risk of negative outcomes than children in intact married families (see Amato, 2005). But this risk is modest and outcomes for most children of separated families are no different from those of most children in intact families. The risk remains a serious concern, however, because the *number* (rather than proportion) of children adversely affected is substantial (Amato, 2005). The differences in children's well-being can be explained by the interaction of many factors including those relating to the child, parent, family (including its resources and functioning), neighborhood, and broader community.[9]

The importance of family functioning to child well-being within separated families has recently been demonstrated in the evaluation of the 2006 family law reforms undertaken by the Australian Institute of Family Studies (Kaspiew et al., 2009). This study showed that separated parents' assessments of their children's well-being varied according to the quality of their relationship with the other parent. Children whose separated parents reported a highly conflictual or fearful inter-parental relationship appeared to be progressing less well over a range of indicators compared with those whose parents held friendly or cooperative relationships (Figure 1.2). These findings echo the past findings of Noller and colleagues (see chapter 8 and chapter 23 in this volume).

The evaluation also suggested that children were at an increased risk of experiencing negative outcomes where there had been a history of family violence, mental health and/or substance abuse problems, and where one parent experienced safety concerns (for themselves or their child) linked with ongoing contact with the other parent. Furthermore, the risk of lowered well-being (as reported by mothers) appeared to be particularly elevated where the children experienced equal time with each parent but the mother held serious concerns for her and/or the children's safety.

Past experiences are also important. For example, parental separation is but a step in the longer process of relationship breakdown and readjustment, and the outcomes for children depend on their experiences during the entire process (Amato, 2000). These experiences relate to the quality of functioning in the family, with family violence, child abuse, and parents' substance abuse being extreme examples of poor functioning that may have contributed to the separation and would have had detrimental effects on the children. Under these circumstances, the children would normally be better off through parental separation.

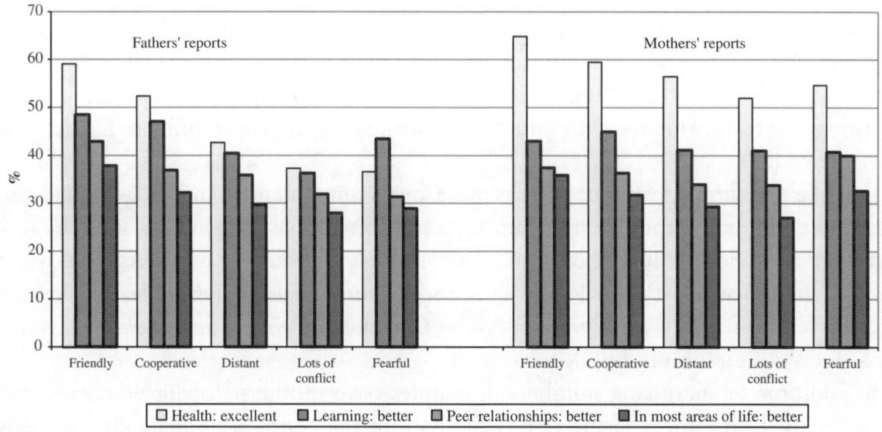

Figure 1.2 Proportion of separated parents who rated their children's health as excellent or doing better than other children in three areas (learning, peer relationships, most areas of life) by perceived quality of inter-parental relationships
Source: Adapted from Kaspiew et al. (2009) based on Figure 11.10

The number and nature of family forms that individuals experience, especially during their childhood, also require monitoring. Recent research suggests that successive changes in family forms require adjustments that can be very difficult for children to handle and increase the risk of negative developmental outcomes (Cherlin, 2008; Teachman, 2008; Wolfinger, 2005). These changes themselves may reflect continuing or successive problems in family functioning to which children may have contributed (e.g., if they are unhappy with the parents' new partner).

Challenges for families and for policy

It is important to point out that family functioning is complex and is influenced by internal and external forces. It reflects the way the families respond to environmental forces, such as shifts in the economy which influence the way they allocate breadwinning and homemaking responsibilities. Such changes have impacts, not only within the family, but also for society. In turn, they also have implications for policy and the provision of supports to families. Two specific issues are explored below.

Breadwinning and homemaking responsibilities. In some ways, life was simpler with a clear division of breadwinning and homemaking responsibilities, although such a situation was by no means ideal for everyone concerned. Nor is such a division the norm these days. For example, in 1983, just over half the couple families with dependent children had only one parent in paid work (whether full-time or part-time) while 40% had both parents in paid work. Over the years, the proportion of dual-earner couple families increased, so that by 2007, 60% of couple families with dependent children had both parents in paid work and only 35% had only one parent in paid work. Couple families with one parent working full-time (father or mother) and the other working part-time are considerably more common than those in which both parents work full-time (36% vs. 24% in 2007). The move of mothers into the workforce also applies to families headed by mothers. The proportion of single mothers with dependent children who are in the workforce increased from 32% in 1983 to 57% in 2007 (ABS, 2007b; Renda, 2003). Such changes have had ripple effects, requiring other adjustments within the home, workplace, and community to facilitate this new way of life.

Outside the family, various policies have been implemented in the workplace and community to accommodate the family commitments of employees, including the introduction of flexible work hours and leave to look after family members, both young and old, the provision of formal child care, and for some, paid maternity leave. However, access to family-friendly work practices varies considerably within and between organizations (Gray & Tuddbull, 2003).

In addition, as increasing numbers of couples have mothers in paid work, pressures have mounted on fathers to increase their share in the couple's homemaking responsibilities. There is now a detectable shift, however, in fathers' behavior consistent with these expectations, although mothers are still doing the lion's share around the home (see Baxter, 2002; Bittman, 2004a, 2004b). It is therefore not surprising that mothers with full-time paid work and with young children are more likely than their counterparts with part-time or no paid work to experience time pressures (see Baxter, Gray, Alexander, Strazdins, & Bittman, 2007).

The above example illustrates one way in which changes in the different strategies for managing parental responsibilities can generate their own set of needs which must be met if the family is to function well. The meeting of these needs is not something that families can do on their own. While some receive support from their extended families, such families also need the support of their workplaces, their communities, and governments.

Impact of the information age. Advances in information technology represent another set of societal changes that have added to the complexity of family life. For example, technology has contributed to a blurring of the boundaries between work and family life. While these changes have enabled some parents to work from home, which may help them better manage their work- and family-life responsibilities, they can also increase the chance that work demands interfere with home life.

These advances in information technology have affected many other aspects of family life, such as the amount of time that family members spend in contact with others via mobile telephones and the Internet. Family members' potential access to pornography, violence, bullying through the Internet, along with all the information that assists them in their work (relating to school or employment), can also have a profound impact on behavior in the home (Donnerstein, 2010).

Conclusion – Pitfalls of Form and Prospects of Functioning

Regardless of family form, there are basic needs common to all families. For instance, parents need to provide their children with the resources to meet their basic requirements for remaining healthy, feeling safe and secure, and growing up to become happy, well-adjusted, and productive members of the community. The meeting of these needs can be enhanced or threatened by a variety of interacting forces relating to characteristics of the family members, the family as a whole (including its form and especially its functioning), and external factors, such as the economic climate, government policies, and technological advancements.

The prevalence of different family forms has changed and some new types of families are emerging. These trends result from broad societal forces and personal circumstances of individuals including their values and aspirations as well as the opportunities available to them. Such trends and their contributing factors need to be monitored closely in order to develop proactive policies.

However, while monitoring the different family forms is important, it is also important to avoid inferring family functioning from family form. In other words, particular attention needs to be given to family functioning (in all its diversity) that occurs within these different forms, and the impact of such functioning on the well-being of family members.

This task is by no means an easy one. It is far simpler to measure family form and socio-demographic characteristics associated with family form, such as the family's household income and residential location—and to compare the well-being of family members in different family forms as these relate to their socio-demographic correlates. Family functioning is important as a mediator between form and these other correlates on the one hand, and well-being outcomes on the other (see Chase-Lansdale, Cherlin, & Kiernan, 1995; Pryor & Rodgers, 2001).

The family needs to be understood in its wider social context, for this context plays a central role in the overall functioning and lifestyle of the family. While "it takes a village to raise a child," a supportive village is also necessary for families to thrive, meet the needs of their members, and thereby enhance the well-being of their village. There are many ways in which Australia now supports its families, including the financial support targeting different groups, and the provision of various services (Gray, Qu, & Weston, 2008). There is a need, however, for policy to take a lifespan development approach to support families whatever their forms. This approach emphasizes the fact that development is a multifaceted, multidirectional, and lifelong process, and highlights factors influencing developmental directions (e.g. Baltes, 1987). Such an approach throws light on the appropriate nature and timing of supports required. Strong support needs to be directed not only at the "front-end" (e.g., early childhood; relationship education), but across the life course, in all its diversity.

Notes

The views expressed in this chapter are those of the authors and may not reflect the views of the Australian Institute of Family Studies or the Australian government.

1. While this lifestyle is foreign to the mainstream Australian families, Schaffer and Emerson (1964) observed that children have networks of attachment that extend beyond the family.
2. Hugo (2001) notes that it is only in recent decades that census information about relationships in the family has been used to organize the data in such a way that the structure and composition of families can be identified.
3. Surrogacy involves a woman having a child for another woman, using the sperm of the partner of the latter ("commissioning" woman). The "commissioning woman's" eggs may be fertilized, with the embryos then being transplanted into the surrogate mother, or the eggs of the surrogate mother may be used. Such procedures are not legal in all states, and the latter procedure may not be practiced.
4. If a single mother and her children live with both her parents, then the ABS treats them as two separate families living in one household.
5. The information based on the 2006 census was computed by the authors using the 2006 TableBuilder.
6. Any number of categories could have been identified from these data.
7. Some of these couples may well separate when their children have left home.
8. Some of the circumstances of single-mother families created by relationship breakdown are discussed later in this chapter.
9. See Bronfenbrenner and Crouter (1983) for an excellent discussion of the ways in which characteristics of the context, process, and individual child interact to affect children's developmental outcomes.

References

Amato, P. (2000). The consequences of divorce for adults and children. *Journal of Marriage and Family, 62*(4), 1269–1287.

Amato, P. (2005). The impact of family formation change on the cognitive, social and emotional well-being of the next generation. *The Future of Children, 15*(2), 75–96.

Amato, P. R., & Booth, A. (2000). *A generation at risk: Growing up in an era of family upheaval.* Cambridge, MA: Harvard University Press.

Ambert, A.-M. (1997). *Parents, children, and adolescents: Interactive relationships and development in context.* New York: Haworth Press.

Australian Bureau of Statistics (2001). *Yearbook Australia, 2001.* (Cat. No. 1301.0). Canberra: ABS.

Australian Bureau of Statistics (2002). *Census of population and housing: Selected social and housing characteristics, Australia 2001.* (Cat. No. 2015.0). Canberra: ABS.

Australian Bureau of Statistics (2005a). *Family, household and income unit variables, 2005.* (Cat. No. 1286.0). Canberra: ABS.

Australian Bureau of Statistics (2005b). *Australian social trends 2005.* (Cat. No. 4102.0). Canberra: ABS.

Australian Bureau of Statistics (2007a). *2006 census of population and housing – Census tables,* (Cat. No. 2068.0). Canberra: ABS.

Australian Bureau of Statistics (2007b). *Labour force status and other characteristics of families (datacube ST FA4).* (Cat. No. 62240.0.55.001.). Canberra: ABS.

Australian Bureau of Statistics (2008). *Family characteristics and transitions, Australia, 2006–07.* (Cat. No. 44442.0). Canberra: ABS.

Baltes, P. B. (1987). Theoretical propositions of life-span developmental psychology: On the dynamics between growth and decline. *Developmental Psychology, 5,* 611–626.

Baxter, J. (1997). Gender equality and participation in housework: A cross-national perspective. *Journal of Comparative Family Studies, 28*(3), 220–247.

Baxter, J. (2002). Patterns of change and stability in the gender division of household labour in Australia, 1986–1997. *Journal of Sociology, 38*(4), 399–424.

Baxter, J., Gray, M., Alexander, M., Strazdins, L., & Bittman, M. (2007). *Mothers and fathers with young children: Paid employment, caring and well-being* (Social Policy Research Paper No. 30). Canberra, ACT: Department of Families, Community Services and Indigenous Affairs.

Bittman, M. (2004a). Parenting and employment: What time-use surveys show. In N. Folbré & M. Bittman (Eds.). *Family time: The social organization of care* (pp. 152–170). London: Routledge.

Bittman, M. (2004b). Parenthood without penalty: Time use and public policy in Australia and Finland. In N. Folbré & M. Bittman (Eds.). *Family time: The social organization of care* (pp. 224–237). London: Routledge.

Bourke, E. (1993). The first Australians: Kinship, family and identity. *Family Matters, 35,* 4–6.

Bronfenbrenner, U., & Crouter, A. C. (1983). The evolution of environmental models in developmental research. In P. H. Mussen (Series Ed.) & W. Kessen (Ed.), *Handbook of child development: Vol. 1 History, theories, and methods* (pp. 357–414). New York: Wiley.

Butler, B. (1993). Aboriginal children: Back to origins. *Family Matters, 35,* 7–12.

Chase-Lansdale, P. L., Cherlin, A. J., & Kiernan, K. E. (1995). The long-term effects of parental divorce on the mental health of young adults: A developmental perspective. *Child Development, 66,* 1614–1634.

Cherlin, A. (2008). Multiple partnerships and children's well-being. *Family Matters, 80,* 33–36.

Cook, W. L. (2010). The comparative study of interpersonal relationships. *Family Science, 1*(1), 37–47.

Crouter, A. C., & Seery, B. (1994). Looking to the future: Diversity in family experience. In L. L'Abate (Ed.), *Handbook of developmental family psychology and psychopathology* (pp. 415–432). New York: Wiley.

de Vaus, D. (2004). *Diversity and change in Australian families: A statistical profile.* Melbourne: Australian Institute of Family Studies.

Donnerstein, E. (2010). *The media and aggression: From TV to the internet.* Paper presented at the 13th Sydney Symposium of Social Psychology: Social Conflict and Aggression, Sydney.

Dunne. E. G., & Kettler, L. J. (2008). Grandparents raising grandchildren in Australia: Exploring psychological health and grandparents' experience of providing kinship care. *International Journal of Social Welfare, 17*(4), 333–345.

Fitzpatrick, M., & Reeve, P. (2003). Grandparents raising grandchildren—A new class of disadvantaged Australians. *Family Matters, 66,* 54–57.

Gilding, M. (2002). Families of the new millennium: Designer babies, cyber sex and virtual communities. *Family Matters, 62,* 4–10.

Gray, M., Qu, L., & Weston, R. (2008). *Fertility and family policy in Australia* (Research Paper No. 41). Melbourne: Australian Institute of Family Studies.

Gray, M. & Tuddball, J. (2003). Family-friendly work practices: Differences within and between workplaces. *Journal of Industrial Relations, 45*(3), 269–291.

Hugo, G. (2001). A century of population change in Australia. In Australian Bureau of Statistics, *Yearbook Australia, 2001* (Cat. No. 1301.0). Canberra: ABS.

Kaspiew, R., Gray, M., Weston, R., Moloney, L., Hand, K., & Qu, L.& the Family Law Evaluation Team (2009). *Evaluation of the 2006 family law reforms.* Melbourne: Australian Institute of Family Studies.

Levin, I., & Trost, J. (1999). Living Apart Together. *Community, Work & Family, 2*(3), 279–294.

McDonald, P. (1995). *Families in Australia: A socio-demographic perspective.* Melbourne: Australian Institute of Family Studies.

Morphy, F. (2006). Lost in translation? Remote indigenous households and definitions of the family. *Family Matters, 73,* 23–31.

Ochiltree, G. (2006). *Grandparents, grandchildren and the generation in between.* Melbourne: ACER Press.

Olson, D. H., McCubbin, H. I., Barnes, H., Larsen, A., Muxen, M., & Wilson, M. (1983). *Families: What makes them work.* Beverly Hills: Sage.

Pryor, J., & Rodgers, B. (2001). *Children in changing families: Life after parental separation.* Oxford: Blackwell Publishers.

Renda, J. (2003). Polarisation of families according to work status. *Family Matters, 64,* 16–21.

Robinson, E. (2009). Sole-parent families: Different needs or a need for different perceptions? *Family Matters, 82,* 47–51.

Schaffer, H. R., & Emerson, P. E. (1964). The development of social attachment in infancy. *Monographs of the Society for Research in Child Development, 29*(3), serial no. 94.

Strohm, C. V., Seltzer, J. A., Cochran, S. D., & Mays, V. M. (2009). "Living Apart Together" relationships in the United States. *Demographic Research, 21*(7), 177–214.

Teachman, J. (2008). Complex life course patterns and the risk of divorce in second marriages. *Journal of Marriage and Family, 70*(2), 294–305.

Weston, R., & Qu, L. (2007). Families in Australia: Continuities and change. In E. Shaw & J. Crawley (Eds.), *Couple therapy in Australia: Issues emerging from practice* (pp. 23–47). Kew, Victoria: PsychOz Publications.

Wolfinger, N. H. (2005). *Understanding the divorce cycle: The children of divorce in their own marriages.* Cambridge: Cambridge University Press.

2

Social Trends and their Impact on Couple and Family Relationships

David de Vaus

Introduction

Fifty years ago the pathways to family formation, the dynamics of family life, and the responsibilities of mothers, fathers, husbands, and wives were clear and prescriptive. It was a brave and "deviant" person who ventured beyond these boundaries. Today people "do" family and relationships very differently, and do so with far less normative prescription and much greater diversity. These changes, which are part of a broader process of profound social change, have been viewed relatively positively by some people (e.g., Giddens, 1992; Stacey, 1996) and denounced by others (e.g., Blankenhorn, 1995; Popenoe, 1988).

This chapter does not aim to identify the full gamut of social changes that affect the way in which contemporary couples form their relationships and families. Instead, I focus on two related features of social change and discuss how these features shape the way we "do relationships and families" at the beginning of the 21st century. The analysis, which is partly speculative and certainly not comprehensive, provides a lens through which to view the nature of contemporary family trends.

The analysis focuses on two interrelated concepts: choice and risk. Simply put, today's society provides for choice in almost every domain of life. Choice is an uncontested "good thing" but we have to manage choice and the freedoms it brings. I outline two ways in which we deal with choice. On the one hand we plan our lives as projects and contain the insecurity and risks of choice by planning and scheduling to avoid the unpredictability that

---

The Wiley-Blackwell Handbook of Couples and Family Relationships, First Edition.
Edited by Patricia Noller and Gery C. Karantzas.

choice can bring. Alternatively we shy away from making choices altogether and encounter a form of paralysis as we seek to keep all our options open. I argue that both these ways of managing choice are reflected in the way we now form families and relationships.

Family and Relationship Trends

Before elaborating these ideas in the context of family change, I will describe some of the main changes in families and relationships over the last half century common to most advanced Western countries. Rather than reporting specific statistics, since these vary between countries, I will describe common (although not always universal) trends that have occurred in families in these nations (see volumes by Adams & Trost, 2005; de Vaus, 2004; Hennon & Wilson, 2008 for further reading).

Marriage and relationships

Lifelong, monogamous, heterosexual marriage has lost its monopoly as a way of establishing intimate sexual relationships and for bearing and raising children. While marriage remains the most popular form of couple relationship in most developed countries it is no longer the exclusive form. Marriage rates have declined as more couples now live together without being married and many couples live together before they marry.

Not only are fewer marrying, those that do so are marrying later than was typical until the early 1970s. As a result of declining marriage rates, later marriage, and more marital separations, adults are now spending a smaller proportion of their lives in marriage (see chapters 1 and 29 in this volume).

When people marry, they do not necessarily remain married. Over the last half century divorce laws have made divorce easier and far more common. Although divorce rates appear to be stabilizing or even declining in some countries, this change is largely because many people who once would have married and divorced are now living together and separating and not appearing in the divorce statistics.

While divorce is not something to which people typically aspire, there is widespread acceptance that divorce does happen and that divorce is better than a miserable marriage. The widespread opprobrium that once accompanied divorce has dissipated as divorce has become more acceptable, even if regrettable. Whether or not a couple stays together is seen primarily as the business of the couple not of the church or the state.

Same-sex relationships are more public than they once were and this situation has further challenged the monopoly of heterosexuality as the only acceptable form of intimate relationship. There is greater acceptance of ways in which to express one's sexual orientation and many individuals are now able to choose whether to "come out" or not. In more and more countries, same-sex relationships are being legally recognized in one form or another.

Nor has marriage retained its monopoly as the only legitimate arrangement within which to have and rear children. While marriage may still be viewed as the preferable arrangement, more and more children are being born to single mothers and unmarried couples. Laws have changed in many developed countries to reflect and enable these changes in marriages and relationships. Divorce laws have been simplified, discrimination against partners in de facto marriages has been substantially eliminated as have laws that discriminate against children born outside of marriage. Currently reform is underway that reduces the scope of discrimination against same-sex couples.

These changes reflect an erosion of the monopoly of marriage as being the only acceptable institution within which sexual relationships, long-term relationships, child-bearing, and childrearing can take place. As prescriptions have weakened, individuals must decide how to create and end relationships. This erosion of an agreed and given way of behaving can be described as the deinstitutionalization of marriage.

This deinstitutionalization of marriage can be observed in other ways—especially the way in which gender shapes how couples build their relationships. Although gender-based domestic division of labor continues, this division is more blurred than it once was. Rigid prescriptions of what is "his" work and "her" work have become more flexible and the notion of sharing domestic work is at least seen as desirable if not always practiced. The key point is that couples have to work out for themselves how they are going to divide the domestic labor rather than simply follow a well-established script.

Changes in the ways couples manage domestic labor are linked to the radical change in families whereby it is now normal for mothers to be in the paid labor force. While marriage and children once meant the effective end of a woman's career, it is now normal for women to maintain a lifelong labor-force attachment. This situation means that couples have to work out how they will arrange their family and work lives to accommodate the employment of both parents. The old single-breadwinner family model meant that there were few decisions to be made. But now, women have to make decisions about whether to have children, how much time to take off when the child is born, when to return to work, whether to work full or part time, how to deal with school holidays, child illnesses, and the like. In making these choices there are few guidelines and couples have to negotiate and work things out as they go.

My intention here is not to decry these changes. Many changes represent improvements to oppressive and unfair practices. The key point is that family change has seen a move from certainty, continuity, predictability, and well-established expectations and roles to an environment in which there is little consensus or prescription. Each couple has to work things out for themselves.

Children

Virtually all countries have experienced a sharp decline in fertility within the last half century. This decline has been possible because women have gained greater control over their fertility, are more educated, and can see wider horizons. While motherhood was once virtually the only pathway for most women, there are now far more possibilities for young women. Childlessness has increased, women have fewer children and can restrict the most demanding time of parenting to a shorter part of the life course. As a consequence, there is more opportunity for mothers to do things in addition to parenting and domestic work.

Fertility is also being delayed and more carefully planned. Women are delaying their fertility for a reason. They are partnering later, or at least settling down with a long-term partner later. They are investing in an education and traveling or getting established in a career. In other words, for people in their 20s there are many alternatives to having children. Sex is not confined to marriage and sex no longer carries a high risk of pregnancy. Many things compete with parenthood which is seen to close off many of the other attractive options. So why not delay?

There are other fertility choices to be made. The revolution in reproductive technologies means that more and more women will need to make decisions if they are unable to conceive without medical interventions. Age once made the decision for women as to the end of their reproductive period but the new technologies extend this period and mean that the line is now blurred. These technologies mean more decisions and more choices.

Once children are born, the options continue where once the alternatives were limited. The issue of child care is now an issue for most parents. How much will child care be used? Will formal or informal care be used? As the notion of the gendered division of domestic labor is challenged, parents must work out and negotiate the respective part that mothers and fathers will play in childrearing.

Within families and the culture more broadly, the language of authority and responsibilities has given way to the language of equality and rights (Stacey, 1996). This change has influenced relationships between partners and the ways in which children are treated in families. In the same way that the roles of men and women in families have become more blurred, so has the place of children. For many parents there is considerable ambiguity regarding how to rear children, what authority parents (and stepparents) should exercise, and what responsibilities parents should shoulder. Where there was once greater clarity there is now a greater element of confusion and disagreement.

Diversity

The changing landscape of families is probably most obvious when we look at the increasing diversity of family types within developed nations. Changing demographics, increased longevity, declining birth rates, and delays in family formation mean that the "typical" nuclear family of two parents and two dependent children has become far less typical. Single-parent families, blended families, couple-only families, and lone-person households have become increasingly common. Since relationship breakdown is common, there are more complex families which contain stepchildren and stepparents and a fluctuating membership as some children are "shared" between households.

The essential point is that the proto-typical family of "mom, dad, and the kids" has lost its monopoly as the way of "doing family" and of raising children. The resulting diversity makes it clear that there are many ways of doing family. Even if some ways are seen as more desirable, there are many acceptable alternatives. Without a single model of family, individuals have to work their way through this diversity and make choices that shape the type of family they build. The constraints of the past no longer dictate the shape of our families.

Diversity is also evident in the order in which family formation events take place. It was not all that long ago that a strict order of events was required: courtship; engagement; marriage/co-residence and sex; children; empty nest; retirement; widowhood. Many of these stages or events have become jumbled and the transitions blurred. Into this mix has been added premarital cohabitation, far more divorce, re-partnering, and the creation of step- and blended families.

The once prescriptive order in which family formation events were expected to take place has been replaced by a culture in which these stages can be, and are, ordered in a wide variety of ways. In the absence of defined pathways we all now go our own way as we each construct our particular method of ordering our life-course events.

The Context of Family Changes

Rather than following a social script, family life is increasingly a matter of constructing our own drama. Rather than learning and acting out the lines written by earlier generations we need to ad lib as we work out how to live in contemporary society.

Social theorists have characterized contemporary society in a variety of ways using terms such as post modernity, liquid modernity (Bauman, 2000), late modernity, high modernity (Giddens, 1991), and individualization (Beck & Beck-Gernsheim, 2002). While not synonymous, these terms highlight the extent to which contemporary society is one where individuals are active participants in shaping their lives and behavior. In this late-modern world, established prescriptions are less powerful and life is constructed rather than given. Social characteristics such as class, gender, ethnicity, religion, and the like are seen to be less determining of life chances and lifestyle. Thus people now have to make many choices between multiple options and this reflects the deinstitutionalization of family life.

While this degree of choice and the capacity to construct one's own pathways may be welcome and liberating for some, it adds complexity to life and for some it is profoundly unsettling. Complexity arises from diversity. Where the old verities of family life have become blurred and contested, everything has to be worked through and negotiated. The blurring of domestic roles means that these have to be negotiated and agreed on—not always an easy task. How is a family to manage childrearing in a two-career family? Couples have to negotiate how to manage this important task. Where there is no set relationship pathway, couples have to agree and negotiate about whether to marry, have children, and the like where once these were more or less taken for granted. While the capacity to negotiate and construct has real advantages, it can also be exhausting and complicated. For some it will be too hard. While tradition can be constraining it can also bring authority and direction which for some is reassuring, and helps them work through complexities that would otherwise be overwhelming.

The transformations in families that have resulted from the erosion of prescriptions and the widening of options and choices are part of a wider social transformation that has produced a culture of choice. While there are many ways of describing these transformations, I want to focus on four social changes that have contributed to the celebration of choice.

Secularization

Secularization is often thought of as the decline in church attendance, the disappearance of religious practices, and the weakening of doctrinal beliefs. But secularization is much more than this. It is about the loss of a religious framework from the fabric of our social institutions and everyday lives. Nowhere is this clearer than in the loss of a broad consensus about what is right or wrong in many domains of life. The loss of a religious framework has meant that the belief in an absolute morality has weakened. Without an external, God-given morality, where is the basis for saying that something is right or wrong? If there is no authoritative God who declares right or wrong then what is right or wrong becomes something that we must work out for ourselves. Morality becomes personal, situational, and gray as we relativize right and wrong. And as soon as we do that, we allow for multiple rights and wrongs and that people can live according to their own light.

In a secularized world we have to work out right and wrong for ourselves—the answers to life cannot be found in a single authoritative place, person, institution, or book. We must work out how we will live, make decisions, and accept responsibility for those choices. This situation means that in a secular world there is no agreed basis on which to say that sex must be confined to marriage, that homosexuality, divorce, and contraception are wrong, that family authority resides in the husband, that children should be obedient, or that marriage is a sacred institution sealed in a church with a vow before God.

Laissez-faire economics

In most of the developed world and much of the developing world, the ideology of the market is dominant. The market model is based on the concept of choice, and the assumption that choice is a primary and self-evident good. Constraints on choice are bad and distort the operation of a free market. The model is based on the belief that ultimately, providing people with choice will produce better outcomes. The market model places enormous faith in people's capacity to make rational choices. This belief in the market drives many policy initiatives where the philosophy of choice is paramount. In policy terms, this belief means that personal taxation should be reduced and government monopoly services should be opened up to private-sector competition so that individuals can make their own choices about how they spend their money and what service providers they use.

Consumerism

There are two elements of our consumer society that contribute to our culture of choice. The first is related to the enormous variety of brands within any particular product segment that produces the experience and expectation of choice. The range of clothes, cars, toilet papers, and just about any popular product line is based on the assumption that people will want to choose and find the product that suits them. The notion of "one size fits all" makes no sense in a consumer culture. The consumer culture is quintessentially a culture of choice and of individuals matching the particular product to themselves.

The second and related element of consumerism is that identity is partly constructed by what we consume (Bauman, 2007; Douglas & Isherwood, 1976; Dunn, 2008; Friedman, 1994; Lasch, 1979; Veblin, 1899). As gender, class, and ethnicity are less defining and confining, we can construct and portray an identity through our consumption. The clothes we wear, the restaurants we visit, the car we drive, and our lifestyle in general are our badges of identity. While we cannot readily change our sex, class, or ethnicity we can shape our consumption and thus invent and reinvent ourselves. So the consumer culture is fundamentally based on the notion of choice and the capacity to make choices enables us to build our own identities rather than simply take on an identity that is more or less assigned by our social characteristics. Consumerism enables us to build a D.I.Y. identity.

Feminism

Feminism has had a major impact in a number of domains of life. One of the most important insights contributed by feminist movements has been the notion that gender and sex are different concepts: while sex is biologically given, gender is socially constructed. If gender is socially constructed then it can be constructed in a variety of ways. This insight has helped many people understand that the way we "do gender" is the result of choices and structures and is open to change. Changing structures can broaden choices and thus transform the ways in which we perform gender.

This insight has profound implications for social institutions, such as the family, that are strongly shaped by gender. It has meant that gender inequality within families is not the natural order but a construction based on the way in which the sex of a person is used to shape their social position. Feminism has stressed the equality of men and women over what some have argued is a natural hierarchy based on sex. This focus on equality in turn has challenged the notion that fathers and husbands naturally should exercise authority in families and has led to an emphasis on decisions within families being based on discussion, negotiation, and agreement rather than on authority. Fundamentally feminist writers have insisted that family organization does not have to be gender based. Since gender is constructed, then arrangements that are structured around gender can change. Since gender is constructed, feminism has given weight to the notion that women should have choices—choices over fertility, roles, employment, and staying in relationships.

Consequences of Choice

The proposition that modern life is lived within a culture of choice where the old frameworks are less constraining has many possible consequences as to how we negotiate and experience relationships. I will focus on just two of these.

Forced into the future

German sociologist, Elisabeth Beck-Gernsheim (2002), argues that the processes that I have described as the "deinstitutionalization" of the family are part of a broader process of "individualization." Individualization is the process whereby old norms and structures dictated by tradition and social characteristics have been eroded to the extent that individuals must invent themselves and construct their lives rather than follow established pathways.

While less constraining, this postmodern world produces what she refers to as "risky freedoms" (2002, p. 42) and which others call "manufactured insecurity" (Beck, 1994; Giddens, 1994).

In the face of these risky freedoms Beck-Gernsheim (2002) argues that we seek security. While freedoms may be liberating they can also produce profound anxiety (see also Giddens, 1992). One way in which we respond to this freedom-based insecurity is to plan our futures to minimize risk and to calm the manufactured insecurity. Planning can help manage choice-induced insecurity and minimize the risks inherent in not knowing what the future holds.

Since the shape of the future is unknown, and far less predictable and controllable than when our lives were shaped by tradition, planning provides a means of making the future more predictable and controllable. Planning becomes our insurance against future risks. Prevention, calculation, and control become part of our everyday lives as we seek to deal with the choices we have to make and the risks they entail. To do otherwise is to be irresponsible and part of adulthood is to assume these responsibilities for planning one's future.

How does the proposition that we have to be active planning agents of our futures help make sense of some of the changes we see in relationships and families? Living together before marriage has become the norm in many developed countries and for many (but not all) this period represents a trial to test compatibility. Since many marriages break down, a pragmatic risk mitigation strategy is to "try before you buy." Premarital relationship education and marriage contracts that specify agreements about how this marriage will operate represent ways of dealing with the uncertainties and options that have grown as the power of tradition has diminished.

Marriage is also delayed so that other things can be fitted into the planned future before settling down. Education, establishing a career, the overseas trip, and saving up for a house all have to be fitted in before marriage. Children are delayed since they need to fit into the plan. Suitable housing, getting "that job," accumulating sufficient leave, and then having children before time runs out reflect the planning that we must undertake. If we don't plan then who knows what will happen? The number of children, their timing, and spacing are planned to fit in around all the other things we must do. And by doing all this preplanning many couples manage to be trying to have children way beyond their peak fertility period as already noted.

Divorce itself may be planned for. Many couples will be aware at some level that their marriage could end. Divorce carries with it big risks that have lifelong consequences. Beck-Gernsheim (2002) argues that some couples adjust their behavior to mitigate the cost of divorce should it happen. According to Beck-Gernsheim people "live in a relationship while keeping the exit door open: this is becoming the new motto" (p. 26). For example, since formal marriage and children complicate divorce, informal marriage and delays in having children provide ways of mitigating the cost of relationship breakdown. For women, a barrier to divorce is the economic dependence that can flow from the effect of children on employment, so it makes sense for a married woman to maintain a good labor force position and thus be prepared should her marriage end. If we have no control over our futures, there is little need to plan it but as we have achieved a greater capacity to shape our futures, we must plan to minimize the risk and insecurity that accompanies choice.

The paradox of choice

Another response to the dilemmas posed by the multitude of choices we confront is to avoid making choices altogether. Psychologist Barry Schwartz (2004) talks about the paradox of choice—that when we have a large number of options many of us are unable to choose between the many options and do nothing. He points to the empirical evidence from social psychological studies that show that beyond a certain point, numerous choices make it too difficult to come to any decision. Too many alternatives overwhelm rather than liberate.

Why might a large number of options paralyze us into indecision? First, if choices commit us for the long term (e.g., marriage, having children) we need to be sure that we have made the right choice. But how can we know for sure before we have actually made these irrevocable decisions? We are faced with plenty of evidence that marriages fail and that childrearing can go badly wrong as is clear from statistics regarding child abuse, youth suicide, and drug abuse (Australian Institute of Health and Welfare, 2007, 2010; Australian Institute for Suicide Research and Prevention, 2003). How can we make decisions now that commit us into the unknown future? So what do some people do? They put off the difficult decision until another day. But that day never comes and nothing gets decided. Commitments and decisions for the long term are replaced by short-term decisions and commitments that can then be changed as the future unfolds.

A second reason why making decisions in a culture of choice is difficult is because making a choice can limit further choices. That is, any choice can lead to limits on opportunity. Where choice is celebrated and is engrained in the fabric of our society it goes against the grain to make a choice that limits future options. To marry, have children, and purchase a house all involve long-term commitments that in turn limit other choices. They "tie us down," limit our longer term options, and mean that we might miss out on other possibilities.

A third reason why choice can lead to indecision, and ultimately to no decision, is that choice contains risks. With so many possibilities from which to choose there is a good chance that we might make a bad decision, or at least later come to believe that we could have made a better decision. Since we are in a position to make decisions rather than slavishly follow established pathways, we must take some responsibility for our decision making and its outcomes. If things work out badly, then the sense of personal failure is heightened. Schwartz (2004) argues that the epidemic of anxiety and depression in contemporary society is partly due to the self-blame that flows from the responsibility we feel when choices don't work out. One response to the responsibility we must bear for our decisions is to make no decision. Delays in partnering and childbearing may be seen in this light. While for some people these delays are part of a deliberate plan, for others they will be the result of indecision. Ultimately the decision is made for them as the pool of potential partners dries up or age precludes having children.

A further dimension of choice making may shed some light on aspects of contemporary relationships. Schwartz argues that a large number of choices heightens our expectations and in turn leads to greater disappointment. Essentially, he argues that where we have many alternatives we choose what we think is the best alternative. If we have no choice we make do. But where we choose, our expectations increase accordingly, and the chances of disappointment increase as well. Where marriage is but one way of partnering and where we freely choose to marry, we expect more of marriage than if we had no choice (e.g., an arranged marriage). In other words, options heighten expectations and heightened expectations set us up for greater disappointment. If a marriage does not live up to expectations, then the disappointment is that much greater, and the desire to try other possibilities becomes more compelling. The high rate of relationship breakdown is likely to be at least partly attributable to the disappointment of heightened expectations that are nurtured in a culture of choice.

Concluding Comments

The ways in which families change, the ways we build relationships, and what we look for in families and relationships are integrally tied up with the culture and society in which we live. Our relationships reflect many of the themes and values in our culture. In periods of rapid social change such as those experienced in recent decades, families and relationships will also change. In this chapter I have highlighted one important dimension of social change—the erosion of many traditional constraints which have shaped behavior and pathways. In its place we live in a world where individuals have to make many choices and take responsibility for these choices.

While providing greater freedoms, these freedoms bring risks. I have argued that this individualized world brings with it "risky freedom" and "manufactured insecurity." I have described two ways in which we respond to these risks and insecurities and have argued that some of the changes we have seen in families and relationships can be interpreted as responses to this world of choice. One response, put forward by Beck-Gernsheim, is to plan as a way of containing risks and managing insecurity. Family behavior that may reflect this response includes delays in family formation, fertility planning, and balancing family activities with many other priorities. The second response is to do nothing in the face of choices. Where there are too many choices, some people will be paralyzed into inaction. For some people at least, delays in family formation and difficulties with commitment, relationship fragility, and family instability can be interpreted as outcomes of not making choices or making highly contingent choices that keep all options open.

References

Adams, B., & Trost, J. (Eds). (2005). *Handbook of world families*. Thousand Oaks: Sage.

Australian Institute of Health and Welfare (AIHW) (2007). *Statistics on drug use in Australia 2006*. Drug Statistics Series No. 18 (Cat. No. PHE 80). Canberra: AIHW.

Australian Institute of Health and Welfare (AIHW) (2010). *Child protection Australia 2008–09*. (Cat. No. CWS 35). Canberra: AIHW.

Australian Institute for Suicide Research and Prevention (2003). *International suicide rates – recent trends and implications for Australia*. Canberra: Australian Government Department of Health and Ageing.

Bauman, Z. (2000). *Liquid modernity*. Cambridge: Polity Press.

Bauman, Z. (2007). *Consuming life*. Cambridge: Polity Press.

Beck, U. (1994). The reinvention of politics: Toward a theory of reflexive modernization. In U. Beck, A. Giddens, & S. Lasch (Eds.), *Reflexive modernization: Politics, tradition and aesthetics in the modern social order* (pp. 56–109). Cambridge: Polity Press.

Beck, U., & Beck-Gernsheim, E. (2002). *Individualization: Institutionalized individualism and its social and political consequences*. London: Sage.

Beck-Gernsheim, E. (2002). *Reinventing the family: In search of new lifestyles*. Cambridge: Polity Press.

Blankenhorn, D. (1995). *Fatherless America: Confronting our most urgent social problem*. New York: Basic Books.

de Vaus, D. A. (2004). *Diversity and change in Australian families*. Melbourne: Australian Institute of Family Studies.

Douglas, M., & Isherwood, B. (1976). *The world of goods: Towards an anthropology of consumption*. London: Routledge.

Dunn, R. (2008). *Identifying consumption: Subjects and objects in consumer society*. Philadelphia: Temple University Press.

Friedman, J. (1994). *Consumption and identity*. Chur, Switzerland: Harwood.

Giddens, A. (1991). *Modernity and self-identity: Self and society in the late modern age*. Cambridge: Polity Press.

Giddens, A. (1992). *The transformation of intimacy*. Stanford: Stanford University Press.

Giddens, A. (1994). Living in a post-traditional society. In U. Beck, A. Giddens, & S. Lasch (Eds.), *Reflexive modernization: Politics, tradition and aesthetics in the modern social order* (pp. 1–55). Cambridge: Polity Press.

Hennon, C. N., & Wilson, S. (Eds.) (2008). *Families in global context*. New York: Routledge.

Lasch, C. (1979). *The culture of narcissism*. New York: W. W. Norton.

Popenoe, D. (1988). *Disturbing the nest: Family change and decline in modern societies*. New York: Aldine.

Schwartz, B. (2004). *The paradox of choice: Why more is less*. New York: Harper.

Stacey, J. (1996). *In the name of the family: Rethinking family values in the postmodern age*. Boston: Beacon Press.

Veblen, T. (1899). *The theory of the leisure class: An economic study of institutions*. New York: Dover.

3

Changing American Families in the 21st Century

Suzanne M. Bianchi, Sara B. Raley, and Lynne M. Casper

Several key changes in the family occurred in developed countries in the latter half of the 20th century, setting the stage for more diverse family forms in the 21st century (see chapters 1, 2, 4 in this volume). Changes in intimate unions include a delay in entering into (legal) marriage, the rise in unmarried (heterosexual and same-sex) cohabitation, and the decline in marriage in many countries and among some population subgroups in the United States. The median age at first marriage rose to 28 years for men and 26 years for women in the United States. In 2009, 67.5 million opposite-sex couples lived together—with about 90% married and the other 10% cohabiting (U.S. Census Bureau, 2010). Gauging the number of same-sex couples is more difficult but the most recent estimates suggest that there are about 750,000 cohabiting same-sex couples in the United States, with 52% gay/male couples and 48% lesbian/female couples (O'Connell & Lofquist, 2009).

Despite the increasingly late start, most Americans do marry during their lifetime. However, those marriages are frequently disrupted. In his book *The Marriage-Go-Round*, Andrew Cherlin (2009) argues that the United States is exceptional among developed countries for its high rates of marrying and divorcing, and its pattern of cohabitation. Whereas in Europe, cohabitations are often very "marriage-like," lasting for years, in the United States cohabitations tend to be short-lived. Cherlin notes that 10% of U.S. women have had three or more husbands or cohabiting partners by the time they reach age 35, more than twice the percentage for countries in Europe with the highest rates of union dissolution (Cherlin, 2009).

Marriage, cohabitation, divorce, and remarriage patterns are not the only family behaviors that distinguish the United States from many other developed countries.

The Wiley-Blackwell Handbook of Couples and Family Relationships, First Edition.
Edited by Patricia Noller and Gery C. Karantzas.

Fertility levels have plummeted in many countries but in the United States the total fertility rate has remained near replacement level for several decades. Of great interest in the United States is the divergence in fertility behavior by social class. Among the highly educated, children are being postponed but most are born to two married parents. Among the less educated, marriage is delayed or foregone but children are not, resulting in a large proportion of births to unmarried women. Partly reflecting these social-class differences, Americans, on average, have children at an earlier age than mothers in many other developed countries. Women also spend more time as lone mothers, rearing children without a father present (Cherlin, 2009).

Some have suggested that the rapid decline in fertility to very low levels in Southern and Eastern Europe and some countries in Asia, most notably Japan, is due to a lack of change in the family-role expectations for women in these countries (McDonald, 2000). In countries where women are still expected to do most of the housework and childcare with little assistance from men, as women's labor market opportunities expand, many women exercise the only choice they see as available to them: They remain childless when work and family roles are too difficult to reconcile. In the United States, an increase in childlessness has occurred among the most highly educated women but there has also been change toward a more egalitarian division of labor in the home (Bianchi, Robinson, & Milkie, 2006).

A final trend altering family life in the United States, and other developed countries as well, is population aging, a result of both the decline in fertility and the increase in life expectancy. In the United States, the proportion of the population aged 65 and over is projected to increase from the current 12% to 20% in 2030 (He, Sengupta, Velkoff, & DeBarros, 2005). Future generations of elderly are likely to have fewer biological children on whom they can rely for care, at the same time as the number of their stepchildren expands due to high levels of union disruption and re-partnering. However, it is not clear that norms of obligation to assist family members are as strong among step-kin as among biological kin (Coleman & Ganong, 2008).

The combination of these demographic trends, including late marriage, increasing cohabitation, high levels of divorce, increasing single parenting, replacement-level fertility and increased life expectancy, have resulted in a decrease in the "family share" of U.S. households. Whereas 40% of households in 1970 were two-parent family households with children, the comparable figure was 23% in 2007 (Kreider & Elliott, 2009). The share of households that include persons living alone increased substantially from 17% in 1970 to 27% in 2007. This growth reflects the delay in family formation at young ages, increases in divorce, the lengthening life expectancy, decline in disability in the elderly, and an increased economic ability to live alone at older ages.

In sum, the contemporary American household looks very different than the mid-20th century baby boom families with their early and near-universal rates of marriage, low rates of divorce, high rates of fertility, and a highly specialized gender division of labor in the home, with men working for pay in the labor force and women working in the home as caregivers and homemakers. In this chapter, we review the current patterns of U.S. family life, beginning with the transition to adulthood, and then moving to changes in marriage and cohabitation, divorce and childbearing. Changes in these domains alter the composition of households and the family circumstances of children. Changing marriage and fertility patterns also interrelate with changes in the labor-force participation of women and men: Trends such as increased father involvement in household tasks compared with previous generations, an increased likelihood of mothers and fathers as co-providers in two-parent families, and of single mothers as sole providers. We assess trends in these areas as well.

Our focus is on the United States, though the general outline of trends is often similar to what is happening in other countries, particularly other English-speaking countries like Canada and Australia. However, as noted above, there are also ways in which the United States differs from these other contexts. For example, Furstenberg (2010) argues that as the transition to adulthood lengthens in the United States, families bear a greater burden of support for adult children relative to their European counterparts where governmental programs invest more heavily in the education, health care, and job prospects of their young people. The lack of government investment in the United States makes for greater diversity and more inequality in young-adult outcomes. Moreover, Cherlin (2009) argues that the high rates of partnering and re-partnering make for a much more turbulent family system in the United States than elsewhere, especially if one takes the perspective of children who experience much family instability. Perhaps in part because of this factor, nowhere else have declines in (legal) marriage been viewed as so problematic and thus worthy of public-policy intervention. Nowhere else have differing "family values" become such a politicized issue.

Young "Emerging" Adulthood

A half century ago, with World War II coming to an end and the baby boom beginning, most Americans were considered full-fledged adults by the time they reached their 20s, or perhaps even their late teens. "Adulthood" entailed completion of high school, stable full-time employment, and marriage and parenthood for most men and women. Not only were those growing up in the post-war era financially independent of their parents, they were also entering parenthood and supporting children of their own. Today, the picture of early adulthood looks markedly different in the United States, perhaps warranting the distinction of a new stage of life (Furstenberg, Kennedy, Mcloyd, Rumbaut, & Settersten, 2004).

The gap between adolescence and adulthood has widened in large part due to the difficulty in attaining full-time employment lucrative enough to support a family. The availability of jobs that paid a "family wage" with good benefits was ample for men with only a high school diploma in the years after World War II, given the availability of government incentives to help integrate veterans back into society as well as a strong manufacturing sector characterized by heavy unionization (Casper & Bianchi, 2002). As the decades wore on, however, male wages slowly declined while inflation increased. Moreover, as the rest of the world recovered from the economic devastation of World War II, global competition grew more intense and technology advanced in such a way that the shrinking manufacturing sector no longer offered a stable source of middle-class employment (Settersen & Ray, 2010).

In addition to these shifts in the national and global economies, changing social roles for men and women influenced expectations for young adulthood. Rising individualism, and increases in choice of lifestyles, prompted men and women to seek avenues of self-development and self-fulfillment outside of the standard breadwinner/homemaker model of adulthood of the 1950s. It also became more acceptable for women to be employed outside the home and for men to do housework and childcare. Whereas in the past men bore the primary—or in most cases, sole—responsibility for breadwinning, stagnating male wages, increasing economic opportunities for women, and shifting standards for consumption, resulted in heightened expectations that women engage in market work (Casper & Bianchi, 2002). Moreover, the instability of marriage, relative to the 1950s, increased concern among women that they have adequate skills to support themselves in the event that they choose not to marry or their marriage dissolves (Edin & Kefalas, 2005).

In light of the considerable social and economic insecurity that young people face, a college education is now viewed as essential for acquiring a desirable job for all men and women. As more young people pursue the training needed to compete for the "good" jobs in the labor market, they are increasingly relying on their families to support them beyond adolescence and the traditional age of entry into adulthood, ages 18 and 21. Economists note that it takes young American men well into their late 20s and early 30s to earn enough to support themselves, let alone other family members (Smeeding & Ross Phillips, 2002).

Although pursuing higher education is an aspiration of most young people, not all have the cultural, social, and economic resources to succeed in completing college. The economic struggle to secure financial independence among those who do not have a college degree is readily apparent. Indeed, the vast majority of those in their early 20s—regardless of whether they are enrolled in school—receive some sort of economic assistance from their parents (Schoeni & Ross Phillips, 2004). This pattern of intergenerational flows from parent to child is a considerable break from the past when co-residential children in their initial stages of employment typically chipped in to help parents.

The unique economic and social conditions that characterize young people's lives at this historical juncture are calling into question the traditional parameters of what constitutes an adult. Consistent with previous decades, most Americans point to education, employment, and financial independence as the primary indicators of adulthood status (Furstenberg et al., 2004). By contrast, the role of the family in determining adulthood status has changed markedly over the past two generations; although the value placed on family, and particularly marriage and children, has remained strong over time, the emphasis on individualism and tolerance of alternative life choices has increased dramatically such that marriage and children are no longer seen as mandatory transitions (despite the fact that the vast majority of Americans ultimately make these transitions) (chapter 2 in this volume; Thornton & Young-Demarco, 2001). In addition, a lengthening lifespan, increased availability and reliability of contraception, and widespread acceptance of premarital sex, mean that men and women have fewer incentives to rush to marry.

Delayed (First) Marriage and Increased Cohabitation before Marriage

The delayed transition to adulthood shifts the family behaviors early in life in three important ways. First, because many young adults marry relatively late, there is greater diversity and fluidity in living arrangements in young adulthood. Second, young adults increasingly enter a cohabiting union before marriage (see chapter 26 in this volume). Third, the trend to later marriage affects childbearing; it tends to delay entry into parenthood and, at the same time, increases the chances that a birth (sometimes planned but more often unintended) occurs before marriage (Bianchi & Casper, 2000; chapters 1, 2 in this volume).

Cohabitation

Among those aged 15 to 44 in 2002, about half have cohabited (Goodwin, Mosher, & Chandra, 2010). The experience of living as an unmarried partner before marrying was rapidly becoming a modal experience for younger cohorts in the United States. For marriages formed between 1997 and 2001, 62% were preceded by cohabitation (Kennedy & Bumpass, 2007). Cohabitation is also increasingly an alternative to remarriage after separation and divorce, and, in several European countries, is often a long-term substitute for marriage. In the United States, long-term cohabitations are still relatively uncommon.

Why has cohabitation increased so much? Researchers have offered several explanations, including increased uncertainty about the stability of marriage, the erosion of norms against cohabitation and sexual relations outside of marriage, the wider availability of reliable birth control, economic changes, and increased individualism and secularization. Youths reaching adulthood in the past two decades are much more likely to have witnessed their parents' divorce than any generation before them. Some have argued that cohabitation allows a couple to experience the benefits of an intimate relationship without committing to marriage. Further, the financial and legal costs of exiting a cohabiting relationship are also much lower than those associated with exiting a marriage (Casper, Haaga, & Jayasundera, 2009).

An increasing proportion of cohabiting households include children—in the United States estimates overall are that about 40% of unmarried households have children (Fields & Casper, 2001), with half of children born to the couple and the other half, the children that one of the parents had prior to entering the cohabiting relationship (Acs & Nelson, 2002). Other estimates from the Fragile Families Study suggest that the figures are even higher for the very youngest children; as many as 50% of the births to an unmarried mother are actually to a couple who is living together. Among couples who are cohabiting at the time of the child's birth, 28% are married by the time the child is aged 5, 28% are still cohabiting, and the rest are no longer living together in the same household (Carlson & McLanahan, 2010).

Fertility

U.S. fertility is characterized by two divergent trends. On the one hand, childbearing is increasingly delayed among the well educated, with an increase in childlessness. On the other hand, among the less educated and among certain racial groups, childbearing often occurs relatively earlier in life, is frequently unplanned, and often takes place outside marriage.

Delayed childbearing and childlessness

Both marriage and children are being postponed to older ages among the better educated segments of the population. Currently in the United States, among women aged 40 to 44, 20% have never had a child, double the percentage of 30 years ago (Dye, 2008). Morgan (2010) finds that the actual total fertility rate of highly educated women was lower (by about one half a child, averaged over the group) than their stated intentions at the beginning of their childrearing years, suggesting that these women may have had difficulty realizing their preferences for motherhood (or that their preferences changed as they grew older).

Nonmarital childbearing

Nonmarital childbearing has sharply increased since the 1960s, when it comprised less than 10% of all births, to the most recent decade where it accounts for nearly 40% of all births (Ventura, 2009). Other developed nations have also experienced increases in births to unmarried mothers, but the U.S. patterns are unique in terms of the socioeconomic situation of unmarried parents as well as the longevity of the parents' commitment to one another (Carlson & McLanahan, 2010). Ellwood and Jencks (2004) show that there has been very little increase in nonmarital childbearing among highly educated U.S. women over the past 40 years, whereas nonmarital childbearing has increased quite significantly among those who have a high school education or less. In addition, nonmarital childbearing varies by race and ethnicity. About 28% of white children are born to unmarried parents compared with 72% of African American children and 51% of Hispanic children (Hamilton, Martin, & Ventura, 2009).

Recent shifts to a greater proportion of childrearing within cohabiting and other nonmarital unions have heightened the awareness that trends in childbearing and childrearing cannot be studied independently of union (marriage and cohabitation) formation and dissolution. Much recent work has focused on why these nonmarital unions, known as "fragile families," are so unstable and why these couples never marry. For example, Carlson and McLanahan (2010) report that most unmarried mothers and fathers are romantically involved at the time of the nonmarital birth, but only about 40% are still romantically involved 5 years after the birth. Indeed, their disadvantaged backgrounds provide a complicated context for relationship stability. Compared with their married counterparts, unmarried fathers are typically much less educated, are in poorer physical and mental health, are more likely to be addicted to alcohol and drugs, and are more likely to be or have been incarcerated. Moreover, unmarried fathers often have other children with prior partners, known as multi-partner fertility, making it difficult for them to provide adequately for additional dependents, and ultimately placing greater strain on their family relationships given the significance of breadwinning to the identity of fathers (Townsend, 2002).

Despite the recent surge in research on unmarried parents, it remains unclear whether unmarried men simply have little intention of long-term commitment to their partners and children, or whether these men are just doing the best they can in the face of constrained economic prospects and complex neighborhood and family situations (Carlson & McLanahan, 2010). Moreover, when biological fathers decrease their contact with their children and the mothers of their children, other men often come into the picture to offer economic and emotional support. This additional role of "step" or "social father" that men play for other men's (biological) children complicates family functioning, and ultimately modern-day conceptualizations of parenthood, even further.

Union Dissolution

Divorce probabilities have not risen in 30 years but they remain high in the United States. The latest estimates from the 2002 National Survey of Family Growth (NSFG), a national study that tracks marriage and cohabitation, are that about two thirds of marriages last at least 10 years and only about half of married couples are still together at their 20th anniversary (Goodwin et al., 2010). Among new parents in the Fragile Families study, who were married at the time of the child's birth, 77% remained married by the time the child was 5 years old. However, among mothers who were not married to the child's father at the time of birth, only 36% lived with the biological father 5 years later (in 17% of cases the couple had married and in 19% they continued to live together) (Carlson & McLanahan, 2010).

Changes in marriage, divorce, and childbearing complicate the intergenerational picture, as financial and care obligations are no longer necessarily dependent on biological or marital ties. In groups where marriage is increasingly fragile, intergenerational ties may supersede nuclear ties in the rearing of children (Bengtson, 2001). Because most American children live with their mothers after relationships dissolve, divorce reduces contact between fathers and their young children and also curtails men's contact with children when those children become adults (Cooney & Uhlenberg, 1990). Children's living arrangements also vary greatly by race. The percentage of children living with two biological parents is 85% for Asian children, 78% for white, non-Hispanic children, 69% for Hispanic children, and only 38% for black children (U.S. Census Bureau, 2010).

There has been enormous growth in step- or blended families, with a substantial increase in the percentage of children who have experienced a stepfamily. The rise in stepfamilies increases the number of persons with whom the typical individual has some familial connection, but, at the same time, may weaken family ties and norms of obligation (Coleman & Ganong, 2008). How these changes affect familial support is still very much an open question.

Single Parenting

Single parenting, particularly single mothering, is of particular interest in the United States given its striking growth over the past several decades (particularly in the 1970s) as well as the unique challenges single parents face relative to two-parent families (Casper & Bianchi, 2002). In 1970, 6% of family households with children were maintained by a single mother, and 1% by a single father. By 2007, these figures were 23% and 5%, respectively. Only in recent years has it been possible to exclude cohabiting parents from these figures, and when such exclusions are made, current estimates suggest single parents account for about one quarter of U.S. households with own children under age 18 (Kreider & Elliott, 2009).

Single mothers in the United States generally face much greater economic strains than other family types. First, they typically assume primary responsibility for both breadwinning and caregiving, though many single mothers receive financial support and help from relatives and from their children's fathers. Second, although single fathers have increased dramatically since the 1970s, now accounting for about 15% of all single parents in 2007 (Kreider & Elliott, 2009), single mothers are still overrepresented among single parents at 85%. Given that women generally earn less than men, and that single mothers are typically younger and less educated than other mothers, single mothers are particularly vulnerable economically. Never-married single mothers are disadvantaged relative to divorced single mothers and married mothers who tend to be older and better educated. Children of never-married single mothers have less than one fourth the family income of children in two-parent families, although the average income of families headed by divorced mothers is also less than half that of families headed by two-parents (Bianchi & Casper, 2000). Part of the economic inequality between never-married single mothers and divorced single mothers is due to the father's propensity to contribute child support. Mothers who never marry the father of their children are less likely to receive child support (with about 20% reporting receiving it regularly) than are divorced or separated mothers (with about 60% reporting receiving some support) (Bianchi & Casper, 2000).

Changing Gender Division of Labor in Two-Parent Families

Because the majority of U.S. children are still reared in two-parent families, perhaps the greatest change to affect family life in the second half of the 20th century is the increase in mothers' labor-force participation, particularly for married mothers. The decline in the one-wage-earner, two-parent family, greatly altered U.S. family life—increasing expectations of fathers' involvement in the home and mothers' economic role in the family (Bianchi, 2000; Casper & Bianchi, 2002).

Time-diary evidence can be used to track changes in unpaid and paid work of mothers and fathers since the 1960s in the United States. Similar trend data are available for a number of other countries in Europe and also in Australia, though often not for such a long time period. Trends in these countries tend to parallel those in the United States. To briefly summarize, as mothers increased market work they reduced their time in housework but not childcare and fathers boosted their time in the home, first in housework and later in childcare. On average, hours of market work reported by mothers in the historical series of time diaries more than doubled (from 8 to 19 hours per week, averaged across all mothers including those with zero hours of paid work) between 1965 and 1985, continued to rise (to an average of 23 hours in 1995), and then leveled off (even declining slightly in recent years). Somewhat lower hours of paid work for mothers after 2000 fueled the debate about whether mothers were increasingly "opting out" of the paid work force (Belkin, 2003; Boushey, 2005; Stone, 2007). The current widespread recession has stopped this slight increase in "stay-at-home" mothers; the number of mothers who did not work outside the home declined from 5.6 million in 2006 to 5.3 million in 2008. (U.S. Census Bureau, 2010).

Where did mothers find the time for increased paid work? Housework hours for mothers declined from an average of 32 hours per week (reported in 1965 time diaries) to just under 19 hours (reported in 2000), a decline of 13 hours, on average (Bianchi et al., 2006). This situation could be viewed as close to an equal trade: mothers averaged 14 more hours of market work in 2000 than in 1965 as they shed 13 hours of housework. Most of the change in mothers' housework was in "core housework" tasks: mothers almost halved the time they spent preparing meals and doing laundry and cut their housecleaning time by more than one third.

In the United States (and elsewhere), mothers' primary childcare time followed a different pattern from housework. As market work rose, mothers' time in childcare activities declined from 10 to 8½ hours per week between 1965 and 1975. After 1985, however, primary childcare time of mothers rose to almost 13 hours per week by 2000 and has remained high in the 2000–2010 decade (American Time Use Survey (ATUS)).

Routine caregiving, the bulk of childcare (e.g., feeding, clothing, bathing, making and keeping doctors appointments), generally remained steady: it dipped between 1965 and 1985 and returned to (and slightly exceeded) 1965 levels by 2000. The more interactive childcare activities (e.g., playing with, reading to, helping with homework, etc.), however, almost tripled from 1.5 hours per week in 1965 to 4.0 hours per week reported in the ATUS. U.S. middle-class parents are increasingly engaged in a very intensive form of childrearing, with children involved in a dizzying array of activities (Lareau, 2003).

As mothers increased their market work and shed housework, how were fathers changing? Time-diary evidence suggests that fathers more than doubled their housework hours between 1965 and 1985, from 4 to 10 hours per week but then housework time for fathers leveled out. Fathers' primary childcare time was stable at about 2½ hours per week in the 1965 through 1985 diaries but then increased substantially. By 2000, fathers had nearly tripled their primary childcare time, reporting almost 7 hours per week, an estimate similar to the 7 hours per week reported in the ATUS since 2003.

To summarize, mothers replaced unpaid housework with market work but they largely "protected" childcare time, even increasing "quality" interactive time. Fathers picked up workload, first by increasing their time in housework, later their time in childcare. Estimates from the ATUS for the 2000–2010 decade are remarkably consistent with earlier smaller-scale U.S. time-diary surveys and suggest that these reallocations of time in the home have remained fairly steady in the past decade.

Conclusion

The United States, like Australia, Canada, Great Britain and many countries in Europe, has witnessed monumental economic, social, cultural, and demographic changes since the 1960s that have altered family forms in the 21st century. Like these other countries, the United States has experienced a postponement of marriage; declines in marriage among some subgroups; increases in divorce, nonmarital childbearing, and cohabitation; a decline in fertility; the aging of the population; and increases in women's labor-force participation and men's family work, resulting in a shift in the household division of labor.

At the same time, the United States appears to be unique in at least three ways. First, the United States has more inequality among young adults, stemming from the uneven chances of obtaining advanced education and the higher likelihood of some young adults postponing childbearing. Second, American families and children experience much more instability in family forms than families in other countries, with Americans churning in and out of marriage and cohabitation. Finally, although fertility in the United States has declined since the 1960s, it remains high relative to other developed countries.

These differences feed into the unique policy and political climate in the United States. In the 1960s when good jobs were plentiful for men, most households with children included two parents, and most mothers were full-time homemakers, the family could support and rear children for the public good. Increasing economic inequality, diversity in family forms, and family instability have raised questions about children's well-being and the ability of families to fulfill this role. The U.S. government invests much less in education, health care, employment, and welfare than other countries. When families are not strong, stable, or economically secure enough to ensure children's well-being, the government tends not to fill the void.

Some observers argue that the family is in decline as a result of moral weakening in family values and increased individualism, whereas others argue that the family is merely changing due to economic restructuring and changing norms. Both agree that the changes in family forms have been detrimental to children and have increased poverty and both have offered solutions to strengthen families and improve child well-being. Some believe that the key to solving the problem is to promote healthy marriages (see chapter 26 in this volume). Toward this end, in 1996, a number of groups worked together to enact welfare reform legislation. Three of the four pillars of this controversial legislation focused on marriage and family formation. States were directed to promote marriage, reduce out-of-wedlock childbearing, and "encourage the formation and maintenance of two-parent families." Beginning in 2000, marriage rose to the top of the domestic policy agenda with President Bush declaring, "my Administration will give unprecedented support to strengthening marriages" (Ooms, 2002). Pundits argued that if more low-income people married and stayed married, child poverty would be reduced, children would have more contact with their fathers, and children's outcomes would improve more generally. Programs were developed to provide marriage and relationship counseling, and communication classes.

Critics argue that although marriage can be desirable in many cases, it may not raise families out of poverty in communities with high unemployment, soaring crime, and high drug and alcohol abuse rates. Among the services these advocates support are job training, programs to increase jobs and pay in the hardest hit areas, financial management classes, and drug and alcohol counseling.

Most of the policy in the first decade of the 21st century has been to encourage and support the formation and maintenance of healthy marriages. Whether this policy will change, as the current deep recession makes clear that many families can become vulnerable to economic loss and unforeseen circumstances, is the important public-policy question for the coming decade in the United States.

References

Acs, G., & Nelson, S. (2002). The kids are alright? Children's well-being and the rise in cohabitation. *New Federalism National Survey of America's Families, B-48*. Washington, DC: Urban Institute.

Belkin, L. (2003). The opt-out revolution. *New York Times Magazine*, pp. 42–86.

Bengtson, V. L. (2001). Beyond the nuclear family: The increasing importance of multigenerational bonds. *Journal of Marriage and Family, 63*, 1–16.

Bianchi, S. M. (2000). Maternal employment and time with children: Dramatic change or surprising continuity? *Demography, 37*, 401–414.

Bianchi, S.M., & Casper, L.M. (2000). American families. *Population Bulletin*. Washington, DC: Population Reference Bureau.

Bianchi, S. M., Robinson, J. P., & Milkie, M. (2006). *Changing rhythms of American family life*. New York: Russell Sage.

Boushey, H. (2005). *Are women opting out? Debunking the myth*. Center for Economic Policy Research Briefing Paper, November.

Carlson, M. J., & McLanahan, S. S. (2010). Fathers in fragile families. In M. E. Lamb (Ed.), *The role of the father in child development* (5th edn.), (pp. 241–269). Hoboken, NJ: Wiley.

Casper, L. M., & Bianchi, S. M. (2002). *Continuity and change in American family lives*. Thousand Oaks: Sage.

Casper, L. M., Haaga, J. G., & Jayasundera, R. R. (2009). Demography and family health. In J. Kaakinen, S. Hanson, & V. Gedaly-Duff (Eds.), *Family health care nursing: Theory, practice and research* (4th edn.). Philadelphia: F. A. Davis.

Cherlin, A. (2009). *The Marriage-Go-Round*. New York: Vintage.

Coleman, M., & Ganong, L. (2008). Normative beliefs about sharing housing with an older family member. *International Journal of Aging and Human Development, 66*(1), 49–72.

Cooney, T., & Uhlenberg, P. (1990). The role of divorce in men's relations with their adult children after mid-life. *Journal of Marriage and the Family, 52*(3), 677–688.

Dye, J. L. (2008). Fertility of American women 2006. *Current Population Reports, P20-558*. Washington, DC: U.S. Census Bureau.

Edin, K., & Kefalas, M. (2005). *Promises I can keep: Why poor women put motherhood before marriage*. Berkeley, CA: University of California Press.

Ellwood, D. T., & Jencks, C. (2004). The uneven spread of single-parent families: What do we know? In K. M. Neckerman (Ed.), *Social inequality* (pp. 3–78). New York: Russell Sage Foundation.

Fields, J., & Casper, L. (2001). America's families and living arrangements: Population characteristics. *Current Population Reports, P20-537*. Washington, DC: U.S. Census Bureau.

Furstenberg, F. F., Jr., (2010). On a new schedule: Transitions to adulthood and family change. *Future of Children, 20*(1), 67–87.

Furstenberg, F. F., Jr., Kennedy, S., Mcloyd, V. C., Rumbaut, R. G., & Settersten, R. A., Jr., (2004). Growing up is harder to do. *Contexts, 3*(3), 33–41.

Goodwin, P. Y., Mosher, W. D., & Chandra, A. (2010). Marriage and cohabitation in the United States: A statistical portrait based on Cycle 6 (2002) of the National Survey of Family Growth. National Center for Health Statistics. *Vital Health Stat, 23* (28).

Hamilton, B. E., Martin, J. A., & Ventura, S. J. (2009). Births: Preliminary data for 2007. *National Vital Statistics Reports, 57*(12). Hyattsville, MD: National Center for Health Statistics.

He, W., Sengupta, M., Velkoff, V., & DeBarros, K. (2005). 65+ in the United States: 2005. *Current Population Reports, P23-209*. Washington, DC: U.S. Census Bureau.

Kennedy, S., & Bumpass, L. (2007). *Cohabitation and children's living arrangements: New estimates from the United States.* Center for Demography and Ecology Working Paper, 2007–20. Madison, WI: University of Wisconsin-Madison.

Kreider, R. M., & Elliott, D. R. (2009). America's families and living arrangements 2007. *Current Population Reports, P20–561*. Washington, DC: U.S. Census Bureau.

Lareau, A. (2003). *Unequal childhoods*. Berkeley, CA: University of California Press.

McDonald, P. (2000). Gender equity in theories of fertility transition. *Population and Development Review, 26*(3), 427–439.

Morgan, S. P. (2010). *Thinking about demographic family differences.* In M. Carlson & P. England (Eds.), *Changing families in an unequal society.* Unpublished book manuscript.

O'Connell, M., & Lofquist, D. (2009). *Counting same-sex couples: Official estimates and unofficial guesses.* Paper presented at the annual meeting of the Population Association of America, Detroit, MI.

Ooms, T. (2002). Marriage and government strange bedfellows? *CLASP Policy Brief Couples and Marriage Series,* No. 1. Washington, DC: Center for Law and Social Policy.

Schoeni, R., & Ross Phillips, K. (2004). Material assistance received from families during the transition to adulthood. In R. Settersen Jr., F. Furstenberg Jr., & R. Rumbaut (Eds.), *On the frontier of adulthood: Theory, research, and public policy.* Chicago: University of Chicago Press.

Settersen, R. A., & Ray, B. (2010). What's going on with young people today? The long and twisting path to adulthood. *Future of Children, 20*(1), 19–41.

Smeeding, T., & Ross Phillips, K. (2002). Cross-national differences in employment and economic sufficiency. *Annals of the American Academy of Political and Social Science, 580,* 103–133.

Stone, P. (2007). *Opting out.* Berkeley, CA: University of California Press.

Thornton, A., & Young-DeMarco, L. (2001). Four decades of trends in attitudes toward family issues in the United States: The 1960s through the 1990s. *Journal of Marriage and the Family, 63,* 1009–10037.

Townsend, N. (2002). *The package deal: Marriage, work, and fatherhood in men's lives.* Philadelphia: Temple University Press.

U.S. Census Bureau (2010). Press release (January 15, 2010). www.census.gov/Press-release/www/releases/archives/families_households/014540.html.

Ventura, S. J. (2009). Changing patterns of nonmarital childbearing in the United States. *NCHS Data Brief No. 18.* Hyattsville, MD: National Center for Health Statistics.

PART II

Families across the Lifespan

4

The Role of the Family across the Lifespan

Toni C. Antonucci, Kristin M. Wong, and Sarah Trinh

In this chapter the role of the family across the lifespan is explored. In particular, we consider how individual lifespan development influences family experiences over time. In addition, we recognize the critical role of the life course (i.e., the context in which individuals develop over their lifetime) in understanding the family, its evolution, and influence on the individual over time. Next, we consider various definitions of the family as well as its changing structure. We review the roles that exist within the family across the lifespan and over the life course; and finally turn to a consideration of policy and societal influences on the lifespan and life course of individuals and families. We conclude with thoughts about the current state of knowledge and implications for future directions.

We begin this chapter with the recognition that while there has been a great deal of pressure in the past to recognize only one form of family, there appears to be increased awareness that multiple forms of the family can lead to positive pathways of success while the traditionally recognized family form is no guarantee of achieving successful life paths for its members.

Lifespan and Life Course

The importance of recognizing the influence of lifespan development (Baltes, Lindenberger, & Staudinger, 2006) and life-course (Elder & Shanahan, 2006) influences on the

The Wiley-Blackwell Handbook of Couples and Family Relationships, First Edition.
Edited by Patricia Noller and Gery C. Karantzas.

individual has been increasingly recognized. Both fundamentally shape the family, its structure and functioning (Fuller-Iglesias, Smith, & Antonucci, 2010).

Lifespan developmental theory critically recognizes that individuals develop over time in a manner that is interdependent with the past, present, and future. The infant has both pressing needs to be fed, sheltered, and loved but also has limited physical, cognitive, and social skills. The developmental period of infancy clearly delineates an individual who is different from and has distinctive characteristics from, for example, the child, adolescent, and adult. It is not difficult to recognize the differences that each individual possesses at each of these stages. Thus, the elementary sensorimotor-cognitive stage of the infant is replaced by the increasingly complex and abstract cognitive abilities of the adolescent and later adult. Similarly, it is not difficult to ascertain how experience in early developmental periods influences later experiences; for an example of such work see Sroufe, Egeland, Carlson, & Collins 2005).

Life-course theory argues that individuals are influenced by macro-level events and broader environmental contexts that the individuals encounter and navigate, which might have a significant influence on the individual's experience. The contexts include culture or ethnic group memberships and organizational structures such as schools, work, and governments. But perhaps the most important and most immediate group to which the individual is exposed is the family. The family is the closest, most long lasting, and commonly, the most important group to which the individual belongs.

Increasingly scientists are recognizing that we can no longer afford the luxury of separately considering the individual or lifespan perspective from the life-course perspective (Fuller-Iglesias et al., 2010). It is now understood that only a limited assessment of the individual can be obtained by examining one or the other and not both. As we consider the role of the family, we argue that maximal understanding of the family can only be achieved by considering the lifespan or individual development of each of its members, and by understanding that a family is a group, like other groups, with notable developmental trajectories that influence each of its members. We turn next to a focus on the family and family roles as they traditionally exist and have been changing over time.

Changing Family Structures

The term family has many meanings and is used in numerous contexts from everyday conversations to research and policy (see chapter 1 in this volume). What does the term family refer to? Traditionally, the term family has referred to the nuclear family with one mother, one father, and their children (Abbott, 2002). As an individual progresses through the lifespan, family can refer to two different social units: (i) the conjugal family where the individual is a parent and has children of his or her own and (ii) the family of origin which includes the individual's parents and siblings. Conventionally, there has been strong support for these definitions of family because it was thought that the only path to positive outcomes involved being part of a traditional family structure, and that all other types of family were disadvantageous. Increasingly, however, researchers have found that these definitions do not capture the diversity in family structures. Some nonconventional family structures lead to positive outcomes, though clearly, other family structures can challenge the positive developmental trajectory of the individual. In recent times, researchers have proposed definitions of family that are broader and more inclusive to incorporate those related by biology, adoption, marriage, dependence, obligation, and affection (Bedford & Blieszner, 1997; Crawford, 1999; Rothausen, 1999; chapter 1 in this volume).

In the traditional view of families, family members are related biologically or through marriage and were thought to be the only or at least the optimal successful family form. Today, this view is no longer consistent with the various family forms as individuals adopt, use others' genetic material, and have fictive family members. Adoption continues to provide an opportunity for parenting. Advances in reproductive technology help individuals with reproductive problems by providing the option of using others' sperm and/or egg. It is also common for individuals to have fictive kin or chosen families. Fictive kin are individuals considered a part of the family unit and fulfill the role of a family member who may or may not be present (Cicirelli, 1994). Chosen families (families made up of chosen nonrelated individuals) are common among individuals with limited biologically related family, including those who have never married, among those who have been rejected by their biologically related family because of lifestyle and life choices, or who have outlived their family members (Muraco, 2006). In some cases these chosen families have been shown to function as well as, if not better than, traditional families (Dykstra & de Jong-Gierveld, 2004), and in some cases, the risks for maladjustment are higher (e.g., Carlson & Corcoran, 2001).

The term family is expanding to include more family members, perhaps because fewer children are being born to each family. Family demographers have shown that the average family size has decreased considerably over the decades, from families where the average number of children was 3 to 7 at the turn of the 19th century, 3 to 4 in the 1950s, and 2 in the beginning of the 21st century (Centers for Disease Control and Prevention, 2000). In certain families, relatives such as grandparents, cousins, and unmarried aunts and uncles are considered as part of the basic family unit (Bures, 2009; Teachman, Tedrow, & Crowder, 2000). This practice is considered normative, especially in cultures where these relatives are more likely to co-reside and are, therefore, available to help with caregiving and household responsibilities. There are also situations where children are raised by other family members because their parents are unable to care for them. An example is grandparents raising their grandchildren due to the death, incarceration, illness, or abandonment of their children by their parents (Caputo, 2000). Increases in longevity and economic constraints are also expanding the family unit. Adults in late midlife may need to support their parents who are widowed or experiencing financial and/or health problems, as well as partially dependent children transitioning into adulthood (Grundy & Henretta, 2006). Elder parents may also become financial resources for their adult children in need (see below).

Due in part to demographic, economic, and social changes such as divorce, remarriage, adoption, as well as advances in reproductive technology, the traditional nuclear family is no longer representative of all families (see chapters 1, 2, 3 in this volume). Changes in marital practices have led to changes in the way families form. A number of family structures are described in chapter 1 in this volume. However, cultural practice continues to influence family structure and the developmental outcomes for family members. Below, we describe two such practices, family co-residency and family immigration.

Family co-residency

The practice of co-residency has been commonly attributed to cultural practices. It has been argued that in cultures where elders are highly valued, it is considered normative to have aging parents in co-residence arrangements. Cultures influenced by Confucian views are said to practice filial piety where adult children live with and care for parents and parents-in-law to reciprocate the care received as children (Antonucci, Blieszner, & Denmark, 2009; Ishii-Kuntz, 1997; Takagai & Silverstein, 2006). Recently, researchers have speculated that attributing co-residency to cultural practices is too simplistic and that co-residency is a result of cultural practices and numerous situational and economic factors (Ishii-Kuntz, 1997; Takagai & Silverstein 2006). One predominant reason for co-residency is the need for instrumental support. In many family situations, an aging parent co-resides with their adult child because they are experiencing health declines and need assistance (Bedford & Blieszner, 2000). In other situations, co-residency provides a system for mutual support with more people contributing to the household with finances, childcare, and/or household activities. Families often live together to pool their resources, because their aging and/or ailing parents cannot live independently, or they need to assist an adult child experiencing financial difficulties (i.e., loss of employment or divorce; Caputo, 1999). Whether or not families practice co-residency is often contingent on whether there are resources to support others and space in the home to accommodate additions to the family.

Many motivations for co-residing create both benefits and conflicts, depending on the family. This pattern was evident in Lowenstein's (2002) study of older immigrants in Israel from the former Soviet Union who co-reside with their adult children. The older immigrants described experiencing both economic and emotional benefits as well as interpersonal tensions, especially when living under the same roof in their new homeland. Co-residency allows for family members to share more household chores across more individuals; however, it also may engender conflict, especially when there are different expectations for the performance of those jobs. For example, a mother may have different views from her adult child about what constitutes a clean house.

Living together allows for the combining of financial resources so that individuals may maximize their money in some cases. In other instances, it creates more problems as family members disagree on appropriate contributions or on how household money should be spent. Another important and common benefit of co-residency is the provision of emotional support, especially in times of stress. The presence of numerous family members, however, may also create complications if family members become too involved in others' relationships. For example, because of co-residency a father may become too involved in how his adult son disciplines his child.

Having multiple generations living together usually leads to decreases in space and privacy, especially in a small house or apartment. Family members have less, if any, personal space, increasing the probability of tension among them.

Family immigration

Family structure is also affected by immigration, with timing of immigration having important influences on the individual's lifespan development and the family's life course. It is common for only some family members to immigrate to a new country while others stay behind (Bures, 2009). Smith, Lalonde, & Johnson (2004) examined the effects of staggered or serial migration on parent–child relationships in Caribbean immigrants. Due to the uncertainties and the economic costs of setting up a new life in a new country, one parent, or in some cases both parents will immigrate first, leaving their children in the care of extended family members in their country of origin. When reunification occurs, both child and parent(s) often have difficulty readjusting as the child may be resentful and have difficulty obeying the parent. The parent's optimistic expectations for reunification are sometimes unmet. This situation is exacerbated by the length of separation and the presence of new family members (e.g. stepparents, half-siblings etc.).

In other cases, parental contact may be infrequent or nonexistent. For example, parents may send their children to live in the United States for better educational opportunities. In these cases, parents will come to the United States, set up a home, arrange for their child to live with relatives and to attend school, and then return to their country of origin. Under these circumstances there may be relatively little family interaction or supervision (Wong, 2007). These immigration experiences affect family roles and functioning, often resulting in family members taking on nontraditional roles and functioning in altered circumstances (Yakushko & Espin, 2009).

In sum, these varied family experiences and structures produce unique lifespan and life-course trajectories that naturally influence the developmental course of the family and its members. Some variations increase the probability of achieving successful pathways through life while others clearly seem to place the individuals and their family at risk.

Roles Across the Lifespan

Across the typology of family structures, roles within the family unit are contextual, dynamic, temporal, and multifaceted. The differential timing of transitions across the lifespan contributes to the evolving nature of family dynamics. This timing impacts role formation, maintenance, alteration, and dissolution. Roles entail duties and expectations, and are multiply shaped by informal (e.g., gender expectations) and formal (e.g., social policy) norms and institutions as well as macro-level (e.g., globalization, migration, and the economy) and micro-level influences (e.g., personality, marital status, and health). However, individuals are also active agents in constructing their roles (Roy, 2008); therefore, family roles are not uniform or static across the lifespan and over the life course. Moreover, roles provide definition to one's identity and serve as a lens through which individuals understand their relationships and one another (Weigel, Bennett, & Ballard-Reisch, 2006). In this chapter we consider multiple family roles including: spouse, parent, child, and grandparent roles.

The role of the spouse

One of the most frequently studied relationship types is the spousal relationship. The spousal role is heavily imbued with evolving societal values and norms and commonly reflects gendered expectations (Marks, Huston, Johnson, & MacDermid, 2001). For example, the breadwinner role was traditionally ascribed to men, while the nurturer role was ascribed to women (Perrone, 2009). With an increasing number of dual-earner households, more spouses are negotiating the responsibilities of money management, especially if they endorse egalitarian gendered beliefs and have higher incomes and educational attainment (Yodanis & Laurer, 2007).

The role of the parent

Given increased life expectancy, the parent–child relationship is one of the most enduring relational ties within the family unit, second only to that of siblings (Cicirelli, 2006). The bidirectional and reciprocal nature of the parent–child relationship, coupled with the differential rate of development and aging of both individuals across the lifespan, yields a complex profile of the multifaceted roles of parents. Collectively, the parent role includes, but is not limited to, providing support, shaping adaptive skills and competencies (Volling, McElwain, Notaro, & Herrera, 2002), instilling values and beliefs (Fuligni, Tseng, & Lam, 1999; Kim & Ward, 2007), as well as socializing and preparing children for potential challenges (Hughes, Rodriguez, Smith, Johnson, Stevenson, & Spicer, 2006). Research on co-parenting highlights ways in which mothers and fathers differentially impact their children's behavior and development. For example, only paternal emotional availability was predictive of children's committed compliance longitudinally in a study of toddlers (Volling et al., 2002). In another study, fathers' use of gentle compliance gaining predicted children's committed compliance only when the mothers used similar techniques (Blandon & Volling, 2008).

The parental role is most frequently studied using mothers (Clark, Kochanskia, & Ready, 2000), although interest in fatherhood is increasing (Goldscheider, Hofferth, Spearin, & Curtin, 2009; Roy, 2008). There is evidence that fathers and stepfathers uniquely impact children's development. This possibility is particularly salient when examining children's development in various marital contexts (Hetherington, Bridges, & Insabella, 1998). For example, boys tend to benefit more than girls from living with a father or stepfather after divorce, yet living with a stepparent is associated with more behavior problems in girls. Additional research on fatherhood in multiple contexts is necessary and there is no doubt that changing norms about divorce and absent fathers influence the experience of the child. Varying contexts include transnational and nonresident fathers, who live apart from their families, and fathers with children from multiple partners (Caldwell, Wright, Zimmerman, Walsemann, Williams, & Ishchei, 2004; Roy, 2008). Mothers can also engage in transnational and nontraditional parenting, for example, working as domestics in other countries, leaving children in their country of origin to be raised by relatives or neighbors (Horton, 2009). These immigration and transnational experiences are becoming increasingly common (Dreby, 2006).

The role of the child

The role of children encompasses a broad range of behaviors, expectations, and beliefs, as they grow and develop from infancy into adulthood. The role of children in families varies extensively depending on the cultural context, societal expectations, and familial circumstances. For example, some older children assume considerable responsibilities for siblings and work to contribute to their family's financial well-being (Rogoff, 1993; Rogoff, Sellers, Pirotta, Fox, & White, 1975). Most children become siblings, and Dunn (2007) asserts that sibling relationships provide a substantial socialization context.

Changes to parent and child roles—a function of growing up and growing old

The end of adolescence thrusts children into a transitional period, commonly called emerging adulthood (Arnett, 2000). This life stage typically brings many changes to family dynamics as parents and children negotiate changing norms and expectations for themselves and others. The extent and type of parental support given to children may vary extensively as they transition into adulthood. For example, some emerging adults want more financial support than emotional support from their parents as they increasingly rely on friends and partners for the latter. There is also evidence that parental support continues to be influential. McIlvane, Ajrouch, and Antonucci (2007) found that older parents were particularly important sources of support to adult children, especially those who were not married but were raising children. Shulman, Kalnitzki, and Shahar (2009) found that only paternal support predicted positive adaptation in emerging adults, and those perceiving their parents as controlling reported greater difficulties in making decisions (Luyckx, Soenens, Vansteenkiste, Goossens, & Berzonsky, 2007). The influence of role perception on familial processes can be particularly salient as parents and children may hold differing criteria for what constitutes adulthood (Nelson, Padilla-Walker, Carroll, Madsen, Barry, & Badger 2007). The transition to adulthood varies in length, and emerging adulthood is likely related to particular cultures and socioeconomic status (Galambos & Martinez 2007).

Complex and changing family dynamics occur at all points in the lifespan and over the entire family lifecycle. As individual and family dynamics have changed so have the stressful challenges faced by family members. For example, as a result of young people having children later and older people living longer, the middle generation is increasingly "sandwiched" between the other two with caregiving responsibilities or concerns for both generations (Riley & Bowen, 2005).

"Care" takes many forms, from hands-on care of completely dependent elders to providing less intensive forms of instrumental support such as help with transportation or household chores. Similarly, younger people are moving from the dependency of childhood, through adolescence and the increasing independence of young adulthood. Although it is relatively rare for complete dependence in both generations and, at least in the United States, it is not common for the sandwich generation to simultaneously co-reside with dependent children and parents, it is increasingly common for adults in the middle generation to simultaneously provide care for partly dependent adolescent or young adult children and their elderly parents (Grundy & Henretta, 2006), reflecting a lifelong pattern of interdependence among family members.

The role of the grandparent

Increasing lifespan has also led to unprecedented longevity in the grandparent–grandchild relationship. The meaning of the grandparent role varies across contexts and cultures. For example, Sandel and colleagues (2006) conducted a qualitative study examining beliefs regarding the grandmother role in the United States and Taiwan. Euro-American grandmothers believed they served as companions to their grandchildren and opposed providing unsolicited advice. Indeed, the traditional conceptualization of the grandparent role, especially in the United States, calls for few responsibilities, considerable enjoyment, and occasional caregiving. Contrary to the Euro-American grandmothers, Taiwanese grandmothers described their roles as temporary caregivers and disciplinarians to grandchildren, exemplifying clear cultural differences in perception of these family roles.

Although grandparents have always provided some care to their grandchildren, the role of grandparents seems to be expanding in response to circumstances such as parental death or incarceration. Grandparents may serve as primary childcare providers or even legal guardians of their grandchildren. About 6.1 million American children live with grandparents, and 2.5 million grandparents parent their grandchildren (U.S. Census Bureau, 2007).

While most grandparents love their grandchildren and enjoy spending time with them, this expanded grandparent role is often associated with multiple stressors (Dellmann-Jenkins, Blankemeyer, & Olesh, 2002). Grandparents who parent grandchildren report greater stress than their counterparts whose roles are less extensive (Lumpkin, 2007). Aside from the demands of parenting, grandparents are more likely to have health problems due to older age and to report financial struggles due to increased likelihood of being on fixed incomes. However, they also report feelings of self-worth and competence.

The role of grandchildren is less elucidated than that of grandparents. Grandchildren are typically studied indirectly through focusing on grandparenting. Hence, the grandchild role is usually examined in terms of being a recipient of care.

Policy and Societal Influences on the Family

Lifespan development and life-course experiences shape the family and are influenced by multiple factors such as policy, geography, economy, and the society at large. In the United States, the role of parent is influenced by both legal parental status and the rights of biological parents which are upheld and prioritized, while the rights of stepparents, adoptive parents, gay and lesbian parents, and grandparents are more tenuous and less protected (Skinner & Kohler, 2002). Family law in many countries is gendered, biased, and typically in favor of women in Western countries and fathers in Eastern countries (Moghadam, 2004). Similarly, the traditional societal conceptualization of fathers as providers rather than caregivers is evident in the punitive laws regarding child support in the United States (Roy, 2008).

General public policies are also influenced by the life course, although are rarely examined from this perspective (Meyer & Pavalko, 1996). Access to health insurance is commonly shaped by marital and employment status, with access and coverage varying across the life course as one marries, divorces, has children, engages in extensive caregiving, or becomes widowed. Public policies reinforce commonly held societal notions regarding roles and what constitutes a family. For example, a traditional two-parent household bias is apparent in the exclusivity of the legal recognition of parental status (Skinner & Kohler, 2002).

The negotiation and definition of roles is embedded in a larger context that includes the influence of society in a specific time and place. For example, during apartheid, many black South African fathers lived apart from their families due to limited job opportunities in the impoverished urban communities where they resided (Roy, 2008). The emerging global economy continues to reduce the number of job opportunities for many individuals around the world, reshaping roles and family relationships (Kofman, 2004). The global economy has resulted in women from poorer countries being encouraged to leave families behind and accept domestic work in affluent countries (Mattingly, 2001). Grandparents, aunts, uncles, older siblings, and other relatives commonly become primary caregivers of children whose parents migrated for job opportunities usually perceived as a benefit to the entire family since resources are shared (Dreby, 2006). For example, some transnational mothers redefine their roles in terms of their provision of emotional and instrumental support by sending money and providing advice (Hondagneu-Sotelo & Avila, 1997).

On a smaller scale, neighborhood context influences family relations and roles. Specifically, ethnic enclaves provide substantial support, particularly to recent immigrants, by serving as an expression of identity (Mazumdar, Mazumdar, Docuyanan, & McLaughlin, 2000) and a source of social support (Kang, Domanski, & Moon, 2009). For example, 38% of Korean immigrants living among the general population in Arizona reported depression in contrast to 24% of their counterparts living in New York's ethnic enclaves (Kang et al., 2009). Minimal English language proficiency was most predictive of depression. Linguistic isolation may increase reliance on family members for aid in immigrant elders living among non-Korean populations. This situation may increase individual and family stress resulting in higher rates of depression. It is not clear whether this effect is due to differences in age, prior health, or current living conditions.

Cultural values, beliefs, and practices influence who is considered part of the family and individuals' roles within the family, for example, Mexican American families where concept of family often includes extended family members. In general, Mexican Americans co-reside with extended family or live near them to provide daily practical support. Females often provide practical support by helping with household activities or childcare while men work outside the home and help with household maintenance (Sarkisian, Gerena, & Gerstel, 2007).

Family roles are often determined by gender, understanding of which is influenced by values, beliefs, and practices. In Asian cultures, males are often said to be more valuable than females as they perpetuate the family lineage and care for their parents in old age (Tang & Dion, 1999). This responsibility is especially true of the first-born son.

Females are expected to marry and have children (East, 1998) as bearers of culture and traditions. Hence, the value of women is sometimes heightened when the family emigrates because they are central in maintaining the family's connection to the culture of their homeland (Espiritu, 2001). Females also maintain interconnectedness among the family and family networks (Espiritu, 2001). In Latino families, especially peasant families, the eldest daughter cares for her younger siblings (Hondagneu-Sotelo & Avila, 1997).

Religion is an example of a common but varying societal influence. Religion encourages certain family structures and functions and the emergence of roles. Furthermore, some religions influence the family-formation process. For example, in Judaism males are encouraged to marry Jewish females as the religion is matrilineal. In Christian denominations, when a baby is baptized, parents may select two individuals to care for and take responsibility for their child if something happened to them. Godparents are also supposed to provide spiritual guidance to the child throughout their life. Godparents may not already be a family member but as a godparent they have a spiritual connection to the parents and the child. The influence of religion, however, is dependent on the individual, the importance of religion in their lives, and their religious practices (Dollahite, Marks, & Goodman, 2004).

The influence of religion may also vary by culture. In Asian cultures influenced by Confucianism, filial piety is important to family ideologies. Families in these cultures are generally patriarchical and practice traditional family roles. When a female marries she becomes part of her husband's family. When a female marries she also inherits the role of caretaker of her husband's parents (Takagai & Silverstein, 2006). In some cultures, religious figures exemplify role ideals. For example, among Latino/a Catholics, La Virgin de Guadalupe represents the mother who sacrifices everything for her children and faith. La Virgin de Guadalupe serves as a model reinforcing the idea that mothers should be in the home dedicating their time to raising the children and not working outside of the home or concerning themselves with matters not specific to childrearing (Hondagneu-Sotelo & Avila, 1997). Thus, the role of mother in a Latino/a Catholic culture can be a source of conflict, especially in families where financial circumstances require the mother to work outside of the home.

Families, like individuals, are influenced by the broader environment and can take multiple pathways over the lifespan. Policy, geographic location, culture, and religion affect the developmental course of the family and each of its members by shaping family roles, relationships, and legal rights. Each of these can optimize or jeopardize the success of the family and its members.

Conclusions and Implications for Future Directions

As this chapter illustrates, the present time is one of evolving family structures and roles, when lifespan development and life-course experiences are developing and changing with the times. Despite these many important changes, families continue to represent a critical factor in the lives of individuals and the societies within which they live. Our review suggests that families in their many forms will continue to exist well into the future.

The literature also indicates that families provide an important resource that can help members meet the many challenges they face. Nevertheless, they can also be a challenge to their members; rather than providing comfort and care, families can be sources of stress and strain.

There are several implications of these findings. There should be legal and social recognition of the multiple forms that families may take. Variations in structure should not be judged but rather embraced—since often individuals in these nontraditional structures receive care and support similar to the more traditional family forms (e.g., Zheng et al. 2008). Similarly, is the recognition that families, regardless of structure, may cause more harm than good. Both research and media have highlighted how deleterious family outcomes are experienced by families of different structures. Thus, not all families are helpful or supportive, not all families have a positive influence on their members. Policy, custom, and tradition must facilitate recognition and release of individuals from negative family influences.

Multiple family structures and different types of families should be recognized under all circumstances. It is increasingly clear that there is no single path to positive outcomes for the individual or the family. Future research should explore the breadth and depth of the most influential family parameters.

And finally, it is important to think globally, but act locally. By thinking globally we will have greater insights into the multiple influences on the family and its members, and direction on treating local families as they are influenced by immigration and transnational migration patterns. Understanding the family customs and expectations of other cultures will improve our understanding of local families. In sum, future research and policy must recognize and examine the impact of lifespan development and life-course experiences in order to achieve a more comprehensive understanding of the family in its many and evolving forms.

Note

This research was supported in part by grants from the National Institute of Mental Health (MH066876) and the National Institute on Aging (AG030569) to T. C. Antonucci and from the National Institute on Aging (K99AG029879). The authors of this research are fully responsible for its content which does not necessarily reflect the views of National Institute of Aging.

References

Abbott, R. K. (2002). The changing definition of "family" *Compensation & Benefits Report, 16*, 3–4.

Antonucci, T. C., Blieszner, R., & Denmark, F. (2009). Psychological perspectives on older women. In H. Landrine & N. F. Russo (Eds.), *Handbook of diversity in feminist psychology*. New York: Springer.

Arnett, J. J. (2000). Emerging adulthood: A theory of development from the late teens through the twenties. *American Psychologist, 55*, 469–480.

Baltes, P., Lindenberger, U., & Staudinger, U. (2006). Lifespan theory in developmental psychology. In R. M. Lerner (Ed.), *Handbook of child psychology* (6th edn.). *Vol. 1: Theoretical models of human development* (pp. 569–664). New York: Wiley.

Bedford, V. H., & Blieszner, R. (1997). Personal relationships in later-life families. In S. Duck (Ed.), *Handbook of personal relationships* (2nd edn.), (pp. 523–530). Chichester: Wiley.

Bedford, V. H., & Blieszner, R. (2000). Personal relationships in later-life families. In R. M. Milardo & S. Duck (Eds.), *Families as relationships* (pp. 157–174). New York: Wiley.

Blandon, A. Y., & Volling, B. L. (2008). Parental gentle guidance and children's compliance within the family: A replication study. *Journal of Family Psychology, 22*, 355–366.

Bures, R. M. (2009). Living arrangements over the life course: Families in the 21st century. *Journal of Family Issues, 30*, 579–585.

Caldwell, C. H., Wright, J. C., Zimmerman, M. A., Walsemann, K. M., Williams, D., & Ishchei, P. A. C. (2004). Enhancing adolescent health behaviors through strengthening non-resident father–son relationships: A model for intervention with African American families. *Health Education Research, 19*, 644–656.

Caputo, J. (1999). Who is Derrida's Zarathustra? Of fraternity, friendship, and a democracy to come. *Research in Phenomenology, 29*, 184–198.

Caputo, J. (2000). *More radical hermeneutics: On not knowing who we are*. Bloomington: Indiana University Press.

Carlson, M. J., & Corcoran, M. E. (2001). Family structure and children's behavioral and cognitive outcomes. *Journal of Marriage and Family, 63*, 779–792.

Centers for Disease Control and Prevention, (2000). Achievements in public health, 1900–1999: Family planning. *Journal of the American Medical Association, 283*(3), 326–331.

Cicirelli, V. G. (1994). Sibling relationships in cross-cultural perspective. *Journal of Marriage and the Family, 56*, 7–20.

Cicirelli, V. G. (2006). Siblings. In R. Schulz (Ed.), *The encyclopedia of aging* (4th edn., Vol. *2*, pp. 1072–1075). New York: Springer.

Clark, L. A., Kochanskia, G., & Ready, R. (2000). Mothers' personality and its interaction with child temperament as predictors of parenting behavior. *Journal of Personality and Social Psychology, 79*, 274–285.

Crawford, J. M. (1999). Co-parent adoption by same-sex couples: From loophole to law. *Families in Society, 80*, 271–278.

Dellmann-Jenkins, M., Blankemeyer, M., & Olesh, M. (2002). Adults in expanded grandparent roles: Considerations for practice, policy, and research. *Educational Gerontology, 28*, 219–235.

Dollahite, D. C., Marks, L. D., & Goodman, M. (2004). Religiosity and families: Relational and spiritual linkages in a diverse and dynamic cultural context. In M. J. Coleman & L. H. Ganong (Eds.), *The handbook of contemporary families* (pp. 411–431). Thousand Oaks, CA: Sage.

Dreby, J. (2006). Honor and virtue: Mexican parenting in the transnational context. *Gender and Society, 20*, 32–59.

Dunn, J. (2007). Siblings and socialization. In J. E. Grusec & P. D. Hastings,(Eds.), *Handbook of socialization: Theory and research* (pp. 309–327). New York: Guilford Press.

Dykstra, P.A. & de Jong-Gierveld, J. (2004). Gender and marital-history differences in emotional and social loneliness among Dutch older adults. *Canadian Journal on Aging/La Revue canadienne du vieillissement, 23*, 141–155.

East, P. L. (1998). Racial and ethnic difference in girls' sexual, marital, and birth expectations. *Journal of Marriage and the Family, 60*, 150–162.

Elder, G. H., Jr., & Shanahan, M. J. (2005). The life course and human development. In R. M. Lerner (Ed.), *Handbook of child psychology* (6th edn.). *Vol. 1: Theoretical models of human development* (pp. 665–715). New York: Wiley.

Espiritu, Y. L. (2001). We don't sleep around like white girls do: Family, culture, and gender in Filipina American lives. *Signs: Journal of Women in Culture and Society, 26*, 415–440.

Fuligni, A., Tseng, V., & Lam, M. (1999). Attitudes toward family obligations among American adolescents with Asian, Latin American, and European backgrounds. *Child Development, 70*, 1030–1044.

Fuller-Iglesias, H., Smith, J., & Antonucci, T. C. (2010). Theoretical perspectives on lifespan and life course development. In T. C. Antonucci & J. S. Jackson (Eds.), *Annual Review of Gerontology and Geriatrics*. New York: Springer.

Galambos, N. L., & Martinez, M. L. (2007). Poised for emerging adulthood in Latin America: A pleasure for the privileged. *Child Development Perspectives, 1*, 109–114.

Goldscheider, F., Hofferth, S., Spearin, C., & Curtin, S. (2009). Fatherhood across two generations: Factors affecting early family roles. *Journal of Family Issues, 30*, 586–604.

Grundy, E., & Henretta, J. C. (2006). Between elderly parents and adult children: A new look at the intergenerational care provided by the "sandwich generation." *Ageing & Society, 26*, 707–722.

Hetherington, M., Bridges, M., & Insabella, G. (1998). What matters? What does not? Five perspectives on the association between marital transitions and children's adjustment. *American Psychologist, 53*, 167–184.

Hondagneu-Sotelo, P., & Avila, E. (1997). I'm here, but I'm there: The meaning of Latina transnational motherhood. *Gender & Society, 11*, 548–571.

Horton, S. (2009). A mother's heart is weighted down with stones: A phenomenological approach to the experience of transnational motherhood. *Culture, Medicine, and Psychiatry, 33*, 21–40.

Hughes, D., Rodriguez, J., Smith, E. P., Johnson, D. J., Stevenson, H. C., & Spicer, P. (2006). Parents' ethnic-racial socialization practices: A review of research and directions for future study. *Developmental Psychology, 42*, 747–770.

Ishii-Kuntz, M. (1997). Intergenerational relationships among Chinese, Japanese, and Korean Americans. *Family Relations, 46*, 23–32.

Kang, S., Domanski, M. D., & Moon, S. S. (2009). Ethnic enclave resources and predictors of depression among Arizona's Korean immigrant elders. *Journal of Gerontological Social Work, 52*, 489–502.

Kim, J., & Ward, L. M. (2007). Silence speaks volumes: Parental sexual communication among Asian American emerging adults. *Journal of Adolescent Research, 22*, 3–31.

Kofman, E. (2004). Gendered global migrations. *International Feminist Journal of Politics, 6*, 643–665.

Lowenstein, A. (2002). Solidarity and conflicts in co-residence of three-generational immigrant families from the former Soviet Union. *Journal of Aging Studies, 16*, 221–241.

Lumpkin, J. R. (2007). Grandparents in a parental or near-parental role: Sources of stress and coping mechanisms. *Journal of Family Issues, 29*, 357–372.

Luyckx, K., Soenens, B., Vansteenkiste, M., Goossens, L., & Berzonsky, M. D. (2007). Parental psychological control and dimensions of identity formation in emerging adulthood. *Journal of Family Psychology, 21*, 546–550.

Marks, S. R., Huston, T. L., Johnson, E. M., & MacDermid, S. M. (2001). Role balance among white married couples. *Journal of Marriage and Family, 63*, 1083–1098.

Mattingly, D. J. (2001). The home and the world: Domestic service and international networks of caring labor. *Annals of the Association of American Geographers, 91*, 370–386.

Mazumdar, S., Mazumdar, S., Docuyanan, F., & McLaughlin, C. M. (2000). Creating a sense of place: Vietnamese-Americans and Little Saigon. *Journal of Environmental Psychology*, 2000, 319–333.

McIlvane, J. M., Ajrouch, K. J., & Antonucci, T. C. (2007). Generational structures and social resources in mid-life: Influences on health and well-being. *Journal of Social Issues*, *63*, 759–773.

Meyer, M. H., & Pavalko, E. K. (1996). Family, work, and access to health insurance among mature women. *Journal of Health and Social Behavior*, *37*, 311–325.

Moghadam, V. M. (2004). Patriarchy in transition: Women and the changing family in the Middle East. *Journal of Comparative Family Studies*, *35*, 137–162.

Muraco, A. (2006). Intentional families: Fictive kin ties between cross-gender, different sexual orientation friends. *Journal of Marriage and Family*, *68*, 1313–1325.

Nelson, L. J., Padilla-Walker, L. M., Carroll, J. S., Madsen, S. D., Barry, C. M., & Badger, S. (2007). "If you want me to treat you like an adult, start acting like one!" Comparing the criteria that emerging adults and their parents have for adulthood. *Journal of Family Psychology*, *21*, 665–674.

Perrone, K. M. (2009). Traditional and nontraditional work and family roles for women and men. *Journal of Career Development*, *36*, 3–7.

Riley, L. D., & Bowen, C. (2005). The sandwich generation: Challenges and coping strategies of multigenerational families. *The Family Journal*, *13*, 52–58.

Rogoff, B. (1993). Children's guided participation and participatory appropriation in sociocultural activity. In R. Wozniak & K. Fischer (Eds.), *Development in context: Acting and thinking in specific environments*, (pp. 121–153). Hillsdale, NJ: Erlbaum.

Rogoff, B., Sellers, M. J., Pirotta, S., Fox, N., & White, S. H. (1975). Age assignment of roles and responsibilities to children: A cross-cultural survey. *Human Development*, *18*, 353–369.

Rothausen, T. J. (1999). "Family" in organizational research: A review and comparison of definitions and measures. *Journal of Organizational Behavior*, *20*, 817–836.

Roy, K. (2008) A life course perspective on fatherhood and family policies in the United States and South Africa. *Fathering*, *6*, 92–112.

Sandel, T. L., Cho, G. E., Miller, P. J., & Wang, S. (2006). What it means to be a grandmother: A cross-cultural study of Taiwanese and Euro-American grandmothers' beliefs. *Journal of Family Communication*, *64*, 255–278.

Sarkisian, N., Gerena, M., & Gerstel, N. (2007). Extended family integration among European and Mexican Americans: Ethnicity, gender, and class. *Journal of Marriage and Family*, *69*, 40–54.

Shulman, S., Kalnitzki, E., & Shahar, G. (2009). Meeting developmental challenges during emerging adulthood: The role of personality and social resources. *Journal of Adolescent Research*, *24*, 242–267.

Skinner, D. A., & Kohler, J. K. (2002). Parental rights in diverse family contexts: Current legal developments. *Family Relations*, *51*, 293–300.

Smith, A., Lalonde, R. N., & Johnson, S. (2004). Serial migration and its implications for the parent–child relationship: A retrospective analysis of the experiences of the children of Caribbean immigrants. *Cultural Diversity and Ethnic Minority Psychology*, *10*, 107–122.

Sroufe, L. A., Egeland, B., Carlson, E., & Collins, W. A. (2005). *The development of the person: The Minnesota study of risk and adaptation from birth to adulthood.* New York: Guilford Press.

Takagai, E., & Silverstein, M. (2006). Intergenerational co-residence of the Japanese elderly: Are cultural norms proactive or reactive? *Research on Aging*, *28*, 473–492.

Tang, T. N., & Dion, K. L. (1999). Gender and acculturation in relation to traditionalism: Perceptions of self and parents among Chinese students. *Sex Roles 41*, 17–29.

Teachman, J. D., Tedrow, L. M., & Crowder, K. D. (2000). The changing demography of America's families. *Journal of Marriage and Family, 62*(4), 1234–1246.

U. S. Census Bureau, (2007). Facts for features: Grandparents' Day 2008. Retrieved March 28, 2010, from www.census.gov/PressRelease/www/releases/archives/facts_for_features_special_editions/012095.html.

Volling, B. L., McElwain, N. L., Notaro, P. C., & Herrera, C. (2002). Parents' emotional availability and infant emotional competence: Predictors of parent–infant attachment and emerging self-regulation. *Journal of Family Psychology, 16*, 447–465.

Weigel, D. J., Bennett, K. K., & Ballard-Reisch, D. S. (2006). Roles and influence in marriages: Both spouses; perceptions contribute to marital commitment. *Family and Consumer Sciences Research Journal, 35*, 74–92.

Wong, B. P. (2007). Immigration, globalization, and the Chinese American family. In J. E. Lansford & K. Deater-Deckard (Eds.), *Immigrant families in contemporary society*, (pp. 212–228). New York: Guilford Press.

Yakushko, O., & Espin, O. M. (2009). The experience of immigrant and refugee women: Psychological issues. In H. Landrine & N. F. Russo (Eds.), *Handbook of diversity in feminist psychology*. New York: Springer.

Yodanis, C., & Lauer, S. (2007). Managing money in marriage: Multilevel and cross-national effects of the breadwinner role. *Journal of Marriage and Family, 69*, 1307–1325.

Zheng, W., Feng, H., & Schimmele, C. M. (2008). Family structure and children's psychosocial outcomes. *Journal of Family Issues, 29*, 1625–1649.

5

Parents and Adolescents

Challenges and Misconceptions

Ross B. Wilkinson

One of the downsides of being a psychologist, and particularly a clinical psychologist like myself, is that you tend to develop a problem-oriented view of human development and behavior. Essentially you are on the lookout for how people might be unhappy, dissatisfied, "maladjusted," or in conflict with the world around them. In other words, how people might be in trouble. Of course this focus comes from a desire to help these people and try to find solutions to their problems. Nevertheless, this approach can generate a negative view of people and their relationships.

Psychologists are not alone in this approach. Other professions like medicine and law, although dealing with different spheres of human activity, are also very focused on locating potential problems. The media, arguably the most influential of all professional groups, are clearly primarily interested in the trials and tribulations that beset the unfortunate because that is what seems to get the public's attention. There are the tidbits of "good" news that are occasionally sprinkled through the newspaper or on the evening television. However, the prime stuff of media reporting and commentary, and this is particularly true with respect to teenagers, seems centered on trouble, bad behavior, and conflict.

The central contention of this chapter is that a predominantly negative and unbalanced view of adolescence and adolescents is promulgated by both the experts, like myself, and by the media. Given that there are approximately one billion individuals in their second decade of life worldwide (Larson & Wilson, 2004), the scale of this issue has some context.

The Wiley-Blackwell Handbook of Couples and Family Relationships, First Edition.
Edited by Patricia Noller and Gery C. Karantzas.

The problems that adolescents do experience, which can be significant for some, may to a large extent be generated by what they see and experience in the relationships around them. While there is a popular tendency to see adolescents as the "problem," it may be that what is happening in their families and their communities is the real problem.

For as long as I have been studying adolescents and young adults there has been a consistent and pessimistic view of them presented in the media in Australia. Thinking back over the past years I can easily recall a long list of "what is wrong with teenagers today." Implicit in this view is that it is adolescents who are at fault and action needs to be taken to "fix" them. Some of their faults that have been the focus of recent attention include:

- They are lazy—there are plenty of jobs out there but they just won't work.
- They are fat—everybody knows there is an obesity epidemic.
- They are illiterate—employers frequently report that young people today can't read and write properly.
- They are alcoholics and drug-crazed—the culture of binge drinking and drug abuse is out of control with young people.
- They are obsessive—teenagers are addicted to their cell phones, and to the Internet.
- They are antisocial risk takers—there is an epidemic of gang violence and dangerous driving.
- They are criminal—the crime rates are rising and it is mostly teenagers at fault.
- They are promiscuous—underage sex and teen pregnancy are rampant.
- They are neurotic and self-obsessed—the rising rates of anxiety and depression in adolescents are because they are self-centered.
- They are oppositional and difficult—they just won't listen to parents and authorities!

Of course it is simplistic to blame the media for this overly negative portrayal because they do largely present what the public wants to hear. This propensity to view adolescence in a negative light, I believe, is really driven by a confirmation bias. Essentially the common view of adolescence—shared by many experts, the media, and the general community—that has emerged in Western societies over the last century is that they are "trouble" and parents can expect them to be difficult, rebellious, oppositional, moody, and downright unpleasant (Stuart, 2007). Thus, we look for evidence to support that view and tend to overlook, or at least only pay transient attention to, information that doesn't support such a perception.

Two Views of Adolescence

At this point I am going to focus on the social and psychological research on adolescence in order to demonstrate our unbalanced view of this important life stage. A number of leading researchers and theoreticians (e.g., Collins & Laursen, 2004) think that there are really two views of adolescence. The first, and dominant view, is that adolescence is really a pathological state. Adolescents are mentally, socially, and emotionally deficient and the period of adolescence is characterized by emotional upheaval, conflict, and distress. The alternative view, that is increasingly gaining ground, is that adolescence is essentially normal, healthy, adaptive change in the face of major biological, social, and environmental challenges.

The "storm and stress" of adolescence

The idea that adolescence is a dark period of life characterized by conflict and distress is well established in both lay and professional beliefs about the transition from childhood to adulthood. G. Stanley Hall (1904) was one of the first influential social researchers to emphasize the tumultuous and transitional nature of adolescence and to encourage the view that adolescence is characterized by "storm and stress." This view fitted well with emerging psychoanalytic models which focused on the extent to which developmental maturation (physical, social, emotional, and cognitive) generates inherently unstable and turbulent interpersonal relationships, particularly in relation to primary caregivers (Collins & Laursen, 2004).

Freudian-based approaches, for example, focused on how biological changes in the sexual system generate intrapsychic conflicts that result in adolescent–parent conflict (Freud, 1949). Later psychoanalytic formulations (e.g., Blos, 1979) focused more on the adolescent's drive to achieve ego identity and autonomy than on conflicts driven by emerging sexuality and impulse-control issues. Nevertheless, conflict remains the central theme of pronouncements about adolescents. Even though subsequent researchers may not be strictly psychoanalytic in approach, the emphasis to a large extent has remained on the conflict and pathology of adolescence.

Erikson's framework of lifespan development (Erikson, 1968) contains within it arguably the most influential theory of adolescent identity development. Erikson essentially encouraged the view that adolescence is a period of "crisis" and he conceptualized the key developmental crisis of adolescence as identity achievement versus identity confusion. Identity refers to a stable sense of self, incorporating values and attitudes. Identity confusion, on the other hand, is the struggle to develop a coherent and integrated sense of self, with challenges in committing to roles, values, and people. The development of a coherent sense of self, however, is seen as a crucial developmental task and when it is not met, identity disturbance may lead to delinquency, difficulty in interpersonal relationships, or psychopathology.

Of particular interest here is Erikson's second major developmental task for adolescence: intimacy versus isolation (Erikson, 1968). Again this task is frequently described as a "crisis"—this time involving the relation of the self to intimate others. The need for the development of stable and committed personal relationships is seen as competing with the desire for social withdrawal and the avoidance of commitment. This conflict is argued as manifesting in the separation–individuation dilemma that generates much of the interpersonal conflict that supposedly characterizes the teenage years.

But is adolescence really typified by crisis? Smetana, Campione-Barr, and Metzger (2006) argue that this negative view of adolescence has persisted despite more than 30 years of overwhelming evidence to the contrary. In fact, they argue that active rejection of adult values, and extreme alienation from parental and authority figures are the exception and not the norm for adolescence. They point out that only between 5–15% of adolescents, depending on the particular study, report high degrees of emotional distress and relationships with parents characterized by extreme conflict. The evidence is also clear that, even when adolescents do have problems, these difficulties usually first emerged prior to the onset of adolescence (Collins & Laursen, 2004; Steinberg, 1990). In other words, adolescents build on their pre-adolescent experience, especially with regard to relationships with parents.

The continuity–discontinuity dialectic

Contemporary theoretical efforts have sought to conceptualize and present a more balanced view of the transition into adulthood. These approaches have focused on the fact that the parent–adolescent bond endures and that adolescence can be viewed as a period of functional adaptation rather than pathological interaction (Collins & Laursen, 2004). Recent evolutionary (Belsky, Steinberg, & Draper, 1991) and developmental (Collins, 1995; Selman, 1980; Smetana, 1988) approaches have emphasized the transformational nature of adolescence while acknowledging the evidence supporting both the conflict and longer term rapprochement in the relationship.

Attachment theory formulations, which consider the role of intimate relationships across the lifespan, have also been focused on adolescence as a period that reflects both relationship continuity and transformation (Allen & Land, 1999; Bowlby, 1997; Hazan & Zeifman 1994). As the adolescent develops cognitively and emotionally, the parent–adolescent relationship is modified by the adolescent's ability to reciprocate in caregiving (Youniss & Smollar, 1985) and the extension of their network of attachment relationships (Goh & Wilkinson, 2009). Nevertheless, through adolescence and into young adulthood it is clear that parents, and mothers in particular, remain important sources of security and support that enable the adolescent to build and explore their social environments (Markiewicz, Lawford, Doyle, & Haggart, 2006).

The continuity of parent–adolescent relationship qualities is further evidenced by the impact that representations of attachment relationships, developed in infancy, still have on children through adolescence and into adulthood (Becker-Stoll & Fremmer-Bombik, 1997).

Collins and Laursen (2004) make the point that the dialectic between continuity and discontinuity is a feature of the parent–child relationship throughout childhood and adolescence and into early adulthood. It may further be argued that, via the representation of early attachment relationships in cognitive "working models," this dynamic is played out through our entire lives (Bowlby, 1989).

A feature of these more contemporary views is that they accept that some degree of parent–child conflict will occur and place it within a context of relationship transformation rather than just identity achievement. For authors such as Collins (1995) this conflict may center on the adolescent's and parents' experience of the violation of expectancies about the relationship and then subsequent realignment of those expectations. From an attachment perspective, the conflict can arise as the adolescent widens their exploration of the social environment further away from the "secure base" of the family and the transfer of attachment functions to those outside the family begins to accelerate (Hazan & Zeifman, 1994; Markiewicz et al., 2006). That adolescent relationships with parents are frequently characterized by low to moderate level conflict involving bickering and disagreements over everyday issues is not disputed. In fact, this level of conflict is seen as healthy, transient, and part of the transformation of the parent–adolescent relationship (Collins & Laursen, 2004). Evidence suggests that moderate levels of conflict with parents are linked to better adjustment than either no conflict or frequent, high level conflict (Adams & Laursen, 2001; Grotevant & Cooper, 1986) and does not affect the subsequent quality of parent–adolescent relationships (Smetana, Metzger, & Campione-Barr, 2004).

Adolescent–parent conflicts, however, should also be considered in the context that longitudinal research demonstrates that individuals do experience an increase in negative mood states as they negotiate adolescence, although by late adolescence this increase in negative mood appears to stabilize (Larson, Moneta, Richards, & Wilson, 2002). Further, theoretical models and empirical evidence support the view that it is normal to expect that the warmth and closeness of the child–parent relationship will diminish during adolescence (Buhrmester & Furman, 1987; Conger & Ge, 1999; Furman & Buhrmester, 1985, 1992). Fortunately for parents, there is also evidence to indicate that at least some of that former closeness is normally regained in late adolescence to early adulthood (Dubas & Petersen, 1996; Wilkinson, 2010a).

Are Adolescent–Parental Relationships Really So Problematic?

Certainly parent–adolescent relationships are not without their problems for many families, but as far back as the late 1960s researchers were questioning the view that adolescents had *predominantly* poor relationships with their parents (Kandel & Lesser, 1969). More recently, reports from a number of longitudinal studies have argued that the general perception that adolescents do not value their parental relationships does not reflect adolescents' actual attitudes. Smart, Sanson, and Toumbourou (2008), reporting on data from the Australian Temperament Project, found that most adolescents reported positive relationships with their parents. Hair, Moore, Hadley, Kaye, Day, & Orthner (2009a), reporting on data from the U.S. National Longitudinal Study of Youth, found that positive parent–adolescent relationships are significantly more common than negative relationships.

On the other hand, it is understandable that parents feel somewhat concerned about the relationship, as there is evidence that the way children communicate with parents changes as they move into adolescence, and that adolescents engage in less communication with parents during teenage years (Collins & Laursen, 2004). This situation may not be a significant indicator of relationship strain, however, as the majority of teenagers still feel they can talk to their parents about personal concerns (Prior, Sanson, Smart, & Oberklaid, 2000) and turn to their parents, particularly their mothers, when they face significant difficulties (Wilkinson, 2010a).

Complicating matters, evidence also indicates that to some extent parents and adolescents experience conflict in their relationships in quite different ways (Noller, 1994). Adolescents are thought to more accurately evaluate negative interactions with their parents than their parents do (Collins & Laursen, 2004). Steinberg (2001) has found that parents, and particularly mothers, tend to underestimate the frequency of conflict but overestimate its severity. Collins and Laursen (2004) argue that parent–child reports of conflict tend to converge in later adolescence suggesting that disagreements are an important part of both communication and the renegotiating of relationships in the family system.

In terms of relationship satisfaction from the adolescent's perspective, there is extensive research over the past five decades indicating that adolescents sampled from the community are generally satisfied with their relationships with their parents. Around 75% of adolescents report high quality relationships with their parents (Douvan & Adelson, 1966; Kandel & Lesser, 1972; Offer, 1969; Rutter, Graham, Chadwick, & Yule, 1976). More recently, Moore, Guzman, Hair, Lippman, and Garrett (2004) found that adolescents, aged 14 to 17 years, who lived with both parents generally reported positive relationships with their parents (Figure 5.1). Results were quite similar for attitudes towards both mothers and fathers. While adolescents were quite strongly positive in their attitudes towards their parents there was a lower tendency to endorse the view that they would want to be like them, perhaps reflecting the adolescent drive for autonomy. Overall, more than four out of five adolescents agreed or strongly agreed that they thought highly of their

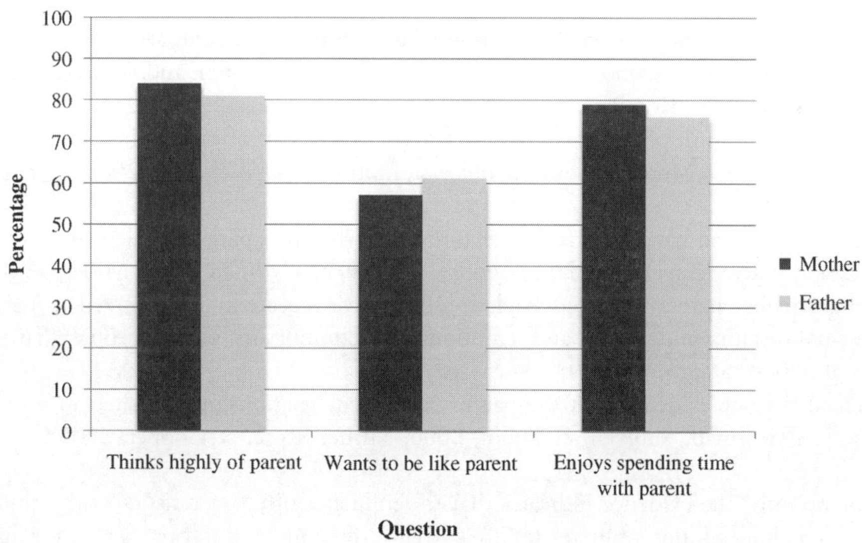

Figure 5.1 Percentage of respondents endorsing positive attitudes towards parents
Source: Based on figure in "Parent-teen relationships and interactions: Far more positive than not," by Kristin A. Moore, Lina Guzman, Elizabeth Hair, Laura Lippman, and Sarah Garrett. Child *Trends Research Brief*, December 2004. Figures 1 and 2, pages 1–2. Retrieved from www.child-trends.org/Files//Child_Trends-2004_12_01_RB_ParentTeen.pdf. doi:2004-25

mother and father and over 75% agreed or strongly agreed that they liked spending time with their mother and father. It is noteworthy that in blended families, however, there was a clear preference for biological rather than stepparents.

Why do Parent–Adolescent Relationships Matter?

Adolescence is perhaps the greatest risk period for the development of psychological disorder (Australian Bureau of Statistics, 2007a) and mental health problems are the leading cause of disability among those aged 15 to 24 years (Australian Institute of Health and Welfare, 2008). Suicide is the now the second leading cause of death for adolescents (Australian Institute of Health and Welfare, 2008) and there is evidence that the incidence of depression for this age group has steadily increased over the last 10 years (Australian Bureau of Statistics, 2007a).

In trying to understand how these significant risks may be reduced, it is crucial to appreciate that the evidence with regard to the link between the quality of relationships with parents and adolescent social, psychological, and health outcomes is substantial and compelling (Collins & Laursen, 2004; Steinberg & Silk, 2002). Importantly the outcomes relate very strongly to those issues that have been identified as the "problem" with adolescents. While a full survey of the literature in this area is beyond the scope of this chapter, below I have highlighted some of the relevant research and its link to social "panics."

- There is substantial evidence that positive relationships with parents are associated with decreased risk of substance use including both drugs and alcohol, and tobacco (Parker & Benson, 2004; Resnick et al., 1997).
- Positive relationships with parents are linked to less risk of criminal or delinquent behaviors (Hair, Moore, Garrett, Kinukawa, Lippman, & Michelson, 2005; Parker & Benson, 2004).
- Adolescents who have high quality relationships with their parents are less likely to be sexually active (Kaye, Day, Hair, Moore, Hadley, & Orthner, 2008; Miller, 1998).
- High quality parent–adolescent relationships have repeatedly been linked to better mental health, and social and emotional functioning in young people (Sawyer et al., 2000; Steinberg, 2001).
- There is some evidence that the parent–adolescent relationship is related to obesity issues (Crossman, Sullivan, & Benin, 2006; Turner, Rose, & Cooper, 2005).

Importantly, the evidence indicates that the influence of characteristics of the child–parent relationship not only relates to current functioning but can carry over into adulthood. Umberson (1992), for example, found that better quality adult child–parent relationships have been associated with lower levels of psychological distress among both adult children and parents. Close relationships with parents during childhood and adolescence have been positively associated with adult children's self-esteem, happiness, and life satisfaction (Amato, 1994). Positive mental and physical health in adulthood has also been positively associated with recollections of early parental support (Shaw, Krause, Chatters, Connell, & Ingersoll-Dayton, 2004).

Adolescent–Parent Attachment

An important aspect of the parent–adolescent relationship that appears to have significant implications for psychological health and adjustment is attachment security. Over the last 20 years, attachment theory has become one of the central theoretical paradigms for understanding relationships and their implications (Cassidy & Shaver, 2008) and a body of research has emerged focused specifically on adolescence. This literature is substantial and growing rapidly, although it is not entirely theoretically or methodologically cohesive. While a complete review is beyond this chapter, I will focus specifically on aspects of my own research that have been centrally concerned with the link between adolescents' parental attachments and psychological health and adjustment.

Over 10 years of our research program at the Australian National University, examining adolescent–parental attachment with over 3000 adolescents, we have shown that only around 25% report any significant dissatisfaction with their relationship with their parents. When the full range of attachment scores are examined, links between the quality of relationships and psychological outcomes, particularly depression, are apparent. Wilkinson and Walford (2001), in a study of late adolescents, found that parental attachment predicted psychological well-being and distress after controlling for personality and life events. In a series of three studies Wilkinson (2004) found that parental attachment predicted both depression and self-esteem in Australian and Norwegian adolescents. Wilkinson and Kraljevic (2008) found further support for the relationship between adolescent depression and parental attachment but failed to find the predicted relationship between parental attachment and adolescent attitudes towards school.

Wilkinson and Parry (2004), in a study of attachment styles, parental attachment, and psychological outcomes, found that both secure and dismissing attachment styles were associated with higher quality of attachment to parents. By measuring attachment to mothers and fathers separately, they also found that even after controlling for attachment style, maternal attachment, but not father attachment, was associated with higher self-esteem. Wilkinson (2006) found age and gender differences in the impact of parental attachment relationships on psychological health in adolescents. The impact of maternal attachment on self-esteem was higher for younger adolescents and there was also some evidence of the same effect for paternal attachment. Importantly both maternal and paternal attachment were linked to depression and this relationship seemed to be stable across the adolescent age groups (13 to 18 years of age). However, there was a nonsignificant trend for the strength of this relationship to be lower for older adolescents. There was also clear evidence supporting a gender identification effect in that maternal attachment was a stronger predictor of psychological adjustment for girls while paternal attachment was a stronger predictor of psychological adjustment for boys. Finally, Wilkinson (2010b), in a study of 13 to 19 year olds, found that both maternal and paternal attachment predicted depression and self-esteem. However, maternal but not paternal attachment predicted school attitude.

This later research is consistent with the finding that relationships with mothers and fathers differ in both quality and importance with regard to adolescent outcomes. A number of studies have demonstrated that across ages, adolescents are generally closer to their mother than to their father (Buhrmester & Furman 1987; Noller, Feeney, Darlington, & Rogers, 2008) and spend more time in direct interaction with their mother (Larson & Richards, 1994). Adolescents also disclose more private issues like dating and sexual attitudes and information with mothers than with fathers (Larson & Richards, 1994; Noller & Callan, 1990). There are clear differences between mothers and fathers with respect to involvement in parenting tasks with adolescents (Paulson & Sputa 1996) and also with respect to the adolescents' perceptions of relationship quality (Wilkinson, 2006).

Challenges

Given the demonstrated importance of parent–adolescent relationships in terms of their association with a raft of risk factors and negative outcomes, factors that threaten those relationships are obvious challenges to adolescent well-being that need to be considered. Arguably the single biggest threat is the dramatic structural changes that have taken place regarding the nature of family composition and duration in recent decades (see chapters 1, 2, 4, 6 in this volume). Although much of the following discussion will focus on the situation in Australia, many of the same trends are evident in other developed, Western countries. There are a number of demographic trends that, when considered together, are the cause of considerable concern. The major issues are: the high proportion of marriage failure; the increase in cohabitation rather than marriage, which has a concomitant higher rate of breakdown; and the increased proportion of adolescents raised in sole-parent families (Australian Bureau of Statistics, 2010).

In terms of the population context in Australia, we know that marriage rates are declining while cohabitation rates are increasing (see chapter 1 in this volume; Qu & Weston 2008). The crude marriage rate (per 1,000) over the last three decades decreased from 7.2 in 1978 to 5.5 in 2006 (Australian Bureau of Statistics, 2007b). Over the same period, the percentage of births outside of marriages has nearly tripled from 11.5% to 32.7% of all births. Australian Bureau of Statistics (2007b) data indicate that there are 1.1 million families in Australia with children aged between 12 and 18 years and that, somewhat alarmingly, 25% are sole-parent families. The percentage of children under 15 years of age living in one-parent families has increased from 14.4% in 1992 to 19.5% in 2006. Sweeper (chapter 24 in this volume) has highlighted the fact that in Australia 50% of all divorces involve children under 18, that there were 44,371 children affected by divorce in 2007, and that up to a third of these children can expect their parents to remain in high conflict.

Family dissolution and outcomes

There is extensive evidence associating family dissolution and single-parent family status with significant problems in adolescent outcomes, although the causal paths are not necessarily clear. In straight demographic terms, the prevalence of significant mental-health problems in children and adolescents are double for those living in step- or blended families and single-parent families compared to those living in the original family unit (Sawyer et al., 2000, Table 5.1). Australian studies show that parental divorce is associated with multiple problems in both adolescence and adulthood including poor academic achievement, low self-esteem, psychological distress, delinquency, recidivism, substance use, sexual precocity, depression, and suicidal behavior (chapter 9 in this volume; Evans, Kelley, & Wanner, 2001; Heckel, Clarke, Barry, McCarthy, & Selikowitz 2009; Rodgers, 1996).

In a meta-analysis of the international literature on the effects of divorce on adjustment, Amato and Keith (1991) found that there were modest differences between intact and divorced families in terms of adolescent outcomes in the domains of academic achievement, conduct, psychological adjustment, self-concept, and parent–child relationships. However, in a later meta-analytic review of studies conducted in the 1990s, Amato (2001) found evidence of an increasing gap in well-being between children from intact and divorced families. Further, he points out that this relative decline compared to the decade of the 1980s occurred despite the growth of school-based interventions, parenting classes for divorcing parents, and divorce mediation.

This effect, however, may be due to poor relationships between parents rather than simple marital status. Noller et al. (2008), for example, found that the adolescents with the lowest levels of adjustment were those whose families were divorced and high in conflict. Hair et al.'s (2009b) examination of the U.S. Longitudinal Survey of Youth data indicated that adolescents in families experiencing poor marital quality were worse off on physical health, mental health, and substance-use indicators. When parents had poor relationships with each other and the adolescent had poor relationships with the parents their situation was even worse. By contrast, adolescents whose parents had a high quality relationship and who had good relationships with both parents consistently had the best outcomes. Hair et al. (2009b) concluded that, overall, relationship quality between parents and between the adolescents and their parents were key predictors of psychological and physical health and substance use.

Table 5.1 Prevalence (%) of Mental Health Problems by Family Type

Mental health	*Original family*		*Step/Blended family*		*Sole-parent family*	
	Males	*Females*	*Males*	*Females*	*Males*	*Females*
Internalizing problems	12.1	9.0	23.0	13.5	20.4	19.5
Externalizing problems	9.5	9.8	23.9	19.9	21.4	24.7
Total problems	11.3	10.7	25.0	19.7	22.2	26.7

Source: Adapted from Sawyer et al. (2000). *Mental health of young people in Australia.* Canberra: Mental Health and Special Programs Branch, Commonwealth Department of Health and Aged Care

Smetana et al. (2006) have argued that structural changes in the family, like divorce and remarriage, lead to a temporary disruption of adolescent–parent relationships, including increased conflict, particularly in the first two years following a divorce and with the new stepparent (Hetherington & Kelly, 2002). However, the evidence of the effects of parental relationship breakdown on the parent–adolescent relationship is somewhat mixed. Collins and Larsen (2004) argue, contrary to Smetana et al.'s (2006) view, that on balance there is no clear evidence that divorce impacts negatively on mother–adolescent relationships in the first few years. However, in their study, Noller et al. (2008) found that there was more conflict experienced in divorcing than married families for all the family members. Interestingly, from an attachment point of view, the impact of negative relationships with the noncustodial father appears to be more severe and more long-lasting, affecting adjustment and relationships even decades later (Burns & Dunlop, 1998; Hetherington, 1999).

Conclusion

Collins and Laursen (2004) argue that of all aspects of adolescent development it is the parent–adolescent relationship that has largely driven both the public and research agenda. Further, it seems that there is a preoccupation with the negative aspects of adolescence that some individuals experience and a tendency to see those problems as representative of adolescence in general. The public perception of adolescence, reinforced by both media coverage and influential psychological and social theories of development, has focused on conflict and the supposed tumult of the transition from child to adult. The bulk of empirical evidence, however, simply does not support the view that adolescents are either rejecting of parents or experience extreme conflict in their relationships with them. Adolescents, who are negotiating the complex tasks of developing autonomy and individuation, generally report high satisfaction with their relationships with parents. Conflict certainly does occur, but this conflict is typically not extreme and represents positive growth and the renegotiating of the child–parent bond. It is normative for this bond to evolve, and changes in this relationship represent neither a "crisis" nor pathology.

The literature is clear that relationships with parents matter to teenagers throughout adolescence and into early adulthood. It appears that it is when these relationships begin to fail that adolescents become at increased risk of all those problems that are of significant concern to society. There is no question that there are major challenges for many adolescents with regard to mental health and social adjustment. However, frequently associated with these problems are poor relationships with parents and, importantly, a poor relationship between parents. The evidence with regard to the higher incidence of problems for adolescents who come from families in which there is high conflict between parents and/or a breakdown of the marital relationship is compelling. Further, there is evidence that adolescents from single-parent households are also at increased risk and that the number of such households is increasing.

It appears to me that the positive aspects of adolescence as a period of growth, transformation, opportunity, and learning have largely been ignored in favor of a culture of complaint against the younger generation. To some extent I believe that this is a result of a failure on behalf of social scientists to communicate the evidence with regard to teenagers and their relationships. If there is prejudice, then it needs to be combated with education about this evidence targeted at policy makers who need to be convinced that a multilevel approach should to be taken that involves intervention, education, and prevention. While adolescents who are in difficulty need to be assisted directly, the evidence also indicates that programs aimed at enhancing the quality of parent–adolescent relationships can be of benefit (Ralph & Sanders, 2006).

Further, in this chapter I have argued that adolescents are not the maladjusted children that we think, and for those that are in trouble it may well be because the older generation is presenting poor role models in terms of how to manage relationships with significant others (see also chapter 9 in this volume). Society-wide changes in the structure of families may be the major contributor to these problems and the biggest challenge is how to deal with the impacts on children and adolescents. While much attention is focused on therapy and interventions for adolescents, perhaps we should be more focused on how to support and assist functional and constructive relationships between their parents. To that end, it may be the case that broad, educational approaches such as Couple Relationship Education (chapter 26 in this volume) may have wider benefits beyond the couple themselves. If as a society we can be persuaded that it is not only in our best interests but in our children's best interests to maintain and foster our intimate interpersonal relationships, then perhaps we can also combat misconceptions of the troubled teen and take up the challenge as the two most important attachment figures in most adolescents' lives—their mother and father.

References

Adams, R., & Laursen, B. (2001). The organization and dynamics of adolescent conflict with parents and friends. *Journal of Marriage and the Family, 63*, 97–110.

Allen, J. P., & Land, D. (1999). Attachment in adolescence. In J. Cassidy & P. R. Shaver (Eds.), *Handbook of attachment: Theory, research, and clinical applications* (pp. 319–335). New York: Guilford Press.

Amato, P. R. (1994). Father–child relations, mother–child relations, and offspring psychological well-being in early adulthood. *Journal of Marriage and the Family, 56*, 1031–1042.

Amato, P. R. (2001). Children of divorce in the 1990s: An update of the Amato and Keith (1991) meta-analysis. *Journal of Family Psychology, 15*, 355–370.

Amato, P. R., & Keith, B. (1991). Parental divorce and the well-being of children: A meta-analysis. *Psychological Bulletin, 110*, 26–46.

Australian Bureau of Statistics (2007a). *National Survey of Mental Health and Wellbeing: Summary of results.* Canberra: Australian Bureau of Statistics.

Australian Bureau of Statistics (2007b). *Lifetime marriage and divorce trends.* Canberra: Australian Bureau of Statistics.

Australian Bureau of Statistics (2010). *Australian social trends.* Retrieved December 2009 from www.Australian Bureau of Statistics.gov.au/AUSSTATS/Australian Bureau of Statistics@.nsf/DetailsPage/4102.0Dec%202009?OpenDocument.

Australian Institute of Health and Welfare (2008). *Australia's health 2008.* Canberra: Australian Institute of Health and Welfare.

Becker-Stoll, F., & Fremmer-Bombik, E. (1997). *Adolescent–mother interaction and attachment: A longitudinal study.* Paper presented at the biennial meeting of the Society for Research in Child Development, Washington, DC.

Belsky, J., Steinberg, L., & Draper, P. (1991). Childhood experience, interpersonal development, and reproductive strategy: An evolutionary theory of socialization. *Child Development, 62*, 647–670.

Blos, P. (1979). *The adolescent passage.* New York: International Universities Press.

Bowlby, J. (1997). *Attachment* (Vol. 1). London: Pimlico. (Original work published 1969)

Bowlby, J. (1989). *The making and breaking of affectional bonds.* London: Routledge. (Original work published 1979)

Buhrmester, D., & Furman, W. (1987). The development of companionships and intimacy. *Child Development, 58*, 1101–1113.

Burns, A., & Dunlop, R. (1998). Parental divorce, parent–child relations, and early adult relationships: A longitudinal Australian study. *Personal Relationships, 5*, 393–407.

Cassidy, J., & Shaver, P. R. (Eds.) (2008). *Handbook of attachment: Theory, research, and clinical applications* (2nd edn.). New York: Guilford Press.

Collins, W. A. (1995). Relationships and development: Family adaptation to individual change. In S. Shulman (Ed.), *Close relationships and socioemotional development* (pp. 128–154). New York: Ablex.

Collins, W. A., & Laursen, B. (2004). Parent–adolescent relationships and influences. In R. M. Lerner & L. Steinberg (Eds.), *Handbook of adolescent psychology* (2nd edn., pp. 331–362). Hoboken, NJ: Wiley.

Conger, R. D., & Ge, X. (1999). Conflict and cohesion in parent–adolescent relations: Changes in emotional expression from early to mid-adolescence. In M. J. Cox & J. Brooks-Gunn (Eds.), *Conflict and cohesion in families: Causes and consequences* (pp. 185–206). Hillsdale, NJ: Erlbaum.

Crossman, A., Sullivan, D. A., & Benin, M. (2006). The family environment and American adolescents' risk of obesity as young adults. *Social Science and Medicine, 63*, 2255–2267.

Douvan, E., & Adelson, J. (1966). *The adolescent experience.* New York: Wiley.

Dubas, J. S., & Petersen, A. C. (1996). Geographical distance from parents and adjustment during adolescence and young adulthood. In J. A. Graber & J. S. Dubas (Eds.), *Leaving home: Understanding the transition to adulthood. New directions for child development* (Vol. *71*, pp. 3–19). San Francisco: Jossey-Bass.

Erikson, E. (1968). *Identity: Youth and crisis.* New York: Norton.

Evans, M. D. R., Kelley, J., & Wanner, R. A. (2001). Educational attainment of the children of divorce: Australia, 1940-90. *Journal of Sociology, 37*, 275–297.

Freud, S. (1949). *An outline of psychoanalysis.* New York: Norton.

Furman, W., & Buhrmester, D. (1985). Children's perceptions of the personal relationships in their social networks. *Developmental Psychology, 21*, 1016–1024.

Furman, W., & Buhrmester, D. (1992). Age and sex differences in perceptions of networks of personal relationships. *Child Development, 63*, 103–115.

Goh, Y. L. D., & Wilkinson, R. B. (2009). *Attachment processes in adolescence.* Paper presented at the 9th Annual Conference of the Australian Psychological Society's Psychology of Relationships Interest Group.

Grotevant, H. D., & Cooper, C. R. (1986). Individuation in family relationships: A perspective on individual differences in the development of identity and role-taking skill in adolescence. *Human Development, 29*, 82–100.

Hair, E. C., Moore, K. A., Garrett, S. B., Kinukawa, A., Lippman, L., & Michelson, E. (2005). The parent–adolescent relationship scale. In L. Lippman (Ed.), *What do children need to flourish?*

Conceptualizing and measuring indicators of positive development (pp. 183–202). New York: Kluwer.

Hair, E. C., Moore, K. A., Hadley, A. M., Kaye, K., Day, R. D., & Orthner, D. K. (2009a). Parent marital quality and the parent–adolescent relationship: Profiles of relationship quality. *Marriage and Family Review, 45*, 189–217.

Hair, E. C., Moore, K. A., Hadley, A. M., Kaye, K., Day, R. D., & Orthner, D. K. (2009b). Parent marital quality and the parent–adolescent relationship: Effects on adolescent and young adult health outcomes *Marriage and Family Review, 45*, 218–248.

Hall, G. S. (1904). *Adolescence: Its psychology and its relations to physiology, anthropology, sociology, sex, crime, religion and education.* New York: Appleton.

Hazan, C., & Zeifman, D. (1994). Sex and the psychological tether. In K. Bartholomew & D. Perlman (Eds.), *Attachment processors in adulthood. Advances in personal relationships* (pp. 151–178). London: Jessica Kingsley.

Heckel, L. D., Clarke, A. R., Barry, R. J., McCarthy, R., & Selikowitz, M. (2009). The relationship between divorce and children with AD/HD of different subtypes and comorbidity: Results from a clinically referred sample. *Journal of Divorce & Remarriage, 50*, 427–443.

Hetherington, E. M. (Ed.) (1999). *Coping with divorce, single parenting, and remarriage: A risk and resiliency perspective.* Mahwah, NJ: Erlbaum.

Hetherington, E. M., & Kelly, J. (2002). *For better or worse: Divorce reconsidered.* New York: Norton.

Kandel, D. B., & Lesser, G. S. (1969). Parental and peer Influences on educational plans of adolescents. *American Sociological Review, 34*, 213–223.

Kandel, D., & Lesser, G. (1972). *Youth in two worlds.* San Francisco: Jossey-Bass.

Kaye, K., Day, R. D., Hair, E. C., Moore, K. A., Hadley, A. M., & Orthner, D. K. (2008). *Marital quality and parent–adolescent relationships: Effects on sexual activity among adolescents and young adults.* Washington, DC: U.S. Department of Health and Human Services.

Larson, R. W., Moneta, G., Richards, M. H., & Wilson, S. (2002). Continuity, stability, and change in daily emotional experience across adolescence. *Child Development, 73*, 1151–1165.

Larson, R. W., & Richards, M. H. (1994). Family emotions: Do young adolescents and their parents experience the same states? *Journal of Research on Adolescence, 4*, 567–583.

Larson, R., & Wilson, S. (2004) Adolescence across place and time: Globalization and the changing pathways to adulthood. In R. M. Lerner & L. Steinberg (Eds.), *Handbook of adolescent psychology* (2nd edn.). Hoboken, NJ: Wiley.

Markiewicz, D., Lawford, H., Doyle, A. B., & Haggart, N. (2006). Developmental differences in adolescents' and young adults' use of mothers, fathers, best friends, and romantic partners to fulfill attachment needs. *Journal of Youth and Adolescence, 35*, 127–140.

Miller, B. C. (1998). *Families matter: A research synthesis of family influences in adolescent pregnancy.* Washington, DC: The National Campaign to Prevent Teen Pregnancy.

Moore, K. A., Guzman, L., Hair, E., Lippman, L., & Garrett, S. (2004). Parent–teen relationships and interactions: Far more positive than not. *Trends in Child Research Brief.* Retrieved from www.childtrends.org/Files//Child_Trends-2004_12_01_RB_ParentTeen.pdf. doi:2004-25.

Noller, P. (1994). Relationships with parents in adolescence: Process and outcome. In R. Montemayor, G. R. Adams, & T. P. Gullotta (Eds.), *Personal relationships during adolescence* (pp. 37–77). Thousand Oaks: Sage.

Noller, P., & Callan, V. J. (1990). Adolescents' perceptions of the nature of their communication with parents. *Journal of Youth and Adolescence, 19*, 349–362.

Noller, P., Feeney, J. A., Darlington, Y., & Rogers, C. (2008). Conflict in divorcing and continuously married families: A study of marital, parent–child and sibling relationships. *Journal of Divorce and Marriage, 49*, 1–24.

Offer, D. (1969). *The psychological world of the teenager.* New York: Basic Books.

Parker, J. S., & Benson, M. J. (2004). Parent–adolescent relations and adolescent functioning: Self-esteem, substance abuse, and delinquency. *Adolescence, 39*, 519–530.

Prior, M., Sanson, A., Smart, D., & Oberklaid, F. (2000). *Pathways from infancy to adolescence: Australian Temperament Project 1983-2000* (No. 4). Melbourne: Australian Institute of Family Studies.

Paulson, S. E., & Sputa, C. L. (1996). Patterns of parenting during adolescence: Perceptions of adolescents and parents. *Adolescence, 31*, 369–381.

Qu, L., & Weston, R. (2008). *Snapshots of family relationships.* Melbourne: Australian Institute of Family Studies.

Ralph, A., & Sanders, M. R. (2006). The "Teen Triple P" Positive Parenting Program: A preliminary evaluation. *Youth Studies Australia, 25*, 41–48.

Resnick, M. D., Bearman, P. S., Blum, R. W., Bauman, K. E., Harris, K. M., Jones, J., et al. (1997). Protecting adolescents from harm: Findings from the National Longitudinal Study on Adolescent Health. *Journal of the American Medical Association, 278*(10), 823–832.

Rodgers, B. (1996). Social and psychological wellbeing of children from divorced families: Australian research findings. *Australian Psychologist, 31*, 174–182.

Rutter, M., Graham, P., Chadwick, O. F. D., & Yule, W. (1976). Adolescent turmoil: Fact or fiction? *Journal of Child Psychology and Psychiatry, 17*, 35–56.

Sawyer, M., et al. (2000). *Mental health of young people in Australia.* Canberra: Mental Health and Special Programs Branch, Commonwealth Department of Health and Aged Care.

Selman, R. (1980). *The development of interpersonal understanding.* New York: Academic Press.

Shaw, B. A., Krause, N., Chatters, L. M., Connell, C. M., & Ingersoll-Dayton, B. (2004). Emotional support from parents early in life, aging, and health. *Psychology and Aging, 19*, 4–12.

Smart, D., Sanson, A., & Toumbourou, J. (2008). How do parents and teenagers get along together? *Family Matters, 78*, 18–27.

Smetana, J. G. (1988). Adolescents' and parents' conceptions of parental authority. *Child Development, 59*, 321–335.

Smetana, J. G., Campione-Barr, N., & Metzger, A. (2006). Adolescent development in interpersonal and societal contexts. *Annual Review of Psychology, 57*, 255–284.

Smetana, J. G., Metzger, A., & Campione-Barr, N. (2004). African American late adolescents' relationships with parents: Developmental transitions and longitudinal patterns. *Child Development, 75*, 932–947.

Steinberg, L. (1990). Autonomy, conflict, and harmony in the family relationship. In S. Feldman & G. Elliot (Eds.), *At the threshold: The developing adolescent* (pp. 255–276). Cambridge, MA: Harvard University Press.

Steinberg, L. (2001). We know some things: Parent–adolescent relationships in retrospect and prospect. *Journal of Research on Adolescence, 11*, 1–19.

Steinberg, L., & Silk, J. S. (2002). Parenting adolescents. In M. H. Bornstein (Ed.), *Handbook of parenting: Children and parenting* (2nd edn., Vol. 1, pp. 103–133). Mahwah, NJ: Erlbaum.

Stuart, J. (2007, January 16). The trouble with teens. *The Independent.* Retrieved June 28, 2010, from www.independent.co.uk/life-style/health-and-families/health-news/the-trouble-with-teens-432366.html.

Turner, H. M., Rose, K. S., & Cooper, M. J. (2005). Schema and parental bonding in overweight and non-overweight female adolescents. *International Journal of Obesity, 29*, 81–87.

Umberson, D. (1992). Relationships between adult children and their parents: Psychological consequences for both generations. *Journal of Marriage and the Family, 54*, 664–674.

Wilkinson, R. B. (2004). The role of parental and peer attachment in the psychological health and self-esteem of adolescents. *Journal of Youth & Adolescence, 33*, 479–493.

Wilkinson, R. B. (2006). Age and sex differences in the influence of attachment relationships on adolescent psychological health. *The Australian Educational and Developmental Psychologist, 23*, 87–104.

Wilkinson, R. B. (2010a). Adolescent best friends as attachment figures: Implications for psychological health and adjustment. In J. Toller (Ed.), *Friendships: Types, cultural variations, and psychological and social aspects*. New York: Nova.

Wilkinson, R. B. (2010b). Best friend attachment versus peer attachment in the prediction of adolescent psychological adjustment. *Journal of Adolescence, 33*, 709–717.

Wilkinson, R. B., & Kraljevic, M. (2004). Adolescent psychological health and school attitudes: The impact of attachment relationships. *Proceedings of the Australian Psychological Society's Psychology of Relationships Interest Group 4th Annual Conference*, pp. 150–155.

Wilkinson, R. B., & Parry, M. M. (2004). Attachment styles, quality of attachment relationships, and components of self-esteem in adolescence. *Proceedings of the 39th Australian Psychological Society Annual Conference*, pp. 301–305.

Wilkinson, R. B., & Walford, W. A. (2001). Attachment and personality in the psychological health of adolescents. *Personality and Individual Differences, 31*, 473–484.

Youniss, J., & Smollar, J. (1985). *Adolescent relations with mothers, fathers, and friends*. Chicago: University of Chicago Press.

6

Family Caregiving

Perspectives of Adult Children and Older Parents

Gery C. Karantzas

Aged care has become a priority for governments across the world (United Nations, 2004). Estimates suggest that by the year 2025 approximately 1.69 billion people will be over the age of 75, with many in this age group requiring care due to a decline in well-being and functional independence (United Nations, 2004). Gerontologists and population economists suggest that governments' inability to keep up with the welfare needs of an aging population has increasingly thrust the responsibility of aged care onto the family unit (Goodnow, Lawrence, Ryan, Karantzas, & King, 2002; Karantzas, Evans, & Foddy, 2010).

However, shifts in the trends that yield different family forms and functioning (see chapters 1, 3, 4 in this volume) have led to changes in the capacity for families to provide the care needed by older parents. For instance, reduced family size and changing family roles (e.g., greater participation of women in the labor force) and shifting gender roles are argued to have impacted on adult children's ability to care for their parents in the modern age (e.g., Himes, 1994; Long & Harris, 2000). More recently, middle-aged adults find themselves part of the "sandwich generation"; a subset of society whose caregiving capacities are particularly taxed as they attend to the needs of their own children as well as the needs of their parents (Grundy & Henretta, 2006). These social changes bring into sharp focus questions regarding how family caregivers assist in the caregiving of older

The Wiley-Blackwell Handbook of Couples and Family Relationships, First Edition.
Edited by Patricia Noller and Gery C. Karantzas.

parents, while negotiating the competing responsibilities typical of today's world. Specifically, questions regarding: (i) what type of caregiving is deemed important and valued by caregivers and care recipients; (ii) how caregiving is and ought to be distributed amongst members of one's family; and (iii) what are the psychological drivers (or motivations) that influence caregiving are important to answer in unpacking the complexity of family caregiving.

In this chapter, I describe various research programs that I have been involved in that have examined each of these three broad questions. In doing so, I draw on research that has examined the perspectives of both caregivers and care recipients. I begin by revisiting the concept of family caregiving—broadening its definition to accommodate the complexities and changing nature of family caregiving in recent decades. I then outline our research programs on family caregiving. In the final section, I discuss how the knowledge drawn from these research programs can be applied to both policy and practice in the aged-care setting.

Defining Family Caregiving

Caring for older parents beyond the frail and ill

Family caregiving has been traditionally defined as the emotional, instrumental (including organizational tasks such as running errands and housekeeping), physical, financial, and social support family members provide to frail, ill, or disabled relatives on a daily or intermittent basis (National Family Caregivers Association, 1998). However, modern medical advances have meant that many adults will live well into older age in relatively good health and maintain fairly independent lives. Nevertheless, older adults may still call on their adult children to render assistance from time to time for such tasks as running the odd errand or helping with physically demanding household repairs. The help rendered to independent older adults challenges the assumption that family caregiving solely involves providing assistance to "frail," "ill," or "disabled" family members. The care afforded to independent older adults extends the definition of family caregiving to encompass the care of older adults in good health.

As a result, researchers have made calls to redress the emphasis placed on carers of older parents experiencing poor health, by concentrating on parents who are relatively healthy, as these care arrangements can result in important knowledge about how family caregiving is conducted during noncrisis periods (Karantzas et al., 2010; Roberto, Allen, & Blieszner, 2001; Sorensen, Webster, & Roggman, 2002).

Caregiving beyond the "here" and "now"

The increasing life expectancy and well-being of older adults has prompted research investigating adult children and independent older parents' willingness to consider, and prepare, for their future care in the event that the health of the older parent declines (e.g.,

Pinquart & Sorensen, 2002; Roberto et al., 2001; Sorensen & Pinquart, 2000). While research investigating adult children's and older parents' prospective decision making around the issue of future care is in the early stages, it is clear that both potential caregivers and care recipients are likely to consider impending care requirements, though there may be great individual variability in the degree to which these issues are contemplated and considered (Bromley & Blieszner, 1997; Sorensen & Pinquart, 2000). This emerging emphasis on anticipatory care broadens the definition of family caregiving to include the care that currently occurs in families, as well as the care that may be needed in the future.

Caregiving as a task-based activity

Much of the research into caregiving has been dogged by "methodological individualism" (Karantzas & Lawrence, 1998) whereby the focus is placed on the primary caregiver's personalized reactions to caregiving experiences, and caregiving is viewed as a single, unitary task (Finch & Mason, 1993). However, if the complexities of family caregiving are to be accounted for adequately, it seems more fruitful to consider the distribution of caregiving for the elderly in terms of an array of specific tasks. Older adults often need assistance with instrumental tasks such as cooking, cleaning and managing the bills, but require the fulfillment of emotional or personalized tasks such as companionship and a shoulder to cry on (Kendig, 1986). Thus, a task-based approach to caregiving not only highlights the importance of tasks often seen as routine domestic activities (Abel, 1990), but enables one to compare the type of care provided by multiple family members other than the primary carer, and the extent to which older parents may choose to seek different types of support from different caregivers. Dwyer, Henretta, Coward, and Barton (1992) noted that siblings can act as an "ensemble" when caring for an older adult, with multiple caregivers coordinating their caregiving responsibilities in meeting the needs of the parent.

If we are to broaden our view of family caregiving to acknowledge shifts in family structures, the caring of parents both frail and of good health, willingness to provide future care, and as an activity involving multiple tasks, then research needs to encompass questions and methods that highlight the merit of considering these aspects of caregiving. In the following sections, I outline research that I have been involved with that examines family caregiving in ways that align with this broadened view.

What Sorts of Caregiving Tasks are Valued?

In the previous section, I outlined that family caregiving should not be seen as a singular all-encompassing activity; rather caregiving is complex and multifaceted involving varying degrees of physical and emotional investment (Goodnow et al., 2002; Ingersoll-Dayton, Starrels, & Dowler, 1996; Karantzas & Lawrence, 1998; Wolf, Freedman, & Soldo, 1997). For example, running an errand requires far less pre-planning than sleeping in a parent's house or attending to the parent's personal hygiene. Furthermore, a task-based approach allows for different care-related tasks to be considered as different forms of resources, which may be valued differently by caregivers and care recipients. The value placed on various tasks may then influence the extent to which some of these tasks remain the sole responsibility of family caregivers, while others may be legitimately moved to more formal paid help.

In an attempt to understand the value that adult children and older parents place on family caregiving we (Karantzas & Lawrence, 1998; Karantzas et al., 2010) took a task-based approach to parental care and examined the extent to which adult children and older parents valued 26 instrumental and emotional caregiving tasks. The 26 tasks were drawn from the literature and extensively piloted with community samples. We also asked the adult children and older parents the extent to which they were willing to substitute family help with particular caregiving tasks for paid assistance. Our research, which included a sample of family caregivers involved in the care of older parents as well as a sample of older adults who were still independent and active in the community, revealed similar findings for the two participant groups. Specifically, emotional caregiving was valued significantly more than instrumental caregiving by both adult children and older parents. Furthermore, adult children and older adults were less willing to replace emotional forms of care than instrumental caregiving tasks with paid help.

We probed participants' substitution of emotional caregiving tasks further, by asking them to rate the extent to which different types of caregiving could be substituted for emotional caregiving. We identified the most valued emotional caregiving task, which was "providing companionship," and asked participants to consider the extent to which it was acceptable to substitute this caregiving task for five tasks that represented different forms of caregiving. These tasks included: (1) providing money for regular goods and services (paid help); (2) taking the parent on outings (an alternative emotional caregiving task); (3) helping with the daily shower (a physical grooming task); (4) cleaning the house (a form of home help); and (5) arranging services and equipment (an organizational task). Our findings revealed that taking the parent on outings was regarded as a significantly more appropriate substitute to providing companionship than all other alternatives. However, this trend was only found for female caregivers. Care recipients and male caregivers did not significantly prefer one type of task over another as a substitution for companionship. Rather, all possible task substitutions were deemed inadequate for these groups.

Who Ought to be a Family Caregiver?

The shifting trends of family structure and form (see chapters 1, 3, 4 in this volume) highlight that the composition of families, and the roles and responsibilities of family members, are likely to influence how caregiving is undertaken in families. That is, the factors that influence family caregiving are likely to be multiple rather than single such as a combination of "proximity, competing responsibilities, interest and willingness to help, gender roles and history of family relationships" (Cicirelli, 1995, p. 133). However, as noted by us (Lawrence, Goodnow, Woods, & Karantzas, 2002) and others (e.g., Brody, 1985; Wolf et al., 1997), it is difficult to implement research designs that examine how the combination of family circumstances influence the ways caregiving is conducted in families. Moreover, unless caregiving is viewed from a task-based perspective, then it is difficult to unpack how caregiving tasks may be distributed amongst family members with differing family roles and competing life responsibilities. In an attempt to fill this gap, we developed a research program that investigated how a mix of family factors may influence caregiving and how differences in the amount and type of contributions made by caregivers can influence family care arrangements.

If differing family situations matter to the way family caregiving is negotiated, then combining/including information about circumstances should influence the impression people have about a situation compared to considering a single circumstance. For example, overlaying knowledge regarding a family caregiver's gender with the type of work they do should matter in the mind of someone who is going to distribute caregiving responsibilities to this member of the family. For instance, an adult daughter who is recently divorced and managing single parenthood alongside full-time work commitments should be perceived as less able to commit to the care of an older parent than a single son who engages in part-time work.

Within studies of caregiving, differences in the extent of contributions made by caregivers have attracted a larger share of attention than differences in type of contribution. Family members, however, are known to vary on both scores as a function of gender (e.g., Cicirelli, 1991). Daughters, for example, typically contribute a larger share of caregiving overall than sons. They also attract more of the work involving "hands-on" personal care, whereas sons attract more of the work involving finances (Dalley, 1996; Miller & Cafasso, 1992). Many argue these differences are embedded in gender roles (e.g., Golombok & Fivush, 1994).

Commitments may also have effects on both amount and type of care provided by daughters and sons. Paid work, for example, can affect both the size of the contribution and the extent of involvement in tasks that make particular demands on one's time (e.g., Brody, 1985). However, on the one hand, commitments can only affect the amount that sons and daughters contribute if some tasks are seen as movable between gendered lines. If none of the tasks are seen as able to be performed by both sons and daughters, it will not matter what commitments are present. If some tasks are seen as able to be performed by either sons or daughters, then the impact of commitments should occur by way of these less sharply gendered tasks. To investigate such a moderating effect, first we need to establish that some tasks are less sharply gendered than others and then we need to determine whether these are the tasks most likely to change hands when commitments are taken into account.

On the other hand it is possible that circumstances influence distributions by way of a process that has been called task specialization (e.g., Litwak, 1985; Messeri, Silverstein, & Litwak, 1993; Penning, 1995). In accounts of this process the distribution of a task to a caregiver is based on the fit between the particular demands of the task and the expertise of an individual in fulfilling the task.

In tackling the issues regarding gender, commitments, and the diversity of caregiving tasks, we conducted a series of studies to examine how caregiving responsibilities could be distributed amongst family caregivers with different life responsibilities (see Goodnow et al., 2002; Karantzas & Lawrence, 1998; Lawrence et al., 2002). Specifically, Lawrence and Campbell (1997) developed an interactive computer program that presented a family vignette involving an older parent (Mrs. Clark) who had recently broken her hip and required home help for approximately 6 weeks after being released from hospital. Being a widow, she required assistance with various caregiving tasks and had four adult children – Helen, George, Carla, and John. The vignette required that 11 caregiving tasks that varied in their links to gender roles, and covered an array of emotional, physical, and organizational tasks, be distributed across the four adult children. The caregiving tasks were provided on the computer screen along with the names of the four adult children. Tasks could be assigned by the participants using a drop-and-drag function, and the list of caregiving tasks distributed to each adult child would appear under their names (see Figure 6.1). Importantly, we used pairwise manipulation (we moved the same commitments to different genders across vignettes) to alter the life circumstances of the adult children resulting in four different scenarios. In addition to the gender of the adult children, the life commitments manipulated were work status, marital status, and family responsibilities. The manipulation of commitments is summarized in Table 6.1 along with the descriptions of the children's commitments in each scenario.

Our findings demonstrated that when the circumstances of the children fitted in with the traditional gender roles (e.g., Helen is a stay-at-home mother, and George is a banker) then gender was clearly the determining factor that shaped the distribution of caregiving responsibilities by both caregivers and care recipients, despite the fact that the stay-at-home mother may have been just as busy as the father who is a banker. However, once the circumstances of the adult children appear to deviate from prototypical gender roles,

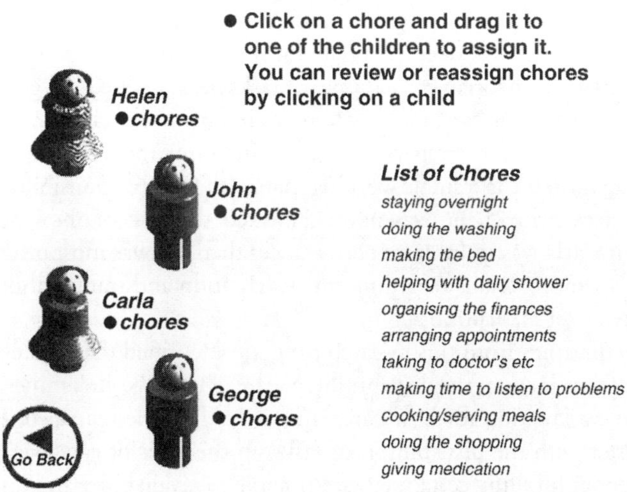

Figure 6.1 Screenshot for the Lawrence and Campbell (1997) caregiving computer interactive task
Source: Lawrence, J. A., Goodnow, J. J., Woods, K., & Karantzas, G. (2002). Distribution of caregiving tasks among family members: The place of gender and availability. *Journal of Family Psychology, 16,* 493–509

Table 6.1 An Outline of the Description of Family Scenarios
Source: Lawrence, J. A., Goodnow, J. J., Woods, K., & Karantzas, G. (2002). Distribution of caregiving tasks among family members: The place of gender and availability. *Journal of Family Psychology, 16,* 493–509

Family	Helen	George	Carla	John
F1	$M\ \overline{W}\ C$[a]	$M\ W\ C$[b]	$\overline{M}\ W\ \overline{C}$[c]	$\overline{M}\ \overline{W}\ C$
F2	$M\ W\ C$	$M\ \overline{W}\ C$	$\overline{M}\ \overline{W}\ C$	$\overline{M}\ W\ \overline{C}$
F3	$M\ \overline{W}\ \overline{C}$	$M\ W\ \overline{C}$	$\overline{M}\ W\ C$	$\overline{M}\ \overline{W}\ \overline{C}$
F4	$M\ W\ \overline{C}$	$M\ \overline{W}\ \overline{C}$	$\overline{M}\ \overline{W}\ \overline{C}$	$\overline{M}\ W\ C$

[a] Married, Not in paid work, with children.

[b] Helen and George are matched pairs across F1 and F2 when they are in paid work as a banker or are a houseperson, with children; and in F3 and F4 where they are without children.

[c] Carla and John are matched pairs across F1 and F2 where they either are in paid work as an office worker or are unemployed, with or without children; and in F3 and F4 where they are either in paid work with children or without either.

competing life demands and the competencies of children to perform particular caregiving tasks (what Litwak, 1985, termed "task specialization") become organizing principles that shape the distribution of caregiving tasks amongst family members. For instance, when Helen was a banker, she was deemed as the most appropriate of the siblings to organize Mrs. Clark's finances. Moreover, it appears tasks less wedded to gendered roles are more transferable between caregivers as family circumstances change, while other tasks are resistant to such transfer irrespective of shifts in family members' responsibilities. For instance, despite John being a single working man with fewer responsibilities than all other adult children (scenario 2), he was never allocated the task of showering Mrs. Clark. However, when Carla was in John's circumstances then she was most often given this task (scenario 1). (For more details regarding the distribution and transferability of caregiving tasks see Lawrence et al., 2002.)

In short, the findings from this research program identified that while gender roles are an important determinant of the distribution of caregiving tasks in families, gender alone is not a sufficient explanation for how caregiving is likely to be managed. Rather, circumstances do matter with the distribution of tasks on the basis of caregiver availability and those most adept at fulfilling certain tasks. Principles of availability and task specialization seem to shape the negotiation of the care of older parents. Interestingly, the views of caregivers and care recipients demonstrate remarkable similarities, with few distinctions in the allocation of tasks across the different scenarios. This lack of difference between adult children and older parents may highlight that caregivers and care recipients may not view caregiving situations that differently.

Motives that Underlie Caregiving and Care Receiving

While the value that adult children and older parents place on caregiving tasks, and the manner in which families distribute and negotiate caregiving will influence how families go about caring for their older parents, the fact remains that caregivers provide care because of some underlying motivation to do so. Walker et al. (1989, 1990) proposed that adult children's care of older parents is driven by obligatory motives (i.e., a sense of duty or responsibility to care) and discretionary motives (i.e., the desire to care). Two widely cited motives of care are filial obligation and attachment.

Filial obligation

Silverstein, Gans, and Yang (2006) define filial obligation as adult children's duty to support their aging parents. According to Finley, Roberts, and Banahan (1988), filial obligation was the basis of family cohesion in the late 19th century, when expectations surrounding instrumental support held primacy over the emotional needs of the caregiver or care recipient. It is suggested that obligatory motives such as filial obligation are central to caregiving because these motives are embedded in cultural and family-based traditions of family functioning (e.g., Dilworth-Anderson, Williams, & Gibson, 2002; Lee & Sung, 1997; Shi, 1993). According to Wallhagen and Yamamoto-Mitani (2006), a moral obligation toward caring for one's parents is a universal theme of elder care across Eastern cultures. For instance, Yue and Ng (1999) found that both Chinese adult children and older parents hold high levels of filial obligation. Research into Western cultures suggests that older parents maintain expectations around calling on adult children as important sources of support during periods of frailty (Blieszner & Mancini, 1987; Burr & Mutchler, 1999; Silverstein et al., 2006). However, issues surrounding filial obligation seem to be explicitly negotiated with greater frequency in Western societies than in Eastern cultures where filial obligation is primarily tacit and responsibilities can be negotiated between an ensemble of caregivers and the care recipient (Finch, 1987; Finch & Mason, 1993).

Despite the emphasis in caregiving research on filial obligation, it has been found to make only modest contributions to caregiving and carer outcomes when included alongside variables representing parent–child relationship quality (e.g., Cicirelli, 1983, 1993). Various social gerontologists have not been surprised by the modest contribution of obligatory motives to caregiving in the 20th and 21st centuries, arguing that society has seen a shift in family caregiving to include an emphasis on affectional bonds and the emotional aspects of caregiving (e.g., Carpenter, 2001; Cicirelli, 1993; Crispi, Schiaffino, & Berman, 1997; Magai & Cohen, 1998). From this perspective attachment theory, a lifespan theory of human bonding and caregiving (Bowlby, 1969), provides an important framework from which to investigate the motives, processes, and consequences of family care arrangements amongst adult children and ailing older parents.

Attachment

Attachment theory is comprehensively described in other chapters of this text and its applications to sexual functioning and caregiving more broadly (see chapters 11, 14 in this volume). The theory has also been applied to explain how attachment bonds between parents and their children may influence familial caregiving in adulthood. Specifically, Cicirelli (1993) and Mikulincer and Shaver (2007), propose that when situations endanger the attachment bond between an adult child and their elderly parent, the child engages in helping behavior as a means of safeguarding the attachment bond. Consequently, as the ailing health of older parents is recognized by their adult children, children engage in caregiving—as a means of delaying the loss of their attachment figure and achieving a sense of felt security. Cicirelli referred to such caregiving attempts as "protective behavior."

However, the degree to which adult children engage in helping their older parents, the type of help they provide, and the amount of carer strain experienced are thought to be influenced by the adult child's attachment style towards their parent. Specifically, attachment style refers to a person's most available mental schemas and behaviors regarding close personal relationships (Mikulincer & Shaver, 2007). As described in other chapters, attachment style is widely regarded as comprising two independent dimensions: attachment anxiety and avoidance (Brennan, Clark, & Shaver, 1998). Attachment anxiety is characterized by a preoccupation about relationships and an excessive need for approval (Brennan et al., 1998). Attachment avoidance is characterized by a discomfort with closeness, a lack of confidence in depending on others, and an excessive self-reliance (Karantzas, Feeney, & Wilkinson, 2010). Attachment security is defined by low scores on both dimensions and is characterized by a comfort with emotional closeness and intimacy, a trust of relationship partners, and a confidence in depending on others in times of need (Brennan et al., 1998; Karantzas, Lawrence, & Ryan, 2010).

While links between attachment and adult children's provision of care to older parents have been proposed, few empirical studies have been conducted in the area of family caregiving. However, of the studies that have been conducted, attachment has been found to be associated with adult children's caregiving behavior and carer outcomes. For example, Thompson and Walker (1984) found that mother–daughter caregiving reciprocity was positively associated with increasing familial attachment strength. Cicirelli (1983, 1993) reported that attachment strength was positively related to adult daughters' care of an older mother, but negatively associated with daughters' perceived burden.

Markiewicz, Reis, and Gold (1997) found that attachment insecurity was associated with the placement of older parents into aged-care facilities, while attachment security was related to carers maintaining community-based help for their parents. In addition, Magai and Cohen (1998) found that caregiver burden was best predicted in adult children caring for demented older parents by pre-morbid attachment. In their study, securely attached family caregivers reported lower levels of burden than insecurely attached adult children. Carpenter (2001) found that secure adult children provided more emotional assistance to an aging parent than did anxiously attached adult children, while also reporting lower levels of burden. Similarly, Crispi et al. (1997) found that adult children with a preoccupied attachment style (a facet of attachment anxiety) experienced more carer burden.

More recently, adult children's attachment style has been associated with anticipatory caregiving. Specifically, Sorensen et al. (2002) found that adult children's consideration of the future care needs of older parents was associated with attachment security. In contrast, insecurely attached individuals characterized by high avoidance limited thoughts about their parent's future care, while adult children high on anxiety worried excessively about the anticipated care and did not develop constructive strategies for dealing with future responsibilities. In summary, the reviewed findings suggest that attachment security increases adult children's tendencies to protect and care for older parents during periods of ill health and in planning for their parents' future care needs.

Even fewer studies have examined the associations between attachment and care receiving. However, these studies also highlight the role of attachment dynamics in receiving support from significant others and associated well-being. For instance, Merz and Consedine (2009) found that compared to insecurely attached older adults, secure older adults who received emotional support reported greater well-being and fewer negative effects on well-being when receiving instrumental support. Kafetsios and Sideridis (2006) found that attachment anxiety was negatively associated with older adults' perceptions of social support, which in turn, were associated with their mental health outcomes.

Obligatory and discretionary motives in caregiving research

Little research investigating the differential role of obligatory and discretionary motives in family caregiving has been carried out over the last three decades. The most widely cited of these studies conducted by Cicirelli (1983, 1993) found that attachment and filial obligation made significant independent contributions to both caregiving behavior and burden. However, Cicirelli found that attachment accounted for over 20% of the variance in both adult children's caregiving behavior and felt burden while filial obligation contributed under 10% of the variance. Specifically, attachment strength (he did not distinguish between attachment styles) was associated with greater caregiving contributions and lower perceived burden. Filial obligation on the other hand increased both caregiving and carer burden.

In a recent study we (Karantzas et al., 2010) further examined the role of filial obligation and attachment in caregiving to older parents and carer outcomes. Importantly, we extended the research in three ways. Firstly, we examine these obligatory and discretionary motives in a sample of caregivers, as well as a sample of care recipients. Secondly, we were interested in how these motives influence caregiving in families where older parents are generally in good health. Thirdly, due to the good health of parents, we investigated these motives in the context of current and future caregiving. When controlling for demographic variables (i.e., gender, socioeconomic status, geographic distance between caregiver and care recipient) and parental needs for assistance, we found that filial obligation was positively associated with adult children's caregiving while older parents' perceptions of children's filial obligation predicted their care receiving. Furthermore, while filial obligation was not directly associated with adult children's perceptions of carer burden, an indirect link was found through caregiving.

Attachment avoidance and anxiety were found to have very different associations for adult children and older parents in terms of current and future caregiving and carer burden. Specifically, attachment avoidance was found to predict adult children's carer burden and willingness to provide parental care in the future. However, attachment avoidance was not associated with adult children's current provisions of care to their parents. Attachment anxiety was found to have no associations with adult children's current and future caregiving or perceptions of carer burden. In contrast, attachment anxiety was found to predict older parents' current receipt of care, future willingness to receive care, and their perceptions of carer burden.

Interestingly, attachment anxiety and filial obligation were positively associated for older parents; and in turn, filial obligation predicted older parents' seeking of current care. We interpret this finding as suggesting that issues of filial obligation may be interlinked with attachment anxiety. As a result, older parents high in attachment anxiety may impose filial responsibilities on their family caregivers as a means of safeguarding their relationship with their adult children. In other words, as a means of defending against feelings of low self-worth and the constant need for validation, anxious care recipients may require their adult children to fulfill various caregiving responsibilities. Overall, these attachment-related findings across both models suggest that parents and children may hold different attachment concerns that yield differences in the seeking and provision of care.

Implications and Conclusion

Across the three types of research programs discussed in this chapter, our findings demonstrate that there exist similarities and differences in the cognitions and attitudes that adult children and older parents hold about family caregiving. Clearly the value placed on caregiving tasks and their distribution amongst family members provide evidence of similarity, and highlight that adult children and older parents share similar understandings and hold similar goals and expectations about current and future parental care.

The value placed on tasks is important. While this premise may seem simple, unless health professionals and policy makers understand which aspects of caregiving are valued similarly or differently by adult children and older parents, then it is difficult to ensure that the right mix of formal and informal help is provided to families. For instance, given the disparity in value placed on emotional and instrumental caregiving by both adult children and older parents, it is clear that the farming out of physical and organizational caregiving tasks to paid services is money well spent. This process allows adult children to engage in care that is important and unsuitable for substitution by a paid helper.

A commonly held belief is that adult children differ in their views of caregiving compared to their older parents (e.g., Miller & Cafasso, 1992). However, this assumption is based on the fact that caregiving is not openly discussed in families, but rather assumptions about people's views of caregiving are not shared openly and caregiving is negotiated on an implicit basis (Finch & Mason, 1993). Thus, it seems that family members "perceive" others within the family as holding different views about caregiving when in fact this may not be the case. These erroneous assumptions may result in family conflict, as family members accuse one another of holding unfair and inaccurate perceptions of one another as caregivers.

Such family conflict can be avoided if families and health professionals are cognizant of the fact that families often hold corresponding views regarding caregiving arrangements. These points of similarity can be used by therapists, social workers, and counsellors to highlight the shared understandings and goals that families have about the welfare of their parents and to use this knowledge as a starting point to then explore possible differences that may exist in family members' opinions of some aspects of the caregiving arrangements.

Gender alone does not determine how caregivers and care recipients will distribute caregiving tasks. Clearly adult children and older parents are mindful of the challenges faced by the "sandwich" generation as they tackle caring for an older parent, while still tending to their own children's needs and striving for a career. Our findings alert practitioners and policy makers to the possibility that some caregiving tasks do cross gendered lines when family members are overcommitted with life responsibilities, or have a particular competency suited to a particular caregiving task. Health professionals and policy makers would do well to develop protocols that provide information about family caregivers' life commitments and specializations, and conduct family meetings that identify the tasks necessary for the caregiving of older parents. Health professionals could then facilitate discussion and negotiation as to how these tasks could be undertaken by various family members based on available time and skill sets.

Our research also highlights that examining the obligatory and discretionary motives that underlie caregiving and care receiving are likely to yield clearer understandings about how filial obligation and attachment issues are deemed important for adult children and older parents (Noller, Feeney, & Peterson, 2001). According to our findings, while the effects of filial obligation as a motive are similar for adult children and older parents, the generations hold different attachment concerns which give rise to differences in the receipt and provision of care (Karantzas et al., 2010). While research in this area is still in the early stages, continued research is likely to result in the identification of family carers who are at risk of carer burnout either prior to undertaking caregiving responsibilities or during the caregiving role.

Furthermore, examining attachment processes in older adults is likely to identify elderly parents who are not adjusting well to the receipt of family care. Most importantly, an attachment perspective may assist health care professionals (i.e., clinicians, counsellors, and social workers) in tailoring the counselling of families through understanding the role of attachment in family dynamics, mental health outcomes, and emotional reactions related to current caregiving and the planning of future care arrangements. For instance, Krause and Haverkamp (1996) argue that insecurely attached individuals seem to possess mental representations of relationships, which are not as accurate as the cognitive models held by securely attached adult individuals. Krause and Haverkamp further suggest that for insecure adult children to deal with the heightened strain of caring for a parent, these carers may require "cognitive or affective revision of the individual's [the adult child's] internal working models towards more positive and accurate expectations of self and others" (p. 86). The consideration of attachment issues may thus improve the efficacy of interventions aimed at reducing family and carer burden, which to date have resulted in modest improvements for carers (Brodaty & Green, 2002; Cooke, McNally, Mulligan, Harrison, & Newman, 2001).

In closing, examining family caregiving in normative and non-normative contexts is of particular importance for social policy. For example, the assumed needs of adult children providing help and older parents receiving help are likely to vary based on the health of the older parent. Therefore, conducting research that investigates the care of frail older parents as well as research investigating the help provided by kin in families where parents are in good health may generate more appropriate social policy, aimed at meeting the needs of caregivers and care receivers across diverse caregiving contexts (Karantzas et al., 2010; Lawrence et al., 2002; Roberto et al., 2001). Furthermore, it is important that research incorporate the view of both the caregiver and the care recipient so that the perspectives of two equally important stakeholder groups are considered—adult children caring for their beloved parents and older parents receiving care from their beloved children.

References

Abel, E. K. (1990). Informal care for the disabled elder: A critique of recent literature. *Research on Ageing, 12*, 139–157.

Blieszner, R., & Mancini, J. A. (1987). Enduring ties: Older adults' parental role and responsibilities. *Family Relations, 36*, 176–180.

Bowlby, J. (1969). *Attachment and loss: Vol. 1 Attachment.* New York: Basic Books.

Brennan, K. A., Clark, C. L., & Shaver, P. R. (1998). Self-report measurement of adult romantic attachment: An integrative overview. In J. A. Simpson & W. S. Rholes (Eds.), *Attachment theory and close relationships* (pp. 46–76). New York: Guilford Press.

Brodaty, H., & Green, A. (2002). Who cares for the carer? The often forgotten patient. *Clinical Practice: Therapeutic Review, 31*(9), 1–4.

Brody, E. M. (1985). Parent care as a normative family stress. *The Gerontologist, 25*, 19–29.

Bromley, M. C., & Blieszner, R. (1997). Planning for long-term care: Filial behavior and relationship quality of adult children with independent parents. *Family Relations, 46*, 155–162.

Burr, E. M., & Mutchler, J. E. (1999). Race and ethnicity variation in norms of filial responsibility among older persons. *Journal of Marriage and the Family, 61*, 674–687.

Carpenter, B. C. (2001). Attachment bonds between adult daughters and their older mothers: Associations with contemporary caregiving. *Journal of Gerontology: Psychological Sciences, 56*, 257–266.

Cicirelli, V. G. (1983). Adult children's attachment and helping behaviour to elderly parents: A path model. *Journal of Marriage and the Family, 45*, 815–822.

Cicirelli, V. G. (1991). *Family caregiving: Autonomous and paternalistic decision-making.* Newbury Park, CA: Sage.

Cicirelli, V. G. (1993). Attachment and obligation as daughters' motives for caregiving behavior and subsequent effects on subjective burden. *Psychology and Aging, 8*, 144–155.

Cooke, D. D., McNally, L., Mulligan, K. T., Harrison, M. J. G., & Newman, S. P. (2001). Psychosocial interventions for caregivers of people with dementia: A systematic review. *Aging and Mental Health, 5*, 120–135.

Crispi, E. L., Schiaffino, K. B., & Berman, W. H. (1997). The contribution of attachment to burden in adult children of institutionalized parents with dementia. *The Gerontologist, 37*(1), 52–60.

Dalley, G. (1996). *Ideologies of caring: Rethinking community and collectivism* (2nd edn.). London: Macmillan.

Dilworth-Anderson, P., Williams, I. C., & Gibson, B. E. (2002). Issues of race, ethnicity, and culture in caregiving research: A 20-year review (1980–2000). *The Gerontologist, 42*, 237–272.

Dwyer, J. W., Henretta, J. C., Coward, R. T., & Barton, A. M. (1992) Changes in the helping behaviors of adult children as caregivers. *Research on Aging, 14*, 351–375.

Finch, J. (1987). Family obligation and the life course. In A. Bryman, B. Bytheway, P. Allatt, & T. Keil (Eds.), *Rethinking the life-cycle*, (pp. 155–169). London: Macmillan.

Finch, J., & Mason, J. (1993). *Negotiating family responsibilities*. London: Tavistock/Routledge.

Finley, N. J., Roberts, M. D., & Banahan, B. F. (1988). Motivators and inhibitors of attitudes of filial obligation toward aging parents. *The Gerontologist, 28*, 73–78.

Golombok, S., & Fivush, R. (1994). *Gender development*. Cambridge: Cambridge University Press.

Goodnow, J. J., Lawrence, J. A., Ryan, J., Karantzas, G., & King, K. (2002). Extending studies of collaborative cognition by way of caregiving situations. *International Journal of Behavioral Development, 26*, 16–25.

Grundy, E., & Henretta, J.C. (2006). Between elderly parents and adult children: A new look at the intergenerational care provided by the "sandwich generation." *Ageing and Society, 26*, 707–722.

Himes, C. L. (1994). Parental caregiving by adult women: A demographic perspective. *Research on Aging, 16*, 191–211.

Ingersoll-Dayton B., Starrels M. E., & Dowler D. (1996). Caregiving for parents and parents-in-law: Is gender important? *The Gerontologist, 36*, 483–491.

Kafetsios, K., & Sideridis, G. D. (2006). Attachment, social support and well-being in young and older adults. *Journal of Health Psychology, 11*, 863–876.

Karantzas, G. C., Evans, L., & Foddy, M. (2010). The role of attachment in current and future parent caregiving. *Journal of Gerontology: Psychological Science, 65*, 573–580.

Karantzas, G. C., & Lawrence, J. A. (1998). *Distributions of caregiving responsibilities made by adults in later life*. Technical report for the National Ageing Research Institute. Melbourne: University of Melbourne.

Karantzas, G. C., Feeney, J. A., & Wilkinson, R. B. (2010). Does less mean more? A confirmatory factor analytic study of the Attachment Style Questionnaire and the Attachment Style Questionnaire – Short Form. *Journal of Social and Personal Relationship, 27*, 749–780.

Karantzas, G. C., Lawrence, J. A., & Ryan, J. (2010). *The value of elder care tasks for older adults and family caregivers*. Manuscript submitted for publication.

Kendig, H. (1986). Intergenerational exchange. In H. Kendig (Ed.), *Ageing and families: A support networks perspective*, (pp. 85–109). Sydney: Allen & Unwin.

Krause, A. M., & Haverkamp, B. E. (1996). Attachment in adult child–older parent relationships: Research, theory and practice. *Journal of Counseling and Development, 75*, 83–92.

Lawrence, J. A., & Campbell, H. (1997). *Assigning responsibilities in families*. Melbourne: University of Melbourne.

Lawrence, J. A., Goodnow, J. J., Woods, K., & Karantzas, G. (2002). Distribution of caregiving tasks among family members: The place of gender and availability. *Journal of Family Psychology, 16*, 493–509.

Lee, Y. R., & Sung, K. T. (1997). Cultural differences in caregiving motivations for demented parents: Korean caregivers versus American caregivers. *International Journal of Ageing and Human Development, 44*, 155–127.

Litwak, E. (1985). *Helping the elderly: The complementary roles of informal and formal systems*. New York: Guilford Press.

Long, S. O., & Harris, P. B. (2000). Gender and elder care: Social change and the role of the caregiver in Japan. *Social Science Japan Journal, 3*, 21–36.

Magai, C., & Cohen, C. I. (1998). Attachment style and emotion regulation in dementia patients and their relation to caregiver burden. *Journal of Gerontology: Psychological Sciences, 53*, 147–154.

Markiewicz, D., Reis, M., & Gold, D. P. (1997). An exploration of attachment styles and personality traits in caregiving for dementia patients. *International Journal of Ageing and Human Development, 45*, 111–132.

Merz, E., & Consedine, N.S. (2009). The association of family support and wellbeing in later life depends on adult attachment style. *Attachment and Human Development, 11*, 203–221.

Messeri, P., Silverstein, M., & Litwak, E. (1993). Choosing optimal support groups: A review and reformulation. *Journal of Health & Social Behavior, 34*, 122–137.

Mikulincer, M., & Shaver, P. R. (2007). *Attachment patterns in adulthood: Structure, dynamics, and change.* New York: Guilford Press.

Miller, B., & Cafasso, L. (1992). Gender differences in caregiving: Fact or artifact? *The Gerontologist, 32*, 498–507.

National Family Caregivers Association (1998). *Caregiving across the life-cycle.* Maryland: National Family Caregivers Association. Retrieved April 12, 2005, from www.thefamilycaregiver.org/who_are_family_caregivers/caregiving_survey.cfm.

Noller, P., Feeney, J. A., & Peterson, C. (2001). *Personal relationships across the life-span.* Philadelphia: Psychology Press.

Penning, M. J. (1995). Cognitive impairment, caregiver burden, and the utilisation of home health services. *Journal of Aging and Health, 7*, 233–253.

Pinquart, M., & Sorensen, S. (2002). Older adults' preferences for informal, formal, and mixed support for future care needs: A comparison of Germany and the United States. *International Journal of Aging and Human Development, 54*, 291–314.

Roberto, K. A., Allen, K. R., & Blieszner, R. (2001). Older adults' preferences for future care: Formal plans and familial support. *Applied Developmental Science, 5*, 112–120.

Shi, L. (1993). Family financial and household support exchange between generations: A survey of Chinese rural elderly. *The Gerontologist, 22*, 468–480.

Silverstein, M., Gans, D., & Yang, F. M. (2006). Intergenerational support to aging parents: The role of norms and needs. *Journal of Family Issues, 27*, 1068–1084.

Sorensen, S., & Pinquart, M. (2000). Vulnerability and access to resources as predictors of preparation for future care needs in the elderly *Journal of Aging and Health, 12*, 275–300.

Sorensen, S., Webster, J. D., & Roggman, L. A. (2002). Adult attachment and preparing to provide care for older relatives. *Attachment & Human Development, 4*, 84–106.

Thompson, L., & Walker, A. J. (1984). Mothers and daughters: Aid patterns and attachment. *Journal of Marriage and the Family, 46*, 313–322.

United Nations (2004). *World population ageing: 1950–2050.* United Nations. Retrieved April 27, 2005, from www.un.org/esa/population/publications/worldageing19502050/.

Walker, A. J., Pratt, C. C., Shin, H. Y., & Jones, L. L. (1989). Why daughters care: Perspectives of mothers and daughters in a caregiving situation. In J. A. Mancini (Ed.), *Aging parents and adult children* (pp. 199–212). Boston: Lexington Books.

Walker, A. J., Pratt, C. C., Shin, H. Y., & Jones, L. L. (1990). Motives for parental caregiving and relationship quality. *Family Relationships, 39*, 51–56.

Wallhagen, M. I., & Yamamoto-Mitani, N. (2006). The meaning of family caregiving in Japan and the United States: A qualitative comparative study. *Journal of Transcultural Nursing, 17*, 65–73.

Wolf, D. A., Freedman, V., & Soldo, B. J. (1997). The division of family labor: Care for elderly parents. *Journals of Gerontology Series B, 52*, 102–109.

Yue, X., & Ng, S. H. (1999). Filial obligations and expectations in China: Current views from young and old people in Beijing. *Asian Journal of Social Psychology, 2*, 215–226.

7

Late-Life Transitions and Interventions

Impacts on Marriage, Remarriage, and Widowhood

Kathleen Piercy

One of the benefits of current longevity patterns are that more couples attain old age, sometimes very old age, together. Marriage rates of older adults differ by gender and race, with men age 65 and older more likely to be married than are women, because women live longer on average than men and older men often remarry younger women. Caucasians in late life are more likely to be married than persons of other races or ethnicities (except for Asian/Pacific Islander men, who are married at slightly higher rates than white men (U.S. Census Bureau, 2005).

Living into old age with a marital partner benefits the health of older adults (Pienta, Hayward, & Jenkins, 2000), particularly when the marriage is of good quality (Umberson, Williams, Powers, Liu, & Needham, 2006). In fact, Umberson and colleagues found that negative marital experiences were associated with a decline in self-rated health among aging married persons over a 9-year period. Thus, simply being married does not confer health benefits; rather, positive marital interaction is necessary to maintain good health in old age.

Furthermore, when health declines, having a spouse as primary caregiver often results in more personalized care and reduced likelihood of institutionalization. Spouse caregivers tend to provide care longer than adult children, and some senior adults who can function independently have moved into assisted living facilities with their spouses to avoid placing them in a nursing home (Kemp, 2008). Other couples turn to homecare providers to assist them with their goal of preserving togetherness when one or both partners experience serious health problems (Piercy, 2007).

The Wiley-Blackwell Handbook of Couples and Family Relationships, First Edition.
Edited by Patricia Noller and Gery C. Karantzas.

Different types of old-age marriage are prevalent. The "survivors of marriage," those in long-term marriages, may be married 40 years or longer by the time they reach age 65, and many live to celebrate 50 years together. However, many older adults' marriages, including some long-term marriages, are remarriages that occur after one or both partners have been widowed or divorced. Although divorce rates are low among today's elders, increasingly, they are divorcing (Clarke, 1995). Given the higher rates of divorce among today's middle-aged cohorts, it is likely that more couples will enter old age in a second or third marriage, or as cohabitants rather than spouses.

Currently, some couples cohabit in late life. Although cohabitation rates are quite low among older Americans, cohabitation has increased among all age groups in recent years (Brown, Lee, & Bulanda, 2006). Characteristics of older cohabiters are mixed in valence; for example, they tend to have more depressive symptoms than married elders, but they rate their relationships as more equitable than married couples and spend more time alone with partners (Calasanti & Kiecolt, 2007). Other nonmarital couples include homosexual partnerships and couples who live apart together. Less is known about these relationships, but they are increasing in prevalence (Calasanti & Kiecolt, 2007; chapter 2 in this volume).

Factors that Contribute to Marital Quality and Satisfaction in Late-Life Marriages

Most late-life marriages are happy ones. However, across different samples, about 1 in 5 couples report marital distress, dissatisfaction, or loneliness (De Jong Gierveld, van Groenou, Hoogendoorn, & Smit, 2009; Henry, Miller, & Giarrusso, 2005; Ko, Berg, Butner, Uchino, & Smith, 2007; Umberson et al., 2006). However, disagreements and distress in late-life marriage may not lead to separation and divorce. Next, I review areas of disagreement and conflict in late-life marriages, as well as individual and couple characteristics that contribute to marital quality and satisfaction in late-life marriage.

Both quantitative and qualitative research has been conducted to examine the strengths of and tensions within enduring marriages. Findings offer insights into what couples believe makes their marriages stable and strong. For example, in marriages of 35 years duration or longer, Levenson, Carstensen, and Gottman (1993) found that the primary precipitants of conflict in these marriages were issues of communication, recreation, money, and children. Chief sources of pleasure in these marriages were children and grandchildren, past good times, memorable vacations, and recent activities.

In Henry and associates' (2005) study, couples identified areas of disagreements and disappointments. An average of 1.4 problems was nominated, with satisfied couples nominating fewer problems. Conflict over leisure activities was the problem most often endorsed (23% of responses), followed by intimacy and communication (13%), financial matters, or no problems at all (both at 11%). A mere 16% of all couples were totally congruent in identified problems. Nonetheless, over 86% of these couples reported being satisfied with their marriages.

Asked what sustained their marriages in good and bad times, couples married 30 years or longer in Robinson and Blanton's (1993) study described intimacy that was balanced with autonomy, commitment, communication, religious orientation, and similar perceptions of their relationship. Likewise, Aleman's (2009) study of couples married over 40 years identified commitment to each other and to the marriage as characteristics that allowed them to remain stable in the face of changes, particularly undesired ones, such as poor health.

As in younger marriages, positive and negative interaction patterns contribute to marital satisfaction in late-life couples (e.g., chapters 9, 10, 29 in this volume). Comparing a sample of middle-aged and older couples who were observed in both disagreements and collaborative tasks, Henry et al. (2007) found that older spouses viewed their partners' behaviors as more positive and less negative than did middle-aged spouses. Relationships between a spouse's positive behavior (warmth, friendliness) and level of marital satisfaction was stronger among older than middle-aged couples. However, older spouses with partners who exhibited more frequent negative (hostile) behaviors were more likely than middle-aged spouses to tie their lower levels of marital satisfaction to partners' negative behaviors.

Those who have negative interactions with spouses in late life may also experience difficulties in their other close relationships. A longitudinal study of 500 elders explored negative interactions with one's social network over a 6-year period. Only half of the sample was married. But those married participants who reported negative interactions with spouses also reported problems with children and friends (Krause & Rook, 2003). Depression contributed to negative interactions among study participants.

Finally, a Dutch study of aging examined the presence of emotional or social loneliness among married elders and examined factors that predicted each type of loneliness (de Jong Gierveld et al., 2009). Overall, nearly 20% of married women rated their emotional loneliness as high; while 18–26% of the sample rated their social loneliness as high (men had higher ratings of social loneliness than women). Higher levels of both types of loneliness were reported in situations in which the spouse had health problems or functional limitations, or the marriage had frequent disagreements, few conversations, or an unsatisfying level of sexual activity. It is evident that a spouse's declining health can have deleterious consequences for interpersonal connections, marital quality, or both.

There are many challenges to couple satisfaction and bonds that occur in late life. Chronic or life-threatening illness for one or both members of the dyad can threaten the couple's bond. Severe illness or death of a middle-aged child can precipitate significant grief that challenges couples to find positive and compatible ways to cope with their losses. A child's divorce leaves an older couple to deal with the loss of valued children-in-law and grandchildren. Children's remarriages thrust them into unfamiliar roles of step-grandparenthood. Eventually, one spouse is widowed and faced with undergoing a process of bereavement and establishing a new identity as a single person. When widows and widowers date and remarry, relationships in their own intergenerational family are affected.

In the rest of this chapter, I discuss challenges to couple closeness brought on by several typical life transitions in late life. These challenges include retirement, health problems, dementia care, widowhood, and remarriage.

Retirement

Most persons withdraw from the paid labor force in mid or late life. For some, retirement because of poor health or corporate downsizing occurs as soon as their early 50s; for others, retirement is postponed until old age. Since 1995, participation in the paid labor force has increased for men both ages 55–64 as well as over age 65 (Purcell, 2008). Since the middle of the 20th century, women's participation in the paid labor force has steadily increased among those nearing and in late life. As of 2007, 12.6% of women age 65 and older in the United States were in the paid labor force (Purcell, 2008). Interestingly, in 2008, over 37% of men aged 55 to 64 who received income from a pension or retirement saving plan were still working part or full time. Thus, retirement occurs later than before, and for some, withdrawal from paid labor is a gradual process, rather than a sudden event.

Much retirement research has focused on couple levels of satisfaction. Most couples express satisfaction with their lives in retirement (Szinovacz & Davey, 2005); however, retirement satisfaction or perceived marital quality in retirement are affected by several factors. Good health and sufficient retirement income and assets have been associated with retirement satisfaction for both men and women retirees (Smith & Moen, 2004; Szinovacz & Davey, 2005). For men who exhibit positive affect and physiological relaxation in their marital interactions pre-retirement, greater levels of retirement happiness were reported (Kupperbusch, Levenson, & Ebling, 2003). However, one or more adult children living in the couple's home is linked to lower levels of relationship quality for retired couples (Chalmers & Milan, 2005).

Couples express preferences for retiring together (Henkens, 1999), and some studies suggest that the quality of the couple's relationship is better when retirement is synchronous (Chalmers & Milan, 2005). However, asynchronous retirement among today's couples is likely to be more prevalent because of economic issues. Because transitions to retirement bring about potential changes to couple roles and responsibilities, couple decision making and influence in retirement decision making has been examined in relation to retirement satisfaction.

Smith and Moen (2004) studied married couples in which one member of the couple had retired to determine what factors were associated with retirement satisfaction in these couples. They found that 77% of those who had retired reported being very satisfied with their retirement; however, only 67% of their spouses were equally satisfied. They also found important gender differences. Couples with retired husbands had more satisfied husbands when their wives had exerted more influence in their decisions to retire; however, retired wives were much more likely to be satisfied with their retirement when their husbands were *not* influential in their retirement decisions (Smith & Moen).

Using a longitudinal design and nationally representative data set (Health and Retirement Survey), Szinovacz and Davey (2005) also investigated the influence of marital decision making (a spouse's relative say in marital decisions) on retirement satisfaction. Retirement satisfaction was generally high in the overall sample. However, retired wives with husbands who still worked and had greater levels of say in the couple's relationship were among the least satisfied of all couples. They also found that retired husbands with working wives who possessed more influence in decisions were less satisfied with their retirement than retired husbands whose wives worked but had lesser amounts of decision-making influence in the marriage. These findings suggest that the retirement transition is a sensitive topic for many couples, and that wives in particular may desire to make independent decisions about the timing and circumstances of their retirement. Given that many of the current cohort of older women may have interrupted or postponed careers for childbearing and childrearing purposes, many may desire to extend their paid employment/careers into late life for both the financial and social benefits that often are acquired with longer employment.

Health Problems

As people age, health status and functional ability generally decline. However, there is great variation in personal health status, as well as the number and severity of health problems experienced by couples in old age. In some dyads, both partners enter old age in good health and remain healthy for a decade or longer; in others, one or both partners has experienced several chronic health conditions by their later years. Functional limitations often increase over time for persons with chronic illnesses such as diabetes, arthritis, or autoimmune disorders such as lupus. Other persons develop life-threatening illnesses such as cancer or heart disease. When one partner is healthy and the other's health declines, the healthier partner likely becomes primary caregiver to the ailing partner. Spouse caregiving often is stressful (Levesque, Ducharme, Zarit, Lachance, & Giroux, 2008); sometimes it is simultaneously rewarding and stressful (Perry & O'Connor, 2002).

Most societies expect spouses to provide care to an ill or impaired partner. Some provide assistance for years, while others undertake care for a few weeks or months. Dementia is a disease about which much research has been conducted. Because of its increasing prevalence and deleterious effects on the health, well-being, and marital quality of close dyads, I focus on it next.

Mild Cognitive Impairment and Dementia

Mild cognitive impairment (MCI) or dementia is increasingly likely to affect one or both members of an elderly dyad. MCI is a diagnostic category that refers to "the transitional state between the cognitive changes of normal aging and very early dementia" (Petersen & Negash, 2008, p. 45). Although not all persons with MCI will progress to dementia, persons with the amnestic type of MCI progress to Alzheimer's disease at the rate of about 10–15% per year (Petersen, Smith, Waring, Ivnik, Tangalos, & Kokmen, 1999). When MCI or dementia is present, couples experience a series of changes that eventually alter their relationships with each other and their existing social networks (Wright, 1991).

Few treatments are available to persons with cognitive impairments. Clinical trials with medicines such as donepezil (Aricept) have found that its use *may* delay a diagnosis of Alzheimer's disease in persons with MCI (Petersen et al., 2005). Donepezil and other acetylcholenesterase inhibitors (AChEIs) also treat persons in early to mid-stage dementia. They may slow but not arrest cognitive decline. In lieu of effective treatment options, both researchers and practitioners have examined how care partners (person with dementia and primary caregiver) manage their situations.

Coping with cognitive impairment

A diagnosis of MCI or dementia can turn a couple's world upside down. Some couples initially deny the implications of the diagnosis, preferring instead to attribute memory problems and apathy in their partner to laziness or a lack of focus (Blieszner, Roberto, Wilcox, Barham, & Winston, 2007). For many of these couples, it is only when presented with dramatic, undeniable evidence of persistent memory loss or unsafe behaviors that they begin to try to cope with these symptoms.

Dementia care is time consuming, expensive, and in some cases, hazardous to the primary caregiver's health. A recent study of coronary heart-disease risk in those caring for a spouse with dementia found that dementia caregivers were at greater risk than non-caregivers of developing heart disease over time, primarily because of higher blood pressure (von Kanel, et al., 2008). Emotional and psychological well-being can be similarly affected. Elevated levels of depressive symptoms have been found in dementia caregivers (Schulz, O'Brien, Bookwala, & Fleissner, 1995). In addition, a U.S. study comparing dementia caregivers with nondementia caregivers found that dementia caregivers were more likely to be spouses and elderly, to invest more hours in weekly care provision, and acknowledge greater levels of physical and emotional strain than nondementia caregivers (Ory, Hoffman, Yee, Tennstedt, & Schulz, 1999).

Despite these risks and difficulties, many persons with dementia have dedicated spouse caregivers who recognize that the illness is part of "living in relationship" (Davies & Gregory, 2007); and many of them persistently seek ways to preserve couplehood and the dignity of the spouse with dementia. Robinson Clare, and Evans's (2005) study showed that both members of the dementia-care dyad immediately began a process of making sense of their circumstances and adjusting to losses that included developing coping strategies. Attentive spouse dementia caregivers exhibit compassion towards their partners (Baikie, 2002), and engage in a process of preserving personhood in the loved one with dementia (Perry & O'Connor, 2002). The primary goal of spouse caregivers was to insure that the spouse with dementia "remain fully present—to himself, to the caregiver, and to others—as a person rather than simply a dementia sufferer" (p. 56). Caregiver strategies included maintaining continuity over time in the relationship, supporting competencies in the spouse with dementia, protecting the spouse from feelings of incompetence, and strategizing public encounters (Perry & O'Connor).

Notwithstanding these positive findings, the progression of MCI and dementia can lead to a lower quality marital relationship, often because upsetting behaviors, apathy, or withdrawal on the part of the person with dementia reduce the amount of interaction and reciprocity between partners (de Vugt et al., 2003; Garand, Dew, Urda, Lingler, DeKosky, & Reynolds, 2007; Wright, 1991). Even so, deVugt and colleagues (2003) noted that most caregivers reported feeling closer to their spouses with dementia than they had in the past.

Having a close relationship both pre- and post-impairment is crucial to the well-being of both members of the dyad. Steadman, Tremont, and Davis (2007) found that a close relationship prior to dementia onset was associated with less perceived burden, less reactivity to cognitive and behavioral problems, and better communication and problem-solving efforts on the part of spousal caregivers. Furthermore, preserving relationship closeness between care partners can influence the course of cognitive and functional decline in the person with dementia. In a longitudinal population study of dementia care dyads, Norton and colleagues (2009) found that the closer the relationship between care partners, the slower the rate of cognitive and functional decline in persons with dementia. The effect of relationship closeness on the rate of decline in dementia was greater for spouse dyads than adult child–parent dyads.

Regardless of relationship quality, many spouses caring for partners with dementia need help to provide care. In the next section I describe effective care management strategies, along with interventions that have been helpful in strengthening couple relationships or managing caregiver burden.

Optimal care management strategies and therapeutic interventions

Choice of caregiver strategies for managing the lifestyle of persons with mild cognitive impairment or dementia may affect the care recipient's behavior. De Vugt et al. (2004) identified three typical care management strategies, based in part on whether or not caregivers accepted the situation they faced. *Non-adapters* did not accept the situation and they characteristically reacted to the person with dementia with impatience, irritation, or anger. They tried to manage behavior problems by confronting or ignoring their spouse.

Caregivers who accepted the situation were called adapters, divided into two types: nurturing and supporting. Nurturers took on most responsibilities in their households, tried to protect the person with dementia, and saw the spouse as childlike, no longer an equal. Supporting caregivers, by contrast, found ways to adapt to demented persons' levels of functioning and allowed them to lead the way. These caregivers talked things over with their spouses, exhibited patience in dealing with dementia-related behavior issues, and tried to encourage their spouses to engage in activities, either alone or together. De Vugt and colleagues (2004) found that over a year, caregivers who used non-adaptive strategies had more behavior problems with their spouses and felt less competent as caregivers than those who were supporters. Non-adapting caregivers also reported higher levels of depression and neuroticism than accepting caregivers. Thus, care strategies utilized play an important role in the well-being of both spouses in a dementia-care situation.

Blieszner et al. (2007) and Blieszner and Roberto (2010) have recommended that interventions be delivered early in the care process to optimize the environment for couples and families facing MCI and dementia. Remarried couples experiencing cognitive impairment in one spouse may be especially in need of such interventions, as evidence suggests that remarried caregivers experience little family involvement in care provision and significant conflict with stepchildren (Sherman & Boss, 2007).

Both education and counseling services have potential to help spouse caregivers deal with changes in relationships with their ill spouses. Some interventions target the primary caregiver, while others target the couple's relationship. An example of a couple-centered intervention was proposed by Quayhagen and Quayhagen (1996) who developed a 4-month dyadic cognitive-remediation intervention. Both spouses were engaged in enhancing communication and conversation skills, along with improving problem solving and cognitive stimulation of the spouse with dementia. After several months, spouse relationships improved as dyads rediscovered quality in their lives.

More recently, a counselor-guided dyadic intervention for persons with early-stage dementia and their family caregivers was offered to help care partners (including nonspouse caregivers) plan for future care needs. This program showed success in attaining concrete plans (Whitlatch, Judge, Zarit, & Femia, 2006). Critical to the success of both of these interventions was a sense that persons with dementia felt listened to and understood by their caregivers.

Other intervention programs teach elders with dementia to perform stimulating activities matched to their current abilities in their homes, and instruct family caregivers how to initiate and carry out these activities (Gitlin, Winter, Burke, Chernett, Dennis, & Hauck, 2008). A randomized trial of this "Tailored Activity Program" demonstrated that caregivers whose relatives received the intervention reported less frequent problem behaviors and greater activity engagement in persons with dementia than in matched controls. Caregivers who received this program felt they were "on duty" less often than before, and also experienced a greater sense of mastery and skill at providing care (Gitlin et al., 2008).

Interventions that increase support for spouse caregivers have also produced positive outcomes. A longitudinal study of spouses assigned to an enhanced counseling and support intervention that included family counseling, a weekly support group, and on-call telephone counseling for crises found that compared with those spouses who received "usual care," spouses who took part in the enhanced intervention reported increases in support-network size, satisfaction with their support networks, and supportive persons increased their involvement with care provision (Roth, Mittelman, Clay, Madan, & Haley, 2005).

All of the described interventions are labor-intensive and require patience and persistence on the part of care partners and interventionists alike. Yet, the stressors of care provision are such that these programs are worth disseminating to wider audiences than they currently reach.

Adjustment to Widowhood

Being widowed is common in old age, particularly for women. As they age, married women are increasingly likely to be widowed compared to married men (He, Sengupta, Velkoff, & DeBarros, 2005). Widowhood generally requires more psychological and social adjustments than any other late-life event (Hatch, 2000), and is linked to elevated mortality rates for both widows and widowers in the first decade of widowhood (Elwert & Christakis, 2008). Yet the majority of persons adjust satisfactorily to widowhood after a period of grieving, although they follow different trajectories of grief and recovery in the months after spousal death (Bonanno, Wortman, & Nesse, 2004). A widow or widower's support network may be crucial in this adjustment.

Loneliness affects most widowed adults. Pinquart's (2003) study of loneliness among German elders found that widowers endorsed higher levels of loneliness than widows, similar to Davidson's (2001) findings with a British sample. To cope with loneliness and grief, widowed persons benefitted from high-quality contact with their adult children (Pinquart, 2003). Other research found that widowed persons received more emotional and instrumental support following their losses than their married counterparts, but that contact with and levels of support from others return to pre-loss levels about 2.5 years after widowhood commences (Guiaux, Van Tilburg, & Broese, 2007).

One's use of a support network prior to widowhood may influence its use after widowhood. In a longitudinal study of American widowed persons, Ha (2008) reported that persons with a confidant prior to widowhood were much more likely to have a confidant post-loss than those with no confidant pre-loss. Ha also found that compared to their married counterparts, those widowed for 18 months reported more emotional support from friends and other relatives. Taking these results together provides strong evidence that while widowed persons are lonelier than those still married, a support network, including family and friends, tends to increase contact and emotional support to bereaved persons in the first 18 months–2.5 years after widowhood.

Can being widowed lead to personal growth? The answer is yes for some men and women, according to Carr (2004a). Using a resilience framework and longitudinal design, she examined pre-loss marital dependence among a sample of widowed men and women. Overall, Carr found that bereaved women reported higher levels of personal growth following spousal loss than did bereaved men. Examining these gender differences, she discovered that the more emotionally dependent a woman was during her marriage, the higher her level of self-esteem was in widowhood. Among widowed men, those "who were most dependent on their wives for home maintenance and financial management tasks experience the greatest personal growth following loss" (Carr, 2004a, p. 220). She concluded that those widows and widowers who learn that they are capable of functioning successfully alone are most likely to attain an increased level of psychological well-being.

Remarriage

Studies of dating and remarriage among older adults are sparse. Though men are more likely to remarry than women, relatively few do so: 2% of older widows and 20% of older widowers remarry (Smith, Zick, & Duncan, 1991). In one study of widows and widowers' desires to date and remarry, Carr (2004b) found that men with low or average levels of social support at 6 months post-loss were more likely than women to report interest in remarrying. At 6 months after their spouse's death, men were more likely than women to desire remarriage (30 vs. 16%), to desire dating (17 vs. 6%), and to be dating at present (15 vs. less than 1%). However, at 18 months post-loss, men and women did not vary in their desire to remarry, although this desire remained below 30% for both sexes. At this 18-month interval, men were more likely than women to desire to date and to actually do it.

Some reasons for these gender differences in desire to date and remarry were offered by Davidson (2001) in her study of widows and widowers conducted at least 2 years post-loss. Widows described themselves as selfish; enjoying their newfound freedom from responsibility for looking after the daily needs of a husband. Few of them dated and most who sought any contact with men wanted only a companion to accompany them to social events. By contrast, a third of the sample of widowers was dating again, with several desirous of marriage. Loneliness in widowhood was a great motivator for courtship and remarriage for these men, although the older and poorer their health, the less likely they were to view remarriage as a possibility.

In support of the notion of loneliness as a motivator for widower remarriage, Carr (2004b) found that social support from friends reduced a widower's desire to remarry. Overall, gender and levels of support from others seem to play an important role in response to dating and remarriage during widowhood.

As in any remarriage, issues related to stepfamily formation and adjustment play a role in the success of the new union (Adler-Baeder & Higginbotham, 2004). Problems in remarriage may occur when one or both partners has not adequately grieved the lost spouse, or continues a relationship with an ex-spouse following divorce. Also, adult children, particularly those who remain financially or emotionally dependent on a parent, may create conflict between partners that threatens the success of their remarriage (Piercy, 2010). Unresolved issues of money and inheritance can create tensions in late-life remarriages. For example, Sherman and Boss (2007) found that even among remarried couples with prenuptial agreements, adult children of remarried men with dementia challenged their stepmothers about ownership of personal or family possessions and inheritance issues. Given these difficulties, couples may be wise to seek counseling prior to a remarriage. In addition, couples with substantial amounts of income and assets may also benefit from a pre-nuptial agreement prior to the wedding.

Implications for Practitioners

Interventions for couples or widowed persons experiencing difficult transitions are important to maintaining well-being. I have presented evidence that targeted interventions for dementia have proved helpful to couples. However, current cohorts of older adults are often reluctant to seek help. For example, Switzer, Wittink, Karsch, and Barg (2006) found that among their sample of depressed elders, personal responsibility, described as pulling oneself up by the bootstraps, was the pervasive approach to managing depression. Moreover, among widowed adults who used hospice services before spousal death, less than half of them accessed bereavement interventions, and most preferred services offered by clergy or medical providers delivered at home (Bergman & Haley, 2009). Given that many current intervention programs are not able to offer flexible delivery options, reaching couples and individuals who might benefit from professional help is a challenge.

Socioemotional selectivity theory (Carstensen, 1995) suggests that as people age, they seek or maintain fewer social contacts, but prefer emotionally close relationships with them. Following this theory, a primary goal in working with older widowed individuals or couples is to help them expand their supportive networks or learn how to make better use of the networks they already have. Practitioners need to look beyond family members to support of friends, neighbors, church members, paid help, and adopted family members (so called "fictive kin;" Stack, 1974). Blieszner and Adams (1992) noted that education programs and formal and informal support groups could help older adults to build new friendships or supplement them.

One way for older adults to develop close, rewarding relationships is through volunteerism and civic engagement. In the United States, over 60% of adults ages 55 and over volunteer through organizations, informally, or in both ways (Zedlewski & Schaner, 2005). Volunteering offers a host of benefits to elders. Volunteering benefits both physical (Hinterlong, Morrow-Howell, & Rozario, 2007) and mental health among older adults (Lum & Lightfoot 2005; Morrow-Howell, Hinterlong, Rozario, & Tang, 2003; Musick & Wilson 2003), especially when volunteer activities are combined with paid employment (Hao, 2008). Older volunteers also report greater well-being than their nonvolunteer peers. Greenfield and Marks (2004) found that older adults who volunteered for formal organizations experienced more positive affect and felt a stronger sense of purpose in life than their nonvolunteer counterparts. This sense of purpose is especially strong in those who serve in religious organizations (Piercy, Cheek, & Teemant, 2010; Stockton-Chilson 2004). Thus, encouraging older adults to engage with their community may be a key factor in ensuring the maintenance of meaningful social ties and safeguarding their emotional well-being.

References

Adler-Baeder, F., & Higginbotham, B. (2004). Implications of remarriage and stepfamily formation for marriage education. *Family Relations, 53*, 448–458.

Aleman, M. W. (December, 2009). *Managing dialectical tension in later life marriage and families.* Retrieved December 29, 2009 from http://journal.oates.org.

Baikie, E. (2002). The impact of dementia on marital relationships. *Sexual and Relationship Therapy, 17*, 289–299.

Bergman, E. J., & Haley, W. E. (2009). Depressive symptoms, social network, and bereavement service utilization and preferences among spouses of former hospice patients. *Journal of Palliative Medicine, 12*, 170–176.

Blieszner, R., & Adams, R. G. (1992). *Adult friendship*. Newbury Park, CA: Sage.

Blieszner, R., & Roberto, K. A. (2010). Care partner responses to the onset of mild cognitive impairment. *The Gerontologist, 50*, 11–22.

Blieszner, R., Roberto, K. A., Wilcox, K. L., Barham, E. J., & Winston, B. L. (2007). Dimensions of ambiguous loss in couples coping with mild cognitive impairment. *Family Relations, 56*, 196–209.

Bonanno, G. A., Wortman, C. B., & Nesse, R. M. (2004). Prospective patterns of resilience and maladjustment during widowhood. *Psychology and Aging, 19*, 260–271.

Brown, S. L., Lee, G. R., & Bulanda, J. R. (2006). Cohabitation among older adults: A national portrait. *Journals of Gerontology: Social Sciences, 61B*, S71–S79.

Calasanti, T., & Kiecolt, K. J. (2007). Diversity among late-life couples. *Generations, 31*(3), 10–17.

Carr, D. (2004a). Gender, preloss marital dependence, and older adults' adjustment to widowhood. *Journal of Marriage and the Family, 66*, 220–235.

Carr, D. (2004b). The desire to date and remarry among older widows and widowers. *Journal of Marriage and the Family, 66*, 1051–1068.

Carstensen, L., (1995). Evidence for a life-span theory of socioemotional selectivity. *Current Directions in Psychological Science, 4*, 151–156.

Chalmers, L., & Milan, A. (spring, 2005). Marital satisfaction during the retirement years. *Canadian Social Trends* (Cat. No. 11-008). Statistics Canada.

Clarke, S. C. (1995). Advance report of final divorce statistics, 1989 and 1990. *Monthly Vital Statistics Report, 43*(8). Hyattsville, MD: National Center for Health Statistics.

Davidson, K. (2001). Late life widowhood, selfishness and new partnership choices: A gendered perspective. *Ageing and Society, 21*, 297–317.

Davies, J., & Gregory, D. (2007). Entering the dialogue: Marriage biographies and dementia care. *Dementia, 6*, 481–488.

de Jong Gierveld, J., van Groenou, M. B., Hoogendoorn, A. W., & Smit, J. H. (2009). Quality of marriages in later life and emotional and social loneliness. *Journals of Gerontology: Social Sciences, 64B*, 497–506.

de Vugt, M. E., Stevens, F., Aalten, P., Lousberg, R., Jaspers, N., Winkens, I., et al. (2003). Behavioral disturbances in dementia patients and quality of the marital relationship. *International Journal of Geriatric Psychiatry, 18*, 149–154.

de Vugt, M. E., Stevens, F., Aalten, P., Lousberg, R., Jaspers, N., Winkens, I., et al. (2004). Do caregiver management strategies influence patient behavior in dementia? *International Journal of Geriatric Psychiatry, 19*, 85–92.

Elwert, F., & Christakis, N. A. (2008). The effect of widowhood on mortality by the causes of death of both spouses. *American Journal of Public Health, 98*, 2092–2098.

Garand, L., Dew, M. A., Urda, B., Lingler, J. H., DeKosky, S. T., & ReynoldsIII, C. F. (2007). Marital quality in the context of mild cognitive impairment. *Western Journal of Nursing Research, 29*, 976–992.

Gitlin, L. N., Winter, L., Burke, J., Chernett, N., Dennis, M. P., & Hauck, W. W. (2008). Tailored activities to manage neuropsychiatric behaviors in persons with dementia and reduce caregiver burden: A randomized pilot study. *American Journal of Geriatric Psychiatry, 16*, 229–239.

Greenfield, E., & Marks, N. (2004). Formal volunteering as a protective factor for older adults' psychological well-being. *Journal of Gerontology: Social Sciences, 59B*, 258–264.

Guiaux, M., Van Tilburg, T., & Broese, M. (2007). Changes in contact and support exchange in personal networks after widowhood. *Personal Relationships, 14*, 457–473.

Hatch, L. R. (2000). *Beyond gender differences: Adaptations to aging in life course perspective.* Amityville, NY: Baywood.

Ha, J. (2008). Changes in support from confidants, children, and friends following widowhood. *Journal of Marriage and the Family, 70*, 306–318.

Hao, Y. (2008). Productive activities and psychological well-being among older adults. *Journal of Gerontology: Social Sciences, 63B*, S64–S72.

He, W., Sengupta, M., Velkoff, V. A., & DeBarros, K. A. (2005). P23-209. *65+ in the United States: 2005.* U.S. Census Bureau Current Population Reports. Washington, DC: Government Printing Office.

Henkens, K. (1999). Retirement intentions and spousal support: A multi-actor approach. *Journal of Gerontology: Social Sciences, 54B*, S63–S74.

Henry, N. J. M., Berg, C. A., Smith, T. W., & Florsheim, P. (2007). Positive and negative characteristics of marital interaction and their association with marital satisfaction in middle-aged and older couples. *Psychology & Aging, 22*, 428–441.

Henry, R. G., Miller, R. B., & Giarrusso, R. (2005). Difficulties, disagreements, and disappointments in late-life marriages. *International Journal of Aging and Human Development, 61*, 243–264.

Hinterlong, J. E., Morrow-Howell, N., & Rozario, P. A. (2007). Productive engagement and late-life physical and mental health: Findings from a nationally representative panel study. *Research on Aging, 29*, 348–370.

Kemp, C. L. (2008). Negotiating transitions in later life: Married couples in assisted living. *Journal of Applied Gerontology, 27*, 231–251.

Ko, K. J., Berg, C. A., Butner, J., Uchino, B. N., & Smith, T. W. (2007). Profiles of successful aging in middle-aged and older adult married couples. *Psychology & Aging, 22*, 705–718.

Krause, N., & Rook, K. S. (2003). Negative interaction in late life: Issues in the stability and generalizability of conflict across relationships. *Journal of Gerontology: Psychological Sciences, 58*, P88–P99.

Kupperbusch, C., Levenson, R. W., & Ebling, R. (2003). Predicting husbands' and wives' retirement satisfaction from the emotional qualities of marital interaction. *Journal of Social and Personal Relationships, 20*, 335–354.

Levenson, R. W., Carstensen, L. L., & Gottman, J. M. (1993). Long-term marriage: Age, gender and satisfaction. *Psychology & Aging, 8*, 301–313.

Levesque, L., Ducharme, F., Zarit, S. H., Lachance, L., & Giroux, F. (2008). Predicting longitudinal patterns of psychological distress in older husband caregivers: Further analysis of existing data. *Aging and Mental Health, 12*, 333–342.

Lum, T. Y., & Lightfoot, E. (2005). The effects of volunteering on the physical and mental health of older people. *Research on Aging, 27*, 31–55.

Morrow-Howell, N., Hinterlong, J., Rozario, P. A., & Tang, F. (2003). Effects of volunteering on the well-being of older adults. *Journal of Gerontology: Social Sciences. 158B*, 137–145.

Musick, M. A., & Wilson, J. (2003). Volunteering and depression: The role of psychological and social resources in different age groups. *Social Science and Medicine 56*: 259–269.

Norton, M. C., Piercy, K. W., Rabins, P. V., Green, R. C., Breitner, J. C. S., Ostbye, T. et al. (2009). Caregiver-recipient closeness and symptom progression in Alzheimer disease. The Cache County Dementia Progression Study. *Journals of Gerontology: Psychological Sciences, 64B*, 560–568.

Ory, M., Hoffman, R. R., Yee, J. L., Tennstedt, S., & Schulz, R. (1999). Prevalence and impact of caregiving: A detailed comparison between dementia and nondementia caregivers. *The Gerontologist, 39*, 177–185.

Perry, J., & O'Connor, D. (2002). Preserving personhood: (Re)Membering the spouse with dementia. *Family Relations, 51*, 55–62.

Petersen, R. C., & Negash, S. (2008). Mild cognitive impairment: An overview. *CNS Spectrum, 13*, 45–53.

Petersen, R. C., Smith, G. E., Waring, S. C., Ivnik, R. J., Tangalos, E. G., & Kokmen, E. (1999). Mild cognitive impairment: Clinical characterization and outcome. *Archives of Neurology, 56*, 303–308.

Petersen, R. C., Thomas, R. G., Grundman, M., Bennett, D., Doody, R., Ferris, S., & Alzheimer's Disease Cooperative Study Group. (2005). Vitamin E and Donepezil for the treatment of mild cognitive impairment. *New England Journal of Medicine, 352*, 2379–2388.

Pienta, A. M., Hayward, M. D., & Jenkins, K. R. (2000). Health consequences of marriage for the retirement years. *Journal of Family Issues, 21*, 559–586.

Piercy, K. W. (2007). Successful collaborations between formal and informal care providers: Paul and Patrice's story. *Generations, 31*(3), 72–73.

Piercy, K. W. (2010). *Working with aging families: Therapeutic solutions for caregivers, spouses, & adult children.* New York: W. W. Norton.

Piercy, K. W., Cheek, C., & Teemant, B. (2010). Perceived challenges, growth, and benefits to older adults in volunteer services with religious organizations. Unpublished manuscript.

Pinquart, M. (2003). Loneliness in married, widowed, divorced, and never-married older adults. *Journal of Social and Personal Relationships, 20,* 31–53.

Purcell, P. (2008). *Older workers: Employment and retirement trends* (RL30629). Washington, DC: Congressional Research Service. Retrieved February 14, 2010 from http://assets.opencrs.com/rpts/RL30629_20080915.pdf.

Quayhagen, M. P., & Quayhagen, M. (1996). Discovering life quality in coping with dementia. *Western Journal of Nursing Research, 18,* 120–135.

Robinson, L. C., & Blanton, P. W. (1993). Marital strengths in enduring marriages. *Family Relations, 42,* 38–45.

Robinson, L., Clare, L., & Evans, K. (2005). Making sense of dementia and adjusting to loss: Psychological reactions to a diagnosis of dementia in couples. *Aging & Mental Health, 9,* 337–347.

Roth, D. L., Mittelman, M. S., Clay, O. J., Madan, A., & Haley, W. E. (2005). Changes in social support as mediators of the impact of a psychosocial intervention for spouse caregivers of persons with Alzheimer's disease. *Psychology and Aging, 20,* 634–644.

Schulz, R., O'Brien, A. T., Bookwala, J., & Fleissner, K. (1995). Psychiatric and physical morbidity effects of dementia caregiving: Prevalence, correlates, and causes. *The Gerontologist, 35,* 771–791.

Sherman, C. W., & Boss, P. (2007). Spousal dementia caregiving in the context of late-life remarriage. *Dementia, 6,* 245–270.

Smith, D. B., & Moen, P. (2004). Retirement satisfaction for retirees and their spouses: Do gender and the retirement decision-making process matter? *Journal of Family Issues, 25,* 262–285.

Smith, K. R., Zick, C. D., & Duncan, G. J. (1991). Remarriage patterns among recent widows and widowers. *Demography, 28,* 361–374.

Stack, C. (1974). *All our kin.* New York: Harper and Row.

Steadman, P. L., Tremont, G., & Davis, J. D. (2007). Premorbid relationship satisfaction and caregiver burden in dementia caregivers. *Journal of Geriatric Psychiatry and Neurology, 20,* 115–119.

Stockton-Chilson, K. E. (2004). A comparative study of giving and volunteering patterns among adults with Seventh-day Adventist and other Christian religious identities. *Dissertation Abstracts International: Section B: The Sciences and Engineering, 64* (Electronic; Print). Retrieved from http://www.csa.com. (2004-99002-323).

Switzer, J. F., Wittink, M. N., Karsch, B. B., & Barg, F. K. (2006). "Pull yourself up by your bootstraps:" A response to depression in older adults. *Qualitative Health Research, 16,* 1207–1216.

Szinovacz, M. E., & Davey, A. (2005). Retirement and marital decision making: Effects on retirement satisfaction. *Journal of Marriage and the Family, 67,* 387–398.

Umberson, D., & Williams, K., Powers, D. A., Liu, H., & Needham, B. (2006). You make me sick: Marital quality and health over the life course. *Journal of Health & Social Behavior, 47,* 1–16.

U.S. Census Bureau (2005). *American community survey 2005 questionnaire.* Washington, DC: U.S. Census Bureau.

Von Kanel, R., Mausback, B. T., Patterson, T. L., Dimsdale, J. E., Aschbacher, K., Mills, P. J., Grant, I. (2008). Increased Framingham coronary heart disease risk score in dementia caregivers relative to non-caregiving controls. *Gerontology, 54,* 131–137.

Whitlatch, C. J., Judge, K., Zarit, S. H., & Femia, E. (2006). Dyadic intervention for family caregivers and care receivers in early-stage dementia. *The Gerontologist, 41*, 462–473.

Wright, L. K. (1991). The impact of Alzheimer's disease on the marital relationship. *The Gerontologist, 31*, 224–237.

Zedlewski, S. R., & Schaner, S. G. (2005). Older adults engaged as volunteers. Retrieved from http://www.urban.org/UploadedPDF/311325_older_volunteers.pdf.

PART III

Communication and Conflict Processes in Couples and Families

8

Conflict Avoidance in Families

Functions, Outcomes, and Applied Implications

John P. Caughlin, Jennifer L. Hardesty, and Ashley V. Middleton

People in families and other close relationships attempt to avoid conflict in a number of distinct ways (Roloff & Ifert, 2000; Sillars, Canary, & Tafoya, 2004). Sometimes they choose not to discuss issues that might lead to conflict; sometimes they withdraw during conflict or try to change the subject; sometimes they leave the setting of an argument. Regardless of the particular strategy used, the general impression one gets from both scholarly and popular writing is that avoiding conflict is harmful.

The Case Against Conflict Avoidance

Scholars and clinicians commonly believe that avoiding conflicts is inherently counterproductive. With respect to marriage, for instance, Wahlroos (1995) advised against avoidance, suggesting, "You must resolve—if you want a truly intimate and trusting relationship with your partner—to be open and honest about your feelings, to level with your partner, and to bring up all significant problems, concerns, and worries" (p. 107). Notarius, Lashley, and Sullivan (1997) claimed that confronting potential problems rather than avoiding them is crucial: "If your partner is doing something that leaves you feeling hurt and angry, it is obviously not constructive simply to ignore the offensive behavior

The Wiley-Blackwell Handbook of Couples and Family Relationships, First Edition.
Edited by Patricia Noller and Gery C. Karantzas.

and hope that it goes away" (p. 235). Withdrawing from a conflict once it has begun is also considered a "danger sign" in marital relationships (Clements, Cordova, Markman, & Laurenceau, 1997; chapters 9, 10 in this volume).

One reason why conflict avoidance is viewed as problematic is the fact that engaging in conflict can serve important functions in families (Koerner & Fitzpatrick, 2006). Conflict can help family members become aware of each other's needs, making it possible to accommodate each other (Koerner & Fitzpatrick, 2006). Conflict also appears to serve developmental functions for younger family members: A common view of parent–adolescent conflict holds "that conflict between mothers and daughters is normative in early adolescence, and that some conflict may be necessary for girls to become more autonomous" (Graber & Brooks-Gunn, 1999 p. 213).

Overall, conflict avoidance typically is associated with poor marital and family outcomes (Noller, Feeney, Bonnell, & Callan, 1994; Meeks, Hendrick, & Hendrick, 1998). In a study of stepfamilies, for example, Golish (2003) found that it was uncommon for adolescents in thriving stepfamilies to report avoiding conflict topics, but adolescents in families who struggled commonly avoided topics that could lead to conflict (e.g., issues surrounding their biological parents' divorce). Also, interventions designed to promote constructive conflict engagement can be effective (e.g., Hahlweg, Markman, Thurnmaier, Engl, & Eckert, 1998).

Reasons to Question Whether Conflict Avoidance is Inherently Problematic

Despite the apparently strong evidence against avoiding conflict, there are reasons to question whether conflict avoidance is inevitably problematic. First, the success of teaching constructive conflict management techniques to distressed couples does not necessarily preclude the possibility that conflict avoidance can be innocuous and even useful. The most consistent communication correlates of marital discord are affectively-negative ones—not avoidant ones (Caughlin & Vangelisti, 2006). Thus, the studies that show benefits of teaching constructive conflict engagement may depend more on family members learning to replace negative behaviors with positive ones; that is, preventing negative behaviors may be more important than preventing avoidant ones.

Second, avoiding conflict is common, even in seemingly functional relationships. Vuchinich (1987) found that even in nondistressed families, the majority of naturally occurring conflicts were not resolved; most conflicts ended in standoffs, which involved a family member simply initiating a nonconflict activity without any clear winner or compromise. Moreover, there is strong evidence that people simply do not raise most potential conflict issues in their marital and family relationships. Even in good relationships, people "often irritate each other on a daily basis" (Roloff & Wright, 2009, p. 321), but only a small minority of those irritations result in an overt conflict episode (Caughlin & Vangelisti, 2006).

Overall then, there does not appear to be convincing evidence that avoiding conflict is inevitably harmful. Unqualified statements about the inadvisability of conflict avoidance are too simplistic. Indeed, avoiding conflicts can be functional in some circumstances (Roloff & Wright, 2009).

Some Potential Benefits of Conflict Avoidance

One reason some scholars give for engaging in (rather than avoiding) conflict is the notion that "the number and type of conflict areas . . . are less important than how couples handle these conflicts" (Clements et al., 1997, p. 342). This mantra is useful for aiding some troubled couples because it draws attention to conflict-management skills, which can be taught. However, there is strong evidence that the number of overt conflict episodes in families does matter. The frequency of conflicts in marriage, for instance, is a known correlate of poor relational quality (Kelly, Huston, & Cate, 1985; Noller & Feeney, 1998, 2002; chapter 9 in this volume), and the number of conflicts couples have as newlyweds forecasts their level of satisfaction 13 years after their wedding (Caughlin & Huston, 1996). Similarly, frequent conflict between parents and adolescents is associated with poor adolescent adjustment, both concurrently (Caughlin & Malis, 2004; chapter 9 in this volume) and over time (Shek, 1998). Given that frequent conflict episodes seem to be problematic in family relationships, avoiding some conflicts might benefit some relationships.

Avoiding conflict may be particularly beneficial if it is used as a means to prevent the noxious effects of certain behaviors. Roberts (2000), for instance, found that the association between husbands' hostility and wives' dissatisfaction was diminished by the husbands' conflict avoidance. As Roberts concluded, "A wife may react positively to her husband's conflict-avoiding behaviors if the alternative is hostile responsiveness" (p. 704).

Given the reasons to believe that conflict avoidance does not always harm couples, it is important to consider when conflict avoidance would be more or less harmful. Based on a review of literature and an analysis of the various possible purposes of conflict and conflict avoidance behaviors (see Caughlin & Scott, 2010), there are at least three types of factors that are likely to determine whether conflict avoidance is helpful, harmful, or innocuous: (a) the form of the conflict avoidance; (b) the meanings of behaviors to family members; and (c) the specific context in which those behaviors are enacted. We discuss each of these factors below before turning to practical implications of such research. Because the vast majority of the extant literature focuses on instances in which conflict avoidance is harmful, we attend primarily to conditions when conflict avoidance may be helpful or innocuous.

Factors that Influence the Effects of Conflict Avoidance

Forms of conflict avoidance

Conflict avoidance may be more or less detrimental to relationships, depending upon how individuals avoid (Sillars et al., 2004). Although most studies of conflict avoidance do not distinguish among various avoidant behaviors, the few studies that do so suggest the importance of examining different forms of conflict avoidance. Roberts (2000), for example, examined partners' perceptions of the frequency of conflict-avoidance behaviors, distinguishing between angry withdrawal and other conflict avoidance. Angry withdrawal, avoidance marked by high levels of hostility, was associated with dissatisfaction and distress, whereas conflict avoidance was only weakly associated with relationship quality (Roberts, 2000). The Roberts' study suggests that conflict avoidance that is marked with negative affect is more detrimental to marital well-being than is avoidance alone.

Another apparently useful distinction was made by Crohan (1996), who differentiated between actively leaving the scene versus passively waiting until the conflict episode has subsided. Individuals who avoid conflict by actively withdrawing, as compared to those who passively avoid by remaining quiet, are more likely to experience decreased satisfaction over time (Crohan, 1996). This finding suggests a conceptual distinction between implicit avoidance (e.g., changing the topic without explicitly refusing to discuss the conflict issue) versus explicit conflict avoidance (e.g., overtly refusing to talk about an issue or physically leaving).

Indeed, Caughlin and Scott (2010) argued that explicit or overt avoidance is more uniformly dissatisfying in marital and family relationships than are more tacit strategies of avoidance. The reason is that if one person wishes to discuss a conflict topic and the other explicitly avoids that topic, such behavior will nearly always be understood as being uncooperative. Avoiding through more implicit means, however, leaves open the possibility that family members can maintain the pretense that they have discussed or would discuss the issues.

We are not suggesting that a person using implicit avoidance strategies will always be successful in maintaining the appearance of open discussion, but there do appear to be occasions when family members avoid talking about topics while successfully maintaining the pretext that they are completely open and engaging with each other. For instance, in a study of Australian parents and adolescents, Kirkman, Rosenthal, and Feldman (2005) found that maintaining a global impression of "openness" was important in families, but that such an impression could be maintained even if explicit discussions of some sexual issues were avoided. Clearly, if such avoidance happens explicitly, it would be harder to maintain the sense of overall openness than if the avoidance is more implicit.

Additionally, Dailey and Palomares (2004) found that the association between relationship satisfaction and strategic topic avoidance varied by the degree to which the avoidance tactic was direct and polite. The use of highly polite and indirect avoidance strategies was positively associated with relationship satisfaction and closeness (for similar findings regarding indirect strategies see chapter 16 in this volume; Roloff & Ifert 1998).

Although the examples discussed thus far concern avoiding communication generally, there are good reasons to believe that this pattern of findings can be extrapolated to conflict avoidance. One instance of conflict avoidance that is inherently explicit is the demand–withdraw pattern of conflict, which occurs when one individual attempts to engage the partner in a discussion, but the partner avoids the issue (Caughlin & Scott, 2010; Christensen & Heavey, 1993; chapters 9, 10 in this volume). Because the demand part of the pattern explicitly introduces the topic to the conversation, the possibility of completely covert conflict avoidance (e.g., when a topic is simply not raised) is precluded (Caughlin &

Scott, 2010). This fact could help explain why demand–withdraw appears to be so consistently related to undesirable outcomes (e.g., Caughlin & Huston, 2002; Denton, Burleson, Hobbs, Von Stein, & Rodriguez, 2001; Malis & Roloff 2006).

Moreover, various off-the-record conflict-avoidance strategies may have benefits. The literature on serial arguing in relationships (Roloff & Johnson, 2002) suggests that it is often more important to foster the impression that a conflict could be resolved than to actually resolve it (Malis & Roloff, 2006). Conventional wisdom, of course, would suggest that not actually engaging in conflicts would only result in the issue causing greater problems later. In contrast, Malis and Roloff (2006) found that coping strategies like selectively ignoring problems are frequently beneficial to relationships. Because ignoring a problem is a cognitive strategy, it is certainly tacit most of the time, and this could be part of the reason why it can be effective in terms of maintaining relational closeness.

Meaning of Avoidance Behaviors

One of the most fundamental tenets of communication scholarship is the fact that communication behaviors do not have inherent meanings (Caughlin, 2010). Individuals' beliefs about other communicators' purposes or goals in conversation, for example, partly determine the meanings that people ascribe to communication behaviors (Wilson, 2002). In marriage, a suggestion to change a spouse's behavior can be considered either "helpful advice" or "nagging," depending on the purposes attributed to the suggestion (Goldsmith, Lindholm, & Bute, 2006).

This fundamental tenet implies that conflict avoidance may not be dysfunctional or functional in its own right. Rather, the meaning ascribed to avoidant behaviors is important for understanding the significance of avoidance. At the most basic level, perceptions help define what constitutes conflict avoidance. If family members having a conversation do not perceive a topic to be an area of disagreement, for example, they would not interpret behaviors like silence or changing the topic to be conflict avoidance (Sillars, 1986). That is, people's perceptions help define the difference between what is seen as an avoided topic of conflict versus the myriad topics not being discussed at the time. Moreover, even if family members recognize some disagreement about a topic, perceptions are still important to defining the importance of the disagreement. The perception that the issue is trivial may allow them to avoid initiating conflicts about the issue without substantive harm to their relationship (Roloff & Ifert, 2000).

Additionally, individuals' beliefs about the specific reasons for the conflict avoidance probably shape the meaning and impact of that avoidance. Buysse and her colleagues (1999, 2000) found that one common reason for avoiding conflicts is the perception that an issue is relationship threatening. Although most research examining conflict avoidance has not examined the specific motivations for the avoidance, the larger literature on avoiding topics suggests that protecting a relationship is one of the most frequently cited reasons for avoiding certain topics (Dailey & Palomares, 2004). For example, adolescents in stepfamilies commonly report that they protect their relationships with their mothers, fathers, and stepparents by avoiding certain topics (Golish & Caughlin, 2002). More important, attributing avoidance to relationship protection can mitigate the connection between avoidance and relational dissatisfaction (Caughlin & Afifi, 2004).

Additionally, broader causal attribution processes may influence the connection between conflict avoidance and relational outcomes. During conflict, individuals form attributions about the other person's behavior (Sillars, Roberts, Leonard, & Dun, 2000; Sillars et al., 2004), and the specific attributions that people make about conflict behaviors are associated with relationship satisfaction (Vangelisti, 1994). For instance, individuals who make external, unstable attributions about another family member's avoidance may be less dissatisfied with their relationship than if they were to determine that the avoidance was due to stable, internal causes. Also, cognitive working models may predispose individuals to perceive features of conflict in particular ways. Individuals with an insecure attachment style tend to view conflict as inherently distressing and problematic (Creasey, 2002; Feeney, 2008); thus, having an insecure attachment may exacerbate any detrimental effects of conflict avoidance.

Similar to internal working models, marital and family schemata also structure the way individuals think about their family relationships, which may influence perceptions of conflict avoidance. Marital schemata are cognitive frameworks that influence the way that individuals interpret behavior in marriage (Koerner & Fitzpatrick, 2002a). Individuals also have schemata pertaining to entire family systems (Koerner & Fitzpatrick, 2002a). According to Fitzpatrick (1988), a defining dimension of such schemata is conflict orientation, or individuals' beliefs about the utility of avoiding conflict. Individuals who are high in avoidance orientation tend to view conflict avoidance in families as normative (Fitzpatrick & Ritchie, 1994; Koerner & Fitzpatrick, 2002b), which means they probably would view conflict avoidance as less dissatisfying than would people low on avoidance orientation. Indeed, in an observational study of married couples, Sillars, Pike, Jones, and Redmon (1983) found that avoidant conflict strategies generally were associated with marital dissatisfaction, but there was no evidence that conflict avoidance was dissatisfying among the group of couples who view conflict avoidance as normative.

The Context of Conflict Avoidance

Scholars who seek to evaluate the sophistication of communication strategies (e.g., Goldsmith, 2004) note that the effectiveness of communication behaviors is inherently linked to particular situations. One cannot make claims about whether a communication behavior or strategy is effective without understanding the interactional circumstances. For instance, episodes in which one person gives advice to another person typically involve certain risks to identity, such as the potential for appearing nosey (Goldsmith, 2004). The salience of that risk, however, depends on contextual factors such as: (a) whether the advice was solicited by the advisee or not; (b) the nature of the relationship between the advisor and advisee; and (c) the nature of the advice given. Thus, one cannot make unqualified statements about the best way to give advice because the risk of appearing intrusive is dependent on the circumstances (see also chapter 16 in this volume).

Because effectiveness depends on context, the impact of any communication behavior also depends on context. There are a number of different aspects of interactional situations that are important. First, like any communicative strategy, conflict avoidance is embedded in a broader conversational context. That is, conflict avoidance must be understood with respect to what occurs before, during, and after the avoidance. For example, outcomes of conflict avoidance can vary with the emotions expressed while avoiding. In conflicts marked by high hostility and negative affect reciprocity, husbands' avoidance is associated with higher satisfaction among wives (Roberts, 2000). That is, husbands' withdrawal appears to buffer wives' distress during hostile conflict.

Second, even when conflict avoidance generally has negative effects, these effects can be offset by other relational behaviors. Gottman (1994) reported that some people in stable marriages engaged in many avoidant behaviors, but this avoidance did not seem problematic when they also attempted to understand their partner and enacted more positive behaviors, such as focusing on the positive aspects of their relationship rather than on disagreements. Similarly, Caughlin and Huston (2002) found that avoidance occurring as part of demand–withdraw was not associated with marital dissatisfaction among couples who were otherwise very affectionate.

Third, the meaning of avoidance (and therefore potential implications for family relationships) may be a function of when it occurs in a given interaction. Fitzpatrick, Fallis, and Vance (1982) examined conflict between spouses and found that conflict avoidance was not consistently perceived to be antisocial or dysfunctional. Sometimes, conflict avoidance was perceived as cooperative. If the meaning of conflict avoidance is dependent on when it occurs (Fitzpatrick et al., 1982), then the outcomes of that conflict avoidance may be tied to when family members choose to engage in avoidance.

Outcomes of avoidance also may be a function of the physical setting in which a conflict occurs. Extant literature suggests that particular communication patterns, such as demand–withdraw, are reliably associated with poor relationship quality (Caughlin & Huston, 2002; chapter 10 in this volume). Despite the wealth of evidence regarding these communication patterns, the very nature of observational studies may preclude examination of a wide array of avoidant behaviors because the setting may limit the ways in which partners can avoid conflict (Caughlin & Scott, 2010; Roberts, 2000). For example, consider an experiment in which two family members are asked to discuss a conflict issue. The scene will generally begin with one person explicitly raising an issue. If the other person wishes to avoid discussing the topic, what options might she or he have, given the setting? Certainly, given the demands of the research study, it would be difficult for a family member to simply leave the scene, even though that happens in actual family conflict episodes (Christensen & Heavey, 1993). Also, because the instructions of the study prompted discussion of the issue, a family member who otherwise might have avoided through indirect means probably would have a more difficult time doing so in the observational setting. Thus, the context might make family members resort to more explicit forms of verbal avoidance, which may make the conflict avoidance more detrimental than if it occurred in another setting.

The type of relationship (e.g., romantic, parent–child, or sibling) may also influence the ways in which conflict avoidance is associated with functioning. When avoidance is considered normative within a particular relationship, individuals may not perceive it as dissatisfying. For example, parents often avoid discussing aspects of their own sex life with children. Rather than being viewed as a threat to the parent–child relationship, such avoidance may be viewed as appropriate and even desirable by the child (see Petronio, 2002). Further, norms that are specific to certain family forms, such as blended or stepfamilies, may preclude discussion of sensitive topics. Overall, if avoiding certain issues is perceived as normative within a given type of relationship, it is feasible that avoidance may not be associated with relationship distress or dissatisfaction (Golish & Caughlin, 2002; Petronio, 2002).

Even within a particular type of family relationship, the dynamics of each specific relationship probably shape the meaning and importance of conflict avoidance. People who are very secure and committed to their relationship may be untroubled by conflict avoidance. For example, Roloff and Ifert (1998) found that explicitly declaring that some topics were to be avoided in a relationship was dissatisfying in low-commitment dating relationships but not highly committed ones. The power dynamics of a relationship also matter. In dating and married couples, being comparatively dependent emotionally on one's partner is associated with the tendency to withhold complaints about the relationship (Solomon, Knobloch, & Fitzpatrick, 2004). For example, in a study of retired couples, Szinovacz and Schaffer (2000) found that spouses who were more dependent on their partner were more likely to avoid conflict by keeping their opinions to themselves. Avoiding due to power deficits can change the meaning of avoidance to partners. People who are low in power often minimize the importance of the topic (Solomon & Samp, 1998), which may be a coping strategy for dealing with unaddressed concerns. Such cognitive coping strategies may allow individuals to maintain their satisfaction with the relationship, at least in the short term (Roloff & Wright, 2009).

Practical Implications

In this chapter, we have argued that there are circumstances when conflict avoidance can be more or less functional in marital and family relations. This viewpoint runs counter to much scholarship on family communication, which often presumes that engaging in conflict is always more beneficial than avoiding it. Because of the often unquestioned bias toward conflict engagement (and against conflict avoidance), there are instances in which individuals in relationships are advised—and sometimes even compelled—to attempt to work through issues, even when this strategy is not ideal.

To illustrate this point clearly, it is useful to consider a particular type of family relationship in which avoiding conflict can have obvious benefits, married couples who are in the process of divorcing (see chapter 24 in this volume). Marital relationships do not end the moment the partners decide to divorce, particularly when the couple has children. Instead of ending, the family relationships are restructured with new rules and boundaries (Emery, 1994). As part of the divorce process, parents must learn how to relate to one another as parents while no longer being partners (Bohannan, 1971; Emery & Dillon, 1994). Ongoing parental conflict after divorce can have detrimental effects on children (Marsiglio, Amato, Day, & Lamb, 2000; chapter 9 in this volume); thus, separating parents are encouraged to develop cooperative relationships with minimal conflict. Policies and intervention programs have been developed to help parents with this transition. For example, many governments in Western countries mandate education classes for divorcing parents that are aimed at strengthening cooperative co-parental relationships and decreasing destructive conflict between parents (e.g., Amato, 2000). The primary purpose is to teach parents the skills to work together to resolve conflicts. While conflict engagement is appropriate for some parents, conflict avoidance may be a more effective approach in some situations.

Avoiding conflict and developing distant relationships may be healthier and safer for divorcing parents with persistently high conflict or a history of marital violence. High conflict divorces are characterized by high rates of litigation, high levels of anger and fear, and lack of trust (Blaisure & Geasler, 2006). These parents (and their children) may benefit more from learning parallel (vs. cooperative) co-parenting skills, in which parents disengage from one another to avoid explicit conflicts. Parallel co-parenting relationships tend to have a businesslike quality (Emery & Dillon, 1994) with more formal and less frequent communication, lower engagement, and more rigid boundaries than cooperative co-parenting relationships. Both types of co-parenting relationships can effectively minimize children's exposure to conflict and contribute to family adjustment after divorce (Kelly & Emery, 2003).

In addition to high conflict, a history of marital violence can make conflict avoidance essential. Women who have left their abusive husbands and are going through divorce have legitimate fears, such as concerns that they or their children remain in danger of violence from their (ex)-husbands (Hardesty & Ganong, 2006; Walker, Logan, Jordan, & Campbell, 2004). Indeed, the period after the initial separation is a time of heightened risk of abuse (Campbell, et al., 2003; Walker et al., 2004). In such circumstances, the need to ensure physical safety ought to take precedence over co-parenting plans and arrangements that rely on cooperation (Hardesty & Chung, 2006).

Unfortunately, there are considerable pressures on women who have left abusive husbands to engage in conflict with their former mates. As noted above, court-mandated parenting programs often assume that open discussion of issues is always warranted, and such programs make it difficult for women to avoid conflict altogether. Even when not directly mandated to participate in a cooperative co-parenting program, women may believe—or even be given legal advice—that their case for custody can be undermined if they are seen as anything other than a friendly and cooperative co-parent (Hardesty & Ganong, 2006). Moreover, many women strongly believe in the value of both parents being involved with children, making it personally difficult for them to cut themselves off from the spouse they are divorcing (Hardesty & Ganong, 2006). Such factors may make it difficult for women with a history of being abused to avoid conflicts with their former partners. Yet, engaging in conflicts around parenting issues could place them at continued risk of physical harm or psychological abuse (Walker et al., 2004).

Despite the barriers to doing so, some abused women have reported using conflict-avoidance strategies to prevent the potential for violence (Hardesty, Khaw, Chung, & Martin, 2008). For example, abused women reported avoiding conflict by setting rigid boundaries that limited the time spent talking with their ex-husbands and the topics about which they communicated (e.g., restricting topics unrelated to the children; Hardesty &

Ganong, 2006; Hardesty et al., 2008). When safety concerns persist after separation, women's efforts to avoid conflict become more explicit (Hardesty & Ganong, 2006). Thus, although it may be constructive to implicitly avoid conflict in general, in situations with violence, indirect strategies for avoidance may be insufficient: explicit conflict avoidance may be necessary to reinforce boundaries that separate parental and former spouse roles. Understanding when conflict avoidance is a protective factor has implications for mental health professionals and the legal system.

First, it must be recognized that legal mandates that are designed to encourage cooperative co-parenting between ex-spouses are not appropriate in all cases. Regardless of how helpful such mandates are in the majority of cases, if the efforts at establishing cooperation put a mother and children at risk for continued violence, the ideal of open discussion of differences should be abandoned in those cases. Thus, courts need to take a history of intimate partner violence very seriously, and they need a way to routinely screen for it in the divorce process (for a more thorough discussion of this issue, see Hardesty & Chung, 2006). Moreover, laws and court rulings must be sensitive to the real harm that can be done in encouraging women with a history of experiencing violence to actively engage with their former partners. There should be, for instance, provisions for identifying abused women, assessing risk, and exempting women from typically mandated programs that may compromise their safety (Hardesty & Chung, 2006).

From a counseling perspective, clinicians and social workers who assist mothers in the divorce process should be aware that many of them will have beliefs about the ideal family that make them reluctant to completely avoid conflict with their co-parent. Mothers may believe that avoiding discussions (and conflict) with the father of their children makes them uncooperative and will harm the relationship of the father with the child. When safety is an issue, however, such concerns serve as obstacles to doing what is best for the mother and the child. In such instances, clinicians would benefit from knowledge about how the meaning of conflict avoidance can be shaped by the inferences people make about avoidance. A mother who is convinced that conflict avoidance is aimed at putting the child's safety and welfare first, for example, will have a different understanding of avoidance than one who believes the avoidance serves a less benevolent purpose. When explicit and extreme conflict avoidance is warranted, counselors should recognize that individuals' willingness and ability to engage in such actions may depend, in part, on their beliefs about what those actions are accomplishing. Helping abused women understand the purposes of avoidance may be as important as suggesting when they should avoid.

The case of abused women provides a clear illustration that proscriptions against conflict avoidance are overly simplistic. There are other family relationships in which conflict avoidance is probably useful in some instances. For example, divorced parents may reasonably be committed to a continuing relationship with one another for the purposes of co-parenting their children. Parents and children may benefit from learning when and how to avoid conflict when it is in the best interests of maintaining healthy and safe relationships. For example, there may be issues that are simply too heated for the parents to discuss constructively, and it may be better to avoid such issues while still maintaining a co-parenting relationship by discussing other issues.

Lest the reader infer that we are suggesting that conflict avoidance is only useful in families negotiating a divorce, similar logic can be used in stable family relationships as well. The emphasis on openness and resolving conflicts involves risks, perhaps leaving family members unprepared for setting boundaries when necessary. Additionally, children are harmed by exposure to conflict (Cummings & Davies, 2002), so married parents who cannot resolve their issues quickly and constructively need to balance any perceived threat to their relationship against the harm that conflict episodes can have on children.

Although conflict avoidance is certainly not ideal in all situations, researchers and practitioners would benefit from understanding that conflict avoidance can be useful at times. Conflict avoidance may come with costs, as implied by the well-known association between conflict avoidance and poor adjustment in family relationships, but conflict avoidance can also have benefits that in some situations outweigh the costs. Rather than focusing only on teaching family members constructive conflict engagement skills, clinicians would do well to teach family members skills related to productive conflict avoidance, such as recognizing when conflict avoidance might be warranted, as well as how to go about avoiding conflict to minimize the risks of conflict avoidance in a given situation.

References

Amato, P. R. (2000). The consequences of divorce for adults and children. *Journal of Marriage and the Family, 62*, 1269–1287.

Blaisure, K. R., & Geasler, M. J. (2006). Educational interventions for separating and divorcing parents and their children. In M. A. Fine & J. H. Harvey (Eds.), *Handbook of divorce and relationship dissolution* (pp. 575–602). Mahwah, NJ: Erlbaum.

Bohannan, P. (1971). *Divorce and after*. New York: Anchor Books.

Buysse, A., De Clercq, A., Verhofstadt, L., Heene, E., Roeyers, H., & Van Oost, P. (2000). Dealing with relational conflict: A picture in milliseconds. *Journal of Social and Personal Relationships, 17*, 574–597.

Buysse, A., & Ickes, W. (1999). Communication patterns in laboratory discussions of safer sex between dating versus nondating partners. *Journal of Sex Research, 36*, 121–134.

Campbell, J., Webster, D., Koziol-McLain, J., Block, C., Campbell, D., Curry, M. et al. (2003). Risk factors for femicide in abusive relationships: Results from a multi-site case control study. *American Journal of Public Health, 93*, 1089–1097.

Caughlin, J. P. (2010). A multiple goals theory of personal relationships: Conceptual integration and program overview. *Journal of Social and Personal Relationships, 27*, 824–848.

Caughlin, J. P., & Afifi, T. D. (2004). When is topic avoidance unsatisfying? Examining moderators of the association between avoidance and satisfaction. *Human Communication Research, 30*, 479–513.

Caughlin, J. P., & Huston, T. L. (1996, November). *The development of conflict: Perception and frequency of conflict among couples with different marital outcomes.* Paper presented at the Annual Convention of the Speech Communication Association, San Diego, CA.

Caughlin, J. P., & Huston, T. L. (2002). A contextual analysis of the association between demand/withdraw and marital satisfaction. *Personal Relationships, 9*, 95–119.

Caughlin, J. P., & Malis, R. S. (2004). Demand/withdraw communication between parents and adolescents: Connections with self-esteem and substance use. *Journal of Social and Personal Relationships, 21*, 125–148.

Caughlin, J. P., & Scott, A. M. (2010). Toward a communication theory of the demand/withdraw pattern of interaction in interpersonal relationships. In S. Smith & S. R. Wilson (Eds.), *New directions in interpersonal communication* (pp. 180–200). Thousand Oaks, CA: Sage.

Caughlin, J. P., & Vangelisti, A. L. (2006). Conflict in dating and marital relationships. In J. G. Oetzel & S. Ting-Toomey (Eds.), *Sage handbook of conflict communication: Integrating theory, research, and practice* (pp. 129–157). Thousand Oaks, CA: Sage.

Christensen, A., & Heavey, C. L. (1993). Gender differences in marital conflict: The demand/withdraw interaction pattern. In S. Oskamp & M. Costanzo (Eds.), *Gender issues in contemporary society* (pp. 113–141). Newbury Park, CA: Sage.

Clements, M. L., Cordova, A. D., Markman, H. J., & Laurenceau, J. (1997). The erosion of marital satisfaction over time and how to prevent it. In R. J. Sternberg & M. Hojjat (Eds.), *Satisfaction in close relationships* (pp. 335–355). New York: Guilford Press.

Creasey, G. (2002). Associations between working models of attachment and conflict management behavior in romantic couples. *Journal of Counseling Psychology, 49*, 365–375.

Crohan, S. E. (1996). Marital quality and conflict across the transition to parenthood in African American and white couples. *Journal of Marriage and the Family, 58*, 933–944.

Cummings, E., M., & Davies, P. T. (2002). Effects of marital conflict on children: Recent advances and emerging themes in process-oriented research. *Journal of Child Psychology & Psychiatry & Allied Disciplines, 43*, 31–63.

Dailey, R. M., & Palomares, N. A. (2004). Strategic topic avoidance: An investigation of topic avoidance frequency, strategies used, and relational correlates. *Communication Monographs, 71*, 471–496.

Denton, W. H., Burleson, B. R., Hobbs, B. V., Von Stein, M., & Rodriguez, C. P. (2001). Cardiovascular reactivity and initiate/avoid patterns of martial communication: A test of Gottman's psychophysiologic model of marital interaction. *Journal of Behavioral Medicine, 24*, 401–421.

Emery, R. E. (1994). *Renegotiating family relationship: Divorce, child custody, and mediation.* New York: Guilford Press.

Emery, R. E., & Dillon, P. (1994). Conceptualizing the divorce process: Renegotiating boundaries of intimacy and power in the divorced family system. *Family Relations, 43*, 374–379.

Feeney, J. A. (2008). Adult romantic attachment: Developments in the study of couple relationships. In J. Cassidy & P.R. Shaver (Eds.), *Handbook of attachment: Theory, research, and clinical applications* (2nd edn., pp. 456–481). New York: Guilford Press.

Fitzpatrick, M. A. (1988). *Between husbands and wives: Communication in marriage.* Newbury Park, CA: Sage.

Fitzpatrick, M. A., Fallis, S., & Vance, L. (1982). Multifunctional coding of conflict resolution strategies in marital dyads. *Family Relations, 31*, 61–70.

Fitzpatrick, M. A., & Ritchie, L. D. (1994). Communication schema within the family. *Human Communication Research, 20*, 275–302.

Goldsmith, D. J. (2004). *Communicating social support.* New York: Cambridge University Press.

Goldsmith, D. J., Lindholm, K. A., & Bute, J. J. (2006). Dilemmas of talking about lifestyle changes among couples coping with a cardiac event. *Social Science and Medicine, 63*, 2079–2090.

Golish, T. D. (2003). Stepfamily communication strengths: Understanding the ties that bind. *Human Communication Research, 29*, 41–80.

Golish, T. D., & Caughlin, J. P. (2002). "I'd rather not talk about it": Adolescents' and young adults' use of topic avoidance in stepfamilies. *Journal of Applied Communication Research, 30*, 78–106.

Gottman, J. M. (1994). *What predicts divorce?* Hillsdale, NJ: Erlbaum.

Graber, J. A., & Brooks-Gunn, J. (1999). "Sometimes I think that you don't like me": How mothers and daughters negotiate the transition into adolescence. In M. J. Cox & J. Brooks-Gunn (Eds.), *Conflict and cohesion in families* (pp. 207–242). Mahwah, NJ: Erlbaum.

Hahlweg, K., Markman, H. J., Thurnmaier, F., Engl, J., & Eckert, V. (1998). Prevention of marital distress: Results of a German prospective longitudinal study. *Journal of Family Psychology, 12*, 543–556.

Hardesty, J. L., & Chung, G. H. (2006). Intimate partner violence, parental divorce, and child custody: Directions for intervention and future research. *Family Relations, 55*, 200–210.

Hardesty, J. L., & Ganong, L. H. (2006). How women make custody decisions and manage coparenting with abusive former husbands. *Journal of Social and Personal Relationships, 23*, 543–563.

Hardesty, J. L., Khaw, L., Chung, G. H., & Martin, J. M. (2008). Coparenting relationships after divorce: Variations by type of marital violence and fathers' role differentiation. *Family Relations, 57*, 479–491.

Kelly, C., Huston, T. L., & Cate, R. M. (1985). Premarital relationship correlates of the erosion of satisfaction in marriage. *Journal of Social and Personal Relationships, 2*, 167–178.

Kelly, J. B., & Emery, R. E. (2003). Children's adjustment following divorce: Risk and resilience perspectives. *Family Relations, 52*, 352–362.

Kirkman, M., Rosenthal, D. A., & Feldman, S. S. (2005). Being open with your mouth shut: The meaning of "openness" in family communication about sexuality. *Sex Education, 5*, 49–66.

Koerner, A. F., & Fitzpatrick, M. A. (2002a). Toward a theory of family communication. *Communication Theory, 12*, 70–91.

Koerner, A. F., & Fitzpatrick, M. A. (2002b). You never leave your family in a fight: The impact of families of origins on conflict behavior in romantic relationships. *Communication Studies, 53*, 234–251.

Koerner, A. F., & Fitzpatrick, M. A. (2006). Family conflict communication. In J. Oetzel & S. Ting-Toomey (Eds.), *The Sage handbook of conflict communication* (pp. 159–183). Thousand Oaks, CA: Sage.

Malis, R. S., & Roloff, M. E. (2006). Features of serial arguing and coping strategies: Links with stress and well-being. In R. M. Dailey & B. A. Le Poire (Eds.), *Applied interpersonal communication matters: Family, health, and community relations* (pp. 39–65). New York: Lang.

Marsiglio, W., Amato, P., Day, R. D., & Lamb, M. E. (2000). Scholarship on fatherhood in the 1990s and beyond. *Journal of Marriage and the Family, 62*, 1173–1191.

Meeks, B. S., Hendrick, S. S., & Hendrick, C. (1998). Communication, love and relationship satisfaction. *Journal of Social and Personal Relationships, 15*, 755–773.

Noller, P., & Feeney, J. A. (1998). Communication in early marriage: Responses to conflict, nonverbal accuracy, and conversational patterns. In T. N. Bradbury (Ed.), *The developmental course of marital dysfunction* (pp. 11–43). New York: Cambridge University Press.

Noller, P., & Feeney, J. A. (2002). Communication, relationship concerns, and satisfaction early in marriage. In A. L. Vangelisti, H. T. Reis, & M. A. Fitzpatrick (Eds.), *Stability and change in relationships* (pp. 129–155). New York: Cambridge University Press.

Noller, P., Feeney, J. A., Bonnell, D., & Callan, V. J. (1994). A longitudinal study of conflict in marriage. *Journal of Social and Personal Relationships, 11*, 233–252.

Notarius, C. I., Lashley, S. L., & Sullivan, D. J. (1997). Angry at your partner? Think again. In R. J. Sternberg & M. Hojjat (Eds.), *Satisfaction in close relationships* (pp. 219–248). New York: Guilford Press.

Petronio, S. (2002). *Boundaries of privacy: Dialectics of disclosure.* Albany, NY: SUNY Press.

Roberts, L. J. (2000). Fire and ice in marital communication: Hostile and distancing behaviors as predictors of marital distress. *Journal of Marriage and the Family, 62*, 693–707.

Roloff, M. E., & Ifert, D. E. (1998). Antecedents and consequences of explicit agreements to declare a topic taboo in dating relationships. *Personal Relationships, 5*, 191–205.

Roloff, M. E., & Ifert, D. E. (2000). Conflict management through avoidance: Withholding complaints, suppressing arguments, and declaring topics taboo. In S. Petronio (Ed.), *Balancing the secrets of private disclosures* (pp. 151–163). Mahwah, NJ: Erlbaum.

Roloff, M. E., & Johnson, K. L. (2002). Serial arguing over the relational life course: Antecedents and consequences. In A. L. Vangelisti, H. T. Reis, & M. A. Fitzpatrick (Eds.), *Stability and change in relationships* (pp. 107–128). New York: Cambridge University Press.

Roloff, M. E., & Wright, C. N. (2009). Conflict avoidance: A functional analysis. In T. D. Afifi & W. A. Afifi (Eds.), *Uncertainty, information management, and disclosure decisions* (pp. 320–340). New York: Routledge.

Shek, D. T. (1998). A longitudinal study of the relations between parent–adolescent conflict and adolescent psychological well-being. *Journal of Genetic Psychology, 159*, 53–67.

Sillars, A. L. (1986). *Procedures for coding interpersonal conflict* (revised manual). Missoula: University of Montana, Department of Interpersonal Communication.

Sillars, A., Canary, D. J., & Tafoya, M. (2004). Communication, conflict, and the quality of family relationships. In A. L. Vangelisti (Ed.), *Handbook of family communication* (pp. 413–446). Mahwah, NJ: Erlbaum.

Sillars, A. L., Pike, G. R., Jones, T. S., & Redmon, K. (1983). Communication and conflict in marriage. *Communication Yearbook, 7*, 414–429.

Sillars, A., Roberts, L. J., Leonard, K. E., & Dun, T. (2000). Cognition during marital conflict: The relationship of thought and talk. *Journal of Social and Personal Relationships, 17*, 479–502.

Solomon, D. H., Knobloch, L. K., & Fitzpatrick, M. A. (2004). Relational power, marital schema, and decisions to withhold complaints: An investigation of the chilling effect on confrontation in marriage. *Communication Studies, 55*, 146–167.

Solomon, D. H., & Samp, J. A. (1998). Power and problem appraisal: Perceptual foundations of the chilling effect in dating relationships. *Journal of Social and Personal Relationships, 15*, 191–209.

Szinovacz, M. E., & Schaffer, A. M. (2000). Effects of retirement on marital conflict tactics. *Journal of Family Issues, 21*, 367–389.

Vangelisti, A. L. (1994). Communication problems in committed relationships: An attributional analysis. In J. H. Harvey, T. L. Orbuch, & A. L. Weber (Eds.), *Attributions, accounts, and close relationships* (pp. 144–164). New York: Springer.

Vuchinich, S. (1987). Starting and stopping spontaneous family conflicts. *Journal of Marriage and the Family, 49*, 591–601.

Wahlroos, S. (1995). *Family communication* (Rev. edn.), Chicago: Contemporary Books.

Walker, R., Logan, T. K., Jordan, C. E., & Campbell, J. C. (2004). Integrative review of separation in the context of victimization: Consequences and implications for women. *Trauma, Violence, & Abuse, 5*, 143–193.

Wilson, S. R. (2002). *Seeking and resisting compliance: Why people say what they do when trying to influence others*. Thousand Oaks, CA: Sage.

9

Conflict in Family Relationships

Patricia Noller

One important principle of family systems theory is circular causality; this principle states that change in one member of the family affects other members and the system as a whole (Hetherington & Clingempeel, 1992; Hinde, 1989; Minuchin, 1988; O'Connor, Hetherington, & Clingempeel, 1997). In addition, family systems theory focuses on the "mutual influences of individuals within a relationship and the mutual influences among relationships" (O'Connor et al., 1997, p. 493).

In this chapter, I will be exploring the associations among different relationships within the family in the context of conflict. In our studies we have frequently explored these associations among different family relationships: links between the marital relationship and the parent–child relationship, between the parent–child relationship and the sibling relationship, and between the marital relationship and the sibling relationship, as well as the effects of siblings on each other (Noller & Feeney, 2004).

Conflict in relationships is inevitable because romantic relationships tend to bring together two people who have had different experiences in their families of origin, and who then have to find ways to live together at least relatively amicably. They also need to agree to some extent about how to parent their children. In addition, families tend to have limited resources, leading to competition and conflict between family members who want to make sure that they obtain their "fair share" of those resources. Because of the strength of feeling among family members and the inevitability of differences, conflict, when it occurs, can be intense and difficult.

The Wiley-Blackwell Handbook of Couples and Family Relationships, First Edition.
Edited by Patricia Noller and Gery C. Karantzas.

Misunderstandings and Conflict in Marriage

Noller and her colleagues (Noller, 1980, 1981, 1984; Noller & Ruzzene, 1991; Robillard & Noller, in press) carried out several studies to explore the link between accuracy in interpreting one another's nonverbal messages and the level of marital satisfaction of couples. All of these studies used standard content methodology where spouses use words that can be interpreted in at least three ways, depending on the nonverbal behavior accompanying the message. "What are you doing?" is a good example of this kind of message because it can have positive, neutral, and negative connotations.

In the Noller (1980) study, there was clear evidence that those in unhappy relationships, but especially husbands, tended to make more errors in both the way they sent the message (encoding) and the way they interpreted a message from their spouse (decoding). In addition, husbands were more likely to make decoding errors in a negative direction, whereas wives tended to make errors in a positive direction (see Noller, 2001). For example, if a wife asked her husband "What are you doing?" he would be likely to see that question as involving criticism of himself, whereas if a husband asked his wife the same question, she would be more likely to see the question in a positive light. It is easy to see how conflicts can stem from these kinds of misunderstandings.

In another study (Guthrie & Noller, 1988), where spouses were asked to report their own intentions in an interaction while their partners made a separate judgment about those intentions, those who were in low satisfaction marriages were less likely to accurately infer their spouse's intentions. In addition, the intentions of those in low satisfaction marriages were rated more negatively by a group of outside observers than were the intentions of those in high satisfaction marriages, suggesting that these low satisfaction spouses were leaking negativity through their nonverbal behavior. All spouses attributed more positive intentions to themselves when they were angry than they attributed to their angry partners. Again, there was evidence in these data for misunderstandings likely to increase the probability of conflict occurring.

Conflict Styles

Of course, family members differ in the ways that they approach conflict and respond to it (Christensen, 1988; Christensen & Heavey, 1990; Sagrestano, Christensen, & Heavey, 1998). Common patterns include mutual discussion of the issue, a coercive approach to the issue, mutual avoidance of the issue, and demand/withdraw (where one partner tries to get the other partner involved in discussion of an issue while the other partner withdraws; Christensen & Heavey, 1990). Family members, especially couples, can also collude to avoid dealing with the issue at all, in a pattern generally referred to as mutual avoidance.

Demand–withdraw as a conflict style

A large amount of research has focused on the demand–withdraw pattern in married couples (Christensen, 1988; Eldridge & Christensen, 2002; chapter 10 in this volume). Noller and

White (1990) used Christensen's Communication Patterns Questionnaire (CPQ; Christensen, 1988) and showed that greater self-reported demand–withdraw communication was associated with lower marital satisfaction. In a study of young newlywed couples recruited before their weddings, Noller and her colleagues (Noller, Feeney, Bonnell, & Callan, 1994) found that spouses who were high in marital satisfaction after 2 years of marriage were less likely to engage in destructive patterns of communication such as demand–withdraw, behaving coercively towards the partner, and avoiding discussion of the conflict.

Feeney, Noller, and Callan (1994) used the same data set to explore the links among attachment security, relationship satisfaction, and conflict communication. Mutuality in communication reported by males was positively associated with comfort with closeness and negatively associated with attachment anxiety, two important aspects of attachment security/insecurity. Attachment anxiety was positively associated with coercion for both males and females at both the first marital assessment and at follow-up, and was associated with destructive process (demand–withdraw) for females at the first marital assessment and for males at follow-up. These findings suggest that at least some conflict styles in marriage are driven by attachment insecurity, particularly anxiety about the relationship and how much the partner really cares.

Withdrawal as a conflict style

Withdrawal is generally seen as a negative behavior in couple interactions because of its consequences (Christensen, 1988; Fruzzetti, 1996; Noller, Feeney, Roberts, & Christensen, 2005). The consequences of withdrawal can include the issue not being resolved and becoming an ongoing and even escalating issue in the relationship, with the lack of resolution creating resentment in the person wanting change, and coldness and distance between the couple. It has also been suggested that withdrawal can lead to ongoing power struggles (Holtzworth-Munroe, Smutzler, & Stuart, 1998).

Of course, withdrawal can be subtle as in becoming silent, turning to look at the TV or the newspaper or changing the topic, or blatant such as in storming out of the room. In terms of Blake and Mouton's (1964) model of interpersonal communication (see Figure 9.1), withdrawal is seen as involving low concern for self (not being willing to push for what one wants) and low concern for the other (due to the apparent lack of concern for resolving the issue for the sake of the relationship with one's partner). Of course, withdrawal can also be positive, especially if a mutual decision is made to put off

Care for One's own Interests	Care for the Relationship High	Low
High	Problem-solving	Aggression
Low	Obliging/Soothing	Avoidance

Figure 9.1 Conflict styles based on Blake and Mouton, 1964
Source: Blake, R. R., & Mouton, J. S. (1964). *The managerial grid.* Houston: Gulf

discussing the issue until the partners have calmed down and are more willing to engage in a rational discussion of the issue. It has also been suggested that withdrawal is not necessarily negative, especially if partners are not introspective and share a strong bond of affection (Raush, Barry, Hertel, & Swain, 1974). (See chapter 8 in this volume for a discussion of positive aspects of conflict avoidance.)

Christensen and Heavey (1990) showed that the use of withdrawal by husbands was related to whose issue was being discussed. Husbands were more likely to withdraw when their wives' issues were being discussed than were wives whose husbands' issues were being discussed. Christensen and Heavey interpreted this finding in terms of the social structure view that focuses on power discrepancies between men and women. According to Noller (1993), men maintain their power by resisting their wives' requests for change and withdrawing from such interactions.

Withdrawal also involves a particular pattern of nonverbal behavior (Noller & Christensen, 1991, in Noller et al., 2005). These researchers found that husbands' withdrawal during discussion of their wives' issue (the clearest pattern in these data) was characterized by a lack of open gestures and gaze and by head down and head turn. Wives were rated as withdrawing during discussion of their own issue when they used few neutral gestures and engaged in head down, and husbands also used head down when withdrawing during discussion of their own issues. These behaviors are, of course, the more subtle versions of withdrawal that one might expect to see when couples are being observed in the laboratory.

Withdrawal in violent couples

Noller and Roberts (2002) compared four groups of couples in terms of their use of withdrawal: nonviolent happy; nonviolent unhappy; violent happy; and violent unhappy. Anxiety/arousal was assessed using both self-report and physiological measures, and withdrawal was rated from video-recordings of two conflict interactions: one proposed by the wife and one proposed by the husband. Overall, men tended to withdraw from conflict interactions more than did women, especially in discussions of the wife's issue and if they described their relationship as unhappy. Withdrawal tended to be used more by couples in violent distressed relationships, especially when the wife's issue was being discussed.

Because this study involved participants reporting on their anxiety/arousal and also having their physiological reactions measured continuously, we were able to use time-series analysis and explore the links between anxiety/arousal and withdrawal. There was an association between the withdrawal of males from conflict interaction and the anxiety of their female partners; in other words, when he withdrew from their interaction, her anxiety increased. This finding suggests that the anxiety of women in violent relationships is driven, at least in part, by the partner's withdrawal from the interaction. Perhaps women interpret male withdrawal as a signal that once the talking has stopped, violence may follow.

In addition, the anxiety/arousal of those men who were in violent relationships was linked to their withdrawing from an interaction with their wives within 30 seconds. Such a finding supports Gottman and Levenson's (1988) proposal that anxiety/arousal actually caused men to withdraw from marital interactions in order to decrease their unpleasant level of arousal. It is important to note, however, that the finding in the Noller and

Roberts (2002) study was specific to men in violent relationships, whereas the Gottman and Levenson (1988) proposal concerned men more generally.

Learning Conflict Patterns in the Family

One issue we were interested in was how these conflict styles are learned in the family. In a sample of families with adolescent siblings, we used different versions of the Communication Patterns Questionnaire (CPQ; Christensen, 1988) to assess communication styles between a married couple, the mother and daughter, the father and daughter, the mother and son, the father and son, and between the two siblings (Noller, Feeney, Peterson, & Sheehan, 1995). We found that the association between conflict styles in the marital relationship and in the parent–child relationship was generally strong (see Table 9.1).

Demand/withdraw ratings in the marital and the parent–child relationships were strongly correlated, especially between the marital and mother–son relationship and between the marital and father–son relationship. It seems that boys, in particular, learn this pattern in interaction with both mothers and fathers, a pattern that they are then likely to repeat in their conflict with their siblings and in their romantic relationships later in life (see Table 9.2).

In the same study, we then compared CPQ reports of conflict styles in the parent–adolescent relationship with reports of conflict styles in the sibling relationship and found moderate correlations between conflict styles in the parent–child and sibling relationships (see Table 9.2). Interestingly, there were no correlations between conflict styles in the marital and sibling relationships, suggesting that conflict styles used in sibling relationships are not modeled directly on the marital relationship, but are learned in interactions with parents (Noller et al., 1995).

Conflict and Family Members' Perceptions of One Another

In another study (Noller, Feeney, Sheehan, & Peterson, 2000), we again used the CPQ to explore the association among reports of conflict behavior in families of adolescent twins

Table 9.1 Correlations Between Marital and Parent–Child Conflict

Conflict style	*Mother*		*Father*	
	Son	*Daughter*	*Son*	*Daughter*
Mutual	.24	.48**	.49**	.54**
Coercion	.58**	.34*	.36*	.34*
Demand/withdraw	.55**	.47**	.54**	.51**

Note: $^{*}p<.05$. $^{**}p<.01$

Source: Based on Noller, P., Feeney, J., Peterson, C., & Sheehan, G. (1995). Learning conflict patterns in the family: Links between marital, parent–child and sibling relationships. In T. J. Socha & G. H. Stamp (Eds.), *Parents, children and communication: Frontiers of theory and research* (pp. 273–298). Hillsdale, NJ: Erlbaum

Table 9.2 Correlations Between Parent–Child and Sibling Conflict

Conflict style	*Mother*		*Father*	
	Son	*Daughter*	*Son*	*Daughter*
Mutual	.29	.35**	.22	.28**
Coercion	.61**	.36**	.40**	.29*
Demand/withdraw	.54**	.30*	.61**	.30*

Note: $^{*}p<.05$. $^{**}\ p<.01$
Source: Based on Noller, P., Feeney, J., Peterson, C., & Sheehan, G. (1995). Learning conflict patterns in the family: Links between marital, parent–child and sibling relationships. In T. J. Socha & G. H. Stamp (Eds.), *Parents, children and communication: Frontiers of theory and research* (pp.273–298). Hillsdale, NJ: Erlbaum

and global ratings made by family members of behavior during a videotaped decision-making interaction that included all four family members. There were no associations found for mothers, but associations were found between marital conflict styles reported by fathers and their ratings of the behavior of their adolescents during the decision-making interaction. Those fathers who reported destructive patterns of conflict in their marital relationship, perceived their adolescent twins more negatively. Thus it seems that fathers' perceptions of their offspring are affected by the quality of their relationship with their wives. It is also possible, of course, that adolescents in families where the parents are highly conflicted are more controlling and rejecting towards their parents than are adolescents whose parents are not so conflicted.

Links were also found between reports of father–child conflict and children's perceptions of one another during the interaction. Where fathers reported destructive patterns of parent–child conflict, adolescents reported more negative perceptions of one another (Noller, Feeney, Sheehan, & Peterson, 2000). It seems that patterns of marital conflict are linked, not only with conflict patterns used in other family relationships but also with family members' perceptions of one another in decision-making situations (e.g., planning a holiday). These findings illustrate the ways in which communication during conflict can impact on family relationships, even for those not directly involved in the conflict.

Conflict Strategies and Relationship Satisfaction

Noller et al. (1994) assessed not only conflict styles or patterns, but also conflict strategies over three time periods in newlywed couples: before the wedding; after approximately 1 year of marriage; and after about 2 years. On each occasion, spouses were asked to work through the videotape of their interaction and to stop the tape when they were aware of a specific strategy they were using and describe what they were trying to do. A six-category system was derived from the literature on compliance-gaining strategies and conflict resolution (e.g., Schaap, Buunk, & Kerkstra, 1988). The six categories included three strategies that would generally be considered positive: reason, assertion, partner support; as

Table 9.3 Definitions and Examples of Six Conflict Strategies

Positive strategies	*Definitions*
Reason	Rational argument, problem solving (use of reason or logic; presenting alternatives or seeking solutions)
Assertion	Direct expression of opinions or wants (clear statement of one's position; redirecting conversation to topic; emphasis by gesture or eye contact)
Partner support	Acknowledgment of partner's views (active listening or questioning; support or agreeing with partner; compromise or concession)
Negative strategies	
Coercion	Seeking control through use of force (threat; blame; sarcasm; physical or verbal aggression)
Manipulation	Attempts to gain compliance by indirect or false means (providing misleading information; attempts to make partner feel guilty/defensive; feigning of moods)
Avoidance	Physical/emotional retreat from the situation (changing or avoiding the topic; avoiding eye contact)

Source: Noller, P., Feeney, J. A., Bonnell, D., & Callan, V. J. (1994). A longitudinal study of conflict in early marriage. *Journal of Social and Personal Relationships, 11*, 233–252.

well as three strategies that would generally be considered negative: coercion, manipulation, and avoidance. See Table 9.3 for definitions of the strategies and examples of the ways they were implemented.

In terms of positive strategies, we found that husbands low in relationship satisfaction increased their use of the reasoning from before marriage to a year or so after marriage, and then reduced their use of reason after 2 years of marriage. Wives low in relationship satisfaction, on the other hand, increased their support of their husbands from before marriage to after a year of marriage and then decreased that support after 2 years. For the negative strategies, both husbands and wives low in relationship satisfaction reported less manipulation and less avoidance after a year of marriage than they did before marriage or after 2 years. It seems that couples make an effort over the first year or so and then give up if they don't get the effect they want. Spouses high in satisfaction after 2 years of marriage were less likely to rely on manipulation, avoidance, and destructive patterns such as demand–withdraw and coercion in dealing with conflicts with their partners.

Conflict in Separated/Divorcing Families

Although people tend to have a general expectation that conflict ends with separation and divorce, that notion seems to be far from the truth. We carried out a study to explore conflict in separated/divorcing families with adolescents, and to compare the levels of conflict in those families with the levels of conflict in stable married families that included the biological parents of the adolescents (Noller, Feeney, Sheehan, Darlington, & Rogers, 2008; Sheehan & Noller, 2002).

Sibling relationships

We focused first on the relationships between siblings because we wanted to know what impact an event such as the separation or divorce of their parents would have on the relationships between siblings. We expected that, rather than their relationships becoming more conflicted (that is, *congruent* with the relationships of their parents), siblings might become closer as a way of *compensating* for the loss of a close relationship with their parents. We did find more sibling conflict in the relationships of siblings in divorcing families than was true for the relationships of siblings in stable married families, and we also found that, whereas siblings from divorcing families reported similar levels of conflict over time, those from stable married families reported decreasing levels of conflict. These findings tend to support the congruence hypothesis.

We also found that siblings in the divorcing families reported using more attacking-type communication in interactions with their sibling at the second data collection (approximately 12 months later) than at the first, whereas siblings in the married families reported less attacking-type communication at the second data collection than at the first. In addition, the difference between the siblings in the two types of families was greater at the second data collection than the first. In other words, the communication between the siblings in the stable married families tended to improve over time, whereas the communication between the siblings in the divorcing families seemed to get worse over time.

Although there is considerable research support for the congruence hypothesis (Boer, Goedhart, & Treffers, 1992; Noller et al., 1995), Sheehan and her colleagues (Sheehan, Darlington, Noller, & Feeney, 2002) argued that congruence and compensation could coexist in sibling relationships in separated/divorcing families. Congruence is possible because sibling relationships tend to be intense (Sulloway, 1996), because adolescents in families in the process of separating or divorcing are likely to be exposed to high levels of conflict between parents (Amato & Keith, 1991) that could be highly stressful (Noller, Feeney, Peterson, & Atkin, 2000). In other words, if the congruence hypothesis is correct, sibling relationships in these families are likely to be quite hostile and conflicted.

On the other hand, the conditions may also exist for compensation to occur. Bank (1992) argued that a lack of parental care and high levels of access to their sibling are likely to increase the probability of adolescents compensating for this lack of parental attention by developing a very close bond with their sibling. Although parents in separating and divorcing families are not knowingly or deliberately neglectful of their children, they are likely to be so absorbed in their own problems that adolescent siblings are left to care for one another and their relationships could become closer and warmer.

We based our study on a typology of sibling relationships developed by McGuire and her colleagues (McGuire, McHale, & Updegraff, 1996) in which sibling relationships were assessed on the two critical dimensions of warmth and hostility. Warmth and hostility were measured using the Sibling Relationship Questionnaire (SRQ; Furman & Buhrmester, 1985).

McGuire et al. (1996) identified four possible types of sibling relationships. In our research, we also found the same four types of sibling relationships found by McGuire et al. (1996): harmonious (high in warmth and low in hostility); hostile (high in hostility and low in warmth); uninvolved (low on both warmth and hostility); and affect-intense

Sibling Hostility	Sibling Warmth	
	High	Low
High	Affect-intense	Hostile
Low	Harmonious	Uninvolved

Figure 9.2 McGuire et al.'s 1996 typology of sibling relationships
Source: Created from McGuire, S., McHale, S.M., & Updegraff, K. (1996). Children's perceptions of the sibling relationship in middle childhood: Connections within and between family relationships. *Personal Relationships, 3*(3), 229–239

(high in both warmth and hostility). A really interesting finding was that the sibling relationships of those adolescents in the separated/divorcing families were twice as likely as those from the stable married families to be affect-intense or high in *both* hostility and warmth (Sheehan et al., 2002; see Figure 9.2.). Affect-intense relationships tended to be as nurturant as harmonious relationships and as dominant as hostile relationships. Sibling relationships in the married families were not all harmonious, but more evenly spread across the four types.

Because we also interviewed individual adolescents about the nature of their sibling relationships, we were able to understand how high levels of warmth and high levels of hostility could coexist in these relationships. A commonly reported scenario was where older siblings provided nurturance and support for younger siblings who weren't always appreciative of this support and sometimes even resented it. For example, a younger sibling might seek support from an older sibling when the parents were fighting and want to stay with him or her, but would resist if they thought that their independence was being threatened or the sibling was being too nurturant. Younger siblings were often ambivalent about the protectiveness of an older sibling and saw such behavior as sometimes good and sometimes bad.

An older brother might believe that he should take on a fathering role towards his younger brother and teach him how to shave etc., but the younger brother might not be totally happy with being "fathered" by his brother and want a more equal role in the relationship. It is important to note that there were also families in which the younger child appreciated the love and support of an older sibling and felt protected because of that support. In addition there were families where the support was mutual (Sheehan et al., 2002). For example some siblings believed that because of the fighting between their parents, they had grown closer and needed to depend on each other more.

Couple conflict

In this same study (Noller et al., 2008) we asked both children and parents in the married and divorcing families to rate inter-parental conflict. The ratings were made with regard to pre- and post-separation for the separated/divorcing couples and at the follow-up for the married families. For both adult and child ratings, it was clear that there was more conflict between parents in the divorcing families than between those in the stable married families, both before and after the separation.

Children in the separated/divorcing families (the only ones interviewed) tended to see their parents' arguments as stupid and trivial and often saw their parents' conflict behavior as childish. Although they may be right at one level, they almost certainly failed to understand the underlying issues. For example arguments that might seem trivial to children may be about power and who has the right to make decisions in that particular area. For example, relatively unimportant arguments about such issues as which restaurant to eat at or which movie to see can be about power and losing face.

Children also saw a lot of arguments as being about financial issues, and they particularly reported on financial issues that affected them. Examples are issues about who would pay school-related expenses such as uniforms and school camps, and who would pay for extracurricular activities such as music lessons and sport.

Children also mentioned conflict around transfers when they were moving between families. These seemed to be times when parents could start arguments with each other around all kinds of issues, particularly child-related issues. And, if all else failed, there was always the telephone. Children reported many arguments between their parents using the telephone. They described parents screaming at each other on the telephone and arguing with each other for hours at a time.

Parent–child conflict

Family members also completed the ICPS Family Functioning Scales (Noller, Seth-Smith, Bouma, & Schweitzer, 1992) as a measure of parent–child conflict and the SRQ as a measure of sibling conflict (note that data from the SRQ have already been reported in the section on sibling relationships.). Both parents and children in the divorcing families reported more parent–child conflict in the divorcing families than in the married families. In addition, the children in the divorcing families reported less family intimacy than those in the stable married families (Noller et al., 2008).

In terms of mother–adolescent conflict, young people described their relationships with their mothers as "up-and-down" before the separation but basically okay. Some, however, reported more conflict with their mothers after the separation than before. They also reported frequent arguments with their mothers about money and admitted that they sometimes provoked conflict by being deliberately annoying towards their mothers who were generally the resident parent.

Fathers were criticized for being too controlling and for not allowing their adolescent sons and daughters enough of the kinds of choices that they would expect at their age. They saw their fathers as being critical of them and not accepting them, and some claimed that their fathers were prone to outbursts of temper during times of conflict. As would be expected, they also complained about problems of organizing time together and being in trouble for planning things or being invited to parties etc. on "his weekend."

Family Conflict and Adolescent Psychological Adjustment

Another important issue related to family conflict concerns the impact of family conflict on the psychological adjustment of younger family members. In the study of divorcing families described above (Noller et al., 2008), we also obtained measures of adjustment: self-esteem, anxiety, and depression. Our analysis was carried out with conflict and family type (married versus divorcing) as the independent variables. We found that across all three measures of adjustment, adolescents in high conflict families were less well adjusted than their counterparts in low conflict families. A similar effect was found for family type, with adolescents in divorcing families being less well adjusted than those in stable married families. In addition, those whose families were both high in conflict and in the process of divorcing were the least well adjusted of all the families.

Differential Parenting and Conflict Between Siblings

We have also carried out studies to explore the links between differential treatment by parents (where one sibling is clearly favored over the other) and conflict in the sibling relationships of stable families. We assessed communication during conflict using self-report questionnaires and by coding videotapes of actual interactions between twin siblings (Sheehan, 2000; Sheehan & Noller, 2002). Links were found between twins' reports of absolute differential treatment (that is, not taking into account who was favored and who was disfavored) and their reports of their conflict interactions. Twins who reported more differential treatment also reported more destructive patterns of conflict in their interactions with one another. They reported more avoidance of conflict, more attacking behavior, more distress following the conflict, and less ability to solve the problems between them. It is important to note here that both twins experienced this negative climate for dealing with conflict, irrespective of whether they were favored or disfavored.

In the interaction task, twins who reported that they were treated differently from their twin by their parents, rated their own and their twin's communication less positively than those who did not report differential treatment. In addition, outsiders' ratings of the communication between the twins were correlated with the twins' reports of differential parenting. For firstborn twins, their reports of differential parenting were associated with outsider ratings of their communication with their twin as unfriendly and rejecting. Thus differential parenting was related to more negative interactions between siblings than was true for families where differential treatment was not reported.

Implications

Conflict that is inevitable in family relationships can be related to misunderstandings, especially in couples, who may misinterpret one another's intentions. Such misunderstandings may be particularly problematic when intentions are interpreted more negatively than they were meant. It may be important for therapists to highlight the importance of the nonverbal behaviors that accompany their statements and that may lead to misinterpretation and arguments.

Family members use different conflict styles, with the main styles being mutual discussion, coercion, demand–withdraw, and withdrawal. Conflict styles are related to attachment insecurity and the quality of the relationship. Withdrawal is generally seen as less effective than other styles because issues tend not to get resolved and there can be a build-up of resentment leading to coldness and distance between the couple. Therapists may find it useful to work on attachment styles with some couples, especially if they engage in a lot of coercive interactions or tend to favor demand–withdraw as a conflict style. Those engaging in pre-marital education may also need to be aware of the importance of the first 2 years of marriage for the development of communication patterns.

Communication styles are learned in the family, especially in interactions between parents and children and these interactions can affect sibling conflicts. Children, and especially sons, seem to learn the demand–withdraw style in interaction with their parents. Given that demand/withdraw is not an effective way of dealing with conflict, those educating parents in conflict management should help them find more constructive strategies for dealing with conflict so that destructive patterns won't be passed on to the next generation.

In violent couples, both husbands' and wives' anxiety seems to be an important driver of their communication patterns. It may be important for therapists to talk with violent couples about this pattern and the role that the anxiety of both the husband and wife plays in the cycle of violence.

Fathers' perceptions of their conflict communication with their wives had an impact on their perceptions of their offspring. In addition, fathers' perceptions of parent–child conflict seemed to affect siblings' perceptions of one another. Parents in conflicted families may need help to understand these processes and the implications for all family relationships.

Divorced or separated families tend to be involved in more conflict than stable married families across marital, parent–child, and sibling relationships. In addition, in those families that were both high in conflict and separated or divorced, the children were the least well-adjusted children in the study. Those counseling divorcing couples may need to help them to deal with their disagreements more effectively, and in ways that do not impact so heavily on the children. Because of the intense emotions that are aroused by family breakdown, this task will not be an easy one (see chapter 24 in this volume).

In families where there is differential treatment, both siblings tend to be involved in more destructive forms of conflict, thus creating a negative climate for their relationship. This finding was supported by both questionnaire results and observation. No one wins in this type of relationship, and the focus needs to be on helping the parents to be more even-handed in their dealings with their children.

Overall, the findings of the studies reported here have implications for marital and family therapists and those who teach communication skills. Many families could be helped to achieve more functional relationships if they were able to learn more constructive ways to communicate in conflict situations.

References

Amato, P., & Keith, B. (1991). Parental divorce and the wellbeing of children: A meta-analysis. *Psychological Bulletin, 110*(1), 26–46.

Bank, S. (1992). Remembering and reinterpreting sibling bonds. In F. Boer & J. Dunn (Eds.), *Children's sibling relationships: Developmental and clinical issues* (pp. 139–151) Hillsdale, NJ: Erlbaum.

Blake, R. R., & Mouton, J. S. (1964). *The managerial grid.* Houston: Gulf.

Boer, F., Goedhart, A. W., & Treffers, P. D. A. (1992). Siblings and their parents. In F. Boer & J. Dunn (Eds.), *Children's sibling relationships: Developmental and clinical issues* (pp. 42–54). Hillsdale, NJ: Erlbaum.

Christensen, A. (1988). Dysfunctional interaction patterns in couples. In P. Noller & M. A. Fitzpatrick (Eds.), *Perspectives on marital interaction* (pp. 31–52). Philadelphia: Multilingual Matters.

Christensen, A., & Heavey, C. L. (1990). Gender, power and marital conflict. *Journal of Personality and Social Psychology, 59*, 73–85.

Eldridge, K. A., & Christensen, A. (2002). *Demand–withdraw communication during couple conflict: A review and analysis.* In P. Noller & J. A. Feeney (Eds.), *Understanding marriage: Developments in the study of couple interaction* (pp. 289–322). New York: Cambridge University Press.

Feeney, J. A., Noller, P., & Callan, V. J. (1994). Attachment style, communication and satisfaction in the early years of marriage. In K. Bartholomew & D. Perlman (Eds.), *Attachment processes in adulthood* (pp. 269–308). London: Jessica Kingsley

Fruzzetti, A. E. (1996). Causes and consequences: Individual distress in the context of couple interactions. *Journal of Consulting and Clinical Psychology, 64*(6), 1192–1201.

Furman, W., & Buhrmester, D. (1985). Children's perceptions of the personal relationships in their social networks. *Developmental Psychology, 21*(6), 1016–1024.

Gottman, J. M., & Levenson, R. L. (1988). The social psychophysiology of marriage. In P. Noller & M. A. Fitzpatrick (Eds.), *Perspectives on marital interaction* (pp. 182–200). Philadelphia: Multilingual Matters.

Guthrie, D. M., & Noller, P. (1988). Spouses' perceptions of one another in emotional situations. In P. Noller & M. A. Fitzpatrick (Eds.), *Perspectives on marital interaction* (pp. 153–181). Philadelphia: Multilingual Matters.

Hetherington, E. M., & Clingempeel, W. G. (1992). Coping with marital transitions: A family systems perspective. *Monographs of the Society for Research in Child Development, 57*(2–3), 1–242.

Hinde, R. A. (1989). Reconciling the family systems and the relationships approaches to child development. In K. Kreppner & R. M. Lerner (Eds.) *Family systems and life-span development* (pp. 149–163). Hillsdale, NJ: Erlbaum.

Holtzworth-Munroe, A., Smutzler, N., & Stuart, G. L. (1998). Demand and withdraw communication among husbands experiencing husband violence. *Journal of Consulting and Clinical Psychology, 66*(5), 731–743.

McGuire, S., McHale, S.M., & Updegraff, K. (1996). Children's perceptions of the sibling relationship in middle childhood: Connections within and between family relationships. *Personal Relationships, 3*(3), 229–239.

Minuchin, P. (1988). Relationships within the family: A systems perspective on development. In R. A. Hinde & J. Stevenson-Hinde (Eds.), *Relationships within families: Mutual influences* (pp. 7–26). Oxford: Clarendon Press.

Noller, P. (1980). Misunderstanding in marital communication: A study of couples' nonverbal communication. *Journal of Personality and Social Psychology, 39*, 1135–1148.

Noller, P. (1981). Gender and marital adjustment level differences in decoding messages from spouses and strangers. *Journal of Personality and Social Psychology, 41*(2), 272–278.

Noller, P. (1984). *Nonverbal communication and marital interaction.* Oxford: Pergamon Press.

Noller, P. (1993). Gender and emotional communication in marriage: Different cultures or differential social power? *Journal of Language and Social Psychology, 12*(1–2), 132–152.

Noller, P. (2001). Using standard content methodology to assess nonverbal sensitivity in dyads. In J. Hall & F. Bernieri (Eds.), *Interpersonal sensitivity: Theory, measurement and applications* (pp. 243–264). Mahwah, NJ: Erlbaum.

Noller, P., & Christensen, A. (1991). *Nonverbal behavior in demanding and withdrawing.* Unpublished manuscript, University of Queensland.

Noller, P., & Feeney, J. A. (2004). Conflict in families with adolescents: How family relationships affect each other. In S.H. Ng, C.N. Candlin, & C.Y. Chiu (Eds.), *Language matters: Communication, identity, and culture* (1st edn., pp. 473–497). Hong Kong: City University of Hong Kong.

Noller, P., Feeney, J. A., Bonnell, D., & Callan, V. J. (1994). A longitudinal study of conflict in early marriage. *Journal of Social and Personal Relationships, 11*(2), 233–252.

Noller, P., Feeney, J. A., Peterson, C., & Atkin, S. (2000). Marital conflict and adolescents. *Family Matters, 55*, 68–73.

Noller, P., Feeney, J. A., Peterson, C., & Sheehan, G. (1995). Learning conflict patterns in the family: Links between marital, parent–child and sibling relationships. In T. J. Socha & G. H. Stamp (Eds.), *Parents, children and communication: Frontiers of theory and research* (pp. 273–298). Hillsdale, NJ: Erlbaum.

Noller, P., Feeney, J. A., Roberts, N. D., & Christensen, A. (2005). Withdrawal in couple interactions: Exploring the causes and consequences. In R. E. Riggio & R. S. Feldman (Eds.), *Applications of nonverbal communication* (pp. 195–213). Mahwah, NJ: Erlbaum.

Noller, P., Feeney, J. A., Sheehan, G., Darlington, Y., & Rogers, C. (2008). Conflict in divorcing and continuously married families: A study of marital, parent–child and sibling relationships. *Journal of Divorce and Remarriage, 49*(1–2), 1–24.

Noller, P., Feeney, J. A., Sheehan, G., & Peterson, C. (2000). Marital conflict patterns: Links with family conflict and family members' perceptions of one another. *Personal Relationships, 7*(1), 79–94.

Noller, P., & Roberts, N. D. (2002). The communication of couples in violent and nonviolent relationships: Temporal associations with own and partners' anxiety/arousal and behaviour. In P. Noller & J. A. Feeney (Eds.), *Understanding marriage: Developments in the study of couple interaction* (pp. 411–436). New York: Cambridge University Press.

Noller, P., & Ruzzene, M. (1991). Communication in marriage: The influence of affect and cognition. In G. O. Fletcher & F. D. Fincham (Eds.), *Cognition in close relationships* (pp. 203–233). Hillsdale, NJ: Erlbaum.

Noller, P., Seth-Smith, M., Bouma, R., & Schweitzer, R. (1992). Parent and adolescent perceptions of family functioning: A comparison of clinic and nonclinic families. *Journal of Adolescence, 15*(2), 101–114.

Noller, P., & White, A. (1990). The validity of the Communication Patterns Questionnaire. *Psychological Assessment: A Journal of Consulting and Clinical Psychology, 2*(4), 478–482.

O'Connor, T. G., Hetherington, E. M., & Clingempeel, W. G. (1997). Systems and bidirectional influences in families. *Journal of Social and Personal Relationships, 14(4)* 491–504.

Raush, H. L., Barry, W. A., Hertel, R. K., & Swain, M. A. (1974). *Communication, conflict and marriage.* San Francisco: Jossey-Bass.

Robillard, L., & Noller, P.(in press). Rejection sensitivity, violence and decoding deficits in married men. In J. L. Smith, W. Ickes, J. Hall, S. Hodges, & W. Gardner (Eds.), Managing interpersonal sensitivity: Knowing when–and when not–to understand others. New York: Nova Science Publishers.

Sagrestano, L., Christensen, A., & Heavey, C.L. (1998). Social influence techniques during marital conflict. *Personal Relationships*, *5*(1), 75–89.

Schaap, C., Buunk, A. P., & Kerkstra, A. (1988). Marital conflict resolution. In P. Noller & M. A. Fitzpatrick (Eds.), *Perspectives on marital interaction* (pp. 203–244). Philadelphia: Multilingual Matters.

Sheehan, G. (2000). *Parental favoritism: Implications for adolescents' family relationships.* Unpublished Ph.D. thesis, University of Queensland, Australia.

Sheehan, G., Darlington, Y., Noller, P., & Feeney, J. A. (2002). Children's perceptions of their sibling relationships during parental separation and divorce. *Journal of Divorce and Remarriage*, *41*(1–2), 69–94.

Sheehan, G., & Noller, P. (2002). Adolescents' perceptions of differential parenting: Links with attachment style and adolescent adjustment. *Personal Relationships*, *9*, 173–190.

Sulloway, F. J. (1996). *Born to rebel: Birth order, family dynamics and creative lives.* New York: Pantheon.

10

Demand–Withdraw Communication in Couples

Recent Developments and Future Directions

Kathleen A. Eldridge, and Brian Baucom

The demand–withdraw interaction pattern has been a focused interest of close relationship researchers and clinicians for several decades. In this pattern, one partner engages in demanding forms of behavior, such as complaints, criticisms, and pressures for changes, while the other partner engages in withdrawing forms of behavior, such as halfhearted involvement, changing the topic, avoiding discussion, or even walking away (Christensen, 1988). Importantly, the pattern is conceptualized as bidirectional: each partner's behavior influences the behavior of the other. For example, demand behavior does not cause withdrawing, instead demanding is both a cause and consequence of withdrawing. Each behavior exacerbates the other in a systemic, dyadic manner such that behaviors become increasingly polarized and rigid over time (Baucom, McFarland, & Christensen, 2010; Eldridge, Sevier, Jones, Atkins, & Christensen, 2007). Further, research has demonstrated that this pattern is distinct from general negativity (Caughlin & Huston, 2002).

Couple therapists have long recognized demand–withdraw communication as a common problem among therapy-seeking couples. Although consistent replication is often difficult to achieve in the social sciences, systematic research on the demand–withdraw pattern is unique, as it contains multiple replications that increase confidence in findings. After a brief description of replicated findings and proposed theories about the pattern, we review in this chapter recent developments in demand–withdraw research by

The Wiley-Blackwell Handbook of Couples and Family Relationships, First Edition.
Edited by Patricia Noller and Gery C. Karantzas.

summarizing the proximal and distal contexts for the pattern, immediate and long-term consequences of demand–withdraw, treatment responsiveness, and ideas for substantive and methodological advancements.

Replicated Findings

Arguably the most robust finding about demand–withdraw is the association with relationship dissatisfaction. Among several types of relationships (married, cohabiting, dating, same-sex, cross-sex, treatment-seeking, and nonclinical samples) and across cultures (North American, Australian, European, Brazilian, Taiwanese, and Pakistani), greater relationship distress is associated with more demand–withdraw communication (see Eldridge & Christensen, 2002, for a review). We are aware of only one study that did not produce this finding (Heffner et al., 2006), possibly due to the size and idiosyncratic nature of this sample (older, longer-married, highly satisfied spouses). This link between demand–withdraw and dissatisfaction carries the greatest concern for clinicians.

One of the most interesting aspects of the demand–withdraw pattern is that, in heterosexual relationships, it can be further specified into male-demand/female-withdraw and female-demand/male-withdraw. Most studies find that the female-demand/male-withdraw pattern is more common than the reverse. However, Christensen and Heavey (1990) first used a two-topic methodology (his issue and her issue) to discover that this gender difference holds true for conversation topics of primary importance to the female, but not for conversation topics of primary importance to the male. Studies employing this two-topic methodology have found that during female-generated topics, female-demand/male-withdraw is more common than the reverse, and during male-generated topics either there is no significant gender difference in demanding or withdrawing (Christensen & Heavey, 1990; Heavey, Layne, & Christensen, 1993; Vogel & Karney, 2003), or there is greater male-demand/female-withdraw than the reverse (Holtzworth-Munroe, Smutzler, & Stuart, 1998; Klinetob & Smith, 1996; McGinn, McFarland, & Christensen, 2009), or the presence of this effect depends on distress level and marriage length (Eldridge et al., 2007). These findings have made clear the central importance of using a two-topic protocol for studying demand–withdraw, as the topic of the conversation strongly influences each partner's behavior.

Theories

There are four explanations for why demand–withdraw occurs: individual differences; social structure; conflict structure; and multiple goals. Each of these explanations, except the most recent multiple goals perspective, attempts to account for the gender linkage in demand and withdraw roles. A lengthy review of each perspective is beyond the scope of this chapter, so each is described briefly below (see Eldridge & Christensen, 2002; and Sagrestano, Heavey, & Christensen, 2006, for more extended coverage).

The *individual differences* perspective posits that physiological or socialization differences between men and women foster the development of demand–withdraw communication behavior, particularly the female-demand/male-withdraw pattern. The *escape conditioning* explanation (Gottman & Levenson, 1988) suggests that men are more aversely affected by the physiological arousal experienced during conflict, making men more inclined to withdraw from conflict to alleviate the aversive arousal. In contrast, *gender role socialization* explanations (Chodorow, 1978; Gilligan, 1982; Noller, 1993; Rubin, 1983; summarized in Sagrestano et al., 2006) focus on the divergent social worlds of men and women that influence personality, identity and values development, communication goals, speech usage, and interpretations of conversations. Generally, women become more relationship-oriented and men become independence-oriented, thus women pursue closeness and connection (demand) while men seek to maintain separation (withdrawal) (Christensen, 1987, 1988; Jacobson, 1989; Jacobson & Margolin, 1979). A third version of the individual differences perspective suggests that differences between people in basic *personality attributes*, not necessarily gender-linked (such as agreeableness, neuroticism, and extraversion), contribute to demand–withdraw through directly influencing one's own communication behavior (self-influence) and/or one's partner's behavior (relational influence) (Caughlin & Vangelisti, 2000; chapters 9, 16 in this volume).

The *social structure* perspective (Christensen & Heavey, 1990; Sagrestano et al., 2006) emphasizes the sociocultural variables associated with gender, such as power and social roles. This explanation suggests that the relational partner with more power and status in society (the male) will want to maintain that position by withdrawing from discussions about changes in the relationship that would reduce his power or status. Similarly, the relational partner with less power (the female) will engage in communication behavior (demand) designed to bring about change in the relationship so that it is defined more according to their interests.

The individual and social structure perspectives focus on enduring and distal characteristics of men and women that influence communication tendencies throughout a relationship. In contrast, the conflict structure and multiple goals approaches allow for more attention to the proximal characteristics of each conversation. The *conflict structure* view suggests that the person seeking change in the issue being discussed will tend to be more demanding whereas the person seeking to maintain the status quo will tend to be more withdrawn. Thus behavior is determined by investment in either change or stability, not by sex or gender (Heavey et al., 1993).

The *multiple goals* approach (Caughlin & Scott, 2010) is similar to the conflict structure viewpoint in that it focuses on the immediate goals at hand in a conversation. However, this approach broadens the potential goals, extending beyond seeking change or consistency, to include primary and secondary goals. Primary goals represent the main objective, while secondary goals influence whether and how primary goals are pursued. Examples of primary goals provided by Caughlin and Scott parallel those in the conflict structure approach, such as wanting to influence the other to change, or wanting to maintain the existing arrangement. However, secondary goals include such examples as wanting to prevent upheaval, wanting to appear reasonable, or not wanting to appear dictatorial. It is assumed that these goals are likely to change over the course of a conversation as well as over longer spans of time. Caughlin and Scott (2010) suggest that this approach is consistent with existing research findings on demand–withdraw, yet offers the possibility of addressing limitations in prior explanations for the pattern.

Several studies reviewed in this chapter have attempted to test these explanations. The results of a large number of cleverly designed and implemented studies make it clear that biological sex alone does not fully explain the gender differences observed in demand–withdraw, and no one theory has yielded more empirical support than the others. As with most relationship phenomena, it is likely that one theory does not fit all couples, and variations within and between samples foster mixed and inconclusive results. Each perspective contains valuable and essential information in understanding demand–withdraw, and none offer a complete explanation. Combined they suggest that, like most relationship phenomena, demand–withdraw is multifactorial. Therefore, a combined model that encompasses both proximal and distal influences is needed to provide a more complete and contextual understanding of demand–withdraw.

The Proximal and Distal Context of Demand–Withdraw Communication

Research has identified several variables associated with demand–withdraw that can be cogently organized into proximal and distal variables. Proximal variables occur very close in time to the behavior and may be more fluid or dynamic. Distal variables, on the other hand, are more stable and enduring characteristics of partners or relationships that are present for longer periods of time and act as more distant antecedents of demand–withdraw.

Distal context: individual, relational, and cultural variables

Individual. Individual variables associated with demand–withdraw include personality characteristics and personal desire for greater closeness or independence in the relationship. Caughlin and Vangelisti (2000) found that desire for closeness and argumentativeness were each positively related to one's own demanding behavior and inversely related to one's own withdrawing. Neuroticism and external locus of control over conflict were positively associated with demand–withdraw, while agreeableness, flexibility, and internal locus of control were inversely associated with demand–withdraw. Christensen and colleagues (Christensen, 1987, 1988; Christensen & Shenk, 1991) demonstrated that the partner desiring more closeness tends to be more demanding during conflict, while the partner desiring more distance tends to be more withdrawing, and greater differences between partners in their desires for closeness and distance predicts greater demand–withdraw (Christensen, Eldridge, Catta-Preta, Lim, & Santagata, 2006).

Relational. As described above, greater relationship distress is consistently associated with more demand–withdraw. Research has begun to extend this finding by examining additional variables that may influence the relationship between distress and demand–withdraw. For example, Caughlin and Huston (2002) demonstrated that this relationship was reduced in the context of an affectionate relationship. Similarly, Weger (2005) reported that feeling understood by one's spouse mediated the association between marital satisfaction and demand–withdraw for husbands and partially mediated it for wives. In contrast, investigators examining couples in which one partner is also depressed have largely found that depression does not uniquely contribute to demand–withdraw when controlling for distress (Baucom et al., 2007; Byrne, Carr, & Clark, 2004).

Cultural. As with all behavior, demand–withdraw must be understood within a cultural context. Recent studies have examined demand–withdraw using a cultural lens. Christensen et al. (2006) examined demand–withdraw behavior in couples from Brazil, Italy, Taiwan, and the United States. These countries represent disparate cultural attitudes, religions, and gendered expectations that are presumed to influence relationship communication. Despite these cultural disparities, findings were consistent across the four cultures and replicated earlier findings. Demand–withdraw was negatively associated with relationship satisfaction, and female-demand/male-withdraw was more likely than male-demand/female-withdraw.

Rehman and Holtzworth-Munroe (2006) examined the influence of social norms about gender and power on demand–withdraw behavior in a study of three cultures with varying degrees of espoused patriarchy: white Americans, immigrant Pakistani couples in America, and Pakistani couples in Pakistan. In all three groups the relationship between demand–withdraw and distress was replicated. However, one of the primary contributions of this study was the examination of the gender linkage in demand–withdraw roles. These authors hypothesized that the gender-stereotyped pattern of female-demand/male-withdraw might not be present to the same degree in patriarchal countries as in more egalitarian ones, but rather that women in patriarchal countries might refrain from culturally incongruent demanding behavior. Likewise men in patriarchal countries might be less likely to withdraw if they are not threatened by wife demands and instead engage in more explicit demanding behavior.

As expected, American couples demonstrated significantly more wife-demand/husband-withdraw than Pakistani couples, with no statistically significant differences between the two Pakistani groups. Further, both Pakistani groups demonstrated significantly greater husband-demand/wife-withdraw than American couples. Pakistani wives demonstrated significantly more unassertive and fewer aggressive demands than American wives, whereas Pakistani and immigrant husbands demonstrated significantly more aggressive demands than their wives while the converse was found for American couples. Finally, unlike American couples, Pakistani wives withdrew significantly more than their husbands and significantly more than American wives.

These results strongly suggest that the roles of men and women in the demand–withdraw pattern are not determined solely by gender, but are clearly influenced by gender role expectations and cultural norms. Even though one approach to understanding the female-demand/male-withdraw pattern has been to hypothesize that women demand due to their reduced power and thus dissatisfaction in the traditional marital structure of American couples, these authors suggest that women with reduced power in patriarchal cultures may tend to withdraw as a result of resignation. These findings demonstrate the importance of understanding the intent, function, or goals behind demanding and withdrawing behavior, and support the utility of the multiple goals approach described above (Caughlin & Scott, 2010).

Although Rehman and Holtzworth-Munroe (2006) did not utilize direct measures of gender roles, two studies examining the links between demand–withdraw, traditionalism, and egalitarianism found similar results. Kluwer et al. (1997) found that during discussions about the division of household labor, traditional wives, and wives with traditional husbands, were more likely to avoid conflict than were egalitarian wives and wives with an egalitarian husband. Kluwer (1998) suggests that traditional wives, and wives with a traditional husband, may find it more difficult to engage in conflict over the division of labor because of strongly held gender role ideologies (DeVault, 1990). Opposing the traditional marital roles is considered inappropriate in such marriages. Interestingly, traditional ideologies may actually reduce the gender-stereotyped wife-demand/husband-withdraw pattern, and instead increase the extent of conflict avoidance among traditional wives and wives with a traditional husband.

Just as certain conflict structures may exacerbate or facilitate the gender-stereotyped pattern of wife-demand/husband-withdraw (such as when the topic is one in which the wife wants change, see chapter 16 in this volume), there are moderating variables, such as gender roles, that may reduce or even reverse this interaction pattern. For example, Eldridge (2000) found that during conflict discussions generated by wives, traditional couples demonstrated greater husband-demand/wife-withdraw than egalitarian couples, and more traditionalism was associated with more husband-demand/wife-withdraw and less wife-demand/husband-withdraw. These studies suggest that type of marital structure and gender roles influence patterns of demand–withdraw behavior.

Another way researchers have examined the relative influence of inherent differences between men and women versus other variables is by comparing cross-sex and same-sex couples (Baucom, Snyder, &, Gordon, 2009; Holley & Levenson, 2010; Kurdek, 2004). One study found that gay (but not lesbian) couples engage in less demand–withdraw than cross-sex married couples with children (but not cross-sex childless married couples, Kurdek, 2004) while another found that same-sex and cross-sex couples engage in similar levels of demand and withdraw, and demand–withdraw polarization (Holley & Levenson, 2010).

Similar to cross-sex couples, same-sex relationship satisfaction is inversely associated with demand–withdraw (Baucom et al., 2009), and differences in amount of change desired by partners predicted expected differences in demanding and withdrawing during conflict (Holley & Levenson, 2010). In the only study to use the two-topic protocol among cross-sex and same-sex couples, Baucom et al. (2009) found that partners' demanding was greater during discussion of their own chosen issue than during discussion of their partners' chosen issue, while withdrawing was greater during discussion of their partners' chosen issue than their own issue. These results suggest that gender differences alone cannot account for the demand–withdraw pattern, while the conflict structure perspective focusing on differences in desired change applies to same-sex couples as it does to cross-sex couples.

Proximal context: immediate antecedents of demand–withdraw

Topic variables. As suggested by the conflict structure view, the amount and type of demand–withdraw are related to the topic of the conflict. One explanation for these findings is that the person who chooses the topic is the one more invested in changing that area of the relationship, and is therefore primed to be more demanding, while the other partner is less invested in change and is thus primed to be more withdrawn. This model suggests that a complete crossover in roles depending on topic should occur. Some studies have found this crossover (Holtzworth-Munroe et al., 1998; Klinetob & Smith, 1996; McGinn et al., 2009), but others have not (Christensen & Heavey, 1990; Heavey et al., 1993; Vogel & Karney, 2003), and one study demonstrated that the crossover occurs among nondistressed couples but not among distressed couples seeking therapy (Eldridge et al., 2007). These discrepancies suggest that proximal and distal variables interact, an issue which we examine later in the chapter.

Other elements of the topic, in addition to who chose it for discussion, have been studied. McGinn et al. (2009) failed to find associations between issue seriousness and demand–withdraw during conflict. Eldridge et al. (2007) found that more previous discussion of a topic was associated with more demand–withdraw during the discussion of that topic, most strongly among distressed couples discussing wife-generated topics (Eldridge, 2000). Topic novelty did not predict discrepancy in demand–withdraw patterns (Eldridge et al., 2007).

Although virtually all demand–withdraw research has been conducted in the context of discussions in which partners are attempting to resolve a conflict or solve a relationship problem, one study (Eldridge et al., 2007) examined demand–withdraw in the context of supportive relationship discussions about partners' personal problems. The unique aspect of these discussions is that the person desiring change and carrying the burden of change are the same. Using the two-topic paradigm, Eldridge et al. (2007) showed that, as expected, there was more demand–withdraw in conflict discussions than support discussions, and this difference was more pronounced for severely distressed couples. Interestingly, wife-demand/husband-withdraw was greater than husband-demand/wife-withdraw in both types of discussions.

Importantly, in the Eldridge et al. (2007) study, seeking change in the husband predicted gender-stereotyped disparity in roles in all discussions. Whenever the discussion centered on the husband changing, whether the change was being sought by the wife (in a wife-chosen problem-solving topic) or by the husband himself (in a husband-chosen social-support topic), this gender-stereotyped difference was present. However, if the discussion was centered on the wife changing, whether husband-imposed (conflict topic) or wife-imposed (support topic), there was little to no gender polarization in demand–withdraw roles. As the authors report, "It is unclear whether the greater disparity is because husbands are more resistant to change than wives, because wives are more insistent on change than husbands, or both" (p. 225). Hence, essential proximal variables in understanding demand–withdraw may revolve around characteristics of the topic like investment in change, resistance to change, and gender of the person who feels pressured to change.

Mood and satisfaction variables. Recently, mood and distress immediately preceding interaction have been inconsistently linked to demanding and withdrawing behaviors. Tashiro and Frazier (2007) found that couples exhibited greater demanding and withdrawing behaviors after a negative mood induction (having the couple discuss presenting problems) than after a positive mood induction (talking about positive aspects of the relationship). Likewise, Afifi et al. (2009) found that greater dissatisfaction reported immediately before an interaction predicted more observationally coded avoidance and greater self-reported perceptions of partner avoidance during the interaction. In contrast, McGinn et al. (2009) failed to find significant associations between level of distress prior to discussion and demand–withdraw behavior during conflict. These null findings may be due to low ratings of upset in their mostly satisfied, nondistressed sample; Tashiro and Frazier (2007) found the impact of negative mood induction on demanding behavior to be enhanced in less satisfied couples.

Immediate goals. Caughlin and Scott (2010) have recently proposed that goals are an important proximal variable to consider. Their recent description of the multiple goals approach contained a transcript analysis of marital and parent–adolescent discussions and determined four qualitatively different forms of demand–withdraw: discuss/exit (one partner seeks discussion while the other overtly exits the conversation, physically or verbally); Socratic question/perfunctory response (one partner asks questions while the other provides dutiful minimal responses); complain/deny (one partner complains about the other, while the other denies the legitimacy of the complaint); and criticize/defend (one partner complains about the other, while the other justifies the criticized behavior). Proximal goals such as avoidance of the discussion can be pursued in various ways depending on other goals such as wanting to appear cooperative (an identity goal) or wanting to maintain harmony (a relational goal). For example, outright exit is one way to avoid discussion, but a perfunctory response serves multiple goals of avoiding true conflict discussion while appearing cooperative and maintaining relationship harmony. This qualitative lens reminds us that type of demand–withdraw, not just amount or gender-linked pattern, is important to consider.

Interaction of proximal and distal variables

Distal variables also influence the association between proximal variables and demand–withdraw. For example, Tashiro and Frazier (2007) demonstrated that the impact of negative mood induction on demanding behavior was stronger for less satisfied couples than for more satisfied couples. Eldridge et al. (2007) demonstrated that the impact of conflict structure (husband or wife topic) on demand–withdraw patterns depended on two distal variables: distress level of the relationship and marriage length. Severely distressed couples remained in gender-stereotyped demand–withdraw roles regardless of conflict structure, whereas moderately distressed and nondistressed couples reversed roles depending on conflict structure. Marriage length interacted with distress level as well, such that couples in shorter marriages reversed roles depending on who chose the topic, whereas among those in longer marriages, only those less distressed couples reversed roles depending on who chose the topic. Longer marriages that were severely distressed remained locked in gender-stereotyped demand–withdraw roles across wife and husband topics, but couples in shorter marriages that were severely distressed demonstrated some role reversal depending on the conflict structure. Together, these two studies suggest that proximal variables such as mood and topic are strongly influenced by distal ones, most clearly level of distress.

Immediate and Long-term Consequences of Demand–Withdraw Communication

What happens to couples when they engage in demanding and withdrawing behavior? How do they feel, think, and behave in response to conflicts that contain demand–withdraw patterns? Research has identified a number of short- and long-term consequences of demand–withdraw.

Immediate consequences

A number of immediate consequences of demand–withdraw have been identified, each with probable long-term implications. Research on general marital conflict has shown that there are significant individual differences in cognitive response to conflict. Some individuals continue thinking about the conflict a great deal while others attempt to avoid thinking about it (e.g., Johnson & Roloff, 1998). Consistent with these findings, Malis and Roloff (2006) found that self-demand/partner-withdraw was positively associated with reports of post-conflict hyper arousal, attempts to avoid recollections and feelings about the episode, intrusive thoughts, feelings, and images related to the episode, and health-related reductions in life activities (work, school, etc.) after the episode. Partner-demand/self-withdraw was also associated with attempts to avoid thinking about the episode and with post-episode appraisals of stressful life events, but not with hyper arousal or health-related reductions in activities.

Using diary methodology, Papp et al. (2009) found that wife-demand/husband-withdraw and husband-demand/wife-withdraw were each associated with less conflict resolution for husbands and wives. McGinn et al. (2009) found that higher levels of demand–withdraw during a discussion predicted less satisfaction with the outcome of the discussion, independent of the actual outcome. Surprisingly, demand–withdraw did not predict resolution frequency, but for those issues that were considered resolved, partner-demand/self-withdraw was associated with less likelihood of coming to agreed-upon changes. Demand–withdraw is also associated with perceived resolvability of the issue, such that demand–withdraw during conflict, and avoidance after conflict, were each inversely correlated with perceived resolvability (Johnson & Roloff, 1998).

Weger (2005) conceptualizes demand–withdraw as an example of disconfirming communication, causing the demanding partner to feel misunderstood and unaccepted by the withdrawing partner. He found that demand–withdraw resulted in spouses feeling less understood by their mates. Feeling misunderstood mediated associations between demand–withdraw and satisfaction for both spouses. Even perceptions of avoidance can have consequences. Afifi et al. (2009) found that perceptions of partner avoidance during a discussion predicted decreases in relationship satisfaction from before to after the interaction.

Longitudinal research

Although cross-sectional research on demand–withdraw has been plentiful and findings have been fairly consistent, longitudinal research has been sparse and findings have sometimes been counter-intuitive. Although there is relatively limited longitudinal research, much of it attempts to determine whether demand–withdraw predicts later dissatisfaction, whether dissatisfaction predicts later demand–withdraw, and if these relationships are bidirectional over time.

Kurdek (2003) found that higher levels of self-report demand–withdraw behavior were related to longitudinal declines in relationship satisfaction in a sample of gay male and lesbian couples. Several observational studies have found that higher levels of wife-demand/husband-withdraw predict decreases in relationship satisfaction over time, particularly for women (Gottman & Levenson, 2000; Heavey et al., 1995). Similarly, husband-withdraw, independent of wife-demand, has been found to predict declines in husband relationship satisfaction over time (Gottman & Krokoff, 1989; Heavey, Christensen, & Malamuth, 1995). Other studies have generated almost diametrically opposed findings. Caughlin and Huston (2002) found that both husband-demand/wife-withdraw and wife-demand/husband-withdraw predicted increases in relationship satisfaction for women. Heavey et al. (1993) also found that husband-demand/wife-withdraw predicted increases in wives' satisfaction. Finally, some studies (e.g. Noller, Feeney, Bonnell, & Callan, 1994) have failed to find any relationship between demand–withdraw behavior and relationship satisfaction over time at all. These inconsistencies have been attributed to methodological and statistical differences across studies (Bradbury & Karney, 1993; Gottman & Krokoff, 1990; Smith, Vivian, & O'Leary, 1991; Woody & Costanzo, 1990).

Treatment Responsiveness

Does treatment reduce demand–withdraw? Given the robust association between demand–withdraw and relationship distress, it is essential to develop treatments that effectively diminish the presence of this pattern in treatment-seeking couples. One study to date has examined the effect of couple therapy on reducing the demand–withdraw pattern. Eldridge (2000) examined reduction in demand–withdraw from pre- to post-therapy among couples seeking therapy in a randomized clinical trial of Traditional Behavioral Couple Therapy (chapters 21, 22 in this volume; Jacobson & Margolin, 1979) and Integrative Behavioral Couple Therapy (chapter 22 in this volume; Christensen & Jacobson, 2000; Jacobson & Christensen, 1996). Results indicated that reported and observed demand–withdraw declined significantly over time, and that female-demand/male-withdraw decreased more than male-demand/female-withdraw. These are hopeful results. However, since these analyses were conducted on a subsample of the couples who had completed treatment at the time, they are preliminary, and the sample size was not large enough to compare differences between the two forms of treatment in their ability to reduce demand–withdraw.

Future Research Directions

The results of recent studies suggest refinements of the existing models of demand–withdraw behavior and identify avenues of exploration that are in need of additional study. One area of research that has seen considerable recent attention is the escape-conditioning model. Early work examining the escape-conditioning model measured emotional arousal through physiological indices such as blood pressure, heart rate, and cortisol. By and large, these measures failed to show associations with demanding and withdrawing behaviors (Denton, Burleson, Hobbs, Von Stein, & Rodroguez, 2001; Kiecolt-Glaser, Newton, Cacioppo, & MacCallum, 1996; Kiecolt-Glaser, Bane, Glaser, & Malarkey, 2003; Loving, Heffner, Kiecolt-Glaser, Glaser, & Malarkey, 2004).

Two recent studies used widely differing measures of emotional arousal and found convergent evidence linking higher levels of emotional arousal to higher levels of demanding and lower levels of withdrawing. Vogel et al. (2008) reported these findings in a sample of heterosexual community couples using skin conductance to measure arousal, and Baucom et al. (2010) documented these associations in samples of treatment-seeking heterosexual, cohabiting heterosexual, gay male, and lesbian community couples using fundamental frequency (a well-accepted vocal measure of emotional arousal that is very highly correlated with perceived pitch; see Juslin & Scherer, 2005) to measure emotional arousal. Baucom et al. (2010) suggest that specific emotions associated with demanding (anger/frustration) and withdrawing (anxiety) may be important to consider in understanding the associations between emotional arousal and demand–withdraw behavior in future studies.

Other substantive areas are just beginning to receive empirical attention, such as the role of demand–withdraw in physical/mental health (Byrne et al., 2004; Papp, et al., 2009) and demand–withdraw during specific developmental stages of the relationship. For example, Smith et al. (2009) found behaviors similar to demand–withdraw occurring in older adults but also note that the form of demanding and withdrawing behaviors may change over the course of a relationship with some significant sex differences in behaviors not emerging until later life. In examining control behavior (which is conceptually similar to demanding) in middle-aged and older adult couples, older adult women used significantly higher levels of hostile controlling behaviors than men. In contrast, older adult men used significantly higher levels of warm control than women but there were no sex differences in these two behaviors in middle-aged couples (Smith et al., 2009). Additional work is needed to explore this possibility as well as to examine demand–withdraw behavior during other salient relationship stages, such as the transitions to marriage, parenthood (Thorp, Krause, Cukrowicz, & Lynch, 2004), and retirement.

Similarly, recent studies have focused on demand–withdraw behavior between parents and adolescents (Caughlin & Malis, 2004; Caughlin & Ramey, 2005; chapter 8 in this volume), and within the family system (Noller, Feeney, Sheehan, & Peterson, 2000; chapter 9 in this volume). The pioneering work in this area documents the occurrence and ramifications of demand–withdraw behavior for parents and children; however, much remains to be learned about the developmental correlates of demand–withdraw behavior for children such as whether demand–withdraw behavior is a mechanism of intergenerational transmission of domestic aggression, risk for divorce, and depression. A final line of research that holds much promise for additional exploration is culture. Rehman and Holtzworth-Munroe's (2006) thought-provoking study of cultural variation in demand–withdraw behavior suggests the need for examination of other cultural norms for behavior, such as the cultural congruence of assertiveness, high/low context communication tendencies, patriarchal tendencies, and the degree of individualism/collectivism.

Conclusion

Recent years have seen exciting expansions in demand–withdraw research. Notably, investigators who examine relationship communication, now often focus specifically on the demand–withdraw pattern, instead of global positive/negative communication. With the amount of knowledge amassed about demand–withdraw in past and recent years, the time is ripe to explore two important avenues in the next decade: (i) careful refinement and combination of demand–withdraw theories into a cohesive proximal-distal model and (ii) extension to clinical practice by examining treatment responsiveness and refining existing therapies to most effectively alleviate this pattern. Couples polarized by this pattern, and therapists working with them, would benefit greatly from focused efforts in these two areas.

References

Afifi, T. D., McManus, T., Steuber, K., & Coho, A. (2009). Verbal avoidance and dissatisfaction in intimate conflict situations. *Human Communication Research, 35*, 357–383.

Baucom, B., Atkins, D., Eldridge, K., Sevier, M., & Christensen, A. (2010). *The language of demand/withdraw: Verbal and vocal correlates of demand/withdraw behavior.* Unpublished manuscript, University of California, Los Angeles.

Baucom, B., Eldridge, K., Jones, J., Sevier, M., Clements, M., Markman, H., Stanley, S., et al. (2007). Contributions of marital distress and depression to communication patterns in distressed couples. *Journal of Social and Clinical Psychology, 26*(6), 689–707.

Baucom, B., McFarland, P., & Christensen, A. (2010). Gender, topic, and time in observed demand/withdraw interaction in cross- and same-sex couples. *Journal of Family Psychology, 25*, 570–580.

Baucom, D. H., Snyder, D. K., & Gordon, K. (2009). *Helping couples get past the affair: A clinician's guide.* New York: Guildford Press.

Bradbury, T. N., & Karney, B. R. (1993). Longitudinal study of marital interaction and dysfunction: Review and analysis. *Clinical Psychology Review, 13*, 15–27.

Byrne, M., Carr, A., & Clark, M. (2004). Power in relationships of women with depression. *Journal of Family Therapy, 26*, 407–429.

Caughlin, J. P., & Huston, T. L. (2002). A contextual analysis of the association between demand/withdraw and marital satisfaction. *Personal Relationships, 9*, 95–119.

Caughlin, J. P., & Malis, R. S. (2004). Demand/withdraw communication between parents and adolescents: Connections with self-esteem and substance use. *Journal of Social and Personal Relationships, 21*, 125–148.

Caughlin, J. P., & Ramey, M. E. (2005). The demand/withdraw pattern of communication in parent–adolescent dyads. *Personal Relationships, 12*, 337–355.

Caughlin, J. P., & Scott, A. M. (2010). Toward a communication theory of the demand/withdraw pattern of interaction in interpersonal relationships. In S. W. Smith & S. R. Wilson (Eds.), *New directions in interpersonal communication research* (pp. 180–200). Thousand Oaks, CA: Sage.

Caughlin, J. P., & Vangelisti, A. L. (2000). An individual difference explanation of why married couples engage in the demand/withdraw pattern of conflict. *Journal of Social and Personal Relationships, 17*, 523–551.

Chodorow, N. (1978). *The reproduction of mothering: Psychoanalysis and the sociology of gender.* Berkeley: University of California Press.

Christensen, A. (1987). Detection of conflict patterns in couples. In K. Hahlweg & M. J. Goldstein (Eds.), *Understanding major mental disorder: The contribution of family interaction research* (pp. 250–265). New York: Family Process Press.

Christensen, A. (1988). Dysfunctional interaction patterns in couples. In P. Noller & M. A. Fitzpatrick (Eds.), *Perspectives on marital interaction* (pp. 31–52). Philadelphia: Multilingual Matters.

Christensen, A., Eldridge, K., Catta-Preta, A. B., Lim, V. R., & Santagata, R. (2006). Cross-cultural consistency of the demand/withdraw interaction in couples. *Journal of Marriage and the Family, 68*, 1029–1044.

Christensen, A., & Heavey, C. L. (1990). Gender and social structure in the demand/withdraw pattern of marital conflict. *Journal of Personality and Social Psychology, 59*, 73–81.

Christensen, A., & Jacobson, N. S. (2000). *Reconcilable differences.* New York: Guilford Press.

Christensen, A., & Shenk, J. L. (1991). Communication, conflict, and psychological distance in nondistressed, clinic, and divorcing couples. *Journal of Consulting and Clinical Psychology, 59*, 458–463.

Denton, W. H., Burleson, B. R., Hobbs, B. V., Von Stein, M., & Rodroguez, C. P. (2001). Cardiovascular reactivity and initiate/avoid patterns of marital communication: A test of Gottman's psychophysiologic model of marital interaction. *Journal of Behavioral Medicine, 24*, 401–421.

DeVault, M. L. (1990). Conflict over housework: The problem that (still) has no name. In L. Kriesberg (Ed.), *Research in social movements, conflict and change* (pp. 189–202). Greenwood, CT: JAI.

Eldridge, K. A. (2000). *Demand–withdraw communication during marital conflict: Relationship satisfaction and gender role considerations.* Unpublished doctoral dissertation, University of California, Los Angeles.

Eldridge, K. A., & Christensen, A. (2002). Demand–withdraw communication during couple conflict: A review and analysis. In P. Noller & J. A. Feeney (Eds.), *Understanding marriage: Developments in the study of couple interaction.* (pp. 289–322). New York: Cambridge University Press.

Eldridge, K. A., Sevier, M., Jones, J., Atkins, D. C., & Christensen, A. (2007). Demand–withdraw communication in severely distressed, moderately distressed, and nondistressed couples: Rigidity and polarity during relationship and personal problem discussions. *Journal of Family Psychology, 21*, 218–226.

Gilligan, C. (1982). *In a different voice: Psychological theory and women's development.* Cambridge, MA: Harvard University Press.

Gottman, J. M., & Krokoff, L. J. (1989). Marital interaction and satisfaction: A longitudinal view. *Journal of Consulting and Clinical Psychology, 57*, 47–52.

Gottman, J. M., & Krokoff, L. J. (1990). Complex statistics are not always clearer than simple statistics: A reply to Woody and Costanzo. *Journal of Consulting and Clinical Psychology, 58*, 502–505.

Gottman, J. M., & Levenson, R. W. (1988). The social psychophysiology of marriage. In P. Noller & M. A. Fitzpatrick (Eds.), *Perspectives on marital interaction* (pp. 182–200). Philadelphia: Multilingual Matters.

Gottman, J. M., & Levenson, R. W. (2000). The timing of divorce: Predicting when a couple will divorce over a 14-year period. *Journal of Marriage and Family, 62*, 737–745.

Heavey, C. L., Christensen, A., & Malamuth, N. M. (1995) The longitudinal impact of demand and withdrawal during marital conflict. *Journal of Consulting and Clinical Psychology, 63*, 797–801.

Heavey, C. L., Layne, C., & Christensen, A. (1993). Gender and conflict structure in marital interaction: A replication and extension. *Journal of Consulting and Clinical Psychology, 61*, 16–27.

Heffner, K., Loving, T., Kiecolt-Glaser, J., Himawan, L., Glaser, R., & Malarkey, W. (2006). Older spouses' cortisol responses to marital conflict: Associations with demand/withdraw communication patterns. *Journal of Behavioral Medicine, 29*, 317–325.

Holley, S., & Levenson, R. (2010). Exploring the basis for gender differences in the demand–withdraw pattern. *Journal of Homosexuality, 57*, 666–684.

Holtzworth-Munroe, A., Smutzler, N., & Stuart, G. L. (1998). Demand and withdraw communication among couples experiencing husband violence. *Journal of Consulting and Clinical Psychology, 66*, 731–743.

Jacobson, N. S. (1989). The politics of intimacy. *Behavior Therapist, 12*, 29–32.

Jacobson, N. S., & Christensen, A. (1996). *Integrative couple therapy: Promoting acceptance and change*. New York: Norton.

Jacobson, N. S., & Margolin, G. (1979). *Marital therapy: Strategies based on social learning and behavior exchange principles*. New York: Brunner/Mazel.

Johnson, K. L., & Roloff, M. E. (1998). Serial arguing and relational quality: Determinants and consequences of perceived resolvability. *Communication Research, 25*, 327–343.

Juslin, P., & Sherer, K. (2005). *Vocal expression of affect*. In J. A. Harrigan, R. Rosenthal, & K. R. Scherer (Eds.), *The new handbook of methods in nonverbal behavioral research* (pp. 65–136). New York: Oxford University Press.

Kiecolt-Glaser, J., Bane, C., Glaser, R., & Malarkey, W. (2003). Love, marriage, and divorce: Newlyweds' stress hormones foreshadow relationship changes. *Journal of Consulting and Clinical Psychology, 71*, 176–188.

Kiecolt-Glaser, J. K., Newton, T., Cacioppo, J. T., & MacCallum, R. C. (1996). Marital conflict and endocrine function: Are men really more physiologically affected than women? *Journal of Consulting and Clinical Psychology, 64*, 324–332.

Klinetob, N. A., & Smith, D. A. (1996). Demand–withdraw communication in marital interaction: Tests of interpersonal contingency and gender role hypotheses. *Journal of Marriage and the Family, 58*, 945–957.

Kluwer, E. S. (1998). *Marital conflict over the division of labor: When partners become parents.* Unpublished doctoral dissertation. Kurt Lewin Institute Dissertation Series, University of Groningen.

Kluwer, E. S., Heesink, J. A., & Van De Vliert, E. (1997). The marital dynamics of conflict over the division of labor. *Journal of Marriage and the Family, 59*, 635–653.

Kurdek, L. A. (2003). Differences between gay and lesbian cohabiting couples. *Journal of Social and Personal Relationships, 20*, 411–436.

Kurdek, L. A. (2004). Are gay and lesbian cohabiting couples really different from heterosexual married couples? *Journal of Marriage and Family, 66*, 880–900.

Loving, T. J., Heffner, K. L., Kiecolt-Glaser, J. K., Glaser, R., & Malarkey, W. B. (2004). Stress hormone changes and marital conflict: Spouses' relative power makes a difference. *Journal of Marriage and Family, 66*(3), 595–612.

Malis, R. S., & Roloff, M. E. (2006). Demand/withdraw patterns in serial arguments: Implications for well-being. *Human Communication Research, 32*, 198–216.

McGinn, M. M., McFarland, P. T., & Christensen, A. (2009). Antecedents and consequences of demand/withdraw. *Journal of Family Psychology, 23*, 749–757.

Noller, P. (1993). Gender and emotional communication in marriage: Different cultures or differential social power? *Journal of Language and Social Psychology, 12*, 132–152.

Noller, P., Feeney, J. A., Bonnell, D., & Callan, V. J. (1994). A longitudinal study of conflict in early marriage. *Journal of Social and Personal Relationships, 11*, 233–252.

Noller, P., Feeney, J. A., Sheehan, G., & Peterson, C. (2000). Marital conflict patterns: Links with family conflict and family members' perceptions of one another. *Personal Relationships, 7*, 79–94.

Papp, L. M., Kouros, C. D., & Cummings, E. M. (2009). Demand–withdraw patterns in marital conflict in the home. *Personal Relationships, 16*, 285–300.

Rehman, U. S., & Holtzworth-Munroe, A. (2006). A cross-cultural analysis of the demand–withdraw marital interaction: Observing couples from a developing country. *Journal of Consulting and Clinical Psychology, 74*, 755–766.

Rubin, L. B. (1983). *Intimate strangers: Men and women together*. New York: Harper & Row.

Sagrestano, L. M., Heavey, C. L., & Christensen, A. (2006). Individual differences versus social structural approaches to explaining demand–withdraw and social influence behaviors. In K. Dindia & D. J. Canary (Eds.), *Sex differences and similarities in communication* (pp. 379–395). Mahwah, NJ: Erlbaum.

Smith, D. A., Vivian, D., & O'Leary, K. D. (1991). The misnomer proposition: A critical reappraisal of the longitudinal status of "negativity" in marital communication. *Behavioral Assessment, 13*, 7–24.

Smith, T. W., Berg, C. A., Florsheim, P., Uchino, B. N., Pearce, G., Hawkins, M., & Olsen-Cerny, C. (2009). Conflict and collaboration in middle-aged and older couples: I. Age differences in agency and communion during marital interaction. *Psychology and Aging, 24*, 259–273.

Tashiro, T., & Frazier, P. (2007). The causal effects of emotion on couples' cognition and behavior. *Journal of Counseling Psychology, 54*, 409–422.

Thorp, S. R., Krause, E. D., Cukrowicz, K. C., & Lynch, T. R. (2004). Postpartum partner support, demand–withdraw communication, and maternal stress. *Psychology of Women Quarterly, 28*, 362–369.

Vogel, D. L., & Karney, B. R. (2003). Demands and withdrawal in newlyweds: Elaborating on the social structure hypothesis. *Journal of Social and Personal Relationships, 19*, 685–701.

Vogel, D. L., Werner-Wilson, R. J., Liang, K., Cutrona, C. E., Seeman, J. C., & Hackler, A.H. (2008). The relationship of physiological arousal with demand and withdraw behavior: Examining the accuracy of the escape-conditioning hypothesis. *Sex Roles, 59*, 871–879.

Weger, H. (2005). Disconfirming communication and self-verification in marriage: Associations among the demand/withdraw interaction pattern, feeling understood, and marital satisfaction. *Journal of Social and Personal Relationships, 22*, 19–31.

Woody, E. Z., & Costanzo, P. R. (1990). Does marital agony precede marital ecstasy? A comment on Gottman and Krokoff's "Marital interaction and satisfaction: A longitudinal view." *Journal of Consulting and Clinical Psychology, 58*, 499–501.

PART IV

Individual Differences Perspectives on Intimacy, Love, and Caregiving

11

Adult Attachment and Sexuality

Attachment Insecurities Bias the Functioning of the Sexual Behavior System

Phillip R. Shaver and Mario Mikulincer

Sigmund Freud, the founder of psychoanalysis, included in his theory of motivation two major drives or instincts: sex and aggression (e.g., Freud, 1955). By the time John Bowlby trained as a psychoanalyst decades later in London, Freud's psychoanalytic theory had morphed into "object relations theory" (e.g., Fairbairn, 1952), which placed greater emphasis on social-relational motives other than sex. Bowlby (1982—a revised version of his 1969 book) built upon object relations theory by focusing on secure emotional "attachments" as a key goal of human motivation. But Bowlby still considered other motivational, or as he called them, "behavioral," systems to be important; and among those other systems was the sexual behavior system.

In the present chapter we summarize what we have learned about the interplay of the attachment and sexual systems. The first of these systems, attachment, was hypothesized by Bowlby (1982) to govern one person's (e.g., an infant's) reliance on another person (e.g., a parent) for protection and support, especially when fear is aroused or help is needed. The second behavioral system, sex, was hypothesized by us (e.g., Mikulincer & Shaver, 2007c; Shaver, Hazan, & Bradshaw, 1988; Shaver & Mikulincer, 2006a) to be the motivational basis of sexual behavior and to explain individual differences in sexual motives, feelings, attitudes, and activities, and in the effects that sexuality has on the formation and maintenance of romantic and marital relationships.

The Wiley-Blackwell Handbook of Couples and Family Relationships, First Edition.
Edited by Patricia Noller and Gery C. Karantzas.

We begin this chapter by explaining Bowlby's behavioral system construct in some detail, and show how it organizes our conception of the functions, goals, and primary and secondary strategies of the attachment and sexual systems. We also summarize the effects that attachment and sex have on relationship quality. We then explain how attachment insecurities can bias the functioning of the sexual system and the effects this bias has on couple relationships. We review various examples of attachment research, focusing on the effects that attachment anxiety and avoidance have on sexual motives, fantasies, feelings, attitudes, and behavior. We then review the still sparse evidence for the distorting effects of attachment insecurities on the link between sex and relationship quality.

A Behavioral Systems Perspective on Attachment and Sex

Although Bowlby (1973, 1980, 1982) devoted attention to the formation of child–parent attachment bonds, he also considered how evolution has shaped brain mechanisms that govern other kinds of human behavior (e.g., exploration, parental caregiving, and sexual mating). He borrowed from ethology the concept of *behavioral system*, a species-universal neural program that organizes an individual's behavior in ways that increase the likelihood of survival and reproductive success. Each behavioral system is organized around a particular goal (e.g., attaining a sense of security) and includes a set of interchangeable, functionally equivalent behaviors that constitute the *primary strategy* of the system for attaining its goal (e.g., proximity seeking). These behaviors are automatically "activated," by situations that make a particular goal salient (e.g., loud noises that signal danger). The behaviors are "terminated" by other stimuli or outcomes that signal attainment of the desired goal. Each behavioral system also includes cognitive operations that facilitate goal attainment and excitatory and inhibitory neurological links with other systems.

Bowlby (1973) believed that, although behavioral systems are innate, experience shapes them in various ways, resulting in systematic individual differences. According to Bowlby, the residues of such experiences are stored in the form of mental representations, or *working models of self and others,* that guide future attempts to attain the goal of a particular behavioral system. With repeated use, these models become automatic and are important sources of within-person continuity in behavioral system functioning throughout development.

The attachment behavioral system

According to Bowlby (1982), the biological function of the attachment system is to protect a person (especially during infancy and childhood) from danger or suffering by ensuring that he or she maintains proximity to loving and supportive others (*attachment figures*). The proximal goal of the system is to attain a subjective sense of security (which Sroufe & Waters, 1977, called "felt security"), which normally terminates the system's activation (Bowlby, 1982). The goal of attaining security is made salient by perceived threats, which drive people to seek actual or symbolic proximity to attachment figures (Bowlby, 1982).

According to Ainsworth, Blehar, Waters, and Wall (1978), during infancy, attachment-system activation includes nonverbal expressions of need and desire for proximity, as well as observable behavior aimed at restoring and maintaining actual proximity (Ainsworth et al.). According to our extension of Bowlby's (1982) theory to adult attachment (Mikulincer and Shaver, 2003, 2007a, 2007b), the primary attachment strategies do not necessarily involve actual proximity-seeking behavior in adulthood, but they can be measured indirectly in the form of reassuring mental representations of past experiences with supportive attachment figures.

Smooth functioning of the attachment system requires that an attachment figure be available in times of need, responsive to the individual's bids for proximity, and effective in alleviating his or her distress. Such positive interactions promote an inner sense of attachment security, which in turn promotes general faith in other people's beneficence; a sense of being loved, and accepted by relationship partners; and optimistic beliefs about one's ability to handle distress. Bowlby (1988) considered attachment security to be a mainstay of emotion regulation, mental health, and social adjustment throughout life. A host of cross-sectional and longitudinal studies support this view (see Feeney, 2008; and Mikulincer & Shaver, 2007a, for reviews).

However, when attachment figures are not reliably available, responsive, and supportive, a sense of attachment security is not attained, negative working models are constructed, worries about self-protection and lovability are heightened, and strategies of affect regulation other than appropriate proximity seeking (strategies that Cassidy & Kobak, 1988, called *secondary attachment strategies*) are adopted. Attachment theorists (e.g., Cassidy & Kobak, 1988; Mikulincer & Shaver, 2007a) emphasize two such secondary strategies: hyperactivation and deactivation of the attachment system. Hyperactivation of the system (which Bowlby, 1982, called "protest") is manifested in energetic, insistent attempts to get a relationship partner to pay more attention and provide better care and support. These strategies include clinging and controlling, cognitive and behavioral efforts to establish not only physical contact but also perceived self–other similarity and "oneness," and overdependence on relationship partners as a source of protection (Shaver & Mikulincer, 2002). Hyperactivation keeps the attachment system chronically activated, thereby exacerbating relational distress and conflicts and interfering with good communication, emotional tranquility, and mature personal development.

Deactivation of the attachment system includes inhibition of proximity seeking and cultivation of what Bowlby (1980) called "compulsive self-reliance" and "detachment." These strategies require denial of attachment need: avoidance of closeness and dependence in relationships; maximization of cognitive, emotional, and physical distance from others; and striving for independence (Shaver & Mikulincer, 2002). They also involve active inattention to threatening events and personal vulnerabilities as well as suppression of thoughts and memories that arouse distress and feelings of vulnerability. These defenses are designed to preclude unwanted activation of the attachment system, associated by avoidants with undesirable outcomes (Mikulincer & Shaver, 2003).

When studying secondary strategies during adolescence and adulthood, attachment researchers have focused mainly on *attachment style*—the systematic pattern of relational expectations and behaviors that results from a particular history of attachment experiences (Shaver & Mikulincer, 2002). Research, beginning with Ainsworth et al. (1978) and continuing through recent studies (reviewed by Mikulincer & Shaver, 2007a), indicates that attachment style can be measured in terms of two independent forms of insecurity: attachment-related *anxiety* and *avoidance* (Brennan, Clark, & Shaver, 1998). Scores on the *avoidant attachment* dimension reflect the extent to which a person distrusts the goodwill of relationship partners and strives to maintain behavioral independence and emotional distance from them. One's score on the *anxious attachment* dimension reflects the degree to which a person worries that a partner will not be available in times of need and therefore engages overzealously in proximity seeking. People who score low on both insecurity dimensions are deemed secure and hold positive beliefs about the self and others. The two dimensions can be measured with reliable and valid self-report scales and are associated in theoretically predictable ways with many other variables, including characteristic emotions, adjustment, relationship-relevant cognitions, and social behaviors (Mikulincer & Shaver, 2007a).

The sexual behavioral system

From an evolutionary perspective, the major function of the sexual system is to pass genes from one generation to the next (Buss & Kenrick, 1998). The goal of this system, at least in heterosexual individuals, is to have sexual intercourse with an opposite-sex partner and either become pregnant (in the case of women) or impregnate a partner (in the case of men). As evolutionary psychologists have explained, however, the proximal motivation for an act (i.e., wishing to have sex with an attractive person) need not be the same as the evolutionary reason for the existence of the motives involved. People can seek sexual pleasure without hoping that pregnancy will result, and modern methods of birth control, as well as homosexuality, make it possible to separate the two goals. Nevertheless, many aspects of sexual motivation and attraction are presumably governed by neural and hormonal systems that evolved for reproductive purposes.

The sexual system is automatically activated by noticing and appraising an attractive, potentially interested, and (in the case of heterosexual attraction) presumably fertile partner (Fisher, 1998). The primary strategy for achieving this goal is to approach such a partner, persuade him or her to have sex, and engage in intercourse. That is, the primary strategy of the sexual system consists of bringing partners together to have sex by heightening sensitivity to signals of sexual interest in a partner, increasing one's attractiveness as a potential sexual partner, and using effective techniques to seduce a potential partner. From a behavioral system perspective (e.g., Shaver, et al., 1988), sexual attraction drives individuals to look for either short-term or long-term mating opportunities with potential sexual partners.

Smooth functioning of the sexual system requires coordination of two partners' motives and behaviors. It depends on the ability to attract a partner and convince him or her to have sex, and on the partner's availability and responsiveness to one's sexual advances. These mutually coordinated interactions can lead to sexual encounters where both partners gratify sexual needs and have enjoyable experiences. Moreover, they produce feelings of vitality and energy (which Ryan & Frederick, 1997, called "subjective vitality"): perception of oneself as attractive and potent; able to attract relationship partners and have sex when desired; feelings of being loved by a partner; and enhanced feelings of love and gratitude, toward the partner (Shaver & Mikulincer, 2006a).

Dysfunctions of the sexual system can be conceptualized in terms of hyperactivating and deactivating strategies. Sexual hyperactivation involves effortful, mentally preoccupying, and even coercive attempts to persuade a partner to have sex. In the process, a person can overemphasize the importance of sexual activities within a relationship, exaggerate appraisals of a partner's sexual needs, and adopt a hypervigilant stance toward a partner's signals of sexual attraction or rejection. In contrast, sexual deactivation is characterized by inhibition of sexual desire and an erotophobic, avoidant attitude toward sex. It includes dismissal of sexual needs, distancing from a partner interested in sex, suppression of sexual thoughts and fantasies, repression of sex-related memories, and inhibition of sexual arousal and orgasmic joy.

We constructed a 24-item self-report scale to tap these secondary strategies of the sexual system, the Sexual Behavioral System Scale (SBSS; Shaver & Mikulincer, 2006b). Factor analyses conducted in the United States and Israel yielded the intended two factors underlying the 24 items. In addition, we found low correlations between the hyperactivation and deactivation scores, indicating that the two strategies are roughly independent, as in our widely used self-report measure of attachment anxiety and avoidance (i.e., the Experiences in Close Relationships [ECR] Scale, Brennan et al., 1998). The SBSS scales have good test–retest reliability, with validity indicated by high correlations between self and partner reports. (This correspondence implies that self-reports are reflected, at least in part, in sexual activities that can be observed by both relationship partners.) We examined the convergent validity of the SBSS by correlating it with preexisting self-report measures of various sexual attitudes and experiences. In general, hyperactivation scores are associated with preexisting measures of intense but anxious sexual feelings and attitudes, and deactivation scores are associated with sexual inhibition (indicated, e.g., by erotophobia).

Effects of attachment and sex on couple relationships

According to our extension of attachment theory to adults (Mikulincer & Shaver, 2007a; Shaver et al. 1988; Shaver & Mikulincer, 2002), individual differences in the parameters of the attachment and sexual systems can affect the quality of romantic relationships. The smooth functioning of these two systems brings relationship partners together, increases physical and emotional closeness, heightens feelings of mutual love and gratitude, and promotes feelings of being valued. The smooth operation of the two systems is often crucial for forming and maintaining intimate, satisfying, and long-lasting couple relationships.

Attachment researchers have generated a large body of theory-consistent findings showing that attachment anxiety and avoidance are associated with lower levels of relationship stability and satisfaction in both dating and married couples (see Mikulincer, Florian, Cowan, & Cowan, 2002; Shaver & Mikulincer, 2007a, for reviews). Research has also revealed associations between avoidant or anxious attachment and lower scores on measures of relationship intimacy and commitment (e.g., Collins & Read, 1990; Simpson, 1990), and with relationship-destructive emotional reactions to a partner's behavior and maladaptive strategies of conflict resolution (e.g., Rholes, Simpson, & Orina, 1999; Scharfe & Bartholomew, 1995). Attachment insecurities are associated with negative expectations about a partner's behavior (e.g., Baldwin, Fehr, Keedian, Seidel, & Thomson, 1993) and relationship-destructive attributions for a partner's disappointing or distressing behaviors (e.g., Collins, 1996).

Unsurprisingly, interactions in which both partners gratify their sexual needs contribute to relationship satisfaction and stability (see Sprecher & Cate, 2004, for a review) and heighten feelings of love and commitment (e.g., Sprecher & Regan, 1998; Waite & Joyner, 2001). Moreover, dysfunctions of the sexual system are often responsible for relational conflict, worries, instability, and eventual relationship dissolution (e.g., Hassebrauck & Fehr, 2002; Sprecher & Cate, 2004). Chronic sexual-system activation accompanied by heightened sex-related anxieties and worries may encourage intrusive or aggressive behavior aimed at coercing a partner to have sex, which can heighten the frequency of sex-related conflicts and result in relationship dissatisfaction (Long, Cate, Fehsenfeld, & Williams, 1996). Adopting a distancing attitude when a partner expresses sexual interest and inhibiting one's own sexual arousal and orgasmic joy can leave a partner sexually frustrated and encourage interest in alternative partners (e.g., Hurlbert, Apt, Hurlbert, & Pierce, 2000). Using the SBSS, Shaver and Mikulincer (2006b) found that higher scores on the SBSS hyperactivation and deactivation scales are associated with lower levels of relationship satisfaction, intimacy, trust, and commitment, and more relationship-destructive emotional reactions to a romantic or marital partner, even after controlling for attachment insecurities.

Gillath, Mikulincer, Birnbaum, and Shaver (2008) provided experimental evidence supporting the hypothesized causal pathway from activation of the sexual system to the maintenance of a close relationship. In five laboratory experiments, Gillath et al. found that participants who were subliminally exposed (for 20 milliseconds) to erotic words or pictures, as compared to participants who were subliminally primed with neutral words or pictures, reported heightened tendencies to initiate and maintain a close relationship. Specifically, subliminal priming of sexually arousing stimuli was associated with increased willingness to disclose intimate information to a romantic partner, to sacrifice for this partner, and to adopt relationship-enhancing strategies during interpersonal conflicts with a romantic partner.

Interplay of the attachment and sexual systems

Shaver et al. (1988) formulated explicit hypotheses about how individual differences in attachment system functioning might bias the operation of the sexual system. Since the attachment system appears first in development (during the first year of life), its pattern of functioning and specific forms of dysfunction (either hyperactivation or deactivation) can affect the sexual system, which appears later in development. Shaver et al.'s (1988) analysis was based on Bowlby's (1982) claim that activation of the attachment system inhibits or distorts the operation of other behavioral systems, such as the exploration system, and interferes with activities associated with those systems. The same kind of inhibition or distortion can occur when a distressed or defensive person encounters an attractive, sexually available prospective relationship partner. For such people, the partner is likely to be appraised as a possible security provider or savior rather than simply as a sexual partner or as a source of potential distress that should be avoided.

Thus Shaver et al. (1988) hypothesized that secure individuals would be attentive to a partner's actual signals of sexual arousal and attraction, perceive the partner's sexual preferences accurately, and therefore engage in mutually satisfying sexual activities. A secure person's comfort with closeness, willingness to self-disclose, and comfort with behavioral and psychological interdependence all help to establish a positive foundation for sexual engagement, one of the most intimate of human activities. In addition, secure people's positive models of others make it relatively easy for them to view a sexual partner as caring and well-intentioned, allowing them to enjoy intimate sex without fear of being exploited or betrayed. Moreover, secure people's positive self-models make it easy to feel desired and esteemed during sexual activities and help to maintain a confidence about being able to gratify one's own and a partner's sexual needs. These positive mental representations allow secure adults to be less preoccupied with sexual performance, thereby facilitating "letting go" sexually and experiencing maximal sexual pleasure.

Insecure adults are likely to have more sexual problems and be less able to relax and enjoy sex. Avoidant people's discomfort with closeness and negative models of others may interfere with psychological intimacy and "letting go" during sex. In addition, avoidant people may be willing to engage in sex mainly when it does not involve emotional closeness and commitment to a long-term relationship. In other words, avoidant attachment may be associated with measurable sexual deactivation, sexual abstinence, or preference for impersonal, uncommitted sex. Moreover, because avoidant strategies are associated with extreme self-reliance and personal control, avoidant people may use sex to maximize control over a partner, gain social prestige, or enhance self-esteem, without much regard for a partner's feelings.

Attachment anxiety is likely to be associated with a complex, ambivalent approach to sex. Because sex is an obvious route to closeness and intimacy, attachment-anxious people can have positive attitudes toward sex and use it as a means of fulfilling unmet needs for security and love. However, while focusing on their own desires for protection and security, they may have difficulty attending accurately to a partner's sexual wishes and preferences. Moreover, anxious individuals' negative models of self and their worries about rejection and disapproval may keep them from relaxing and "letting go" sexually, thereby reducing sexual pleasure and tainting it with discomfort and distress. Thus, although anxious people are likely to place a high value on sex, often for reasons beyond sex itself, they may still have personal sexual problems and difficulties with sexual partners.

Anxious and avoidant attachment may also affect the construal of the role of sex in close relationships. Avoidant people's preference for interpersonal distance and emotional detachment favor viewing sex and romantic relationships as distinct. In contrast, anxious individuals' unmet attachment needs and their compulsive need for love and security may cause them to equate sex with romantic love and to use sexual interest and sexual activities as a "barometer" of relationship quality (Davis, Shaver, & Vernon, 2004). That is, they may interpret good or frequent sex as an indication of their partner's love and commitment, and interpret a partner's lack of sexual desire or refusal to engage in sexual activities as an indication of insufficient love.

In the remainder of this chapter, we review studies that have tested these theoretical ideas. In the immediately subsequent section, we briefly review evidence concerning the ways in which attachment insecurities shape a person's sexual motives, fantasies, feelings, attitudes, and behaviors. We then present findings on the ways in which attachment insecurities distort the relational effects of sexual activities.

Attachment Insecurities and Sexual System Functioning

Several studies have found that avoidant attachment is associated with less frequent sexual intercourse (e.g., Brassard, Shaver, & Lussier, 2007; Tracy, Shaver, Albino, & Cooper, 2003) and with more positive attitudes toward casual rather than committed sex (e.g., Brennan & Shaver, 1995; Gentzler & Kerns, 2004). Moreover, several studies have found that avoidant individuals are more interested in emotionless sex, are less likely to be involved in sexually exclusive relationships, and are more likely to have sex with a stranger and engage in "one-night stands" and mate poaching (e.g., Bogaert & Sadava, 2002, Cooper, Shaver, & Collins, 1998; Schachner & Shaver, 2002). In a series of laboratory experiments, Gillath and Schachner (2006) found that self-reports of attachment-related avoidance were associated with preference for a short-term rather than a long-term mating strategy, and that contextual priming of avoidance (thinking about a relationship in which one felt avoidant) increased interest in a short-term rather than a long-term sexual relationship.

Research has also shown that both attachment anxiety and avoidance are associated with lowered expectations of gratifying one's sexual needs (Tracy et al., 2003), lower sexual self-esteem (Shafer, 2001), more negative feelings during sex (e.g., Birnbaum, Reis, Mikulincer, Gillath, & Orpaz, 2006), and less open communication about sexual issues (e.g., Feeney, Hohaus, Noller, & Alexander, 2001). However, whereas avoidant individuals tend to dismiss the importance of sex and fail to express feelings of love and affection for their partner in sexual fantasies or during sexual intercourse, anxious individuals typically express a strong desire for their partner's emotional involvement during sex, together with strong sex-related worries (Birnbaum, 2007a, 2007b, in press; Birnbaum et al., 2006).

Several studies have examined the association between attachment insecurities and sexual motives, consistently finding that these insecurities bias people's reasons for engaging in sex (e.g., Davis et al., 2004; Schachner & Shaver, 2004; Tracy et al., 2003). Whereas anxiously-attached individuals are more likely to report having sex to foster closeness, gain a partner's reassurance, and prevent rejection by a partner, avoidant individuals are less likely to report having sex as a means of fostering closeness or expressing love for a partner and more likely to have sex to fit in with their social group, to comply with peer pressure, or to brag about it. Overall, these findings suggest that the main sexual goal for anxious and avoidant individuals is not to enjoy sex per se, but to use it as a means to achieve other goals.

Attachment insecurities have also been implicated in sexual coercion. Specifically, higher attachment anxiety and avoidance scores are associated with higher rates of physical coercion of sexual partners and more involvement in unwanted sex (e.g., Gentzler & Kerns, 2004; Tracy et al., 2003). Impett and Peplau (2002) found that anxiety and avoidance were related to different reasons for women's acceptance of unwanted sex. Whereas anxiously-attached women more often accepted unwanted sex to reduce relational conflicts and avoid rejection or abandonment, avoidant women more often had unwanted sex to avoid intimate and self-disclosing discussions about relational issues. Fournier, Brassard, and Shaver (in press) found, in a recent study of 55 men undergoing counseling for relationship difficulties, including domestic violence, that attachment anxiety was associated with being aggressive (both physically and psychologically), and that the association was partially mediated by a man-demand/woman-withdraw pattern of sexual interactions.

Overall, research indicates that attachment anxiety and avoidance are both associated with theoretically predictable patterns of sexual motives, cognitions, and behaviors. Anxious individuals tend to sexualize their desire for love and security, thereby conflating sexual desire with their hunger for secure attachment. Unfortunately, this subordination of sexuality to attachment goes hand in hand with lack of sexual self-confidence and the use of coercion, which in turn, ironically, increase the likelihood of disappointing sexual encounters and the eventual breakup of a couple relationship. Avoidant people's discomfort with closeness and negative models of others sometimes cause them to abstain from sexual intercourse, engage in casual, uncommitted sex, experience various forms of discomfort during sex, forego mutual sexual exploration, and use sex to bolster their self-esteem and reputation among peers.

Attachment Insecurities and the Role of Sex in Relationships

Beyond biasing, sexual system functioning can interfere with the potentially beneficial effects of sexual feelings and activities on a relationship. Birnbaum et al. (2006) asked both members of heterosexual cohabiting couples to complete daily-diary measures of interactions with their partner and the quality of their relationship over a period of 42 days. Each time they had sex during that period, participants were asked to report on their thoughts and feelings related to the sexual episode. It turned out that attachment anxiety amplified the effects of sexual experiences on relationship quality: Having sex or experiencing positive feelings during sexual intercourse on one day had a positive effect on interactions with the partner the next day, and on appraisals of relationship quality among highly anxious participants but not among less anxious ones. Avoidant attachment, in contrast, dampened the effects—either positive or negative—of sexual experiences on perceived relationship quality.

As a whole, Birnbaum et al.'s (2006) findings, like those of Davis et al. (2004) mentioned earlier, indicate that anxious people use sexual activity as a "barometer" of relationship quality. Attachment-anxious people seem to conflate sex and love, making it likely that feelings about sex will get translated into feelings about the relationship in general. In contrast, avoidant attachment favors detachment of sex from love, reducing the effects of sexual interactions on relationship satisfaction.

Implications for Therapy

In this section, we briefly consider implications of attachment theory and research for individual and couple therapy with clients who present with sexual complaints or difficulties (see Obegi & Berant, 2008, for an in-depth treatment of attachment-oriented psychotherapy, and Johnson, 2008, for an accessible overview of couple therapy from an attachment perspective). Insights from attachment theory are useful in the early phase of therapy, when clients' problems are assessed and a treatment plan is formulated. Therapists can use any of the simple measures of attachment orientations (included in the appendix of Mikulincer & Shaver, 2007a) to assess clients' mental representations of self and others and goals and fears in sexual relationships.

People with different attachment patterns require different approaches (e.g., as outlined by Mallinckrodt, 2010). The relatively secure ones can fairly easily discuss their thoughts and feelings, and are likely to develop confidence in a therapist's good intentions fairly quickly. Those who are high in attachment anxiety are likely to be very emotional and verbal, and a therapist will need to indulge this tendency at first and then gradually move toward a calmer, more constructive consideration of a client's difficulties. Those who are high on avoidance will require longer to let down defenses and begin to trust the therapist. In couple therapy, a pair of anxious partners can be expected to become easily hurt or angry by a partner's comments, and they are likely to have a history of intense arguments, bouts of jealousy, and doubts about their partners' commitment. A pair of avoidant partners are likely to be distant, cautious, and perhaps cynical or dismissing with regard to their own and their partner's feelings. When one partner is anxious and the other is avoidant, there is likely to be a history of pursuing and distancing, as described by Bartholomew and Allison (2006).

Bowlby, the originator of attachment theory, was himself a psychotherapist. In his 1988 book, *A Secure Base: Clinical Applications of Attachment Theory*, he explained that favorable therapeutic outcomes depend on the extent to which a climate of security is created within the clinical setting, a climate that encourages clients to identify, clarify, question, revise, and transform insecure mental representations and associated feelings into more secure ones. More specifically, he outlined five important therapeutic tasks, the first of which is to provide clients with a secure base from which they can begin to explore painful memories and emotions. The second task is to encourage and assist clients in learning about maladaptive consequences of their characteristic patterns of relating. The third task is to encourage clients to examine their relationship with the therapist, which will inevitably include the projection of long-established "working models" (mental representations) onto the therapeutic relationship. The fourth, and related, task is to encourage clients to reflect on how their representations of self and others are rooted in previous experiences with relationship partners, beginning with parental figures. The fifth task is to help clients consider ways in which negative representations of self and others can be revised and updated to improve current relationships.

Expanding on Bowlby's (1988) ideas, several treatment strategies have been designed for couple therapy (e.g., Johnson, 2003, 2008; chapter 23 in this volume; emotionally focused couple therapy). These interventions explicitly focus on the trauma caused by rejections, separations, contempt from partners, and losses in the present relationship as well as previous ones. Johnson (2003, 2008) calls these "attachment injuries." Research has shown that an attachment-oriented approach to couple therapy is more effective than cognitive-behavioral approaches in reducing relationship distress (e.g., Clothier, Manion, Gordon-Walker, & Johnson, 2002). Further development of this approach based on the still-expanding body of empirical research on attachment-related mental and social processes can be expected.

Concluding Remarks

Bowlby devoted a great deal of thought to the parent–child relationship and wrote relatively little about sexuality, explicitly separating himself from Freud's ideas about the supposedly sexual nature of all close relationships. But of course he did not deny the obvious role of sexuality in evolution and in adolescent and adult relationships. He viewed sex as one of several core behavioral systems besides attachment, and in this chapter we have used his behavioral system concept to organize research on connections between the attachment and sexual systems. Researchers who study adult attachment have produced many valuable insights into the effects of attachment orientations on sexual motives and sexual behavior, and on the impact of attachment and sexuality on the quality and emotional rewards and difficulties of couple relationships. These insights are important to adults' self-understanding and to couples' attempts, including working with couple therapists, to improve their relationships, a goal that is important to all individuals, couples, families, and societies.

References

Ainsworth, M. D. S., Blehar, M. C., Waters, E., & Wall, S. (1978). *Patterns of attachment: Assessed in the strange situation and at home.* Hillsdale, NJ: Erlbaum.

Baldwin, M. W., Fehr, B., Keedian, E., Seidel, M., & Thomson, D. W. (1993). An exploration of the relational schemata underlying attachment styles: Self-report and lexical decision approaches. *Personality and Social Psychology Bulletin, 19,* 746–754.

Bartholomew, K., & Allison, C. J. (2006). An attachment perspective on abusive dynamics in intimate relationships. In M. Mikulincer & G. S. Goodman (Eds.), *Dynamics of romantic love: Attachment, caregiving, and sex* (pp. 102–127). New York: Guilford Press.

Birnbaum, G. E. (2007a). Attachment orientations, sexual functioning, and relationship satisfaction in a community sample of women. *Journal of Social and Personal Relationships, 24,* 21–35.

Birnbaum, G. E. (2007b). Beyond the borders of reality: Attachment orientations and sexual fantasies. *Personal Relationships, 14,* 321–342.

Birnbaum, G. E. (in press). Bound to interact: The divergent goals and complex interplay of attachment and sex within romantic relationships. *Journal of Social and Personal Relationships.*

Birnbaum, G. E., Reis, H. T., Mikulincer, M., Gillath, O., & Orpaz, A. (2006). When sex is more than just sex: Attachment orientations, sexual experience, and relationship quality. *Journal of Personality and Social Psychology, 91,* 929–943.

Bogaert, A. F., & Sadava, S. (2002). Adult attachment and sexual behavior. *Personal Relationships, 9*, 191–204.

Bowlby, J. (1973). *Attachment and loss: Vol. 2 Separation: Anxiety and anger*. New York: Basic Books.

Bowlby, J. (1980). *Attachment and loss: Vol. 3 Sadness and depression*. New York: Basic Books.

Bowlby, J. (1982). *Attachment and loss: Vol. 1 Attachment* (2nd edn.). New York: Basic Books.

Bowlby, J. (1988). *A secure base: Clinical applications of attachment theory*. London: Routledge.

Brassard, A., Shaver, P. R., & Lussier, Y. (2007). Attachment, sexual experience, and sexual pressure in romantic relationships: A dyadic approach. *Personal Relationships, 14*, 475–494.

Brennan, K. A., Clark, C. L., & Shaver, P. R. (1998). *Self-report measurement of adult attachment: An integrative overview*. In J. A. Simpson & W. S. Rholes (Eds.), *Attachment theory and close relationships* (pp. 46–76). New York: Guilford Press.

Brennan, K. A., & Shaver, P. R. (1995). Dimensions of adult attachment, affect regulation, and romantic relationship functioning. *Personality and Social Psychology Bulletin, 21*, 267–283.

Buss, D. M., & Kenrick, D. T. (1998). Evolutionary social psychology. In D. T. Gilbert, S. T. Fiske, & G. Lindzey (Eds.), *Handbook of social psychology* (Vol. *2*, pp. 982–1026). New York: McGraw-Hill.

Cassidy, J., & Kobak, R. R. (1988). Avoidance and its relationship with other defensive processes. In J. Belsky & T. Nezworski (Eds.), *Clinical implications of attachment* (pp. 300–323). Hillsdale, NJ: Erlbaum.

Clothier, P., Manion, I., Gordon-Walker, J., & Johnson, S. M. (2002). Emotionally-focused interventions for couple with chronically ill children: A two-year follow-up. *Journal of Marital and Family Therapy, 28*, 391–398.

Collins, N. L. (1996). Working models of attachment: Implications for explanation, emotion, and behavior. *Journal of Personality and Social Psychology, 71*, 810–832.

Collins, N. L., & Read, S. J. (1990). Adult attachment, working models, and relationship quality in dating couples. *Journal of Personality and Social Psychology, 58*, 644–663.

Cooper, M. L., Shaver, P. R., & Collins, N. L. (1998). Attachment styles, emotion regulation, and adjustment in adolescence. *Journal of Personality and Social Psychology, 74*, 1380–1397.

Davis, D., Shaver, P. R., & Vernon, M. L. (2004). Attachment style and subjective motivations for sex. *Personality and Social Psychology Bulletin, 30*, 1076–1090.

Fairbairn, W. R. D. (1952). *An object-relations theory of the personality*. New York: Basic Books.

Feeney, J. A. (2008). Adult romantic attachment: Developments in the study of couple relationships. In J. Cassidy & P. R. Shaver (Eds.), *Handbook of attachment: Theory, research, and clinical applications (*2nd edn., pp. 456–481). New York: Guilford Press.

Feeney, J. A., Hohaus, L., Noller, P., & Alexander, R. P. (2001). *Becoming parents: Exploring the bonds between mothers, fathers, and their infants*. New York: Cambridge University Press.

Fisher, H. E. (1998). Lust, attraction, and attachment in mammalian reproduction. *Human Nature, 9*, 23–52.

Fournier, B., Brassard, A., & Shaver, P. R. (in press). Adult attachment and male aggression in couple relationships: The demand-withdraw communication pattern and relationship satisfaction as mediators. *Journal of Interpersonal Violence*.

Freud, S. (1955). *Beyond the pleasure principle* (2nd edn.). London: Hogarth Press.

Gentzler, A. L., & Kerns, K. A. (2004). Associations between insecure attachment and sexual experiences. *Personal Relationships, 11*, 249–265.

Gillath, O., Mikulincer, M., Birnbaum, G., & Shaver, P. R. (2008). When sex primes love: Subliminal sexual priming motivates relationship goal pursuit. *Personality and Social Psychology Bulletin, 34*, 1057–1069.

Gillath, O., & Schachner, D. A. (2006). How do sexuality and attachment interact? Goals, motives, and strategies. In M. Mikulincer & G. S. Goodman (Eds.), *Dynamics of love: Attachment, caregiving, and sex* (pp. 337–355). New York: Guilford Press.

Hassebrauck, M., & Fehr, B. (2002). Dimensions of relationship quality. *Personal Relationships, 9*, 253–270.

Hurlbert, D. F., Apt, C., Hurlbert, M. K., & Pierce, A. P. (2000). Sexual compatibility and the sexual desire-motivation relation in females with hypoactive sexual desire disorder. *Behavior Modification, 24*, 325–347.

Impett, E. A., & Peplau, L. A. (2002). Why some women consent to unwanted sex with a dating partner: Insights from attachment theory. *Psychology of Women Quarterly, 26*, 360–370.

Johnson, S. M. (2003). Attachment theory: A guide for couple therapy. In S. M. Johnson, & V. E. Whiffen (Eds.), *Attachment processes in couple and family therapy* (pp. 103–123). New York: Guilford Press.

Johnson, S. M. (2008). *Hold me tight: Seven conversations for a lifetime of love*. New York: Little, Brown.

Long, E. C. J., Cate, R. M., Fehsenfeld, D. A., & Williams, K. M. (1996). A longitudinal assessment of a measure of premarital sexual conflict. *Family Relations, 45*, 302–308.

Mallinckrodt, B. (2010). The psychotherapy relationship as attachment: Evidence and implications. *Journal of Social and Personal Relationships, 27*, 262–270.

Mikulincer, M., Florian, V., Cowan, P. A., & Cowan, C. P. (2002). Attachment security in couple relationships: A systemic model and its implications for family dynamics. *Family Process, 41*, 405–434.

Mikulincer, M., & Shaver, P. R. (2003). The attachment behavioral system in adulthood: Activation, psychodynamics, and interpersonal processes. In M. P. Zanna (Ed.), *Advances in experimental social psychology* (Vol. *35*, pp. 53–152). New York: Academic Press.

Mikulincer, M., & Shaver, P. R. (2007a). *Attachment in adulthood: Structure, dynamics, and change*. New York: Guilford Press.

Mikulincer, M., & Shaver, P. R. (2007b). Boosting attachment security to promote mental health, prosocial values, and inter-group tolerance. *Psychological Inquiry, 18*, 139–156.

Mikulincer, M., & Shaver, P. R. (2007c). A behavioral systems perspective on the psychodynamics of attachment and sexuality. In D. Diamond, S. J. Blatt, & J. D. Lichtenberg (Eds.), *Attachment and sexuality* (pp. 51–78). New York: Analytic Press.

Obegi, J. H., & Berant, E. (Eds.). (2008). *Attachment theory and research in clinical work with adults*. New York: Guilford Press.

Ryan, R. M., & Frederick, C. (1997). On energy, personality, and health: Subjective vitality as a dynamic reflection of well-being. *Journal of Personality, 65*, 529–565.

Rholes, W. S., Simpson, J. A., & Orina, M. M. (1999). Attachment and anger in an anxiety-provoking situation. *Journal of Personality and Social Psychology, 76*, 940–957.

Schachner, D. A., & Shaver, P. R. (2002). Attachment style and human mate poaching. *New Review of Social Psychology, 1*, 122–129.

Schachner, D. A., & Shaver, P. R. (2004). Attachment dimensions and motives for sex. *Personal Relationships, 11*, 179–195.

Scharfe, E., & Bartholomew, K. (1995). Accommodation and attachment representations in couples. *Journal of Social and Personal Relationships, 12*, 389–401.

Shafer, A. B. (2001). The big five and sexuality trait terms as predictors of relationships and sex. *Journal of Research in Personality, 35*, 313–338.

Shaver, P. R., Hazan, C., & Bradshaw, D. (1988). Love as attachment: The integration of three behavioral systems. In R. J. Sternberg & M. Barnes (Eds.), *The psychology of love* (pp. 68–99). New Haven, CT: Yale University Press.

Shaver, P. R., & Mikulincer, M. (2002). Attachment-related psychodynamics. *Attachment and Human Development, 4*, 133–161.

Shaver, P. R., & Mikulincer, M. (2006a). A behavioral systems approach to romantic love relationships: Attachment, caregiving, and sex. In R. J. Sternberg & K. Weis (Eds.), *The new psychology of love* (pp. 35–64). New Haven, CT: Yale University Press.

Shaver, P. R., & Mikulincer, M. (2006b). *Conceptualization and operationalization of individual differences in the functioning of the sexual behavioral system.* Paper presented at the International Association for Relationship Research Biannual Conference, Crete, Greece.

Simpson, J. A. (1990). Influence of attachment styles on romantic relationships. *Journal of Personality and Social Psychology, 59*, 871–980.

Sprecher, S., & Cate, R. M. (2004). Sexual satisfaction and sexual expression as predictors of relationship satisfaction and stability. In J. H. Harvey, A. Wenzel, & S. Sprecher (Eds.), *Handbook of sexuality in close relationships* (pp. 235–256). Mahwah, NJ: Erlbaum.

Sprecher, S., & Regan, P. C. (1998). Passionate and companionate love in courting and young married couples. *Sociological Inquiry, 68*, 163–185.

Sroufe, L. A., & Waters, E. (1977). Attachment as an organizational construct. *Child Development, 48*, 1184–1199.

Tracy, J. L., Shaver, P. R., Albino, A. W., & Cooper, M. L. (2003). Attachment styles and adolescent sexuality. In P. Florsheim (Ed.), *Adolescent romance and sexual behavior: Theory, research, and practical implications* (pp. 137–159). Mahwah, NJ: Erlbaum.

Waite, L. J., & Joyner, K. (2001). Emotional satisfaction and physical pleasure in sexual unions: Time horizon, sexual behavior, and sexual exclusivity. *Journal of Marriage and the Family, 63*, 247–264.

12

Sexual Dysfunction in Intimate Heterosexual Relationships

Denisa Goldhammer and Marita P. McCabe

Sexual activity provides couples with a means by which to express intimacy and affection within their relationship, as well as being a way of achieving physical pleasure and tension reduction (Arrington, Cofrancesco, & Wu, 2004; Wise, 1999). McCarthy (1999) proposed that when sexuality functions well in a relationship, it reinforces the bond between partners; however, sexual dysfunction plays an inordinately powerful role, draining the couple relationship of its intimacy and vitality.

Whereas men generally place greater emphasis on sexual activity compared to women (Mathias, O'Leary, Henning, Pasta, Fromm, & Rosen, 1999; Patton & Waring, 1985), having a healthy, satisfying sex life is regarded as an important component in overall relationship and life satisfaction for both genders (Chesney, Blakeney, Cole, & Chan, 1981), and has also been noted as a key element of successful relationships (Costa & Brody, 2007; Dean, de Boer, Graziottin, Hatzichristou, Heaton, & Tailor, 2006b; McCabe, 1999). Growing evidence suggests that sexual relationships can have a positive influence on health and general well-being, with (good) sex being linked to health and happiness (Dunn, Croft, & Hackett, 1999). As such, disrupted sexual function can have an adverse impact on the state of the overall relationship between romantic partners (Latini et al., 2002; Riley, 2002).

Sexual problems and dysfunctions are common within the general population. Lifetime prevalence estimates suggest that up to 50% of individuals will experience some level of

The Wiley-Blackwell Handbook of Couples and Family Relationships, First Edition.
Edited by Patricia Noller and Gery C. Karantzas.

sexual dysfunction at one or more points in their lives (Feldman, Goldstein, Hatzichristou, Krane, & McKinlay, 1994; Heiman, 2002). Widely referenced community sample data from the United States indicated that approximately 31% of men and 43% of women experience sexual difficulties in any one year (Laumann, Paik, & Rosen, 1999).

The relationship that an individual has with their sexual partner provides the context within which sexual health concerns occur (Bancroft, Loftus, & Long, 2003; Fisher, Rosen, Eardley, Sand, & Goldstein, 2005). Yet research on the impact that sexual difficulties have on interpersonal functioning and general relationship satisfaction has thus far been limited. In this chapter, we outline current knowledge with respect to the psychological and interpersonal impact of sexual dysfunction within intimate heterosexual relationships. Empirical research findings for men and women are discussed separately. The literature presented here focuses primarily on erectile dysfunction (ED) for men, and hypoactive sexual desire disorder (HSDD) for women, as these are two of the most prevalent sexual problems reported for each gender (Laumann et al., 1999; Shifren, Monz, Russo, Segretti, & Johannes, 2008). The effect of one partner's sexual dysfunction on the sexual functioning of the other is also considered throughout the chapter, with the clinical implications of these research findings discussed. We begin by briefly describing the current classification of male and female sexual dysfunction.

The Classification of Male and Female Sexual Dysfunction

Sexual problems are conceptualized as arising from an impairment or disturbance in one of the primary stages of sexual response identified by Masters and Johnson (1966) and later refined by Kaplan (1977, 1979). These stages are desire, arousal, and orgasm. According to this model, the sexual response occurs as a linear progression through these stages, irrespective of occasion or context. Desire is defined as the interest one has in being sexual and in having sexual relations by oneself (i.e., masturbation) or with a partner (Wincze & Carey, 2001). Arousal refers to the various changes (physiological, cognitive, and affective) that serve to prepare men and women for sexual activity (Wincze & Carey, 2001). Finally, orgasm is defined as the peaking of sexual pleasure; in men, this is often associated with the ejaculation of sperm.

Conceptually, disruption to individual sexual response can occur at any one of these proposed stages, in both men and women. The most recent revision of the *Diagnostic and Statistical Manual of Mental Disorders*, produced by the American Psychiatric Association (APA), describes the common forms of sexual dysfunction associated with each of these stages of sexual response, and also includes a sexual pain category. Table 12.1 displays the classification system that appears within the DSM-IV-TR (APA, 2000).

As shown in Table 12.1, the various sexual dysfunctions are regarded by the APA as fitting neatly within the stages of sexual response. However, there exists much contention within the literature regarding the accuracy of this simplistic, categorical model; epidemiological studies report frequent comorbidity between sexual disorders among both men and women (Laumann et al., 1999; Simons & Carey, 2001; West, D'Aloisio, Agans,

Table 12.1 The DSM-IV-TR Classification of Sexual Dysfunction in Men and Women

Stage of sexual response cycle affected	*Dysfunction in men*	*Dysfunction in women*
Desire	Hypoactive sexual desire disorder (HSDD) Sexual aversion disorder	Hypoactive sexual desire disorder (HSDD) Sexual aversion disorder
Arousal	Male erectile dysfunction (ED)	Female sexual arousal disorder (FSAD)
Orgasm	Male orgasmic disorder premature ejaculation (PE)	Female orgasmic disorder (FOD)
Pain	Dyspareunia	Dyspareunia Vaginismus

Kalsbeek, Borisov, & Thorp, 2008). This finding suggests that the three-stage model may not be an accurate representation of the complexities of the human sexual response (Wincze & Carey, 2001). In particular, the model has been criticized as an inaccurate representation of a woman's sexual response pattern (Basson, 2000; Tiefer, 1991), with many women reporting that they tend not to differentiate between sexual desire and sexual arousal, for example (Goldhammer & McCabe, 2011; Graham, Sanders, Milhausen, & McBride, 2004). Such qualitative findings are furthermore reflected in the high comorbidity rate that is often found between HSDD and female sexual arousal disorder (Dennerstein, Koochaki, Barton, & Graziottin, 2006; Graziottin, 2007; Hayes, Dennerstein, Bennett, & Fairley, 2008; Heiman, 2002; Segraves & Segraves, 1991; West et al., 2008), suggesting that a model of sexual response that combines these two elements (sexual desire and sexual arousal) may be more representative of a woman's sexual response (Giles & McCabe, 2009; Sand & Fisher, 2007).

The current diagnostic approach to sexual disorders is strongly informed by research with an emphasis on the biological aspects of sexual health/dysfunction and the physiological changes that occur within each sexual-response stage. This biological focus has led to an understanding of the underlying physiological mechanisms and lifestyle factors that can contribute to the development of certain sexual dysfunctions and how medical therapies can assist in their treatment. However, this approach has been criticized for its emphasis on (dys)function, and the relative neglect of the numerous other factors involved in an individual's sexual well-being (O'Donohue & Geer, 1993; Simons & Carey, 2001; Wincze & Carey, 2001). Both psychological and interpersonal factors may contribute to the development of a sexual dysfunction and, equally, may be affected when a sexual dysfunction develops; thus, an understanding of such factors is crucial in developing treatments that comprehensively address the individuals' (and the couples') needs. The following discussion concentrates on the psychological and interpersonal factors associated with male and female sexual dysfunction, and the effect of sexual dysfunction on intimate heterosexual relationships.

Male Sexual Dysfunction and Intimate Relationship Correlates and Outcomes

Erectile dysfunction (ED) is one of the most pervasive sexual disorders among men (McDowell, Snellgrove, & Bond, 2001; Snow, 2004), with a lifetime prevalence estimate of 50% (Feldman et al., 1994). It has also been reported as the most common chronic medical condition affecting men over the age of 40 (Carson, 2002). ED occurs in men during the arousal phase of the sexual response, and is defined as the partial or complete inability to attain or maintain an erection that is sufficient for sexual intercourse to occur (APA, 2000).

Following a recent nationwide survey of the sex lives of Australian men, researchers estimated that 10% of men within the general population would have experienced some level of ED for at least one month in the prior year (Richters, Grulich, de Visser, Smith, & Rissel, 2003). Other national estimates have indicated that ED ranges in prevalence from 3% (for men aged 40–49 years) to 64% (for men aged 70–79 years) in a community sample (Pinnock, Stapleton, & Marshall, 1999), and 39% in men of various ages attending general medical practices (Chew, Earle, Stuckey, Jamrozik, & Keogh, 2000). A strong relationship has been found between increasing age and lowered erectile response (Feldman et al., 1994; Nicolosi, Moreira, Shirai, Tambi, & Glasser, 2003; Rosen, Fisher, Eardley, Niederberger, Nadel, & Sand, 2004), although it should also be noted that the importance of sex in men's lives declines with age, and sex often becomes a less significant component of men's overall life satisfaction (Hinchcliff & Gott, 2004; Laumann et al., 1999; Moore, Strauss, Herman, & Donatucci, 2003; Trudel, 2002).

Sexuality generally forms an integral part of a man's sense of identity, with men attaching a great deal of importance to their sexual performance and functioning; men who experience ED often report a diminished sense of masculinity (Potts, Grace, Gavey, & Vares, 2004). This loss of masculinity can generalize to an overall decline in self-esteem (Levine, 2003; Potts, 2000), and possibly to more serious psychological distress (Araujo, Mohr, & McKinlay, 2004), in addition to declines in overall quality of life (Latini et al., 2002, 2003; Stolk & Busschbach, 2003).

Adequate sexual functioning is an important component not only in the physical and psychological well-being of men, but is also a prerequisite for sexual, interpersonal, and general life satisfaction (Althof, 2002; Donnelly, 1993; Hartman, 1983; Hoch, Safir, Peres, & Shepher, 1981). The impact of ED has widespread implications for the relationships of affected men that extend beyond the bedroom (Korenman, 1998). Communication deficits, relationship dissatisfaction, and reductions in both frequency of sexual activity and levels of intimacy with one's partner are common among couples who experience this disorder (Cameron, Rosen, & Swindle, 2005; Hawton, Catalan, & Fagg, 1992; McCabe, 1994, 1997; McCabe & Cobain, 1998).

Men with ED often report decreased levels of sexual intimacy, which may contribute to a decline in their overall relationship satisfaction (Bokhour, Clark, Inui, Silliman, & Talcott, 2001; Carroll & Bagley, 1990; McCabe, 1997, 1999; Pontin, Porter, & McDonagh, 2002; Speckens, Hengeveld, Lychlama á Nijeholt, van Hemert, & Hawton, 1995). Several qualitative studies have explored the impact of ED on men who had been treated for prostate cancer, indicating that the presence of ED alters the role of sex within the relationship and leads to a decline in levels of intimacy (Bokhour et al.; Pontin et al.). The inability to achieve an erection sufficient for penetration not only impacts on the mechanical aspects of sex, but also the possibility of having an intimate experience that is satisfying for both the man and his partner (Bokhour et al.). It has been found that men with ED have less intimate relationships with their partners, both sexually and more broadly, than those without ED (McCabe, 1997).

In an Internet-based study investigating factors related to ED, Cameron et al. (2005) reported that relationship satisfaction was significantly lower among men with ED compared to men without ED. Other interpersonal factors have been associated with the development and maintenance of ED (Wincze & Carey, 2001); for example, an association has been demonstrated between communication deficits and erectile failure, with research demonstrating that conflict is more frequent between partners experiencing ED compared to couples reporting no ED (e.g. McCabe & Cobain, 1998; Metz & Epstein, 2002; Roffe & Britte, 1981). Furthermore, Hawton et al. (1992) found that the strongest predictor of successful therapy outcome for men with ED was the ability of the couple to communicate effectively.

There appears to be a lack of willingness among men affected by ED to discuss their problem and take the necessary steps to seek treatment; a recent Italian study found that 40% of men with ED of at least three years' duration had not discussed their condition with either their physician or their partner (Mirone et al., 2002). The result of a decline in effective communication and a rise in general relationship conflict may lead to relationship difficulties that extend far beyond the sexual relationship and the sexual dysfunction. Part of the reason that ED has such an impact on the lives of affected men is that these men wait a long time before seeking treatment (Hawton, 1992), and thus they (and their partners) adapt their lives around the presence of the problem. For example, the couple learns to live without having an intimate sexual interaction as part of their relationship, and the woman frequently develops a lack of interest in sex (Fisher et al., 2005). Consequently, regaining the ability to attain and maintain an erection following treatment may require a period of adjustment for some men and their partners (Leiblum, 2002; Phelps, Jain, & Monga, 2004), with this change in sexual functioning not always welcomed by female partners due to renewed pressures to engage in sexual intercourse (Potts et al., 2004).

It is difficult to determine whether interpersonal factors are a cause or consequence of ED; however, it is evident that many complex dyadic issues are associated with this disorder, and numerous areas of interpersonal functioning are affected by the presence of ED. Studies have indicated that men with ED are more likely to experience relationship instability, extra-marital relationships, conflict, poor communication with their partners, and less frequent sexual activity compared to sexually functional men (Feldman et al., 1994; Mathias et al., 1999; McCabe & Cobain, 1998).

The importance of considering a man's partner and the overall relationship when ED develops is gaining increasing recognition within the literature. Recently, several studies have sought to directly explore the impact of ED in the (sexual) lives of partners of affected men (e.g. Carroll & Bagley, 1990; Chevret, Jaudinot, Sullivan, Marrel, & Solesse de Gendre, 2004; Dunn, Croft, & Hackett, 2000; Fisher et al., 2005). It has been found that women who are in a relationship with men suffering from ED experience a decline in intimacy levels, as well as personal levels of sexual satisfaction and subsequent relationship satisfaction (Bokhour et al., 2001; Carroll & Bagley, 1990; Mathias et al., 1999; Pontin et al., 2002; Speckens et al., 1995). While declines in relationship functioning and satisfaction do not appear to be inevitable following the onset of ED (e.g., Dunn et al., 1999; Simkins-Bullock, Wildman, & Sugrue, 1992), the potential for such problems to develop subsequent to the man's ED demonstrates the impact that this dysfunction can have on the relationship. Research has furthermore indicated that a woman may experience a decline in her own sexual functioning, particularly decreases in levels of sexual desire/ interest, following the onset of ED in her partner (Carroll & Bagley, 1990; Fisher et al., 2005; Riley, 2002; Riley & Riley, 2000). Conversely, successful treatment of ED in men has been found to have significant positive effects on the sexual functioning of the female partner (Cayan, Bozlu, Canpolat, & Akbay, 2004; Goldstein et al., 2005).

What appears to be most important in determining how the presence of ED affects a couple is the way in which they react to the dysfunction and the meaning they attach to it (Chesney et al., 1981; Frank, Anderson, & Rubenstein, 1978; McCabe & Cobain, 1998; Spector & Boyle, 1986). For instance, couples who magnify the effect of a sexual problem by reacting to it with fear, anger, and anxiety also display increased relationship conflict and poorer communication in general (Korenman, 1998). Emerging evidence indicates that ED is not a condition that can be assessed and treated in isolation from the man's relationship. Even in cases where the ED is primarily caused by biological factors, psychological and interpersonal factors are likely to be maintaining this disorder, with more favorable outcomes likely to be achieved when medical treatment is supplemented with psychological interventions (Ackerman & Carey, 1995; Bass, 2001; Dean, de Boer, Graziottin, Hatzichristou, Heaton, & Tailor, 2006a; Hudson-Allez, 1998; Rosen & Leiblum, 1993). A purely medical approach may perpetuate performance anxiety among men with ED by strengthening the belief that they must achieve a perfect erection (Bass, 2001; McCarthy & Fucito, 2005).

Oral medications to treat ED (e.g. sildenafil citrate marketed as Viagra™) have demonstrated their effectiveness in being able to induce a physiological arousal response in the majority of men; yet there are high dissatisfaction and discontinuation rates among men who are treated using these mainline pharmacological therapies, with some studies reporting discontinuation rates of around 50–60% (Althof et al., 2003; Seftel, 2002). The inability of these medical treatments to address the broader individual psychological and interpersonal factors that are involved in many cases of ED may be largely responsible for the high level of patient discontinuation (Althof, 2002; Carpiano, 2001).

Implications for the treatment of male sexual dysfunction

As our understanding of the physiology and pathophysiology of ED develops, there exists a growing temptation to bypass attending to the related psychological and interpersonal issues in the assessment and treatment of this condition (Basson, 1998). However, the dissatisfaction seen among a large percentage of ED medication users suggests that exclusively targeting the physical component of ED may be insufficient as a treatment approach for this condition (Bancroft, 1970; Carpiano, 2001; Rosen, 1996; Wincze &

Carey, 2001). In many cases it is unlikely that improved sexual responsiveness alone will adequately resolve some of the complex and often longstanding psychological and interpersonal issues that couples experiencing ED may be affected by (Heiman & Meston, 1997; Leiblum, 2002; McDowell et al., 2001; Mohr & Beutler, 1990). However, the outcome of pharmacological interventions and reported satisfaction with ED medications has been found to be significantly enhanced by involving partners in the assessment and treatment process (Dean et al., 2006a; Rosen & Leiblum, 1993). It is therefore indicated that the assessment and treatment of ED should habitually include a thorough individual and couple assessment in order to understand the psychosocial context in which the ED is occurring and tailor an intervention that comprehensively addresses the couple's needs.

Female Sexual Dysfunction and Intimate Relationship Correlates and Outcomes

Sexual desire is considered to be a core aspect of healthy sexuality (McCarthy, Ginsberg, & Fucito, 2006), although substantial debate exists regarding the conceptualization, operationalization, and measurement of this attribute within the literature (Meana, 2010). Hypoactive sexual desire disorder (HSDD) constitutes the most common category of female sexual dysfunction (FSD) in epidemiological studies from the United States, Europe, and Australia (Fugl-Meyer & Fugl-Meyer, 1999; Giles & McCabe, 2009; Hayes, Bennett, Fairley, & Dennerstein, 2006; Laumann et al., 1999; Najman, Dunne, Boyle, Cook, & Purdie, 2003; Richters et al., 2003; Simons & Carey, 2001).

The prevalence of HSDD in women is currently unclear (Basson, 2007), with numerous changes in DSM criteria for this disorder over time posing obstacles to determining prevalence (Brotto, 2010). Recent prevalence rates have ranged from 8% to as high as an average of 64% among clinical populations (Avis, Zhao, Johannes, Ory, Brockwell, & Greendale, 2005; Deeks & McCabe, 2001; Fugl-Meyer & Fugl-Meyer, 1999; Hayes et al., 2008; Laumann et al., 1999; Richters et al., 2003). It is furthermore suggested that the prevalence of this disorder has increased over time (Spector & Carey, 1990), and that a low level of desire is frequently accompanied by low levels of arousal, infrequent orgasm, and sexual dissatisfaction (Basson, 2006). As noted previously, while sexual desire is conceptually distinct from the physiological process of genitally based changes that comprise sexual arousal, including vaginal lubrication (Masters, Johnson, & Kolodny, 1994), there is growing evidence that women may not experience sexual desire and sexual arousal as distinct phases, but rather as aspects of the same experience (e.g. Giles & McCabe, 2009; Sand & Fisher, 2007).

Biological, psychological, and interpersonal factors may all affect a woman's normal sexual functioning/response and consequently contribute to the development and maintenance of FSD. A recent Australian study found that interpersonal factors were more important to women's experience of sexual desire, whereas biological and individual (psychological) characteristics were more strongly associated with genital arousal and orgasmic function (Hayes et al., 2008).

A substantial body of literature suggests that sexual and interpersonal functioning is strongly associated for women. Sexual dysfunction may be a symptom of a larger relationship dysfunction (McCabe, 1991), and women may still report sexual dissatisfaction even if they are able to follow a "normal" sexual response pattern (McCabe, 1999). In a recent study conducted by King, Holt, and Nazareth (2007), the most commonly perceived causes of sexual difficulties cited by women, regardless of whether they were assigned a diagnosis of FSD, were relationship difficulties. Research has furthermore indicated that women diagnosed with HSDD are more likely to have negative feelings about the quality of their relationship, particularly related to poor interpersonal communication and a lack of intimacy within their relationship in general (Atwood & Dershowitz, 1992; Donahey & Carroll, 1993; Trudel, Boulos, & Matte, 1993; Trudel, Marchand, Ravart, Aubin, Turgeon, & Fortier, 2001).

It has been shown that, in general, women place greater emphasis on relationships as a context for sexual feelings and behaviors than do men (Peplau, 2003), and interpersonal factors have been found to be more strongly associated with sexual dysfunction for women than for men (McCabe & Cobain, 1998). This emphasis may be a result of differences in socialization between genders; women are socialized with an emphasis on emotional connection (with a partner) as a prerequisite for sexual expression (Baumeister & Vohs, 2004).

Several studies have reported a positive association between sexual desire in women and their perception of relationship quality, as determined by measures of relationship satisfaction (Brezsnyak & Whisman, 2004; Dunn et al., 1999; Hurlbert & Apt, 1994; McCabe, 1999; McCabe & Cobain, 1998; Witting et al., 2008). A poor relationship with a partner has been linked to low sexual desire for women (Byers, 2001; Hallstrom & Samuelsson, 1990). One hypothesis attempting to explain this association proposes that low sexual desire is produced by the negative affect and cognitions resulting from an unsatisfactory interpersonal context (Hallstrom & Samuelsson, 1990). For example, experiencing feelings of anger has been correlated with significantly reduced sexual desire levels for women (Beck & Bozman, 1995).

The causal association between low sexual desire and relationship satisfaction remains elusive at present. Whereas desire problems can lead to interpersonal conflict (Althof et al., 2005), a poor relationship with a partner predicts low levels of sexual desire (Stuart, Hammond, & Pett, 1987). Research findings often suggest a bidirectional association between interpersonal factors such as relationship and sexual satisfaction, intimacy, communication, unresolved conflict, and partner sexual dysfunction, and a woman's sexual desire (Metz & Epstein, 2002). Clearly then, there is a need to acknowledge and address such factors when assessing this aspect of women's sexuality.

Effective communication between partners has frequently been associated with sexual functioning for women (Chesney et al., 1981; Ferroni & Taffe, 1997; McCabe, 1999). However, research that has examined the specific nature of communication problems experienced by sexually dysfunctional couples is limited. Kelly, Strassberg, and Turner (2004) proposed that effective sexual stimulation may be facilitated by women communicating their sexual needs to their partner, in addition to having a partner who is receptive to this expression. Numerous authors have also proposed that self-disclosing desired and undesired sexual techniques to a partner is associated with the experience of fewer sexual problems (Byers & Demmons, 1999; Metts & Cupach, 1989; Russell, 1990).

Clinical observations have consistently indicated a strong association between relationship conflict and the development and maintenance of sexual dysfunction (Heiman, LoPiccolo, & LoPiccolo, 1981; McCarthy, 1998, 1999; Metz & Dwyer, 1993; Rosen & Leiblum, 1992). Research has also indicated that sexually dysfunctional couples employ distinct conflict resolution styles in comparison to controls, although the direction of association between these variables is not conclusive. For example, a comparison of conflict resolution in sexually functional and dysfunctional couples indicated that dysfunctional women were more verbally aggressive and demonstrated more engaging behavior, while their partner was avoiding or withdrawing from the interaction (Metz & Dwyer). In comparison to sexually functional couples, sexually dysfunctional couples' conflict resolution styles were characterized by higher levels of aggression and withdrawal and lower levels of assertion and negotiation (Metz & Epstein, 2002). A bidirectional causal link has been proposed to exist between sexual dysfunction and unresolved relationship conflict (Metz & Epstein, 2002).

Emotional intimacy between partners serves as a foundation for healthy sexual functioning and may be one of the primary interpersonal factors contributing to a woman's sexual response (McCarthy & Thestrup, 2008). A study evaluating the association between sexual functioning and relationship intimacy found that women with disorders of sexual desire reported lower levels of sexual intimacy than sexually functional controls (McCabe, 1997). Higher levels of intimacy have furthermore been associated with greater levels of sexual satisfaction and orgasm among heterosexual couples in long-term relationships (Costa & Brody, 2007; Haning, O'Keefe, Randall, Kommor, Baker, & Wilson, 2007).

A critical task in the primary evaluation of sexual dysfunction has been to promote a transition towards a couple sexual style that has emotional intimacy as a core process (McCarthy & Thestrup, 2008). Some authors have suggested that the relatively poor treatment success for problems in sexual desire is due to an inadequate recognition of, and attention to, the relational aspects of these problems (Talmadge & Talmadge, 1996). Research findings demonstrating that the quality of the relationship between partners improves following successful treatment of the disorder in sexual desire supports this assertion (Trudel et al., 2001).

Implications for the treatment of female sexual dysfunction

Developments in the area of sexual pharmacology, particularly following the introduction of Viagra™ by Pfizer onto the market for the treatment of ED in 1998, have arguably led to biological reductionism of FSD, with an emphasis on physiological processes and a focus on women's genital performance (Balon & Segraves, 2005). Sex therapists warn that taking a purely medical approach to the treatment of female sexual problems is unlikely to be successful, if psychosocial and interpersonal contributors remain unexamined (Goldberg & Pervin, 2006).

A major barrier to the development of clinical research and practice has been the absence of a well-defined, broadly accepted diagnostic framework and classification for

FSD (Basson et al., 2000), and this problem is also reflected in the fact that fewer treatment options are currently available for women than for men (Segraves & Balon, 2005). It has been suggested that including an assessment of a woman's emotional experience within her sexual context is necessary to facilitate a complete understanding of sexual dysfunction (Everaerd, Both, & Laan, 2006). That is, as for men, an evaluation of the context in which sexual interactions occur or do not currently occur (i.e. the interpersonal relationship between a woman and her partner) is necessary in order to tailor an effective treatment intervention that addresses the multitude of factors associated with the woman's sexual (dys)function.

Conclusion and Recommendations for Clinical Practice

The need for sexual problems to be viewed in context rather than simply as physiological phenomena occurring in isolation from psychological and interpersonal experiences has been repeatedly emphasized (e.g., Balon, 2008; Bancroft et al., 2003; Basson et al. 2004; Clayton, 2007; Hayes, 2008). An individual's sexual functioning is shaped by biological, psychological, interpersonal, and sociocultural/contextual influences, all of which must be considered in order to intervene effectively when a sexual problem emerges (Basson, 2005; Levine, 1992). In this chapter, we have discussed empirical findings with respect to the association between psychological/interpersonal factors and sexual dysfunction within intimate heterosexual relationships. Although considerable research remains to be conducted in this area, it is evident that sexual dysfunction impacts extensively on personal and interpersonal functioning in both men and women.

Given the pervasive negative effects of sexual dysfunction on both the individual and his/her intimate relationship, it is important that effective intervention strategies are developed. Despite the frequent involvement of psychological and interpersonal characteristics as precipitating and maintaining factors for sexual dysfunction, as discussed above, in recent years pharmacological treatments have gained favor over psychological interventions for such problems (Levine, 1992). However, given the demonstrated potential for sexual dysfunction to impact on the psychological well-being and interpersonal functioning of the affected individual, the adequacy of pharmacological treatments to address the inherent complexity of sexual dysfunction must be questioned.

The failure of pharmacological treatment approaches to address the broader issues involved in male and female sexual dysfunction necessitates consideration of psychologically based treatments to fill the gaps. Unfortunately less attention has been directed toward developing psychological and interpersonal approaches for treating sexual dysfunctions, meaning that there have been relatively few innovative, psychologically based treatment approaches developed in recent years. Given the critical role of psychological and interpersonal factors, even in cases of a clear-cut biological etiology for sexual dysfunction (e.g., in some cases of ED), the failure to attend to these issues is unlikely to lead to successful management and treatment of the sexual dysfunction.

McCabe (1991) proposed a model based on cognitive theory to explain the development of sexual dysfunction by an individual in a relationship. This model suggests that an interaction of intergenerational, individual (psychological), and interpersonal factors contribute to the development and maintenance of sexual dysfunction, with each of these factors evaluated by both individuals involved in the relationship. Depending on the evaluation that is made, the individual reacts in a particular way, which may lead to the development of a sexual dysfunction. This model indicates that any treatment approach must take into account and address each of these three categories of factors in order to be successful. It furthermore implies that any intervention approach is unlikely to be successful unless both partners are involved in the treatment process, with both individuals' needs as well as their interpersonal needs addressed. It is therefore recommended that clinicians determine and address both the individual and interpersonal needs of the couple in approaching the treatment of any sexual dysfunction. In particular, communication patterns and any unresolved conflicts that exist between partners need to be assessed and addressed.

References

Ackerman, M. D., & Carey, M. P. (1995). Psychology's role in the assessment of erectile dysfunction: Historical precedents, current knowledge, and methods. *Journal of Consulting and Clinical Psychology*, *63*, 862–876.

Althof, S. E. (2002). When an erection alone is not enough: Biopsychosocial obstacles to lovemaking. *International Journal of Impotence Research*, *14*, S99–S104.

Althof, S. E., Cappelleri, J. C., Shpilsky, A. et al. (2003). Treatment responsiveness of the Self-Esteem and Relationship Questionnaire in erectile dysfunction. *Urology*, *61*, 888–892.

Althof, S. E., Leiblum, S. R., Chevret-Measson, M. et al. (2005). Psychological and interpersonal dimensions of sexual function and dysfunction. *Journal of Sexual Medicine*, *2*, 793–800.

American Psychiatric Association (2000). *Diagnostic and statistical manual of mental disorders.* (4th edn., text revision). Washington, DC: American Psychiatric Association.

Araujo, A. B., Mohr, B. A., & McKinlay, J. B. (2004). Changes in sexual function in middle-aged and older men: Longitudinal data from the Massachusetts Male Aging Study. *Journal of the American Geriatric Society*, *52*, 1502–1509.

Arrington, R., Cofrancesco, J., & Wu, A. W. (2004). Questionnaires to measure sexual quality of life. *Quality of Life Research: An International Journal of Quality of Life Aspects of Treatment, Care and Rehabilitation*, *13*, 1643–1658.

Atwood, J. D., & Dershowitz, S. (1992). Constructing a sex and marital therapy frame: Ways to help couples deconstruct sexual problems. *Journal of Sex and Marital Therapy*, *18*, 196–219.

Avis, N. E., Zhao, X., Johannes, C. B., Ory, M., Brockwell, S., & Greendale, G. A. (2005). Correlates of sexual function among multi-ethnic middle-aged women: results from the Study of Women's Health Across the Nation (SWAN). *Menopause*, *12*, 385–398.

Balon, R. (2008). The DSM criteria of sexual dysfunction: Need for a change. *Journal of Sex and Marital Therapy*, *34*, 186–197.

Balon, R., & Segraves, R. T. (Eds.) (2005). *Handbook of sexual dysfunction*. Boca Raton: Taylor & Francis.

Bancroft, J. (1970). Disorders of sexual potency. In O. W. Hill (Ed.), *Modern trends in psychosomatic medicine* (pp. 246–261). London: Butterworths.

Bancroft, J., Loftus, J., & Long, J. S. (2003). Distress about sex: A national survey of women in heterosexual relationships. *Archives of Sexual Behavior*, *32*, 193–208.

Bass, B. A. (2001). The sexual performance perfection industry and the medicalization of male sexuality. *The Family Journal: Counseling and Therapy for Couples and Families, 9*, 337–340.

Basson, R. (1998). Integrating new biomedical treatments into the assessment and management of erectile dysfunction. *Canadian Journal of Human Sexuality, 7*, 213–229.

Basson, R. (2000). The female sexual response: A different model. *Journal of Sex and Marital Therapy, 26*, 51–65.

Basson, R. (2005). Women's sexual dysfunction: Revised and expanded definitions. *Canadian Medical Association Journal, 172*, 1327–1333.

Basson, R. (2006). Sexual desire and arousal disorders in women. *New England Journal of Medicine, 354*, 1497–1506.

Basson, R. (2007). Sexual desire/arousal disorders in women. In S. R. Leiblum (Ed.), *Principles and practice of sex therapy* (4th edn., pp. 25–53). New York: Guilford Press.

Basson, R., Berman, J., Burnett, A. et al. (2000). Report of the International Consensus Development Conference on female sexual dysfunction: Definitions and classifications. *Journal of Urology, 163*, 888–893.

Basson, R., Leiblum, S., Brotto, L. et al. (2004). Revised definitions of women's sexual dysfunction. *Journal of Sexual Medicine, 1*, 40–48.

Baumeister, R. F., & Vohs, K. D. (2004). Sexual economics: Sex as female resource for social exchange in heterosexual interactions. *Personality and Social Psychology Review, 8*, 339–363.

Beck, J. G., & Bozman, A. W. (1995). Gender differences in sexual desire: The effects of anger and anxiety. *Archives of Sexual Behavior, 24*, 595–612.

Bokhour, B. G., Clark, J. A., Inui, T. S., Silliman, R. A., & Talcott, J. A. (2001). Sexuality and treatment for early prostate cancer. Exploring the meaning of "erectile dysfunction." *Journal of General Internal Medicine, 16*, 649–655.

Brezsnyak, M., & Whisman, M. A. (2004). Sexual desire and relationship functioning: The effects of marital satisfaction and power. *Journal of Sex and Marital Therapy, 30*, 199–217.

Brotto, L. A. (2010). The DSM diagnostic criteria for hypoactive sexual desire disorder in women. *Archives of Sexual Behavior, 39*, 221–239.

Byers, E. S. (2001). Evidence for the importance of relationship satisfaction for women's sexual functioning. In E. Kaschak & L. Tiefer (Eds.), *A new view of women's sexual problems* (pp. 23–26). Binghamton: Hawthorn Press.

Byers, E. S., & Demmons, S. (1999). Sexual satisfaction and sexual self-disclosure within dating relationships. *Journal of Sex Research, 36*, 180–189.

Cameron, A., Rosen, R. C., & Swindle, R. W. (2005). Sexual and relationship characteristics among an internet-based sample of US men with and without erectile dysfunction. *Journal of Sex and Marital Therapy, 31*, 229–242.

Carpiano, R. M. (2001). Passive medicalization: The case of Viagra and erectile dysfunction. *Sociological Spectrum, 21*, 441–450.

Carroll, J. L., & Bagley, D. H. (1990). Evaluation of sexual satisfaction in partners of men experiencing erectile failure. *Journal of Sex and Marital Therapy, 16*, 70–78.

Carson, C. C. (2002). Erectile dysfunction in the 21st century: Whom can we treat, whom we cannot treat and patient education. *International Journal of Impotence Research, 14*, S29–S34.

Cayan, S., Bozlu, M., Canpolat, B., & Akbay, E. (2004). The assessment of sexual function in women with male partners complaining of erectile dysfunction: Does treatment of male sexual dysfunction improve female partner's sexual functions? *Journal of Sex and Marital Therapy, 30*, 333–341.

Chesney, A. P., Blakeney, P. E., Cole, C. M., & Chan, F. A. (1981). A comparison of couples who have sought sex therapy with couples who have not. *Journal of Sex and Marital Therapy, 7*, 131–140.

Chevret, M., Jaudinot, E., Sullivan, K., Marrel, A., & Solesse de Gendre, A. (2004). Impact of erectile dysfunction (ED) on sexual life of female partners: Assessment with the Index of Sexual Life (ISL) questionnaire. *Journal of Sex and Marital Therapy, 30*, 157–172.

Chew, K. K., Earle, C. M., Stuckey, B. G. A., Jamrozik, K., & Keogh, E. J. (2000). Erectile dysfunction in general medical practice: Prevalence and clinical correlates. *International Journal of Impotence Research, 12*, 41–45.

Clayton, A. H. (2007). Epidemiology and neurobiology of female sexual dysfunction. *Journal of Sexual Medicine, 4*, 260–268.

Costa, R. M., & Brody, S. (2007). Women's relationship quality is associated with specifically penile-vaginal intercourse orgasm and frequency. *Journal of Sex and Marital Therapy, 33*, 319–327.

Dean, J., de Boer, B., Graziottin, A., Hatzichristou, D., Heaton, J., & Tailor, *A.* (2006a). Partner satisfaction and successful treatment outcomes for men with erectile dysfunction. *European Journal of Urology, 5*, 779–785.

Dean, J., de Boer, B., Graziottin, A., Hatzichristou, D., Heaton, J., & Tailor, *A.* (2006b). Psychological, social, and behavioural benefits for men following effective erectile dysfunction treatment: Men who enjoy better sex experience improved psychological well-being. *European Journal of Urology, 5*, 773–778.

Deeks, A., & McCabe, M. P. (2001). Sexual function and the menopausal woman: The importance of age and partner's sexual functioning. *Journal of Sex Research, 38*, 219–225.

Dennerstein, L., Koochaki, P., Barton, I., & Graziottin, A. (2006). Hypoactive sexual desire disorder in menopausal women: A survey of Western European women. *Journal of Sexual Medicine, 3*, 212–222.

Donahey, K. M., & Carroll, R. A. (1993). Gender differences in factors associated with hypoactive sexual desire. *Journal of Sex and Marital Therapy, 19*, 25–40.

Donnelly, D. A. (1993). Sexually inactive marriages. *Journal of Sex Research, 30*, 171–179.

Dunn, K. M., Croft, P. R., & Hackett, G. I. (1999). Association of sexual problems with social, psychological, and physical problems in men and women: A cross sectional survey. *Journal of Epidemiology and Community Health, 53*, 144–148.

Dunn, K. M., Croft, P. R., & Hackett, G. I. (2000). Satisfaction in the sex life of a general population sample. *Journal of Sex and Marital Therapy, 26*, 141–151.

Everaerd, W., Both, S., & Laan, E. (2006). The experience of sexual emotions. *Annual Review of Sex Research, 17*, 183–199.

Feldman, H. A., Goldstein, I., Hatzichristou, G., Krane, R. J., & McKinlay, J. B. (1994). Impotence and its medical and psychosocial correlates: Results of the Massachusetts male aging study. *Journal of Urology, 151*, 54–61.

Ferroni, P., & Taffe, J. (1997). Women's emotional well-being: The importance of communicating sexual needs. *Sexual and Marital Therapy, 12*, 127–138.

Fisher, W. A., Rosen, R. C., Eardley, I., Sand, M., & Goldstein, I. (2005). Sexual experience of female partners of men with erectile dysfunction: The female experience of men's attitudes to life events and sexuality (FEMALES) study. *Journal of Sexual Medicine, 2*, 675–684.

Frank, E., Anderson, A., & Rubenstein, D. (1978). Frequency of sexual dysfunction in "normal" couples. *New England Journal of Medicine, 299*, 111–115.

Fugl-Meyer, A. R., & Fugl-Meyer, K. S. (1999). Sexual disabilities, problems and satisfaction in 18–74 year old Swedes. *Scandinavian Journal of Sexology, 2*, 79–105.

Giles, K. R., & McCabe, M. P. (2009). Conceptualizing women's sexual function: Linear vs. circular models of sexual response. *Journal of Sexual Medicine, 6*, 2761–2771.

Goldberg, D. C., & Pervin, L. A. (2006). Progress in the treatment of sexual desire disorders. PsycCRITIQUES, *35*, 786–787.

Goldhammer, D. L., & McCabe, M. P. (2011). A qualitative exploration of the meaning and experience of sexual desire for partnered heterosexual women. *Canadian Journal of Human Sexuality, 20*, 19–29.

Goldstein, I., Fisher, W. A., Sand, M. et al. (2005). Women's sexual function improves when partners are administered vardenafil for erectile dysfunction: A prospective, randomized, double-blind, placebo-controlled trial. *Journal of Sexual Medicine, 2*, 819–832.

Graham, C. A., Sanders, S. A., Milhausen, R. R., & McBride, K. R. (2004). Turning on and turning off: A focus group study of the factors that affect women's sexual arousal. *Archives of Sexual Behavior, 33*, 527–538.

Graziottin, A. (2007). Prevalence and evaluation of sexual health problems–HSDD in Europe. *Journal of Sexual Medicine, 4*, 211–219.

Hallstrom, T., & Samuelsson, S. (1990). Changes in women's sexual desire in middle life: The longitudinal study of women in Gothenburg. *Archives of Sexual Behavior, 19*, 259–268.

Haning, R. V., O'Keefe, S. L., Randall, E. J., Kommor, M. J., Baker, E., & Wilson, R. (2007). Intimacy, orgasm likelihood, and conflict predict sexual satisfaction in heterosexual male and female respondents. *Journal of Sex and Marital Therapy, 33*, 93–113.

Hartman, L. M. (1983). Effects of sex and marital therapy on sexual interaction and marital happiness. *Journal of Sex and Marital Therapy, 9*, 137–151.

Hawton, K. (1992). Sex therapy research: Has it withered on the vine? *Annual Review of Sex Research, 3*, 49–72.

Hawton, K., Catalan, J., & Fagg, J. (1992). Sex therapy for erectile dysfunction: Characteristics of couples, treatment outcome, and prognostic factors. *Archives of Sexual Behavior, 21*, 161–175.

Hayes, R. D. (2008). Assessing female sexual dysfunction in epidemiological studies: Why is it necessary to measure both low sexual function and sexually-related distress? *Sexual Health, 5*, 215–218.

Hayes, R. D., Bennett, C. M., Fairley, C. K., & Dennerstein, L. (2006). What can prevalence studies tell us about female sexual difficulty and dysfunction? *Journal of Sexual Medicine, 3*, 589–595.

Hayes, R. D., Dennerstein, L., Bennett, C. M., & Fairley, C. K. (2008). What is the "true" prevalence of female sexual dysfunctions and does the way we assess these conditions have an impact? *Journal of Sexual Medicine, 5*(4), 777–787.

Heiman, J. R. (2002). Sexual dysfunction: Overview of prevalence, etiological factors, and treatments. *Journal of Sex Research, 39*, 73–78.

Heiman, J. R., LoPiccolo, L., & LoPiccolo, J. (1981). The treatment of sexual dysfunction. In A. S. Gurman & D. P. Kinskern (Eds.), *Handbook of family therapy* (pp. 592–627). New York: Brunner-Mazel.

Heiman, J. R., & Meston, C. M. (1997). Empirically validated treatment for sexual dysfunction. *Annual Review of Sex Research, 8*, 148–195.

Hinchcliff, S., & Gott, M. (2004). Perceptions of well-being in sexual ill health: What role does age play? *Journal of Health Psychology, 9*, 649–660.

Hoch, Z., Safir, M. P., Peres, Y., & Shepher, J. (1981). An evaluation of sexual performance–Comparison between sexually dysfunctional and functional couples. *Journal of Sex and Marital Therapy, 7*, 195–206.

Hudson-Allez, G. (1998). The interface between psychogenic and organic difficulties in men with erectile dysfunction. *Sexual and Marital Therapy, 13*, 285–293.
Hurlbert, D. F., & Apt, C. (1994). What constitutes sexual satisfaction? Directions for future research. *Sexual and Relationship Therapy, 9*, 285–289.
Kaplan, H. S. (1977). Hypoactive sexual desire. *Journal of Sex and Marital Therapy, 3*, 3–9.
Kaplan, H. S. (1979). *Disorders of sexual desire*. New York: Brunner/Mazel.
Kelly, M. P., Strassberg, D. S., & Turner, C. M. (2004). Communication and associated relationship issues in female anorgasmia. *Journal of Sex and Marital Therapy, 30*, 263–276.
King, M., Holt, V., & Nazareth, I. (2007). Women's views of their sexual difficulties: Agreement and disagreement with clinical diagnoses. *Archives of Sexual Behavior, 36*, 281–288.
Korenman, S. G. (1998). New insights into erectile dysfunction: A practical approach. *American Journal of Medicine, 10*, 135–144.
Latini, D. M., Penson, D. F., Colwell, H. H. et al. (2002). Psychological impact of erectile dysfunction: Validation of a new health related quality of life measure for patients with erectile dysfunction. *Journal of Urology, 168*, 2086–2091.
Latini, D. M., Penson, D. F., Lubeck, D. P., Wallace, K. L., Henning, J. M., & Lue, T. F. (2003). Longitudinal differences in disease specific quality of life in men with erectile dysfunction: Results from the exploratory comprehensive evaluation of erectile dysfunction study. *Journal of Urology, 169*, 1437–1442.
Laumann, E. O., Paik, A., & Rosen, R. C. (1999). Sexual dysfunction in the United States: Prevalence and predictors. *Journal of the American Medical Association, 281*, 537–544.
Leiblum, S. R. (2002). After sildenafil: Bridging the gap between pharmacological treatment and satisfying sexual relationships. *Journal of Clinical Psychiatry, 63*, S17–S22.
Levine, S. B. (1992). *Sexual life: A clinician's guide*. New York: Plenum Press.
Levine, S. B. (2003). Erectile dysfunction: Why drug therapy isn't always enough. *Cleveland Clinical Journal of Medicine, 70*, 241–246.
Meana, M. (2010). Elucidating women's (hetero)sexual desire: Definitional challenges and content expansion. *Journal of Sex Research, 47*, 104–122.
Masters, W., & Johnson, V. (1966). *Human sexual response*. Boston: Little Brown.
Masters, W. H., Johnson, V. E., & Kolodny, R. C. (1994). *Heterosexuality*. New York: HarperCollins.
Mathias, S. D., O'Leary, M. P., Henning, J. M., Pasta, D. J., Fromm, S., & Rosen, R. C. (1999). A comparison of patient and partner responses to a brief sexual function questionnaire. *Journal of Urology, 162*, 1999–2002.
McCabe, M. P. (1991). The development and maintenance of sexual dysfunction: An explanation based on cognitive theory. *Sexual and Marital Therapy, 6*, 245–260.
McCabe, M. P. (1994). The influence of the quality of relationship on sexual dysfunction. *Australian Journal of Marriage and Family, 15*, 2–8.
McCabe, M. P. (1997). Intimacy and quality of life among sexually dysfunctional men and women. *Journal of Sex and Marital Therapy, 23*, 276–290.
McCabe, M. P. (1999). The interrelationship between intimacy, relationship functioning, and sexuality among men and women in committed relationships. *Canadian Journal of Human Sexuality, 8*, 31–38.
McCabe, M. P., & Cobain, M. J. (1998). The impact of individual and relationship factors on sexual dysfunction among males and females. *Sexual and Marital Therapy, 13*, 131–143.
McCarthy, B. W. (1998). Sex in the first two years of marriage. *Journal of Family Psychotherapy, 9*, 1–11.
McCarthy, B. W. (1999). Marital style and its effects on sexual desire and functioning. *Journal of Family Psychotherapy, 10*, 1–12.

McCarthy, B. W., & Fucito, L. M. (2005). Integrating medication, realistic expectations, and therapeutic interventions in the treatment of male sexual dysfunction. *Journal of Sex and Marital Therapy, 31*, 319–328.

McCarthy, B. W., Ginsberg, R. L., & Fucito, L. M. (2006). Resilient sexual desire in heterosexual couples. *Family Journal: Counseling and Therapy for Couples and Families, 14*, 59–64.

McCarthy, B. W., & Thestrup, M. (2008). Integrating sex therapy interventions with couple therapy. *Journal of Contemporary Psychotherapy, 38*, 139–149.

McDowell, A. J., Snellgrove, C. A., & Bond, M. J. (2001). Beyond Viagra: Psychological issues in the assessment and treatment of erectile dysfunction. *Australian Family Physician, 30*, 867–873.

Metts, S., & Cupach, W. R. (1989). The role of communication in human sexuality. In K. McKinney & S. Sprecher (Eds.), *Human sexuality: The societal and interpersonal context* (pp. 139–161). New Jersey: Ablex.

Metz, M. E., & Dwyer, S. M. (1993). Differences in conflict management styles between sex dysfunction, sex offender, and satisfied couples. *Journal of Sex and Marital Therapy, 19*, 104–122.

Metz, M. E., & Epstein, N. (2002). Assessing the role of relationship conflict in sexual dysfunction. *Journal of Sex and Marital Therapy, 28*, 139–164.

Mirone, V., Gentile, V., Zizzo, G. et al. (2002). Did men with erectile dysfunction discuss their condition with partner and physicians? A survey of men attending a free call information service. *International Journal of Impotence Research, 14*, 256–258.

Mohr, D. C., & Beutler, L. E. (1990). Erectile dysfunction: A review of diagnostic and treatment procedures. *Clinical Psychology Review, 10*, 123–150.

Moore, T. M., Strauss, J. L., Herman, S., & Donatucci, C. F. (2003). Erectile dysfunction in early, middle, and late adulthood: Symptom patterns and psychosocial correlates. *Journal of Sex and Marital Therapy, 29*, 318–399.

Najman, J. M., Dunne, M. P., Boyle, F. M., Cook, M. D., & Purdie, D. M. (2003). Sexual dysfunction in the Australian population. *Australian Family Physician, 32*, 951–954.

Nicolosi, A., Moreira, E. D., Shirai, M., Tambi, M. I. B. M., & Glasser, D. B. (2003). Epidemiology of erectile dysfunction in four countries: Cross-national study of the prevalence and correlates of erectile dysfunction. *Urology, 61*, 201–206.

O'Donohue, W. T., & Geer, J. H. (1993). Research issues in the sexual dysfunctions. In W. T. O'Donohue & J. G. Geer (Eds.), *Handbook of the assessment and treatment of the sexual dysfunctions* (pp. 1–14). Boston: Allyn & Bacon.

Patton, D., & Waring, E. M. (1985). Sex and marital intimacy. *Journal of Sex and Marital Therapy, 11*, 176–184.

Peplau, L. A. (2003). Human sexuality: How do men and women differ? *Current Directions in Psychological Science, 12*, 37–40.

Phelps, J. S., Jain, A., & Monga, M. (2004). The PsychoedPlusMed approach to erectile dysfunction treatment: The impact of combining a psychoeducational intervention with sildenafil. *Journal of Sex and Marital Therapy, 30*, 305–314.

Pinnock, C. B., Stapleton, A. M. F., & Marshall, V. R. (1999). Erectile dysfunction in the community: A prevalence study. *Medical Journal of Australia, 171*, 353–357.

Pontin, D., Porter, T., & McDonagh, R. (2002). Investigating the effect of erectile dysfunction on the lives of men: A qualitative research study. *Journal of Clinical Nursing, 11*, 264–272.

Potts, A. (2000). "The essence of the hard on". Hegemonic masculinity and the cultural construction of "erectile dysfunction." *Men and Masculinities, 3*, 85–103.

Potts, A., Grace, V., Gavey, N., & Vares, T. (2004). "Viagra stories": Challenging "erectile dysfunction." *Social Science and Medicine, 59*, 489–499.

Richters, J., Grulich, A. E., de Visser, R. O., Smith, A. M., & Rissel, C. E. (2003). Sex in Australia: Sexual difficulties in a representative sample of adults. *Australian and New Zealand Journal of Public Health, 27,* 164–170.

Riley, A. (2002). The role of the partner in erectile dysfunction and its treatment. *International Journal of Impotence Research, 14,* S105–S109.

Riley, A., & Riley, E. (2000). Behavioural and clinical findings in couples where the man presents with erectile disorder: A retrospective study. *International Journal of Clinical Practice, 54,* 220–224.

Roffe, M. W., & Britt, B. C. (1981). A typology of marital interaction for sexually dysfunctional couples. *Journal of Sex and Marital Therapy, 7,* 207–222.

Rosen, R. C. (1996). Erectile dysfunction: The medicalization of male sexuality. *Clinical Psychology Review, 16,* 497–519.

Rosen, R. C., Fisher, W., Eardley, I., Niederberger, C., Nadel, A., & Sand, M. (2004). The multinational men's attitudes to life events and sexuality (MALES) study I: Prevalence of erectile dysfunction and related health concerns in the general population. *Current Medical Research Opinion, 20,* 607–617.

Rosen, R. C., & Leiblum, S. R. (1992). *Erectile disorders: Assessment and treatment.* New York: Guilford Press.

Rosen, R. C., & Leiblum, S. R. (1993). Treatment of male erectile disorder: Current options and dilemmas. *Sexual and Marital Therapy, 8,* 5–8.

Russell, I. (1990). Sex and couples therapy: A method of treatment to enhance physical and emotional intimacy. *Journal of Sex and Marital Therapy, 16,* 111–120.

Sand, M., & Fisher, W. A. (2007). Women's endorsement of models of female sexual response: The nurse's sexuality study. *Journal of Sexual Medicine, 4,* 708–719.

Seftel, A. D. (2002). Challenges in oral therapy for erectile dysfunction. *Journal of Andrology, 23,* 729–736.

Segraves, K. B., & Segraves, R. T. (1991). Hypoactive sexual desire disorder: Prevalence and comorbidity in 906 subjects. *Journal of Sex and Marital Therapy, 17,* 55–58.

Segraves, R. T., & Balon, R. (2005). Introduction: Treatment of sexual disorders in the 21st century. In R. Balon & R. T. Segraves (Eds.), *Handbook of sexual dysfunction* (pp. 1–11). Boca Raton: Taylor & Francis.

Shifren, J. L., Monz, B. U., Russo, P. A., Segretti, A., & Johannes, C. B. (2008). Sexual problems and distress in United States women: Prevalence and correlates. *Obstetrics and Gynecology, 112,* 970–978.

Simkins-Bullock, J., Wildman, B. G., & Sugrue, D. P. (1992). Etiological attributions, responsibility attributions, and marital adjustment in erectile dysfunction patients. *Journal of Sex and Marital Therapy, 18,* 83–103.

Simons, J., & Carey, M. (2001). Prevalence of sexual dysfunction: Results from a decade of research. *Archives of Sexual Behavior, 30,* 177–219.

Snow, K. J. (2004). Erectile dysfunction: A review and update. *Formulary, 39,* 261–268.

Speckens, A. E. M., Hengeveld, M. W., Lychlama á Nijeholt, G., van Hemert, A. M., & Hawton, K. E. (1995). Psychosexual functioning of partners of men with presumed non-organic erectile dysfunction: Cause or consequence of the disorder? *Archives of Sexual Behavior, 24,* 157–172.

Spector, I. P., & Carey, M. P. (1990). Incidence and prevalence of the sexual dysfunctions: A critical review of the empirical literature. *Archives of Sexual Behavior, 19,* 389–408.

Spector, K. R., & Boyle, M. (1986). The prevalence and perceived aetiology of male sexual problems in a non-clinical sample. *British Journal of Medical Psychology, 59,* 351–358.

Stolk, E. A., & Busschbach, J. V. B. (2003). Are patient and the general public like-minded about the effect of erectile dysfunction on quality of life? *Urology, 61*, 810–815.

Stuart, F. M., Hammond, D. C., & Pett, M. A. (1987). Inhibited sexual desire in women. *Archives of Sexual Behavior, 16*, 91–106.

Talmadge, L. D., & Talmadge, W. C. (1996). Relational sexuality: An understanding of low sexual desire. In *The Hatherleigh guide to marriage and family therapy* (pp. 191–218) New York: Hatherleigh Press.

Tiefer, L. (1991). Historical, scientific, clinical and feminist criticisms of the human sexual response cycle model. *Annual Review of Sex Research, 2*, 1–23.

Trudel, G. (2002). Sexuality and marital life: Results of a survey. *Journal of Sex and Marital Therapy, 28*, 229–249.

Trudel, G., Boulos, L., & Matte, B. (1993). Dyadic adjustment in couples with hypoactive sexual desire. *Journal of Sex Education and Therapy, 19*, 31–36.

Trudel, G., Marchand, A., Ravart, M., Aubin, S., Turgeon, L., & Fortier, P. (2001). The effect of a cognitive-behavioral group treatment program on hypoactive sexual desire in women. *Sexual and Relationship Therapy, 16*, 145–164.

West, S. L., D'Aloisio, A. A., Agans, R. P., Kalsbeek, W. D., Borisov, N. N., & Thorp, J. M. (2008). Prevalence of low sexual desire and hypoactive sexual desire disorder in a nationally representative sample of US women. *Archives of Internal Medicine, 168*, 1441–1449.

Wincze, J. P., & Carey, M. P. (2001). *Sexual dysfunction: A guide for assessment and treatment.* (2nd edn). New York: Guildford Press.

Wise, T. (1999). Psychosocial side effects of sildenafil therapy for erectile dysfunction. *Journal of Sex and Marital Therapy, 25*, 145–150.

Witting, K., Santtila, P., Alanko, K. et al. (2008). Female sexual function and its associations with number of children, pregnancy, and relationship satisfaction. *Journal of Sex and Marital Therapy, 34*, 89–106.

13

Regulating Incentives and Threats in Close Relationships

Approach and Avoidance Motivation

Shelly L. Gable

Consider the following descriptions of two equally dissatisfied couples.

Ben and Barb: Ben and Barb met in college and married a few years after graduation. They have enjoyed a comfortable and secure relationship over the years. They make it a point not to argue, and each one trusts the other not to intentionally harm or criticize them. However, both feel as if something has been missing for quite some time. They seem to have drifted apart and become increasing less intimate. Each enjoys his or her own activities and they seldom laugh together or have interesting conversations. They are considering separating.

Jack and Jane: Jack and Jane also met in college and married a few years after graduation. They have enjoyed many fun activities together and lots of intimate conversations over the years. Many of their friends have commented on how much they seem to enjoy each other's company and still have that passionate spark of the newly married. However, they often criticize one another and complain about each other's habits. Indeed, the littlest disagreements seem to escalate into major brawls and neither feels completely secure that the other will be there in tough times or will not intentionally cause emotional pain for the other. They are considering separating.

The Wiley-Blackwell Handbook of Couples and Family Relationships, First Edition.
Edited by Patricia Noller and Gery C. Karantzas.

Close relationships are sources of pleasure and pain. There are valuable potential rewards in close relationships, such as companionship, passion, and intimacy. There are also important potential dangers, such as betrayal, jealousy, and criticism. In response to this reality, people are motivated to both obtain the incentives in relationships *and* avoid the threats. Ben and Barb seem to be successfully avoiding the threats in relationships but they do not seem to be adept at obtaining the incentives. On the other hand, Jack and Jane seem to be doing just fine in the incentive category but are having difficulty avoiding the threats. In the following sections, I briefly summarize the evidence that relationships are fundamental to human existence but expose people to consequential incentives as well as threats. I then present a model of close relationship motivation that is both incentive and threat-based, and describe evidence in support of this model.

Incentives and Threats in Relationships

Human beings have a fundamental need to form and maintain stable interpersonal relationships (e.g., Baumeister & Leary, 1995; Berscheid & Reis, 1998; Reis, Collins, & Berscheid 2000). This assertion is based on a great deal of empirical evidence which shows that people easily form attachments and resist dissolving them; several behavioral and affective processes are focused on the formation and maintenance of relationships (see chapters 16, 17 in this volume); and decrements in health, adjustment, and well-being are seen when people are unable to form and maintain relationships (see Baumeister & Leary, 1995). Perhaps one reason that people show a need for close relationships is that they provide important rewards difficult to obtain outside of such relationships.

For example, people more often than not cite relationships when asked what currently gives their lives meaning (Klinger, 1977; Little, 1989). And, when looking back on life, relationships with family members and close friends are often cited as major sources of life satisfaction (e.g., Sears, 1977). Also, perceiving that one has supportive others to turn to in times of stress has beneficial effects on endocrine, cardiovascular, and immune function (see Uchino, Cacioppo, & Kiecolt-Glaser, 1996, for a review).

Despite these potential benefits, research has clearly shown that relationships can be a major source of distress and dysfunction. For example, when asked what was the last "bad thing" that happened in their lives, the majority of people in a national survey listed the conflict or dissolution of a significant relationship (Veroff, Douvan, & Kulka, 1981) and close relationship difficulties are routinely the impetus for people seeking psychotherapy (Pinsker, Nepps, Redfield, & Winston, 1985). Indeed, relationship conflict and hostility are associated with physiological reactions known to have significant health consequences (e.g., immune responses, cardiovascular reactivity; Kiecolt-Glaser, 1999; Uchino, Holt-Lunstad, Uno, & Flinders, 2001). The strongly touted belief that marriage is good for your health only holds if the marriage is happy and nondistressed (e.g., Kiecolt-Glaser & Newton, 2001). Finally, at an extreme end, abusive relationships have detrimental effects and pose a social and economic challenge to the community at large (Dutton, 1996).

Approach and Avoidance Motivation in Close Relationships

Although it is apparent that people are motivated to approach interpersonal incentives and avoid interpersonal threats, close relationship processes have rarely been examined from a motivation or goal-theory perspective. Recently, my colleagues and I have proposed and tested a model outlining processes associated with the establishment, maintenance, and dissolution of close relationships that is based on motivation and goal theory (Gable, 2006; Gable & Berkman, 2008; Gable & Poore, 2008; Impett, Gordon, Kogan, Oveis, Gable, & Keltner, in press). Our theoretical and empirical work has highlighted a critical dimension of motivation and behavior regulation—the focus of goals.

Relationship goals can be approach based (focused on a rewarding or desired end state) or avoidance based (focused on a punishing, undesired end state; Gable, 2006). The vast majority of research in close relationships has been concerned with either the rewarding aspects (e.g., attraction, intimacy) or the punishing aspects (e.g., insecurity, conflict, see chapters 9, 11, 14, 24 in this volume), but has not examined them in tandem. However, because close relationships present potential threats and incentives, we have taken the stance that models of close relationship functioning are incomplete unless both approach and avoidance dimensions are considered. These dimensions in turn have important implications for attention, cognition, emotions, and behavior in the relationship context.

The importance of the approach–avoidance distinction has long been recognized in other domains such as achievement, power, and affiliation (e.g., Atkinson, 1958; Miller, 1959; Schneirla, 1959). And even though the existence of incentives and threats in relationships is well known (for reviews see Gable & Reis, 2001; Reis & Gable, 2003), less attention has been given to the approach–avoidance motivational distinction in close relationships. Early related work on social behavior (although not concerned with close relationships, per se) was conducted by Atkinson, Heyns, and Veroff (1954), Boyatzis (1973), and Mehrabian (1976), who examined both incentive-focused social motivation (e.g., need for affiliation) and threat-focused social motivation (e.g., fear of rejection). Later, McAdams and colleagues conducted research that is more relevant to reciprocal and ongoing relationships (e.g., McAdams, Healy, & Krause, 1984), which they referred to as intimacy motivation. However, McAdams did not separately examine incentive-based intimacy motives and threat-based intimacy motives in this line of research.

Model of approach and avoidance goals in close relationships

Recently, Gable (2006) proposed an approach–avoidance model of social motivation of close relationship processes. The model is hierarchical, similar to existing models of approach–avoidance motivation (e.g., Elliot, 2006). As shown in Figure 13.1, the model posits that individual differences in dispositional threat and incentive sensitivities (e.g., relatively stable traits) and the current social environment (e.g., recent events in a particular close relationship) predict the goals individuals adopt—approach and avoidance goals—and the strength of those goals. Specifically, approach social motives (e.g., hope for

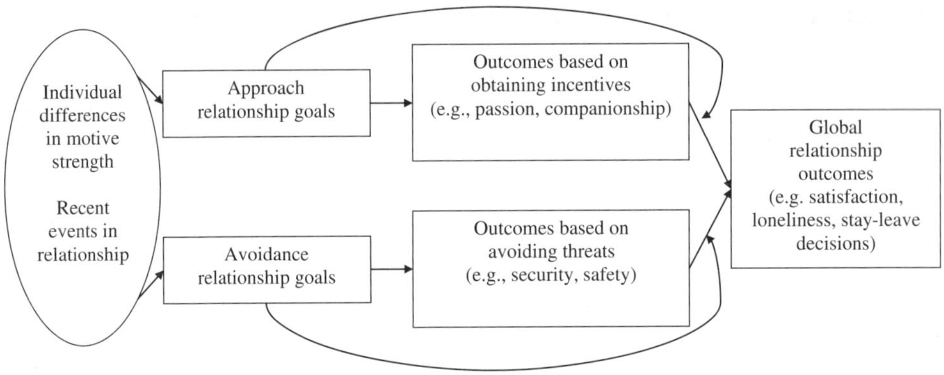

Figure 13.1 Model of approach–avoidance relationship motivation
Source: Gable, S. L. (2006). Approach and avoidance social motives and goals. *Journal of Personality, 71*, 175–222

affiliation) and the potential for incentives in the current social environment are positively associated with the adoption of short-term approach relationship goals; and avoidance social motives (e.g., fear of rejection) and the potential for current threats in the social environment are positively associated with the adoption of avoidance-relationship goals. As evidence for this portion of the model Gable (2006) found that individual differences in distal motives predicted more proximal goals such that individuals with strong approach motives were more likely to adopt short-term approach social goals (e.g., "Make new friends") and those with strong avoidance motives were more likely to adopt short-term avoidance social goals (e.g., "Not be lonely").

For example, in a newly established romantic relationship, Jake, who has a strong approach motive of hope for affiliation and has just had several interesting and fun dates with Jessie, is likely to adopt approach goals regarding intimacy: "I want to have a good time and show her my best side on our next few dates." On the other hand, if Jake had a strong avoidance motive of fear of rejection or if he and Jessie had some awkward moments on their initial dates, he would be more likely to adopt avoidance goals, such as "I don't want to do something boring or make a fool of myself on our next few dates." Or, for example, in a discussion on the household budget, a husband who has strong approach social motives and recently has had several fun and loving interactions with his wife would be more likely to adopt approach goals, such as "I want us to have a relaxed discussion and for both of us to be satisfied with the outcome"; whereas a husband who has strong avoidance motives and has recently had a series of misunderstandings with his wife would be more likely to adopt avoidance goals, such as "I want to avoid any harsh feelings and for neither of us to be dissatisfied with the outcome." Although the goal content in these examples is similar, the focus of the goal matters.

Specifically, as the hierarchical model in Figure 13.1 shows, approach and avoidance goals should be linked to different relationship outcomes. Approach relationship goals are incentive based and thus should be strongly associated with outcomes defined by the presence of social rewards, such as passion and intimacy. Therefore for individuals who have strong approach goals in their relationships, positive interactions and relationship qualities are defined as those which provide such rewards as positive emotions, closeness, and companionship; negative interactions and relationships are those that fail to provide these rewards.

Avoidance relationship goals are threat-based and thus should be strongly associated with outcomes defined by the presence of punishments, such as criticism, rejection, and conflict. For individuals who have strong avoidance goals in their relationship, positive interactions and relationships are defined as those that lack criticism, disagreement, rejection, and anxiety; negative interactions and relationships are those that have these qualities.

Moreover, approach and avoidance goals are independent of one another. People can have strong approach and weak avoidance relationship goals, weak approach and strong avoidance relationships goals, strong approach and strong avoidance relationship goals, or weak approach and weak avoidance relationship goals. For example, if a person has strong approach and avoidance relationship goals, positive interactions and relationships are those that provide rewards and lack any threatening aspects.

Another characteristic of the model is that different processes are predicted to mediate the association between approach goals and outcomes and the association between avoidance goals and outcomes. Therefore, the processes that account for the link between approach goals and passion, for example, may be different from the processes that account for the link between avoidance goals and security. Finally, individuals form global assessments about relationship quality and make dissolution–continuance decisions based on a combination of reward-based and threat-based relationship outcomes (i.e., intimacy, security).

There are two unique features of the model that are not readily apparent in Figure 13.1. First, close relationships are dyadic. Unlike traditional research on motivation which only considers the individual as the unit of analysis, motivational approaches to relationships must go beyond the person and account for the other half of the dyad. Therefore, in the context of a close relationship it is crucial to investigate not only the goals of one individual, but also those of the partner; and the unique interaction of the two. The second aspect of the model that is distinctive in a motivational model of close relationships is that by their very definition close relationships exist over time. As a result, relationship goals are expected to fluctuate dynamically over time, responding to progress assessments and changes in the partner and the relationship environment. I now turn to the existing evidence that supports the links between approach and avoidance relationship goals and outcomes.

Linking Approach and Avoidance Goals to Relationship Outcomes

Several studies have examined the links between approach and avoidance goals and social and relationship outcomes. Some of these studies have focused on the goals people have for their close relationships in general (e.g., "Deepening my relationships with my friends," "Avoiding being hurt by my friends") and others have examined the goals people have for a specific relationship, such as a romantic relationship (e.g., "Enhance the intimacy in my romantic relationship"). Gable (2006) examined the strength of goals individuals had for a variety of their existing close relationships (family, friends, romantic partner) in three studies. Consistent with hypotheses, approach and avoidance motives and goals were associated with different outcomes. Specifically, the strength of approach motives and goals positively predicted positive affect toward partners and satisfaction with close relationships, both concurrently and over time. The strength of avoidance motives and goals positively predicted negative affect toward relationship partners and relationship insecurity, concurrently and over time. These studies also showed that approach and avoidance goals and motives jointly predicted loneliness. Loneliness is an outcome defined by both a lack of incentives (meaningful ties) and avoidance of threats (insecurity).

Moreover, relationship-specific motives and goals were unique predictors that accounted for significant variance in outcomes above and beyond general sensitivity to reward and punishment (e.g., individual differences in behavioral activation system (BAS) and behavioral inhibition system (BIS) sensitivities; Carver & White, 1994; Gray, 1990). Elliot, Gable, and Mapes (2006) conducted another set of studies focused on approach and avoidance goals for existing friendships. Parallel to Gable's (2006) results, they found that strong approach-friendship goals were positively associated with social satisfaction and negatively associated with loneliness. In addition, approach-friendship goals were associated with positive changes in well-being over time and avoidance-friendship goals were associated with increased physical symptoms over time.

Several studies have focused on romantic relationships and have shown that approach and avoidance goals for a specific relationship (or specific interactions) are also associated with distinct outcomes. In the first such study, Gable (2000) found that married couples who had strong avoidance goals also reported greater insecurity than those with weaker avoidance goals. On the other hand, the strength of approach goals was positively associated with more positive affect during marital interactions on a daily basis. Impett, Strachman, Finkel, and Gable (2008) also found that approach goals (but not avoidance goals) were strongly related to sexual desire in romantic relationships. In three studies they found that those who adopted strong (relative to weak) approach goals in their romantic relationships also reported greater sexual desire over time. The results also showed that approach relationship goals buffered against typical declines in sexual desire over time and were associated with more sexual desire during sexual interactions. These associations were even stronger for women than men.

In terms of overall global satisfaction, in a daily diary study Gable and Poore (2008) found that individuals with strong approach goals were more satisfied on a daily basis (i.e., "Overall, how was your relationship today?"—answered on a scale ranging from terrible to terrific) than those with weak approach goals. In this study they also found that individuals with strong avoidance goals were less satisfied than those with weak avoidance goals at the end of the day. It was not surprising that overall satisfaction was predicted by both approach and avoidance goals because like loneliness, global relationship satisfaction is thought to be a combination of both the presence of rewards and the absence of threats.

In another series of studies, Impett and colleagues (in press) examined the links between approach and avoidance goals in dating couples and relationship satisfaction (daily and changes in global levels across time). The results showed that people with stronger approach goals for their relationships reported higher levels of daily relationship satisfaction and greater satisfaction over time than those with weaker approach goals for their relationships. But, reflecting the dyadic nature of relationship goals, the greatest satisfaction levels were found in couples in which both partners had strong approach goals. In these studies they also found that those with stronger avoidance goals for their relationships reported less satisfaction over time than those with weaker avoidance goals for their relationships; those who had a partner who had strong avoidance goals were also less satisfied over time.

Approach and avoidance goals may also be specific to particular interactions. In a study that examined the goals that individuals have for specific interactions with their partners, the results showed that approach and avoidance motives for singular behaviors also predict outcomes (Impett, Gable, & Peplau, 2005). Specifically, dating couples reported concerning their motives for enacting for the sake of their partner's behaviors that they themselves did not prefer (i.e., everyday relationship sacrifices, Van Lange, et al., 1997; such as accompanying a partner to a dull work function, or not spending time with friends). When participants sacrificed for approach motives (e.g., to promote intimacy), they reported greater positive affect and relationship satisfaction. However, when they enacted the same behaviors for avoidance motives (e.g., to prevent my partner from becoming upset), they reported greater negative affect, lower relationship satisfaction, and more conflict. Sacrificing for avoidance motives was particularly detrimental to relationships over time: The results showed that even when controlling for initial satisfaction, the more individuals sacrificed for avoidance motives over the course of the study, the less satisfied they were with their relationships at the follow-up assessment 6 weeks later and the more likely they were to have broken up.

In summary, several studies have examined the links between approach and avoidance relationship motivation and outcomes. Studies that used diverse methods (cross-sectional, daily experience, and longitudinal data) and assessed a spectrum of close relationships (such as friendships, romantic relationships, family ties) found that approach and avoidance motives and goals were associated with important relationship outcomes. Moreover, as predicted by the model, approach goals were more strongly associated with outcomes defined by the presence of incentives (e.g., positive affect, sexual desire) than avoidance goals. Avoidance goals were more strongly associated with outcomes defined by the absence of threats (e.g., negative affect, security) than approach goals. Outcomes that involve both incentives and threats, such as global satisfaction and loneliness, were correlated with both approach and avoidance relationship motivation. In the next section, I review recent research that has examined the cognitive, behavioral, and affective processes that mediate the links between motives and outcomes.

Mediating Processes Linking Goals to Outcomes

What processes account for the links between relationship goals and outcomes? We have investigated these mediating processes in several studies. Because approach and avoidance relationship goals are relatively independent, the processes that link approach goals to outcomes are not necessarily the same processes that link avoidance goals to outcomes. An example of this distinction was found in studies linking approach and avoidance goals to variation in the experience of social events (e.g., Gable, Reis, & Elliot, 2000). Gable (2006) found that that approach social motives and goals were associated with increased exposure to positive social events; strong approach relationship motives and goals predicted increased frequency of the occurrence of positive social events. Approach relationship motives and goals did not predict the frequency of negative social events. The frequency of positive events mediated the link between approach relationship motives and outcomes.

Avoidance relationship motives and goals were correlated with increased reactivity to negative social events; when negative social events did occur, those with strong avoidance relationship motives and goals rated them as more important and showed more changes in their well-being than those with weak avoidance goals (Elliot et al., 2006; Gable, 2006). Avoidance goals did not predict reactivity to positive social events, nor did approach goals predict reactivity to negative social events. These studies showed that a process of exposure to positive social events mediated the association between approach relationship goals and outcomes whereas a process of reactivity to negative social events linked avoidance relationship goals to outcomes. These results mirrored parallel work on domain-general incentive and punishment motivations (individual differences in behavioral activation and behavioral inhibition systems; Gable et al., 2000). More recent research on social goals has examined how relationship goals predict outcomes through social cognitive and affective processes, such as biases in memory and interpretation of ambiguous information, the experience of positive emotions, and the algorithms used to weight different information in global evaluations.

Memory and interpretation of ambiguous information

Memory bias in the recall of social information is likely to be important in relationships. For example, Neuberg's (e.g., 1996) work has clearly shown that expectancy–confirmation processes affect information seeking, behavior during an interaction with another, and even the other's behavior. In close relationships, people have repeated interactions with the same partner and thus have ample opportunity to form memories and expectancies regarding that partner. Thus, knowing how relationship goals may influence memories and the interpretation of new information seem particularly important. There it was hypothesized that social goals would influence the interpretation of ambiguous social information and later recall of that information. Specifically, approach goals should bias people to be more aware of and expectant toward the potential incentives in their social environment and recall this information more readily. Avoidance goals should bias people to be more aware of and expectant toward the potential threats in their social environment and recall this information more readily.

Strachman and Gable (2006) tested these hypotheses in two studies. In the first study, individual differences in the strength of goals for current friendships were assessed prior to participants reading a story that contained positive, negative, and neutral information about two relationship partners. The results indicated that those with strong avoidance goals recalled more of the negative information in the story than those with weak avoidance goals (Strachman & Gable, 2006, Study 1). In another study, participants were randomly assigned either an approach or avoidance social goal for an upcoming interaction with a stranger; half of the participants were given approach goals for a get-acquainted conversation and half were given avoidance goals (e.g., try to make a good impression, try not to make a bad impression, respectively). After being given a self-description ostensibly written by the other person, those in the avoidance-goal condition remembered more negative information about, and expressed more dislike for, the other person than those in the approach-goal condition. Both studies showed that memory for social information is influenced by the focus of relationship goals (i.e., on incentives or threats).

However, recall of events and interactions are dependent on the initial interpretation of that information. For example, when a romantic partner declines an invitation to dinner is it indicative of a hectic work schedule or declining interest in the relationship? Strachman and Gable (2006) also analyzed how participants interpreted the positive, negative, and neutral information by examining how people reproduced the information from the story. People with strong avoidance goals were more likely to interpret neutral and positive information from the story more negatively that those with weak avoidance goals. For example, a seemingly neutral statement in the story like "he picked her up at 10:00," was likely to be interpreted by those with high avoidance goals as being picked up late.

Affective experience in close relationships

Previous research on domain-general threat and reward sensitivity showed that the strength of the approach motivation predicted reports of positive affect—strong approach motives were associated with higher levels of positive affect on a daily basis than weak approach motives. Avoidance motivation predicted reports of negative affect—strong avoidance motives were associated with more negative affect on a daily basis than weak avoidance motives. More importantly, approach goals did not predict negative affect and avoidance goals did not predict positive affect (Gable et al., 2000).[1]

Similarly in the relationship domain, Impett and colleagues (in press) conducted two studies investigating the mediation role of positive emotion goals in the link between goals and satisfaction in dating couples. They found that the strength of approach (but not avoidance) goals was positively associated with general positive affect on a daily basis (Impett et al., in press, Study 1) and relationship-specific positive emotions such as gratitude, love, and compassion (Impett et al., in press, Study 2). Moreover, they found that the strength of participants' approach goals also predicted partners' reports of positive emotions in the same direction. Finally, the experience of positive emotions mediated the link between approach goals and relationship satisfaction. More research is needed to understand how avoidance goals and negative emotions might mediate the link between avoidance goals and relationship outcomes.

Weight of social information

Another important aspect of the relationship goals model depicted in Figure 13.1 is how incentive-based outcomes such as passion, and threat-based outcomes such as security, combine to form more global evaluations in relationships. In a study by Gable and Poore (2008), it was hypothesized that strong approach goals should lead to weighing the presence (or absence) of incentives in relationships more heavily in global evaluations than would weak approach goals. Strong avoidance goals should lead to weighing the presence (or absence) of threats in relationships more heavily when making global evaluations than would weak avoidance goals.

Gable and Poore (2008) conducted a signal-contingent daily-experience study of people in dating relationships to test these hypotheses. Participants were signaled at several random intervals throughout the day and reported their feelings of passion for, and security with, their relationship partners at that very moment. They also reported their overall satisfaction with their relationships (i.e., terrible to terrific) at the end of each day. The results showed that individuals with strong approach goals weighed passion more heavily than those low in approach goals in their end-of-day reports of relationship satisfaction. Those with strong avoidance goals weighed security more than those with weaker avoidance goals in their end-of-day reports of satisfaction. The implication of these findings is that on the days that people feel more passion than they typically feel, they will only report increased relationship satisfaction if they have strong approach relationship goals; and on the days that they feel more insecure than they typically feel they will only report less relationship satisfaction if they have strong avoidance relationship goals. In short, the very definition of satisfaction (the presence of incentives or the absence of threats) was influenced by goals. These results parallel findings of Updegraff, Gable, and Taylor (2004) on general approach and avoidance goals and the weighting of positive and negative emotions.

Summary and Future Directions

Existing research has provided clear evidence that there are significant incentives and threats in close relationships, thus the domain of close relationships is particularly in need of a model that simultaneously addresses the regulation of both outcomes. In this chapter, I presented a model of close relationship processes that addresses the regulation of both incentives and threats inherent in social bonds. As research on incentive and threat regulation in relationships continues there are three areas that future investigations need to address.

First, because close relationships are those that persist over time, work is needed to examine how relationship partners evaluate progress on their approach and avoidance goals over time. As predicted by Carver and Scheier's (1982, 1990) control-process model, it is very likely that a fundamental contributor to behavior and the cognitive and affective experience of people in close relationships would be their evaluation of goal progress and rate of that progress. However, the cues of progress and rate of progress are likely to be assessed differently for approach goals than avoidance frameworks. For example, the husband who has the goal of not criticizing his wife is only one stray comment away from failure at any given time, regardless of how many compliments he gives her. However, a husband who has an approach goal of appreciating his wife's positive qualities grows closer to his goal with recognition of her strengths.

Future research also needs to focus explicitly on the dyadic influence of partners' motives and goals. The question of how one partner's approach and avoidance goals affect the other partner remains open but previous research suggests it is important. For example, Impett et al. (2005) found that when one partner perceived that the other was making everyday sacrifices for avoidance motives they reported less well-being and lower relationship quality than when they perceived the same sacrifices were made for approach reasons. Finally, to date, research on approach and avoidance goals in relationships has focused exclusively on explicit or consciously accessible goals. However, work from several other researchers on the power that seemingly nonconscious goal pursuit has on behavior in close relationships is compelling (e.g., Anderson, Reznik, & Manzella, 1996; Baldwin, Carrell, & Lopez, 1990; Fitzsimons & Bargh, 2003; Mikulincer, 1998; Scinta & Gable, 2007). For example, Fitzsimons and Fishbach (2010) recently reported that people feel closer to relationship partners who are instrumental to personal goal pursuit. However, people go on to feel less close to relationship partners once their partners have assisted them in making progress towards personal goals. Future studies need to understand the implication of nonconscious motivation on approach and avoidance models.

Concluding Comments

Although the approach and avoidance motivation distinction has a long and prolific history in several domains in the psychological literature, it has not been applied to close relationships research until recently. The approach–avoidance framework explicitly addresses the simultaneous regulation of the inherent incentives and threats in close relationships. This approach is likely a more realistic representation of the reality of people's social lives and may offer insights into both of the couples introduced in the opening of this chapter: Ben and Barb and Jack and Jane. For example, Ben and Barb's current relationship environment lacks incentives. Jack and Jane's current relationship environment is teaming with threats. The goals that each has for the relationship are likely to be a reflection of their individual differences in threat and reward sensitivity and perceptions of their relationships. Moreover, their goals are likely contributing to their current state through biases in cognitive, affective, and behavioral processes. Attempts to better Ben and Barb's relationship need to address their lack of rewarding interactions, and attempts to better Jack and Jane's relationship need to address their threatening interactions. The model proposed in this chapter, while in need of further research, offers a new insight into how therapists and counselors can view the motivations and associated behaviors, cognitions, and emotions of couples. In turn, the framework can shape the approach taken by therapists in assisting distressed couples to navigate the rewards and punishments of their relationships as well as helping those couples wishing to enhance their relationship functioning.

Note

Preparation of this chapter was facilitated by CAREER Grant #BCS 0444129 from the National Science Foundation.

1. There is recent evidence that approach motivation is associated with approach (versus withdrawal) emotions, most but not all of which are positive; and avoidance motivation is associated with withdrawal emotions, not all of which are negative. For example, anger is an emotion related to approach motivation (for review see Carver & Harmon-Jones, 2009) and relief is an emotion related to avoidance motivation (Carver, 2009).

References

Anderson, S. M., Reznik, I., & Manzella, L. M. (1996). Eliciting facial affect, motivation, and expectancies in transference: Significant-other representations in social relations. *Journal of Personality and Social Psychology, 71*, 1108–1129.

Atkinson, J. W. (Ed.). (1958). *Motives in fantasy, action and society*. Princeton, NJ: Van Nostrand.

Atkinson, J. W., Heyns, R. W., & Veroff, J. (1954). The effect of experimental arousal of the affiliation motive on thematic apperception. *Journal of Abnormal and Social Psychology, 49*(3), 405–410.

Baldwin, M. W., Carrell, S. E., & Lopez, D. F. (1990). Priming relationship schemas—My adviser and the pope are watching me from the back of my mind. *Journal of Experimental Social Psychology, 26*, 435–454.

Baumeister, R. F., & Leary, M. R. (1995). The need to belong: Desire for interpersonal attachments as a fundamental human motivation. *Psychological Bulletin, 117*, 497–529.

Berscheid, E., & Reis, H. T. (1998). Attraction and close relationships. In D. T. Gilbert, S. T. Fiske, & G. Lindzey (Eds.), *The handbook of social psychology* (4th edn., vol. 2, pp. 193–281). New York: McGraw-Hill.

Boyatzis, R. E. (1973). Affiliation motivation. In D. C. McClelland & R. S. Steele, (Eds.), *Human motivation: A book of readings* (pp. 252–276). Morristown, NJ: General Learning Press.

Carver, C. S. (2009). Threat sensitivity, incentive sensitivity, and the experience of relief. *Journal of Personality, 77*(1), 125–138.

Carver, C. S., & White, T. L. (1994). Behavioral inhibition, behavioral activation, and affective responses to impending reward and punishment: The BIS/BAS scales. *Journal of Personality and Social Psychology, 67*, 319–333.

Carver, C. S., & Harmon-Jones, E. (2009). Anger is an approach-related affect: Evidence and implications. *Psychological Bulletin, 135*(2), 183–204.

Carver, C. S., & Scheier, M. F. (1982). Control theory: A useful conceptual framework for personality-social, clinical, and health psychology. *Psychological Bulletin, 92*, 111–135.

Carver, C. S., & Scheier, M. F. (1990). Origins and functions of positive and negative affect: A control-process view. *Psychological Review, 97*, 19–35.

Dutton, D. G. (1996). *The domestic assault of women*. Vancouver: University of British Columbia Press.

Elliot, A. J. (2006). A hierarchical model of approach and avoidance motivation. *Motivation and Emotion, 30*, 111–116.

Elliot, A. J., Gable, S. L., & Mapes, R. R. (2006). Approach and avoidance motivation in the social domain. *Personality and Social Psychology Bulletin, 32*, 378–391.

Fitzsimons, G. M., & Bargh, J. A. (2003). Thinking of you: Nonconscious pursuit of interpersonal goals associated with relationship partners. *Journal of Personality and Social Psychology, 84*, 148–164.

Fitzsimons, G. M., & Fishbach, A. (2010). Shifting closeness: Interpersonal effects of personal goal progress. *Journal of Personality and Social Psychology, 98*(4), 535–549.

Gable, S. L. (2000). *Appetitive and aversive social motivation.* Unpublished doctoral dissertation, University of Rochester.

Gable, S. L. (2006). Approach and avoidance social motives and goals. *Journal of Personality, 71*, 175–222.

Gable, S. L., & Berkman, E. T. (2008). Making connections and avoiding loneliness: Approach and avoidance social motives. In A. J. Elliot (Ed.), *Handbook of approach and avoidance motivation* (pp. 203–216). Mahwah, NJ: Erlbaum.

Gable, S. L., & Poore, J. (2008). Which thoughts count? Algorithms for evaluating satisfaction in relationships. *Psychological Science, 19*, 1030–1036.

Gable, S. L., & Reis, H. T. (2001). Appetitive and aversive social interaction. In J. H. Harvey & A. E. Wenzel (Eds.), *Close romantic relationship maintenance and enhancement* (pp. 169–194). Mahwah, NJ: Erlbaum.

Gable, S. L., Reis, H. T., & Elliot, A. J. (2000). Behavioral activation and inhibition in everyday life. *Journal of Personality and Social Psychology, 78*, 1135–1149.

Gray, J. A. (1990). Brain systems that mediate both emotion and cognition. *Cognition and Emotion, 4*, 269–288.

Impett, E., Gable, S. L., & Peplau, L. A. (2005). Giving up and giving in: The costs and benefits of daily sacrifice in intimate relationships. *Journal of Personality and Social Psychology, 89*, 327–344.

Impett, E. A., Gordon, A. M., Kogan, A., Oveis, C., Gable, S. L., & Keltner, D. (in press). Approaching happiness: Daily and long-term consequences of approach and avoidance goals in romantic relationships. *Journal of Personality and Social Psychology.*

Impett, E., Strachman, A., Finkel, E. & Gable, S. L. (2008). Maintaining sexual desire in intimate relationships: The importance of approach goals. *Journal of Personality and Social Psychology, 94*, 808–823.

Kiecolt-Glaser, J. K. (1999). Stress, personal relationships, and immune function: Health implications. *Brain, Behavior and Immunity, 13*(1), 61–72.

Kiecolt-Glaser, J. K., & Newton, T. L. (2001). Marriage and health: His and hers. *Psychological Bulletin, 127*(4), 472–503.

Klinger, E. (1977). *Meaning & void: Inner experience and the incentives in people's lives.* Minneapolis: University of Minnesota Press.

Little, B. R. (1989). Personal projects analysis: Trivial pursuits, magnificent obsessions and the search for coherence. In D. M. Buss & N. Cantor (Eds.), *Personality psychology: Recent trends and emerging directions* (pp. 15–31). New York: Springer-Verlag.

McAdams, D. P., Healy, S., & Krause, S. (1984). Social motives and patterns of friendship. *Journal of Personality and Social Psychology, 47*, 828–838.

Mehrabian, A. (1976). Questionnaire measures of affiliative tendency and sensitivity to rejection. *Psychological Reports, 38*, 199–209.

Mikulincer, M. (1998). Attachment working models and the sense of trust: An exploration of interaction goals and affect regulation. *Journal of Personality and Social Psychology, 74*, 1209–1224.

Miller, N. E. (1959). Liberalization of basic S-R concepts: Extensions to conflict behavior, motivation, and social learning. In S. Koch (Ed.), *Psychology: A study of science, Study 1* (pp. 198–292). New York: McGraw-Hill.

Neuberg, S. L (1996). Expectancy influences in social interaction: The moderating role of social goals. In P. M. Gollwitzer & J. A. Bargh, (Eds.), *The psychology of action: Linking cognition and motivation to behavior* (pp. 529–552). New York: Guilford Press.

Pinsker, H., Nepps, P., Redfield, J., & Winston, A. (1985). Applicants for short-term dynamic psychotherapy. In A. Winston (Ed.), *Clinical and research issues in short-term dynamic psychotherapy* (pp. 104–116). Washington, DC: American Psychiatric Association.

Reis, H. T., Collins, W. A., & Berscheid, E. (2000). The relationship context of human behavior and development. *Psychological Bulletin, 126*, 844–872.

Reis, H. T., & Gable, S. L. (2003). Toward a positive psychology of relationships. In C. L. Keyes & J. Haidt (Eds.), *Flourishing: The positive person and the good life* (pp. 129–159). Washington DC: American Psychological Association.

Schneirla, T. C. (1959). An evolutionary and developmental theory of biphasic processes underlying approach and withdrawal. *Nebraska Symposium on Motivation*, Vol. 7, (pp. 1–43). Lincoln, NE: University of Nebraska Press.

Scinta, A., & Gable, S. L. (2007). Automatic and self-reported attitudes in romantic relationships. *Personality and Social Psychology Bulletin, 33*(7), 1008–1022.

Sears, R. R. (1977). Sources of life satisfactions of the Terman gifted men. *American Psychologist, 32*, 119–128.

Strachman, A., & Gable, S. L. (2006). What you want (and don't want) affects what you see (and don't see): Avoidance social goals and social events. *Personality and Social Psychology Bulletin, 32*, 1446–1458.

Uchino, B. N., Cacioppo, J. T., & Kiecolt-Glaser, J. K. (1996). The relationship between social support and physiological processes: A review with emphasis on underlying mechanisms and implications for health. *Psychological Bulletin, 119*, 488–531.

Uchino, B. N., Holt-Lunstad, J., Uno, D., & Flinders, J. B. (2001). Heterogeneity in the social networks of young and older adults: Prediction of mental health and cardiovascular reactivity during acute stress. *Journal of Behavioral Medicine, 24*(4), 361–382.

Updegraff, J. A., Gable, S. L., & Taylor, S. E. (2004). What makes experiences satisfying? The interaction of approach–avoidance motivations and emotions in well-being. *Journal of Personality and Social Psychology, 86*, 496–504.

Van Lange, P. A. M., Rusbult, C. E., Drigotas, S. M., Arriaga, X. B., Witcher, B. S., & Cox, C. L. (1997). Willingness to sacrifice in close relationships. *Journal of Personality and Social Psychology, 72*, 1373–1395.

Veroff, J., Douvan, E., & Kulka, R. A. (1981). *Mental health in America: Patterns of help-seeking from 1957 to 1976.* New York: Basic Books.

14

Attachment and Caregiving

Functions, Interactions, and Implications

Melanie Canterberry and Omri Gillath

Caregiving involves helping others who are in need. Help may consist of various behaviors such as giving money, holding the door open for another, lending an ear in times of trouble, or providing encouragement in the face of life's challenges. Help may be required for different lengths of time (one instance or an extended period), and can be provided to a range of people (from close friends and family members to strangers). Different theories have been used to explain: why some people help those in need and others do not; the quality of help rendered; and the consequences of care provided (for a review see Penner, Dovidio, Piliavin, & Schroeder, 2005). Recently, attachment theory and methodologies stemming from this theoretical approach have been employed to study and explain people's tendency to help, motivations for helping, outcomes of help provision, and ways to change people's helping or caregiving tendencies (e.g., Collins & Feeney, 2010; Mikulincer, Shaver, Gillath, & Nitzberg, 2005).

In this chapter, we begin by describing the two behavioral systems of attachment and caregiving, followed by a review of research investigating the association between the two systems. We then propose a model of caregiving system dynamics and describe how enhancing a person's attachment security influences their caregiving behavior in the context of couple and family relationships. We conclude with the possible therapeutic implications of invoking attachment security in helping and supporting people to become more sensitive and responsive caregivers.

The Wiley-Blackwell Handbook of Couples and Family Relationships, First Edition.
Edited by Patricia Noller and Gery C. Karantzas.

Attachment Theory and Research

Attachment theory, as advanced by Bowlby (1982) and Ainsworth (e.g., Ainsworth, Blehar, Waters, & Wall, 1978), stipulates that humans have evolved a behavioral system that encompasses a repertoire of behaviors that assure proximity to a "stronger and wiser" other (an *attachment figure*) in order to increase chances of survival. Thus, in situations where a person's safety is threatened, or the person is unable to care for him or herself, the attachment system is activated, motivating the person to seek proximity to an attachment figure. This attachment figure, who is usually one's primary caregiver in infancy and childhood, can provide protection, guidance, and support thereby assisting in the regulation of the person's distress and helping to re-establish a sense of security. Thus, the attachment system is most important early in life when humans are most vulnerable and dependent on others for survival. Bowlby (1988), however, claimed that the system remains important throughout life. As such, the attachment system will mobilize adults to seek proximity in times of need during adulthood (e.g., Cassidy & Shaver, 2008; Mikulincer & Shaver, 2007a; chapters 6, 13 in this volume).

Over time, repeated interactions with an attachment figure lead to the development of mental representations of others and of the self (Bartholomew & Horowitz, 1991). Positive views of others as loving, caring, and trusting, and of the self as a capable and confident individual also worthy of love and support, result in the development attachment security. This sense of security (or feeling protected) in one's relationships is known to be associated with emotional stability, development of a positive self-image, and formation of positive attitudes toward relationship partners and close relationships in general (e.g., Hazan & Shaver, 1987; Feeney & Noller, 1990; Mikulincer & Florian, 1998). Moreover, attachment security is thought to broaden people's relationship skills and views of relationships, providing them with a larger pool of cognitive, affective, and behavioral resources from which to draw in dealing with the ups and downs of relationships. Furthermore, having a sense of security is also known to facilitate the operation of other complementary behavioral systems articulated by Bowlby (1982) such as the caregiving system (e.g., Gillath et al., 2005a, 2005b).

Individual differences in attachment

Not all children experience the same types of interactions with their caregivers. In the previous section we described how a supportive and sensitive relationship between a child and his or her caregiver is associated with a sense of security, which Ainsworth et al. (1978) argued is a central feature of a secure *attachment style*. However, if a person's attachment figures are not reliably available and supportive then people are more likely to develop an insecure attachment style (i.e., high levels of attachment anxiety and/or avoidance).

Experiences with a caregiver who engages in inconsistent and/or intrusive caregiving is thought to result in higher levels of attachment anxiety (for a review, see Mikulincer & Shaver, 2007a). Attachment anxiety reflects the degree to which a person worries about rejection or the unavailability of their attachment figure in times of need. It is also thought to reflect the tendency to be hypervigilant to threat and clingy when threat is present. People high on anxiety tend to adopt a hyperactivating strategy, which involves a chronic activation of the attachment system and a tendency to present oneself as vulnerable and in constant need of help.

Conversely, attachment avoidance is thought to result from childhood experiences with cold and rejecting caregivers resulting in the child needing to cope with distressing events on his or her own. Attachment avoidance is thought to reflect a person's distrust in relationship partners and the tendency to maintain behavioral independence and emotional distance from relationship partners. People high on avoidance tend to adopt a deactivating strategy in dealing with attachment-related distress involving an increased threshold for threat and constant attempts at downplaying the importance of potential threats and the need for emotional closeness or help (compulsive self-reliance).

People low on both anxiety and avoidance are said to be secure or to have a secure attachment style. While throughout this chapter we refer to people as secure, anxious, or avoidant, we use these terms not to denote discrete categories or types of people, but rather to connote people's relative positioning along the primary attachment dimensions of anxiety and avoidance.

To this point, we have briefly described the attachment behavioral system, its structure, functioning, and dynamics. We now turn to describing a related behavioral system—the caregiving system.

The Caregiving System

The term caregiving refers to a broad array of behaviors designed to reduce suffering or foster growth and development in a significant other such as a child or relationship partner. Thus, unlike the goal of the attachment system which is the attainment of felt security, the goal of the caregiving system is to attend another person's need for felt security by providing sensitive and responsive care. Consequently, the caregiving system is activated whenever a significant other is perceived to be in need, and deactivated when the need is met, or the care recipient appears to be protected and in a secure state. Bowlby (1982) regarded the attachment and caregiving systems as evolutionary and complementary behavioral systems. Despite the importance of the caregiving system and its proposed association with the attachment behavioral system, relatively little is known about the components, dynamics, and functioning of this system. In the remainder of this section we propose a behavioral systems model of caregiving, similar to Mikulincer and colleagues' (Mikulincer et al., 2003; Mikulincer & Shaver, 2007a) behavioral systems model of attachment (see also chapter 11 in this volume) that depicts one possible way in which the caregiving system functions.

Specifically, we suggest that when a person is alerted to the signs of another in need (such as witnessing someone in distress), the caregiving system of that person is activated (see Figure 14.1). Similar to attachment system functioning (see chapter 11 in this volume), there are likely to exist individual differences in people's tendencies to: (i) perceive such distress cues; (ii) understand or interpret them; and (iii) act upon them (we

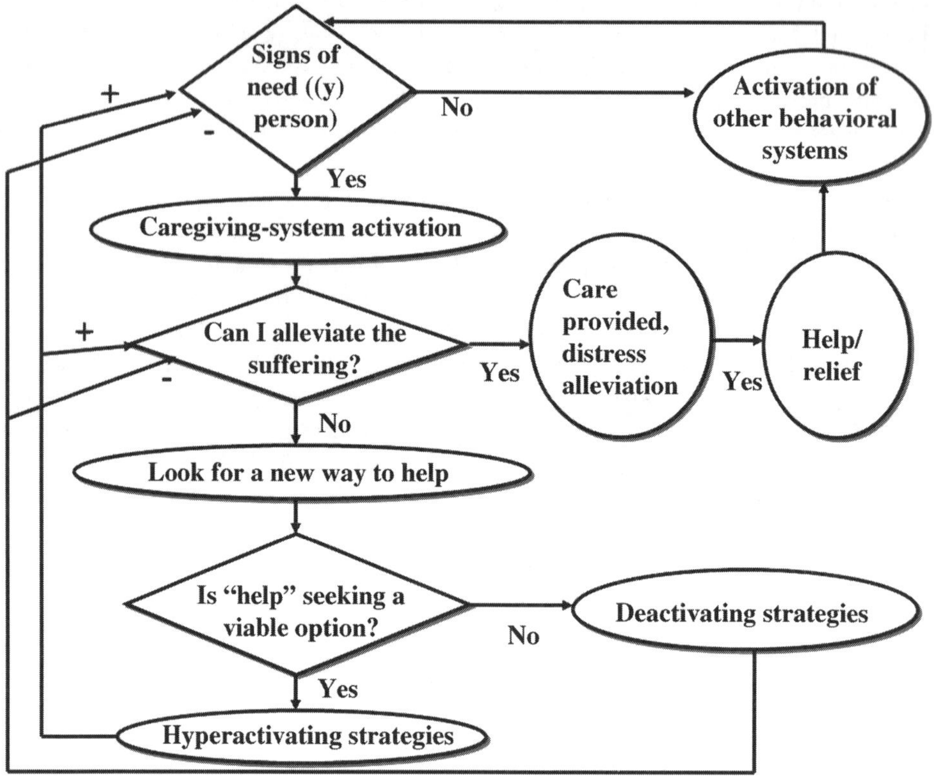

Figure 14.1 A model of the caregiving behavioral system activation and dynamics

discuss individual differences in caregiving tendencies later in this chapter). After sensing distress, the helper is required to make a decision as to whether they can provide immediate help. If the person can help and alleviate another's suffering, aid is likely to be provided (e.g., parent soothes a crying baby). Once the needy person's suffering is alleviated, the caregiving system is deactivated in the helper. If one cannot render immediate assistance, or the help provided does not alleviate the suffering of the person in need (e.g., the baby is still crying), the helper is required to make a further decision regarding whether the provision of help is a viable option at all (e.g., Can I get someone else to assist, or will a repeated attempt(s) to render assistance likely result in alleviation of the person's suffering?). If the answer to this question is yes, the helper is likely to continue to try to provide help (either by re-engaging in helping behavior or by seeking additional help). These persistent attempts to render help are thought to hyperactivate the caregiving system resulting in more effortful caregiving behaviors. If subsequent attempts at helping are deemed not feasible, people are likely to engage in deactivating strategies geared towards distancing themselves from the situation in an attempt to reduce the activation of the caregiving system.

This model shares similarities with the attachment behavioral systems model suggested by Mikulincer and Shaver (2007a; chapter 11 in this volume) and models of helping behavior articulated within the literature on prosocial behavior (e.g., Collins &

Feeney, 2010; Latané & Darley, 1970). The new model has some advantages over existing models of helping behavior. Firstly, the model focuses on the caregiving behavioral system and its functioning. Secondly, it provides a simple depiction of the decision-making process involved in helping/caregiving. Thirdly, it outlines the corresponding dynamics of the attachment and caregiving systems and the associations between the two systems. The operation of the caregiving system as depicted in the model presented in Figure 14.1 is most evident in the emotional and behavioral reactions of parents in response to their children's signals of need or distress; however, the model can also be used to describe helping situations among adult romantic partners, friends, and even strangers drawn to the pain, need, or distress of another (Mikulincer & Shaver, 2007a).

In support of the proposed model, Feeney and Collins (2001) found that anxiously attached people, who are known to adopt a hyperactivating strategy in their attachment system, also seem to adopt such a strategy with their caregiving system. Thus, anxiously attached people were likely to provide help to their partners when the partner was involved in both low and high stress situations. In other words, regardless of whether their partner needed help or not—help was provided. We suggest this behavior reflects the hyperactivation of helping strategies in the caregiving model discussed above. Conversely, avoidant individuals were less likely to provide emotional support to their partner, especially when the partner was highly stressed, or in great need for assistance. We argue that avoidant individuals' lack of caregiving was driven by deactivating behavioral and cognitive-affective responses across both the attachment and caregiving systems.

Individual differences in caregiving

Several different approaches have been used to explain why some people help and others do not, as well as the kind of help people provide. Among these approaches many have focused on the process level rather than the individual differences level, such as the decision-making models (e.g., Latané & Darley, 1970) or the cost–reward models (e.g., Piliavin, Dovidio, Gaertner, & Clark, 1981). Nevertheless, some approaches have used personality models, based on traits such as agreeableness (e.g., Graziano, Habashi, Sheese, & Tobin, 2007), prosocial predisposition (Penner, Fritzsche, Craiger, & Freifeld, 1995), or dispositional compassion (e.g., Unger & Thumuluri, 1997), and more recently attachment security (e.g., Gillath et al., 2005b) to explain differences in the tendency to provide care.

Kunce and Shaver (1994) were the first to suggest a way to measure such differences. Their measure includes four subscales of caregiving: proximity versus distance; sensitivity versus insensitivity; cooperation versus control; and compulsive caregiving. The scale classifies people into three patterns of caregiving: responsive, controlling, and compulsive, which are linked with individual differences in attachment style. Thus, secure individuals tend to be high on proximity and sensitivity, reflective of responsive caregiving, and low on compulsive caregiving. Anxious individuals tend to be high on both proximity and compulsive caregiving (potentially related to their hyperactivated system) and low on sensitivity as compared with secure individuals. Avoidant individuals tend to be low on proximity and compulsive caregiving. These findings reflect patterns of caregiving behavior that are in line with what is known about attachment styles and relationship experiences. Following Kunce and Shaver's work, in recent years more attention has been given to the links between caregiving and individual differences in attachment (see Mikulincer & Goodman, 2006; Mikulincer & Shaver, 2007a; chapter 11 in this volume for reviews).

For example, Feeney and Collins (2003) investigated how partner perceptions of caregiving affect the relationship, highlighting the importance of caregiving style for relationship functioning. Perceiving the partner to have a responsive style was associated with higher relationship satisfaction; whereas, perceiving the partner as having a compulsive caregiving style was associated with a decline in relationship satisfaction. This finding was also true for people's self-ratings of compulsive caregiving, such that people reporting a compulsive style reported less relationship satisfaction over time.

In addition to individual differences in styles and tactics of caregiving, research by Feeney and Collins (2001, 2003) emphasized the importance of different motives for helping people, while also examining the association with attachment style. For instance, providing care to benefit from it or because you feel obligated, which are more egotistic reasons for helping, were more common among insecurely attached people. However, anxious people also helped because they enjoyed helping, felt that providing care benefits the relationship or that their partner needs them. Although people high in avoidance had few reasons for providing care, they had numerous motivations for not providing care, such as avoiding stressful situations and feeling a lack of concern for their partner's problems. Low levels of trust and interdependence, and low levels of knowledge about how to effectively provide care were also associated with lower motivation to help among avoidant people.

Feeney's and Collins's work mainly focuses on the interaction between attachment and caregiving within romantic relationships. Below we further discuss this interaction, while generalizing it to other contexts. This discussion will later allow us to draw implications from this body of research on attachment and caregiving more broadly.

The Interplay between Attachment and Caregiving

While the caregiving system is functionally different from the attachment system, attachment researchers argue that the operation of one system influences the functioning of the alternate system (e.g., George & Solomon, 1999; Mikulincer & Shaver, 2009). Furthermore, the interaction of these behavioral systems has been found to shape people's behavior in close relationships (e.g., Collins, Guichard, Ford, & Feeney, 2006). More specifically, we (e.g., Gillath et al., 2005a, 2005b) and others (e.g., Feeney & Collins, 2001) have argued that while people have a natural tendency to provide care to dependent or needy others, the normative operation of the caregiving system can be suppressed or overridden by non-normative functioning of the attachment system—specifically attachment insecurity.

For example, in a situation where siblings David and Peter experience distress, both siblings may focus on their own distress and call on the other for support and comfort. Alternatively, each sibling may focus on the other sibling's signs of distress, and attempt to provide their brother with care and support. These two possible reactions by the siblings may result from differences in attachment security, which are thought to influence the available mental resources of each sibling to attend compassionately to the other's need for help. Mikulincer and Shaver (2004) argue that secure individuals have the mental resources and the flexibility to direct attention away from their own concerns, thereby temporarily suppressing their attachment needs, and activating their caregiving system to attend to the needs of others. In rendering assistance, secure individuals are thought to regulate their own emotions ensuring that their own personal distress does not impede their effective helping of others (e.g., Batson, Fultz, & Schoenrade, 1987; Fredrickson, 2001). Furthermore, it is argued that secure individuals' past experiences with sensitive and responsive caregivers influence the development of models of how to be an effective caregiver (Kunce & Shaver, 1994).

In contrast, Mikulincer and Shaver (2004) contend that insecure individuals lack the mental resources and/or the attentive capacity to detect and respond to the signals of others in need. As a result, insecure individuals are unlikely to have the mental flexibility to divert attention away from their own personal distress to that of others. Alternatively, insecure individuals' past experiences with rejecting or inept caregivers may have mitigated the development of coherent mental representations of how to respond to others in need. Thus, insecure individuals may notice the distress of others but do not know how to render assistance (Collins & Feeney, 2000; Kunce & Shaver, 1994; Mikulincer & Shaver, 2004). Therefore, individuals' interactions with caregivers may not only shape their attachment style but also influence the development of their caregiving style.

The links between attachment and caregiving have been demonstrated in different types of relationships and contexts. For example, in the realm of volunteering, secure individuals were found to spend more time volunteering, to engage in more volunteering activities, and to report more altruistic reasons for volunteering as compared with people scoring high on attachment avoidance or anxiety (e.g., Gillath et al., 2005b). Similarly, Priel, Mitrany, and Shahar (1998) found that high school students high on anxiety or avoidance were perceived by peers as less supportive than their secure classmates and were less likely to engage in reciprocally supportive relationships than secure peers. Finally, Sörensen and colleagues (2002) found that low scores on the dimensions of anxiety and avoidance (i.e., secure attachment) predicted adult children's planning to care for their older parents, suggesting that secure adult children are care-oriented even before care is explicitly called for (see also chapter 6 in this volume; Karantzas, Evans, & Foddy, 2010). Because attachment security has been linked with numerous positive caregiving-related outcomes, orienting people toward a secure attachment style or more secure behaviors is likely to result in increased caregiving by individuals, and less caregiving-related strain. We next review the literature on the enhancement of attachment security.

Enhancing the sense of attachment security

It has been argued that attachment security can be enhanced through therapy, a long-term committed relationship, or via experimental manipulations (e.g., Mikulincer & Shaver, 2007b; Gillath, Selcuk, & Shaver, 2008). In our studies, we used various subliminal (implicit) and supraliminal (explicit) methods to invoke/prime attachment security. These methods have included: the presentation of pictures implying attachment-figure availability (e.g., a Picasso drawing of a mother cradling an infant in her arms, or a couple holding hands and gazing into each other's eyes); the presentation of the names of security-providing attachment figures or words associated with the sense of security provided by an attachment figure (e.g., love, hug, comfort); and guided imagery concerning either the availability and supportiveness of attachment figures or security-enhancing interactions (e.g., describing a time when one received comfort and support from a loved one; Mikulincer & Shaver, 2007b).

These *security primes* seem to temporarily activate mental representations of attachment figures and the support and comfort they provide, increasing an individual's sense of attachment security and positively affecting behaviors and cognitions. Various studies have compared the effects of security priming with other types of priming to further ascertain beneficial qualities of security priming relative to other forms of affect-enhancing primes. Thus, security priming has been compared to emotionally positive but attachment-unrelated stimuli (e.g., pictures of a large amount of money, the names of close others who are viewed positively but do not serve attachment needs) or self-esteem-related stimuli (e.g., words that describe positive events related to one's sense of self; e.g., Gillath, Hart, Noftle, & Stockdale, 2009). Such studies have consistently found that attachment-related stimuli yield positive mental health outcomes such as greater sense of well-being, lower aggression, and lower mental health symptoms above and beyond other nonattachment-related positive stimuli. The positive outcomes of security priming have been demonstrated even in studies when the security primes were presented in conjunction with threatening situations (Mikulincer, Gillath, Halevy, Avihou, Avidan, & Eshkoli, 2001). Furthermore, these positive effects of security priming have also been found to be long lasting (Gillath et al., 2008), suggesting that priming may yield shifts in people's insecure attachment styles.

When it comes to caregiving-related behaviors, experimentally increasing people's sense of attachment security was found to increase compassionate responses to others' suffering even among insecure individuals (Mikulincer et al., 2005). People high on attachment avoidance typically have less empathic reactions to others' suffering, and are unwilling to help a distressed person. However, when exposed to a security prime, avoidantly attached people tend to be more prosocial, compassionate, and helpful in their behavior. Similarly, although people high on attachment anxiety tend to react emotionally to a person in need, their reaction tends to be more inwardly focused, marked by higher levels of personal distress, and is not associated with actual helping behavior. However, when exposed to a security prime, anxiously attached people show increased levels of caregiving (for similar findings see Mikulincer et al., 2001; Mikulincer et al., 2003). These findings provide evidence for a causal link between attachment security and the tendency to care, such that enhancing one's sense of attachment security increases a person's tendency to be more compassionate and behave in a more prosocial and caring manner.

Implications

What does all this tell us about care provision in the real world? As reviewed in previous sections of this chapter, survey and experimental data have helped to elucidate attachment-related factors associated with the likelihood of providing care and the effects of doing (or not doing) so. The use of attachment theory as a framework, and methodologies used in testing the predictions derived from this framework, have improved our understanding of how caregiving may be enhanced through various priming techniques. This understanding, in turn, has the potential to improve caregiving in the real world and aid in the counseling of those in caregiving situations. In this last section we suggest some ways in which academic knowledge can be applied to therapy and caregiving in real life.

The first step in this application process involves examining whether findings obtained in the laboratory are replicated in caregiving contexts outside the laboratory. The few studies that have investigated the links between attachment and real-world caregiving suggest that indeed the associations between attachment and caregiving hold. For example, one study examining couples where one partner was diagnosed with metastatic cancer found that attachment security was associated with decreased difficulty in providing care, whereas attachment avoidance was associated with increased difficulty in providing emotional support to one's spouse (Kim & Carver, 2007). Similarly, Braun and colleagues (Braun, Mikulincer, Rydall, Walsh, & Rodin, 2007) found that attachment anxiety was related to greater difficulty in providing care to a spouse with cancer and to perceptions of more time spent engaging in caregiving tasks.

Attachment style also seems to predict the emotional well-being of an individual when caring for another. For instance, spousal caregivers reporting high levels of attachment anxiety and avoidance were also found to report high levels of depression (Braun et al., 2007; Rodin et al., 2007). Recently, Gillath and colleagues (in press) reported similar findings, such that attachment insecurity, especially attachment avoidance, was associated with greater depression and loneliness among older adults who provide care for their romantic partner. Together these findings suggest that the associations found between attachment and caregiving in laboratory studies are consistent with the findings of studies investigating the associations between these behavioral systems in real-world caregiving contexts.

The second step in linking academic knowledge to practice involves applying the priming methods used to increase security in the laboratory to enhance caregiving in the real world. For instance, engaging in cognitive or affective therapies that repeatedly draw on examples of positive relationship experiences may induce a sense of security and positive mood that may lead to greater openness in therapy dealing with attachment insecurities and difficulties in being a sensitive and responsive caregiver for others. Moreover, frequent reminders of positive past relationship experiences can be used to help clients generate more positive representations of attachment figures and relationships in general, and may, over time, improve their attachment orientations and their caregiving tendencies and abilities. It may be that getting clients to think about the positive aspects of past attachment relationships, or recalling examples of positive encounters with attachment figures, no matter how fleeting or infrequent, can be particularly important in therapeutic approaches such as narrative therapy. In this form of therapy, the therapist acts as a collaborator in helping the client re-author past disparate and unresolved relationship experiences. In this role, the therapist may prime security in clients through having them recall positive relationship experiences—helping insecurely attached people rewrite their narratives of past relationships in such a way that they arrive at a more healthy view of these relationships.

These revised narratives, facilitated in part through security priming, can then influence the way the client acts as a caregiver in current and subsequent relationships.

Other scholars have highlighted the importance of heightening feelings of attachment security in therapy in dealing with relationship issues such as spousal support, forgiveness, and couple conflict (e.g., Johnson & Whiffen, 2003; Obegi & Berant, 2009; chapters 20, 23 in this volume). For example, emotionally focused therapy for couples (see chapter 23 in this volume) is geared toward having partners develop a secure base with the therapist and with one another, thereby improving the couple's sense of attachment security, which is expected to improve the quality of their relationship, including caregiving and care receiving. The therapeutic session is thought to provide a safe haven and a secure base for the couples to explore and tend to relationship hurts and traumas. By invoking a sense of safety and security in clients during the therapy session, couples are able to attend to challenging and hurtful relationship issues that they otherwise would not. Furthermore, the therapist is thought to act as a model of how to engage sensitive and responsive caregiving thereby demonstrating to couples how to be an effective and loving caregiver.

Specific interventions based on attachment theory have been developed aimed at improving parent–child relationships by reducing parental insensitivity and increasing children's attachment security and improving the quality of adult familial attachment relationships (see Bakermans-Kranenburg, Van Hzendoorn, & Juffer, 2003; Egeland, Weinfield, Bosquet, & Cheng, 2000; van Ijzendoorn, Juffer, & Duyvesteyn, 1995). These interventions often involve psycho-education regarding the qualities and benefits of developing attachment security and strategies on how individuals can recognize their own insecure cognitions and behaviors and correct such thoughts and actions. Some of these interventions also assist insecurely attached individuals to become more sensitive to the attachment needs of others. Such interventions have been successfully tried with families of cancer patients and incarcerated parents (e.g., Makariev & Shaver, 2010; Zaider & Kissane, 2010). Using such interventions that educate people about attachment security and insecurity while providing them with strategies to enhance their sense of attachment security are likely to increase insecurely attached people's capacity to help others, improve the quality of help they provide, improve their mental well-being, and possibly reduce carer burnout.

In the spirit of the interventions outlined above, less formal psycho-education can be provided to insecurely attached clients in therapy, teaching clients about the associations derived from research between attachment and caregiving styles. As noted in the literature, avoidant individuals report poor knowledge about how to provide care, while anxious individuals tend to be overbearing in their attempts to render assistance. As a result, therapists can provide practical information to insecure clients, such as teaching them ways to correctly notice signs of need in others and strategies on how to offer help that meets a person's needs without providing too much help. Findings by Gillath et al. (2005b) suggest that helping behavior has a facilitative component, whereby nonaltruistic helping can promote a sense of attachment security, which in turn is likely to promote further caregiving driven by altruistic motives. Thus, encouraging insecurely attached people to help others may foster attachment security and subsequent prosocial behavior.

In conclusion, our chapter describes the associations between the attachment and caregiving systems. Moreover, experimental research suggests that caregiving-related processes can be affected by changes made to one's sense of attachment security. Specifically, enhancing one's sense of security can result in prosocial outcomes including the increase in sensitive and responsive caregiving behaviors. We have argued that security priming has a place beyond the laboratory and has the potential to influence attachment-based approaches to therapy targeted at increasing people's attachment security and improving their capacities to be loving and supportive caregivers. The research and implications for therapy we discussed in this chapter should be useful to psychologists, therapists, educators, and policy makers who are invested in improving the quality of caregiving dyads—whether these be parent and child, a pair of siblings, two best friends, or a romantic couple.

References

Ainsworth, M. D. S., Blehar, M. C., Waters, E., & Wall, S. (1978). *Patterns of attachment: Assessed in the strange situation and at home.* Hillsdale, NJ: Erlbaum.

Bakermans-Kranenburg, M. J., Van Hzendoorn, M. H., & Juffer, F. (2003). Less is more: Meta-analyses of sensitivity and attachment interventions in early childhood. *Psychological Bulletin, 129,* 195–215.

Bartholomew, K., & Horowitz, L. M. (1991). Attachment styles among young adults: A test of a four-category model. *Journal of Personality and Social Psychology, 61,* 226–244.

Batson, C. D., Fultz, J., & Schoenrade, P. A. (1987). Distress and empathy: Two qualitatively distinct vicarious emotions with different motivational consequences. *Journal of Personality, 55,* 19–39.

Bowlby, J. (1982). *Attachment and loss: Vol. 1 Attachment* (2nd edn.). New York: Basic Books. (Original work published 1969)

Bowlby, J. (1988). *A secure base: Clinical applications of attachment theory.* London: Routledge.

Braun, M., Mikulincer, M., Rydall, A., Walsh, A., & Rodin, G. (2007). Hidden morbidity in cancer: Spouse caregivers. *Journal of Clinical Oncology, 25,* 4829–4834.

Cassidy, J., & Shaver, P. R. (Eds.) (2008). *Handbook of attachment: Theory, research, and clinical applications* (2nd edn.). New York: Guilford Press.

Collins, N. L., & Feeney, B. C. (2000). A safe haven: An attachment theory perspective on support seeking and caregiving in intimate relationships. *Journal of Personality and Social Psychology, 78,* 1053–1073.

Collins, N. L., & Feeney, B. C. (2010). An attachment theoretical perspective on social support dynamics in couples: Normative processes and individual differences. In K. Sullivan & J. Davila (Eds.), *Support processes in intimate relationships* (pp. 89–120). New York: Oxford University Press.

Collins, N. L., Guichard, A. C., Ford, M. B., & Feeney, B. C. (2006). Responding to need in intimate relationships: Normative processes and individual differences. In M. Mikulincer & G. S. Goodman (Eds.), *Dynamics of romantic love: Attachment, caregiving, and sex* (pp. 149–189). New York: Guilford Press.

Egeland, B., Weinfield, N. S., Bosquet, M., & Cheng, V. K. (2000). Remembering, repeating, and working through: Lessons from attachment-based interventions. In J. D. Osofsky & H. E. Fitzgerald (Eds.), Infant Mental Health in Groups at High Risk. *WAIMH Handbook of infant mental health, Vol. 4* (pp. 35–89). New York: Wiley.

Feeney, B. C., & Collins, N. L. (2001). Predictors of caregiving in adult intimate relationships: An attachment theoretical perspective. *Journal of Personality and Social Psychology, 80*, 972–994.

Feeney, B. C., & Collins, N. L. (2003). Motivations for caregiving in adult intimate relationships: Influences on caregiving behavior and relationship functioning. *Personality and Social Psychology Bulletin, 29*, 950–968.

Feeney, J. A., & Noller, P. (1990). Attachment style as a predictor of adult romantic relationships. *Journal of Personality and Social Psychology, 58*, 281–291.

Fredrickson, B. L. (2001). The role of positive emotions in positive psychology: The broaden-and-build theory of positive emotions. *American Psychologist, 56*, 218–226.

George, C., & Solomon, J. (1999). Attachment and caregiving: The caregiving behavioral system. In J. Cassidy & P. R. Shaver (Eds.), *Handbook of attachment: Theory, research, and clinical applications* (pp. 649–670). New York: Guilford Press.

Gillath, O., Hart, J., Noftle, E. E., & Stockdale, G. D. (2009). Development and validation of a state adult attachment measure (SAAM). *Journal of Research in Personality, 43*, 362–373.

Gillath, O., Johnson, D. K., Selcuk, E., & Teel, C. S. (in press). Attachment style and network management skills moderate the links between social networks and mental health among older adults. *Journal of Social and Personal Relationships.*

Gillath, O., Selcuk, E., & Shaver, P. R. (2008). Moving toward a secure attachment style: Can repeated security priming help? *Social and Personality Psychology Compass, 2/4*, 1651–1666.

Gillath, O., Shaver, P. R., & Mikulincer, M. (2005a). An attachment-theoretical approach to compassion and altruism. In P. Gilbert (Ed.), *Compassion: Conceptualizations, research, and use in psychotherapy* (pp. 121–147). London: Brunner-Routledge.

Gillath, O., Shaver, P. R., Mikulincer, M., Nitzberg, R. E., Erez, A., & van IJzendoorn, M. H. (2005b). Attachment, caregiving, and volunteering: Placing volunteerism in an attachment-theoretical framework. *Personal Relationships, 12*, 425–446.

Graziano, W. G., Habashi, M., Sheese, B., & Tobin, R. M. (2007). Agreeableness, empathy, and helping: A person X situation perspective. *Journal of Personality and Social Psychology, 93*, 583–599.

Hazan, C., & Shaver, P. R. (1987). Romantic love conceptualized as an attachment process. *Journal of Personality and Social Psychology, 52*, 511–524.

Hazan, C., & Shaver, P. R. (1994). Attachment as an organizational framework for research on close relationships. *Psychological Inquiry, 5*, 1–22.

Johnson, S. M., & Whiffen, V. (2003). *Attachment processes in couples and families.* New York: Guilford Press.

Karantzas, G. C., Evans, L., & Foddy, M. (2010). The role of attachment in current and future parent caregiving. *Journals of Gerontology: Psychological Science, 65*, 573–580.

Kim, Y., & Carver, C. S. (2007). Frequency and difficulty in caregiving among spouses of individuals with cancer: Effects of adult attachment and gender. *Psycho-Oncology, 16*, 714–723.

Kunce, L. J., & Shaver, P. R. (1994). An attachment-theoretical approach to caregiving in romantic relationships. In K. Bartholomew & D. Perlman (Eds.), *Advances in personal relationships: Attachment processes in adulthood* (Vol. 5, pp. 205–237). London: Jessica Kingsley.

Latané, B., & Darley, J. (1970). *The unresponsive bystander: Why doesn't he help?* New York: Appleton-Century-Crofts.

Makariev, D. W., & Shaver, P. R. (2010). Attachment, parental incarceration and possibilities for intervention: An overview. *Attachment and Human Development, 12*, 311–331.

Mikulincer, M., & Florian, V. (1998). The relationship between adult attachment styles and emotional and cognitive reactions to stressful events. In J. A. Simpson & W. S. Rholes (Eds.), *Attachment theory and close relationships* (pp. 143–165). New York: Guilford Press.

Mikulincer, M., Gillath, O., Halevy, V., Avihou, N., Avidan, S., & Eshkoli, N. (2001). Attachment theory and reactions to others' needs: Evidence that activation of the sense of attachment security promotes empathic responses. *Journal of Personality and Social Psychology, 81*, 1205–1224.

Mikulincer, M., Gillath, O., Sapir-Lavid, Y., Yaakobi, E., Arias, K., Tal-Aloni, L. & Bor, G. (2003). Attachment theory and concern for others' welfare: Evidence that activation of the sense of secure base promotes endorsement of self-transcendence values. *Basic and Applied Social Psychology, 25*, 299–312.

Mikulincer, M., & Goodman, G. S. (Eds.) (2006). *Dynamics of romantic love: Attachment, caregiving, and sex*. New York: Guilford Press.

Mikulincer, M., & Shaver, P. R. (2004). Security-based self-representations in adulthood: Contents and processes. In W. S. Rholes & J. A. Simpson (Eds.), *Adult attachment: Theory, research, and clinical implications* (pp. 159–195). New York: Guilford Press.

Mikulincer, M., & Shaver, P. R. (2007a). *Attachment in adulthood: Structure, dynamics, and change*. New York: Guilford Press.

Mikulincer, M., & Shaver, P.R. (2007b). Boosting attachment security to promote mental health, prosocial values, and inter-group tolerance. *Psychological Inquiry, 18*, 139–156.

Mikulincer, M., & Shaver, P. R. (2009). An attachment and behavioral systems perspective on social support. *Journal of Social and Personal Relationships, 26*, 7–19.

Mikulincer, M., Shaver, P. R., Gillath, O., & Nitzberg, R. A. (2005). Attachment, caregiving, and altruism: Boosting attachment security increases compassion and helping. *Journal of Personality and Social Psychology, 89*, 817–839.

Obegi, J. H., & Berant, E. (Eds.) (2009). *Internal working models and change*. New York: Guilford Press.

Penner, L., Dovidio, J., Piliavin, J., & Schroeder, D. (2005). Prosocial behavior: Multilevel perspectives. *Annual Review of Psychology, 56*, 365–392.

Penner, L. A., Fritzsche, B. A., Craiger, J. P., & Freifeld, T. R. (1995). Measuring the prosocial personality. In J. Butcher & C. D. Spielberger (Eds.), *Advances in personality assessment* (Vol. 10, pp. 147–163). Hillsdale, NJ: Erlbaum.

Piliavin, J. A., Dovidio, J. F., Gaertner, S. L., & Clark, R. D. III (1981). *Emergency intervention*. New York: Academic Press.

Priel, B., Mitrany, D., & Shahar, G. (1998). Closeness, support, and reciprocity: A study of attachment styles in adolescence. *Personality and Individual Differences, 25*, 1183–1197.

Rodin, G., Walsh, A., Zimmermann, C., Gagliese, L., Jones, J., Shepherd, F. A., Moore, M., Braun, M., Donner, A., & Mikulincer, M. (2007). The contribution of attachment security and social support to depressive symptoms in patients with metastatic cancer. *Psycho-Oncology, 16*, 1080–1097.

Sörensen, S., Webster, J. D., & Roggman, L. A. (2002). Adult attachment and preparing to provide care for older relatives. *Attachment and Human Development, 4*, 84–106.

Unger, L. S., & Thumuluri, L. K. (1997). Trait empathy and continuous helping: The case of voluntarism. *Journal of Social Behavior and Personality, 12*, 785–800.

van IJzendoorn, M. H., Juffer, F., & Duyvesteyn, M. G. (1995). Breaking the intergenerational cycle of insecure attachment: A review of the effects of attachment-based interventions on maternal sensitivity and infant security. *Journal of Child Psychology and Psychiatry, 36*, 225–248.

Zaider, T. I., & Kissane, D. W. (2010). Psychosocial interventions for couples and families coping with cancer. In J. C. Holland, W. S. Breitbart, P. B. Jacobsen, M. S. Lederberg, M. J. Loscalzo, & R. S. McCorkle (Eds.), *Psycho-Oncology* (2nd edn., pp. 483–488). New York: Oxford University Press.

PART V

Cognitive and Affective Processes in Couple Relationships

15

Attachment Insecurities and Relationship Self-Regulation

An Investigation of the Mediational Role of Attributions for Negative Partner Behavior

Zoë J. Hazelwood

Attributions in Relationships

Attribution theory provides a useful heuristic for describing intimate partners' cognitive processes, processes that contribute both negatively and positively to relationship quality (e.g. Sumer & Cozzarelli, 2004; Tashiro & Frazier, 2003). Attributions provide relationship partners with the perception that they are better able to predict future behavior by contributing to an understanding of the perceived cause or intent of partner behavior (Bradbury & Fincham, 1990a; Fincham, Harold, & Gano Phillips, 2000). Causal attributions address the need to understand why a behavior or event has occurred; when a person makes a causal attribution, he or she makes a judgment as to the locus, stability, and globality of the perceived cause of the event or behavior. Responsibility attributions tap into the belief that someone, or something, should be held accountable for the behavior; judgments are made as to the intent of the behavior and whether it was a selfish or blameworthy act.

Attributions in relationships are most likely to occur when partner behavior is seen as unpredictable, novel, or important to the observer (Fletcher, Fincham, Cramer, & Heron, 1987). The novel or surprising element of the behavior is likely to cause the

The Wiley-Blackwell Handbook of Couples and Family Relationships, First Edition.
Edited by Patricia Noller and Gery C. Karantzas.

partner to pay more attention to the behavior and try to understand why it occurred, thus attributions are made that potentially serve to improve this understanding. In satisfied partnerships, a lengthy attribution process occurs when behavior is viewed as negative (Bradbury & Fincham, 1990b). In these situations, negative behavior is contrary to expectations and therefore poses an unexpected phenomenon that requires explanation, whereas positive partner behavior would be consistent with expectations. For example, to a satisfied partner, the cause of a partner's unexpected, hurtful statement may be viewed as external to the partner ("He/she is frustrated with something at work"), unstable ("He/she doesn't usually talk to me this way"), and situation-specific ("He/she must be having a bad day"). The behavior would be viewed as unintentional and unselfish and therefore not requiring blame. Conversely, if the hurtful statement was uttered to someone who experiences poor relationship satisfaction, this person may view their partner's hurtful statement as consistent with their (negative) expectations of the partner (Fletcher, 1993). The dissatisfied person would be likely to attribute the cause of their partner's statement as internal to the partner ("He/she is being rude"), and stable and global in nature ("He/she always does this"). The behavior would be likely to be viewed as intentional, selfish, and blameworthy.

This type of negative explanatory style erodes relationship satisfaction and can perpetuate distress (Chatav & Whisman, 2009; Schaefer-Porter & Hendrick, 2000). Furthermore, longitudinal research using growth-curve analysis suggests this relationship is unidirectional (Karney & Bradbury, 2000). It is unlikely that diminished relationship satisfaction contributes to the generation of internal, stable attributions for negative partner behavior as much as these attributions serve to diminish relationship satisfaction. This evidence for the unidirectional relationship between attributions and satisfaction has led researchers to identify variables that may explain how a biased attribution style could form in relationship partners in the first instance. One possible precursor to the development of maladaptive attributions is adult romantic attachment style.

Attachment and Attributions

The research exploring adult romantic attachment style stems from Bowlby's (Bowlby, 1998) assertions that an infant's bond with their caregiver provides a secure base from which to navigate a path through the world. Hazan and Shaver's (1987) seminal work argued that intimate relationships of adults can be conceptualized in a similar manner (for detailed descriptions of attachment theory and attachment style, see chapters 11, 14, 26 in this volume).

Securely attached people are confident that their relationship partners will be available for them, they are comfortable with others' attempts to get close, and they can tolerate absences and separations because they are secure in the knowledge their partner will return to them (Mikulincer, 1998). Anxiously attached individuals are also comfortable with others' attempts at closeness but this feeling is accompanied by concerns about rejection and fears of being abandoned or unloved. Conversely, avoidantly attached people prefer to distance themselves emotionally from others and prefer to remain autonomous

(Mikulincer, Shaver, Sapir-Lavid, & Avihou-Kanza, 2009). Avoidant individuals can be distrustful of their relationship partners or fearful of getting hurt in the relationship (Bartholomew & Horowitz, 1991).

Feeney and Noller (1996) argue that the personal scripts or internal working models that contribute to the development of both anxious and avoidant attachment behaviors have as their basis "attentional processes," where a person's attention is either directed toward or away from a stimulus depending on their attachment security. Thus attachment security guides a person to selectively attend to behavior that confirms his or her beliefs about him or herself and the world. This proposition bears striking similarity to conceptualizations of the attribution process—attributions occur as a result of a person's perception of an event and the subsequent search for an explanation for that event (Fincham, Bradbury, & Grych, 1990). This explanation will be based on the information a person extracts from paying attention to something, in some cases using biased selective attention. Using this rationale, the attachment style of each partner in an intimate relationship can be seen to play a role in predicting the types of attributions a person formulates to explain partner behavior.

This hypothesis has been tested by empirical studies that have found support for the notion that anxious and avoidant attachment styles are linked to the formation of maladaptive or unhelpful and irrational attributions for negative partner behavior. Pearce and Halford (2008) used a community sample of couples to explore the relationship between insecure attachment and negative attributions and found negative causal and responsibility attributions partially mediated the association between attachment anxiety and avoidance and self-reported couple communication. Sumer and Cozzarelli (2004) found security of attachment predicts the extent to which a person makes causal and responsibility attributions for their partner's negative behavior, with anxious and avoidantly attached people making more negative causal and responsibility attributions compared to securely attached people. Similar results have been found elsewhere (Collins Ford, Guichard, & Allard, 2006; Gallo & Smith, 2001) and together these studies lend support to the argument that attachment anxiety and avoidance can produce biased attentional processes (Feeney & Noller, 1996) that subsequently influence the cognitive processing of events, providing the potential for biased or skewed causal explanations of events.

Biased explanations of relationship-salient events may impact on how couples behave in their relationship. For example, we know that attributions can mediate the association between anxious and avoidant attachment and self-reported negative couple communication (Pearce & Halford, 2008), and between anxious and avoidant attachment and perceptions of social support and conflict in the relationship (Gallo & Smith, 2001). The present research aims to explore the extent to which attributions can mediate the relationship between attachment insecurities and each partner's behavioral self-regulation.

Self-Regulation in Relationships

The concept of relationship self-regulation stems from Karoly's (1993) early writings on self-regulation and self-control. Karoly defined self-regulation as an individual's capacity or efforts to undertake goal-directed activities with a view to evoking change in one's circumstances. "The processes of self-regulation are initiated when routinized activity is impeded or when goal-directedness is otherwise made salient (e.g. the appearance of a challenge, the failure of habitual action patterns, etc.)" (Karoly, 1993, p. 25). Thus self-regulation is about working at achieving self-directed change and regulating one's behavior.

Self-regulation in intimate relationships refers to the actions or behaviors undertaken by each partner to enhance the relationship (Halford, Sanders, & Behrens, 1994). Relationship self-regulation consists of an individual's identification of change-enabling strategies for the relationship, and an assessment of the effort they have injected into the relationship to undertake these strategies. These behaviors are collectively viewed as working at a relationship and have been found to account for as much as 30% of the variance in the cross-sectional assessment of relationship satisfaction (Wilson, Charker, Alizzio, Kalford, & Kimlin, 2005).

Relationship self-regulation has not been explored to the same extent as other relationship-salient variables but there is growing interest in this construct as an important correlate of well-being and satisfaction in relationships. Finkel et al.'s (2009) research found that partners who were high in self-regulatory processes such as dispositional self-control and self-regulatory strength were able to refrain from acting on violent impulses and primed to recall a serious argument or fight with a romantic partner. When self-regulation or regulatory strength was manipulated by exposing participants to an insulting or jealousy-provoking hypothetical partner, participants were more likely to experience a violent impulse compared to situations where self-regulatory processes weren't manipulated or interfered with. Halford et al. (2010) have also explored aggression and violence in intimate relationships and found that in couples where aggression and violence were less frequent, behavioral self-regulation was high. Ritter and colleagues have used a "self-regulation depletion" methodology similar to Finkel et al. (2009) to determine the extent to which self-regulation can stop a romantically involved person from looking favorably at opposite-sex alternatives. They found that when a person's self-regulatory processes were high (i.e., not experimentally depleted), romantic partners showed less interest in images of attractive opposite-sex people compared to people who were not romantically involved with anyone. Conversely, when self-regulatory efforts had been experimentally depleted, romantically involved people and uninvolved people showed the same level of interest in the images of opposite-sex people.

Attachment, Attributions, and Self-Regulation

To date there has been no empirical investigation of the extent to which attributions mediate the relationship between attachment insecurity and each partner's behavioral self-regulation, although the theoretical links suggest this model deserves exploration. The model tested here proposes that perceived threats to the relationship activate attachment insecurities and promote the generation of attributions to understand this threat. This cognitive process has the capacity to influence the behavioral reaction a partner displays to manage this perceived threat. These behavioral reactions take the form of self-regulatory actions that, in satisfying relationships, seek to maintain or improve the quality of the relationship. In relationships where satisfaction is low, it is argued that behavioral self-regulation will occur less often. This assumption is partly due to the fact that self-regulation involves cognitive appraisals of the relationship and the identification of cognitions, affect, and behavior that need to be changed in order to improve relationship functioning. In distressed relationships, poor relationship self-appraisals that stem from biased attributions may hinder a partner's perception of their efforts to work at the relationship (Halford, Wilson, Lizzio, & Moore, 2002). Thus, the hypothesis that stems from this model proposes that attributions for negative partner behavior will mediate the association between attachment anxiety and avoidance and behavioral self-regulation.

Testing Attributions as a Mediator of the Association between Attachment and Perceptions of Partner Self-Regulation

To investigate the mediating role of attributions in explaining the association between attachment and perceptions of partner self-regulation, I gathered data from 59 middle-aged couples recruited via media outreach for a larger study of relationships. Approximately half of the couples were married with the remaining couples involved in a de facto relationship. The mean length of relationship was 12 years.

Couples filled in a self-report measure on attachment (Experiences in Close Relationships Scale; Brennan, Clark, & Shaver, 1998) yielding an assessment of each partner's attachment anxiety and avoidance with higher scores indicating greater attachment insecurity. Participants' perceptions of own and of partner's self-regulation were assessed using the Behavioral Self-Regulation for Effective Relationships Scale (Halford et al., 1994) with higher scores reflecting a greater perception of positive self-regulation behavior of self and partners. The attributions reported by each partner in response to hypothetical partner behavior were assessed with the Relationship Attribution Measure (RAM; Fincham & Bradbury, 1992). Respondents rated their agreement with six attribution statements assessing the dimensions of cause and responsibility. As the overall negativity of attributions was of more interest here, scores on each subscale were totaled and a scenario-based average was recorded. Higher scores reflected a greater degree of negative attributions.

Testing the Mediation Hypotheses

To test the proposed mediation hypothesis, the data were analyzed according to the Actor-Partner Interdependence Model (APIM), which uses the couple as the unit of measurement (Campbell & Kashy, 2002). The fit of each model was tested using path analyses in AMOS 13.0, with the error terms for the men's and women's endogenous and exogenous variables correlated to account for the dependence in the dyadic data (Kenny, Kashy, & Cook, 2006).

Determining the extent to which negative attributions mediated the relationship between attachment anxiety and avoidance and self-regulation required the formulation of four actor-partner interdependence models, two (anxiety and avoidance) for the self dimension of perceived self-regulation, and two (anxiety and avoidance) for the partner dimension of self-regulation. The first model, testing whether attributions mediated the association between avoidant attachment and perceptions of one's own self-regulation, resulted in a marginal to good fit, χ^2 (2, $N = 59$) = 2.747, $p = .253$; Comparative Fit Index (CFI) = 0.985; Tucker Lewis Index (TLI) = 0.888; Root Mean Square Error of Approximation (RMSEA) = .080; Standardized Root Mean Squared Residual (SRMR) = .034. Post-hoc examination of the model did not identify any need to modify the model. Women's avoidant attachment was significantly associated with their own attributions ($\beta = .25$), their own reported self-regulation efforts ($\beta = -.48$), and men's self-regulation ($\beta = -.29$). Men's avoidant attachment was significantly associated with their own self-regulation ($\beta = -.26$). Given that there were no significant associations between attributions and self-regulation, no mediation analyses could be conducted.

Similar direct effects were found with anxious attachment, χ^2 (2, $N = 59$) = 4.084, $p = .130$; CFI = 0.950; TLI = 0.626; RMSEA = .134; SRMR = .043. Women's anxious attachment significantly predicted women's attributions ($\beta = .39$) and men's attributions ($\beta = .29$), but did not significantly predict self-regulation. Conversely, there was a direct effect of men's anxious attachment on their own self-regulation ($\beta = -.34$), and men's anxious attachment also significantly predicted men's attributions ($\beta = .28$). As with the first model, there were no significant associations between attributions and self-regulation so no mediation analyses were carried out.

The next model tested whether attributions mediated the association between avoidant attachment and perceptions of one's partner's self-regulation behavior. The first path analysis resulted in an excellent fit, χ^2 (2, $N = 59$) = 0.811, $p = .667$; CFI = 1.000; TLI = 1.106; RMSEA = .000; SRMR = .020. As illustrated in Figure 15.1, women's avoidant attachment directly predicted perceptions of partner self-regulation, and appeared to impact on men's perceptions of partner self-regulation as well. Women's

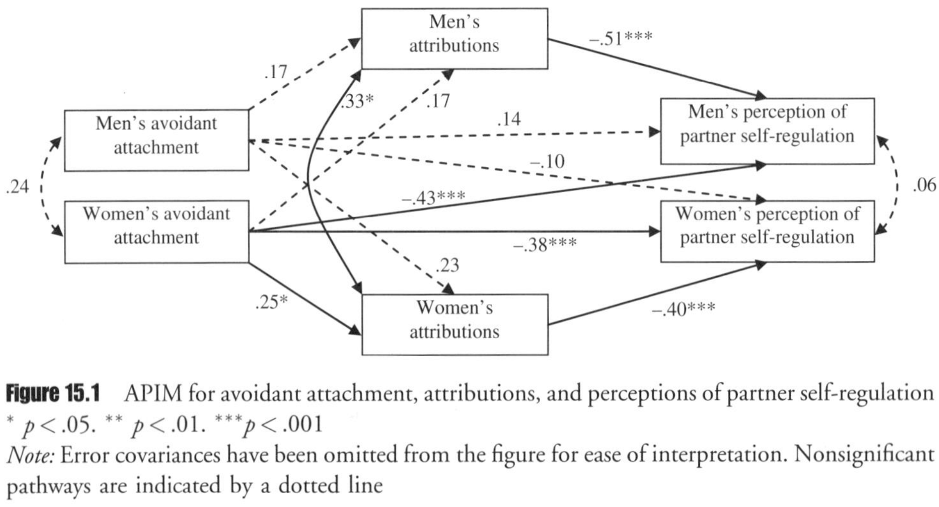

Figure 15.1 APIM for avoidant attachment, attributions, and perceptions of partner self-regulation
$^{*}\ p < .05.\ ^{**}\ p < .01.\ ^{***}p < .001$
Note: Error covariances have been omitted from the figure for ease of interpretation. Nonsignificant pathways are indicated by a dotted line

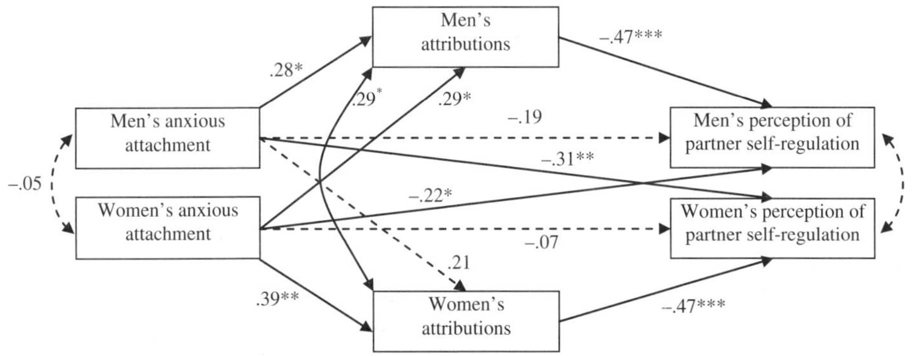

Figure 15.2 APIM for anxious attachment, attributions, and perceptions of partner self-regulation
* $p < .05$. ** $p < .01$. *** $p < .001$
Note: Error covariances have been omitted from the figure for ease of interpretation. Nonsignificant pathways are indicated by a dotted line

avoidant attachment was also significantly associated with their own attributions, which in turn were associated with perceptions of partner self-regulation. Mediation was tested by bootstrapping the sample to 5,000 replications, and estimating the specific indirect effects with bias-corrected 95% confidence intervals (for details regarding the estimation of indirect effects see Mackinnon, 2008; Preacher & Hayes, 2008). The mediated effect of women's avoidant attachment on perceptions of their partner's self-regulation through attributions was supported, ($\beta = -.10$, $p < .05$; 95% CI [−.23, −.01]). Mediation was not tested for men as their avoidant attachment was not associated with attributions.

The final APIM tested the same predictions for anxious attachment, and resulted in an excellent fit, χ^2 (2, $N = 59$) = 1.408, $p = .495$; CFI = 1.000; TLI = 1.061; RMSEA = .000; SRMR = .027. Figure 15.2 illustrates a significant positive association between women's anxious attachment and attributions, and between women's attributions and perceptions of partner self-regulation behavior, but there were no direct effects between anxious attachment and perceptions of partner self-regulation for either women or men. Both men's and women's anxious attachment impacted on men's attributions, and there was a significant inverse association between men's attributions and perceptions of partner self-regulation. As there was a significant association between women's anxious attachment and men's attributions, between women's anxious attachment and men's perceptions of partner self-regulation, and between men's attributions and perceptions of partner self-regulation, the potential mediated effect was tested, and found to be significant ($\beta = -.14$, $p < .05$; 95% CI [−.28, −.03]).

Interpreting the Findings

The research presented here sought to test the hypothesis that attributions for negative partner behavior mediate the relationship between attachment anxiety and avoidance and relationship self-regulation. This hypothesis was tested using perceptions of own self-regulatory behavior and perceptions of partner self-regulatory behavior as dependent variables. The results provide partial support for the hypothesis; when perceptions of own self-regulatory behavior was the dependent variable, we saw mainly direct effects of attachment on self-regulation with little evidence for mediation of this effect by attributions. When perceptions of partner self-regulation behavior was the dependent variable, the potential for biased cognitions had a more noticeable impact. These results support the notion that, in general, the greater a person's anxious attachment, the more negative causal and responsibility attributions are made for negative partner behavior. In turn, these negative attributions lead to the perception that the partner has put less work into the relationship. This finding was true for both men and women. Avoidant attachment in women was also related to more negative attributions and, in turn, lowered perceptions of partner self-regulation behavior for enhancing the relationship.

There was also evidence of a direct effect of attachment anxiety and avoidance on perceptions of both own and partner self-regulation, suggesting the association between attachment and self-regulation independent of attributions cannot be ignored and mediation is likely to be partial. As Shaver and Mikulincer (2002) argue, a major function of the attachment system is to regulate emotion. For example, in times of threat or distress, proximity seeking is an attachment behavior that acts as a regulatory behavior by mobilizing the person to be near their attachment figure thereby experiencing a sense of security (Zimmermann, 1999). However, in situations where the attachment figure is not available and proximity seeking is not viable, avoidant or anxious behavior follow in the form of secondary self-regulatory strategies of deactivation or hyperactivation (see chapter 14 in this volume for a description of these behavioral strategies).

The results of the present research lend support to the notion that perceptions of regulatory behavior within romantic relationships are also related to the attachment system, where both attachment anxiety and avoidance can be linked to perceptions that a person is exerting less effort or being less effective in regulating their relationship. This issue will no doubt be a promising avenue of investigation for future research.

There was a fairly robust association between attachment and attributions. Both men's and women's attachment anxiety and women's avoidance were significantly associated with attributions for negative partner behavior across all four models tested. This finding lends support to previous empirical research (e.g. Gallo & Smith, 2001; Sumer & Cozzarelli, 2004) showing that attachment insecurity can predict the extent to which a person makes negative attributions for negative partner behavior. These findings add weight to the theoretical argument that negative attributions may stem from the biased, selective-attentional processes that often accompany attachment insecurities (Feeney & Noller, 1996).

The lack of support for mediation models utilizing the assessment of own behavioral self-regulation is likely to be the result of adopting an approach to the measurement of attributions that focused on partner behavior more so than own behavior. The utilization of an attribution measure asking participants to provide explanations for their partner's potential negative hypothetical behavior and not asking them to comment on their own behavior in each situation may explain the lack of relationship found between attributions and own self-regulatory behavior.

Relationship attributions are largely viewed from the perspective of explaining a partner's behavior (Sumer & Cozzarelli, 2004). Thus it follows there would be a more robust association between attributions for negative partner behavior and perceptions of partner self-regulation compared to perceptions of own self-regulation. Self-attributions have been explored in the past (e.g. Fincham, Beach, & Baucom, 1987) and have been found to differ in nature from partner attributions in distressed relationships, with less altruism displayed by distressed partners compared to nondistressed partners when exploring the causes of negative events and attributing these to self or partner behavior. It would be an interesting avenue of further exploration to see if self-attributions predict perceptions of own self-regulatory behavior more reliably than partner attributions.

Therapeutic Practice Implications

The fact that attributions may partially mediate the relationship between attachment insecurity and perceptions of a partner's self-regulation with regard to the relationship has a number of important practice implications, for practitioners of therapies such as emotion-focused couples therapy (EFT; Johnson & Denton, 2002; chapter 23 in this volume). In EFT, therapists reframe relationship distress in terms of attachment needs and the fears partners have of expressing these needs. As therapy progresses, therapists teach the clients to better communicate their attachment insecurities and problem-solve their differences. However, the findings presented in this chapter suggest that therapeutic gains in EFT are most likely to occur when therapy *also* targets the attributions associated with the expressed attachment insecurities. Simply targeting attachment insecurity may not be enough to produce long-term changes in relationships; for EFT to be maximally effective it may also need to target the modification of partners' negative attributions.

A consideration of the important contribution of attributions to couples therapy is also relevant to practitioners of self-regulatory couples therapy (SRCT; Halford, 2001). Here the goal is for partners to learn how to appraise their relationship, identify personal goals for change, and implement and evaluate these goals. The goals for changing target behavior, cognition or affect, and the data presented here, suggest it may be important to also consider a person's cognitive-processing style—both attachment insecurity and attributions may lead a person towards biased information processing, and this may be especially relevant when considering a person's perceptions of their partner's self-regulatory relationship behavior. The implications of predicting a partner's perceived self-regulation behavior are also related to the regulation of partner behavior as discussed in chapter 16 in this volume.

Conclusions

In this chapter, I discussed a program of research that illustrated how attributions about negative partner behavior play a role in mediating the association between attachment anxiety and avoidance and relationship self-regulation, in a community sample of couples. In addition to strengthening the argument that attachment orientations involve a biased-attentional, cognitive-processing element, the current research also contributed to our understanding of relationship self-regulation, notably that an individual's perception of their partner's regulatory efforts and strategies can be partially explained by the presence of attachment insecurity and attributions for negative partner behavior. The implications of the results were discussed from a therapeutic position, suggesting EFT and SRCT would benefit from understanding that attachment orientations and attributions cannot be ignored when presenting couple interventions designed to ameliorate relationship distress.

References

Bartholomew, K., & Horowitz, L. M. (1991). Attachment styles among young adults: A test of a four-category model. *Journal of Personality and Social Psychology, 61*, 226–244.

Bowlby, J. (1998). *Attachment and loss: Vol. 2 Separation: Anxiety and anger*. London: Pimlico. (Original work published 1973).

Bradbury, T. N., & Fincham, F. D. (1990a). Preventing marital dysfunction: Review and analysis. In F. D. Fincham & T. N. Bradbury (Eds.), *The psychology of marriage: Basic issues and applications* (pp. 375–401). New York: Guilford Press.

Bradbury, T. N., & Fincham, F. D. (1990b). Attributions in marriage: Review and critique. *Psychological Bulletin, 107*, 3–33.

Brennan, K. A., Clark, C. L., & Shaver, P. R. (1998). Self-report measurement of adult attachment: An integrative overview. In J. A. Simpson & W. S. Rholes (Eds.), *Attachment theory and close relationships* (pp. 44–76). New York: Guilford Press.

Campbell, L., & Kashy, D. A. (2002). Estimating actor, partner, and interaction effects for dyadic data using proc mixed and hlm: A user-friendly guide. *Personal Relationships, 9*, 327–342.

Chatav, Y., & Whisman, M. A. (2009). Partner schemas and relationship functioning: A states of mind analysis. *Behavior Therapy, 40*, 50–56.

Collins, N. L., Ford, M. B., Guichard, A. C., & Allard, L. M. (2006). Working models of attachment and attribution processes in intimate relationships. *Personality and Social Psychology Bulletin, 32*, 201–219.

Feeney, J. A., & Noller, P. (1996). *Adult attachment*. Thousand Oaks, CA: Sage.

Fincham, F. D., Beach, S. R., & Baucom, D. H. (1987). Attribution processes in distressed and nondistressed couples: 4. Self-partner attribution differences. *Journal of Personality and Social Psychology, 52*, 739–748.

Fincham, F. D., & Bradbury, T. N. (1992). Assessing attributions in marriage: The relationship attribution measure. *Journal of Personality and Social Psychology, 62*, 457–468.

Fincham, F. D., Bradbury, T. N., & Grych, J. H. (1990). Conflict in close relationships: The role of intrapersonal phenomena. In S. Graham & V. S. Folkes (Eds.), *Attribution theory: Applications to achievement, mental health, and interpersonal conflict* (pp. 161–184). Hillsdale, NJ: Erlbaum.

Fincham, F. D., Harold, G. T., & Gano Phillips, S. (2000). The longitudinal association between attributions and marital satisfaction: Direction of effects and role of efficacy expectations. *Journal of Family Psychology, 14*, 267–285.

Finkel, E. J., Dewall, C. N., Slotter, E. B., Oaten, M., & Foshee, V. A. (2009). Self-regulatory failure and intimate partner violence perpetration. *Journal of Personality and Social Psychology, 97*, 483–499.

Fletcher, G. J., Fincham, F. D., Cramer, L., & Heron, N. (1987). The role of attributions in the development of dating relationships. *Journal of Personality and Social Psychology, 53*, 481–489.

Fletcher, G. J. O. (1993). Cognition in close relationships. *New Zealand Journal of Psychology, 22*, 69–81.

Gallo, L. C., & Smith, T. W. (2001). Attachment style in marriage: Adjustment and responses to interaction. *Journal of Social and Personal Relationships, 18*, 263–289.

Halford, K. W., Sanders, M. R., & Behrens, B. C. (1994). Self-regulation in behavioral couples' therapy. *Behavior Therapy, 25*, 431–452.

Halford, K. W., Wilson, K. L., Lizzio, A., & Moore, E. (2002). Does working at a relationship work? Relationship self-regulation and relationship outcomes. In P. Noller & J. A. Feeney (Eds.), *Understanding marriage: Developments in the study of couple interaction* (pp. 493–517). Cambridge, U.K.: Cambridge University Press.

Halford, W. K. (2001). *Brief therapy for couples: Helping partners help themselves*. New York: Guilford Press.

Halford, W. K., Farrugia, C., Lizzio, A., & Wilson, K. (2010). Relationship aggression, violence and self-regulation in Australian newlywed couples. *Australian Journal of Psychology, 62*, 82–92.

Hazan, C., & Shaver, P. (1987). Romantic love conceptualized as an attachment process. *Journal of Personality and Social Psychology, 52*, 511–524.

Johnson, S. M., & Denton, W. H. (2002). Emotionally focused couple therapy: Creating secure connections. In A. S. Gurman & N. S. Jacobson (Eds.), *Clinical handbook of couple therapy* (pp. 221–250). New York: Guilford Press.

Karney, B. R., & Bradbury, T. N. (2000). Attributions in marriage: State or trait? A growth curve analysis. *Journal of Personality and Social Psychology, 78*, 295–309.

Karoly, P. (1993). Mechanisms of self-regulation: A systems view. *Annual Review of Psychology, 44*, 23–52.

Kenny, D. A., Kashy, D. A., & Cook, W. L. (2006). *Dyadic data analysis*. New York: Guilford Press.

Mackinnon, D. P. (2008). *Introduction to statistical mediation analysis*. New York: Taylor & Francis.

Mikulincer, M. (1998). Adult attachment style and affect regulation: Strategic variations in self-appraisals. *Journal of Personality and Social Psychology, 75*, 420–435.

Mikulincer, M., Shaver, P. R., Sapir-Lavid, Y., & Avihou-Kanza, N. (2009). What's inside the minds of securely and insecurely attached people? The secure-base script and its associations with attachment-style dimensions. *Journal of Personality and Social Psychology, 97*, 615–633.

Pearce, Z. J., & Halford, W. K. (2008). Do attributions mediate the association between attachment and negative couple communication? *Personal Relationships, 15*, 155–170.

Preacher, K. J., & Hayes, A. F. (2008). Asymptotic and resampling strategies for assessing and comparing indirect effects in multiple mediator models. *Behavior Research Methods, 40*, 879–891.

Schaefer-Porter, R. L., & Hendrick, S. S. (2000). Attributions, behavioral reactions and relationship satisfaction. *Family Therapy, 27*, 1–18.

Shaver, P. R., & Mikulincer, M. (2002). Attachment-related psychodynamics. *Attachment and Human Development, 4*, 133–161.

Sumer, N., & Cozzarelli, C. (2004). The impact of adult attachment on partner and self-attributions and relationship quality. *Personal Relationships, 11*, 355–371.

Tashiro, T., & Frazier, P. (2003). "I'll never be in a relationship like that again": Personal growth following romantic relationship breakups. *Personal Relationships, 10*, 113–128.

Wilson, K. L., Charker, J., Alizzio, A., Kalford, K., & Kimlin, S. (2005). Assessing how much couples work at their relationship: The behavioral self-regulation for effective relationships scale. *Journal of Family Psychology, 19*, 385–393.

Zimmermann, P. (1999). Structure and functions of internal working models of attachment and their role for emotion regulation. *Attachment & Human Development, 1*, 291–306.

16

The Costs and Benefits of Trying to Change Intimate Partners

Nickola C. Overall

As people's relationships develop into committed partnerships, individuals hand over some control of their own well-being to their partners (Kelly & Thibaut, 1978). Mary's future dreams and happiness, for example, depend on John's continued investment in their relationship. Mary's goals and desires on a day-to-day basis also depend on John's behavior, and vice versa. Take the following common situations: John wants to spend time together but Mary is working overtime, Mary wants the house tidier but John thinks it is clean enough, Mary wants to save for house renovations but John wants to enjoy life now, John desires more physical intimacy but Mary is rarely in the mood, Mary wants John to pay less attention to an attractive work colleague but John doesn't see any harm in flirting, and John likes to go the pub on Friday nights but Mary feels stuck at home with the kids.

Most couples continue to confront these types of problems throughout their relationship, including conflict over amount and quality of time spent together, disputes over money and dividing up domestic responsibilities, jealousy, and difficult topics like sex, drugs, and alcohol (Papp, Cummings, & Goeke-Morey, 2009; Storaasli & Markman, 1990). These common problems highlight that at the heart of conflict is a desire for the partner to think and behave in ways more consistent with personal goals—intimates want their partner to devote more time to shared activities, spend less or share more money, participate equally in household chores and childcare, desire more sex, and so on. Thus, central to people's efforts to resolve conflict is a focus on changing the partner's attitudes and behavior.

The Wiley-Blackwell Handbook of Couples and Family Relationships, First Edition.
Edited by Patricia Noller and Gery C. Karantzas.

Supporting the proposition that people attempt to change their partners, Overall, Fletcher, and Simpson (2006) found that people often try to improve their relationship by trying to alter attributes of their partners that are failing to meet expectations—a process they called partner regulation. Indeed, despite being relatively happy in their relationships, over 95% of participants across samples reported attempting to change or regulate some aspect of their partner, including features fundamental to the common problems listed above, such as intimacy, sensitivity, understanding, finances, vitality, and trustworthiness.

Unfortunately, however, Overall et al. (2006) also found that, instead of improving the relationship, more strenuous partner regulation was associated with lower relationship quality of both partners. Analyses suggested two reasons for this effect. First, greater attempts to change the partner were associated with the partner feeling less valued and accepted. The more John tries to get Mary to be more intimate, the more it will dawn on Mary that John is evaluating her poorly. Second, agents of change generally believed their regulation attempts were ineffective and, therefore, perceived their partner and their relationship more negatively. If John tries hard to spend more time together but Mary works instead, this situation signals to John that Mary is not committed to their relationship and he becomes more dissatisfied. When regulatory efforts are relatively successful, however, intimates evaluate their partners and relationship more positively.

Despite a huge body of research examining how couples attempt to resolve conflict (see chapters 8, 9, 10 in this volume), there has been minimal empirical work outlining the mechanisms through which different problem-solving strategies influence relationship outcomes (Bradbury, Rogge, & Lawrence, 2001). The findings by Overall et al. (2006) suggest two central ways partner regulation attempts—and other conflict resolution strategies—will impact relationship functioning. Demonstrating the interdependent nature of relationships, these mechanisms center on the partner, including (i) how accepted and valued the partner feels, and (ii) whether the partner changes targeted qualities or behaviors.

In the remainder of this chapter I explore these mechanisms in more detail and describe research demonstrating the outcomes of partner regulation attempts across time. In the final section, the chapter focuses on practical implications, such as how couples should approach conflict within their relationships.

Partner Regulation Attempts and Perceived Regard

How people believe they are evaluated by their partners plays a pivotal role in the functioning of intimate relationships (Murray, Holmes, & Collins, 2006; Reis, Clark, & Holmes, 2004). People who think they are positively regarded by their partner, trust in their partner's continued commitment and cope constructively with relationship difficulties by trying to restore closeness. Individuals who negatively evaluate their partner's regard experience poor relationship satisfaction and protect themselves from expected rejection by devaluing and withdrawing from their partner (Murray, Bellavia, Rose, & Griffin, 2003).

People's perceptions of their partner's regard, referred to as perceived regard, is powerfully shaped by how the partner behaves toward the self. For example, when partners respond in an accommodative and forgiving fashion to poor behavior, this attitude conveys commitment. Accordingly, intimates become more trustful and invested over time (Weiselquist, Rusbult, Foster, & Agnew 1999). Similarly, when partners respond more positively to self-disclosures, this behavior increases perceived regard and acceptance (Laurenceau, Feldman Barrett, & Pietromonaco, 1998). Thus, caring partner behavior communicates high regard and fosters faith in the partner's continued investment in the relationship.

When partners try to change aspects of the self, in contrast, this behavior communicates dissatisfaction and low regard. Overall et al. (2006) found that receiving regulation attempts from the partner was associated with intimates inferring that they did not live up to their partners' standards. Assessing the impact of regulation attempts longitudinally, Overall and Fletcher (2010) also demonstrated that the more partners tried to change self-attributes central to evaluations in long-term intimate relationship contexts—warmth and trustworthiness, attractiveness and vitality, and status and resources—the more targeted partners evaluated their partner's regard of these specific qualities negatively 6 months later.

By reducing perceived regard, regulation attempts will have important and detrimental effects on the targeted partner. First, consistent with prior work demonstrating that perceiving positive regard by the partner is crucial in feeling secure within relationships (see Murray et al., 2006), Overall and Fletcher (2010) found that decreases in perceived regard were associated with lower relationship quality. Second, by reducing perceived regard, partners' attempts to change self-attributes produced more negative self-perceptions of the specific features targeted as well as more negative evaluations of global self-worth across time.

In sum, the more Mary tries to enhance John's ability to communicate more sensitively, the more John (i) realizes that Mary is dissatisfied with his level of understanding and sensitivity, and John therefore (ii) becomes less satisfied with the relationship and (iii) begins to evaluate himself more negatively. These findings underscore the vulnerability of the targeted partner when faced with their partner's regulation attempts.

Partner Regulation Strategies and Perceived Regard

The negative impact of partners' regulation on the targeted partner should depend on the strategies used to produce change. Three decades of research investigating communication within problem-solving interactions has shown that engaging in hostile, critical, or demanding behavior leads to lower relationship satisfaction over time (for reviews, see chapter 10 in this volume; Gottman, 1998; Gottman & Notarius, 2000; Karney & Bradbury, 1995; Weiss & Heyman, 1997). These destructive effects might primarily arise because of the impact negative communication strategies have on the targeted partner. For example, blaming and demanding communication from the person who wants change often elicits defensive withdrawal, and this demand–withdraw pattern predicts reduced relationship satisfaction (chapters 9, 10 in this volume; Christensen & Heavey, 1990; Heavey, Christensen, & Malamuth, 1995; Klinetob & Smith, 1996). Negative strategies, like guilt induction, pressures for change, and coercive derogation, have also been linked with greater hostility, defensiveness and resistance by the targeted partner (Gottman, 1998; Lewis & Rook, 1999; Oriña, Wood, & Simpson, 2002).

Accordingly, negative regulation strategies may produce more pronounced reductions in perceived regard and, in turn, lower self and relationship evaluations. In contrast, more positive regulation strategies, such as reasoning and expressing love and affection, should communicate concern and respect, and, as a result, induce favourable evaluations by the target. Consistently, cross-sectional analyses by Overall and Fletcher (2010) revealed that when partners engaged in hostile and critical regulation strategies, targeted intimates experienced more severe drops in perceived regard and evaluated their relationships more negatively. Over time, however, greater receipt of positive strategies generally predicted more positive inferences regarding the partner's regard.

Taken together, Overall and Fletcher's (2010) findings demonstrate that one key mechanism through which different conflict strategies will impact the relationship is the degree to which that behavior signals care and esteem versus contempt and disregard. Moreover, although trying to change intimate partners has a corrosive effect on the way targeted partners feel regarded and evaluate their own self-worth, positive regulation strategies, such as expressing affection and validation during regulation attempts, might offset these negative effects by communicating that the partner cares for and loves the target.

Overall and Fletcher (2010) also found another positive side to partner regulation. Targets directly responded to their partner's regulation efforts by attempting to change targeted characteristics. The more Mary tries to change John's sensitivity, the more John will try to be more sensitive and understanding, despite the fact that he is also feeling less regarded by Mary. Targets were also more receptive and responded with greater effort to change when their partners engaged in more positive regulation strategies, but were generally more resistant to change when their partners used more negative regulation strategies.

These latter findings lead back to the second route through which partner regulation will impact on the relationship—whether attempts to change the partner are successful. As the pattern above indicates, the degree to which targeted partners will change should be influenced by how desire for change is communicated.

Communication Strategies and Success in Producing Change

Negative strategies, such as Mary nagging or demanding change, are likely to be poorly received by John and don't really motivate John to listen more attentively to Mary. Accordingly, these strategies may be ineffective at producing desired change compared to more positive strategies, such as using humor and affection to soften regulation attempts. This assumption fits with the findings and prior literature already described in this chapter.

However, although greater expression of negative affect (e.g., anger) and communicative behavior (e.g., blame and hostility) during conflict interactions are negatively associated with concurrent relationship satisfaction in many studies, a handful of investigations have found that negative strategies predict relative *increases* in relationship satisfaction across time (Cohan & Bradbury, 1997; Gottman & Krokoff, 1989; Heavey, Layne, & Christensen, 1993; Karney & Bradbury, 1997). In these four studies, active negative communication behavior such as disagreeing, criticizing, blaming, pressuring for change, and expressing anger during problem-solving discussions were associated with relatively greater relationship satisfaction across time periods of 1 to 4 years. Cohan and Bradbury (1997) and Gottman and Krokoff (1989) also found that positive forms of communication, such as agreement and humor, predicted greater probability of divorce or more negative long-term relationship evaluations.

One explanation for these opposing findings is that directly confronting the problem and engaging in conflict is more successful in resolving problems because it motivates partners to bring about desired change (see Gottman & Krokoff, 1989; Heavey et al., 1993, 1995; Holmes & Murray, 1996). Consistent with this proposition, the majority of negative behaviors linked with positive longitudinal outcomes are active, direct, and partner-focused (e.g., criticism, blame, and rejection), whereas the positive behaviors tied to poorer outcomes are soft and minimize overt conflict (e.g., through the use of humor). Thus, distinguishing communication strategies according to both valence (positive and negative) and directness (direct versus indirect) may be pivotal in clarifying the short-term versus longitudinal impact of conflict behavior.

Figure 16.1 presents communication strategies that are commonly assessed within the conflict literature and can be distinguished according to both valence and directness. Direct communication strategies are explicit, overt, and partner-focused, such as providing rational reasons for change, weighing up the pros and cons of behavior, and offering solutions (positive) or demanding change and derogating, blaming, or threatening one's

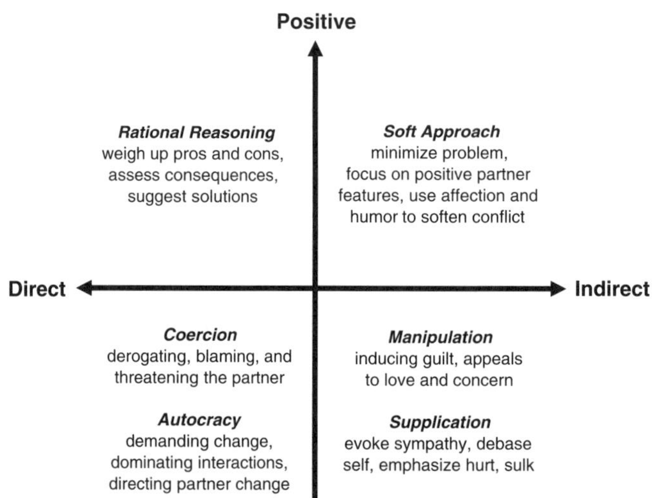

Figure 16.1 Communication strategies that vary in valence (positive and negative) and directness (direct versus indirect)

partner (negative) (see Figure 16.1). These tactics explicitly express discontent and directly impress upon the target the need for change. In the short term, a direct approach might produce defensiveness and negative affect in the targeted partner, such as reduced perceived regard. However, by clearly communicating the nature and seriousness of the problem, direct strategies might also lead to greater efforts to change by the targeted partner and therefore might be more successful at producing change over time.

Indirect strategies, by comparison, are passive or covert ways to resolve issues and bring about change, such as using humor (positive) or evoking guilt (negative) (see Figure 16.1). These tactics are likely to be much less efficient in generating change. For example, minimizing the problem, focusing on more positive partner features, and using positive affect to soften conflict might downplay the severity of the problem and need for change. In the short term, this behavior should reduce conflict and convey perceived regard. In the long term, however, soft positive strategies might do little to spur partner change.

To test these ideas, Overall, Fletcher, Simpson, and Sibley (2009) recorded couples discussing aspects of each other they wanted to change. Features targeted for change included interpersonal qualities like commitment, trust, and intimacy (55%); being self-confident, active, and outgoing (23%); personal attributes such as physical appearance, finances, and ambition (12%); and annoying habits such as tidiness and sleeping patterns (10%).

To test which of the four types of strategies were successful in producing change in the target, the agent's (the person wanting change) behavior was coded according to the communication strategies in Figure 16.1. Immediately following the discussion both partners rated how successful the discussion and the agent were in bringing about change or intention to change, and then couples were followed up multiple times over the course of a year to assess how much partners produced change in the targeted features.

As predicted, the different communication strategies presented in Figure 16.1 had different short-term versus long-term consequences. When agents utilized more negative-direct regulation strategies, such as being coercive and demanding change, the discussion was perceived to be relatively ineffective at motivating change. Positive-direct strategies, such as explicitly discussing the consequences of partner behavior, also predicted lower ratings of immediate success. Thus, frank and explicit attempts to change the partner, even if expressed without anger and hostility, seem to produce ill feelings in the relationship that temporarily exacerbate conflict.

The short-term failure of direct strategies probably occurs because open and candid communication makes it abundantly clear to the target that the partner's regard is waning. This feedback is likely to provoke reciprocation of negative affect and defensive reactions (Gottman, 1994, 1998) and reduce openness and willingness to change, thereby diminishing relationship satisfaction for both partners. For example, the use of more negative-direct communication produced greater tension and upset during the discussion and elicited greater negative-direct behavior by the target. Moreover, targets who responded more bluntly and negatively demonstrated slower progress in change over time.

Despite being a bitter pill to swallow initially, however, both positive and negative direct strategies predicted greater change in targeted features over the following year. Thus, a direct approach increases negativity and conflict immediately but because direct strategies clearly communicate the nature and severity of the problem, the target is more likely to grasp the need for change and be motivated to attempt changing the self.

In contrast, although greater use of positive-indirect strategies was associated with initial perceptions of greater success and less distress in the interactions, there was no connection between the use of positive-indirect strategies and change across time. A soft tactful approach may protect felt-regard in the short term but these tactics probably lessen the salience and visibility of the problem and thus the targeted partner is likely to remain blithely unaware of the extent of the problem (also see Drigotas, Whitney, & Rusbult, 1995). In reality, a soft approach may communicate that changes in attitudes and behavior are unnecessary, and therefore fail to motivate change in targeted traits or behaviors.

Viewed together, the studies presented illustrate that specific types of communication strategies will have different, and sometimes opposing, consequences depending on their valence and directness. For example, a critical blaming approach (negative-direct behavior) should be more likely to prompt change (as a result of directness) but should also be accompanied by the souring of perceived regard and relationship evaluations (due to valence). Such negative effects associated with coercive and hostile communication are unlikely to be fleeting, and the positive changes that are produced by direct strategies may counterbalance but *not* reverse the negative impact of these behaviors. Accordingly, in the Overall et al. (2009) study, greater negative-direct strategies and associated target change did not predict improvements in relationship quality over time. Instead, the costs and benefits of negative-direct strategies likely cancelled each other out.

Practical Implications: Considerations for Therapists and Couples

The more frequently couples face relationship problems and conflict the more their satisfaction with their relationship declines over time and the more likely they will break up or divorce (Kluwer & Johnson, 2007; Murray, Holmes, & Griffin, 1996; Orbuch, Veroff, Hassan, & Horrocks, 2002). How intimates respond to and negotiate relationship problems also has major implications for relationship well-being. The way couples communicate about their relationship difficulties is one of the most common and pressing problems couples identify (Broderick, 1981; Papp et al., 2009; Storaasli & Markman, 1990). Relationship therapists also report that dysfunctional communication is the most common complaint but the most damaging and difficult to treat problem (Geiss & O'Leary, 1981). And not surprisingly, all relationship therapies emphasize improving communication (see Jacobson & Gurman, 1995).

By examining how communication influences important outcomes, such as by motivating the partner to change or reducing trust and felt regard, research on partner regulation offers valuable direction regarding the types of resolution strategies couples should be encouraged to use. First, partner regulation, particularly if direct strategies are employed, does tend to motivate target change and therefore should improve relationships. Second, however, partner regulation, particularly if negative and direct strategies are used, signals to the partner that they are regarded poorly, undermining relationship satisfaction and deflating the target's self-worth. Thus, the increases in problem resolution arising from direct regulation strategies might be best accomplished when using tactics that also communicate care and regard, such as directly discussing problems and suggesting solutions, as long as the message is not gift-wrapped to the point that it appears as if the communicator does not greatly care whether the problem is fixed or not.

The ultimate impact of different communication behaviors will, however, depend on the type and severity of the problem couples are dealing with. In the context of more serious problems, it is more important to resolve relationship difficulties and thus employ direct communication that produces change, even if that means expressing negative affect like anger. In contrast, hostile communication might be uniformly damaging when minor difficulties do not warrant such a tough no-holds-barred approach.

A recent study by McNulty and Russell (2010) provides supporting evidence. They found that blaming, commanding, and rejecting the partner during problem-solving discussions predicted more stable and satisfying relationships for those couples who were initially dealing with more serious problems. In contrast, couples who engaged in more blame and criticism but were not threatened by severe problems suffered growing problems and in turn declines in satisfaction across time. Importantly, negative behaviors that did not target the problem directly, such as avoiding responsibility and sarcasm, were linked with negative outcomes regardless of problem severity. In sum, only negative behaviors that represent direct efforts to get the problem changed are beneficial for relationships, and only when something really needs to be changed.

Likewise, a positive approach such as generating positive and benign attributions, expecting that problems can be resolved, and forgiving partners should only be beneficial if partners cease to behave negatively and problems do improve. McNulty, O'Mara, and Karney (2008), for example, found that more forgiving explanations for negative partner behavior led to relative increases in satisfaction only when couples were dealing with comparatively minor problems. When couples were facing severe problems, tolerant attributions predicted greater declines in satisfaction precisely because problems continued to worsen over time. Similarly, McNulty (2008) found that forgiveness maintained satisfaction only when partners deserved it. When intimates were more forgiving to partners who often behaved negatively, relationship problems continued to grow and satisfaction persistently declined.

As a whole, the research indicates that couples need to adjust communication strategies and behaviors to the demands of the problem. Partners who adopt a direct and negative regulation strategy or a soft and positive approach as a consistent default strategy might (i) do irreparable damage to their relationship when direct and heated communication is disproportionate to issue severity, or (ii) never overcome relationship hurdles when smothering negative feelings and actions means issues remain unaddressed.

The trick to helping couples, therefore, might be teaching intimates how and when to use different communication strategies. When couples need to be in conflict resolution mode, the expression of anger and even hostility has some benefits. In this context, a direct approach communicates to the partner that "I am not a doormat, this is serious, and you need to change your behavior." Reassurance of regard will also be important, however, in counteracting targets' injured feelings of value and acceptance (see chapter 20 in this volume). In response to more minor problems, a softer approach will more likely preserve felt-security and regard in the relationship, as long as minor problems do not escalate in severity. In that event, partners will need to switch to a more positive-direct strategy.

A few disclaimers are necessary here. Presumably there is a level at which criticism and hostility reach the point where it creates so much acrimony that it destroys the relationship before change can be made. The level of negativity evident in the research discussed here is likely to be mild compared to the high levels of conflict couples might experience before seeking help. When couples are experiencing major relationship difficulties, negative-direct communication may simply reaffirm that the relationship has become untenable. Moreover, major presenting problems like infidelity might rock relationship foundations so greatly that any further damages to perceived regard and closeness negate any benefit negative-direct communication might produce.

Finally, there is not a researcher in the world who would argue that constant criticism or hostility, high levels of very hurtful behavior, or verbal and physical aggression is good for relationships. The negative-direct communication that produced positive changes in this research included expressions of anger, dissatisfaction, blame, and criticism while couples discussed issues in a relatively composed manner. Thus, the important message is not to be critical and hostile but to directly convey anger and dissatisfaction to ensure partners get an accurate assessment of the problem and are motivated to change. Furthermore, to reiterate, the best strategy will be one that enhances understanding of the nature and severity of the problem while also reassuring targeted partners that they are valued and cared for.

Alternatives to partner regulation

The practical implications discussed above might appear to contradict respected and successful therapeutic approaches such as acceptance therapy. Partner change might not be the only route to relationship improvement and accepting relationship problems is another viable strategy. However, fostering acceptance as a therapeutic technique is an addition to traditional couples therapy focusing on behavioral change and pursues acceptance of problems that cannot be resolved (Jacobson & Christensen, 1998). Thus, acceptance might be the only way relationships can be maintained if problem-related partner attributes and behavior are unalterable. Moreover, acceptance therapy primarily focuses on changing how partners express emotion and communicate about problems, and successfully increases positive communication patterns during and immediately post therapy (Christensen, Atkins, Berns, Wheeler, Baucom, & Simpson, 2004). Consistent with the above arguments, reducing partner blame and hostility will minimize many costs associated with partner regulation. Nevertheless, over the long term, positive communication will only be effective if tactics also directly target the problem. Positive-indirect strategies that do not produce change, in contrast, risk damaging the relationship over time by leaving problems unresolved.

This dilemma highlights an important distinction between target outcomes (such as perceived regard) and agent outcomes (including improving areas of dissatisfaction). Positive communication is beneficial for targets because it conveys positive regard and builds trust and commitment. Too soft an approach, however, leaves targets happily oblivious to their partner's dissatisfaction. Although benefiting the target of change, because targets do not understand the need to change and alter very little, the partner who wants improvement might become increasingly dissatisfied. Assessing the consequences of positive-indirect behavior for the agent using two social interaction diaries, Overall, Sibley, and Travaglia (2010) found that positive-indirect strategies were less noticed by targeted partners and, hence, had little impact on the problem, with targets failing to modify negative behavior. Of importance, this lack of recognition and reciprocation left agents feeling less valued and less close to their partners.

It takes great effort and motivation to overcome anger and hurt feelings in order to accept problematic partner behavior, forgive and forget, minimize problems, and concentrate on more positive partner features (see chapter 20 in this volume). It is not surprising that when these efforts go unrecognized and unacknowledged individuals feel undervalued and disconnected from their partners. Moreover, by not generating positive partner responses, closeness, and perceived regard, a soft accepting approach may foster disappointment and resentment if relationship maintenance attempts continually fail to pay off. At its worse, positive-indirect attempts that go ignored may reduce chronic feelings of regard and erode agents' satisfaction and commitment because they face recurring problems that do not improve.

Another, and perhaps more successful, means of improving relationships without the costs associated with partner regulation, is changing the self in order to improve the relationship. Halford et al. (1994) argue that the low efficacy and high relapse rates associated with traditional behavioral couples therapy may be because emphasis is placed on promoting changes in the partner's behaviors. Accordingly, Halford et al. (1994) incorporate a focus on self-regulation within couple therapy, including the appraisal of the individual's own behaviors and consequent behavioral change goals. Positive assessments of this approach suggest that promoting self-evaluation and personal change enhances relationship satisfaction and stability (Halford et al. 2004; also see Halford, 2001). In addition, greater relationship-related self-regulation is linked with higher concurrent satisfaction (Halford et al. 2007; Wilson et al., 2005).

Hira and Overall (2010) also recently found that the consequences of relationship improvement attempts depended on whether intimates targeted the partner versus the self to produce change. First, blaming and focusing improvement attempts on the partner were associated with lower perceptions of success in producing desired relationship changes and lower relationship quality (although this study did not track the change that was produced across time). Second, successful change of self-attributes was associated with greater improvement of targeted attributes of the relationship but was not linked with more global evaluations of relationship quality and satisfaction.

Why might successful self-change that improves problematic aspects of the relationship not generate more favorable evaluations of relationship quality? The most likely explanation rests on the interdependence that exists between couples; improving relationship problems requires both partners. Any improvement the individual makes is likely to feel hollow if the partner does not recognize or play a role in the change. As with positive-indirect strategies, therefore, individuals could be left believing they are doing all the work without the crucial payoff if the partner's contribution to the problem is not modified.

Supporting this reasoning, when *partners* were perceived to be trying to change the self and were more successful in their self-regulation attempts, individuals reported greater relationship improvement and they evaluated their relationship more positively. Thus, as in the prior work, successful relationship improvement and associated judgments of relationship quality hinged on whether the partner engaged in successful change attempts. Focusing again on the agents' outcomes, attempts to produce desired changes not only improve the relationship but signal to the agent that the targeted partner is invested in the relationship, regards and values the agent, and is responsive to the agent's needs (see Reis et al., 2004). Thus, partner regulation communicates low regard to the target of change but the target's responsiveness to the agent's regulation attempts conveys commitment and regard to the partner who wanted change.

To recap, highlighting the difficulties in maintaining relationships, successful self-change is unlikely to bring about vast improvements in relationship quality unless persistent self-regulation efforts trigger the partner's cooperation in improving specific relationship problems. Instead, encouraging couples to engage in self-regulation to improve their relationships may be beneficial because the change individuals make enhances the satisfaction of their partners (and vice versa). Moreover, expressing a desire for partner change may not be detrimental if both couple members are taught skills to (a) communicate this need positively with reassurance of regard; (b) improve self-attributes that are contributing to relationship problems; and (c) recognize their partner's efforts to resolve relationship issues. This type of approach may promote reciprocal self-change efforts by both partners while maintaining feelings of value and intimacy.

Conclusion

Like it or not, couples often want, and try, to change each other. Moreover, regardless of how hard Mary attempts to improve her relationship with John, desired changes can only be ultimately achieved if John also cooperates to produce change. Finding the best way to help couples, therefore, will involve identifying ways in which partners can motivate each other to change, while offsetting reactance, hurt feelings, and defensiveness. Whether the problems are severe or only minor irritations, a positive but direct approach seems to offer the optimum balance. Direct communication provides the understanding and incentive necessary for targets to alter problem-inducing attitudes and behavior. Successful changes by the target, in turn, improve conditions and display commitment and responsiveness, boosting the satisfaction of the partner who wanted change. By conveying care and regard, positive-direct communication achieves all this without damaging the targeted partner's felt-security and self-worth. Nevertheless, "it takes two." Both partners need to be responsive and work to sustain and improve their relationship, both partners need to communicate directly with love and regard, and both partners need to recognize the other's efforts.

References

Bradbury, T. N., Rogge, R. D., & Lawrence, E. (2001). Reconsidering the role of conflict in marriage. In A. Booth, N. Crouter, & M. Clements (Eds.) *Couples in conflict* (pp. 59–81). Hillsdale, NJ: Erlbaum.

Broderick, J. E. (1981). A method for derivation of areas of assessment in marital relationships. *American Journal of Family Therapy, 9*, 25–34.

Christensen, A., Atkins, D. C., Berns, S., Wheeler, J., Baucom, D. H., & Simpson, L. E. (2004). Traditional versus integrative behavioral couple therapy for significantly and chronically distressed married couples. *Journal of Consulting and Clinical Psychology, 72*, 176–191.

Christensen, A., & Heavey, C. L. (1990). Gender and social structure in the demand/withdraw pattern of marital conflict. *Journal of Personality and Social Psychology, 59*, 73–81.

Cohan, C. L., & Bradbury, T. N. (1997). Negative life events, marital interaction, and the longitudinal course of newlywed marriage. *Journal of Personality and Social Psychology, 73*, 114–128.

Drigotas, S. M., Whitney, G. A., & Rusbult, C. E. (1995). On the peculiarities of loyalty: A diary study of responses to dissatisfaction in everyday life. *Personality and Social Psychology Bulletin, 21*, 596–609.

Geiss, S. K., & O'Leary, K. D. (1981). Therapist ratings of frequency and severity of marital problems: Implications for research. *Journal of Marital and Family Therapy, 7*, 515–520.

Gottman, J. M. (1994). *What predicts divorce?* Hillsdale, NJ: Erlbaum.

Gottman, J. M. (1998). Psychology and the study of marital processes. *Annual Review of Psychology, 49*, 169–197.

Gottman, J. M. & Krokoff, L. J. (1989). Marital interaction and satisfaction: A longitudinal view. *Journal of Consulting and Clinical Psychology, 57*, 47–52.

Gottman, J. M. & Notarius, C. I. (2000). Decade review: Observing marital interaction. *Journal of Marriage and the Family, 62*, 927–947.

Halford, W. K. (2001). *Brief Couple Therapy*. New York: Guilford Press.

Halford, W. K., Lizzio, A., Wilson, K. L., Occhipinti, S. (2007). Does working at your marriage help? Couple relationship self-regulation and satisfaction in the first 4 years of marriage. *Journal of Family Psychology, 21*, 185–194.

Halford, W. K., Moore, E. M., Wilson, K. L., Dyer, C., & Farrugia, C. (2004). Benefits of a flexible delivery relationship education: An evaluation of the Couple CARE program. *Family Relations, 53*, 469–476.

Halford., W. K., Sanders, M. R., & Behrens, B. C. (1994). Self-regulation in behavioral couples' therapy. *Behavior Therapy, 25*, 431–452.

Heavey, C. L., Christensen, A., & Malamuth, N. M. (1995). The longitudinal impact of demand and withdrawal during marital conflict. *Journal of Consulting and Clinical Psychology, 63*, 797–801.

Heavey, C. L., Layne, C., & Christensen, A. (1993). Gender and conflict structure in marital interaction: A replication and extension. *Journal of Consulting and Clinical Psychology, 61*, 16–27.

Hira, N. S., & Overall, N. C. (2010). Improving intimate relationships: Targeting the partner versus changing the self. Manuscript submitted for publication.

Holmes, J. G., & Murray, S. L. (1996). Conflict in close relationships. In E. T. Higgins & A. Kruglanski (Eds.), *Social psychology: Handbook of basic principles* (pp. 622–654). New York: Guilford Press.

Jacobson, N. S., & Christensen, A. (1998). *Acceptance and change in couple therapy: A therapist's guide to transforming relationships*. New York: Norton.

Jacobson, N. S., & Gurman, A. S. (Eds.). (1995). *Clinical handbook of couple therapy* (2nd edn.). New York: Guilford Press.

Karney, B. R., & Bradbury, T. N. (1995). The longitudinal course of marital quality and stability: A review of theory, method and research. *Psychological Bulletin, 118*, 3–34.

Karney, B. R., & Bradbury, T. N. (1997). Neuroticism, marital interaction, and the trajectory of marital satisfaction. *Journal of Personality and Social Psychology, 72*, 1075–1092.

Kelly, H. H., & Thibaut, J. W. (1978). *Interpersonal relations*. New York: Wiley.

Klinetob, N. A., & Smith, D. A. (1996). Demand–withdraw communication in marital interaction: Tests of interpersonal contingency and gender role hypotheses. *Journal of Marriage and the Family, 58*, 945–957.

Kluwer, E. S., & Johnson, M. D. (2007). Conflict frequency and relationship quality across the transition to parenthood. *Journal of Marriage and the Family, 69*, 1089–1106.

Laurenceau, J. P., Feldman Barrett, L., & Pietromonaco, P. R. (1998). Intimacy as an interpersonal process: The importance of self-disclosure, partner disclosure, and perceived partner responsiveness in interpersonal exchanges. *Journal of Personality and Social Psychology, 74*, 1238–1251.

Lewis, M. A., & Rook, K. S. (1999). Social control in personal relationships: Impact on health behavior and psychological distress. *Health Psychology, 18*, 63–71.

McNulty, J. K. (2008). Tendencies to forgive in marriage: Putting the benefits into context. *Journal of Family Psychology, 22*, 171–175.

McNulty, J. K., O'Mara, E. M., & Karney B. R. (2008). Benevolent cognitions as a strategy of relationship maintenance: Don't sweat the small stuff . . . but it's not all small stuff. *Journal of Personality and Social Psychology, 94*, 631–646.

McNulty, J. K., & Russell, V. M. (2010). When "negative" behaviors are positive: A contextual analysis of the long-term effects of interpersonal communication. *Journal of Personality and Social Psychology, 98*, 587–604.

Murray, S. L., Bellavia, G. M., Rose, P., & Griffin, D. W. (2003). Once hurt, twice hurtful: How perceived regard regulates daily marital interactions. *Journal of Personality and Social Psychology, 84*, 126–147.

Murray, S. L., Holmes, J. G., & Collins, N. L. (2006). Optimizing assurance: The risk regulation system in relationships. *Psychological Bulletin, 132*, 641–666.

Murray, S. L., Holmes, J. G., & Griffin, D. W. (1996). The self-fulfilling nature of positive illusions in romantic relationships: Love is not blind, but prescient. *Journal of Personality and Social Psychology, 71*, 1155–1180.

Orbuch, T. L., Veroff, J., Hassan, H., & Horrocks, J. (2002). Who will divorce: A 14-year longitudinal study of black couples and white couples. *Journal of Social and Personal Relationships, 19*, 179–202.

Oriña, M. M., Wood, W., & Simpson, J. A. (2002). Strategies of influence in close relationships. *Journal of Experimental Social Psychology, 38*, 459–472.

Overall, N. C., & Fletcher, G. J. O. (2010). Perceiving regulation from intimate relationships: Reflected appraisal and self-regulation processes in close relationships. *Personal Relationships, 17*, 433–456.

Overall, N. C., Fletcher, G. J. O., & Simpson, J. A. (2006). Regulation processes in intimate relationships: The role of ideal standards. *Journal of Personality and Social Psychology, 91*, 662–685.

Overall, N. C., Fletcher, G. J. O., Simpson, J. A., & Sibley, C. G. (2009). Regulating partners in intimate relationships: The costs and benefits of different communication strategies. *Journal of Personality and Social Psychology, 96*, 620–639.

Overall, N. C., & Sibley, C. G., & Travaglia, L. K. (2010). Loyal but ignored: The benefits and costs of constructive communication behavior. *Personal Relationships, 17*, 127–148.

Papp, L. M., Cummings, E. M., & Goeke-Morey, M. C. (2009). For richer, for poorer: Money as a topic of marital conflict in the home. *Family Relations, 58*, 91–103.

Reis, H. T., Clark, M. S., & Holmes, J. (2004). Perceived partner responsiveness as an organizing construct in the study of intimacy and closeness. In D. J. Mashek & A. Aron (Eds.), *Handbook of closeness and intimacy* (pp. 201–225). Mahwah, NJ: Erlbaum.

Storaasli, R. D., & Markman, H. J. (1990). Relationship problems in the early stages of marriage: A longitudinal investigation. *Journal of Family Psychology, 4*, 80–98.

Weiss, R. L., & Heyman, R. E. (1997). A clinical-research overview of couple's interactions. In W. K. Halford & H. J. Markman (Eds.), *Clinical handbook of marriage and couples interventions* (pp. 13–41). Chichester, England: Wiley.

Wilson, K. L., Charker, J., Lizzio, A., Halford, K., & Kimlin, S. (2005). Assessing how much couples work at their relationship: The Behavioral Self-Regulation for Effective Relationships Scale. *Journal of Family Psychology, 19*, 385–393.

Weiselquist, J., Rusbult, C. E., Foster, C. A., & Agnew, C. R. (1999). Commitment, pro-relationship behavior, and trust in close relationships. *Journal of Personality and Social Psychology, 77*, 942–966.

17

Through the Eyes of Love

Bias and Accuracy in Intimate Relationships

Garth J. O. Fletcher and Patrick S. G. Kerr

> Love sees not with the eyes, but with the mind;
> And therefore is wing'd Cupid painted blind.
> William Shakespeare

Romantic love is often characterized as shot through with illusions and driven by strong emotions and wishful thinking—as "painted blind" to use Shakespeare's phrase. This thesis is theoretically plausible. From an evolutionary standpoint, romantic love is typically viewed as a commitment device designed to lead men and women to substantially invest for long periods of time in one another, and accordingly support any resultant offspring (Gonzaga & Haselton, 2008). The leap of faith required for long-term romantic commitments is thus likely to be powered by strong biologically based attachment emotions, which in turn, predispose individuals to put a charitable spin on judgments of their partners and relationships.

The theoretical credibility of this thesis is supported by a wealth of empirical evidence. For example, people routinely rate the chances of their own marriages as failing as considerably less than their perceptions of the population base rates (Fowers, Lyons, Montel, & Shaked, 2001), and keep their relationship doubts at bay by restructuring judgments or rewriting their relationship stories (see Murray, 2001). And, as love prospers and grows more intense, individuals increasingly exaggerate their similarity with their partners (Murray, Holmes, Bellavia, Griffin, & Dolderman., 2002), the extent to which

The Wiley-Blackwell Handbook of Couples and Family Relationships, First Edition.
Edited by Patricia Noller and Gery C. Karantzas.

their relationships have improved over time (Karney & Frye, 2002), and the extent to which their real-life partners resemble archetypal ideals (Murray, Holmes, & Griffin, 1996a, 1996b).

There are, however, strong arguments against the "love is blind" hypothesis. The simple fact that many long-term romantic relationships dissolve suggests that the motivating power of love to promote positive bias has its limitations. In addition, the use of evolutionary psychology to support this thesis is a double-edged sword. Evolutionary psychology rests on the Darwinian assumption that mate-selection criteria in species (including humans), and their associated attributes, evolved according to natural and sexual selection. The force of sexual selection to produce the cumbersome, dazzling tail of the peacock relies on the ability of the peahen to accurately perceive the size and quality of the peacock's tail. What typically goes unnoticed is that this Darwinian assumption also requires that human judgments of important attributes in the mating game, such as attractiveness, status, and kindness or trustworthiness, are assessed with reasonable accuracy. If instead, such judgments of potential or actual partners are (or were in our ancestral environment) hopelessly awry, then their use could not have played a role in the development or evolution of such attributes. Thus, the "love is blind" thesis, taken to extremes, undercuts a key assumption in evolutionary psychology.

Moreover, a broad array of empirical evidence suggests that lay judgments of partners and relationships are firmly tied to reality. For example, relationship evaluations quite strongly predict both interactive behavior (e.g., Fletcher & Thomas, 2000) and relationship dissolution (see Karney & Bradbury, 1995), and are shared across partners (e.g., Campbell, Simpson, Kashy, & Fletcher, 2001). Further, studies using a range of external criteria or benchmarks (including self-reports of the partner, observer ratings of interactive behavior, and the predicted future or recalled past states of the relationship) reveal quite good levels of accuracy in relationship and partner judgments (for a recent review see Fletcher & Kerr, in press).

Thus, we are left with an apparent paradox—love is both blind and firmly rooted in the real world. Few (if any) psychologists have argued that love is completely free of reality constraints or that judgments in intimate relationships are not biased in various ways. This observation reasonably suggests that both sides of the argument have some validity, but still leaves the conundrum unsolved. In this chapter we offer three solutions, and, in the process, draw some conclusions about how lay social cognition functions in intimate relationship contexts.

The three resolutions we offer can be summarized thus: bias can be (and often is) rational; bias can (and does) coexist with reality tracking; and couples may be aware of (and welcome) bias. We discuss each factor in turn.

Bias Can be (and Often is) Rational

The concept of "bias" in social judgment has a range of meanings, but the most important general ones addressed in the study of relationships, and social judgments more broadly, comprise (a) the undue influence that prior beliefs, lay theories, or emotional states (e.g., love) exert on specific judgments or perceptions (sometimes termed belief perseverance); and (b) the tendency for individuals to project their own beliefs and views onto their partner. We take each category in turn, and show that each process can be regarded as quite rational.

The "undue" influence of prior beliefs or theories

As noted, one way of defining bias is in terms of the way in which prior (lay) theories influence the way in which new information is processed. Indeed, it is a truism (with countless research examples) that laypeople's judgments are influenced by their prior beliefs, attitudes, and lay theories, with countless demonstrations, for example, that evaluations of relationships bias judgments of all kinds including attributions, predictions, and memories (for reviews see Fletcher & Boyes, 2008; Fletcher & Kerr, in press).

However, demonstrations of such bias do not show that people are systematically irrational, blind to the truth, or unscientific in any way. Scientists of all stripes quite properly use their theories to explain or interpret data routinely and pervasively (Fletcher, 1995), and weight the import of the data accordingly (a variant of Bayes' theorem which deals with conditional probabilities). In the same fashion, laypeople make judgments under conditions of uncertainty that reflect both the nature of the incoming data and their extant relationship theories (both local and general). For example, if Melissa is asked to make judgments about how similar she is to Owen along some personality dimensions, she will do so (in part) by accessing both her general and her local partner and relationship theories. If Melissa is in a very happy relationship, and she believes that more similarity in relationships produces more successful relationships (a common belief), this will quite rationally lead to biased judgments. In short, theory-guided judgments, either scientific or lay, are (by definition) biased judgments.

Of course, if individuals routinely ignored the incoming data (e.g., behavior from their partners) and relied completely on their pre-existent beliefs or lay theories (including relationship evaluations), then this would certainly show love is blind (and that laypeople are irrational). But the research evidence does not support this proposition. Instead it reveals that specific judgments and decisions in relationships are jointly determined by both pre-existent knowledge or lay theories and new information, and that relationship evaluations, beliefs, and so forth are not set in concrete but change in the face of new information (see Fletcher, 2002; Fletcher & Kerr, in press).

Take as an example a commonly cited article by Murray and Holmes (1993) in which participants were persuaded to think (by reading bogus *Psychology Today* articles) that either open disagreement (Study 1) or recognizing differences between partners (Study 2) are crucial to the development of intimacy in romantic relationships. Prior to these experimental manipulations, participants completed short exercises designed to buttress perceptions of their partners as rarely initiating disagreement or as being very similar to the self, respectively. The results convincingly showed how participants (relative to controls) resolved their freshly minted doubts by either embellishing the presence of open disagreement or couple differences, or by emphasizing or reinterpreting other aspects of their relationship to counter the suddenly apparent weakness. In short, the participants seemed to crush doubt and maintain their rose-tinted views by simply rewriting history and altering some key relationship perceptions—a process that looks at face value as anything but scientific or rational.

Note that this study cleverly engineered a lack of fit between local relationship theories and general theories. The highlighted results showed that participants commonly responded by altering some detailed components of their local relationship accounts. However, other results (that were not the primary focus) suggested that some participants developed more negative relationship evaluations, that some rejected the experimenter-supplied general theory completely, and that the manipulation (not surprisingly) did not work for participants who possessed prior local and relationship theories that were close to the manipulated versions. Thus, the participants overall seemed to have been principally motivated to maintain consistency between their local theories, their general theories, and their relationship judgments—an eminently rational, even scientific, process.

Projection

Another judgmental process sometimes referred to as a bias (e.g., Kenny & Acitelli, 2001) concerns the extent to which individuals project the self when making partner judgments. Projection is sometimes viewed as an artifact and therefore as something to be statistically controlled for. For example, it is possible that higher levels of relationship satisfaction are associated with either tracking accuracy or mean-level bias because happier couples tend to project more and also happen to be more similar. On the other hand, projection can also be viewed as a heuristic that individuals use to attain accuracy. If couples are similar to varying degrees on certain traits or dimensions, then projecting appropriately on these traits should lead to more accuracy.

Indeed, an examination of the results produced by Kenny and Acitelli (2001) and Schul and Vinokur (2000) appear to confirm this latter suggestion, with projection reaching substantial proportions for attributions like closeness, enjoying sex, family life events, relationship satisfaction, and financial strain, but (sensibly) being relatively weak for health, job satisfaction, or hours spent at work (for a more comprehensive review of the research that reaches the same conclusions see Fletcher & Kerr, in press).

Bias Can (and Does) Coexist with Reality Tracking

Accuracy of judgments can initially be defined simply in terms of their correspondence with reality. But, as psychologists have long known, the empirical investigation of accuracy quickly turns such an apparently straightforward definition into a sea of complexity. A fundamental beginning point is to distinguish between two kinds of accuracy: mean-level bias and tracking accuracy. This distinction is not new, having been pointed out by several authors over the years both in the relationship domain (Fletcher, 2002; Gagné & Lydon, 2004) and in other areas of research (Cronbach, 1955; Epley & Dunning, 2006; Fletcher, Reeder, & Bull, 1990; Funder & Colvin, 1997; Kenny & Albright, 1987). However, as noted by Epley and Dunning, its importance has largely gone unrecognized, and the distinction is often blurred or ignored in empirical articles.

Mean-level bias can be defined as differences in mean levels of a sample for a specific judgment and then comparing the judgment with some benchmark. Tracking accuracy can be formally defined as the association (typically a correlation) between a judgment or set of judgments and a relevant benchmark or set of benchmarks.

Consider the following example (adapted from Fletcher, 2002). As shown in Table 17.1, imagine that for a group of four couples, each man rates his female partner on the trait of warmth, and that we have gold-standard criteria showing that, in reality, Mary is 5 on warmth, Joanne 4, Iris 4, and Anna 3 (all on 7-point scales). If we take the first column of possible judgments (set a), it can be seen that all four male partners score a direct hit. Thus, the sample overall would produce no mean-level bias and attain perfect tracking accuracy. The next pattern of male ratings (set b) shows an elevated pattern of positive bias, but because each man rates his female partner at two units above her actual level of kindness, the sample shows perfect tracking accuracy ($r = 1.0$). Following the same logic, the remaining two sets (c and d) show patterns of low tracking accuracy and high positive bias, and low tracking accuracy and no bias, respectively.

Fletcher and Kerr (in press) carried out a meta-analysis of published studies of heterosexual romantic relationships, which used external benchmarks of some kind, and reported levels of tracking accuracy (98 studies) and/or mean-level bias (48 studies). They

Table 17.1 An Example Illustrating the Potential Independence of Mean-level Bias and Tracking. Accuracy of Partner Judgments across One Trait in a Sample of Four Couples

	Male perceptions of partner's trait (warmth)			
Benchmark ratings of female targets	*High accuracy No bias (a)*	*High accuracy High bias (b)*	*Low accuracy High bias (c)*	*Low accuracy No bias (d)*
Mary 5	5	7	6	2
Joanne 4	4	6	7	2
Iris 4	4	6	5	6
Anna 3	3	5	6	6
Mean-level bias				
Mean rating 4 across group	4	6	6	4
Tracking accuracy Correlations between perceptions and benchmarks across group	1.0	1.0	.00	−.71

Note: The above example assumes a scale of 1 to 7, where 1 = cold and 7 = warm.

reported that the relevant research could be reliably categorized into six distinct categories: (1) judgments of partner personality traits; (2) judgments of negative attitudes, beliefs, or behaviors (e.g., aggression or criticism) directed to the partner or relationship; (3) judgments of positive attitudes, beliefs, or behaviors that are specifically directed to the partner or relationship, such as love or forgiveness; (4) mind-reading judgments (e.g., intentions and emotional states) advanced during interaction; (5) memories of past events or relationship states; and (6) predictions of future events or relationship states such as relationship satisfaction or longevity.

The results revealed robust overall effect sizes for both tracking accuracy ($r = .47$) and positive, mean-level bias ($r = .09$). Moreover, Fletcher and Kerr (in press) identified 38 studies that reported both positive mean-level bias and tracking accuracy (using the same samples and variables). Consistent with the prior model and discussion, the results showed that these two forms of accuracy were independent—the two kinds of effect size derived from the same set of 38 studies produced a correlation close to zero.

To illustrate these findings, consider some recent research on the so-called affective forecasting error in relationship contexts (Eastwick, Finkel, Krishnamurti, & Loewenstein, 2008). Prior evidence has indicated a robust tendency in nonrelationship contexts for people to predict greater levels of negative or positive affect, following negative or positive events, than actually eventuate (an example of mean-level bias). The research by Eastwick et al. found the same effect when individuals first predicted then experienced the affective outcomes associated with a dating relationship break up; people experienced significantly less distress than they predicted concerning the relationship break up (effect size $r = .66$). However, they also evinced significant tracking accuracy of their emotional reactions ($r = .44$). And the forecasting (mean-level) error disappeared for those who were not in love with their partners, indicating that it was likely they would start a new romantic relationship a few weeks prior to the break up, or initiated the break up.

In short, in the study by Eastwick et al. (2008) only those who were significantly invested in the relationship predicted more distress than they experienced when the relationship actually dissolved. It is hard to resist the interpretation that this particular bias has a functional basis, given that it should motivate individuals who have much at stake to maintain and improve their romantic relationship, and perhaps retain their mates.

Couples May be Aware of (and Welcome) Bias

People express strong desires for authentic, open, and honest relationships (Fletcher, Simpson, Thomas, & Giles, 1999). Research testing self-verification theory has consistently suggested that, at least for married couples, individuals in romantic relationships prefer to have their partners think of them in ways consistent with their self perceptions, even when such attributions are negative (De La Ronde & Swann, 1998; Swann, De La Ronde, & Hixon, 1994). However, there is also evidence that partners welcome positive mean-level bias, especially in judgments that are central to intimate relationships, such as warmth, attractiveness, and status (Boyes & Fletcher, 2007; Swann, Bosson, & Pelham, 2002).

This apparent contradiction is nicely resolved by the distinction drawn in the current chapter, and the associated proposal that intimates may prefer judgments from their partners about themselves that are both positively biased and high in tracking accuracy. This hypothesis has been tested by Lackenbauer, Campbell, Fletcher, and Rubin (in press) who experimentally manipulated the views that partners in romantic relationships had of each other in terms of two independent dimensions—high versus low mean-level positive bias and high versus low tracking accuracy. The results showed that the effects were additive, with the maximum satisfaction attained when the feedback from the partner was both positively biased and accurate.

A separate question concerns the extent to which individuals are normally aware of the amounts of mean-level bias and tracking accuracy in intimate relationships. Swann and Gill (1997) found that people were more confident of the accuracy of their judgments (using questions assessing a wide range of attitudes and behaviors) if their relationships were longer and the lay theories of their partners were more complex and integrated. Unfortunately, there was a minimal link between confidence ratings and accuracy. In a similar vein, Thomas, Fletcher, and Lange (1997) reported that there was no significant association between the accuracy of mind-reading attained during problem-solving interactions and the confidence expressed in the attributions.

In contrast, there is evidence that people can accurately gauge the amounts of mean-level bias in their relationships. Barelds-Dijkstra and Barelds (2008) reported the familiar findings of overall positive mean-level bias when comparing attractiveness judgments made of relationship partners with the self-judgments of the same partners. However, when participants were asked to judge how attractive other people found their partner, the mean-level bias significantly dropped suggesting that individuals were aware to some extent of the bias inherent in their own perceptions. More directly, Boyes and Fletcher (2007) found that men and women in romantic relationships were quite accurate in assessing the amounts of positive mean-level bias in warmth, attractiveness, and status, both in terms of their own judgments of their partners and the bias inherent in their partner's judgments of them. Moreover, these effects were not a function of relationship satisfaction or self-esteem, and so were unlikely to be driven simply by halo effects.

Rusbult, Van Lange, Wildschut, Yovetich, and Verette (2000) showed that when people were given accuracy instructions, this procedure weakened the amounts of positive bias they showed (measured as a within-participant variable), when describing their relationships. This result suggests that people are able to control the production of mean-level bias, depending on which goals are primed. Moreover, the correlation between relationship commitment and positive bias was strongest in a threat condition (.61), moderate in the control condition (.37), and weakest when an accuracy goal was primed (.17). These results support the argument that more positive relationship evaluations motivate greater positive mean-level bias, but that the extent to which they do will be linked to the goals that are primed.

Given the sparse research on these topics, caution should be exercised in drawing firm conclusions. However, the results do raise the question of why individuals may possess better meta-cognition about mean-level bias than tracking accuracy.

Boyes and Fletcher (2007) argue there are two conditions for meta-accuracy of such judgments to flourish. First, there needs to exist a familiar, accessible, and relevant lay theory, such as (in this case) the notion that "love is blind." Second, the existence of such biased judgments needs to be expressed and observable during behavioral interactions. Indeed, there is good evidence that partners in intimate relationships often try to change each other on central relationship dimensions such as warmth, attractiveness, and status (chapter 16 in this volume; Overall, Fletcher, & Simpson, 2006; Overall, Fletcher, Simpson, & Sibley, 2009), and couples will often work collaboratively to improve themselves, such as going on a diet or joining a gym together to lose weight. And, it seems likely that individuals in romantic relationships may often communicate their respective (positively- or negatively-biased) views to each other verbally and nonverbally. If Mary asks Stephen if she looks fat in her new dress, Stephen's reply will be diagnostic about his (biased) perceptions of Mary's attractiveness. Thus, individuals in relationships are likely to have abundant evidence available to help judge the amounts of mean-level bias inherent in partner judgments of specific, relationship-central traits.

In contrast, developing accurate meta-perceptions of the tracking accuracy of mind-reading or personality traits may be more difficult, and perhaps beyond the cognitive resources of many individuals, because of the relative difficulty of the task. For example, with respect to mind-reading, the quality of feedback may be poor (partly because individuals often mask their own emotions and cognitions), the processes involved are often rapid, fleeting, and unconscious, and, finally, unlike mean-level bias, the perceiver is not making relatively simple, comparative assessments between a judgment and a benchmark of some kind (see Ickes, 1993).

Integration and Conclusions

To begin integrating these findings in a powerful explanatory fashion, it is helpful to locate them in the general context of what else we know about intimate relationships, and to apply standard approaches that have already proved their mettle in the scientific marketplace, including evolutionary and social psychological theories.

First, a psychological-evolutionary approach suggests that we should look to the possible functions of endemic biases in social perception (see Haselton & Nettle, 2006). From an evolutionary approach, love is an evolved mechanism that bonds individuals together in a powerful and committed fashion in order to enhance the support and care given to offspring, and thus increase the chances that the parents' genes are sent into the future (Gonzaga & Haselton, 2008). The rose-tinted, optimistic eyes of love are, on this account, simply part of this bonding mechanism. On the other hand, an evolutionary approach would also suggest that when the costs of getting decisions wrong are momentous (as they surely are in mate selection or retention contexts), then people should be motivated towards achieving accurate and balanced judgments of their partners and relationships.

Second, the picture generated by the research is consistent with a social-psychological approach that emphasizes the centrality of interactions between the person and the situation in explaining and predicting affect, behavior, and cognition. Indeed, the research suggests that interactions are par for the course. To pick one example, the link between relationship satisfaction and mean-level bias appears to be moderated by the length of the relationship—at the early stages of relationships more bias is strongly associated with more happiness, but at the later stages this link becomes attenuated (see Fletcher & Kerr, in press). To pick another example, the presence of threat in a close relationship (e.g., the presence of an attractive and available alternative mate for one's partner) motivates securely attached individuals to misread their partners' thoughts and feelings, whereas anxiously attached individuals become more devastatingly accurate in such mind-readings (Simpson, Ickes, & Blackstone, 1995).

Third, the distinction we made between bias and accuracy, and the associated research, goes some way towards resolving this conundrum. Individuals can (and often do) embrace a charitable, optimistic view of their partners, while simultaneously keeping a realistic track of their partners' traits and qualities. People can apparently be cheerleaders and seekers of the truth simultaneously.

Fourth, there exists a long list of conditions that seem to restrict the operation of biases. There is evidence, for example, that such rose-tinted biases are largely confined to traits that are highly relevant to the success of intimate relationships (such as warmth, attractiveness, and ambition) and may not extend to any and all traits and characteristics. In addition, there is evidence that individuals (even those in love) are capable of reverting to a more rational and realistic way of thinking, depending on the conditions and the goals of the perceiver (see chapter 13 in this volume regarding relationship goals). Thus, being asked to move to another city and give up an existing job (a substantial elevation in commitment) by one's partner in the throes of a romantic fling may well motivate a detailed and even exhaustive analysis rather than prompt an immediate romantic leap into the unknown (see Fletcher & Kerr, in press). Finally, individuals involved in romantic liaisons seem to be aware at some level that their perceptions are biased and not entirely veridical, which implies that a cognitive retreat to a more realistic set of appraisals is always a possibility.

To conclude, it seems clear that the confidence and ability to commit to long-term sexual relationships are facilitated by the production of positively-biased interpretations, personality attributions, and mind-readings of the partner and relationship. However, it is equally apparent that people in happy and successful relationships also typically develop accurate and prescient beliefs and perceptions of their partners, with the ability (at least for some people) to remove their rose-colored glasses when the need arises. Investigating the ways in which people manage the feat of being both a cheerleader and a seeker of the truth about their partners and relationships promises to reveal important insights into the nature of the minds of those involved in intimate relationships.

References

Barelds-Dijkstra, P., & Barelds, D. P. H. (2008). Positive illusions about one's partner's physical attractiveness. *Body Image*, *5*, 99–108.

Boyes, A. D., & Fletcher, G. J. O. (2007). Metaperceptions of bias in intimate relationships. *Journal of Personality and Social Psychology*, *92*, 286–306.

Campbell, L., Simpson, J. A., Kashy, D. A., & Fletcher, G. J. O. (2001). Ideal standards, the self, and flexibility of ideals in close relationships. *Personality and Social Psychology Bulletin*, *27*, 447–462.

Cronbach, L. J. (1955). Processes affecting scores on "understanding of others" and "assumed similarity." *Psychological Bulletin, 52*, 177–193.

De La Ronde, C., & Swann, W. B. (1998). Partner verification: Restoring shattered images of our intimates. *Journal of Personality and Social Psychology, 75*, 374–382.

Eastwick, P. W., Finkel, E. K., Krishnamurti, T., & Loewenstein, G. (2008). Mispredicting distress following romantic breakup: Revealing the time course of the affective forecasting error. *Journal of Experimental Social Psychology, 44*, 800–807.

Epley, N., & Dunning, D. (2006). The mixed blessings of self-knowledge in behavioral prediction: Enhanced discrimination but exacerbated bias. *Personality and Social Psychology Bulletin, 32*, 641–655.

Fletcher, G. J. O. (1995). *The scientific credibility of folk psychology*. Hillsdale, NJ: Erlbaum.

Fletcher, G. J. O. (2002). *The new science of intimate relationships*. Malden, MA: Blackwell.

Fletcher, G. J. O., & Boyes, A. D. (2008). Is love blind? Reality and illusion in intimate relationships. In J. Forgas & J. Fitness (Eds.), *Social relationships: cognitive, affective and motivational processes* (pp. 101–114). Cambridge, England: Cambridge University Press.

Fletcher, G. J. O., & Kerr, P. S. G. (in press). Through the eyes of love: Reality and illusion in intimate relationships. *Personality and Social Psychology Bulletin.*

Fletcher, G. J. O., Reeder, G., & Bull, V. (1990). Bias and accuracy in attitude attribution: The role of attributional complexity. *Journal of Experimental Social Psychology, 26*, 275–288.

Fletcher, G. J. O., Simpson, J. A., Thomas, G., & Giles, L. (1999). Ideals in intimate relationships. *Journal of Personality and Social Psychology, 76*, 72–89.

Fletcher, G. J. O., & Thomas, G. (2000). Behavior and on-line cognition in marital interaction. *Personal Relationships, 7*, 111–130.

Fowers, B. J., Lyons, E., Montel, K. H., & Shaked, N. (2001). Positive illusions about marriage among married and single individuals. *Journal of Family Psychology, 15*, 95–109.

Funder, D. C., & Colvin, C. R. (1997). Congruence of others' and self-judgments of personality. In R. Hogan, J. Johnson, & S. Briggs (Eds.), *Handbook of personality psychology*. San Diego: Academic Press.

Gagné, F. M., & Lydon, J. E. (2004). Bias and accuracy in close relationships: An integrative review. *Personality and Social Psychology Review, 8*, 322–338.

Gonzaga, G. C., & Haselton, M. G. (2008). The evolution of love and long-term bonds. In J. P. Forgas & J. Fitness (Eds.), *Social relationships: Cognitive, affective and motivational processes* (pp. 39–54). Cambridge, England: Cambridge University Press.

Haselton, M. G., & Nettle, D. (2006). The paranoid optimist: An integrative evolutionary model of cognitive biases. *Personality and Social Psychology Review, 10*, 47–66.

Ickes, W. (1993). Empathic accuracy. *Journal of Personality, 61*, 587–610.

Karney, B. R., & Bradbury, T. N. (1995). The longitudinal course of marital quality and stability: A review of theory, methods, and research. *Psychological Bulletin, 118*, 3–34.

Karney, B. R., & Frye, N. E. (2002). "But we've been getting better lately": Comparing prospective and retrospective views of relationship development. *Journal of Personality and Social Psychology, 82*, 222–238.

Kenny, D. A., & Acitelli, L. K. (2001). Accuracy and bias in the perception of the partner in a close relationship. *Journal of Personality and Social Psychology, 80*, 439–448.

Kenny, D. A., & Albright, L. (1987). Accuracy in interpersonal perception: A social relations analysis. *Psychological Bulletin, 102*, 390–402.

Lackenbauer, S. D., Campbell, L., Fletcher, G. J. O., & Rubin, H. (in press). Seeing clearly through rose-colored glasses: The unique and combined benefits of being perceived accurately and in a positively biased manner by romantic partners. *Personal Relationships.*

Murray, S. L. (2001). Seeking a sense of conviction: Motivated cognition in close relationships. In G. J. O. Fletcher & M. S. Clark (Eds.), *Blackwell handbook of social psychology: Interpersonal processes* (pp. 107–126). Malden, MA: Blackwell.

Murray, S. L., & Holmes, J. G. (1993). Seeing virtues in faults: Negativity and the transformation of interpersonal narratives in close relationships. *Journal of Personality and Social Psychology, 65*, 707–722.

Murray, S. L., Holmes, J. G., Bellavia, G., Griffin, D. W., & Dolderman, D. (2002). Kindred spirits? The benefits of egocentrism in close relationships. *Journal of Personality and Social Psychology, 82*, 563–581.

Murray, S. L., Holmes, J. G., & Griffin, D. W. (1996a). The benefits of positive illusions: Idealization and the construction of satisfaction in close relationships. *Journal of Personality and Social Psychology, 70*, 79–98.

Murray, S. L., Holmes, J. G., & Griffin, D. W. (1996b). The self-fulfilling nature of positive illusions in romantic relationships: Love is not blind, but prescient. *Journal of Personality and Social Psychology, 71*, 1155–1180.

Overall, N. C., Fletcher, G. J. O., & Simpson, J. A. (2006). Regulation processes in intimate relationships: The role of ideal standards. *Journal of Personality and Social Psychology, 91*(4), 662–685.

Overall, N. C., Fletcher, G. J. O., Simpson, J. A., & Sibley, C. G. (2009). Regulating partners in intimate relationships: The costs and benefits of different communication strategies. *Journal of Personality and Social Psychology, 96*, 620–639.

Rusbult, C. E., Van Lange, P. A. M., Wildschut, T., Yovetich, N. A., & Verette, J. (2000). Perceived superiority in close relationships: Why it exists and persists. *Journal of Personality and Social Psychology, 79*, 521–545.

Schul, Y., & Vinokur, A. D. (2000). Projection in person perception among spouses as a function of the similarity in their shared experiences. *Personality and Social Psychology Bulletin, 26*, 987–1001.

Simpson, J. A., Ickes, W., & Blackstone, T. (1995). When the head protects the heart: Empathic accuracy in dating relationships. *Journal of Personality and Social Psychology, 69*, 629–641.

Swann, W. B., Bosson, J. K., & Pelham, B. W. (2002). Different partners, different selves: Strategic verification of circumscribed identities. *Personality and Social Psychology Bulletin, 28*, 1215–1228.

Swann, W. B., De La Ronde, C., & Hixon, G. (1994). Authenticity and positivity strivings in marriage and courtship. *Journal of Personality and Social Psychology, 66*, 857–869.

Swann, W. B., & Gill, M. J. (1997). Confidence and accuracy in person perception: Do we know what we think we know about our relationship partners? *Journal of Personality and Social Psychology, 73*, 747–757.

Thomas, G., Fletcher, G. J. O., & Lange, C. (1997). On-line empathic accuracy in marital interaction. *Journal of Personality and Social Psychology, 72*, 839–850.

18

Betrayal and Forgiveness in Couple Relationships

Exploring the Roles of Pain and Punishment in Relational Breakdown and Repair

Julie Fitness

Human beings are born with a fundamental need for close, loving relationships with people who will care for and protect them, and who will value their existence and promote their welfare, both physical and psychological. This primary need for love and protection is most evident in infancy and childhood; however, adults, too, have strong needs for love, security, and support from others as they cope with the many challenges of living (see chapters 6, 11, 14, 26, 28 in this volume). In Western cultures, at least, the majority of adults seek to meet these needs within a loving pair-bond, or couple relationship, which (when it goes well) can be the source of great joy, companionship, and mutual fulfillment.

Even in the most loving couple relationships, however, partners will sometimes fail to meet each other's needs, desires, and expectations, and these failures may generate strong feelings of betrayal, hurt, and anger (see chapters 20, 23 in this volume). Such feelings, in turn, may cause relationship conflict and over time, erode partners' happiness and commitment, both to each other and to their relationship. An important question, then, concerns the extent to which the painful consequences of a perceived relationship betrayal can be managed in a way that facilitates recovery and relationship repair, with partners committed to dealing constructively with the episode, as opposed to giving up on one another and heading for the divorce court.

The Wiley-Blackwell Handbook of Couples and Family Relationships, First Edition.
Edited by Patricia Noller and Gery C. Karantzas.

My aim in this chapter is to briefly review and discuss research on the features and outcomes of betrayal in couple relationships, and the processes involved in forgiving (or not) such betrayals. The results of an empirical study demonstrating the power of betrayal to elicit strong, ongoing emotional pain will be discussed, along with a consideration of potentially adaptive responses, such as forgiveness, to such pain. In particular, I will consider the role of punishment as an appropriate response to partner betrayal, and as not incompatible with eventual forgiveness and relationship repair. Finally, I will argue that even the most serious betrayals need not destroy couple relationships, and that relationship repair can be facilitated by clinicians and counselors with an understanding of the psychology of punishment and forgiveness.

The Nature of Betrayal

Most standard English dictionaries offer definitions of betrayal that include behaviors such as treason, deception, disloyalty, and desertion (e.g., see *The Macquarie Dictionary*, 2002). For relationship researchers, however, the most crucial aspect of betrayal is that for the most part, it exists in the eye of the beholder. That is, betrayal involves "the *perceived* violation of an implicit or explicit relationship-relevant norm" (Hannon, Rusbult, Finkel, & Kamashiro, 2010, p. 254), and of course, relationship partners may or may not agree on what constitutes a relationship norm or rule. The strength of this conceptualization of betrayal is that it subsumes the kinds of behaviors described by dictionary compilers while also leaving room for relationship-specific betrayals that may, to an objective observer, appear relatively innocuous. This distinction is important because any behavior, such as spending the mortgage money or repainting the kitchen without consulting one's partner about the color, may be construed by a relationship partner as a betrayal if it violates what he or she holds to be an important rule (e.g., about trust or consultation).

Thinking about betrayal in terms of relationship rule violations also clarifies the point that betrayal is a quintessentially relational phenomenon. It is within our closest relationships that we open ourselves to one another, sharing our secrets and vulnerabilities, and depending on one another for love and loyalty, even (and especially) when times are tough. Ironically, it is this very intimacy and interdependence that makes partners vulnerable to betrayal. When loved ones break relationship rules and behave in ways that favor their own interests (e.g., by having an affair) at the expense of our interests, we feel at best disappointed, and at worst, deeply shocked and hurt. In essence, our expectation that our partner will truly care about our needs and desires is violated, and we perceive that they care more about themselves than about us, or our relationship.

Emotional responses to betrayal

The discovery that one has been betrayed by one's partner may be a shocking and deeply painful experience. In a recent example of just how painful the experience can be, researchers in Australia and the United States conducted a series of studies in which participants were asked to recall and relive, as if it were happening in the present, an experience of either physical pain or betrayal-generated emotional pain (Chen, Williams, Fitness, & Newton, 2008). Participants' reports of their pain, both at the time of the event and while reliving their experiences, were measured on a "Pain Slide," or ruler marked with a 10-point scale ranging from 1 (no pain) to 10 (intense pain). The results provided a powerful demonstration of the power of betrayal to hurt, and keep on hurting. Specifically, both physical and emotional pain experiences were recalled as highly painful when the events happened, but participants' reports of actual pain while reliving the betrayal were significantly stronger than their reports of pain while reliving the physical injury. Calling to mind a past betrayal generated fresh pain (and made several participants tearful). In a fascinating follow-up to this study, De Wall et al. (2010) have reported that, along with curing headaches, acetaminophen (Tylenol or paracetamol) can also soothe the heartache associated with emotional pain.

Of course, hurt is not the only emotional reaction to betrayal in couple relationships. Other frequently reported emotional reactions include anger, sadness, anxiety, and jealousy, depending on how the betrayed partner appraises, or interprets, what has happened (Fitness, 2001; Fitness & Warburton, 2009). Anger, for example, is associated with appraisals of unfairness, injustice, and strong partner-blame for the betrayal, while sadness is associated with appraisals of helplessness and hopelessness for what is perceived to be an irrevocable loss. Anxiety is associated with appraisals of uncertainty and threat, while jealousy may involve all of these appraisals at different times, depending on which aspect of the betrayal is in focus; i.e., its injustice, the painful loss of trust, or the potential relationship threat. Each of these emotions, in turn, is associated with particular motivations, such as the urge to lash out in anger, to seek comfort when sad, and to freeze or flee when frightened. Note, too, that the betraying partner may also experience a bewildering range of emotions when confronted by a victim's hurt, including guilt and shame, perhaps relief at "being caught," and even anger as a result of feeling misunderstood and too harshly judged.

In summary, the experience of relationship betrayal is painful and has the potential, if it breaks a fundamental relationship rule such as fidelity, to destroy a couple's relationship. Even so, this is not an inevitable outcome. Many couples weather stormy periods in their relationships and cope with both minor and major betrayals over the course of their lives together. Less well understood are partners' strategies for dealing with relationship betrayals, and the extent to which they cope by ignoring, denying, or minimizing the impact of such painful events (e.g., see Roloff & Cloven, 1994), or by confronting betrayals and working through the emotional consequences together in ways that lead to recovery and relationship repair. In the next section of this chapter I will discuss forgiveness as a potentially adaptive response to betrayal, and describe the results of both qualitative and experimental research on the role of punishment in facilitating forgiveness.

Forgiveness, Punishment, and Relationship Repair

Throughout recorded history, moral philosophers and theologians have had much to say about the virtues and desirability of forgiveness, including the Christian advice to "turn the other cheek" in response to an interpersonal offense. More recently, social and clinical psychologists with an interest in forgiveness have been careful to point out that forgiving does not mean excusing, condoning, accepting, or inviting more bad behavior (Fincham, Hall, & Beach, 2005; Freedman, Enright, & Knutson, 2005). Rather, forgiveness is typically defined by these and other researchers in terms of a victim's "willingness to a) forego vengeance and demands for retribution and b) react to the betrayal in a constructive, less judgmental manner" (Hannon et al., 2010, p. 254). Further, theorists have argued that the prime emotional motivators of forgiveness are empathy and compassion for the offender (McCullough, Worthington, & Rachal, 1997).

These conceptualizations of forgiveness raise an interesting question. Specifically, and as noted by evolutionary scholars, forgiveness is adaptive in the sense that human beings depend on each other for their survival. Accordingly, maintaining close and supportive relationships with one another is critical, and requires a certain degree of willingness to "get over" perceived offenses and betrayals (Luebbert, 1999). If, over the course of evolution, humans had only ever responded to perceived interpersonal offenses with retaliation and revenge, the species would long ago have become extinct. Other clues to the survival benefits of forgiveness may be found in research demonstrating its relationship with a variety of positive health outcomes. For example, Lawler et al. (2003) interviewed 108 college students about two betrayal incidents, one concerning a parent and one concerning a friend or partner. They collected data on dispositional forgivingness (having a forgiving personality) and state forgiveness (specifically in relation to the betrayals discussed), along with measures of stress, hostility, empathy, and self-reported illness symptoms. These researchers found that trait forgiveness was associated with lower levels of blood pressure and fewer illness symptoms, while state forgiveness was associated with faster recovery from the stressful interviews. Socially, too, forgiveness may be considered a benefit, with cross-cultural research demonstrating that it helps to maintain social harmony (e.g., Fu, Watkins, & Hui, 2004).

However, there is something of a paradox here, in that too much forgiveness is, potentially, as dangerous for humans as too little. Again, and as noted by both evolutionary and social psychologists, over the course of evolutionary history, humans who never retaliated or threatened retaliation to those who harmed them would have become extinct in a "dog-eat-dog" environment (Frijda, 2007; Pinker, 1997). Simply put, retaliation discourages people who have harmed us from doing it again, thereby keeping us safe and enhancing our chances of survival. Further, retaliation means moving from a passive, victim position to an active, in-control position, which feels good and can boost self-esteem (Baumeister, 1997). Hence, there seems to be an important role for retaliation in human social interactions, and there is no reason to believe that this principle does not also apply to couple relationships. The challenge is in knowing how much and what kind of retaliation is potentially functional, and when it is wise to "shut the book" on an interpersonal offense and forgive an offender.

It is important at this point to consider the conceptual differences between the terms "revenge" and "punishment." Psychologists and laypeople alike tend to use the terms synonymously, but they can be teased apart, and the distinctions are potentially important in relation to the process of forgiveness. Specifically, scholarly definitions of forgiveness typically make reference to forgoing vengeance or revenge, and refer to feelings of bitterness and resentment as driving such retributive behaviors (Baumeister, 1997;

chapter 20 in this volume). However, Frijda (1994) found that although laypeople reported day-dreaming about taking creative and ghastly revenge on wrongdoers, they were actually unlikely to ever enact such behaviors (or at least, to report having done so). Even so, the results may have been different had respondents been asked if they had ever punished, rather than taken revenge on, wrongdoers. Punishment refers to the imposition of a penalty for bad behavior that can potentially be rationalized and morally justified, just as parents may rationalize the punishment of children. Accordingly, laypeople may be more willing to admit punishing rule violators than taking revenge on them, and this issue has potentially important implications for forgiveness. Just as parents may believe that bad behavior needs to be corrected by way of punishment, so too may relationship partners consider some degree of punishment for a betrayal, or rule violation, to be perfectly appropriate in the course of negotiating relationship repair.

Of course, the boundaries between these two concepts may be fuzzy and depend on the perspectives of the relationship partners. In particular, punishers may believe their penalties are fair and reasonable, while the punished may perceive the penalties inflicted to be harsh, vindictive, and unwarranted (Kim & Smith, 1993; Zaibert, 2006). This possibility in turn suggests that relationship partners whose perceptions are congruent about the appropriateness of a particular type and degree of punishment in response to a betrayal may be better equipped to achieve forgiveness and relationship repair than partners whose perceptions of both the betrayal and the price to be paid for it are decidedly incongruent.

One study that attempted to explore and clarify the role of punishment in forgiveness was conducted with 90 long-term married and 70 divorced individuals (Fitness, 2001). Participants were asked to recall and write about either a partner-caused or a self-caused marital offense, with divorced participants describing an unforgiven offense, and married participants writing about a forgiven offense. Participants were asked explicitly to report on whether or not they had punished their partners or been punished by their partners for their marital offenses, and to describe the kinds of punishments that had been administered.

No significant differences were found between the long-term married and divorced participants in relation to the reported seriousness of the marital offense they described; similarly, betrayal types (e.g., infidelity, injustice, deception) did not differ between married and divorced participants. There was, however, a striking difference between self-caused and partner-caused offenses with respect to perceived culpability. Specifically, participants reporting on self-caused offenses tended to justify their behaviors as accidental, or due to misunderstandings or provocation. Participants reporting on partner-caused offenses, however, tended to attribute their causes to the deliberate and malicious intentions of the offenders. These findings are in line with social cognitive research that tends to find evidence of self-serving biases in victim versus perpetrator accounts of offenses; simply put, we can all find justifications for our own bad behavior because we are aware of all possible mitigating factors. However, we tend to be less charitable about the reasons for other people's bad behavior, assuming that it is a function of their flawed personalities rather than situational forces that they cannot control (Baumeister, Stillwell, & Wotman, 1990; Fletcher, Overall, & Friesen, 2006).

With respect to forgiveness, as might have been expected, long-term married participants' marital happiness was positively associated with the reported ease of forgiving, or having been forgiven for, self- and partner-caused offenses. Surprisingly, however, marital happiness and ease of forgiving were not associated with the extent to which the victim had reportedly punished or been punished by his or her partner. In fact, the majority of respondents, forgiven and unforgiven, claimed they had punished their partners or been punished by them. These punishments differed in severity according to marital happiness (with divorced respondents reporting the most severe examples), and ranged from reminders, withdrawal, teasing, and discussing the offense with others, to physical abuse, destroying possessions, and even abandonment. Further, punishment was not administered blindly or randomly; participants were able to clearly articulate their motivations for punishing their partners or having been punished by them. Specifically, they reported that punishments served to communicate the depth of the victim's hurt, and to discourage reoffending (in line with evolutionary theorizing). Punishments were also administered to restore the balance of power in the relationship, and to test the commitment of the punished partner.

Overall, these data clearly suggest that punishment is not at all antithetical to forgiveness, and that even happy partners do not necessarily inhibit punitive responses to partner provocations. Rather, whether the final outcome of a relationship conflict is forgiveness or not, punishment is likely to have occurred along the way. However, these data were obtained via self-report, and so may be subject to potential memory distortions. A question remains, then, as to whether or not couples, especially happy couples, actually do punish one another in response to betrayals.

A real-time demonstration of the potency of punishment in the context of relationship betrayal was obtained in an empirical study (Peterson, 2008). Advertised as a "food choices" study, the experiment involved 64 men and women (32 couples) whose ages ranged from 17 to 55 years with a mean of 24.7 years. Partners had been involved in their relationships for an average of 3.7 years (range 0.7 months–24.5 years). After coming into the laboratory, couples were randomly (and unknowingly) allocated to an experimental or control group.

Participants were then separated and completed a number of questionnaires measuring, among other variables (including their own and their partners' food preferences and allergies), their relationship satisfaction. Partners in the experimental group were then asked to recall and write about an instance in which their partner had betrayed them or broken their trust, while participants in the control group were asked to write about "something that happened yesterday." Next, all participants were then given an opportunity to take an aggressive, punitive action against their partners via the allocation of a painfully hot, chili sauce for the partners to consume (an aggression-measuring technique pioneered by McGregor et al., 1998). All participants understood that their partners would be required to consume all of the allocated chili sauce as part of a "taste experiment" (though no sauce was actually to be consumed). Participants also tasted a tiny amount of chili sauce prior to allocation, to ensure they understood how painfully hot it was.

The results of this study were unequivocal with respect to participants' desires to punish perceived partner-caused rule violations. Specifically, participants in the experimental group who had been primed by recalling a partner-related betrayal allocated significantly more painfully hot sauce to their partners than did participants in the control group. Further, participants in the betrayal condition allocated significantly more painfully hot sauce to their partners than to a bogus "other participant" that they did not meet. The study also found that the relationship happiness of betrayed participants was negatively associated with the amount of hot sauce they allocated to their partners. Interestingly, more severe levels of punishment also occurred when betrayed participants' partners reported lower levels of relationship satisfaction.

In a second phase of this study, semi-structured interviews were conducted with 25 couples about the role of punishment in their relationships. Every participant reported having punished his or her partner in the past, and argued that punishment was a legitimate response to bad behavior in the same way that parents need to punish children in order to discourage them from further offending. Two primary forms of punishment were identified: ignoring the partner and withdrawing rewards; and active confrontation, including the infliction of verbal, and occasionally physical, aggression. Some women also reported that they discussed appropriate punishments with their friends, and described a range of penalties, including attempts to make their partners feel guilty or jealous, and (sometimes creative) demands for compensation.

In summary, punishment was considered by respondents in both studies to form an important part of the forgiveness process, because it informs the offending partner that an important relationship rule has been violated, and that the victim is suffering as a consequence of that violation. Punishment also redistributes some of the victim's pain and potentially discourages the offender from reoffending. Importantly, punishment can serve as a commitment test, because a punished partner who responds with remorse rather than retaliation clearly cares about the needs of the betrayed partner. In this respect, punishment sends a signal to a betraying partner that an acknowledgment of the victim's suffering is required; along with appropriate amends (see also Hannon et al., 2010). However, punishers need to carefully monitor the level and length of punishment imposed, since an overly harsh penalty itself constitutes a rule violation, and becomes legitimate grounds for the punished to inflict punishment in turn.

Implications for Couple Counseling

As noted in the introduction, betrayal is a relational event. It involves two partners with their own relationship rules, expectations, and perceptions of what has happened and what it means. Following betrayal, both partners may experience powerful, painful emotions that push and pull them in different directions, including victim impulses to retaliate and punish while also perhaps experiencing feelings of empathy and compassion for the betrayer. In addition, betrayers are likely to experience the need to make amends and repair the damaged relationship while also perhaps experiencing feelings of shame and anger toward the victim. Ultimately, it is the positive emotions of empathy and compassion, remorse and humility that make forgiveness and relationship repair possible. However, the more painful emotions and motivations also need to be acknowledged and dealt with if the process is not to be short-changed and leave one or both participants silently seething, distrustful, and unhappy with their relationship.

The studies reported here and in the forgiveness literature affirm that the first crucial step in the forgiveness process is for betrayers to acknowledge that they have broken an important relationship rule, without attempting to make self-serving excuses for their behavior. They must acknowledge that their behavior has caused their partner pain and suffering, and express sincere sorrow and remorse for it. They must also promise to make amends and, as suggested by the data reported in this chapter, be willing to accept some negative consequences (punishment) for their behavior.

None of this is easy to do. Admitting wrongdoing without excuse is shaming and makes one vulnerable to the poor opinion of another; little wonder, then, that shamed individuals frequently lash out in retaliatory rage (Tangney, 1995). Clinicians are also aware of the negative, retaliatory spirals that characterize unhappy couple conflicts (e.g., Gottman, 1994), including particularly destructive anger–shame spirals characterized by reciprocated accusations, humiliations, and expressions of contempt (Retzinger, 1991). Similarly, in a study of hypothetical relationship betrayals, Hodgins, Liebeskind, and Schwartz (1996) found it was the most blameworthy offenders who told more lies and gave the shortest and least apologetic explanations for their behaviors, suggesting that they were more motivated to save face than to resolve relationship conflict or be forgiven.

It is also important to note that, although verbal apologies are a necessary component of the forgiveness process, they are not sufficient (Zechmeister, Garcia, Romero, & Vas, 2004). In the Fitness (2001) study described earlier, true contrition was considered to go far beyond verbal apologies, which may be relatively easy to make. Showing true remorse may take months or even years of paying the price for a betrayal and demonstrating true commitment to one's partner and the relationship (e.g., by giving up problem drinking, gambling, or affairs). Further, there is no guarantee that, even when an offender is truly remorseful, victims will forgive the betrayal. In the ideal case, a betrayed partner may consider that justice has been done and forgiveness is warranted. However, not all offenses may be considered forgivable, and some respondents in the marital forgiveness study argued that they would never forgive their partners because only "weak" people forgive and leave themselves open to further exploitation. Others claimed that forgiving involves giving up a moral advantage and may even serve to legitimize a betrayal by appearing to diminish its long-term impact. Importantly and sadly, however, several divorced respondents noted that an offense they had considered unforgivable at the time no longer seemed so extreme, and they realized with great regret that in fact, they could have "worked through it," had either or both partners had sufficient patience, insight, and support. The implications here are clear: forgiveness takes time, perseverance, patience, and trust that the relationship is worth the struggle. Indeed, researchers have found that relationship commitment is a powerful predictor of forgiveness—truly a case of "for better or for worse" (Finkel, Rusbult, Kumashiro, & Hannon, 2002).

No doubt many couples have discovered over time how to balance the need to punish an offending partner and discourage the possibility of future betrayal, with the need to forgive and maintain a close, rewarding relationship. Many marriages do survive infidelity and other crises of faith. However, the spiraling marital separation and divorce rates suggest that many other couples are not particularly skilled at working through these issues.

How, then, can counselors and clinicians support couples in this process? The first point to note is that, as stressed throughout this chapter, betrayal, punishment, and forgiveness are dyadic processes, which means that therapy needs to involve the couple, rather than individual partners. Second, partners need support to tell their stories and to hear and understand each other's needs, beliefs, and expectations. They need encouragement to acknowledge each other's feelings and emotions; to agree to disagree, if necessary, on the distribution of blame for a relationship betrayal; and to resolve to work through the process of forgiveness together because they value their relationship and want not just to maintain it, but to strengthen and enrich it (see chapter 20 in this volume for an example of a such an intervention).

This process implies an educative role for counselors as much as an emotionally supportive and facilitative one. For example, as noted earlier in this chapter, people tend to make self-serving attributions for their own offenses while attributing partner offenses to partner-related flaws. However, couples in happy marriages explain their own and their partner's behaviors a little differently. Specifically, although they still tend to minimize the impact of their own negative behaviors, they do not tend to maximize the impact of their partner's negative behaviors, or attribute malicious motives to their partners (chapter 18 in this volume; Kearns & Fincham, 2005). Rather, they tend to make relationship-enhancing attributions in which the partner is given full credit for good behavior, and given the benefit of the doubt for bad (Fletcher et al., 2006; chapter 17 in this volume). This kind of cognitive reframing can be explained and taught to couples, who come to realize that to an extent, relationship happiness is "all in their heads" and can be a result of conscious choice and a change of focus.

Even so, no amount of cognitive reframing and positive spin makes it easy to mend a broken heart, especially in the recent aftermath of a betrayal. As respondents in the study reported earlier noted, forgiveness involves the heart and the head, and sometimes the heart is not so ready to forgive, despite what the head has decided (Fitness, 2001). Further, and as noted in Chen et al.'s (2008) pain study, even thinking about a past betrayal can elicit fresh feelings of pain and distress. McCullough, Bono, and Root (2007) also found in a longitudinal study that ruminating about offenses reignites anger and actually makes forgiveness more difficult.

One potentially important factor that may be relevant in this context is so-called emotional intelligence (also known as emotional competence; see Fitness, 2006). The results of a study exploring emotional intelligence and forgiveness showed that emotion clarity, or the ability to accurately recognize and reason about one's own and other's emotional states, was positively associated with ease of forgiveness, and negatively associated with both shame intensity and imagined partner hate in response to a self-caused offense (Fitness & Mathews, 1998). These findings suggest that individuals with a deep and nuanced understanding of their own and others' emotions may feel more guilt than shame in relation to their own betrayals and so are more motivated to make amends than to return hurt for hurt in a spiral of humiliated rage. Further, they may correctly perceive their partners as angry, hurt, and having a legitimate right to inflict punishment. Less emotionally competent offenders, on the other hand, may feel more shame than guilt about their own betrayals and perceive their partner's emotions as signaling hatred for them; consequently, they may act defensively, destructively, and without apparent remorse. Moreover, it may be that more emotionally competent victims are better able to judge when their partners are "sorry enough" and/or have been sufficiently punished to warrant forgiveness.

Again, there is a clear role here for clinicians and counselors to help couples develop such emotional competence. Emotion-focused therapy, for example, is an approach that explicitly takes account of the informational value of emotions, with therapists helping couples to access, understand, and communicate their needs and emotions in a safe, supportive, and educative environment (see chapters 20, 23 in this volume; Greenberg & Goldman, 2008). The development of emotional intelligence is a primary aim of therapy, and the approach clearly has strong relevance to the emotion-laden context of couple betrayal, punishment, and forgiveness. However, a therapist does not have to be exclusively "emotion-focused" to provide insights and support to partners who find their emotions difficult to understand, articulate, or effectively communicate. Rather, the best therapeutic approach may be integrative and eclectic, with counselors able to support and guide couples in relation to their cognitions, motivations, and emotions at all stages of the forgiveness process.

Concluding Comments

The research discussed in this chapter suggests that, not only is some form of painful consequence for bad behavior not incompatible with forgiveness, in the context of ongoing, happy couple relationships it may even be a necessity. However, we still know very little about how close relationship partners go about forgiving one another's rule violations, including whether or not it is ever possible to completely forget what has been forgiven. There is also much to learn about the features and functions of punishment in both happy and unhappy relationships, and about the ways in which victims of betrayal may moderate their urges for punishment even while experiencing strong feelings of pain and anger. Hopefully, researchers will continue to explore these fascinating issues, and advances in our knowledge will help equip both clinicians and laypeople with the skills needed to nourish that most important source of human health and happiness: our close, loving relationships with one another.

References

Baumeister, R. F. (1997). *Evil: Inside human cruelty and violence.* New York: W. H. Freeman.

Baumeister, R. F., Stillwell, A. M., & Wotman, S. R. (1990). Victim and perpetrator accounts of interpersonal conflict: Autobiographical narratives about anger. *Journal of Personality and Social Psychology, 59,* 994–1005.

Chen, Z., Williams, K., Fitness, J., & Newton, N. (2008). When hurt will not heal: Exploring the capacity to relive social and physical pain. *Psychological Science, 19,* 789–795.

De Wall, N. C., MacDonald, G., Masten, C. L., Baumeister, R. F., Powell, C., Combs, D., Schurtz, D., Stillman, T. F., Tice, D. M., & Eisenberger, N. I. (2010). Tylenol reduces social pain: Behavioral and neural evidence. *Psychological Science, 21,* 931–937.

Fincham, F. D., Hall, J., & Beach, S. (2005). "Til lack of forgiveness doth us part": Forgiveness and marriage. In E. Worthington (Ed.), *Handbook of forgiveness* (pp. 207–226). New York: Routledge.

Finkel, E., Rusbult, C., Kumashiro, M., & Hannon, P. A. (2002). Dealing with betrayal in close relationships: Does commitment promote forgiveness? *Journal of Personality and Social Psychology, 82*, 956–974.

Fitness, J. (2001). Betrayal, rejection, revenge and forgiveness: An interpersonal script approach. In M. Leary (Ed.), *Interpersonal rejection* (pp. 73–103). New York: Oxford University Press.

Fitness, J. (2006). The emotionally intelligent marriage. In J. Ciarrochi, J. P. Forgas, & J. Mayer (Eds.), *Emotional intelligence in everyday life: A scientific inquiry* (2nd edn, pp. 129–139). New York: Psychology Press.

Fitness, J., & Mathews, S (1998). *Emotions, emotional intelligence, and forgiveness in marriage.* Paper presented at the 9th International Conference on Personal Relationships, Saratoga Springs, New York.

Fitness, J., & Warburton, W. A. (2009). Thinking the unthinkable: Cognitive appraisals and hurt feelings. In A. Vangelisti (Ed.), *Feeling hurt in close relationships* (pp. 34–49). New York: Cambridge University Press.

Fletcher, G. J. O., Overall, N. C., & Friesen, M. D. (2006) Social cognition in intimate relationships. In A. Vangelisti & D. Perlman (Eds.), *The Cambridge handbook of personal relationships* (pp. 353–568). Cambridge, England: Cambridge University Press.

Freedman, S., Enright, R., & Knutson, J. (2005). A progress report on the process model of forgiveness. In E. Worthington (Ed.), *Handbook of forgiveness* (pp. 393–406). New York: Routledge.

Frijda, N. (1994). The Lex Talionis: On vengeance. In S. H. van Goozen, N. E. van de Poll, & J. Sergeant (Eds.), *Emotions: Essays on emotion theory* (pp. 263–289). Mahwah, NJ: Erlbaum.

Frijda, N. (2007). *The laws of emotion.* Cambridge, England: Cambridge University Press.

Fu, H., Watkins, D., & Hui, E. (2004). Personality correlates of the disposition towards interpersonal forgiveness: A Chinese perspective. *International Journal of Psychology, 39*, 305–316.

Gottman, J. (1994). *What predicts divorce? The relationship between marital processes and marital outcomes.* Mahwah, NJ: Erlbaum.

Greenberg, L. S., & Goldman, R. (2008). *Emotion-focused couples therapy: The dynamics of emotion, love and power.* Washington, DC: American Psychological Association.

Hannon, P., Rusbult, C., Finkel, E., & Kamashiro, M. (2010). In the wake of betrayal: Amends, forgiveness, and the resolution of betrayal. *Personal Relationships, 17*, 253–278.

Hodgins, H. S., Liebeskind, E., & Schwartz, W. (1996). Getting out of hot water: Facework in social predicaments. *Journal of Personality and Social Psychology, 71*, 300–314.

Kearns, J., & Fincham, F. D. (2005). Victim and perpetrator accounts of interpersonal transgressions: Self-serving or relationship-serving biases. *Personality and Social Psychology Bulletin, 31*, 321–333.

Kim, S., & Smith, R. (1993). Revenge and conflict escalation. *Negotiation Journal, 9*, 37–43.

Lawler, K. A., Younger, J. W., Piferi, R. L., Billington, E., Jobe, R., Edmondson, K., & Jones, W. H. (2003). A change of heart: Cardiovascular correlates of forgiveness in response to cardiovascular fitness. *Journal of Behavioral Medicine, 26*, 373–393.

Luebbert, M. C. (1999). The survival value of forgiveness. In D. Rosen & M. C. Luebbert (Eds.), *Evolution of the psyche* (pp. 169–187). Westport, CT: Praeger Press.

McCullough, M. E., Bono, G., & Root, L. (2007). Rumination, emotion, and forgiveness: Three longitudinal studies. *Journal of Personality and Social Psychology, 92*, 490–505.

McCullough, M. E., & Worthington, E. L., & Rachal, K. C. (1997). Interpersonal forgiving in close relationships. *Journal of Personality and Social Psychology, 73*, 321–336.

McGregor, H. A., Lieberman, J. D., Greenberg, J., Solomon, S., Arndt, J., Simon, L., & Pyszczynski, T. (1998). Terror management and aggression: Evidence that mortality salience motivates aggression against worldview-threatening others. *Journal of Personality and Social Psychology, 74*, 590–605.

Peterson, J. (2008). *Exploring punishment in close relationships.* Department of Clinical Psychology, Macquarie University.

Pinker, S. (1997). *How the mind works.* New York: W. W. Norton.

Retzinger, S. (1991). *Violent emotions: Shame and rage in marital quarrels.* Newbury Park, CA: Sage.

Roloff, M. E., & Cloven, D. H. (1994). When partners transgress: Maintaining violated relationships. In M. E. Roloff & D. H. Cloven (Eds.), *Communication and relational maintenance* (pp. 23–43). San Diego: Academic Press.

Tangney, J. P. (1995). Shame and guilt in interpersonal relationships. In J. P. Tangney & K. Fischer (Eds.), *Self-conscious emotions: The psychology of shame, guilt, embarrassment and pride* (pp. 114–139). New York: Guilford Press.

Zaibert, L. (2006). Punishment and revenge. *Law and Philosophy, 25*, 81–118.

Zechmeister, J. S., Garcia, S., Romero, C., & Vas, S. (2004). Don't apologize unless you mean it: A laboratory investigation of forgiveness and retaliation. *Journal of Social and Clinical Psychology, 23*, 532–564.

PART VI

Education and Intervention in Couple and Family Relationships

19

Taking it to the Streets (and Information Super Highways)

Using Technology to Enhance the Reach and Impact of Marriage and Relationship Education

W. Kim Halford and Samira Hayes

Rob (36) and Jess (32) are farmers who live about 250 km (160 miles) from the nearest town. They have been living together for 2 years, and are planning to marry in 6 months to start a family. Rob and Jess like the idea of doing relationship education, but think that getting to sessions is too difficult. Nerida (27) is an office worker and Tian (38) works in a bank. They have been living together for a couple of months. Nerida and Tian are concerned that Nerida's 2 children from an earlier relationship are not getting on well with Tian. They are keen to attend couple relationship education but arranging child care is difficult.

These two examples illustrate some potential barriers to couples attending couple relationship education (CRE). This chapter shows how information technology (IT) can be used to enhance couples' access to CRE. We begin with a description of the nature of CRE, and an analysis of the evidence on the efficacy of CRE. Then there is analysis of the limited impact of CRE, which can be attributed substantially to the modest reach of CRE. We review some of the potential advantages of using IT to address the challenge of reach, and illustrate how IT can be applied in CRE, with a description of an exemplar program.

The Wiley-Blackwell Handbook of Couples and Family Relationships, First Edition.
Edited by Patricia Noller and Gery C. Karantzas.

What is Couple Relationship Education?

Couple relationship education (CRE) is the provision of structured learning experiences to help couples develop their relationship knowledge, attitude, and skills. CRE typically is targeted at couples who identify themselves as currently satisfied with their relationship, and builds on strengths in the relationship to enhance commitment and healthy interaction (Halford, Markman, & Stanley, 2008). The key goals of CRE are to help couples sustain a healthy committed relationship, to prevent the erosion of relationship satisfaction, and to reduce the considerable personal and social costs of relationship distress and separation.

Most couples have high relationship satisfaction early in their relationship, but average satisfaction declines across time (Glenn, 1998; Holman, 2001). CRE is designed to reduce or eliminate this decline. The average decline can be attributed to a complex interplay of factors including the abatement of the initial, intense attraction; deficits in couples' communication and conflict management skills; insufficient couple focus and working on their relationship; and the deleterious effects of life stresses (Bradbury & Karney, 2004; Halford, Lizzio, Wilson, & Occhipinti, 2007; Holman, 2001). Of these factors, the interaction between the partners is the strongest predictor of future relationship satisfaction (Bradbury & Karney, 2004). For example, low reported effort in sustaining and enhancing the relationship strongly predicts future deterioration in relationship satisfaction (Halford et al., 2007). Similarly, ineffective communication characterized by elevated negativity predicts deterioration in couple relationship satisfaction (Johnson, et al., 2005; Kiecolt-Glaser, Bane, Glaser, & Malarkey, 2003).

CRE is intended to assist couples to develop the relationship knowledge and skills that will enable them to have healthy patterns of interaction that sustain high relationship satisfaction. CRE is distinct from couple therapy in that CRE targets couples currently satisfied in their relationship. CRE builds upon the high level of positive emotion typical of currently satisfied couples, placing a strong emphasis on building the positive foundations for a great life together. There is less stigma attached to CRE when compared with couple therapy, making it appealing to community members who might not seek therapeutic services (Markman & Halford, 2005). The majority of CRE programs are conducted over a fixed number of sessions, ranging between 6 and 10 (Halford, Markman, & Stanley, 2008).

Approaches to couple relationship education

CRE evolved from the work of religious marriage celebrants, such as priests and ministers in the 1950s, who offered advice and guidance to premarital couples in the hope of strengthening those marriages (Hunt, Hof, & DeMaria, 1998). By the late 1990s between one quarter to one third of premarital couples in the United States, Australia, and Great Britain were attending some form of relationship education (Stanley, 2001). Many CRE programs currently offered have not been empirically evaluated, as CRE providers developed their own programs in response to perceived local needs. Moreover, most are not documented in a manner that can be evaluated (Halford & Simons, 2005). However, since the 1990s there has been an increasing use of evidence-based CRE by providers (Markman & Halford, 2005).

Research on the efficacy of CRE began in the 1970s (Hunt et al., 1998) and a large body of evidence has amassed on the effects of some forms of CRE. There are two commonly used CRE approaches that have been evaluated in randomized controlled trials: assessment with feedback; and curriculum-based knowledge and skill training. The assessment and feedback approach typically uses structured inventory-based assessments, followed by a feedback session, which informs couples about their current relationship strengths and challenges (Larson, Newell, Topham, & Nichols, 2002). This approach is based on the assumption that feedback can guide couples to sustain relationship strengths and to take remedial action to address challenges. The most widely used inventories are PREPARE (Olsen, Fournier, & Druck, 1996), the Facilitating Open Couple Communication Understanding and Study (FOCCUS) (Markey & Micheletto, 1997), and Relationship Evaluation (RELATE) (Busby, Holman, & Taniguchi, 2001). Each of these inventories provides scores across a number of dimensions including: shared realistic relationship expectations; effective communication and conflict resolution skills; emotional health; and effective individual stress management. Scores on these questionnaires predict newlywed couples' future relationship satisfaction and stability (Larson et al., 2002), showing that they assess aspects of couple relationships relevant to future relationship satisfaction.

Curriculum-based CRE focuses on the active training of key relationship skills, although significant emphasis is also placed on building knowledge (Stanley, 2001). One recently developed program also combined assessment feedback with skill training (Halford et al., 2010). Curriculum-based CRE typically consists of 12–15 hours of face-to-face contact and provides opportunities to learn skills via modeling, practice, and feedback. Examples of such programs include: Relationship Enhancement (RE; Guerney & Maxson, 1990); Premarital Relationship Enhancement Program (PREP; Renick, Blumberg, & Markman, 1992); Couple Commitment and Relationship Enhancement (Couple CARE; Halford, Moore, Wilson, Dyer, & Farrugia, 2006); Couples Communication Program (CCP; Miller, Miller, Nunnally, & Wackman, 1992); and Couples Coping Enhancement Training (CCET; Bodenmann & Shantinath, 2004).

The curriculum-based CRE programs have a number of content areas in common. For example, skills training in positive communication, conflict management, and positive expression of affection are included in RE, PREP, Couple CARE, CCP, and CCET. There also are significant variations. For example, in PREP there are multiple foci of intervention, but most time is devoted to the prevention of destructive conflict, believed to be central to the prevention of relationship problems (Markman, Floyd, Stanley, & Storaasli, 1988). In RE, the development of partner empathy receives strong emphasis (Guerney, 1977), while this aspect receives less emphasis in PREP. Coping with life stress, which receives little attention in other programs except for Couple CARE, is a major component of CCET. In Couple CARE the development of relationship self-regulation, involving each partner identifying and implementing personal self-change plans, is a core focus not included in other programs.

A major strength of the curriculum-based approach is that training is focused on variables that predict relationship outcomes. In particular, teaching couple communication is a key focus of all curriculum-based approaches, and effective communication predicts sustained relationship satisfaction, at least over the first 5–10 years of marriage (Gottman, Coan, Carrere, & Swanson, 1998; Markman, 1981; Pasch & Bradbury, 1998).

Efficacy of couple relationship education

There have been four published studies evaluating the effects of inventory-based assessment and feedback CRE on couple relationships. In a quasi-experimental study Knutson and Olsen (2003) found feedback based on the PREPARE inventory improved premarital couples' relationship satisfaction. Three randomized controlled trials evaluated the Internet-based RELATE inventory. Larson, Vatter, Galbraith, Holman, and Stahmann (2007) found RELATE feedback produced immediate increases in relationship satisfaction and commitment in early-stage committed couples' relationships, but there was no follow-up to evaluate the maintenance of effects. A combination of RELATE feedback with 6 sessions of curriculum-based CRE significantly enhanced relationship satisfaction, and this effect was maintained to 6-month follow-up (Busby, Ivey, Harris, & Ates, 2007). However, whether the effects were attributable to the feedback or the curriculum-based skills training could not be established. Halford, Farrugia, Lizzio, and Wilson (2010) compared RELATE feedback alone, with feedback coupled with the Couple Care skill-training curriculum. Adding Couple CARE to RELATE significantly enhanced couples' communication and improved maintenance of relationship satisfaction over the next 12 months for women, suggesting greater benefits from curriculum-based CRE than from feedback alone.

Four other studies have evaluated assessment and feedback as a brief intervention with couples. Two quasi-experimental studies (Cordova, Warren, & Gee, 2001; Halford, Osgarby, & Kelly, 1996) and two randomized control trials (Cordova, Scott, Dorian, Mirgain, Yaeger, & Groot, 2005; Worthington, McCullough, Shortz, Mindes, Sandage, & Chartrand, 1995) showed that assessment and feedback increased relationship satisfaction for at least some months after intervention. In all four studies assessment occurred across two or three sessions; and involved the completion of self-report inventories, structured interviews, completion of behavioral tasks like communication, and self-monitoring of relationship interaction. This intensive assessment was more comprehensive than the single-inventory assessment typically used in CRE. In addition, in the Cordova et al. (2001, 2005) and Halford et al. (1996) studies, the couples were mildly to moderately distressed. Consequently, these studies evaluated brief couple therapy rather than CRE. Nonetheless, all four studies found that assessment and feedback improved couples' relationship satisfaction.

A meta-analysis of the large number of trials of curriculum-based CRE showed that this program reliably teaches positive couple communication, an effect which is maintained for some years after training (Blanchard, Hawkins, Baldwin, & Fawcett, 2009; Halford et al., 2008). CRE also reliably produces small, short-term increases in relationship satisfaction (Hawkins, Blanchard, Baldwin, & Fawcett, 2008). The small immediate effects likely reflect a ceiling effect, with highly satisfied couples having little scope for increasing satisfaction.

The crucial test of CRE is whether it prevents erosion of couples' relationship satisfaction over time. There are eight published trials evaluating CRE effects with follow-ups of more than one year. Three were quasi-experimental studies showing a long-term (3–4 year) universal benefit for couples from curriculum-based CRE (Bodenmann, Pihet, Shantinath, Cina, & Widmer, 2006; Hahlweg, Markman, Thurmaier, Engl, & Eckert, 1998; Markman et al., 1988). However, self-selection by couples to receive CRE may account for these results (Halford et al., 2008). There are five published randomized controlled trials, and in four of these studies curriculum-based CRE helped couples sustain high relationship satisfaction (Halford, Sanders, & Behrens, 2001; Halford, Petch, & Creedy, 2010; Kaiser, Hahlweg, Fehm-Wolfsdrof, & Groth, 1998; Shultz, Cowan, & Cowan, 2006), although this finding was not replicated in one study (van Widenfelt, Hosman, Schaap, & Van der Staak, 1996).

The largely positive findings on the efficacy of curriculum-based CRE do not mean that all couples gain a long-term benefit from CRE. Of the four trials that found benefits of CRE extending beyond 12 months, Halford et al. (2001) found that only couples at high risk for future relationship problems benefited from CRE. Two studies were with couples making the transition into parenthood, who are known to be at high risk for deteriorating relationship satisfaction (Halford et al., 2010; Shultz et al., 2006), and one study was with couples who were experiencing some relationship distress (Kaiser et al., 1998). Many low-risk couples have mutually satisfying relationships without CRE, and the major benefits of curriculum-based CRE might only be evident in high-risk couples (Larson and Halford, in press).

One major caveat on the efficacy of CRE is that almost all evaluations to date have been conducted on white, middle-class, premarital couples. The efficacy of CRE with low-income, socially disadvantaged couples and couples from non-English speaking backgrounds is largely untested. However, there is considerable ongoing research evaluating CRE with these groups (Hawkins, Wilson, Ooms, Nock, Malone-Colon, & Cohen, 2009).

Impact of Couple Relationship Education

The impact of CRE is the change in rates of relationship distress, or couple separations, attributable to CRE. The impact of CRE is dependent on two factors: the reach and effectiveness of CRE. The reach of CRE is the number of people in the population accessing a service. Effectiveness of CRE is the effects of intervention on couples who receive it within usual service-delivery conditions. There is an important distinction between efficacy and effectiveness (Chambless & Ollendick, 2001). Efficacy refers to the effects of a psychological intervention within tightly controlled trials of the intervention, where often the people delivering the intervention are highly trained and closely supervised, such as in the many randomized controlled trials that have been done of curriculum-based CRE. A range of factors can make effectiveness substantially lower than efficacy, particularly if the intervention is not well supported in the service-delivery organization (Society for Prevention Research, 2004). In the sections that follow we discuss specific strategies to enhance the reach and effectiveness of CRE.

Enhancing the limited reach of couple relationship education

The focus of evidence-based CRE has now extended well beyond couples planning to marry, and programs have been developed for couples at diverse stages in their relationship including: relationship enrichment for couples who have been together for some years (Kaiser et al., 1998); assistance for couples making the transition to parenthood (Petch & Halford, 2008); helping couples adjust to a serious illness affecting one partner (e.g. Baucom et al., 2009); people re-partnering to form stepfamilies (e.g. Nicholson, Phillips, Whitton, Halford, & Sanders, 2007); and even couples separated by one partner being jailed (Einhorn, Williams, Stanley, Wunderlin, Markman, & Eason, 2008). Despite these innovations, premarital education continues to be the most common route whereby couples access CRE (Markman & Halford, 2005; Stanley, Amato, Johnson, & Markman, 2006). Furthermore, religious organizations offering premarital CRE continue to be the major providers of CRE. In the United States and Australia, couples who marry in religious settings are much more likely to access premarital CRE than couples marrying in secular settings (Halford, O'Donnell, Lizzio, & Wilson, 2006; Stanley et al., 2006). Interestingly, those who are not religious are at higher risk of future marital problems than religious couples (Mahoney, Pargament, Tarakeshwar, & Swank, 2001).

The role of religious organizations as pioneers in offering premarital CRE has been crucial in the evolution of the field. However, even with their efforts only about 30% of marrying couples attend CRE (Halford, O'Donnell et al., 2006; Stanley et al., 2006). Rates of attending premarital CRE have increased from the 1950s through to the early 2000s, but the increase has been entirely in couples marrying for the first time (Doss, Rhoades, Stanley, Markman, & Johnson, 2009). Couples that include a previously divorced partner are underrepresented in those attending CRE, yet these couples are at high risk of future relationship problems (Doss, Rhoades, Stanley, & Markman, 2009). Extending the reach of CRE to remarrying partners, and to those married by a secular marriage celebrant is important, and achieving this goal might require other service providers offering CRE to complement the existing offerings by religious organizations.

Marriage *used* to be a clear marker of the beginning of committed couple relationships, and premarital CRE was an effective way of offering education to most couples early in their relationship. However, the patterns of forming committed relationships have changed substantially in many Western countries (see chapters 1, 2 this volume). Currently cohabiting couples make up over 8% of couple households in the United States (United States Census Bureau [USCB], 2003), 16% of couple households in Australia (Australian Bureau of Statistics [ABS], (2008), and 16% in Canada (Statistics Canada, 2001). The majority of couples cohabit before marrying, with over 70% of U.S. and 85% of Australian couples living with their partner before marrying (ABS, 2008; USCB, 2003). Couples choosing long-term cohabitation are somewhat different from married couples, and more likely to have experienced disruption in their parents' marriages, to have been married previously, to have lower levels of education, and to have low income (chapter 3 in this volume; de Vaus, Qu, & Weston, 2003). All these factors predict high risk for future relationship problems (Bradbury & Karney, 2004). Thus, making CRE accessible to cohabiting couples—a group at elevated risk of future problems—is important.

Curriculum-based CRE is most widely offered as face-to-face programs for small groups of couples (Wilson & Halford, 2008). Surveys of couples not accessing CRE identify a number of barriers to attending CRE in this mode. One key barrier is that attendance at face-to-face sessions is inconvenient, requiring commitment to attend a series of evenings or a weekend (Halford & Simons, 2005). For people who live in rural or remote areas, or who have dependent children and limited access to child care, or who have changing shifts of employment, attendance at regular scheduled sessions across multiple weeks may be very difficult. Furthermore, many couples see their relationships as private, and are uncomfortable with the idea of CRE groups (Halford & Simons, 2005). The reach of CRE could potentially be enhanced if a more diverse range of methods for accessing it existed, and IT has a potentially important role to play in diversifying the modes of CRE delivery.

Enhancing the effectiveness of couple relationship education

CRE research has focused heavily on the efficacy of interventions (Halford, Farrugia, Lizzio, & Wilson, 2010), with less attention being paid to the effectiveness of CRE programs. Only four studies have examined the effectiveness in routine service delivery of CRE on relationship satisfaction and stability (Birch, Weed, & Olsen, 2004; Schumm, Resnick, Silliman, & Bell, 1998; Stanley et al., 2006; Sullivan & Bradbury, 1997). Although each study involved significant methodological limitations (e.g., limited information on content or format of the CRE), all reported a modest positive association between attendance at CRE and later marital satisfaction or stability. However, Stanley et al. (2006) also found that much of what current providers of CRE offer is too brief to be effective. Moreover, many CRE providers do not give couples active skill training (Halford & Simons, 2005), which is the component of evidence-based CRE with the strongest evidence for its efficacy.

A limitation on the effectiveness of most curriculum-based CRE is it being offered in a one-size-fits-all manner, whereby content is standardized without taking into account the diversity of couples' backgrounds, knowledge, or relationship skills (Larson & Halford, in press). This approach has three major drawbacks. First, it fails to direct relationship education to those who might benefit the most such as high-risk couples. Second, standardized CRE curricula fail to address the unique needs, risks, and protective factors of couples. Not all couples need all components of a program, and couples report finding working through materials not directly applicable to their relationship needs unhelpful (Busby et al., 2007). Reviewing less personally relevant concepts and skills can de-motivate learners to participate in other curriculum components more relevant to their needs (Duncan & Goddard, 2005).

A third drawback of offering a fixed CRE curriculum is that, while CRE is targeted to currently satisfied couples, a substantial minority of couples seeking out CRE are distressed (DeMaria, 2005). Distressed couples might benefit from CRE, but also might need programs tailored to their particular relationship challenges. For example, relationship distress covaries with a range of individual psychological disorders (Whisman, 2007), which might require professional treatment.

A challenge in offering customized CRE is that many current providers of relationship education do not have the professional skills to carry out the assessments that might guide customization (Doherty & Anderson, 2004). The effective provision and uptake of tailored CRE is likely to be dependent on ease of delivery and accessibility. In other words, if assessment is used to tailor CRE, that assessment needs to be easy to access and interpret. If skill training is to be a core component of CRE in routine delivery, which is not currently the case, then systems need to be developed to make such skill training easy to deliver. The available information technology provides an exciting opportunity to develop cost-effective CRE that incorporates assessment and skills training tailored to suit the needs of couples.

Technology to Enhance Couple Relationship Education Impact

IT is currently being used to deliver a wide range of psychological services using such devices as mobile (cell) phones, personal digital assistants, DVDs, Internet-based video- and web-conferencing, e-mail, and social media (e.g. Facebook, Twitter; Casey & Halford, 2010). Examples of applications of IT include assessment and treatment for anxiety and depression (Spek, Cuijpers, Nyklicek, Riper, Keyzer, & Pop, 2007), problem gambling (Tavares, Martins, Zilberman, & el Gue, 2002), and coping with major health problems like cancer and heart disease (Lieberman & Goldstein, 2005). The advantages of using IT for service delivery are abundant and include: accessibility, flexibility, cost effectiveness, and service reliability.

Across diverse applications of adult education, programs structured to incorporate ease of access and to promote self-directed learning are termed "flexible delivery" programs, and flexible delivery can greatly enhance the reach of educational programs to target populations (Laurillard, 2002). Flexible delivery could enhance the reach of CRE, as couples can access CRE at times and places that suit them. Internet web sites, smart phone-based services, and audiovisual education programs completed at home, can remove the inconvenience of travel, as well as the concern over self-disclosure about one's relationship, perceived by many couples as barriers to attending group CRE sessions (Halford & Simons, 2005). In addition, IT offers access to CRE for couples with disabilities or social disadvantage. Computer and mobile phone software can provide, via screen magnifiers and audiovisual presentations, opportunities for these people to access CRE. Similarly, subtitled audiovisual materials can enhance access to CRE for people with hearing disabilities.

IT-based CRE also allows the process of learning to be tailored to meet specific couples' preferred learning styles. Web sites can be constructed to provide diverse ways of accessing information. For example, one couple might prefer to watch an audiovisual lecture, another couple might prefer to read text, while a third couple might prefer an interactive Internet-based contact with a professional. All three options can be offered to couples through an Internet site. Participants can review the material as many times as they like, which is not practicable in a group environment. Participants can be given feedback on their learning via interactive quizzes or reviews with educators by telephone or Internet video-conference and then assisted to identify productive learning processes to address learning needs. Thus, IT allows a tailoring of learning processes used in CRE beyond the capacity of current face-to-face modes of delivery.

IT-based CRE can also involve tailoring content for a particular couple. For example, the Internet-based RELATE assessment has key branching questions built into its design. If someone reports that they have a child living with them from a previous relationship then that triggers a set of questions specific to the challenges confronting stepfamilies. Education materials specific to those challenges can be made available to the couple. Similar branching questions can assess the relevance of material on relationship violence, concerns about finances, relationships with extended family, and so forth.

All possible advantages of IT-enhanced CRE would be moot if couples were unwilling to engage with such programs, but it seems many couples do use such programs effectively. A number of randomized controlled trials (e.g., Braithwaite & Fincham, 2009; Halford, Moore, Wilson, Dyer, & Farrugia, 2004; Halford, Farrugia, Lizzio, & Wilson, 2010; Larson et al., 2007) found that couples engage with and complete IT-based CRE that utilizes either Internet or DVD-based content. Moreover these same studies found IT-based CRE produced short-term improvements in couple satisfaction and stability, and benefits sustained for at least 1 year (Braithwaite & Fincham, 2009; Halford, Farrugia, Lizzio, & Wilson, 2010).

Providing contact with a professional is often the largest expense in delivering psychological interventions, and one issue is what level of professional contact—if any—is needed to achieve desired outcomes with CRE. The research on other IT-based psychological interventions has findings relevant to CRE. In a meta-analysis of 12 randomized controlled trials of Internet-based cognitive-behavioral treatment for anxiety and depression with therapist support demonstrated a large mean effect size, while interventions without therapist support displayed a small mean effect size (Spek et al., 2007). Similarly, Busby et al. (2007) and Larson et al. (2007) found higher consumer satisfaction and more gains in relationship satisfaction from CRE, when a telephone-based discussion with a therapist was added to the provision of a computer-generated couple relationship report. Together, findings suggest that some professional contact is important in CRE delivery, although this can be done remotely with IT, rather than face to face.

Relate with Couple CARE Program

An illustrative example of flexible-delivery, tailored CRE is the RELATE with Couple CARE Program (Halford, Farrugia, Lizzio, & Wilson, 2010). This program combines the Internet-based RELATE assessment with the Couple CARE relationship-skills training program. RELATE (Busby et al., 2001) provides a downloadable, computer-generated report on couple relationship strengths and challenges, and an interpretation of those designed to be easily understood by couples. The factors assessed by RELATE predict relationship satisfaction in couples (Holman, 2001), and are used in RELATE with Couple CARE to guide a decision on whether a couple needs intensive, skill-based CRE and what relationship domains might be most important to focus upon. While some professionals might wonder about the validity of reports based on computer assessments, it has been long established that people's reports of personal material to computer-based assessments are often more disclosing and reliable than that given to a professional interviewer (Garb, 2007).

Couple CARE consists of three components: (a) a DVD that presents key ideas and models core relationship skills; (b) a guidebook presenting a series of structured tasks for the couple that applies the key ideas to their relationship and helps partners engage in self-change; and (c) a series of sessions with a relationship educator to review progress and troubleshoot problems, which can be conducted by telephone or via Internet video-conference. Couple CARE was designed to allow flexible delivery so that the program can be completed by couples in their own homes, though couples also can use the resource materials as part of attending a face-to-face CRE program (Halford, 2011). Couple CARE utilizes a framework of self-directed learning (Wilson & Halford, 2008). Specifically, partners are assisted to evaluate their current behavior, identify goals for change, and implement self-change plans to enhance their relationship (Halford et al., 2004). Thus, rather than teach particular forms of couple interaction, Couple CARE encourages reflection, goal setting, and self-change (Wilson & Halford, 2008). The RELATE assessment forms part of the information provided to couples to guide this self-reflection.

Couple CARE for Parents program (CCP)

The use of IT can be combined with more traditional face-to-face delivery of CRE. For example, CCP consists of 6 units, using a combination of face-to-face and flexible delivery (Halford et al., 2010). CCP is focused on the promotion of positive couple adjustment to parenthood via skill training in key relationship skills, supplemented with infant care information.

The structure of CCP was designed to make access easy for couples, given how busy couples usually are when caring for a young infant. Unit 1 is a 6-hour face-to-face antenatal workshop, and includes couple activities, brief didactic presentations, video demonstrations, and skill training for groups of 3–4 couples. The remaining 5 CCP units are completed in the couple's home. Units 2 and 3 are home visits, conducted before and after the birth, respectively. Units 4 through 6 are in flexible-delivery mode and involve the couple watching a 10–12-minute DVD, completing exercises described in a guidebook, and having a telephone call with the CCP educator to review the unit and provide skill training. Thus, all the units after the birth are conducted in the couple's home and at times that are flexible to accommodate infant care demands. CCP enhances couple communication, and helps couples sustain high relationship satisfaction across the transition to parenthood (Halford et al., 2010).

Expanding Relationship Education Services

Technology can expand the range of CRE services in important ways. As noted in the example of CCP, flexible delivery can be used to assist couples when time demands make travel and attendance at face-to-face sessions difficult. Another example of the use of IT and flexible delivery for couples is providing CRE to couples having a health crisis. Halford, Chambers, & Clutton (2010) describe a couple-based education program for couples in which one partner was recently diagnosed with cancer. The program combines use of DVD-based educational material with telephone- or Internet-based contact with a professional. The program aims to help couples make key treatment decisions, develop active coping strategies, communicate effectively about their feelings, and provide each other with effective mutual support in managing the stresses of cancer diagnosis and treatment.

There are multiple other windows of opportunity for couples to access CRE using IT. One possibility is to develop CRE for users of online dating, which is booming in popularity. More than 40 million Internet users visit online dating sites per year in the United States alone, which is approximately half of all single adults in the United States (Mulrine, 2003). Despite the vast numbers of people using online dating, scholarly work is only just beginning to emerge regarding online relationships (Lucid, 2009).

Recent research has revealed that online daters often hold high and unrealistic expectations as to the potential mate they might attract (Whitty, 2008). These expectations may occur because individuals fill gaps in information about online partners with unrealistically positive assumptions, combined with the effect of having a large number of potential mates to select from online (Whitty, 2008). Upon meeting face to face, online daters report their dates often do not match their online profile and such mismatches are a frequent source of disappointment (Whitty, 2008).

CRE could expand into online dating systems to assist users to develop realistic expectations, make informed decisions about whom they wish to converse with online, and develop relationships in a safe and healthy manner. Such CRE could utilize existing evidence-based research on factors that predict potential attraction and long-term relationship satisfaction (Bradbury & Karney, 2004), and content could evolve as more is learned about online relationships.

Conclusion

At present CRE is provided primarily in face-to-face modalities to premarital couples. Despite the efforts of many clergy, professionals, and government to encourage couples' participation in CRE, only 30% of couples access existing services. Many couples report not accessing CRE due to the inconvenience of attending face-to-face sessions, or a desire for privacy. The wide availability of computers, DVD players, and high-technology telephones make CRE potentially more accessible than ever before. These technologies also can be used to make assessment- and curriculum-based CRE delivery easier, as illustrated with the RELATE with Couple CARE Program. Whole new areas of CRE delivery can be developed in which technology plays a key role, such as within online dating sites. Utilizing technology in creative ways can increase outreach to couples, provide accessible CRE cheaply and efficiently, and enhance the tailoring of programs to couples' learning styles and identified learning needs. In brief, IT in CRE can help more couples to realize their potential for a long-lasting, mutually fulfilling relationship.

Note

Preparation of this chapter was supported by Australian Research Council Grant DP1095507, *The effects of home-based couple relationship education on couple relationships, mental health and work performance*, to W. Kim Halford, Keithia L. Wilson, K. Dean Busby, Jeffry Larson, and Thomas Holman.

References

Australian Bureau of Statistics (2008). *Social trends.* http://www.abs.gov.au.

Baucom, D. H., Porter, L., Kirby, J., Grenmore, T., Wiesenthal, N., Aldridge, W., Friedman, S., Stanton, S. E., Scott, J. L., Halford, W. K., & Keefe, F. J. (2009). A couple-based intervention for female breast cancer. *Psycho-Oncology, 18*, 276–283.

Birch, P., Weed, S., & Olsen, J. (2004). Assessing the impact of community marriage policies on county divorce rates. *Family Relations, 53*, 495–503.

Blanchard, V. L., Hawkins, A. J., Baldwin, S. A., & Fawcett, E. B. (2009). Investigating the effects of marriage and relationship education on couples' communication skills: A meta-analytic study. *Journal of Family Psychology, 23*, 203–214.

Bodenmann, G., & Shantinath, S. D. (2004). The Bodenmann Couples Coping Enhancement Training (CCET): A new approach to prevention of marital distress based upon stress and coping. *Family Relations, 53*, 477–484.

Bodenmann, G., Pihet, S., Shantinath, S. D., Cina, A., & Widmer, K. (2006). Improving dyadic coping in couples with a stress-oriented approach: A 2-year longitudinal study. *Behaviour Modification, 30*, 571–597.

Bradbury, T. N., & Karney, B. R. (2004). Understanding and altering the longitudinal course of marriage. *Journal of Marriage and the Family, 66*, 862–879.

Braithwaite, S. R., & Fincham, F. D. (2009). A randomized clinical trial of a computer based preventive intervention: Replication and extension of ePREP. *Journal of Family Psychology, 23*, 32–28.

Busby, D. M., Holman, T. B., & Taniguchi, N. (2001). RELATE: Relationship evaluation of the individual, family, cultural and couple contexts. *Family Relations, 50*, 308–317.

Busby, D. M., Ivey, D. C., Harris, S. M., & Ates, C. (2007). Self-directed, therapist-directed, and assessment based interventions for premarital couples. *Family Relations, 56*, 279–290.

Casey, L. M., & Halford, W. K. (2010). Couples and the silicon chip: Applying information technology to couple relationship services. In. K. Hahlweg, D. Baucom, & M. Grawe-Gerber (Eds.), *Enhancing couples: The shape of couple therapy to come* (pp. 216–230). Cambridge, England: Hogrefe.

Chambless, D. L., & Ollendick, T. (2001). Empirically supported psychological interventions: Controversies and evidence. *Annual Review of Psychology, 52*, 685–716.

Cordova, J. V., Scott, R. L., Dorian, M., Mirgain, S., Yaeger, D., & Groot, A. (2005). The marriage checkup: An indicated preventive intervention for treatment-avoidant couples at risk for marital deterioration. *Behaviour Therapy, 36*, 301–309.

Cordova, J. V., Warren, L. Z., & Gee, C. B. (2001). Motivational interviewing as an intervention for at-risk couples. *Journal of Marital and Family Therapy, 27*, 315–326.

de Vaus, D., Qu. L., & Weston, T. (2003). Changing patterns of partnering. *Family Matters, 64*, 34–39.

DeMaria, R. M. (2005). Distressed couples and marriage education. *Family Relations, 54*, 242–253.

Doherty, W. J., & Anderson, J. R. (2004). Community marriage initiatives. *Family Relations, 53*, 425–432.

Doss, B. D., Rhoades, G., Stanley, S., & Markman, H. J. (2009). Marital therapy, retreats, and books: The who, what, when and why of relationship help-seeking. *Journal of Marital and Family Therapy, 35*, 18–29.

Doss, B. D., Rhoades, G., Stanley, S., Markman, H. J., & Johnson, C. A. (2009). Differential use of premarriage education in first and second marriages. *Journal of Family Psychology, 23*, 268–273.

Duncan, S. F., & Goddard, H. W. (Eds.) (2005). *Family life education: Principles and practices for effective outreach*. Thousand Oaks, CA: Sage.

Einhorn, L., Williams, T., Stanley, S., Wunderlin, N., Markman H. J., & Eason, J. (2008). PREP inside and out: Marriage education for inmates. *Family Process, 47*, 341–356.

Garb, H. N. (2007). Computer-administered interviews and rating scales. *Psychological Assessment, 19*, 4–13.

Glenn, N. D. (1998). The course of marital success and failure in five American 10-year cohorts. *Journal of Marriage and the Family, 60*, 269–282.

Gottman, J. M., Coan, J., Carrere, S., & Swanson, C. (1998). Predicting marital happiness and stability from newlywed interactions. *Journal of Marriage and the Family, 60*, 5–22.

Guerney, B. G., Jr.,(Ed.). (1977). *Relationship enhancement: Skill training programs for therapy, problem prevention, and enrichment*. San Francisco: Jossey-Bass.

Guerney, B. G., Jr., & Maxson, P. (1990). Marital and family enrichment research: A decade review and look ahead. *Journal of Marriage and the Family, 52*, 1127–1137.

Hahlweg, K., Markman, H. J., Thurmaier, F., Engl, J., & Eckert, V. (1998). Prevention of marital distress: Results of a German prospective longitudinal study. *Journal of Family Psychology, 12*, 543–556.

Halford, W. K. (2011). *Marriage and relationship education: What works and how to provide it*. New York: Guilford Press.

Halford, W. K., Chambers, S., & Clutton, S. (2010). *Couples coping with cancer*. In: N. A. Pachana, K. Laidlaw, & B. Knight (Eds.). *Casebook in clinical geropsychology: International perspectives on practice* (pp. 73–90). Oxford, England: Oxford University Press.

Halford, W. K., Farrugia, C., Lizzio, A., & Wilson, K. L. (2010). Relationship aggression, violence and self-regulation in Australian newlywed couples. *Australian Journal of Psychology, 62*, 82–92.

Halford, W. K., Lizzio, A., Wilson, K. L., & Occhipinti, S. (2007). Does working at your relationship help? Couple relationship self-regulation and satisfaction in the first 4 years of marriage. *Journal of Family Psychology, 21*, 185–194.

Halford, W. K., Markman, H. J., & Stanley, S. (2008). Strengthening couples' relationships with education: Social policy and public health perspectives. *Journal of Family Psychology, 22*, 497–505.

Halford, W. K., Moore, E. M., Wilson, K. L., Dyer, C., & Farrugia, C. (2004). Benefits of a flexible delivery relationship education: An evaluation of the Couple CARE program. *Family Relations, 53*, 469–476.

Halford, W. K., Moore, E. M., Wilson, K. L., Dyer, C., & Farrugia, C. (2006). *Couple commitment and relationship enhancement*. Brisbane: Australian Academic Press.

Halford, W. K., O'Donnell, C., Lizzio, A. J., & Wilson, K. L. (2006). Do couples at high risk of relationship problems attend pre-marriage education? *Journal of Family Psychology, 92*, 160–163.

Halford, W. K., Osgarby, S. M., & Kelly, A. B. (1996). Brief behavioural marital therapy: A preliminary quasi-experimental evaluation. *Behavioural and Cognitive Psychotherapy, 24*, 263–273.

Halford, W. K., Petch, J., & Creedy, D. (2010). Promoting a positive transition to parenthood: A randomized clinical trial of couple relationship education. *Prevention Science, 11*, 89–100.

Halford, W. K., Sanders, M. R., & Behrens, B. C. (2001). Can skills training prevent relationship problems in at-risk couples? Four-year effects of a behavioural relationship education program. *Journal of Family Psychology, 14*, 750–768.

Halford, W. K., & Simons, M. (2005). Couple relationship education in Australia. *Family Process, 44*, 147–259.

Halford, W. K., Markman, H. J., & Stanley, S. (2008). Public health perspectives on family interventions. *Journal of Family Psychology, 22*, 497–505.

Halford, W. K., Wilson, K., Watson, B., Verner, T., Larson, J., Busby, D., & Holman, T. (2010). Couple relationship education at home: Does skill training enhance relationship assessment and feedback? *Journal of Family Psychology, 24*, 188–196.

Hawkins, A. J., Blanchard, V. L., Baldwin, S. A., & Fawcett, E. B. (2008). Does marriage and relationship education work? A meta-analytic study. *Journal of Consulting and Clinical Psychology, 76*, 723–734.

Hawkins, A. J., Wilson, R. F., Ooms, T., Nock, S. L., Malone-Colon, L., & Cohen, L. (2009). Recent government reforms related to marital formation, maintenance and dissolution in the United States: A primer. *Journal of Couple and Relationship Therapy, 8*, 264–281.

Holman, T. B. (Ed.) (2001). *Premarital prediction of marital quality or break up. Research, theory and practice*. New York: Kluwer.

Hunt, R., Hof, I., & DeMaria, R. (Eds.) (1998). *Marriage enrichment: Preparation, mentoring and outreach*. Philadelphia: Brunner/Mazel.

Johnson, M. D., Cohan, C. L., Davilla, J., Lawrence, E., Rogge, R., & Karney, B., et al. (2005). Problem-solving skills and affective expression as predictors of change in marital satisfaction. *Journal of Consulting and Clinical Psychology, 73*, 15–27.

Kaiser, A., Halweg, K., Fehm-Wolfsdorf, G., & Groth, T. (1998). The efficacy of a compact psycho-educational group training programme for married couples. *Journal of Consulting and Clinical Psychology, 66*, 753–760.

Kiecolt-Glaser, J. K., Bane, C., Glaser, R., & Malarkey, W. B. (2003). Love, marriage, and divorce: newlyweds' stress hormones foreshadow relationship changes. *Journal of Consulting and Clinical Psychology, 71*, 176–188.

Knutson, L., & Olsen, D. H. (2003). Effectiveness of PREPARE Program with premarital couples in a community setting. *Marriage and Family, 6*, 529–646.

Larson, J. H., & Halford, W. K. (in press). One size does not fit all: Customizing couple relationship education for unique couple needs. *Journal of Couple and Relationship Therapy*.

Larson, J. H., Newell, K., Topham, G., & Nichols, S. (2002). A review of three comprehensive premarital assessment questionnaires *Journal of Marital and Family Therapy, 28*, 233–239.

Larson, J. H., Vatter, R. S., Galbraith, R. C., Holman, T. B., & Stahmann, R. F. (2007). The relationship evaluation (RELATE) with therapist-assisted interpretation: Short-term effects on premarital relationships. *Journal of Marital and Family Therapy, 33*, 364–374.

Laurillard, D. (2002). *Rethinking university teaching: A framework for the effective use of learning technologies*. London: Routledge Falmer.

Lieberman, M. A., & Goldstein, B. A. (2005). Self-help online: An outcome evaluation of breast cancer bulletin boards. *Journal of Health Psychology, 10*, 855–862.

Lucid, L. (2009). Misrepresenting the self in online dating. *Mind Matters: The Wesleyan Journal of Psychology, 4*, 37–49.

Mahoney, A., Pargament, K., Tarakeshwar, N., & Swank, A. (2001). Religion in the home in the 1980s and 1990s: A meta-analytic review and conceptual analysis of links between religion, marriage, and parenting. *Journal of Family Psychology, 15*, 559–596.

Markey, B., & Micheletto, M. (Eds.) (1997). *Instructor manual for FOCCUS*. Omaha, NE: Archdiocese of Omaha.

Markman, H. J. (1981). Prediction of marital distress: A 5-year follow-up. *Journal of Consulting and Clinical Psychology, 49*, 760–762.

Markman, H. J., Floyd, F. J., Stanley, S. M., & Storaasli, R. D. (1988). Prevention of marital distress: A longitudinal investigation. *Journal of Consulting and Clinical Psychology, 56*, 210–217.

Markman, H. J., & Halford, W. K. (2005). International perspectives on couple relationship education. *Family Process, 44*, 139–146.

Miller, S. L., Miller, P. A., Nunnally, E. W., & Wackman, D. B. (Eds.) (1992). *Couple communication instructor manual*. Denver-Littleton, CO: Interpersonal Communication Programs.

Mulrine, A. (2003, September 29). Love.com: For better or for worse, the Internet is radically changing the dating scene in America, *U.S. News & World Report*.

Nicholson, J. M., Phillips, M., Whitton, S. W., Halford, W. K., & Sanders, M. R. (2007). Promoting healthy stepfamilies: Couples' reasons for seeking help and perceived benefits from intervention. *Family Matters, 77*, 48–57.

Olsen, D. H., Fournier, D. G., & Druck, J. M. (Eds.) (1996). *PREPARE*. Minneapolis: Life Innovations.

Pasch, L. A., & Bradbury, T. N. (1998). Social support, conflict, and the development of marital dysfunction. *Journal of Consulting and Clinical Psychology, 66*, 219–230.

Petch, J., & Halford, W. K. (2008). Psycho-education to enhance couples' transition to parenthood. *Clinical Psychology Review, 28*, 1125–1137.

Renick, M. J., Blumberg, S., & Markman, H.J. (1992). The Prevention and Relationship Enhancement Program (PREP): An empirically based preventive intervention program for couples. *Family Relations, 41*, 141–147.

Schumm, W. R., Resnick, G., Silliman, B., & Bell, D. B. (1998). Premarital counselling and marital satisfaction among civilian wives of military service members. *Journal of Sex and Marital Therapy, 24*, 21–28.

Shultz, M. S., Cowan, C. P., & Cowan, P. A. (2006). Promoting healthy beginnings: A randomized controlled trial of preventive intervention to preserve marriage quality during the transition to parenthood. *Journal of Consulting and Clinical Psychology, 74*, 20–31.

Society for Prevention Research (2004). *Standards of evidence: Criteria for efficacy, effectiveness and dissemination*. Fall Church, VA: Society for Prevention Research.

Spek, V., Cuijpers, P., Nyklicek, I., Riper, H., Keyzer, J., & Pop, V. (2007). Internet-based cognitive behaviour therapy for symptoms of anxiety and depression: a meta-analysis. *Psychological Medicine, 37*, 319–328.

Stanley, S. M. (2001). Making the case for premarital training. *Family Relations, 50*, 272–280.

Stanley, S. M., Amato, P. R., Johnson, C. A., & Markman, H. J. (2006). Pre-marital education, marital quality, and marital stability: Findings from a large, random, household survey. *Journal of Family Psychology 20*, 117–126.

Sullivan, K. T., & Bradbury, T. N. (1997). Are premarital prevention programs reaching couples at risk for marital dysfunction? *Journal of Consulting and Clinical Psychology, 65*, 24–30.

Statistics Canada (2001). *Social trends*. www.statcan.gc.ca/start-debut-eng.html.

Tavares, H., Martins, S. S., Zilberman, M. L., & el Guebaly, N. (2002). Gamblers seeking treatment: Why haven't they come earlier? *Addictive Disorders and Their Treatment, 1*, 65–69.

United States Census Bureau (2003). *Social trends*. http://www.census.gov.

van Widenfelt, B., Hosman, C., Schaap, C., & van der Staak, C. (1996). The prevention of relationship distress for couples at risk: A controlled evaluation with nine-month and two-year follow-ups. *Family Relations, 45*, 156–165.

Whisman, M. A. (2007). Marital distress and DSM-IV psychiatric disorders in a population-based national survey. *Journal of Abnormal Psychology, 116*, 638–643.

Whitty, M. (2008). Revealing the "real" me, searching for the "actual" you: Presentations of self on an internet dating site. *Computers in Human Behaviour, 24*, 1707–1723.

Wilson, K. L., & Halford, W. K. (2008). Processes of change in the flexible delivery of couple relationship education. *Family Relations, 57*, 625–635.

Worthington, E. L., McCullough, M. E., Shortz, J. L., Mindes, E. J., Sandage, S. J., & Chartrand, J. M. (1995). Can couples assessment and feedback improve relationships? Assessment as a brief relationship enrichment procedure. *Journal of Counselling Psychology, 42*, 466–475.

20

Relationship Education

Facilitating Apology, Forgiveness, and Relationship Security Following Hurtful Events

Judith A. Feeney and Jennifer Fitzgerald

Love Hurts
Love Really Hurts Without You
Love is a Battlefield
Love and Other Bruises

As the song titles listed above suggest, we do not have to look far, in terms of popular culture, to meet the idea that love relationships can be hurtful. Psychological research tends to support this idea, although it does not accord with the extreme version which regards all partners in love relationships as doomed to a life of pain and suffering. Rather, research suggests that hurt feelings do arise, with varying regularity, in ongoing couple relationships (Feeney & Hill, 2006). Further, research indicates that the resolution of these events is important both to the self-esteem of the injured party and to the future of the relationship (Caughlin, Scott, & Miller, 2009; Feeney, 2004; Fitness & Warburton, 2009).

With regard to resolving hurtful events, both popular culture and psychological theory suggest that victims face some basic dilemmas, in terms of competing response tendencies. For example, victims may be tempted to retaliate (take revenge, "get even"), while at the

The Wiley-Blackwell Handbook of Couples and Family Relationships, First Edition.
Edited by Patricia Noller and Gery C. Karantzas.

same time thinking that restraint may be the better course of action (see chapter 18 in this volume). In addition, victims may find themselves feeling wary towards the offender ("once bitten, twice shy"), while nevertheless wanting to regain the degree of openness and trust that characterized the relationship previously. Finally, following hurtful events, victims may debate the relative merits of focusing on protecting themselves from further hurt versus nurturing the couple relationship (although these alternatives are not necessarily mutually exclusive). These dilemmas can be linked to contemporary views of forgiveness, which recognize the importance of the hurt party relinquishing the tendencies toward revenge and avoidance, and re-establishing a sense of goodwill toward the offender (e.g., Fincham, 2000; Gordon & Baucom, 1998; McCullough, Rachal, Sandage, Worthington, Brown, & Hight, 1998; chapter 18 in this volume).

In the remainder of this chapter, we discuss some key issues pertaining to hurtful events in couple relationships, and then outline a program of relationship education designed to facilitate apology, forgiveness, and security. First, we briefly raise four issues linked to the broad question: What is hurtful in couple relationships, and why does hurt require forgiveness?

What Types of Events are Hurtful?

Hurt feelings can be elicited by many different events. In a retrospective study conducted by Leary and colleagues (Leary, Springer, Negel, Ansell, & Evans, 1998), victims' accounts of hurtful events could be grouped into six categories: active disassociation (explicit rejection, abandonment, or ostracism); passive disassociation (implicit rejection, such as ignoring the partner); criticism; betrayal; teasing; and feeling unappreciated, used, or taken for granted. The utility of distinguishing between the different types of events is highlighted by the finding that these categories differed in levels of hurt and in appraisals of rejection: on both these indices, for example, criticism was seen as less serious than acts of disassociation and betrayal.

More recently, we offered a critique of this typology and adapted it specifically for couple (romantic) relationships (Feeney, 2004). This study found support for five types of hurtful events: active disassociation (denying or retracting feelings of love and commitment); passive disassociation (ignoring or excluding partner from plans and activities); criticism; sexual infidelity; and deception (lying, breaking promises and confidences). Again, these categories showed systematic differences. For instance, infidelity was generally seen as very serious, with victims reporting high levels of hurt (including intentional hurt) and powerlessness, and long-term negative effects on their self-confidence and on the couple relationship. Conversely, on average, criticism was seen as less serious. However, the five types of hurtful events do *not* represent a simple continuum of seriousness. For example, victims of all these events tended to perceive moderately high levels of rejection. Further, although passive disassociation was less immediately hurtful than infidelity and active disassociation, it had severe long-term effects on the victim's self-confidence (Feeney, 2004).

Although many hurtful events are minor and easily resolved, some researchers have focused their attention on more serious events. Of particular importance to the long-term adjustment of the victim are *attachment injuries*, which Johnson and colleagues defined as serious acts of abandonment or betrayal of trust that maintain distress, because the injured party continues to view the other as unreliable (Johnson, Makinen, & Millikin, 2001; chapter 23 in this volume). This concept can apply to most, if not all, of the types of events just discussed. Attachment injuries can be responsible for ongoing distress on the part of the target, and for impasses that block attempts to repair the relationship; it is as though the victim has decided "I'll never allow myself to need you so much again." Johnson's emotion-focused therapy draws heavily on attachment principles, and is designed to help couples deal with attachment injuries (see chapters 11, 14 in this volume for detailed descriptions of attachment theory).

Relevance of the Broader Context

The broader context of the offender's behavior is also relevant to issues of hurt and forgiveness. Although researchers who study hurt feelings often choose to focus on one particular relationship event, it is clear that individuals interpret such events in the light of their relationship history and their global evaluations of relationship quality, rather than as isolated acts. Relevant questions include: Was this a first offense, or part of an ongoing pattern of hurtful behavior? And is the problem behavior perceived as specific to the episode in question, or as part of a wider relationship problem, such as failing to show respect or consideration for the partner?

Questions of this sort are relevant to the attributions that targets make for the offending behavior, as well as to their perceptions of offender remorse (Allan & Harrison, 2009). In turn, attributions for the offense, and perceptions of offender remorse, are crucial to the process of resolving hurtful events. For example, there is considerable evidence that successful resolution is hampered when the hurtful behavior is perceived as intentional (rather than accidental) and as driven by malice, and when the offender is not regarded as being "truly sorry" for the hurt they have caused (Feeney, 2004; Fitness, 2001; Vangelisti & Young, 2000).

Emotional Turmoil

Following one of the classic themes in psychology, issues of hurt and forgiveness require us to consider not only the hurtful behaviors themselves, but also the associated emotions and cognitions. With regard to emotion, it is clear that in some extreme cases of attachment injuries, targets may present with intense fear and helplessness (Johnson, 2003; Kobak, Cassidy, & Zir, 2004). Even in less severe instances, "hurt," by definition, is experienced as painful. This concept is highlighted by neuroimaging data that link responses to rejection with those to physical pain (Eisenberger, Lieberman, & Williams, 2003; chapter 18 in this volume).

Researchers have debated the exact nature of the emotional experience of "hurt feelings." In a prototype study of the hierarchical organization of emotion concepts, cluster analysis placed "hurt" within the basic emotion of sadness, in a sub-cluster of terms (e.g., "agony," "anguish") reflecting the theme of suffering (Shaver, Schwartz, Kirson, & O'Connor, 1987). However, hurt is often regarded as a blend of emotions. For example, Vangelisti (2001; Vangelisti & Young, 2000) has proposed that hurt involves a combination of sadness (at a felt loss) and fear (of being vulnerable to harm). In a somewhat different approach, Leary and Springer (2001) suggested that hurt may be a unique emotion in its own right; that is, hurt feelings are not simply reducible to other negative emotions, although they are often accompanied by them. A recent study by Fitness and Warburton (2009) in which respondents were asked to recall separate events that had elicited hurt, sadness, and anger supports this suggestion. In this study, respondents were able to differentiate between the three types of events, with hurtful events being characterized as very unexpected and difficult to understand, as eliciting strong feelings of confusion and distress, and as resulting in urges to cry and to leave the situation.

Analysis of victims' open-ended accounts of hurtful events in couple relationships indicates that common elements include sadness, fear, and anger (Feeney, 2005). Further, the emotional experience often shifts over time, and in somewhat unpredictable ways. For example, some victims report that an initial surge of anger gradually gave way to a growing sense of sadness, whereas others report the reverse pattern. Despite these elements of sadness, fear, and anger, the dominant theme in respondents' accounts of hurtful events was a sense of pain and injury, providing further support for the view that hurt is a unique emotion.

What Does the Hurtful Act Seem to Signify?

What specific cognitive appraisals elicit hurt feelings? Several overlapping views have been put forward. One view (Leary, 2001) links hurt to perceived *relational devaluation*; that is, to the perception that the offender regards the relationship as less valuable or important than the target would like. In another approach, Vangelisti (2001) proposed that the defining feature of hurt feelings is *relational transgression*; that is, the offender is seen as having broken a relationship rule, and the target appraises his or her own role in the interaction as that of victim. More recently, we have suggested that hurt feelings stem from relational transgressions that involve a sense of *personal injury* to one's self-worth or basic trust in others (Feeney, 2005). That is, consistent with attachment theory, hurt results when partners' behavior threatens positive working models of self and/or others. In a slight amendment to this view, Shaver and colleagues have proposed that a key feature of hurtful events is their capacity to destroy an individual's sense of safety and security, which is deep, visceral, and generally unconscious (Shaver, Mikulincer, Lavy, & Cassidy, 2009).

A Complicating Factor: Differences in Perceptions and Responses

Before we consider our approach to intervention, we would like to briefly highlight the fact that people differ in their perceptions of, and reactions to, hurtful events. For the purposes of this chapter, we will mention just two sources of such differences.

First, we need to consider the role the individual has played in the event; that is, as victim or offender. As researchers have noted, instances of wrongdoing carry different implications for victims and offenders (Mikula, Athenstaedt, Heschgl, & Heimgartner, 1998; Schutz, 1999). Specifically, victims may seek to preserve their self-concept and social image as good people, and to justify punishing the perpetrator; hence, they tend to adopt an *accusing* stance. In contrast, offenders may be motivated to restore their self-concept and social image as just and moral, and to protect themselves from blame and punishment; hence, they tend to adopt a *defensive* stance. The result of such biases is that victims evaluate transgressions more negatively than do perpetrators (Baumeister, Stillwell, & Wotman, 1990; Cameron, Ross, & Holmes, 2002; Leary et al., 1998; Zechmeister & Romero, 2002). We see these biases reflected particularly in the language people use to "tell the story" of hurtful events. For example, for a couple in one of our studies (Feeney & Hill, 2006), the contentious issue was the destruction of a photo frame, which the female had given to the male, and which had subsequently been belittled by the female's ex-partner. The female (the offender) simply stated, "the frame smashed." The male elaborated, "the frame was a symbol of all the things I love about her—and partners should not throw things at each other's heads!"

Interestingly, diary data from that study showed that in everyday life, offenders often fail to perceive the partner's sense of hurt. This finding probably reflects the indirect and ambiguous nature of much couple communication, as failure to perceive partner's hurt was more likely to occur when the hurtful event was inferred rather than clearly evident (e.g., involving a "sin of omission," or pertaining to nonverbal behavior that accompanied a message). Further, in some instances, both partners perceived themselves as the victim, an effect that may reflect the complexity of intimate relationships and the different ways in which ongoing interactions can be "punctuated" (Feeney & Hill, 2006).

A second important source of differences in perceptions and responses to hurtful events are individual differences in attachment security. For example, individuals who are anxious about relationships respond to hurtful partner behavior with high levels of distress and self-blame; these immediate responses tend to maintain, or even exacerbate, their fears and self-doubts (Feeney, 2004). In addition, avoidant individuals tend to perceive their partners as lacking remorse for hurtful behavior; this perception serves to fuel relationship conflict and impede relationship repair (Feeney, 2004). These findings are consistent with a broader body of research into attachment-style differences in affect regulation (see Shaver et al., 2009), and further highlight the relevance of attachment issues to the outcomes of hurtful events.

How Do Couples "Get Over" Hurtful Events?

To investigate the process of successfully resolving hurtful events, we gathered data from a community-based sample of 107 couples (dating, cohabiting, or married) regarding the resolution of their relationship hurts. Such an approach acknowledges the value of gathering "insider" information (Noller & Guthrie, 1991); that is, couples' own insights into their relationship histories of hurt and resolution, and their perceptions of their successes and failures. "Outsiders" can then evaluate these suggestions in the light of established research into couple communication, conflict, and relational outcomes.

The couples, who overall reported high levels of relationship satisfaction, were asked to consider factors they found helpful and unhelpful in resolving hurtful episodes, and factors they believed made resolution difficult or affected the partner's responses to hurt. An audiovisual recording was made of each couple as they briefly discussed their responses to these questions. A thematic analysis of their responses was then conducted.

Comments regarding resolution of hurtful events were categorized into six distinct domains: helpful/unhelpful actor (perpetrator) and target (victim) behaviors; and helpful/unhelpful couple interactions. A summary of couples' comments appears in Table 20.1.

Throughout the couples' discussions, the issue of appropriate timing of conversations about the hurtful episode was raised spontaneously by more than half the sample. While there was general agreement that it was important to talk about the episode, couples varied in their opinions as to *when* that talking should take place. Broadly, some couples emphasized the value of waiting or taking time before talking over the issue, while others suggested that the issue should be given priority and addressed quickly. Within-couple differences were also found: Some couples described one partner's need to resolve hurtful issues quickly, and the other's need to calm down and think before talking. The difficulty of working with such a tension was evident in these couples' conversations; for example, one husband exclaimed, "But I just *have* to know what I've done to hurt you!" to which his wife rather grimly replied, "And you know that I have to sulk for at least two days before I am ready to talk."

Table 20.1 Resolving Hurtful Events: Frequently Suggested Helpful and Unhelpful Behaviors (With Frequencies)

Type of behavior	*Recommendations*
Helpful actor	Acknowledge the hurt caused and apologize (29.97%)
	Understand partner's needs, feelings, and perspective (16.82%)
	Listen, allow partner to express feelings (14.95%)
	Explain intention (11.21%)
Helpful target	Openly discuss (46.72%)
	Clearly express feelings (29.90%)
	Calm down before talking (22.43%)
	Keep the size of the event in perspective (14.95%)
Helpful couple interaction	Discuss in a calm, respectful, and honest manner; end on a positive note (53.27%)
	Consider each partner's needs, feelings, and point of view (30.84%)
	Be motivated to resolve and willing to compromise (10.28%)
Unhelpful actor	Ignore partner's needs and feelings (18.69%)
	Defend oneself loudly, irritably (10.28%)
Unhelpful target	Be silent, sulk, bottle up feelings (56.07%)
	Express hurt forcefully (41.12%)
	Ruminate (10.28%)
Unhelpful couple interaction	Avoid: the issue, each partner's point of view, each other (23.36%)
	Retaliate: drag in other complaints, store up hurts, threaten to leave (18.64%)

Table 20.2 Frequently Suggested Factors Impeding Resolution of Hurt

Individual factors	*Frequencies*	*Contextual factors*	*Frequencies*
Strong emotions: anger, jealousy, fear	15.88%	Separation or distance: phone, long work hours, leaving the house in anger	12.13%
Personality: moody, inexpressive	8.41%	Presence of family, children, or friends	10.28%
Sulking; refusing to talk or change	8.41%	"Baggage" from other relationships	4.67%
Hypersensitivity	5.6%	Influence of alcohol and other substances	3.73%
Loss of perspective	3.73%	Fatigue, feeling unwell, taking medications	2.8%
One partner likes to express feelings/other doesn't	2.8%		
Refusal to let go of issue/having "fixed points"	1.86%		

Overall, couples' suggestions reflected a confidence in constructive communication as a tool for resolving hurt, with the critical ingredients including effective listening and speaking skills, emotional regulation, and a motivation to find a mutually satisfying resolution. Mutual understanding of each other's perspectives emerged as a central theme.

The importance of actors' apologies or acknowledgments was also mentioned as a helpful factor by a substantial proportion of the couples. This effect may occur because an apology is likely to convey that the actor has already suffered (Ohbuchi, Kameda, & Agarie, 1989), or that the actor intends to behave better in the future (Weiner, 1995); indeed, apology may reduce the likelihood of the target punishing the offender (McLaughlin, Cody, & O'Hair, 1983). When resolving more serious hurtful events that involve attachment injuries, Makinen and Johnson (2006) underscore the importance of offenders' understanding and acknowledging the impact of the hurtful events for their partners, a step which can then result in expressions of sincere remorse.

Not surprisingly, strong negative emotions (such as anger, jealousy, and fear) were noted as a particular barrier to the resolution process. This finding highlights the importance of addressing emotions in couple therapy and relationship education (chapter 23 in this volume). Table 20.2 summarizes factors perceived as making resolution difficult.

Can Education Help Newly Committed Couples to Prevent and Resolve Hurtful Events?

The negative consequences of hurtful events for victims and for couple relationships highlight the need for couples to develop awareness and skills in preventing and resolving hurt. Consistent with the focus of prevention science (e.g., Coie et al., 1993), we expected that a relationship education program that aimed to strengthen skills in relationship repair processes would be particularly beneficial for at-risk couples in the early years of commitment. Given earlier research indicating that the interaction of the two partners' attachment styles was important in determining couples' marital satisfaction (Feeney, 1994; Senchak & Leonard, 1992), we anticipated that a dyadic configuration of insecure attachment styles would be useful in identifying at-risk couples. Thus, drawing on the work of Banse (2004), couples in the study described below were categorized as "secure2" if the female partner self-nominated as secure in attachment style and her male partner self-nominated as either secure or dismissing-avoidant; "insecure" couples included dyadic configurations involving preoccupied, dismissing avoidant, or fearful avoidant styles.

The findings from our initial study of couples (described above) were used to guide the development of a 1-day 6-hour educational workshop for couples, which aimed to prevent and resolve hurtful events in couples' relationships. A controlled-effectiveness trial evaluated the longitudinal impact of the workshop for 69 couples in the first 5 years of commitment, recruited from the University of Queensland, Australia, and the wider community. This educational workshop integrated current research in couple communication, psychological hurt, and forgiveness. Unlike many other interventions designed to facilitate forgiveness, this workshop promoted relationship well-being by addressing *both* targets' hurt and actors' guilt and shame. Further, this program focused on emotions more broadly, with the aim of assisting couples to understand and regulate their negative emotions.

Content and process of the workshop

A Hurtful Event Record (based on the work of Feeney, 2004) was administered at the beginning of each of the nine workshops that were conducted. The number of participants at each workshop varied from 2 to 10 couples. For the larger workshops, trained assistants were present to support couples in their reflections and within-couple discussions. Couples were asked to choose two events in their relationship, one in which the male had been hurtful and the other in which the female had been hurtful. Both partners were then asked to reflect on and write about their individual perspectives regarding *both* these hurtful events (Hurtful Event Record; HER). Completing this exercise and referring to these events in the couple exercises throughout the day gave couples an opportunity to explore the relevance of the material to their own relationship concerns. Thus, this record of personal experiences made relevant, or "customized," the educational material for each couple; the material was also standardized across workshops through the use of workbooks, slide presentations, and prepared exercises (Carroll & Doherty, 2003). It was made clear at the start of the workshops that there would be no large-group sharing of hurtful events; individual reflection and within-couple communication were encouraged at frequent intervals and supported by the facilitator and assistants. All events described in the HERs could be coded according to Feeney's typology (see examples in Table 20.3).

Table 20.3 Feeney's (2004) Typology of Hurtful Events: Examples from the Hurtful Event Records

Event	*Example*
Active disassociation	Female told partner they should sell their home and separate
Implicit rejection	Male went out to a bar and spent a lot of money, leaving wife and baby home alone for a longer period of time than was arranged
Criticism	Male learned that his fiancée was talking to her friends, calling him names which implied that he was weak and useless
Third-party involvement	Female went overseas and had a sexual relationship with someone else
Other acts of betrayal	Male lied about taking his children to an expensive restaurant for his daughter's birthday, and about meeting his ex-wife in a public place when collecting the children for the party

Just as attachment theory offers marital therapists a "map to the terrain of adult love relationships" (Johnson, 2004, p. 8), we hypothesized that attachment concepts would provide a helpful guide for relationship educators as well. Partners were invited to think of their relationship as an *attachment bond,* and reflect on ways in which each partner does and could provide a "safe haven" and "secure base" for the other (for a detailed description of attachment bonds see chapters 11, 14 in this volume). The core attachment concepts of availability and responsiveness were developed throughout the workshop; for example, in exercises which promoted effective listening and disclosing, perspective taking, and understanding own and partners' emotional experience.

It was suggested that *understanding* painful emotions is an important step in managing emotional distress. Hence, the workshop provided information about emotions more broadly; for example, adaptive versus maladaptive functions and primary versus secondary emotions were discussed (Greenberg & Paivio, 1997). Interactive exercises provided opportunity for partners to reflect on their experiences of sadness, anger, fear, and hurt; questions prompted reflection and discussion about typical triggers, bodily experiences, associated thoughts, and action tendencies of each of these emotions (Arnold, 1960; Fitness & Fletcher, 1993). Strategies were suggested for increasing emotional regulation, such as attention to felt experience, self-soothing techniques, and "softened start up" (Gottman, 1994) for discussion of sensitive topics.

After the concepts of attachment needs, listening and speaking techniques, perspective taking, and emotional understanding had been carefully explained and explored, the workshop focused on more specific skills of relationship repair: namely, apology and forgiveness. Table 20.4 displays an overview of the content of the workshop.

Program evaluation: Design

The impact of the workshops was evaluated in two ways. First, general measures of relationship functioning (e.g., relationship satisfaction, emotional control, self- and partner efficacy to handle hurtful events) were mailed to both intervention group and wait-list control group couples at three time points: 1 week before the scheduled

Table 20.4 Sections of the Workshop, Designed to Promote Relationship Security

Towards greater security through...	*Themes*
Respectful communication: skills to build a secure relationship	Four common communication problems Effective listening Expressing thoughts and feelings
Mutual understanding	Early influences on beliefs and expectations about self and close relationships Differing styles of adult attachment
Effective relationship repair	Helpful and unhelpful responses to hurtful events Timing of discussions Calming down
Understanding and managing emotions	Function of emotions Sadness, anger, and fear Problems of over- and under-control
Understanding partner perspectives	Role-related differences in story telling Partner perspective taking
Forgiveness	Definition and clarification Granting and seeking forgiveness Self-forgiveness
Practical demonstrations of love and care	Patient, persistent efforts to demonstrate sincere remorse
Committing to a reconciliation plan	Eight steps to build a bridge to reconciliation

workshops (pre-intervention), 2 weeks after the intervention group had undertaken the workshop (post-intervention), and 6 months after the intervention group had undertaken the workshop (follow-up). Second, HERs were included in the post-intervention and follow-up data collection for the intervention group only (owing to constraints from the University Ethics Committee). At follow-up (which was designed to assess generalization of skills), 17 of the 23 intervention-group couples who returned questionnaires indicated that there had been no hurtful events since the workshop. Of the remaining six couples, four did not follow instructions accurately and reported on the same events as at the workshop, leaving no meaningful HER data at follow-up. Wait-list couples attended workshops after all three data collection points were completed.

Impact of the workshop

Quantitative analyses assessing the impact of the intervention focused on the general measures of relationship functioning and responses to the HERs. Table 20.5 summarizes significant findings from these analyses.

General measures of relationship functioning. For relationship satisfaction, females in the intervention group only reported greater satisfaction post-intervention ($M=6.87$, $SD=1.52$) than pre-intervention ($M=6.45$, $SD=1.50$). This improvement was

Table 20.5 Summary of Significant Results from Intervention Study

General measures (group × time analyses)	
Relationship satisfaction	Females: group × time, F (2, 32) = 2.58, $p < .1$ ($\eta^2 = .13$) Females: group × time × risk, F (2, 31) = 4.74, $p < .05$ ($\eta^2 = .23$)
Targets' self-efficacy	Females: group × time, F(2, 36) = 4.32, $p < .05$ ($\eta^2 = .20$)
Partner efficacy as target	Females: group × time, F(2, 36) = 3.09, $p = .06$ ($\eta^2 = .15$)
Emotional control	Males: time, F (2,26) = 3.22, $p = .06$ ($\eta^2 = .20$)
Hurtful Event Record (role × time analyses)	
Emotional tone	Male-perpetrated events: time, F (1.25) = 6.19, $p < .05$; role, F (1,25) = 24.79; time × role, F (1.25) = 33.14, $p < .001$ ($\eta^2 = .57$) Female-perpetrated events: role, F(1,26) = 19.72, $p < .001$
Targets' forgiveness/Partners' perceptions of forgiveness	Male-perpetrated events: time, F (1,23) = 33.19, $p < .001$ ($\eta^2 = .59$); time × role, F (1,23) = 5.68, $p < .05$ ($\eta^2 = .20$) Female-perpetrated events: time, F (1,22) = 28.80, $p < .001$ ($\eta^2 = .57$)
Actors' remorse/Partners' perceptions of remorse	Male-perpetrated events: time, F (1,23) = 16.11, $p < .01$ ($\eta^2 = .41$) Female-perpetrated events: time, F (1,23) = 32.72, $p < .001$ ($\eta^2 = .59$); role, F (1,23) = 5.59, $p < .05$
Attributions of intentionality	Female-perpetrated events: time, F (1,23) = 3.02, $p < .1$ ($\eta^2 = .12$)
Distress-maintaining attributions	Male-perpetrated events: time, F (1,23) = 3.50, $p < .1$ ($\eta^2 = .12$)

sustained at follow-up ($M = 6.54$, $SD = 1.33$). Further, and supporting the relevance of attachment configurations, relationship satisfaction increased from pre-intervention to follow-up for females in insecure dyads, in contrast to females in secure or control dyads. Specifically, females' relationship satisfaction in insecure dyads at 6-month follow-up ($M = 6.5$, $SD = 1.48$) was higher than at pre-intervention ($M = 5.62$, $SD = 1.58$, see Figure 20.1). This finding warrants replication with larger samples.

Females in the intervention group also reported improvements in own and partner's efficacy (as targets) to handle hurtful events. Specifically, their reported self-efficacy increased from pre-intervention ($M = 7.45$, $SD = 1.64$) to post-intervention ($M = 8.24$, $SD = 1.62$), although it decreased at follow-up ($M = 7.88$, $SD = 1.48$). Again, for intervention-group females only, perceptions of partner-efficacy to handle hurtful events increased from pre-intervention ($M = 7.31$, $SD = 2.12$) to post-intervention ($M = 8.20$, $SD = 1.74$), and this change was sustained at follow-up ($M = 7.91$, $SD = 1.87$).

For males, only one result for the general measures of relationship functioning approached significance. Specifically, intervention-group males tended to be less controlling of negative emotions at follow-up ($M = 2.60$, $SD = .95$) than pre-intervention ($M = 3.24$, $SD = 1.16$).

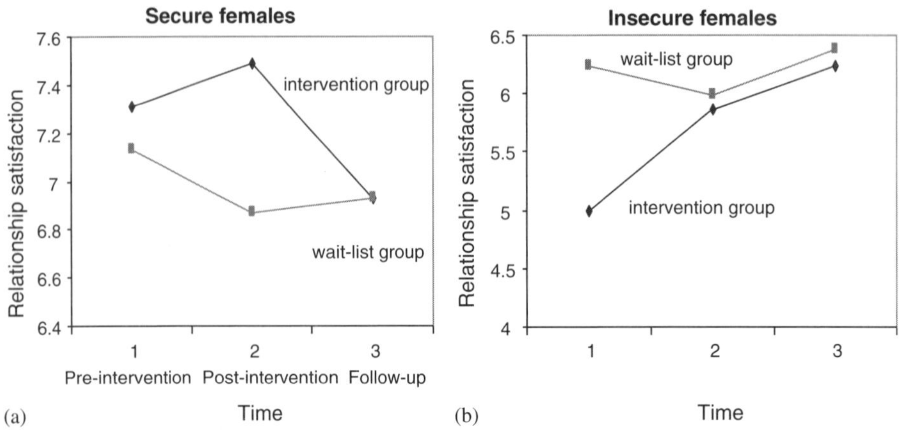

Figure 20.1 Interaction of time by group by "at-risk" status for females' relationship satisfaction, for (a) secure couples and (b) insecure couples

Responses to the hurtful event records. Role by time analyses of couples' accounts of hurtful events in their relationship (HER data; see lower section of Table 20.5) showed an increase in both targets' forgiveness and actors' remorse from pre-intervention to post-intervention. Importantly, these self-reported changes were verified by *partners'* perceptions of changes in forgiveness and remorse. For male-perpetrated events, a role by time interaction showed that targets reported more forgiveness post-intervention ($M = 5.55$, $SD = .61$) than pre-intervention ($M = 4.68$, $SD = .91$), and to a slightly lesser degree, their partners perceived more forgiveness post-intervention ($M = 5.48$, $SD = .78$) than pre-intervention ($M = 4.74$, $SD = .88$). For female-perpetrated events, a main effect of time emerged, with more forgiveness reported post-intervention ($M = 5.41$, $SD = .78$) than pre-intervention ($M = 4.85$, $SD = .85$).

Actors' remorse and targets' perceptions of remorse also showed positive changes. For male-perpetrated events, perceptions of remorse were greater post-intervention ($M = 5.30$, $SD = 1.22$) than pre-intervention ($M = 4.64$, $SD = 1.45$). Similarly, for female-perpetrated events, perceptions of remorse were higher post-intervention ($M = 5.19$, $SD = 1.22$) than pre-intervention ($M = 4.13$, $SD = 1.60$). In addition, female actors ($M = 5.02$, $SD = 1.36$) reported expressing more remorse than their partners perceived ($M = 4.31$, $SD = 1.48$).

For attributions regarding hurtful behavior, male targets tended to attribute less intentionality to their partners' negative behavior post-intervention ($M = 1.52$, $SD = 1.0$) than pre-intervention ($M = 1.75$, $SD = .90$). Similarly, female targets tended to make fewer distress-maintaining attributions for partners' behavior post-intervention ($M = 2.39$, $SD = 1.23$) than pre-intervention, ($M = 2.88$, $SD = 1.55$).

We offer further comments regarding role-related differences in the HERs of the couples participating in our intervention; these analyses address issues relating to the links among emotional regulation, perspective taking, and forgiveness. HERs of both intervention and control groups (collected at the start of the workshops) were pooled and analyzed for role-related differences in reporting. Specifically, we hypothesized that levels

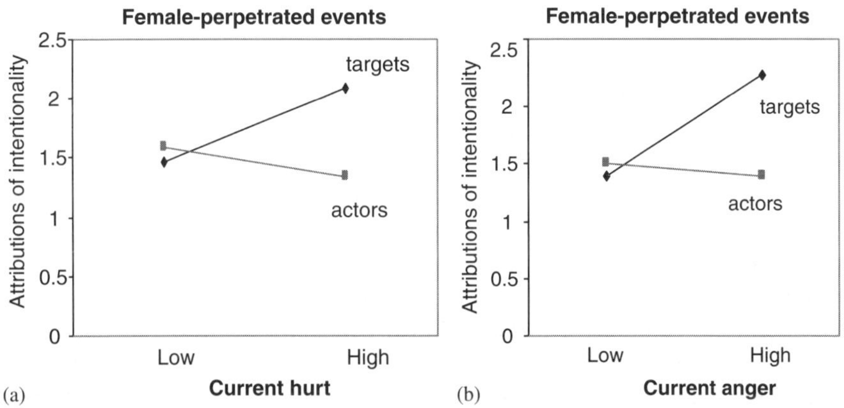

Figure 20.2 Interactions of role by hurt (a) and role by anger (b) for attributions of intentionality

of emotion (i.e., high or low levels of anger or hurt) at the time of completing the HER would moderate role-related differences in reporting.

Results supported this hypothesis, as analyses revealed several role (target/actor) by emotion (high/low) interactions. For attributions of intentionality for female-perpetrated events, there was a significant role by hurt interaction, $F\ (1,\ 54) = 7.52,\ p < .01$ (see Figure 20.2a); and a role by anger interaction, $F\ (1,\ 54) = 10.97,\ p < .01$ (see Figure 20.2b). At low levels of hurt, there was no effect of role, $F\ (1,\ 24) = .28$, *ns*. At higher levels of hurt, the effect of role was significant, $F\ (1,\ 30) = 11.76,\ p < .01$; targets ($M = 2.09$, $SD = 1.27$) rated more intentionality than did actors ($M = 1.34$, $SD = .54$). Similarly, at low levels of anger, there was no effect of role, $F\ (1,\ 28) = .46$, *ns*. At higher levels of anger, an effect of role emerged, $F\ (1,\ 26) = 13.35,\ p < .01$; targets ($M = 2.28$, $SD = 1.33$) again attributed more intentionality than did actors ($M = 1.39$, $SD = .59$). Similar results were found for the moderating effects of hurt and anger on emotional tone, and effect of hurt on perceptions of remorse for male-perpetrated events.

These results point to the constricting effect of unresolved negative emotion on perspective taking in the context of hurtful events. Further, these findings, and previously mentioned couples' reports that strong emotions can be a barrier to relationship repair, fit with recent research indicating the value of emotional regulation for forgiveness of relationship transgressions. Hodgson and Wertheim (2007) reported that ability to manage and repair emotions predicted a greater disposition to forgive, in their sample of university students and community volunteers. Moreover, perspective taking mediated the relationship between emotion management and forgiveness of others.

Clinical implications

Taken together, these findings carry significant clinical implications. First, it is clear that relationship therapists cannot afford to "turn a blind eye" to hurtful events in couple or family relationships. Hurtful events, especially more serious events that tear at the fabric of the couple's attachment bond, invariably lead to emotional pain for targets; the expression of this distress can elicit further negative responses in offending partners. Couples are then vulnerable to negative cycles of criticism/attack and defend/withdraw, which both reflect and perpetuate their distress. At worst, hurtful events can seriously undermine trust and perceptions of safety in the relationship, which can result in relationship dissolution. Feeney's typology of hurtful events alerts couple therapists to the experience of psychological hurt; these events, and their significance for particular couples, should not be overlooked.

Second, distressed couples dealing with hurtful relationship events may need considerable assistance in emotionally processing their psychological pain. Some partners may need support to attend to and label primary hurt, sadness and fear (in contrast to more surface reactive anger), as well as to communicate that emotional experience effectively to the partner. Likewise, receiving information about a partner's emotional experience can be challenging, with many individuals needing support to tolerate the associated guilt or shame. Importantly, a dyadic approach to resolution appears to be most effective; therapists need to balance carefully the concurrent tasks of promoting respect and support for the hurt partner's emotional distress, while supporting the offending spouse's efforts to engage constructively in clear acknowledgment of injury, management of shame/guilt, and apology. Perspective taking, forgiveness, and restoration of trust, crucial steps in relationship repair, take time and effort; paying careful attention to the primary emotional experience of both partners is a sound place for relationship therapists to start.

Conclusions

In this chapter we have focused on the importance of hurtful events in couple relationships. Types of hurtful events have been described, along with associated issues such as the tension that arises between individual and relationship well-being, role-related differences in reporting hurtful events, and suggested strategies to assist resolution of hurtful events. A relationship education program has been described that focused on emotional understanding, communication skills, and apology and forgiveness. Evaluation of this educational intervention pointed to its particular benefit in the longer term for insecurely attached couples. Some clinical implications of our findings are discussed, with recommendations for relationship educators and therapists to support emotional regulation as an aid to perspective taking, forgiveness, and rebuilding of trust.

References

Allan, G., & Harrison, K. (2009). Affairs and infidelity. In A. L. Vangelisti (Ed.), *Feeling hurt in close relationships* (pp. 191–208). New York: Cambridge University Press.

Arnold, M. (1960). *Emotion and personality.* New York: Columbia University Press.

Banse, R. (2004). Adult attachment and marital satisfaction: Evidence for dyadic configuration effects. *Journal of Social and Personal Relationships, 21*, 273–282.

Baumeister, R. F., Stillwell, A., & Wotman, S. R. (1990). Victim and perpetrator accounts of interpersonal conflict. *Journal of Personality and Social Psychology, 59*, 994–1005.

Cameron, J. J., Ross, M., & Holmes, J. G. (2002). Loving the one you hurt: Positive effects of recounting a transgression against an intimate partner. *Journal of Experimental Social Psychology, 38*, 307–314.

Carroll, J., & Doherty, W. (2003). Evaluating the effectiveness of premarital prevention programs: A meta analytic review of outcome research. *Family Relations, 52*, 105–118.

Caughlin, J. P., Scott, A. M., & Miller, L. E. (2009). Conflict and hurt in close relationships. In A. L. Vangelisti (Ed.), *Feeling hurt in close relationships* (pp. 143–166). New York: Cambridge University Press.

Coie, J. D., Watt, N. F., West, S. G., Hawkins, J. D., Asarnow, J. R., Markman, H. J., Ramey, S. L., Shure, M. B., & Long, B. (1993). The science of prevention: A conceptual framework and some directions for a National Research Program. *American Psychologist, 48*, 1013–1022.

Eisenberger, N. I., Lieberman, M. D., & Williams, K. D. (2003). Does rejection hurt? An fMRI study of social exclusion. *Science, 302*, 290–292.

Feeney, J. A. (1994). Attachment style, communication patterns, and satisfaction across the life cycle of marriage. *Personal Relationships, 1*, 333–348.

Feeney, J. A. (2004). Hurt feelings in couple relationships: Towards integrative models of the negative effects of hurtful events. *Journal of Social and Personal Relationships, 21*, 487–508.

Feeney, J. A. (2005). Hurt feelings in couple relationships: Exploring the role of attachment and perceptions of personal injury. *Personal Relationships, 12*, 253–271.

Feeney, J. A., & Hill, A. (2006). Victim perpetrator differences in reports of hurtful events. *Journal of Social and Personal Relationships, 23*, 587–608.

Fincham, F. D. (2000). The kiss of the porcupines: From attributing responsibility to forgiving. *Personal Relationships, 7*, 1–23.

Fitness, J. (2001). Betrayal, rejection, revenge, and forgiveness: An interpersonal script approach. In M. R. Leary (Ed.), *Interpersonal rejection* (pp. 73–103). New York: Oxford University Press.

Fitness, J., & Fletcher, G. (1993). Love, hate, anger, and jealousy in close relationships: A prototype and cognitive appraisal analysis. *Journal of Personality and Social Psychology, 65*, 942–958.

Fitness, J., & Warburton, W. (2009). Thinking the unthinkable: Cognitive appraisals and hurt feelings. In A. L. Vangelisti (Ed.), *Feeling hurt in close relationships* (pp. 34–49). New York: Cambridge University Press.

Gordon, K. C., & Baucom, D. H. (1998). Understanding betrayals in marriage: A synthesized model of forgiveness. *Family Process, 37*, 425–449.

Gottman, J. (1994). *What predicts divorce?* Hillsdale, NJ: Erlbaum.

Greenberg, L., & Paivio, S. (1997). *Working with emotions in psychotherapy*. New York: Guilford Press.

Hodgson, L. K., & Wertheim, E. H. (2007). Does good emotion management aid forgiving? Multiple dimensions of empathy, emotion management and forgiveness of self and others. *Journal of Social and Personal Relationships, 24*, 931–949.

Johnson, S. M. (2003). Attachment theory: A guide for couple therapy. In S. M. Johnson & V. E. Whiffen (Eds.), *Attachment processes in couple and family therapy* (pp. 103–123). New York: Guilford.

Johnson, S. M. (2004). *The practice of emotionally-focused couple therapy: creating connection*. New York: Brunner-Routledge.

Johnson, S. M., Makinen, J. A., & Millikin, J. W. (2001). Attachment injuries in couple relationships: A new perspective on impasses in couples therapy. *Journal of Marital and Family Therapy, 27*, 145–155.

Kobak, R., Cassidy, J., & Zir, Y. (2004). Attachment-related trauma and posttraumatic stress disorder: Implications for adult adaptation. In W. S. Rholes & J. A. Simpson (Eds.), *Adult attachment: Theory, research, and clinical implications* (pp. 388–407). New York: Guilford Press.

Leary, M. R. (2001). Toward a conceptualization or interpersonal rejection. In M. R. Leary (Ed.), *Interpersonal rejection* (pp. 3–20). New York: Oxford University Press.

Leary, M. R., & Springer, C. A. (2001). Hurt feelings: The neglected emotion. In R. M. Kowalski (Ed.), *Behaving badly: Aversive behaviors in interpersonal relationships* (pp. 151–175). Washington, DC: American Psychological Association.

Leary, M. R., Springer, C., Negel, L. A., Ansell, E., & Evans, K. (1998). The causes, phenomenology, and consequences of hurt feelings. *Journal of Personality and Social Psychology, 74*, 1225–1237.

Makinen, J., & Johnson, S. (2006). Resolving attachment injuries in couples using emotionally-focused therapy: Steps toward forgiveness and reconciliation. *Journal of Consulting and Clinical Psychology, 74*, 1055–1064.

McCullough, M. E., Rachal, K. C., Sandage, S. J., Worthington, E. L., Jr., Brown, S. W., & Hight, T. L. (1998). Interpersonal forgiving in close relationships: II. Theoretical elaboration and measurement. *Journal of Personality and Social Psychology, 75*, 1586–1603.

McLaughlin, M. L., Cody, M. J., & O'Hair, H. D. (1983). The management of failure events: Some contextual determinants of accounting behaviour. *Human Communication Research, 9*, 208–224.

Mikula, G., Athenstaedt, U., Heschgl, S., & Heimgartner, A. (1998). Does it only depend on the point of view? Perspective-related differences in justice evaluations of negative incidents in personal relationships. *European Journal of Social Psychology, 28*, 931–962.

Noller, P., & Guthrie, D. (1991). Studying communication in marriage: An integration and critical evaluation. *Advances in Personal Relationships, 3*, 37–73.

Ohbuchi, K., Kameda, M., & Agarie, N. (1989). Apology as aggression control: Its role in mediating appraisal of and response to harm. *Journal of Personality and Social Psychology, 56*, 219–227.

Senchak, M., & Leonard, K. E. (1992). Attachment styles and marital adjustment among newlywed couples. *Journal of Social and Personal Relationships, 9*, 51–64.

Schutz, A. (1999). It was your fault! Self-serving biases in autobiographical accounts of conflicts in married couples. *Journal of Social and Personal Relationships, 13*, 193–208.

Shaver, P. R., Mikulincer, M., Lavy, S., & Cassidy, J. (2009). Understanding and altering hurt feelings: An attachment-theoretical perspective on the generation and regulation of emotions. In A. L. Vangelisti (Ed.), *Feeling hurt in close relationships* (pp. 92–119). New York: Cambridge University Press.

Shaver, P., Schwartz, J., Kirson, D., & O'Connor, C. (1987). Emotion knowledge: Further exploration of a prototype approach. *Journal of Personality and Social Psychology, 52*, 1061–1086.

Vangelisti, A. L. (2001). Making sense of hurtful interactions in close relationships. In V. Manusov & J. H. Harvey (Eds.), *Attribution, communication behavior, and close relationships* (pp. 38–58). Cambridge, England: Cambridge University Press.

Vangelisti, A. L., & Young, S. L. (2000). When words hurt: The effects of perceived intentionality on interpersonal relationships. *Journal of Social and Personal Relationships, 17*, 393–424.

Weiner, B. (1995). *Judgments of responsibility: A foundation for a theory of social conduct*. New York: Guilford Press.

Zechmeister, J. S., & Romero, C. (2002). Victim and offender accounts of interpersonal conflict: Autobiographical narratives of forgiveness and unforgiveness. *Journal of Personality and Social Psychology, 82*, 675–686.

21

A Common Factors Perspective of Relationship Counseling

Ruth Ingrid Sturmey, Patricia Noller, and Gery C. Karantzas

The most common form of professional assistance available for those experiencing unhappy, distressed intimate relationships is relationship counseling. At the heart of relationship counseling is the psychology of relationships and the practice of couple therapy. Couple therapy involves working with relationship partners to limit and soften negative patterns of response that become entrenched over time, and to build more positive responses that strengthen the couple's emotional bonds (Davis & Piercy, 2007; chapters 22, 23 in this volume). For a therapist, knowing how relationships work, how best to form a good working alliance with both partners, and what to do to assist change is the science and art of effective couple therapy.

Based on a comparative study of psychological healing, Frank (1961) claimed that the person delivering the treatment and the expectancy effects around their power to heal were more potent factors in successful healing than the interventions themselves. Despite this claim by Frank, much of the empirical research into the effectiveness of therapy has ignored or minimized the influence of therapist and client characteristics in an effort to establish the effectiveness of a given therapeutic model. While studies investigating the efficacy of particular couple therapies have provided evidence to support the utility of these therapies (e.g., Christensen, Atkins, Berns, Wheeler, Baucom, & Simpson, 2004; Snyder & Wills, 1989; chapter 22 in this volume), others have argued that the amount of client change attributed to the therapeutic model when common factors are included in the assessment is modest (e.g., Messer & Wampold, 2006). Lambert (1992) and Wampold

The Wiley-Blackwell Handbook of Couples and Family Relationships, First Edition.
Edited by Patricia Noller and Gery C. Karantzas.

(2001) argue that such findings highlight the importance of contextual factors common across treatments in explaining therapeutic change, rather than the unique aspects associated with a given therapeutic model.

In this chapter, we provide a brief review of the research on what makes couple therapy effective from a broad common factors perspective (Sprenkle, Davis, & Lebow, 2009). The focus is on factors other than the unique aspects of the different treatment models to explain effectiveness. We argue that there exists sufficient research evidence to support the common factors view that the quality of the collaborative relationship between clients and therapist is an important determinant of the effectiveness of couple therapy. Specifically, we discuss the therapeutic alliance; therapist and client characteristics, and the match between these characteristics; and client expectations regarding therapy outcomes as importance common factors that effect therapeutic change. We also discuss the importance for therapists of ensuring that their practice is guided by relationship research. Lastly, we discuss the implications of considering common factors in the practice and service delivery of couple and family therapy.

The Therapeutic Alliance

One of the most significant factors accounting for the effectiveness of therapy, whether with individuals (Bachelor & Horvath, 1999; Horvath & Luborsky, 1993; Norcross, 2002) or with couples and families (Sprenkle et al., 2009) is the therapeutic alliance (also called the working alliance). In couple therapy the proportion of variance in outcome attributed to the therapeutic alliance ranges from 5% to 22% (Bourgeois, Sabourin, & Wright, 1990; Brown & O'Leary, 2000; Holtzworth-Munroe, Jacobson, DeKlyen, & Whisman, 1989; Johnson & Talitman, 1997; Symonds & Horvath, 2004).

The concept of the therapeutic alliance has changed since the 1960s. Under the influence of behaviorism and more solution-focused approaches to therapy, it came to be seen more as an agreed contract for working together between therapist and client (Sprenkle et al., 2009). Now it is seen as a composite of several factors involving: (i) a positive emotional *bond* between therapist and client, in which the client trusts and respects the therapist and feels safe, understood, and supported; (ii) an agreed understanding of the *goals* of the therapy; and (iii) comfort with the therapeutic *tasks* set by the therapist, i.e., the tasks make sense (Bordin, 1979; Sprenkle et al., 2009).

Rait (2000) argues that the therapeutic alliance is central to therapy for couple and family relationships, but suggests that this alliance differs from the working alliance characteristic of individual therapy. Rait notes that unlike in individual therapy, the therapist must establish multiple alliances between couple and family members. Not only must working alliances be established between therapist and clients and the clients themselves, but an alliance must be established between the therapist and the couple as a collective (i.e., the "identified patient" in systemic terms; Pinsof, 1995; Pinsof, Zinbarg, & Knobloch-Fedders, 2008; Rait, 2000). Creating and maintaining a strong alliance requires negotiating the differing levels of commitment to the working relationship between the parties involved in therapy, the differing agendas for change, and differing expectancies regarding counseling. Hence, much of the early work of couple therapy is about strengthening motivation and hopefulness in one (or both) partners and helping them agree on an agenda regarding the issues to be tackled in therapy and the manner in which this therapy will occur.

In addition to establishing multiple alliances in family therapy, Knobloch-Fedders, Pinsof, and Mann (2004, 2007) indicate that tracking therapeutic alliance scores over time is a useful way of measuring therapeutic change. Specifically, Knobloch-Fedders et al. found that the female client's rating of the therapist's alliance with the couple at mid therapy was the strongest predictor of the therapy outcome. The second strongest predictor was the male's personal alliance with the therapist mid therapy, (supporting the widespread belief that men are harder to engage and that the strength of their engagement is a more accurate measure of the likely success of therapy). It is argued, however, that once therapists have kept their clients positively engaged for at least 6 sessions, they are likely to remain positively engaged throughout the therapeutic relationship (normally no more than 25 sessions) due to the effects of such phenomena as positive sentiment override (Weiss, 1980).

Therapist and Client Factors

Therapist factors

Recently, common factors researchers have resurrected Frank's (1961) claim that the therapist is still the major factor in the strength of the alliance and the effectiveness of couple therapy (Blow, Sprenkle, & Davis, 2007). It is the responsibility of the therapist to keep clients engaged, identify opportunities for change, and assist clients to choose more effective responses (Blow et al.). Although research on the significance of therapists actions' and the quality of their presence, independent of the therapeutic model being applied, has been out of vogue for the last 20 years, a number of researchers have found evidence to support Frank and Frank's (1991) contextual view that the person delivering the treatment is more potent than the specific ingredients of the treatment (Blatt, Sanislow, Zuroff, & Pilkonis, 1996; Crits-Christoph et al., 1991; Luborsky et al., 1986; Wampold, 2001).

As a case in point, Blatt et al. (1996) and Elkin et al. (1989) reported on a National Institute of Mental Health study comparing the effects of cognitive-behavioral therapy, interpersonal therapy, drug therapy, and a placebo "attention-without-intervention" condition on the treatment of depression. Findings revealed that the therapist effects were larger than and independent of the treatment effects across all forms of therapy, even when accounting for the setting for the treatment and therapist experience (Blatt et al., 1996; Elkin et al., 1989).

In unpacking the specific qualities that made therapists effective across a range of clients and presenting problems, Holmes (2006) found that highly effective therapists demonstrated abilities to: (i) cope with strong emotional arousal within themselves and their clients; (ii) integrate therapeutic knowledge from different domains and perspectives; and

(iii) make the personal adjustments needed to stay in a positive influential relationship with several people at once (Holmes, 2006; see also Muir, Schwartz, & Szapocznik, 2004).

Similarly, Beutler et al.'s (2004) and Blow et al.'s (2007) reviews of the research into the qualities of an effective therapist revealed similar therapist characteristics. According to these reviews, the characteristics shown to have the most impact on the effectiveness of therapy are: positivity/friendliness; the ability to be highly directive in order to interrupt escalating conflict and hostility and manage the process; the ability to work with and regulate emotion; nondefensiveness (under conditions of arousal); the ability to focus attention on the client's needs (i.e., to be "attuned" to others rather than be self-focused); the ability to draw on different perspectives in dealing with a situation; and the ability to alter (adapt) the therapeutic approach in response to a lack of progress in, or adherence to, therapy.

An element of therapist effectiveness that emerges through the work of Blatt et al. (1996), Elkin et al. (1989), Holmes (2006), and others is that a therapist needs to be adaptable in working with clients. According to Norcross (2002) and Sprenkle et al. (2009), therapists need to ensure that their style of relating and use of interventions fit "well enough" with clients' expectations, personalities, values, cultural mores, and "diagnosed problems." For example, better outcomes are achieved with highly resistant clients when minimal direction and interventions favoring self-control are applied; whereas better outcomes are achieved with clients low in resistance by directive instruction and using interventions that favor explicit guidance (Miller, 2000; Waldron, Turner, Barton, Alexander, & Cline, 1997).

Some argue that the outcomes of therapy, as predicted by therapist characteristics, bring into question the importance of clinical experience and training. For instance, in his controversial book, *House of Cards: Psychology and psychotherapy built on myth*, Dawes (1994) points to numerous studies and reviews showing that clinical experience does not improve therapeutic performance; rather, other therapist characteristics are more likely to influence therapy outcomes. More recently, a number of the studies cited by Dawes and others contending that therapy experience does not matter have been criticized on methodological grounds. For instance, Leon, Martinovich, Lutz, and Lyons (2005) suggest the lack of difference between more and less experienced therapists stems from a failure to control such factors as the socio-demographic characteristics of the patient, the number of patient contact hours of the therapist, and the therapy used by the practitioner. In controlling for such factors Driscoll, Cukrowicz, Reitzel, Hernandez, Petty, and Joiner (2003) found that experience was significantly associated with treatment outcomes—a finding replicated by Powell, Hunter, Beasley, and Vernberg (2010). Thus, it seems that both therapist characteristics and clinical experience and training are factors that significantly influence therapy outcomes, especially with more difficult and more distressed clients (Beutler, 1998; Hupert et al., 2001).

In summary, the evidence on the differential effectiveness of different therapists has led common factors researchers and those specifically interested in the therapeutic process to claim that it is just as valid to talk about "empirically-validated therapists" or "empirically-validated therapeutic relationships" as "empirically-validated therapies" (Blow et al., 2007; Norcross, 2002). While the extent to which such statements are true is yet to be determined, the research does point to the important role that the therapist, as an agent of change, plays in helping couples and families improve their relationship outcomes.

Client factors

While therapist characteristics are likely to influence therapeutic outcomes, so too can client characteristics shape the therapeutic alliance and the effectiveness of therapy (Bachelor & Horvath, 1999; Bergin & Lambert, 1978). Research investigating the effect of client characteristics demonstrates that the client's approach to therapy and various intra-individual factors can influence therapy outcomes independently of the strategies employed by the therapist (Tallman & Bohart, 1999). Furthermore, therapists can be seen as poor judges of what works for clients and are at times surprised to learn that clients' evaluations of therapeutic efficacy differ from those of the therapist (e.g., Helmeke & Sprenkle, 2000).

Attempts have been made to delineate the type of client characteristics that are most likely to influence therapy. For instance, Lambert (1992) and Hubble, Duncan, and Miller (1999) proposed motivation, commitment to change, inner strength, religious faith, stressful life events, community involvement, and the receipt of social support as examples of important client characteristics. Furthermore, the interaction between client characteristics, particular types of couple/family problems, and different therapies have been examined to better understand how these factors come together to influence clinical outcomes. For example, couples who are young, emotionally engaged, flexible in their gender role prescriptions, and not depressed are most likely to benefit from Behavioral Marital Therapy and Insight-oriented Couple Therapy (Jacobson & Addis, 1993).

Snyder and colleagues concluded in the early 1990s that the more severe the presenting problem, the less effective the purely cognitive- and behaviorally-based couple therapies were in producing change (Snyder, Wills, & Grady-Fletcher, 1991; Snyder, Mangrum, & Wills, 1993). However, Johnson and colleagues assert that their research on the efficacy of emotionally focused couple therapy (EFCT) demonstrates that it is equally effective with older couples experiencing high amounts of emotional disengagement and conflict, and with couples with a child suffering a chronic health condition but without serious issues around violence and control (Johnson, 2002; see also chapter 23 in this volume). Gottman (1994, 1999) maintains that the state of a couple's relationship can have a major impact on the outcome of therapy. Clients who have withdrawn from each other emotionally and physically and lost the desire to change their situation are the most difficult to work with, at least among nonviolent couples or those engaging in minimal violence.

Another important client factor argued to influence therapeutic outcomes is client motivation to engage in therapy. Despite the emphasis placed on client characteristics, this issue has been largely neglected in couple therapy research (Sprenkle et al., 2009). Effective couple therapy requires both partners to be sufficiently committed to their relationship and to be motivated to want to improve it. Yet split agendas, where one wants in and the other wants out, different levels of motivation, and cultural and gendered beliefs around who should take responsibility for making the relationship "work" create particular difficulties in relationship counseling. Couple therapists need to pay much more attention to the motivations of their clients in therapy than they currently do. Couple therapists are not normally trained to think in terms of a stages-of-change model like that of Prochaska and DiClemente (1982; Prochaska, DiClemente, & Norcoss 1992), which would help them deal systematically with issues of motivation before launching into couple work. However, this procedure is now being suggested by common factors researchers such as Sprenkle et al. (2009). They suggest that the use of motivational interviewing techniques be brought into couple therapy in order to deal with reluctant partners (Miller & Rollnick, 2002).

The match between therapist and client characteristics

Studies indicate that significant increases can occur in the effectiveness of therapy when treatments and the relationship style of the therapist match both the clients' relating styles and their way of dealing with problems (Barber & Muenz, 1996; Beutler, 1991; Blatt et al., 1996; Blatt & Folsen, 1993; Blatt & Ford, 1994). A more cognitive approach probably works better for more avoidant clients, and training in emotion regulation or emotion-focused therapy for impulsive, chronically angry clients. Oppositional clients are likely to respond better to a therapist who exerts little direct control, and works collaboratively on joint tasks (Beutler & Consoli, 1993). The therapist's ability to respond as needed in a particular instance is vital to the overall effectiveness of the therapist over a range of clients and client problems.

Expectancy Effects

Another aspect of research into the common factors approach to therapy has examined clients' expectations regarding the outcomes of therapy. Lambert (1992) estimated that hope/expectancy accounted for more than 15% of the outcome variance in individual therapy—as much as is accounted for by the model of therapy used. Three studies have shown that the role of hope/expectancy in couple therapy is highly influenced by the therapist's ability to present their approach to therapy in a way that restores their clients' hope that things can be different (Crane, Griffin, & Hill, 1986; Johnson & Talitman, 1997; Kuehl, Newfield, & Joanning, 1990). Clients normally seek help when they have lost hope of changing their relationship by themselves. In similar vein, Howard, Moras, Brill, Martinovich, and Lutz (1996) have suggested that the process of restoring hope (which they call re-moralization) is vital to engaging clients in therapy and is likely to be reflected in the strength of the therapeutic alliance.

Relationship Research: Current Findings, Future Trends, and Therapist Uptake

While the common factors perspective highlights the importance of therapist and client characteristics, as well as the therapeutic alliance, and expectancy regarding treatment effects, we also believe that therapists' efficacy is likely to be informed by the extent to which they use research to inform their therapeutic practice. While many couple therapists implement therapeutic approaches such as traditional behavioral couples therapy (TBCT), integrative behavioral couples therapy (ICBT), and EFCT, some do not, and as a result undertake an atheoretical approach to the treatment of couple and family issues. Moreover, even those who do use evidence-based therapy models would be served well by drawing on the latest research in relationships to further inform and refine their therapeutic practices. In this section, we briefly outline some of the major past and current research findings and future trends in relationship research. We also discuss the importance of therapists using this research to inform practice.

Over the past 20 years, research in the area of relationships has steadily grown to the point that much has been learnt about the processes that shape the formation, maintenance, and dissolution of couple and family relationships. Much of this knowledge has been gained through the application of theories pertaining to attachment bonds (see Cassidy & Shaver, 2008; Mikulincer & Shaver, 2007), social interdependence (e.g., Rusbult, Arriaga, & Agnew, 2001; Rusbult & Van Lange, 1996), communication (Christensen, 1988; Christensen & Jacobson, 2000; chapters 8, 9, 10 in this volume), intimacy and trust (Reis & Shaver, 1988; Rempel, Holmes, & Zanna, 1985), emotions and hurt feelings (e.g., Feeney, 2004; Frijda, 2007; McCullough, Bono, & Root, 2007; chapters 18, 20 in this volume), and the functional aspects of cognitive processes and relationship motivations (e.g., Campbell, Simpson, Kashy, & Fletcher, 2001; Murray, 2001; chapters 13, 17 in this volume). Furthermore, more general theories that attempt to link contextual factors with individual difference variables and relationship outcomes such as Karney and Bradbury's (1995) Vulnerability Stress Adaptation (VSA) model have also been developed. Evidence to support models such as the VSA is now emerging (e.g., Cohan & Bradbury, 1997; Hanzal & Segrin, 2009; Langer, Lawrence, & Barry, 2008).

The new directions for relationship research point to the integration of knowledge across the disciplines of relationship research. Social neuroscience and developmental science are being integrated with social psychological research on relationships, as are communication and sociological perspectives. For instance, Damazio (1999) and Panksepp (2009) have demonstrated the neuropsychological correlates of various emotions and argue that emotions such as fear and lust organize complex reactions to social situations that activate or inhibit various autonomic, hormonal, and somatic reactions, which in turn, influence behavior. In another example, Coan (2008) and Gillath, Bunge, Shaver, Wendelken, and Mikulincer (2005) have found that attachment styles are differentially associated with anterior cingulated cortex activity. This growing body of neuroscientific knowledge is important to a modern understanding of how relational response patterns become expressed in adult relationships. These response patterns result from the consolidation and calibration of neural circuitry during childhood. Reviews of this research and its implications for assisting families and couples can be found in the writings of Fishbane (2007); Fosha, Siegel, and Solomon (2009); and Snyder, Simpson, and Hughes (2006).

Developmental, social psychological, and sociological perspectives have also influenced the way relationships are studied. For instance, the observational and longitudinal research designs and analytical methods used by these disciplines have significantly shaped, and continue to shape, our understanding of intimate processes. For example, Christensen and colleagues (e.g., Christensen, 1987, 1988; Eldridge, Sevier, Jones, Atkins, & Christensen, 2007) and Simpson et al. (e.g., 1992, 1996, 2002) have repeatedly video-recorded couple interactions during stress-provoking situations or during the discussion of conflict. The research resulting from these methods has informed our understanding of how social support and communication patterns are exchanged between relationship partners. Gottman's (1994) longitudinal research observing the behavioral and emotional responses of couples in vivo, coupled with the collection of physiological data from partners, revealed the importance of the ratio of positive to negative affective exchanges in predicting relationship outcomes (Gottman, 1999). Using mathematical modeling borrowed from the environmental and developmental sciences (e.g., Murray, 1989; Nesselroade & Boker, 1994), Gottman, Murray, Swanson, Tyson, and Swanson (2005) have also shown that intimate relationships function as complex and dynamic systems that follow nonlinear relationship trajectories. Huston and colleagues have demonstrated how the relationship patterns in newlyweds can predict relationship satisfaction a decade later. Huston, Caughlin, Houts, Smith, and George (2001) identified that an abatement of overt love and affection and perceptions of a decline in spousal responsiveness, and an increase in ambivalence significantly heightened the risks of marital dissolution.

We believe that knowledge about relationship research is important in guiding couple and family therapists in their work with clients. Just as Sprenkle et al. (2009) argue that therapeutic models give coherence and direction to the therapist's work with clients, we claim that awareness of relationship research is a vehicle that can drive therapists' approaches to couple and family therapy. For instance, the work by Christensen and colleagues (e.g., Christensen, 1987, 1988; Christensen & Jacobson, 2000; Eldridge et al., 2007) and Gottman (1994) has identified the specific couple communication patterns most deleterious to couple functioning (see also chapters 9, 10 in this volume). Practitioners' knowledge of this research can then guide their therapeutic practice so that they target specific communication patterns such as demand–withdraw when working with couples experiencing conflict. More recently, the work investigating the role of affect and its neuropsychological correlates in relationship processes alerts therapists to consider models of therapy that target emotions (e.g., EFCT) as opposed to cognition or behavior. Thus, therapists' awareness of relationship research can influence what they choose to focus on in therapy, and the therapeutic model(s) that they choose to implement.

Implications for Practice and Service Delivery

In this chapter, we have specifically examined the common factors that have been known to influence therapeutic outcomes. We have also alerted readers to the importance of becoming acquainted with relationship research in order to inform their practice. We, however, qualify our view of common factors by noting that therapeutic efficacy is in part driven by the common factors that cut across various models of therapy, but is also influenced by the therapeutic model of choice. We, like Sprenkle et al. (2009), take a moderate view of common factors in which therapeutic "paradigms can be viewed as the vehicles through which common factors operate" (p. 5). So what recommendations can we give from a moderate common factors perspective to assist therapists with promoting effective relationship counseling?

Firstly, we believe that relationship counselors should engage in the scientist-practitioner model. In doing so, therapists should do their best to stay abreast of relationship research that can be integrated into practice. Furthermore, therapists should ensure that they are aware of the research supporting various therapeutic models and that the models they use in practice are the most validated. Secondly, providers of couple and family counseling services should ensure that relationship counselors are selected on the basis of their skills in establishing a strong therapeutic alliance with clients; their ability to adapt their style of relating, and choice of interventions, to suit the client characteristics; and the capacity to effectively regulate their own emotions and those of clients during therapy.

Thirdly, practitioners involved in the professional development and training of couple and family therapists should ensure that training places a renewed emphasis on recognizing and working with the emotions in addition to the cognitions and behaviors that contribute to the maintenance of dysfunctional relationship patterns. Such a multi-modal approach has been highlighted by common factors researchers as important in effecting therapeutic change (Davis & Piercy, 2007).

Fourthly, we encourage practitioners to remain mindful of the need to maintain couples' and families' motivation for change by adopting a positive approach to therapy that engenders hope and negotiating a therapeutic agenda that all stakeholders can agree to. Implicit in taking such an approach to enhancing client motivation is the importance of agreeing on the tasks and goals of therapy—two critical elements of the therapeutic alliance. However, while agreeing on goals and tasks around therapy, the therapist must also attend to establishing, maintaining, checking, and, if necessary, repairing the bond with their clients to ensure that a good working alliance underlies the therapy. The task of establishing a good therapeutic alliance is difficult, especially for couples and families that are emotionally detached or in conflict, and therapists need to appreciate that the challenge involves maintaining both a task-focused and client-focused approach to the therapeutic process. Therapists also need to be mindful of clients' expectations regarding therapy. Consequently, therapists should seek regular feedback from clients about their attitudes regarding therapy progress and the working alliance. This feedback should be attended to nondefensively and therapists should be open to adapting their way of working, at least to some extent, based on this feedback (Waldron et al., 1997).

Finally, therapists should ensure that their approach to couple and family therapy is characteristic of a modern relational approach. Their focus should include: (a) encouraging clients to take responsibility for their interpersonal behavior; (b) assisting clients to conceptualize difficulties in relational rather than individual terms; (c) educating clients on how affect, cognition, and behavior are associated and how these associations influence clients' patterns of relating; (d) helping clients learn to disrupt or contain aversive, dysfunctional cycles of problem-maintaining behaviors under conditions that elicit negative affect; and (e) teaching clients an expanded set of skills regarding communication, emotion regulation, and problem solving to manage themselves and resolve interpersonal issues.

Conclusion

Our review of the common factors approach to therapy highlights the importance of common factors to therapeutic outcomes. In particular, we highlight the significance of the therapeutic alliance and emphasize that the therapeutic alliance is multidimensional and more complex to establish and navigate in the couple and family therapy contexts than in individual therapy. Drawing on more recent relationship research, we also note that therapists are more likely to work effectively if they treat relationships (whether between couples and family members or themselves and their clients) as complex, dynamic, and nonlinear in their nature that need nurturing in ways that sustain positive connection. It is rare that the journey of (re)establishing and then maintaining a good relationship follows a simple linear path.

Finally, we point out that common factors such as therapist and client characteristics and client expectancies regarding therapy should not be viewed as discrete, independent factors, but as related factors that will differentially contribute to therapy outcomes at different times and in different circumstances. For example, in some instances, a couple with high relationship commitment may do well in therapy with a warm, empathic therapist who is poor at outlining therapeutic goals and tasks, whereas the same combination of factors will not work if the couple has a strong need for structure and success and looks to concrete tasks to maintain focus and change their problematic behaviors.

The complex interplay between common factors and the therapeutic models used by practitioners highlights just how challenging it is for therapists to support couples and families in achieving positive relationship outcomes. Despite these challenges, many therapists are highly effective in bringing about client change. We hope that in this chapter, we have alerted therapists and service providers to the common factors that can assist in enhancing therapeutic efficacy and the need to maintain a watchful eye on developments in relationship research to inform practice.

References

Bachelor, A., & Horvath, A. (1999). The therapeutic relationship. In M. A. Hubble, B. L. Duncan, & S. D. Miller, (Eds.), *The heart and soul of change: What works in therapy*. Washington, DC: American Psychological Association.

Barber, J. P., & Muenz, L. R. (1996). The role of avoidance and obsessiveness in matching patients to cognitive and interpersonal psychotherapy: Empirical findings from the treatment for depression and collaborative research program. *Journal of Consulting and Clinical Psychology*, *64*(5), 951–958.

Bergin, A. E., & Lambert, M. J. (1978). The evaluation of therapeutic outcome. In A. E. Bergin & S. L. Garfield (Eds.), *Handbook of psychotherapy and behavior change* (2nd edn.). New York: John Wiley.

Beutler, L. E. (1991). Have all won and must all have prizes? Revisiting Luborsky et al.'s verdict. *Journal of Consulting and Clinical Psychology*, *59*(2), 226–232.

Beutler, L. E. (1998). Identifying empirically supported treatments: What if we didn't? *Journal of Consulting and Clinical Psychology*, *66*(1), 113–120.

Beutler, L. E., & Consoli, A. J. (1993). Matching the therapist's interpersonal stance to clients' characteristics: Contributions from systematic eclectic psychotherapy, *Psychotherapy, 30*(3), 417–422.

Beutler, L. E., Malik, M., Alimohamed, S., Harwood, T. M., Talebi, H., Noble, S., & Wong, E. (2004). Therapist variables. In M. J. Lambert (Ed.), *Bergin and Garfield's handbook of psychotherapy and behavior change* (5th Ed.). New York: Wiley.

Blatt, S. J. (1992). The differential effect of psychotherapy and psychoanalysis with anaclitic and introjective patients: The Menninger Psychotherapy Research Project revisited. *Journal of the American Psychoanalytic Association, 40*, 691–724.

Blatt, S. J., & Folsen, I. (1993). Different kinds of folks may need different kinds of strokes: The effect of patient's characteristics on therapeutic process and outcome. *Psychotherapy Research, 3*, 245–259.

Blatt, S. J., & Ford, R. O. (1994). *Therapeutic change: An object relations perspective.* New York: Plenum.

Blatt, S. J., Sanislow, C. A., Zuroff, D. C., & Pilkonis, P. A. (1996). Characteristics of effective counsellors: Further analyses of data from the National Institute of Mental Health treatment of depression collaborative research program. *Journal of Consulting and Clinical Psychology, 64*, 1276–1284.

Blow, A., Sprenkle, D. H., & Davis, S. D. (2007). Is who delivers the treatment more important than the treatment itself? The role of the counsellor in common factors. *Journal of Marital and Family Therapy, 33*, 298–317.

Bordin, E. S. (1979). The generalizability of the psychoanalytic concept of the working alliance. *Psychotherapy: Theory, Research and Practice, 16*, 252–260.

Bourgeois, L., Sabourin, S., & Wright, J. (1990). Predictive validity of therapeutic alliance in group marital therapy. *Journal of Consulting and Clinical Psychology, 58*(5), 608–613.

Brown, P. D., & O'Leary, K. D. (2000). Therapeutic alliance: Predicting continuance and success in group treatment for spouse abuse. *Journal of Consulting and Clinical Psychology, 68*, 340–345.

Campbell, L., Simpson, J. A., Kashy, D. A., & Fletcher, G. J. O. (2001). Ideal standards, the self, and flexibility of ideals in close relationships. *Personality and Social Psychology Bulletin, 27*, 447–462.

Cassidy, J., & Shaver, P. R. (Eds.) (2008). *Handbook of attachment: Theory, research, and clinical applications* (2nd edn.). New York: Guilford Press.

Christensen, A. (1987). Detection of conflict patterns in couples. In K. Hahlweg & M. J. Goldstein (Eds.), *Understanding major mental disorder: The contribution of family interaction research* (pp. 250–265). New York: Family Process Press.

Christensen, A. (1988). Dysfunctional interaction patterns in couples. In P. Noller & M. A. Fitzpatrick (Eds.), *Perspectives on marital interaction* (pp. 31–52). Philadelphia: Multilingual Matters.

Christensen, A., Atkins, D. C., Berns, S., Wheeler, J., Baucom, D. H., & Simpson, L. E. (2004). Traditional versus Integrative Behavioral Couple Therapy for significantly and chronically distressed married couples. *Journal of Consulting and Clinical Psychology, 72*, 176–191.

Christensen, A., & Jacobson, N. S. (2000). *Reconcilable differences.* New York: Guilford Press.

Coan, J. A. (2008). Towards a neuroscience of attachment. In J. Cassidy & P. R. Shaver (Eds.), *Handbook of attachment: Theory, research, and clinical applications* (2nd edn., pp. 241–265). New York: Guilford Press.

Cohan, C. L., & Bradbury, T. N. (1997). Negative life events, marital interaction, and the longitudinal course of newlywed marriage. *Journal of Personality and Social Psychology, 73*, 114–128.

Crane, D. R., Griffin, W., & Hill, R. D. (1986). Influence of therapist skills on client perceptions of marriage and family therapy outcome: Implications for supervision. *Journal of Marital and Family Therapy, 12*(1), 91–96.

Crits-Christoph, P., Baranackie, K., Kurcias, J. A. et al. (1991). Meta-analysis of therapist effects in psychotherapy outcome studies. *Psychotherapy Research, 2*, 81–91.

Damasio, A. R. (1999). *The feeling of what happens: Body and emotion in the making of consciousness.* New York: Harcourt.

Davis, S. D., & Piercy, F. P. (2007). What clients of couple therapy model developers and their former students say about change. Part I: Model-dependent common factors across three models. *Journal of Marital and Family Therapy, 33*, 318–343.

Dawes, R. M. (1994). *House of cards: Psychology and psychotherapy built on myth.* New York: The Free Press.

Driscoll, K. A., Cukrowicz, K. C., Reitzel, L. R., Hernandez, A., Petty, S. C., & Joiner, T. E., Jr., (2003). The effect of trainee experience in psychotherapy on client treatment outcome. *Behavior Therapy, 34*, 165–177.

Eldridge, K. A., Sevier, M., Jones, J., Atkins, D. C., & Christensen, A. (2007). Demand–withdraw communication in severely distressed, moderately distressed, and nondistressed couples: Rigidity and polarity during relationship and personal problem discussions. *Journal of Family Psychology, 21*, 218–226.

Elkin, I., Shea, T., Watkins, J. T., Imber, S. D. et al. (1989). National Institute of Mental Health treatment of depression collaborative research program: General effectiveness of treatments. *Archives of General Psychiatry, 46*, 971–982.

Feeney, J. (2004). Hurt feelings in couple relationships: Towards integrative models of the negative effects of hurtful events. *Journal of Social and Personal Relationships, 21*(4), 487–508.

Fishbane, M. D. (2007). Wired to connect: Neuroscience, relationships and therapy. *Family Process, 46*(3), 395–412.

Fosha, D., Siegel, D. J., & Solomon, M. F. (2009). *The healing power of emotion: Affective neuroscience, development and clinical practice.* New York: W.W. Norton.

Frank, J. D. (1961). *Persuasion and healing: A comparative study of psychotherapy.* Baltimore: Johns Hopkins University Press.

Frank, J. D., & Frank, J. B. (1991). *Persuasion and healing: A comparative study of psychotherapy* (3rd Ed.). Baltimore: John Hopkins University Press.

Frijda, N. H. (2007). *The laws of emotion.* Mahwah, NJ: Erlbaum.

Gillath, O., Bunge, S. A., Shaver, P. R., Wendelken, C., & Mikulincer, M. (2005). Attachment style differences in the ability to suppress negative thoughts: Exploring the neural correlates. *NeuroImage, 28*(4), 835–847.

Gottman, J. M. (1994). *What predicts divorce? The relationship between marital processes and marital outcomes*, Hillsdale, NJ: Erlbaum.

Gottman, J. M. (1999). *The marriage clinic: A scientifically-based marital therapy.* New York: W.W. Norton.

Gottman, J. M., Murray, J. D. Swanson, C. C. Tyson, R., & Swanson, K., (2005). *The mathematics of marriage: Dynamic, non-linear models*, Cambridge, MA: MIT Press.

Hanzal, A., & Segrin, C. (2009). The role of conflict resolution styles in mediating the relationship between enduring vulnerabilities and marital quality. *Journal of Family Communication, 9*, 150–169.

Helmeke, K. B., & Sprenkle, D. H. (2000). Clients' perceptions of pivotal moments in couple therapy: A qualitative study of change in therapy. *Journal of Marital and Family Therapy, 26*, 469–484.

Holmes, S. B. (2006). Becoming the best possible family counsellor of family mediator: What expertise research has to say. *Journal of Family Studies, 12*(1), 113–122.

Holtzworth-Munroe, A., Jacobson, N. S., DeKlyen, M., & Whisman, M. (1989). Relationship between behavioural marital therapy outcome and process variables. *Journal of Consulting and Clinical Psychology, 57*, 658–662.

Horvath, A. O., & Luborsky L. (1993). The role of the therapeutic alliance in psychotherapy. *Journal of Consulting and Clinical Psychology, 61*(4), 561–573.

Howard, K. I., Moras, K., Brill, P. L., Martinovich, Z., & Lutz, W. (1996). The evaluation of psychotherapy: Efficacy, effectiveness and patient progress. *American Psychologist, 51*, 1059–1064.

Hubble, M. A., Duncan, B. L., & Miller, S. D. (Eds.) (1999). *The heart and soul of change: What works in therapy*. Washington, DC: American Psychological Association.

Hupert, J. D., Bufka, L. F., Barlow, D. H., Gorman, J. M., Shear, M. K., & Woods, S. W. (2001). Therapists, therapist variables and CBT outcomes for panic disorder: Results from a multi-centre trial. *Journal of Consulting and Clinical Psychology, 69*, 747–755.

Huston, T. L., Caughlin, J. P., Houts, R. M., Smith, S. E., & George, L. J. (2001). The connubial crucible: Newlywed years as predictors of marital delight, distress, and divorce. *Journal of Personality and Social Psychology, 80*, 237–252.

Jacobson, N. S., & Addis, M. E. (1993). Research on couple therapy: What do we know? Where are we going? *Journal of Consulting and Clinical Psychology, 61*(1), 85–93.

Johnson, S. M. (2002). Marital problems. In D.H. Sprenkle (Ed.), *Effectiveness research in marriage and family therapy*. Alexandria, VA: AAMFT.

Johnson, S. M., & Talitman, E. (1997). Predictors of success in emotionally focussed marital therapy. *Journal of Marital and Family Therapy, 23*, 135–152.

Karney, B. R., & Bradbury, T. N. (1995). The longitudinal course of marital quality and stability: A review of theory, method, and research. *Psychological Bulletin, 118*, 3–34.

Knobloch-Fedders, L. M., Pinsof, W., & Mann, B. J. (2004). The formation of the therapeutic alliance in couple therapy. *Family Process, 43*, 425–442.

Knobloch-Fedders, L. M., Pinsof, W., & Mann, B. J. (2007). Therapeutic alliance and treatment progress in couple psychotherapy. *Journal of Marital and Family Therapy, 33*, 245–257.

Kuehl, B. P., Newfield, N. A., & Joanning, H. (1990). A client-based description of family therapy. *Journal of Family Psychology, 3*, 310–321.

Lambert, M. J. (1992). Psychotherapy outcome research: Implications for integrative and eclectic therapists. In J. C. Norcross & R. M. Goldfried (Eds.), *Handbook of psychotherapy integration* (pp. 94–129). New York: Basic Books.

Langer, A., Lawrence, E., & Barry, R. A. (2008). Using a vulnerability-stress-adaptation framework to predict physical aggression trajectories in newlywed marriage. *Journal of Consulting and Clinical Psychology, 76*, 756–768.

Leon, S. C., Martinovich, Z., Lutz, W., & Lyons, J. S. (2005). The effect of therapist experience on psychotherapy outcomes. *Clinical Psychology and Psychotherapy, 12*, 417–426.

Luborsky, L., Crits-Christoph, P., McLellan, A. T., Woody, G., Piper, W. et al. (1986). Do therapists vary much in their success? Findings from four outcome studies. *American Journal of Orthopsychiatry, 56*(4), 501–512.

McCullough, M. E., Bono, G., & Root, L. (2007). Rumination, emotion, and forgiveness: Three longitudinal studies. *Journal of Personality and Social Psychology, 92*, 490–505.

Messer, S. B., & Wampold, B. E. (2002). Let's face facts: Common factors are more important potent than specific therapy ingredients, *Clinical Psychology: Science and Practice, 9*, 21–25.

Mikulincer, M., & Shaver, P. R. (2007). *Attachment patterns in adulthood: Structure, dynamics, and change*. New York: Guilford Press.

Miller, W. R. (2000). Motivational Interviewing: IV. Some parallels with horse whispering. *Behavioural and Cognitive Psychotherapy, 28*, 285–292.

Miller, W. R., & Rollnick, S. (2002). *Motivational interviewing: Preparing people for change* (2nd edn.). New York: Guilford Press.

Muir, J. A., Schwartz, S. J., & Szapocznik, J. (2004). A program research with Hispanic and African American families: Three decades of intervention development and testing influenced by the changing cultural context of Miami. *Journal of Marital and Family Therapy, 30*, 113–120.

Murray, J. D. (1989). *Mathematical biology*. Berlin: Springer-Verlag.

Murray, S. L. (2001). Seeking a sense of conviction: Motivated cognition in close relationships. In G. J. O. Fletcher & M. S. Clark (Eds.), *Blackwell handbook of social psychology: Interpersonal processes* (pp. 107–126). Malden, MA: Blackwell.

Nesselroade, J. R., & Boker, S. M. (1994). Assessing constancy and change. In T. F. Heatherton & J. L. Weinberger (Eds.), *Can personality change?* (pp. 121–147). Washington, DC: American Psychological Association.

Norcross, J. C. (Ed.) (2002). *Psychotherapy relationships that work: Therapist contributions and responsiveness to patients*. New York: Oxford University Press.

Panksepp, J. (2009). Brain emotional systems and qualities of mental life: From animal models of affect to implications for psychotherapeutics. In D. Fosha, D. J. Siegel, & M. F. Solomon (Eds.), *The healing power of emotion: Affective neuroscience, development and clinical practice*. New York: W.W. Norton.

Pinsof, W. M. (1995). *Integrative problem-centered therapy*. New York: Basic Books.

Pinsof, W. M., Zinbarg, R., & Knobloch-Fedders, L. M. (2008). Factorial and construct validity of the revised short form integrative psychotherapy alliance scales for family, couple and individual therapy. *Family Process, 47*, 281–301.

Powell, J. L., Hunter, H. L., Beasley, L. O., & Vernberg, E. M. (2010). Using fine-grained indexes of therapists' experience and training to predict treatment outcomes in a university-based training clinic for children and families. *Training and Education in Professional Psychology, 4*, 138–144.

Prochaska, J. O., & DiClemente, C. C. (1982). Transtheoretical therapy: Toward a more integrative model of change. *Psychotherapy Theory Research and Practice, 19*, 276–288.

Prochaska, J. O., DiClemente, C. C., & Norcoss, J. C. (1992). In search of how people change: Applications to addictive behaviors. *American Psychologist, 47*, 1102–1114.

Rait, D. S. (2000). The therapeutic alliance in couple and family therapy. *Journal of Clinical Psychology, 56*(2), 211–224.

Reis, H. T., & Shaver, P. R. (1988). Intimacy as an interpersonal process. In S. Duck (Ed.), *Handbook of research in personal relationships* (pp. 367–389). Chichester, England: Wiley.

Rempel, J. K., Holmes, J. G., & Zanna, M. P. (1985). Trust in close personal relationships. *Journal of Personality and Social Psychology, 49*, 95–112.

Rusbult, C. E., Arriaga, X., & Agnew, C. (2001). Interdependence in close relationships. In G. J. O. Fletcher & M. S. Clark (Eds.), *Blackwell handbook of social psychology: Interpersonal processes* (pp. 359–387). Malden, MA: Blackwell.

Rusbult, C. E., & Van Lange, P. A. M. (1996). Interdependence processes. In E. T. Higgins & A. Kruglanski (Eds.), *Social psychology: Handbook of basic principles* (pp. 564–596). New York: Guilford Press.

Simpson, J. A., Rholes, W. S., & Nelligan, J. S. (1992). Support seeking and support giving within couples in an anxiety-provoking situation: The role of attachment styles. *Journal of Personality and Social Psychology, 62*, 434–446.

Simpson, J. A., Rholes, W. S., Orina, M., & Grich, J. (2002). Working models of attachment, support giving, and support seeking in a stressful situation. *Personality and Social Psychology Bulletin, 28,* 598–608.

Simpson, J. A., Rholes, W. S., & Phillips, D. (1996). Conflict in close relationships: An attachment perspective. *Journal of Personality and Social Psychology, 71,* 899–914.

Snyder, D. K., Mangrum, L. F., & Wills, R. M. (1993). Predicting couples' response to marital therapy: A comparison of short- and long-term predictors. *Journal of Consulting and Clinical Psychology, 61,* 61–69.

Snyder, D. K., Simpson, J. A., & Hughes, J. N. (2006). *Emotion regulation in couples and families: Pathways to dysfunction and health.* Washington, DC: American Psychological Association.

Snyder, D. K., & Wills, R. M. (1989). Behavioral versus insight-oriented marital therapy: Effects on individual and interspousal functioning. *Journal of Consulting and Clinical Psychology, 57,* 39–46.

Snyder, D. K., Wills, R. M., & Grady-Fletcher, A. (1991). Long-term effectiveness of behavioral versus insight-oriented marital therapy: A 4-year follow-up study. *Journal of Consulting and Clinical Psychology, 59,* 138–141.

Sprenkle, D. H., Davis, S. D., & Lebow, J. L. (2009). *Common factors in couple and family therapy: The overlooked foundation for effective practice.* New York: Guilford Press.

Symonds, D., & Horvath, A. O. (2004). Optimizing the alliance in couple therapy. *Family Process, 43*(4), 443–456.

Tallman, K., & Bohart, A. C. (1999). The client as common factor: Clients as self-healers. In M. A. Hubble, B. L. Duncan, & S. D. Miller (Eds.), *The heart and soul of change: What works in therapy.* Washington, DC: American Psychological Association.

Waldron, H. B., Turner, C. W., Barton, C., Alexander, J. F., & Cline, V. B. (1997). Therapist defensiveness and marital therapy process and outcome. *American Journal of Family Therapy, 25,* 233–243.

Wampold, B. E. (2001). *The great psychotherapy debate: Models, methods and findings.* Mahwah, NJ: Erlbaum.

Weiss, R. L. (1980). Strategic behavioral marital therapy: Toward a model for assessment and intervention. In J. P. Vincent (Ed.), *Advances in family intervention, assessment and theory* (Vol. 1, pp. 229–271). Greenwich, CT: JAI Press.

22

The Efficacy of Evidence-Based Couple Therapy

Peter Howell

Few of the best accepted couple therapies are derived from evidence-based practice or have strong empirical support (Gurman, 2008a). Therefore, it is likely that a significant proportion of couple therapists may not be familiar with the philosophies or issues associated with evidence-based practice. Couple therapists of all persuasions are invited to consider the principles and growing importance of evidence-based practice (Nathan & Gorman, 1998).

In this chapter I describe what evidence-based practice is and review issues related to efficacy. I also provide a brief description of two of the three best empirically supported couple therapies, cognitive-behavioral couple therapy (CBCT; Baucom, Epstein, La Taillade, & Kirby, 2008) and integrative behavioral couple therapy (IBCT; Jacobson & Christensen, 1998). The third, emotionally-focused couple therapy (Johnson, 2004), is addressed by Johnson and Rheem in chapter 23 of this volume.

Couple Therapy and Relationship Functions and Outcomes

Couple therapy refers to psychotherapy aimed at improving a relationship and involves both partners of a committed relationship. The term marital therapy has been largely replaced in the literature by the term couple therapy so as to include unmarried cohabiting couples (Gurman, 2008a). Although very little relationship and couple-therapy research has investigated cohabiting couples, it is assumed that the principles and practices

The Wiley-Blackwell Handbook of Couples and Family Relationships, First Edition.
Edited by Patricia Noller and Gery C. Karantzas.

applicable to married couples also apply to other committed couples. It should also be explicitly stated that couple therapy is not individual therapy focused on improving a relationship. Some models of couple therapy include individual sessions during the assessment phase of treatment, but then therapy is delivered via conjoint sessions (Gurman, 2008a).

In spite of changing expectations about marriage and the permanency of committed relationships in Western societies (see chapters 1, 2 in this volume), individuals still seek to meet their companionship and intimacy needs through marriage or other forms of committed relationships. The importance of such relationships is supported by research suggesting numerous psychological and physical health benefits associated with being in a successful committed relationship (Brannon & Feist, 1997). There is also evidence of the serious adverse consequences of relationship conflict and divorce upon psychological functioning and physical health (Bloom, Asher, & White, 1978; Brannon & Feist, 1997; chapters 9, 10 in this volume). Relationship conflict has been associated with a number of psychiatric disorders such as depression, bipolar disorder, and alcohol abuse (Christensen & Heavey, 1999). Parental conflict is also a risk factor for the development of childhood psychiatric problems such as conduct disorders and depression (Christensen & Heavey, 1999). "Whether through actual divorce or chronic conflict and distress, the breakdown of marital relationships exacts enormous costs" (Gurman, 2008a, p. 3). Although differentiating between the effects of divorce and relationship conflict is complex and controversial, the research appears to suggest that conflict may have a more profound and longer-lasting adverse effect than relationship dissolution itself (Lebow, 2008).

Couple therapy is an intervention which can ameliorate some of the negative social, psychological, and health consequences associated with relationship distress (Gurman, 2008a). Couple therapy can reduce relationship conflict and sometimes prevent relationship breakdown, but it is important to note that relationship dissolution may sometimes be the most appropriate outcome for some distressed relationships (Lebow, 2008). Some partners are so poorly matched or have so much negativity in their relationship history that there is little chance of resolution. In some cases separation is best for the safety and well-being of adults and children alike (O'Leary, 2008).

What is Evidence-Based Practice and Why is it Important?

Evidence-based practice refers to the philosophy that practitioners should use intervention approaches which are supported by scientific research. It also includes the idea that therapists can be more accountable for their work by evaluating the effectiveness of their interventions (Lambert, 2009). It can be argued that to ignore the use of scientifically supported interventions or to fail to evaluate therapeutic change is unethical and not in the best interest of clients (Lambert, 2009; Nathan & Gorman, 1998).

Broadly, there are three sources of evidence upon which psychotherapists might base their practice. Firstly, controlled treatment trials are crucial for evaluating the effectiveness of different treatments. Research which randomly assigns participants to various treatment conditions is the most stringent version of the controlled-treatment trial as it reduces the risk of results being biased by participants' differences. There are also less well-controlled studies which form a part of the evidence base.

Secondly, evidence to guide practice may also come from "patient evaluations in uncontrolled, naturalistic clinical practice contexts" (Gurman, 2008a, p. 23). The idea that practitioners can gather such data and evaluate their clinical practice in a scientific manner has been around since the middle of last century (Barlow, Hayes, & Nelson, 1984). The descriptive and case-study data gathered by practitioners can often provide researchers with subject matter to evaluate clinical practice in a stringent manner. In the couple-therapy field, the work of Susan Johnson, who developed emotionally-focused couple therapy (EFCT), is an impressive example of this process (Johnson, 2004). She developed EFCT by reviewing many hours of herself doing couple therapy and by identifying the strategies and responses which appeared to be effective (Johnson & Denton, 2002; chapter 23 in this volume). Since its development EFCT has been evaluated many times and has been found to be an effective couple therapy (Johnson, 2008).

The third source of evidence which should be used to guide theory and practice is the large body of general descriptive research on relationships. For example, relationship research reveals valuable information on communication patterns (Gurman, 2008b; Roberto-Forman, 2008; chapter 9 in this volume), gender differences (Knudson-Martin, 2008), relationship formation patterns (see chapters 1, 2 in this volume), multicultural relationship patterns (Hardy & Laszloffy, 2002), and family violence (O'Leary, 2008). Thus, scientifically supported evidence, whether from controlled treatment trials, client evaluations in clinical settings or the general research on relationships, should be heeded and applied in the best interest of clients.

The introduction of managed-care models in health service delivery and the expectation that mental-health practitioners become more accountable for the efficacy of their work have contributed to the increasing importance of evidence-based practice (Nathan & Gorman, 1998). Evidence-based practice ideas and the scientist-practitioner model (Barlow et al., 1984) are more historically and philosophically connected to the behavioral and cognitive-behavioral schools of therapy. However, most legitimate forms of psychotherapy are now seeking to describe their approaches operationally and subject them to scientific scrutiny. The recently published *Clinical Handbook of Couple Therapy* (Gurman, 2008a) reviews, describes, and compares 12 prominent forms of couple therapy from 6 perspectives (behavioral; humanistic-existential; psychodynamic and trans-generational; social constructionist; systemic; and integrative approaches). All of the 12 approaches have published case studies to support their efficacy but only 4 (cognitive-behavioral couple therapy; integrative-behavioral couple therapy; emotionally-focused couple therapy; and affective-reconstructive therapy which was previously called insight-oriented couple therapy) are supported by more than one controlled research study. It is lamentable that some very prominent and widely used models of couple therapy such as the systemic approaches (strategic couple therapy and structural couple therapy) have no controlled treatment trials supporting their efficacy in reducing couple distress. As a result, practitioners need to generalize their efficacy from outcome studies which apply these approaches to different clinical problems (Simon, 2008).

Historically there has been disconnection and friction between practitioners and researchers, with practitioners claiming researchers are out of touch with the real world of therapy and researchers claiming that practitioners are not using scientifically supported interventions (Gurman, 2008a). In fact, there is validity to both sides of this argument. Increased focus on and commitment to evidence-based practice may help to resolve such discord.

Common Factors among Different Couple Therapies

"A major controversy in individual psychotherapy and, more recently, in couple therapy is whether change is brought about more by specific ingredients of therapy or factors common to all therapies" (Gurman, 2008a, p. 20). In the past, common factors have also been referred to as nonspecific therapeutic factors or therapeutic relationship variables.

Therapists using the familiar evidence-based model of psychotherapy argue that the specific therapeutic interventions produce the clinical changes. Examples of specific ingredients in a therapy include strategies such as cognitive restructuring, psychoeducation, empathic reflection, problem solving, role playing, and communication training. This approach is similar to the medical model where a specific treatment is applied to a problem to achieve improvement or cure. Evidence-based models which emphasize the importance of the therapy ingredients do not ignore nonspecific therapy characteristics or the factors that are common across different therapies. Rather they see them as necessary prerequisites to delivering the substantive content or therapy interventions effectively. For example, Cormier and Nurius (2003) describe the basic skills and interventions of cognitive-behavior therapy. They include common factors in therapy such as characteristics of effective helpers (self-awareness, interpersonal awareness, and critical thinking), other issues affecting helpers (values, diversity, and ethics), ingredients of an effective helping relationship (empathy or accurate understanding, genuineness, and positive regard), and building an effective helping alliance (Cormier & Nurius, 2003).

An alternative research group argues that the different ingredients or techniques in various therapies may not be the critical factors involved in producing clinical change (Hubble, Duncan, Miller, & Wampold, 2009; see also chapter 21 in this volume). Rather, there may be central processes common to all effective therapies that are responsible for change. This proposition has been fuelled by the consistent research finding that when effective couple therapies are compared, no one therapy appears to be statistically superior to another (Christensen & Heavey, 1999; Gurman, 2008a; Hubble et al., 2009). Hubble et al. (2009) reported research that identified four therapeutic change factors and estimated the percentage contribution of each factor to therapeutic change: extra-therapeutic variables or nontherapy influences (40%); common factors or therapeutic relationship (30%); hope, expectancy, and placebo (15%); and the therapy model or technique (15%). This analysis also revealed that the differences between treatment approaches accounted for only 1% of the variance in outcome (Hubble et al., 2009, p. 33). Thus common factor researchers argue that improving the efficacy of treatments will be better achieved by encouraging therapist accountability rather than continuing to search for superior treatments (Hubble et al., 2009). Further, they argue that therapist accountability is best achieved through the collection of practice-based evidence and they recommend that all therapists should evaluate the outcomes of the therapy they provide (Lambert, 2009). This suggestion is reminiscent of the ideas proposed by the scientist-practitioner model (Barlow et al., 1984).

However, there is a significant body of research which demonstrates and argues the alternative view that there are in fact some therapy models which are superior in the treatment of certain conditions (Nathan & Gorman, 1998). It is not necessary to take a polemic stance between these two positions. Although researchers will continue to evaluate and compare different theoretical and intervention models, they should also seek to identify more clearly the core principles or mechanisms of change (Beutler, 2003; Gurman, 2008a). One part of this research effort might involve evaluating the comparative effectiveness of the techniques and components within a therapeutic approach. Such research could develop understanding about why different treatment models might be equally efficacious and which effective techniques need to be adopted by all therapies. "For example, a core (relationship) change mechanism may involve a changed experience of one's partner that leads to an increased sense of emotional safety and collaboration within the couple. Such a change may be activated by the use of techniques from such varied therapy models as cognitive-behavioral (e.g., reattribution methods), object relations (e.g., interpretations used to disrupt projective processes), and emotionally-focused therapy (e.g., restructuring interactions by accessing unacknowledged emotions in problematic partner cycles)" (Gurman, 2008a, p. 21). Unfortunately there is little couple therapy research currently available that examines the comparative effectiveness of components of therapies (Christensen & Heavey, 1999).

Is Couple Therapy Effective?

In a comprehensive review of couple-therapy research Christensen and Heavey (1999) concluded that dozens of treatment studies showed that relationship satisfaction is higher when both partners received couple therapy as opposed to no treatment. Christensen and Heavey concluded that behavior therapy, cognitive-behavior therapy, and emotion-focused therapy were the three couple therapies with the strongest empirical support.

Nevertheless, statistical improvements in satisfaction scores do not necessarily translate to clinically significant change. One meta-analysis concluded that only 41% of couples moved from the distressed to the nondistressed range by the end of therapy (Shadish, Montgomery, Wilson, Wilson, Bright, & Okwumabua, 1993). Jacobson and Addis (1993) similarly reported a 35% success rate. Christensen and Heavey (1999) also claimed that while treatment effects were maintained at the 6-month follow-up these effects faded over a longer period of time. One of the most comprehensive follow-up studies of its time by Snyder and Wills (1989), found that at the 4-year follow-up only 50% of the behavior therapy couples were classified as happy as opposed to 70% of the insight-oriented therapy couples. The latter finding has not been replicated.

Since the Christensen and Heavey (1999) review of couple-therapy research, there have been several significant developments which have improved the efficacy of couple therapies. Firstly, traditional behavioral couple therapy (TBCT; Jacobson & Margolin, 1979) is seldom practiced alone without being incorporated into other therapy approaches. This development came from research findings that revealed TBCT was not effective for many distressed couples (Jacobson & Addis, 1993). Couples who do benefit from TBCT are less distressed, younger, not emotionally disengaged, not experiencing concurrent individual psychiatric problems, and are less likely to have a relationship based on traditional gender roles (Jacobson & Addis, 1993). A second important addition to the field is the development of integrative behavioral couple therapy (IBCT), which has now received significant empirical support and which incorporates strategies to promote acceptance and tolerance (Dimidjian, Martell, & Christensen, 2008; Jacobson & Christensen, 1996). A third movement in the field has been toward more integration and cross-fertilization between approaches. For example, CBCT has extended its focus to include emotion management and has employed strategies from EFCT and dialectical behavior therapy (Baucom et al., 2008). EFCT is itself an integration of humanistic-experiential and systemic approaches with major influence from attachment theory (Johnson, 2008; chapter 23 in this volume). These developments have increased the efficacy of couple therapy interventions.

A recent appraisal of couple therapy suggests it has strong empirical support as an intervention for relationship problems (Gurman, 2008a). The majority of evidence comes from evaluations of the three most researched couple therapy approaches. Firstly, CBCT is the most widely evaluated treatment for couple distress with over 20 controlled-treatment outcome studies. Between 33% and 67% of couples reach the nondistressed range after receiving this treatment (Baucom et al., 2008). Although these results are maintained at 6- to 12-month follow-up, long-term follow-up results to date are not so encouraging with as many as 30% of the recovered couples relapsing (Jacobson, Schmaling, & Holtzworth-Munroe, 1987). Secondly, three controlled-treatment trials have examined the efficacy of IBCT and have found that as many as 80% of couples either improved or recovered (Dimidjian et al., 2008). At a 2-year follow-up 69% of couples remained in the nondistressed range. Thirdly, there is a large and growing body of outcome research showing that EFCT moves 70–75% of couples to the nondistressed range after treatment and that these couples may be less likely to relapse than couples receiving other forms of couple therapy (Johnson, 2008).

CBCT, IBCT, and EFCT each show significant improvements in efficacy and lower relapse rates at follow-up compared to the earlier TBCT (Gurman, 2008a). Although there is no research explaining the exact reasons for this improved efficacy, it seems logical to assume that the inclusion of treatment strategies that directly address the effects of distressing and dysfunctional interaction patterns may be important. It may also be that these interventions provide experiences within couple sessions that generalize beyond sessions (Gurman, 2008a). There is no evidence to date that explains the different levels of efficacy between CBCT, IBCT, and EFCT even though the researchers offer some hypotheses (Baucom et al., 2008; Dimidjian et al., 2008; Johnson, 2008).

The Clinical Handbook of Couple Therapy (4th Edition) provides detailed descriptions and comparisons of 12 couple-therapy approaches (Gurman, 2008a). Two approaches, both with strong empirical support, are reviewed below.

Cognitive-Behavioral Couple Therapy (CBCT)

CBCT theory, causes of relationship dysfunction and change

CBCT evolved out of traditional behavioral couple therapy (TBCT) and thus is strongly influenced by learning theory with additional focus on cognitive theory (Baucom et al., 2008). Several research findings about distressed couples underpin its theory and practice. Distressed couples exhibit a high frequency of negative interactions (Jacobson & Margolin, 1979), and have been found to be deficient in their communication and problem-solving skills (Baucom et al., 2008). Research into cognitive aspects of troubled relationships suggests that distressed couples are more likely than nondistressed couples to notice negative behavior (selective tracking), to interpret such behavior in a negative way (attributions), and to reciprocate with negative behaviors (Baucom et al., 2008). Thus three important objectives of CBCT are to increase the ratio of positive to negative behaviors exchanged in the relationship, to help couples learn and implement more effective communication skills, and to alter distorted cognitions associated with relationship distress.

CBCT theory suggests that self-perpetuating negative cycles develop in couples because aversive interactions are interpreted in a distorted way which then leads to more negative interactions. This kind of interaction cycle can both create and maintain relationship distress. Frequent repetition of such cycles leads to what practitioners of CBCT describe as "global negative emotions" (Baucom et al., 2008, p. 36). The demand–withdraw pattern is an example of one such dysfunctional cycle (see chapters 9, 10 in this volume). For example, one partner may want to confront problems and resolve them quickly while the other finds conflict intolerable. When a problem is raised in a sharp or angry tone the conflict-avoidant partner feels attacked and withdraws, but the confronting partner does not feel heard and so may intensify his/her commitment to confront the concern so the problem may be resolved. Thus, withdrawing intensifies demanding behavior and demanding behavior elicits more withdrawal (see chapters 9, 10 in this volume regarding this conflict pattern). This cycle can escalate and partners can unwittingly train each other to enact the very behaviors they hate the most. Hence both behavioral and cognitive components of these cycles reinforce and maintain distress. CBCT practitioners attempt to interrupt and interfere with these dysfunctional cycles.

Baucom et al. (2008) describe some developments in what they call an enhanced CBCT model that extends attention beyond the interaction processes to the themes of discussions or arguments (content). These themes may be at the root of relationship conflict and are thought to stem from individual and relationship needs. Individual needs for autonomy, control, and achievement, and relationship needs for intimacy, support, and attention may create distress when these needs or expectations come in conflict with the partner's different needs and expectations (Baucom et al., 2008). Also, CBCT now includes strategies to manage emotions and borrows tenets and practices from EFCT.

CBCT therapeutic approach and strategies

Baucom et al. (2008) divided CBCT interventions into those used to modify behaviors, those used to modify cognitions, and those used to modify emotions. The two primary behavior-change treatment strategies are guided behavior change and skills training. Guided behavior change is a more recent development of the earlier behavioral exchange of TBCT (Jacobson & Margolin, 1979). It involves a therapist leading a couple in discussions about the problem behaviors or interpersonal patterns. After identifying critical issues, the parties are encouraged to commit themselves to start making changes irrespective of their partner's behavior or responses. Thus, guided behavior change is different from behavioral exchange in that it does not rely on conditional reciprocal exchanges and does not encourage a rule-governed model (Baucom et al., 2008). This strategy can also be used to work on some of the themes identified in the assessment. For example, if one partner needs more autonomy in order to feel happier within the relationship, then the other partner can work on providing more of this factor in the ways identified during the guided behavior change discussion. For example, the partner may provide more child care or domestic support to allow the other to have time and energy to meet important personal needs.

The CBCT skills-based interventions include: skills for sharing thoughts and emotions; listening skills; ways to respond to a partner; and guidelines for decision-making conversations (Baucom et al., 2008). Not all couples who benefit from communication training have deficits in these skills. Some have simply ceased to use more effective communication that they used earlier in the relationship and may still use effectively in other contexts. In such cases, communication training may serve as a tool to help break some of the dysfunctional cycles mentioned earlier and re-establish more effective communication patterns. Skills training is delivered via didactic discussions but can also be aided by the use of videos and reading material. During communication training, therapists focus on the process but use opportunities to further explore the themes associated with couple distress.

The cognitive therapy component of CBCT focuses on helping couples reassess their cognitions about relationship behaviors rather than focusing on behavior change (Baucom et al., 2008). The focus is not so much on negative interpretations or cognitions but on distortions that mediate dissatisfaction, dysfunctional behavior, and negative emotions. Several types of cognitive distortions can impact negatively upon relationships. These include selective attention, negative attributions (meaning or inferences), expectancies (predictions), assumptions (what the relationship is like), and standards (what the relationship should be like) (Epstein & Baucom, 2002). If one partner tries to be more caring but their partner interprets their changed behavior as an attempt to get, for example, more sex (selfish motive), the caring behavior will not produce increased satisfaction for the recipient.

CBCT uses a variety of cognitive strategies which broadly encompass two approaches, those of Socratic questioning and guided discovery (Epstein & Baucom, 2002). Socratic questioning simply involves asking a series of questions to help a client reevaluate the logic of their thinking. Guided discovery is a more experiential strategy where a therapist helps to create an experience for the couple that leads them to question their assumptions about the relationship.

CBCT includes interventions to manage two types of emotional experience and expression. Firstly, the CBCT therapist will use strategies borrowed from EFCT (Johnson, 2004; Johnson & Greenberg, 1987) to help couples access and heighten their emotions when one or both exhibit restricted or minimized emotional experience or expression. Secondly, the CBCT therapist will help couples contain the experience and expression of emotion when they are excessive and destructive to the relationship (Baucom et al., 2008). Containment strategies have been adapted from the work of Marsha Linehan (1993) and include scheduling times for emotional discussions, practicing healthy compartmentalization, seeking alternative means for communicating feelings, seeking support, and distress tolerance strategies (Kirby & Baucom, 2007).

Integrative Behavioral Couple Therapy (IBCT)

IBCT theory, causes of relationship dysfunction and change

After more than a decade of research into why TBCT is less effective for distressed couples, Jacobson and Christensen (1998) concluded that exclusively focusing on change appears to exacerbate couple distress. They developed IBCT which focuses on and integrates acceptance and change. Acceptance is not defined as tolerance of a poor relationship but rather as a hopeful alternative method by which "couples use problems—once experienced as divisive and damaging—as vehicles for greater intimacy and closeness" (Dimidjian et al., 2008, p. 74). The basis of the IBCT theory of couple distress is that differences, disagreements, and conflicts are a normal and inevitable part of any relationship. Rather than being caused by the differences themselves, IBCT proposes that couple distress is caused by the destructive ways couples respond to these differences. Partner characteristics or differences which are initially found to be attractive may later be differences over which conflict emerges.

Differences are more likely to become problematic when they are associated with individual vulnerabilities and thus reactions to these differences may elicit intense emotions and destructive interaction patterns. The coercive cycles spoken of within IBCT are similar to the self-perpetuating cycles already described in CBCT. Over time, attempts to change undesirable partner behaviors become more extreme and coercive to the point that the partners start to view differences as defects (Dimidjian et al., 2008). A partner who is initially viewed as direct and assertive might now be viewed as a bully, or one who was initially viewed as easy going is now seen as lazy or unmotivated. These judgments are used to justify continued attempts to reform the partner. Over time, the differences become a major source of conflict and the ongoing attempts to change each other intensify distress, and increase the distance between the couple.

TBCT focuses on helping partners change unhelpful relationship patterns through behavioral exchange. If a partner shows little affection she/he is encouraged to show more affection. IBCT expands this behavioral exchange method "by focusing as much or more on the recipient of behavior as on the agent of behavior" (Dimidjian et al., 2008, p. 76; Jacobson & Christensen, 1996). IBCT practitioners seek to change the context of the relationship by encouraging the couple to change their behavior as well as to receive the behavior of their partner in a more effective way. Being more accepting of negativity from one's partner and learning not to take this negativity so personally is an example of receiving a negative behavior in a different way.

This shift in emphasis can be explained by several factors. Firstly, there are some differences in relationships that are simply unsolvable. Secondly, and paradoxically, increased acceptance (reduced pressure to change) may sometimes actually promote increased change. Feeling under pressure to change complex or engrained patterns immediately can be discouraging or even aversive. Having time and patience from a partner might allow a more gradual and realistic process of change. "Thirdly . . . in most cases the reaction to an offending behavior is as much a problem as the offending behavior itself" (Dimidjian et al., 2008, p. 76). As not taking negative behavior so personally is receiving the behavior differently, not reacting defensively or seeking clarification are different ways to respond.

IBCT therapeutic approach and strategies

Acceptance strategies, tolerance strategies, and change strategies are the three types of IBCT interventions (Dimidjian et al., 2008; Jacobson & Christensen, 1996). The behavior change strategies (behavior exchange, communication and problem-solving training) need not be mentioned again as they are referred to in the description of CBCT. The two acceptance strategies of empathic joining and unified detachment are designed to help partners gain greater emotional intimacy over matters that previously divided them. During empathic joining the therapist facilitates the expression of pain without accusation. The therapist listens to each partner describe particular issues, reformulates these issues in light of the themes identified during the assessment, and then reflects these back to the couple in a nonblaming way (see chapter 23 in this volume). Another empathic-joining strategy involves encouraging softer rather than harder emotions or disclosures (Dimidjian et al., 2008). This technique may not only soften the speaker but also the listener. The second acceptance strategy is called unified detachment. When using this strategy the therapist is encouraging an intellectual rather than emotional discussion about a particular problem. This focus can be achieved by continually referring back to the major themes, having the couple describe the pattern in a particular conflict, or getting the partners to compare incidents (Dimidjian et al., 2008).

The object of tolerance-building strategies is to help couples reduce their futile efforts to change each other. Specific tolerance strategies include: pointing out positive aspects of negative behavior; practicing negative behaviors in therapy sessions; faking negative behaviors outside of sessions; and promoting tolerance through self-care (Dimidjian et al., 2008). It is important to note here that there are some behaviors, such as physical violence, which should not be accepted or tolerated.

Although the IBCT therapist flexibly moves between these interventions within sessions, based on the context at the time, Jacobson and Christensen (1998) recommend that therapists start with the acceptance strategies and use the tolerance strategies when couples face issues that are strongly resistant to change. Change techniques are sometimes not used at all, are sometimes dispersed within the therapy, and occasionally if the couple is not very distressed may even be the starting point.

Conclusion

Reviewing these two brief summaries of CBCT and IBCT may be affirming to therapists who use many of these strategies. It may also be frustrating to others who recognize that similar therapeutic strategies are used by other approaches although described and theorized differently. Thus, there is potential for scientific research to produce greater integration in the practice of couple therapy as it teases out the effective strategies and core essential processes of change. Couple therapists are encouraged to become familiar with the empirically supported couple therapies and to acquaint themselves with the descriptive relationship research. Such research is of little value unless it is used by practitioners to provide increasingly more effective couple therapy.

An implication from the common factor research is that couple therapists may justify not abandoning their theoretical and practical approaches in favor of the three therapy approaches with strongest empirical support. Evidence-based practice and therapist accountability can also be achieved by evaluating the effectiveness of interventions. The APA Presidential Task Force (2006) defined evidence-based practice in psychology as "the integration of the best available research with clinical expertise in the context of patient characteristics, culture, and preferences. Ongoing monitoring of patient progress and adjustment of treatment as needed are essential. Monitoring outcome and adjusting accordingly on the basis of client feedback—practice-based evidence—must become routine" (Hubble et al., 2009, p. 29). Couple therapists are thus encouraged to consider ways they may apply the principles of evidence-based practice to improve the efficacy of their efforts to help distressed couples.

References

Barlow, D. H., Hayes, S. C., & Nelson, R. O. (1984). *The scientist practitioner: Research and accountability in clinical and educational settings.* New York: Pergamon Press.

Baucom, D. H., Epstein, N. B., La Taillade, J. J., & Kirby, J. S. (2008). Cognitive-behavioral couple therapy. In A. S. Gurman (Ed.), *Clinical handbook of couple therapy* (4th edn., pp. 31–72). New York: Guilford Press.

Beutler, L. E. (2003). David and Goliath: When empirical and clinical standards of practice meet. *American Psychologist, 55*, 997–1007.

Bloom, B. L., Asher, S. J., & White, S. W. (1978). Marital disruption as a stressor: A review and analysis. *Psychological Bulletin, 85*, 867–894.

Brannon, L., & Feist, J. (1997). *Health psychology: An introduction to behavior and health* (3rd edn.). Pacific Grove, CA: Brooks/Cole.

Christensen, A., & Heavey, C. L. (1999). Interventions for couples. *Annual Review of Psychology, 50*, 165–190.

Cormier, S., & Nurius, P. S. (2003). *Interviewing and change strategies for helpers: Fundamental skills and cognitive behavioral interventions* (5th edn.). Pacific Grove, CA: Brooks/Cole-Thomson Learning.

Dimidjian, S., Martell, C. R., & Christensen, A. (2008). Integrative behavioral couple therapy. In A. S. Gurman (Ed.), *Clinical handbook of couple therapy* (4th edn.). New York: Guilford Press.

Epstein, N., & Baucom, D. H. (2002). *Enhanced cognitive-behavioral therapy for couples: A contextual approach*. Washington, DC: American Psychological Association.

Gurman, A. S. (2008a). A framework for the comparative study of couple therapy: History, models, and applications. In A. S. Gurman (Ed.), *Clinical handbook of couple therapy* (4th edn., pp. 1–26). New York: Guilford Press.

Gurman, A. S. (2008b). Integrative couple therapy: A depth-behavioral approach. In A. S. Gurman (Ed.), *Clinical handbook of couple therapy* (4th edn., pp. 383–423). New York: Guilford Press.

Hardy, K. V., & Laszloffy, T. A. (2002). Couple therapy using a multicultural perspective. In A. S. Gurman (Ed.), *Clinical handbook of couple therapy* (4th edn., pp. 569–596). New York: Guilford Press.

Hubble, M. A., Duncan, B. L., Miller, S. D., & Wampold, B. E. (2009). Introduction. In B. L. Duncan, S. D. Miller, B. E. Wampold, & M. A. Hubble (Eds.), *The heart and soul of change: Delivering what works in therapy* (2nd edn., pp. 23–46). Washington, DC: American Psychological Association.

Jacobson, N. S., & Addis, M. E. (1993). Research on couples and couple therapy: What do we know? Where are we going? *Journal of Consulting and Clinical Psychology, 61*(1), 85–93.

Jacobson, N. S., & Christensen, A. (1996). *Integrative couple therapy: Promoting acceptance and change*. New York: W. W. Norton.

Jacobson, N. S., & Christensen, A. (1998). *Acceptance and change in couple therapy: A therapist's guide to transforming relationships*. New York: W. W. Norton.

Jacobson, N. S., & Margolin, G. (1979). *Marital therapy: Strategies based on social learning and behavior exchange principles*. New York: Mazel.

Jacobson, N. S., Schmaling, K. B., & Holtzworth-Munroe, A. (1987). A component analysis of behavioral marital therapy: Two-year follow-up and prediction of relapse. *Journal of Marital and Family Therapy, 13*, 187–195.

Johnson, S. M. (2004). *The practice of emotionally focused couple therapy: Creating connection* (2nd edn.). New York: Brunner/Routledge.

Johnson, S. M. (2008). Emotionally focused couple therapy. In A. S. Gurman (Ed.), *Clinical handbook of couple therapy* (4th edn., pp. 107–137). New York: Guilford Press.

Johnson, S. M., & Denton, W. (2002). Emotionally focused couple therapy: Creating secure connections. In A. S. Gurman & N. S. Jacobson (Eds.), *Clinical handbook of couple therapy* (3rd edn., pp. 221–250). New York: Guilford Press.

Kirby, J. S., & Baucom, D. H. (2007). Treating emotional dysregulation in a couples context: A pilot study of couples skills group intervention. *Journal of Marital and Family Therapy, 33*, 1–17.

Knudson-Martin, C. (2008). Gender issues in the practice of couple therapy. In A. S. Gurman (Ed.), *Clinical handbook of couple therapy* (4th edn., pp. 641–661). New York: Guilford Press.

Lambert, M. J. (2009). "Yes, it is time for clinicians to routinely monitor treatment outcome." In B. L. Duncan, S. D. Miller, B. E. Wampold, & M. A. Hubble (Eds.), *The heart and soul of change: Delivering what works in therapy* (2nd edn., pp. 239–266). Washington, DC: American Psychological Association.

Lebow, J. (2008). Separation and divorce issues in couple therapy. In A. S. Gurman (Ed.), *Clinical handbook of couple therapy* (4th edn., pp. 459–476). New York: Guilford Press.

Linehan, M. (1993). *Cognitive-behavioral treatment of borderline personality disorder.* New York: Guilford Press.

Nathan, P. E., & Gorman, J. M. (1998). Treatments that work—And what convinces us they do. In P. E. Nathan & J. M. Gorman (Eds.), *A guide to treatments that work.* New York: Oxford University Press.

O'Leary, K. D. (2008). Couple therapy and physical aggression. In A. S. Gurman (Ed.), *Clinical handbook of couple therapy* (4th edn., pp. 478–497). New York: Guilford Press.

Roberto-Forman, L. (2008). Transgenerational couple therapy. In A. S. Gurman (Ed.), *Clinical handbook of couple therapy* (4th edn., pp. 196–228). New York: Guilford Press.

Shadish, W. R., Montgomery, L. M., Wilson, P., Wilson, M. R., Bright, I., & Okwumabua, T. (1993). Effects of family and marital psychotherapies: A meta-analysis. *Journal of Consulting and Clinical Psychology, 61*(6), 992–1002.

Simon, G. M. (2008). Structural couple therapy. In A. S. Gurman (Ed.), *Clinical handbook of couple therapy* (4th edn., pp. 323–351). New York: Guilford Press.

Snyder, D. K., & Wills, R. M. (1989). Behavioral versus insight-oriented marital therapy: Effects on individual and inter-spousal functioning. *Journal of Consulting and Clinical Psychology, 57*(1), 39–46.

23

Surviving Trauma

Susan M. Johnson and Kathryn D. Rheem

The association between secure attachment and resilience in the face of adversity has been clearly established (Mikulincer & Shaver, 2007). To offer a clear recent example, survivors of 9/11 who were securely attached were significantly less symptomatic and were able to deal with this trauma in a more growth-oriented manner than more insecure survivors (Fraley, Fazzari, Bonanno, & Dekel, 2006).

Thus, how exactly might a secure connection with a loved one translate into resilience in the face of adversity? The first and most obvious factor is that secure attachment fosters the ability to effectively regulate affect during times of anxiety and stress. Secure individuals are more in tune and able to reflect on their own distress without fear of losing control or becoming overwhelmed (Mikulincer, 1995; Mikulincer & Florian, 1995). A sense of supportive connection with another can change the way threat is actually perceived and encoded in the brain. For example, securely attached women have been shown to be less reactive physiologically to the threat of electric shock when their husbands hold their hand (Coan, Schaefer, & Davidson, 2006). Also, the soothing and reassuring responses of the attachment figure become integrated into self-soothing and self-caregiving routines (Neff, 2003) that are easily accessed during times of stress.

The second obvious link is that being able to actively turn to others for support and comfort when stress is potentially overwhelming mitigates the impact of traumatic events. In fact, the impact of traumatic experience is most often best predicted, not by trauma history, but by whether survivors can seek comfort in the arms of another (van der Kolk, Perry, & Herman, 1991), that is, whether they have a bond that offers them a safe haven and a secure base (chapters 11, 14 in this volume). On the other hand, emotional

The Wiley-Blackwell Handbook of Couples and Family Relationships, First Edition.
Edited by Patricia Noller and Gery C. Karantzas.

isolation exacerbates any kind of stress, trauma, and less functional affect-regulation strategies such as numbing (Johnson, 2002; Mikulincer & Shaver, 2007).

A third possible factor may be the positive and efficacious sense of self that results from secure attachment relationships (Mikulincer, 1995). Secure relationships allow a person to see all experience as "workable," as challenges to be mastered, and so a descent into helplessness (a main element of post-traumatic stress) is less likely. A fourth factor may be that secure attachment allows for the accessing of positive emotions even in the midst of stress. This process minimizes distress and interrupts negative emotions and arousal (Frederickson, 2001).

A fifth and more general factor may simply be one of flexibility of response. Repression and avoidance (which is not typical of secure attachment) can also be effective in the short run and can be necessary in some situations (Bonanno, 2004). However extreme self-reliance and cool invulnerability have their limits. These strategies break down under intense or prolonged stress (Johnson, 2002; Mikulncer & Shaver, 2007). Secure people, because they are more flexible in their approach to problems, are more likely to be able to choose a coping strategy that suits a particular situation. All these explanations are expressions of one of the most basic tenets of attachment theory and research: that we are infinitely stronger when emotionally connected with a significant other who will be there when we need them (Bowlby, 1969).

Couple therapy that actively focuses on the regulation, processing, and integration of affect and the creation of a more secure bond between partners has the potential to aid in the containment of the negative effects of traumatic experience and to create a safe haven and secure base that expedites healing in both partners (Johnson, 2002). This focus is central to emotion focused therapy (EFT) described in the next section.

The EFT Model of Intervention

EFT combines an experiential, intrapsychic focus with a systemic focus on cyclical interactional responses and patterns (Johnson, 2004). The process of change in EFT has been delineated in nine steps within three stages. The first stage is assessment and de-escalation of a couple's negative interactional cycle, such as critical blaming followed by defensive withdrawing, so that the couple can step out of this cycle which plunges them into attachment hurts and fears, and begin to view the cycle as their joint enemy. Stage Two focuses on restructuring the couple's bond in which a positive cycle of mutual emotional accessibility and responsiveness is created, ending in withdrawn partners becoming emotionally re-engaged and blaming partners softening their stance. Both partners can then ask for attachment needs to be met and respond reassuringly in meeting each other's fears and vulnerabilities. This process constitutes what Bowlby (1969) terms effective dependency, where each partner can offer the other a safe haven and a secure base. The third stage is consolidation in which partners integrate their new views of themselves, supported by the partner, to create a coherent story of their descent into distress and their ascent into a place of love and safety. As this story emerges for the couple, they are encouraged to address problems that were once a minefield of attachment anxieties but are now viewed as manageable and solvable problems.

Attachment theory (Bowlby, 1969) provides EFT with a developmental nonpathologizing theoretical context for understanding the importance of emotional bonds, interdependency, and adult love and intimacy. EFT combines a focus on what Bowlby called the inner ring of experience—each partner's key emotional and intrapsychic experiences including working models of self and other—as well as the outer ring of patterned interactions with others. Both rings intersect, creating and maintaining the other. Emotions, linking self and system, drive the strategies and habitual moves partners make within the frame of their attachment relationship (Johnson, 2003, 2004).

Background of EFT

The focus of EFT is consonant with recent research on the nature of relationship distress. For example, EFT addresses the toxic relationship pattern of demand–withdraw that predicts divorce (chapters 9, 10 in this volume). Furthermore, EFT choreographs the emotional responsiveness between partners—a powerful predictor of relationship satisfaction across time (Huston, Caughlin, Houts, Smith, & George, 2001). The theory and general process of change in EFT has been validated in process research (Bradley & Furrow, 2004) and in research on specific EFT tasks such as forgiveness (chapter 21 in this volume; Makinen & Johnson, 2006). Change in EFT is associated with a positive collaborative alliance, a deepening of emotional experience, and the ability to create affiliative interactions or enactments where partners can reach for each other, share anxieties, and ask for attachment needs to be met (Johnson, 2008).

EFT is the only model of couple therapy based on a rich, clear, and tested theory of adult love and bonding, namely attachment theory (Bowlby, 1969; see also chapters 11, 14 in this volume). This theory provides a map to the internal emotional realities of clients and unpacks "the moves in a couple's dance" as well as the impact of this dance on the nature of the relationship. Negative interactional patterns are seen within EFT as expressions of the deprivation of attachment needs, loss of a secure emotional connection with a significant other, and less functional ways of dealing with separation distress.

The goal in EFT is to address the need for a safe haven and secure base and to build interactions that characterize a secure bond (see chapter 21 in this volume). In such interactions, partners can recognize their loss of connection, tune into and manage their distress and attachment fears in a manner that does not trigger instant withdrawal, emotional numbing, or aggressive criticism. They can also send clear attachment signals to their partner in a manner that elicits caring and responsiveness. When their partner responds with care they can trust the partner's responsiveness, accept it, and use it to help find emotional balance. When emotionally balanced, they can turn and reciprocate a caring partner response. The goal is then the creation of more emotional engagement and secure bonding, rather than the teaching of communication skills, insight into the past, or problem-solving skills.

Attachment theory and EFT, like many interventions for traumatic stress, prioritize the management of fear; in the case of EFT, the therapist prioritizes the fear of abandonment and rejection and the accompanying vulnerability and emotional isolation that heightens the reminders of trauma. Negative responses, such as emotional withdrawal and responsiveness, angry criticism, or attacking behavior, are seen as manifestations of attachment anxiety (Johnson, 2004). In EFT, partners change each other as each learns to offer the other a safe haven and secure base where both partners can be open and trusting of one another and help each other grow and heal.

The principles of EFT are that the therapist stays focused in the present (traumatic cues and triggers arise and inevitably bring the past into the present in the session). The EFT therapist focuses on the process of interaction and the experiencing of emotions rather than addressing content issues. From an EFT standpoint, it is *how* the couple talk about an issue and the underlying attachment emotions and distorted messages contained in an issue, not that the couple has different ways of dealing with an issue. As a process consultant, the therapist also helps partners move from surface reactions such as defensive numbing or angrily blaming the partner into experiencing more primary emotions such as sadness, fear, helplessness, and shame. When the level of emotional experience changes, so too do the signals sent to the partner change, opening the door for new responses to occur.

EFT Interventions

In terms of EFT interventions, the therapist uses empathic reflection, constant validation, and evocative questioning to expand on the client's experience, thereby increasing clarity about the problem and making what was implicit explicit. The therapist also heightens the client's experience through the use of images and replays, and subtle reinterpretations of language. For example, a statement including the term "difficulty" might be stated more concretely and vividly as "scary." The fit of such interpretations of the experience is then checked with the client. The therapist also reflects patterns of interaction between relationship partners and reframes interactions and responses in terms of attachment theory; for example, framing withdrawal as a response to the impact a complaining partner has on the withdrawer, rather than as indifference or hostility towards the complaining partner.

Enactments are then constructed in every session where new awareness of distilled emotional experience is shaped into new signals to a partner. These enactments become more focused and intense in Stage Two of therapy. There are more specific interventions than enactments that are particularly needed for more fragile, traumatized couples. For example, the "slicing it thinner" intervention is used to minimize the experience of overwhelming fear by partners when discussing a sensitive issue (Johnson, 2004). So if the therapist asks a partner to share his or her fear with the other and this partner balks, the therapist will minimize the risk by backing up and exploring how hard it is to share in this way and then ask that the partner merely share this awareness. This reduces the risk that the client is asked to take, metaphorically slicing the emotional risk and fear more thinly. This example of a specific intervention highlights that defenses are respected and validated in EFT as these defenses have already saved these partners' lives.

Another intervention or process used in EFT is that of "unpacking" vague, denied, unformulated, or chaotic emotional responses (Johnson, 2004). Here the therapist focuses on the elements of emotion: their cues, initial perception, body response, negative or catastrophic appraisals, meanings, and action tendencies, as well as how these tendencies play into interactional cycles. As the therapist creates a sense of safety in exploring these emotional elements, the client is able to tune into their unregulated emotional experience in an effort to make it more coherent and to lead them in their relational dance. By slowing down and unpacking the process of an unregulated emotional response, both the client and the therapist are better able to grasp the raw elements of the emotional process and put them in context with the relationship's interactional patterns. For example, Dan, a numbed-out veteran, is able to grasp the trigger for his shutting down (the look of disappointment on her face), and its impact (this is bad, dangerous). He can then explore his body (my chest goes tight and I freeze up) and his thoughts (I have lost her already—I am a loser; a screw up. No point in trying). He acknowledges how this emotion moves him: he acts cold and detached and often leaves her crying. He sees how this then triggers rage and despair in her and fuels her criticism of him. In this process, difficult, dysregulated emotional experience is made coherent and workable.

Relationships and Post-Traumatic Stress

Post-traumatic stress disorder (PTSD) and depression are the two mental-health problems that most often accompany significant relationship distress (Whisman, 1999). As Foa and Rothbaum point out (1998), PTSD poses a serious health problem in North America. Over 9% of people in an urban suburb have been documented as suffering from PTSD (Breslau, Davis, Andreski, & Peterson, 1991). Given the long-term negative impact of PTSD symptoms on survivors and on their relationships, it is clear that couple therapists are likely to see, in their practices, a significant number of trauma survivors who have experienced a variety of traumatic events. In fact, couple therapists increasingly see distressed couples who are also dealing with the impact of illness (such as recurring breast cancer), violent events such as rape, or catastrophes such as fires or car accidents, past events such as childhood sexual abuse, or trauma that occurs as the result of war or engagement in police or fire-fighting duties. These events heighten the need for safe emotional engagement with a partner and intensify the personal and relational consequences when this engagement is not possible.

One of the first trauma theorists, Henry Krystal (1978), noted that trauma results in a "de-differentiation of affect" that results in the loss of the ability to identify specific emotions and to use emotions as guides to appropriate action. Given that the regulation of emotion and the sending of clear emotional signals are essential organizing elements, if not the defining features of the dance between intimates (Johnson, 2004), it is not difficult to understand that traumatic stress scrambles the signals between partners at a time when the survivor needs a positive relationship most urgently.

All the classic PTSD symptoms, as well as the toxic "solutions" to these symptoms such as substance abuse or cutting one's body to exit states of numbness and dissociation, become a "trap" (Shalev, 1993). One level of impairment acts as a trap by blocking self-regulatory and relational healing processes from occurring on other levels. For instance, when the survivor numbs by turning to alcohol, this shuts out the partner and inhibits relationship intimacy. The survivor then feels more abandonment and is more likely to have traumatic symptoms and becomes more obsessed with escaping into alcohol. It is easy to see why so many trauma survivors tend to seek out the help of couple therapists. Relationship distress and emotional isolation exacerbate post-traumatic symptoms, and these symptoms then actively create ongoing relationship distress. The survivor and his or her partner become trapped in an escalating spiral of alienation, loss, anxiety, and hopelessness. As a result of this trauma trap, partners often show symptoms of secondary traumatic stress (Nelson & Wampler, 2000).

As the impact of trauma on a survivor's relationships has become more and more apparent, and as couple interventions such as EFT that focus on the creation of a secure healing bond have become systematized and tested (Johnson, 2004), the use of couple therapy as part of an effective treatment approach to trauma has become more and more accepted. Apart from studies demonstrating the effectiveness of EFT in helping couples recover from distress and build intimacy and trust and the maintained improvements in couple functioning even in couples facing ongoing stress and at high risk for relapse (Clothier, Manion, Gordon Walker, & Johnson, 2002; Johnson, Hunsley, Greenberg, & Schlindler, 1999); there have been recent studies showing that this intervention can significantly improve the relationships of traumatized couples. These studies show that EFT can also impact PTSD symptoms (Dalton, Johnson, & Classen, in prep.; Macintosh & Johnson, 2008; Naaman, Johnson, & Radwan, in press) in breast cancer survivors, and in the victims of childhood sexual abuse.

EFT with Traumatized Couples

When working with traumatized couples, adjustments are made in the application of EFT (Johnson, 2002). Most often, traumatized partners have completed some individual work on their trauma before coming to couple therapy. Nevertheless, there is a need to pay particular attention to issues such as rage, the potential for abusive behavior, self-injury, and addictions that the survivor may use for reducing PTSD-related distress. A prerequisite for EFT is that the therapist can create emotional and physical safety in the session and work with couples without increasing the risk of heightening the trauma for couples between sessions (Johnson & Makinen, 2003). If a survivor copes with traumatic stress by becoming abusive then EFT may not be appropriate. General guidelines for working with potentially abusive couples apply here (Bograd & Mederos, 1999). At the very least, the survivor must take responsibility for his or her abusiveness and comply with rules to contain this behavior.

With trauma couples, the therapist also needs to gradually educate partners about the impact of trauma on close relationships. For example, most survivors of child abuse do not feel entitled to comfort and care and are too ashamed to speak of their needs—even to their partner. The survivor's partner may also need support to understand the nature of trauma and how it impacts on his or her partner's ability to respond to relationship cues. The therapist has to include education about traumatic stress in the beginning stages of therapy and explicate how the symptoms of PTSD impact the relationship and render experiences that partners usually find rewarding, such as lovemaking, problematic.

Since these couples are often severely distressed, the therapist needs to expect more crises and emotional storms during the therapeutic process. Responses such as aggressive blaming or defensive distancing tend to be more extreme than in nontraumatized couples and the therapist has to be able to contain these responses while maintaining an alliance with the partners. In setting the goals of therapy the therapist has to take the imprint of trauma into account (i.e., the emotional and physical responses associated with recall of the traumatic event). As a result, a survivor of childhood sexual abuse may need to shape very specific and more limited goals around sexuality and confiding in others than partners who have not been so traumatized. A war veteran may need to turn to his battle buddies occasionally rather than his wife to deal with aspects of the imprint of the trauma.

The therapist also needs to consult with other therapists who may be providing individual therapy with a traumatized partner and integrate the goals and process of EFT couple therapy with these other therapies. Finally, and most importantly, the alliance with the therapist tends to be more fragile and has to be constantly monitored. In the beginning of therapy, it is crucial to emphasize the collaborative nature of the alliance and maximize the safety and predictability of the therapeutic process.

It is important that the therapist be as genuine and as transparent as possible so that the sessions can quickly become a safe haven and secure base for both clients, even when they are facing their most overwhelming fears. The therapist uses reflection of the client's own words, soft slow voice, simple words, and repetition to slow down the in-session process and soothe clients while also asking them to risk tuning into their emotions and reaching for their partner while facing their emotional difficulties.

Therapy with these couples is usually longer in duration than therapy with non-traumatized partners (perhaps 30 sessions). The risks associated with having couples connect with difficult emotional experiences and to have partners support each other through this process means that the therapy needs to be broken down into smaller steps. Complex PTSD (Herman, 1992), where individuals have experienced violation by attachment figures, usually requires that the change process proceed very slowly where routine minor relapses are to be expected and managed. In spite of these considerations, couples have taught us that the natural tendency is for traumatized people to want to turn to their attachment figure in times of danger, and partners desire to protect their traumatized loved ones from further hurt. These attachment dynamics are very powerful allies in the treatment process providing that the therapist knows how to evoke and work with these attachment behavioral tendencies.

Held Together by Scotch Tape

In the following case example, the therapist is working in Stage Two of EFT with a couple coping with the echoes of battle. Steve, an army soldier diagnosed with PTSD who had just completed two tours in Iraq, and his wife Camilla, came for therapy after he received word that he would be deployed again. Steve had been emotionally withdrawn and numb as he coped with PTSD and reintegration issues. Camilla was becoming more and more critical as she feared she and the kids were becoming less important to him. With two young children, Camilla reported that Steve's avoidance and irritability had left her "walking on eggshells." The therapist's goal was to help each partner access more primary emotions in order to have a corrective emotional experience.

STEVE: It's true. I'm like a caged animal. After more than two years eating, drinking, sleeping the war, I'm more comfortable with the guys than I am with her and the kids. I don't like being home. Home, for me, is over there.

THERAPIST: Being home isn't comfortable ... It's become unfamiliar and foreign. It's hard to let your guard down?

THERAPIST: It's hard to let your guard down. Hard to relax. Hard to take this time away from the war. Hard to know who you are now?

STEVE: Well, I know who I am—I'm a soldier—but at home, I'm not a soldier. I'm a screw up (defeat, resignation).

THERAPIST: A screw up...

CAMILLA: He's not a screw up but he acts like he doesn't care. We're not the guys. We're not over there. I'm trying to preserve our home life and he acts like it's not important. Like me and the kids aren't important (anger). So, I do tell him what to do, otherwise he would be on the couch all day and at the bar all night. I'm so tired.

THERAPIST: (to wife) You feel so tired and unimportant. You never know when he'll be there, when he wants to connect, play with the kids, hang out with you. Of course, you're tired, you've been holding it together at home for a long time now. Maybe you feel lonely too—tired of feeling so alone?

CAMILLA: Yea, I am tired of being so alone (sadness). I mean, I have the kids and they're wonderful but I'm alone still.

THERAPIST: You'd like Steve to come close? Talk to you? Do you miss him?

CAMILLA: Yes, I do miss him. I miss the old him. I miss the old us. We used to have so much fun together.

THERAPIST: (to husband) You miss talking with your wife? Do you miss the fun you used to have together?

STEVE: (nodding) I do miss it—I did miss it. Now, it seems like a distant memory. It's hard to remember those times. Almost like it was another person back then. So much has happened since then.

THERAPIST: Right, yes, you've been through a lot. Your life has changed but your wife is still here. Your wife is right here talking about missing you. You're here together fighting for your relationship. What happens for you when your wife says she misses you?

STEVE: I kind of freeze. Like my breath catches in the cold. She misses the old me. I don't think she'd like who I've become.

THERAPIST: So, you freeze, your breath catches, you stay distant . . . you keep your distance so she won't come close. You keep your guard up . . . you're worried she won't like who you've become?

STEVE: Yea, I guess I am worried she won't like me. I mean, I'm held together by scotch tape. The only thing keeping me going is hanging out with my buddies. They are the only ones who know, understand. Nobody else will ever understand. Why bother?

THERAPIST: Why bother turning to your wife, you mean? Why bother talking to her? Why bother letting her come close?

STEVE: Right, why risk it? She already tells me how much I screw things up so why bother. I'm not sure she wants to get close to me anyway.

CAMILLA: I do want to be close to you. I do (starts crying). I have wanted to be close to you since you got home but your Kevlar is still on. I thought you just needed more time and I tried to be patient. Tried to give you time. But you stayed distant and I ran out of patience. But, I have missed you. I've missed you a lot but didn't think you cared anymore.

THERAPIST: (to husband, softly evoking) Steve, how are you hearing this? When your wife says she misses you a lot. She wants to be close. Can you see her face (her face is soft, earnest. Eyes wet)?

STEVE: (tentatively looks at wife) Yea, I see her face.

THERAPIST: When she says, "I want to be close" to you, that she has missed you a lot—how does that touch you?

STEVE: Well, um, I didn't know that. I didn't know that she misses me; that she wants to be close to me.

THERAPIST: On the inside, how do you feel?

STEVE: . . . it feels good that she misses me. I didn't know that. It feels good to know that. I didn't think she missed me.

THERAPIST: It feels good knowing she has been missing you; that she wants to come close and be with you. It touches you?

STEVE: (pensively, softly) Um hmm. Yea, it does feel good. It does touch me . . . I didn't think I could be "touched" anymore.

THERAPIST: You mean, after combat, with your Kevlar on, nothing would touch you, nothing would get to you?

STEVE: Right, like I was numb, nothing would touch me, not even my wife . . .

THERAPIST: But now, with your wife right here, missing you, wanting to be close to you, you're touched?

STEVE: Yea, yea, I am. I am.

THERAPIST: What's this moment like—realizing you're being touched, you do feel, you're not numb? What's this "being touched" like for you?

STEVE: It's amazing, actually (water in his eyes). I thought I had lost this forever.

THERAPIST: Like you would never feel again?

STEVE: (slowly) Yea, like I wouldn't feel again. Or, if I felt again, I'd be a raging lunatic.

THERAPIST: So, you've been stuck in this place of not feeling to ensure you won't become a raging lunatic? It's been real risky to feel after being numb, like you might go from one extreme (not feeling) to the other (raging lunatic). But, right here, right now, you are feeling again. You are touched. What is it that you're feeling?

STEVE: Well, I feel sad; it's sad. Sad that she's been missing me this whole time and I didn't know it.

THERAPIST: Sad . . . right. Sad that you've both been alone even when you're back from Iraq. Sad that it's been hard to connect. Really sad that you haven't known how important you are to each other.

STEVE: (water in his eyes) Yea, sad that I've missed so much with her even though I've been home for a while now.

THERAPIST: (softly) Can you turn towards your wife . . . can you tell her how sad you feel that she has been missing you and you didn't know it? Sad that you've both been alone . . .

STEVE (TURNS TO WIFE WITH A BIT OF RELUCTANCE): It's true . . . I am sad now that I know you've been missing me. I didn't know (softly).

THERAPIST: It is sad that she's been missing you. (Both nod affirmingly.) Steve, have you missed your wife too? We know she has missed you and you feel sad that she's been missing you and you haven't known it until now. Have you been missing her too?

STEVE: Yea, actually, now that we're talking about it, I have been missing her.

THERAPIST: What it's like on the inside to realize you've been missing her too?

STEVE: Even sadder, I guess, just more sadness (looking down).

THERAPIST: (to wife) What's it like to have Steve share his sadness with you? To tell you he has been missing you too?

CAMILLA: (water in her eyes, smiling too) It feels good; it's a relief because I was really worried. I didn't think he missed me anymore and now I hear that he has been missing me and also that he didn't know that I was missing him.

THERAPIST: Right, it feels good, a relief, to know you both have been missing each other and haven't known how to talk about it. With all these scrambled signals going back and forth between you, it's been hard to say, "I miss you," or "I'm feeling sad that we're not hanging out." And, now after sharing Steve, how are you feeling?

STEVE: I'm feeling more human than I've felt in a long time. It feels good. Like I'm glad my wife has been missing me (smiles) and that I can say that I've been missing her too.

Conclusion

Since "a secure bond is the primary defense against trauma-induced psychopathology" (Finkelhor & Browne, 1984, p. 36), the relevance of couple interventions for traumatic stress is clear, especially if interventions focus on affect regulation and integration and creating a more secure attachment. The ability for couples to turn toward each other for comfort and care is a key part of creating accessibility and responsiveness—the core elements of a secure bond. For a couple coping with the echoes of trauma, reaching for the other in a moment of need is like leaping across an abyss while not knowing if the landing will be soft. Attachment-oriented interventions provide a safe way for these couples to risk that leap and find themselves in a safe haven. Within this safety, an environment of recovery is created within the couple.

References

Bograd, M., & Mederos, F. (1999). Battering and couples therapy: Universal screening and selection of treatment modality. *Journal of Marital and Family Therapy, 25*, 291–312.

Bonanno, G. (2004). Loss, trauma and human resilience: Have we underestimated the human capacity to thrive after extremely aversive events? *American Psychologist, 59*, 20–28.

Bowlby, J. (1969). *Attachment and loss: Vol. 1 Attachment.* New York: Basic Books.

Bradley, B., & Furrow, J. L. (2004). Toward a mini-theory of the blamer-softening event: Tracking the moment-by-moment process. *Journal of Marital and Family Therapy, 30*(2), 233–246.

Breslau, N., Davis, G. C. D., Andreski, P., & Peterson, E. (1991). Traumatic events and posttraumatic stress disorder in an urban population of young adults. *Archives of General Psychiatry, 48*, 218–222.

Clothier, P. F., Manion, I., Gordon Walker, J., & Johnson, S. M. (2002) Emotionally-focused interventions for couples with chronically-ill children: A two year follow-up. *Journal of Marital and Family Therapy, 28*, 391–398.

Coan, J. A., Schaefer, H. S., & Davidson, R. J. (2006). Lending a hand: Social regulation of the neural response to threat. *Psychological Science, 17*, 1032–1039.

Dalton, E. J., Johnson, S. M., & Classen, C. (in prep.). Emotionally focused couple therapy for relationship distress among survivors of childhood abuse: A randomized controlled trial.

Finkelhor, D., & Browne, A., (1984). The traumatic impact of child sexual abuse: A conceptualization. *American Journal of Orthopsychiatry, 55*, 530–541.

Foa, E. B., & Rothbaum, B. O. (1998). *Treating the trauma of rape: Cognitive behavioral therapy for PTSD.* New York: Guilford Press.

Fraley, C., Fazzari, D., Bonanno, G., & Dekel, S. (2006). Attachment and psychological adaptation in high exposure survivors of the September 11th attack on the World Trade Center. *Personality and Social Psychology Bulletin, 32*, 538–551.

Frederickson, B. L. (2001). The role of positive emotions in positive psychology: The broaden and build theory of positive emotions. *American Psychologist, 56*, 218–226.

Herman, J. L. (1992). *Trauma and recovery.* New York: Basic Books.

Huston, T. L., Caughlin, J. P., Houts, R. M., Smith, S. E., & George, L. J. (2001). The connubial crucible: Newly-wed years as predictors of delight, distress, and divorce. *Journal of Personality and Social Psychology, 80*, 237–252.

Johnson, S. M. (2002). *Emotionally focused couple therapy with trauma survivors: Strengthening attachment bonds.* New York: Guilford Press.

Johnson, S. M. (2003). The revolution in couple therapy: A practitioner-scientist perspective. *Journal of Marital and Family Therapy, 29*, 365–384.

Johnson, S. M. (2004). *The practice of emotionally focused couple therapy: Creating connection* (2nd edn.). New York: Brunner-Routledge.

Johnson, S. M. (2008). *Hold me tight: Seven conversations for a lifetime of love.* New York: Little, Brown.

Johnson, S. M., Hunsley, J., Greenberg, L., & Schlindler, D. (1999). Emotionally focused couples therapy: Status and challenges. *Clinical Psychology; Science and Practice, 6*, 67–79.

Johnson, S. M., & Makinen, J. (2003). Creating a safe haven and a secure base: Couples therapy as a vital element in the treatment of post-traumatic stress disorder. In D. Snyder & M. Whisman (Eds.), *Treating difficult couples* (pp. 308–329). New York: Guilford Press.

Krystal, H. (1978). Trauma and effects. *Psychoanalytic Study of the Child, 33*, 81–116.

Mikulincer, M. (1995). Attachment style and the mental representation of the self. *Journal of Personality and Social Psychology, 69*, 1203–1215.

Mikulincer, M., & Florian, V. (1995). Appraisal of and coping with a real-life stressful situation: The contribution of attachment styles. *Personality and Social Psychology Bulletin, 21*, 406–414.
Mikulincer, M., & Shaver, P. R. (2007). *Attachment in adulthood: Structure, dynamics and change.* New York: Guilford Press.
Macintosh, H. B., & Johnson, S. M. (2008). Emotionally focused therapy for couples and childhood sexual abuse survivors. *Journal of Marital and Family Therapy, 34*, 298–315.
Makinen, J., & Johnson, S. M. (2006). Resolving attachment injuries in couples using EFT: Steps towards forgiveness and reconciliation. *Journal of Consulting and Clinical Psychology, 74*, 1055–1064.
Naaman, S., Johnson, S. M., & Radwan, K. (in press). Evaluation of the clinical efficacy of emotionally focused therapy on psychological adjustment of couples facing early breast cancer. *Psychiatry, Biological and Interpersonal Processes.*
Neff, K. D. (2003). Self-compassion: An alternative conceptualization of a healthy attitude towards self. *Self and Identity, 2*, 85–102.
Nelson, B. S., & Wampler, K. S. (2000). Systemic effects of trauma in clinic couples: An exploratory study of secondary trauma resulting from childhood abuse. *Journal of Marital and Family Therapy, 26*, 171–183.
Shalev, A. Y. (1993). Stress versus traumatic stress: From acute homeostatic reactions to chronic psychopathology. In B. van der Kolk, A. McFarlane, & L. Weisaeth (Eds.), *Traumatic stress* (pp. 77–101). New York: Guilford Press.
van der Kolk, B. A., Perry, C., & Herman, J. L. (1991). Childhood origins of self-destructive behavior. *American Journal of Psychiatry, 148*, 1665–1671.
Whisman, M. A. (1999). Marital dissatisfaction and psychiatric disorders: Results from the National Comorbidity Survey. *Journal of Abnormal Psychology, 108*, 701–706.

24

Children's Adjustment after Parental Separation

Investigating a Clinical Shift from Reducing Parental Conflict to Improving the Parent–Child Relationship

Susie Sweeper

Over the last couple of decades there has been much research and clinical attention on the detrimental effects of parental conflict on children in both marriages and after relationship separation (see Amato, 2001 for a review; Noller, Feeney, Sheehan, Darlington, & Rogers, 2008). It is indisputable that witnessing parental conflict is bad for children and generally the evidence shows that it is pretty intransigent. For instance, Noller's pioneering and career-long research is testament to the ill-effects of parental conflict on children (see chapter 9 in this volume). In recent research, Noller and colleagues assessed the longitudinal effects of conflict in both separated and intact families. They found at multiple time points that psychological adjustment was lowest for children and adolescents in high-conflict separating families (Noller et al., 2008). Organizations worldwide have subsequently spent much time, money, and other valuable resources in treatment efforts to reduce parental conflict. Theoretically, it is expected that children's levels of adjustment will be mediated by the level of parental conflict and that reducing parental conflict, via treatment programs, will indirectly improve children's well-being. Unfortunately, reducing parental conflict has proved quite a difficult and costly task, and reductions in parental conflict have not always been associated with improvements in children's well-being (Kramer & Washo, 1993).

The Wiley-Blackwell Handbook of Couples and Family Relationships, First Edition.
Edited by Patricia Noller and Gery C. Karantzas.

In this chapter I will argue that we need to refocus clinical attention away from efforts at reducing parental conflict to increasing treatment resources that enhance the parent–child relationship. As a clinician and research psychologist, the beginning of this shift in my thinking has come out of my frustration with regard to how difficult it is to improve child outcomes by helping separated parents reduce their conflict. For this reason, I have for some time been thinking of different, more efficient (and less frustrating) ways to improve children's adjustment than focusing on parental conflict.

In this chapter I will discuss the nature of parenting conflict, and its impact on children's adjustment, and review the efficacy of parenting programs aimed at reducing parental conflict. While the focus of the chapter will be on conflict in separating families, data will also be presented on high-conflict intact families. Finally, a different focus, namely improving the parent–child relationship as a treatment focus, will be discussed as a way to enhance children's adjustment post parental separation.

The Nature of Parental Conflict

Research shows that parental conflict is often high after a relationship separation. Buchanan and Heiges (2001) report that up to 25% of couples continue to experience moderate to high conflict. Longitudinal studies of parental conflict demonstrate that parental conflict is also stable over time after a relationship breakdown (chapter 9 in this volume; Ambert, 1989; Maccoby & Mnookin 1992; Noller et al., 2008; Sweeper & Halford, 2006). For instance Sweeper (2004) found no changes in parental conflict between the time of separation and over the following 2 years. Often high conflict after a separation is associated with high conflict prior to the separation (Coysh, Johnston, Tschann, Wallerstein, & Kline, 1989). Additionally, Johnston (1998) found a 79% concordance rate between domestic violence during the relationship and high levels of post-separation conflict. The content of parental conflict post separation usually involves child-related matters, such as contact arrangements or financial support for the child (Buchanan & Heiges, 2001).

Children are often exposed to the conflict and violence of their parents. For example, 37% of adults who reported they were assaulted by a spouse also reported that their children had heard or seen the violence take place (Dauvergne & Johnson, 2001). Parents often underreport the conflict children witness. For instance, parents often report that their children were unaware of the parental conflict and violence, despite children reporting awareness of it (Jaffe, Wolfe, & Wilson, 1990; O'Brien, John, Margolin, & Erel, 1994). Parents will often report that their children were in bed asleep or that the conflict with their former partner occurred over the telephone and were unaware that their children were listening to the phone call or were awake in bed during the conflict.

Children of separated parents who remain in high conflict have disturbed patterns of emotional arousal, affect-regulation difficulties, show little empathy (Lieberman & Vanderhorn, 1998; Margolin & Gordis, 2000), experience heightened aggression, impulsivity, anxiety, and emotional problems (Cummings & Davies, 1994), and increased physiological arousal in response to conflict (McLoyd, Harper, & Copeland, 2001).

Exposure to conflict affects the child's view of the world, themselves, and their expectation of happiness (Garbarino, Dubrow, Kostelyn, & Prado, 1992). High conflict can also alter the child's view that their home is a safe place and that their parents will be available to care for them physically and emotionally. A poor ability to socialize or concentrate at school and an inability to form trusting and secure attachments (Garbarino et al., 1992; Janoff-Bulman, 1992) can also result from witnessing destructive parental conflict. Socialization, concentration, and trust problems are particularly pertinent to school-aged children as they adapt to the school environment and try to establish relationships with peers.

As a result of its longevity and its indisputable consistent negative impacts on children's adjustment, researchers and practitioners alike have quite sensibly put much effort into developing treatment protocols aimed at reducing parental conflict. The argument is that if high conflict is responsible for child adjustment problems then if parents reduce their conflict the child adjustment problems will also reduce. As sensible and reasonable as this approach appears, for a number of reasons it has not worked. In the following section of the chapter, I will critique efforts and success rates at reducing parental conflict and its impact on children.

Difficulties in Reducing Parental Conflict

First, it should be noted that there is only a limited number of published research studies that provide rigorous methodological testing of programs aimed at reducing parenting conflict. Lauri and Kowal (2005) note that although there have been many programs developed to assist divorcing parents, very few have been subjected to empirical evaluations. Pedro-Carroll (2005) reports that most evaluations conducted were limited to parent-satisfaction data (i.e., how satisfied they were with the program). Whilst satisfaction data is useful in gauging how much they liked the program, satisfaction data alone gives no indication of whether the program was responsible for any clinical change.

It appears that when a large body of research evidence pointed to the negative impacts of parental conflict on children in the early 1990s (e.g. Grych & Fincham, 1990), service providers were quick to develop programs aimed at reducing conflict without adequately testing their effectiveness. The legal system in particular took note of this research and began to inundate service providers with court-referred parents mandated to undertake post-separation parenting programs (Geasler & Blaisure, 1998). Hence, it is likely that programs were developed somewhat hastily with little effort to evaluate whether in fact reducing parental conflict was achieved and whether that reduction led to better child outcomes.

In the handful of evaluations that do adhere to scientific practices in treatment evaluation, research shows that reducing conflict in separated parents is difficult. In a thorough review of programs aimed at parents post separation, Goodman, Bonds, Sandler, and Braver (2004) appeared to be underwhelmed by the evidence for change in parental conflict in both short-term (i.e., 6 hours or less) and longer-term (i.e., over 6 hours) treatment protocols.

In their evaluation table of the effectiveness of long-term programs, Goodman et al. (2004) report that no studies demonstrated significant change in interpersonal conflict.

Specifically in regards to longer-term programs, Kramer, Arbuthnot, Gordon, Rousis, and Hoza (1998) compared two popular programs both aimed at reducing parental conflict and improving parental communication after relationship separation. Each program was 10 sessions long with one being skills-based while the other was more information-based. They reported that neither program had effects on domestic violence, actual parental conflict, or child behavior problems. Similarly, Stolberg and Garrison (1985) also evaluating a 10-session program showed no differences between the experimental and control groups in parenting skills or measures of child adjustment for separated parents.

As previously stated, the purpose of reducing parental conflict is the expectation that such a reduction will lead to increases in child adjustment. However, evidence suggests that when in fact conflict does reduce, subsequent impact on child adjustment may not occur. For instance, Kramer and Washo (1993) reported that parental conflict did reduce after their treatment program, however, participation in the program was not associated with improvements in child-rearing behavior or parent–child relationship quality. This finding suggests that targeting variables other than parental conflict might have more impact on children's adjustment after parental separation.

Why are treatments less successful for parents in high conflict?

A number of researchers have speculated on the reasons why post-separation parenting programs may not be successful for high-conflict parents. Kramer et al. (1998) suggest the emotional, social, and financial trauma faced by some couples post separation mitigate the capacity of couples to engage with programs. McKenzie and Bacon (2002) surmised that high-conflict parents can be seen as difficult and unlikely to learn as much as low-conflict parents from post-separation parenting programs. Thus, parents in high conflict after a separation may be having significant personal issues in relation to adjusting to the separation, which prevent them from focusing on reducing their parental conflict.

In the first 2 years after separation most parents experience an increase in adjustment problems, with many of these parents having difficulties with depression, anxiety, and stress (Sweeper & Halford, 2006). Therefore, learning new skills to reduce conflict with their former partner might be seen as too hard, given their personal distress. A lot of treatment programs for separated parents provide very little information on assisting the parents with their own personal adjustment. It is likely that neglecting or minimizing the needs and adjustment issues of the adults will negatively affect any intervention aimed at reducing parenting conflict. In essence, they may need to have some individual assistance to increase their personal adjustment before they can focus on reducing their conflict with their former partner.

Change in conflict is often difficult because it relies on both parents to some extent to have a commitment to reducing the conflict. Research shows that often parents can be at different stages in the adjustment process (Sweeper & Halford, 2006) and while one parent might be eager to reduce conflict, the other parent may still feel the need to continue "the fight" with their former partner. In essence, for two partners who have been in high conflict for a long time, and/or have been through a difficult separation, and/or one or both members are having difficulty adjusting to the end of the relationship, and/or the conflict revolves around what is most precious to them (i.e., their children), it is not surprising that speaking respectfully to one another is a difficult thing to do, even when treatment is provided, particularly if they did not show respect to one another before the separation.

Finally, another reason why treatment programs may not be successful in effecting changes in parental conflict and child adjustment problems is that rather than focusing on the children's needs (as encouraged by the international movement to "focus on the children" and legally do what is in "the best interest of the child"), the content of programs keeps the focus on the parents' relationship when attempting to teach skills of conflict management. In essence, programs focused on parenting conflict keep the focus on the parents, their relationship with each other, and their "fight" as opposed to focusing primarily on the child, their relationship with their child, and their child's needs.

Parent conflict is not solely responsible for child outcomes

In the following section of this chapter, I review other factors, besides parental conflict, that might be responsible for children's adjustment problems after parental separation. Children's reactions to parenting conflict are very complex and it may indeed not be the conflict per se that directly causes child adjustment problems. For instance, not all children from high-conflict situations display emotional or behavioral adjustment problems. In fact, Hanson (1999) in a nationwide longitudinal study also found that parental conflict was by no means the variable solely explaining the association between divorce and child welfare. Furthermore, Fincham and Osborne (1993), while acknowledging the relationship between family conflict and child problems, report that this relationship is by no means large. They indicate that the vast majority of the data show that family conflict and child adjustment problems share less than 10% of the variance. These findings suggest that other variables, apart from family conflict, are responsible for creating child adjustment problems and may be a reason why reducing parenting conflict might not always be sufficient for improving child outcomes.

Grych and Fincham (1990) discuss child-related variables that might help to explain child adjustment problems in the context of parental conflict and why children may respond differently in the face of parental conflict. They argue, from a cognitive-contextual model, that it is how children appraise the causes and consequences of the conflict that determines whether the conflict is detrimental to their well-being. There is a solid body of research supporting this model. It is well documented that cognitive factors such as children's perceptions of the threat posed by conflict mediate the relationship between parental conflict and children's adjustment (Grych, Harold & Miles, 2003). More specifically, Stocker, Richmond, Low, Alexander, and Elias (2003), in a sample of a 136-school-aged children and their parents, found that children's feelings of being to blame for marital conflict and being threatened by it, mediated the association between parental conflict and children's anxiety and depression. Hence, targeting other variables such as child threat appraisals may assist in increasing child adjustment in the context of high-conflict parental separations.

High parental conflict needs to be seen within the larger family context and stressors within the family. Laor, Wolmer, and Cohen (2001) suggest that, in general, acute events that produce relatively little change in social structures tend to carry lower risks than either chronic, ongoing traumatic events, or traumatic events that lead to long-term disruptions in children's social environments. Martinez and Forgatch (2002) found that accumulation of family transitions and stressful changes in divorcing families was associated with poorer school performance, increased externalizing behavior, and problematic emotional adjustment in boys. When parents separate, children's social structures are often altered greatly due to financial pressures resulting from property settlements (Amato, 2000). There is often a need to move to a poorer, more affordable neighborhood often necessitating a change in school and therefore a change in friendships. In this way, parental conflict may need to be considered a risk factor within the context of many other risk factors, such as multiple stressful changes, that occur when parents separate.

Parental separation weakens the parent–child relationship. There is a vast body of research showing that after a relationship separation parents have less positive parent–child relationships and show a greater decline in the quality of parental practices and discipline than parents from intact families (Amato & Booth, 1996; Beelmann & Schmidt-Denter, 2009; Buchanan & Heiges, 2001; Coiro & Emery, 1998; Hanson, McLanahan, & Thomson, 1998; Hetherington, Cox, & Cox, 1982). The quality of the parent–child relationship has been associated with children's behavioral difficulties, psychological and subjective well-being, academic achievement, and relationships to other family members (chapters 5, 25 in this volume; Amato & Booth, 1996; Fagen, Cowen, Wyman, & Work, 1996). The effect of relations between parents and children continues to be important as the child reaches early adulthood, with research showing that it can impact their relationship formation, satisfaction, and the duration of their intimate relationships (Cartwright, 2006).

To summarize, thus far I have reviewed evidence that suggests that high parental conflict is not uncommon in separated families and that children are often exposed to it. Treatment efforts to reduce high conflictual behavior in separated parents is difficult, possibly because one or both parents are in significant distress and unable to cooperate with their former partner. However, it is likely that reductions in conflict will not prove to be the panacea for children's good mental health as other variables such as children's own appraisals of threat in regard to their parents' conflict, the accumulation of stressors associated with parental separation, and the quality of the parent–child relationship seem to predict children's adjustment outcomes. In the second half of this chapter, I will provide evidence to suggest a shift away from focusing on parental conflict in order to improve child outcomes to improving the quality of the parent–child relationship.

The relationship between parent conflict, parent–child relationship quality, and child adjustment

Theoretically, there are very good reasons why we should focus on the parent–child relationship in treatments where parents are in high conflict. John Bowlby, a pioneer in attachment theory, discussed how children's attachment relationships or internal working models of themselves in relation to attachment figures (most often the child's parents) are a result of the interaction quality they have experienced and the emotional openness they have received in that relationship, especially in times of hardship. Hence, applying Bowlby's theory to the separated family, it is argued that a trusting, nurturing, predictable, and secure parent–child relationship is likely to provide protection to the child against significantly harmful levels of parental conflict. Likewise, Davies and Cummings (1994) developed the emotional security perspective which outlines that stressful situations may or may not be damaging to the child's adjustment depending on whether the child believes that their emotional needs will continue to be met by their important attachment figures. In this way, after a relationship separation, it is argued that child adjustment will be more the result of continued positive attachment bonds rather than just the level of parental conflict to which the child is exposed.

Research seems to provide evidence for both Bowlby's (1973) and Davies and Cummings' (1994) assertions in regard to the benefits for children of having a secure attachment relationship with one or more parents when experiencing stress, namely parental conflict (for descriptions regarding attachment theory see chapters 11, 14 in this volume). Hetherington et al. (1982) about 30 years ago found a buffering effect against the damaging nature of post-separation parental conflict when parents soothed their children and engendered trust and encouraged self-regulation. Later, Cummings and Davies (1996) found that a secure mother–child relationship appeared to moderate the distressing nature of conflict for children. In this way the impact of exposure to parental conflict was more benign in terms of: (a) its possible impact of the child feeling threatened by the parental conflict and (b) the child's longer-term adjustment problems when a good mother–child relationship was present.

More recent research continues to show that a secure parent–child relationship can protect children against the damaging effects of parent conflict (e.g., Atkinson, 2004). In fact, for boys, Atkinson and Dadds (2009) found that the quality of the mother–son relationship was the only variable that consistently predicted boys' appraisals of the threat of interparental conflict. This finding suggests that the parent–child relationship (particularly for boys) might be more important for their adjustment than the influence of the parental relationship in terms of conflict. In essence, the quality of the parent–child relationship shaped the child's fear that the parental conflict would escalate and would disrupt the attachment relationship with one or both parents.

Research shows gender differences for parents in the quality of the parent–child relationship in the context of family conflict. Sobolewski and Amato (2007) found that children feel closer to their mother than their father when family stress is present. Similarly, Atkinson (2004) reported that the protective value of the parent–child relationship in the context of high parental conflict is more likely awarded to the mother–child relationship. She found that when boys and girls experienced more warmth and care in their relationship with mothers, they were less likely to exhibit both internalizing and externalizing problems, and more likely to utilize negotiation behaviors to resolve conflict with their brothers and sisters. According to Atkinson and Dadds (2009), mothers were seen as more caring than fathers. Atkinson and colleagues' research, however, did show that a close father–child relationship also had benefits, particularly for girls. The quality of the father–daughter relationship predicted the girl's conflict style, in that the closer daughters felt to their dads, the less likely they were to engage in attacking behaviors to resolve sibling conflict.

Even in "at risk" communities there is evidence to suggest that a good parent–child relationship and/or good parenting behavior moderates the relationship between family conflict and child adjustment. For instance, Formosa, Gonzales, and Aiken (2000) found some evidence that within a low-income, multiethnic sample of adolescents, parental attachment and parental monitoring (i.e., supervision of their child's behavior), moderated the link between family conflict and conduct problems. In addition, children who witnessed violence, but who had more positive relationships with a parent reported fewer symptoms than children who witnessed violence but reported poor parent–child relationships (Boney-McCoy & Finkelhor, 1996).

There are other post-separation stressors, other than parental conflict, that a secure and nurturing parent–child relationship might protect against. As discussed earlier, parental separation can be associated with much change for the child in regard to moving house (often to a poorer neighborhood), moving school, developing new social networks, etc. Martinez and Forgatch (2002) found that effective parenting practices and parental encouragement mediated the relationship between changes associated with the parent's separation and children's adjustment with regard to acting-out behavior and emotional adjustment.

In sum, when reviewing the theoretical arguments proposed and the research data, it appears that the quality of the parent–child relationship mediates the impact of exposure to high parental conflict (and possibly other stressors, such as accumulated changes) associated with parental separation on the child's adjustment—this mediation model is presented in Figure 24.1. Additionally, having a secure parent–child relationship shapes the child's attributions of the threat associated with parental conflict. Hence, in families where there is ongoing high conflict, having a secure, close, and nurturing relationship with a parent is likely to afford some level of protection against the threat of parental conflict or the perceived impact that the parental conflict will have on the child. This assertion would then suggest that in high-conflict families, improving the parent–child relationship should be a target for treatment.

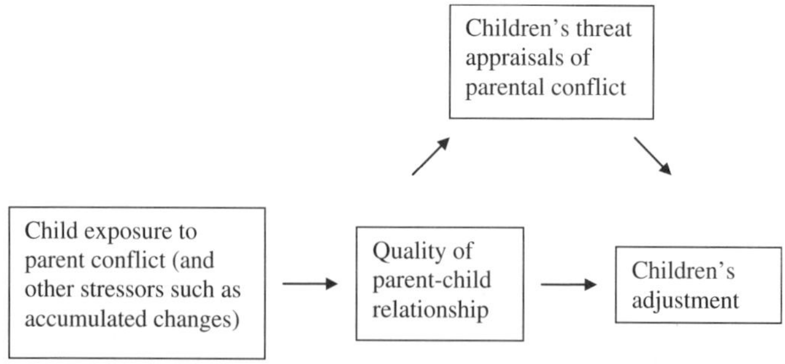

Figure 24.1 Theoretical and research evidence showing the relationship between parent conflict, parent–child relationship, and children's adjustment after parental separation

Clinical Interventions for Improving the Parent–Child Relationship in the Context of High Parental Conflict

I would like to propose an alternate approach to improving children's adjustment to parental conflict and separation. This approach is not new, but I will argue that the focus of our research and interventions needs to change. I argue that in treating high-conflict families after relationship separation we need to focus less on improving the parental relationship and reducing parent conflict, and more on improving the parent–child relationship as a means to improve children's adjustment after parental separation.

Identifying potentially modifiable variables that are associated with children's post-separation adjustment presents an opportunity to develop and deliver treatment to families experiencing difficulties after separation. Evidence has been presented thus far in this chapter arguing that the parent–child relationship might be an important mediating variable between stressors associated with relationship separation, such as parental conflict, and children's adjustment.

In practical terms, it is argued that in order to improve the parent–child relationship, intervention should be targeted at the parent. Grych and Fincham (1992) note that programs directly aimed at children may be limited in their ability to create meaningful change because of the greater influence of the family and other environmental factors on the child's adjustment. Additionally, Wolchik et al. (1993) argues that the potentially modifiable variables likely to lead to improvements in children's adjustment (e.g., parenting behaviors) are in the parents' control and therefore parents are the logical change agent. Consequently, interventions should be targeted directly toward them. Fortunately, there is ample research showing that parenting is a modifiable protective factor and that children's adjustment increases when parental improvement occurs (see Taylor & Biglan, 1998 for a review).

In relation to the separated family, over the last 20 years, two different groups of researchers on the Western side of the United States, one in Oregon (Forgatch and colleagues) and the other in Arizona (Wolchik and colleagues) have developed empirically tested, and published trials investigating ways of improving parenting and parent–child relationships to improve children's adjustment post separation. The content of both the New Beginnings Program (NBP; Wolchik et al., 2000) and the Parenting Through Change Program (PCTP; Forgatch & DeGarmo, 1999) is very similar. An overview of these programs is provided in Table 24.1.

Both Wolchik et al. (1993) and Forgatch and DeGarmo (1999) specifically referred to the influence of Gerald Patterson and his seminal work on parent-training programs (Patterson, 1982), and Wolchik et al. (1993) also referred to the work by Guerney (1977) on relationship-enhancement skills training for parents and children when designing their manual. Each program was designed to teach skills in effective discipline of the child and in improving the quality of the relationship with the child. While these two variables made up the majority of the content of both programs, each program did introduce some other topics. In regards to the PTCP, skills to encourage children's academic ability such as encouraging homework, and to improve individual adult adjustment such as managing emotions and balancing work and play were introduced. Both programs provided some

Table 24.1 Summary of Content of Interventions to Improve Parenting Variables after Relationship Separation

Parenting variable targeted	*Intervention technique*	
	New Beginnings Program	*Parenting Through Change*
Discipline/Monitoring	Clear expectations and rules Use of effective consequences (e.g., time out, reinforcement) Increased consistency	Giving directions Setting limits Time out Work chores Privilege removal Monitoring children's activities
Quality of mother–child relationship/Positive involvement	Positive family activities One-on-one time Attention for appropriate behavior Listening skills	Contingent positive reinforcement Communication with children
Quality of father–child relationship	Education about importance of father–child relationship Reduction of obstacles to visitation	
Skills encouragement		Homework reinforcement
Adult individual adjustment		Managing emotions Balancing work and play
Conflict		
Inter-parental	Anger management skills	Problem solving
Inter-personal	Listening skills	Managing conflict

content on conflict, with the NBP being more specific to inter-parental conflict and the PTCP being more general to inter-personal conflict skill acquisition. Both programs were long term (13 and 14 sessions each: NBP and PTCP, respectively).

Importantly, both studies employed randomized experimental longitudinal designs to evaluate treatment effects. Both studies employed multi-method assessments including self-report, teacher report, and observational/interactional data. The participants in the PTCP consisted of 238 residential mothers and their young sons (aged between 6 and 10). The participants in the NBP consisted of 218 parents (over 90% females with the majority being the resident parent) who had children aged between 9 and 12 years.

In relation to the NBP, 6-year follow-up results showed that adolescents of mothers who participated in the program compared to adolescents of mothers in the control group had reduced rates and symptoms of mental disorders, levels of conduct problems, drug use (including marijuana and alcohol), and number of sexual partners (Wolchik et al., 2002). In addition, they found that those children at highest risk (as defined by mothers and children with initially poor scores on discipline, parent–child relationship quality, and externalizing problems) prior to their mothers' intervention, seemed to have benefited most from the program 6 years later (Dawson-McClure, Sandler, Wolchik, & Millsap Roger, 2004).

This study also employed an additional experimental condition which involved the children. In the additional experimental condition, as well as the mothers receiving treatment, their children also received treatment which aimed to improve their coping with their parents' separation. Results showed no significant treatment differences between the mother-only condition and the condition that also provided treatment to the children. This finding provides more evidence suggesting that the parent is the most successful agent for change.

In relation to the PTCP, $2^1/_2$ years after intervention results showed reductions in coercive parenting and boys' noncompliance as well as improvements in positive parenting. In fact they found over 5 assessment time-points that the experimental group maintained stable outcome trajectories while those in the control condition deteriorated (Martinez & Forgatch, 2001). Additionally, those mothers who reported improvements in better quality parenting also reported significant reductions in depression over time (Patterson, DeGarmo, & Forgatch, 2004). This finding is really important given that parental mental-health problems have been repeatedly linked to children's coping abilities post separation (Clarke-Stewart & Hayward, 1996). In a 9-year follow-up of the PTCP, improvements in parenting significantly reduced teacher-reported delinquency and police arrests for the adolescent boys (Forgatch, Patterson, Degarmo, & Beldavs, 2009).

Conclusion and Future Directions

In sum, there is compelling research evidence, based on methodologically rigorous treatment-outcome studies to suggest that improvements in children's adjustment occurs in programs where the content is based on improved parenting and parent–child relations. The NBP and PTCP programs provided very little information on parenting conflict and in fact gave little emphasis to the relationship with the former partner. In essence, these programs do not necessarily rely on both parents engaging in cooperative parenting. It seems it might be easier for a parent to engage in skills such as spending 10 minutes of one-on-one time with their children each day, rather than having to sit down with their former partner and discuss parenting plans. Enhancing the parent–child relationship means that the parent does not necessarily have to improve their relationship with their former partner in order to assist their child's adjustment.

It should be noted that the above two programs are based mostly on the mothers' relationships with their children. The efficacy of the programs to improve the father–child relationship, which in turn would improve child adjustment, is untested. Additionally, the PTCP is based on only mothers and sons, and while it is hard to consider why it would not work with mothers and daughters, the possibility of improvements to the mother–-daughter relationship remains untested for this program.

In the chapter I have presented data to suggest that (a) improving the parent–child relationship will moderate the negative effects of parental conflict on children's adjustment, and (b) it is very difficult to turn conflictual parents into cooperative parents. Based on these tenets, I have proposed a renewed focus on developing and administering treatment protocols to enhance the parent–child relationship for families where parents remain in high conflict after a relationship separation. I am certainly not suggesting that we "throw the towel in" or "put the white flag up" with regard to discussing, researching, or treating parental conflict. In fact, there are many other reasons, apart from assisting children's adjustment, which suggest that reducing conflict is desirable. For instance, immunology data show the negative effects of stressful conflict on physical health (Glaser & Kiecolt-Glaser, 2005). However, with regard to improving child outcomes when parents have separated and remain in high conflict, the evidence suggests we put more of our research and clinical dollars into enhancing the parent–child relationship.

References

Amato, P. R. (2000). The consequences of divorce for adults and children. *Journal of Marriage and the Family, 62*, 1269–1287.

Amato, P. R. (2001). Children of divorce in the 1990s: An update of the Amato and Keith (1991) meta-analysis. *Journal of Family Psychology, 15*, 355–370.

Amato, P. R., & Booth, A. (1996). A prospective study of divorce and parent–child relationships. *Journal of Marriage and the Family, 58*, 356–365.

Ambert, A.-M. (1989). *Ex-spouses and new spouses: A study of relationships*. Greenwich, CT: JAI Press.

Atkinson, E. (2004). *The role of children's threat perceptions in the relationship between interparental conflict and child adjustment*. Unpublished Clinical Ph.D. thesis, Griffith University.

Atkinson, E., & Dadds, M. R. (2009). Threat is a multidimensional construct: Exploring the role of children's threat appraisals in the relationship between interparental conflict and child adjustment. *Journal of Abnormal Child Psychology, 37*, 281–292.

Beelmann, W., & Schmidt-Denter, U. (2009). Mother–child interaction following marital separation: A longitudinal observation study. *European Psychologist, 14*, 307–319.

Boney-McCoy, S., & Finkelhor, D. (1996). Is youth victimization related to trauma symptoms and depression after controlling for prior symptoms and family relationships? A longitudinal, prospective study. *Journal of Consulting and Clinical Psychology, 64*, 1406–1416.

Bowlby, J. (1973). *Attachment and loss: Vol. 2 Separation, anxiety and anger*. New York: Basic Books.

Buchanan, C. M., & Heiges, K. L. (2001). When conflict continues after marriage ends: Effects of postdivorce conflict on children. In J. H. Grych & F. D. Fincham (Eds.), *Interparental conflict and child development: Theory, research, and application* (pp. 337–362) New York: Cambridge University Press.

Cartwright, C. (2006). You want to know how it affected me: Young adults' perceptions of the impact of parental divorce. *Journal of Divorce and Remarriage, 44*, 125–143.

Clarke-Stewart, K. A., & Hayward, C. (1996). Advantages of father custody and contact for the psychological well-being of school-age children. *Journal of Applied Developmental Psychology, 17*, 239–270.

Coiro, M. J., & Emery, R. (1998). Do marriage problems affect fathering more than mothering? A quantitative and qualitative review. *Clinical Child and Family Psychology Review, 1*, 23–40.

Coysh, W. S., Johnston, J. R., Tschann, J. M., Wallerstein, J. S., & Kline, M. (1989). Parental postdivorce adjustment in joint and sole physical custody families. *Journal of Family Issues, 10*, 52–71.

Cummings, E. M., & Davies, P. T. (1994). *Children and marital conflict: The impact of family dispute and resolution.* New York: Guilford Press.

Cummings, E. M., & Davies, P. T. (1996). Emotional security as a regulatory process in normal development and the development of psychopathology. *Development and Psychopathology, 8*, 123–139.

Dauvergne, M., & Johnson, H. (2001). *Children witnessing family violence.* Juristat, Ottawa: Statistics Canada.

Davies, P. T., & Cummings, E. M. (1994). Marital conflict and child adjustment: An emotional security hypothesis. *Psychological Bulletin, 116*(3), 387–411.

Dawson-McClure, S. R., Sandler, I. N., Wolchik, S. A., & Millsap Roger, E. (2004). Risk as a moderator of the effects of prevention programs for children from divorced families: A six-year longitudinal study. *Journal of Abnormal Child Psychology, 32*(2) 175–190.

Fagen, D. B., Cowen, E. L., Wyman, P. A., & Work, W. C. (1996). Relationships between parent–child relational variables and child-test variables in highly stressed urban children. *Child Study Journal, 26*, 87–108.

Fincham, F. D., & Osborne, L. N. (1993). Marital conflict and children: Retrospect and prospect. *Clinical Psychology Review, 13*, 75–88.

Forgatch, M. S., & DeGarmo, D. S. (1999) Parenting through change: An effective prevention program for single mothers. *Journal of Consulting and Clinical Psychology, 67*, 711–724.

Forgatch, M. S., Patterson, G. R., Degarmo, D. S., & Beldavs, Z. G. (2009). Testing the Oregon delinquency model with 9-year follow-up of the Oregon Divorce Study. *Development and Psychopathology, 21*, 637–660.

Formosa, D., Gonzales, N., & Aiken, L. (2000). Family conflict and children's internalizing and externalizing behavior: Protective factors. *American Journal of Community Psychology, 28*, 175–199.

Garbarino, J., Dubrow, N., Kostelyn, K., & Prado, C. (1992). *Children in danger: Coping with the consequences of community violence.* San Francisco, CA: Jossey-Bass.

Geasler, M. J., & Blaisure, K. R. (1998). A review of divorce education materials. *Family Relations, 47*, 167–175.

Glaser, R., & Kiecolt-Glaser, J. R. (2005). Stress-induced immune dysfunction: Implications for health. *Nature Reviews. Immunology, 5*, 243–251.

Goodman, M., Bonds, D., Sandler, I., & Braver, S. (2004). Parent psychoeducational programs and reducing the negative effects of interparental conflict following divorce. *Family Court Review, 42*, 1–17.

Grych, J. H., & Fincham, F. D. (1990). Marital conflict and children's adjustment: A cognitive-contextual framework. *Psychological Bulletin, 108*, 267–290.

Grych, J. H., & Fincham, F. D. (Eds.) (2001). *Interparental conflict and child development.* New York: Cambridge University Press.

Grych, J. H., Harold, G. T., & Miles, C. J. (2003). A prospective investigation of appraisals as mediators of the link between interparental conflict and child adjustment. *Child Development, 7*, 1176–1193.

Guerney, B. G. (1977). *Relationship enhancement: Skill-training programs for therapy problem prevention and enrichment.* San Francisco: Jossey-Bass.

Hanson, T. L. (1999). Does parental conflict explain why divorce is negatively associated with child welfare? *Social Forces, 77*, 1283–1315.

Hanson, T. L., McLanahan, S. S., & Thomson, E. (1998). Windows on divorce: Before and after. *Social Science Research, 27*, 329–349.

Hetherington, E. M., Cox, M., & Cox, R. (1982). Effects of divorce on parents and children. In M. Lamb (Ed.), *Nontraditional families* (pp. 233–288). Hillsdale, NJ: Erlbaum.

Jaffe, P. G., Wolfe, D. A., & Wilson, S. K. (1990). *Children of battered women.* Newbury Park, CA: Sage.

Janoff-Bulman, R. (1992). *Shattered assumptions: Towards a new psychology of trauma.* New York: Free Press.

Johnston, J. R. (1998). *Developing and testing a group intervention for families at impasse.* Unpublished report. San Francisco: Center for the Family in Transition.

Kramer, K. M., Arbuthnot, J., Gordon, D. A., Rousis, N. J., & Hoza, J. (1998). Effects of skill-based versus information-based divorce education programs on domestic violence and parental communication. *Family and Conciliation Courts Review, 36*, 9–31.

Kramer, L., & Washo, C. A. (1993). Evaluation of a court-mandated prevention program for divorcing parents: The Children First program. *Family Relations, 42*, 179–186.

Laor, N., Wolmer, L., & Cohen, D. J. (2001). Mothers' functioning and children's symptoms 5 years after a SCUD missile attack. *American Journal of Psychiatry, 158*, 1020–1026.

Lauri, K., & Kowal, A. (2005). Long-term follow-up of a court-based intervention for divorcing parents. *Family Court Review, 36*, 452–465.

Lieberman, A. F., & Van Horn, P. (1998). Attachment, trauma, and domestic violence: Implications for child custody. *Child and Adolescent Psychiatric Clinics of North America, 7*, 423–443.

Maccoby, E. E., & Mnookin, R. (1992). *Dividing the child.* Cambridge, MA: Harvard University Press.

Margolin, G., & Gordis, E. B. (2000). The effect of family and community violence on children. *Annual Review of Psychology, 51*, 445–479.

Martinez, C. R., & Forgatch, M. S. (2001). Preventing problems with boys' noncompliance: Effects of a parent training intervention for divorcing mothers. *Journal of Consulting and Clinical Psychology, 69*, 416–428.

Martinez, C. R., & Forgatch, M. S. (2002). Adjusting to change: Linking family structure transitions with parenting and boys' adjustment. *Journal of Family Psychology, 16*, 107–117.

McKenzie, B., & Bacon, B. (2002). Parent education after separation: Results from a multi-site study on best practices. *Canadian Journal of Community Mental Health, 4*, 73–88.

McLoyd, V., Harper, C., & Copeland, N. K. (2001). Does gender moderate the effects of marital conflict on children? In J. Grych & F. Fincham (Eds.). *Interparental conflict and child development* (pp. 9–38). New York: Cambridge University Press.

Noller, P., Feeney, J. A., Sheehan, G. Darlington, Y., & Rogers, C. (2008). Conflict in divorcing and continuously married families: A study of marital, parent-child and sibling relationship. *Journal of Divorce and Remarriage, 49*, 1–24.

O'Brien, M., John, R. S., Margolin, G., & Erel, O. (1994). Reliability and diagnostic efficacy of parents' reports regarding children's exposure to marital aggression. *Violence and Victims, 9*, 45–62.

Patterson, G. R. (1982). *A social learning approach: Coercive family process.* Eugene, OR: Castalia.

Patterson, G. R., DeGarmo, D., & Forgatch, M. S. (2004). Systematic changes in families following prevention trials. *Journal of Abnormal Child Psychology, 32*, 621–633.

Pedro-Carroll, J. L. (2005). Fostering children's resilience in the aftermath of divorce: The role of evidence-based programs for children. *Family Court Review, 43*, 52–64.

Peterson, J. L., & Zill, N. (1986). Marital disruption, parent–child relationships, and behavioral problems in children. *Journal of Marriage and the Family, 48*, 295–307.

Sobolewski, J. M., & Amato, P. R. (2007). Parents' discord and divorce, parent–child relationships and subjective well-being in early adulthood: Is feeling close to two parents always better than feeling close to one? *Social Forces, 85*, 1105–1124.

Stocker, C. M., Richmond, M. K., Low, S. M., Alexander, E. K., & Elias, N. M. (2003). Marital conflict and children's adjustment: Parental hostility and children's interpretations as mediators. *Social Development, 12*, 149–161.

Stolberg, A. L., & Garrison, K. M. (1985). Evaluating a primary prevention program for children of divorce: The divorce adjustment project. *American Journal of Community Psychology, 13*, 111–124.

Sweeper, S. (2004). *Adult adjustment to relationship separation.* Unpublished Clinical Ph.D. thesis, Griffith University.

Sweeper, S., & Halford, W. K. (2006). Assessing adult adjustment to relationship separation: The Psychological Adjustment to Separation Test (PAST). *Journal of Family Psychology, 20*, 632–640.

Taylor, T., & Biglan, A. (1998). Behavioral family interventions for improving childrearing: A review of the literature for clinicians and policy makers. *Clinical Child and Family Psychology Review, 1*, 41–60.

Wolchik, S. A., Sandler I. N., Millsap, R. E., Plummer, B. A., Greene S. M. et al. (2002). Six-year follow-up of preventive interventions for children of divorce: A randomized controlled trial. *Journal of the American Medical Association, 288*, 1874–1881.

Wolchik, S. A., West, S. G., Sandler, I. N., Tein, J., Coatsworth, D., Lengua, L. et al. (2000). An experimental evaluation of theory-based mother and mother–child programs for children of divorce. *Journal of Consulting and Clinical Psychology, 68*, 843–856.

Wolchik, S. A., West, S. G., Westover, S., Sandler, I. N., Martin, A., Lustig, J. et al. (1993). The children of divorce parenting intervention: Outcome evaluation of an empirically based program. *American Journal of Community Psychology, 21*, 293–231.

PART VII

Interpersonal Processes, Families, and Mental Health

25

Depression and Self-Harming in Adolescence

A Family-Centered Approach

Kerryn Hurd and Patricia Noller

> I get on with some people okay but others not at all. I don't get on with girls that often too good but most people I seem to find okay. I don't get on with my Dad at all but my Mum I sort of get on with. I get nervous when I am around my Dad and he is always drunk. I am a caring person but I worry a lot and am anxious and I like to be friends with people. I tend not to deal with my problems, I sort of back out of them. I don't want to face them (Peter, 14 years old).

Five years later at 19 years of age this boy became one of 446 Australians aged between 15 and 19 years who completed suicide that year. He was one of approximately 40% of adolescent suicide completers who had made a previous attempt, and one of 1–9% of male adolescent suicide attempters who eventually die from suicide (Shaffer, 1988). Although he was one of the 20–50% of attempters who present to medical health services (Burless and De Leo, 2001), he still died. He said when he was 14 years old that the reason he took an overdose was because he wanted to die. He had three major risk factors for suicide: (a) a history of depression (de Wilde, Kienhorst, & Diekstra, 2001); (b) previous suicide attempts (Brent et al., 1993); and (c) significant family conflict (Kosky, Silburn, & Zubrick, 1990; Seroczynski, Jacquez, & Cole, 2003).

In line with the risk factors that precipitated Peter's suicide, Kosky et al. (1990) identified three factors that differentiated children and adolescents (mean age of 12.9

The Wiley-Blackwell Handbook of Couples and Family Relationships, First Edition.
Edited by Patricia Noller and Gery C. Karantzas.

years) who attempted suicide (87% had symptoms of depression) from children and adolescents who had suicide ideation (meaning that they thought about suicide and how they might kill themselves; 94% of this group had symptoms of depression). These factors were: (a) chronic family discord; (b) substance abuse; and (c) for males, loss of major attachment figures in the previous 12 months.

In this chapter, we present our research that expands on the findings of Kosky et al. (1990) by exploring and identifying the aspects of family functioning and attachment that are related to self-harming and suicidal behavior in depressed adolescents. Unlike Kosky et al.'s study, the present study included a nonclinical control group as well as a clinical control group and focused only on adolescents (13–17 years). The reason for including the clinical control group was so that we could compare those who were depressed but did not attempt suicide with those who did attempt suicide.

Family Functioning and Suicide Attempts

Kosky, Silburn, and Zubrick (1986) compared 481 children and adolescents aged 15 years or less, who had symptoms of depression without suicide ideation, with 147 children who had depression and suicide ideation. They found that suicide ideation was associated with disturbed, hostile family relationships. In fact, the suicide ideation group was more likely than the depressed (no suicide ideation reported) group to have disturbances in child–father and child–sibling relationships, although both groups showed a high level of disturbance in child–mother relationships. In the suicide ideation group, however, these disturbed relationships were more likely to be characterized by persistent discord and child abuse, and the child was more likely to suffer from feelings of persecution and hostility. There were no differences between the two groups in the proportion coming from divorced families.

Previous longitudinal and cross-sectional studies have shown that family dysfunction is consistently correlated with adolescent suicide ideation and suicidal behavior for both normative and clinical samples (Borowsky, Ireland, & Resnick, 2001; Bridge, Goldstein, & Brent, 2006; Brinkman-Sull, Overholser, & Silverman, 2000; Gould, Greenberg, Velting, & Shaffer, 2003; Kuhlberg, Peria, & Zayas, 2010; Rubenstein et al., 1989). Family dysfunction has also been shown to differentiate between suicidal and nonsuicidal clinical adolescents (Asarnow, 1992; King, Segal, Naylor, & Evans, 1993; Morano, Cisler, & Lemerond, 1993), between adolescents who are depressed without suicide ideation and those who are depressed with suicide ideation (Kosky et al., 1986), and between adolescents with suicide ideation and those who have made suicide attempts (Kosky et al., 1990).

The cross-sectional studies that have directly assessed family functioning and suicidal behavior in children and adolescents have shown that parent–child discord, family conflict, and poor family adjustment are related to increased risk of suicide in adolescents (Brent et al., 1994; de Wilde, Keinhorst, Diekstra, & Wolters, 1993; Gould, Fisher, Flory, & Shaffer, 1996; Kosky et al., 1990; Lewinsohn, Rohde, & Seeley, 1996). Manifestations of family dysfunction, for example, family conflict and poor family problem solving, have been reported by approximately 50% of suicidal adolescents as precipitating their suicidal behavior (Berman & Schwartz, 1990; Hawton, Fagg, & Simkin, 1996).

Prospective studies

A review of the literature has revealed only two studies that have used prospective designs. Lewinsohn, Roberts, Seeley, Rohde, Gotlib, and Hops (1994) used self-report questionnaires aimed at assessing a variety of potential risk factors and a diagnostic interview to assess 1,507 high school students. These students were assessed at two points in time, spaced 1 year apart. At Time 1, students were asked questions about how many suicide attempts they had made in their lifetime and at Time 2, they were asked about suicidal behavior since Time 1. The results indicated that higher levels of family support were negatively associated with adolescent suicide attempts made during the year between Time 1 and Time 2. This association remained significant when the researchers controlled for depression, but was not significant when they controlled for whether the adolescent had previously made a suicide attempt.

In another prospective study, King, Segal, Kaminski, Naylor, Ghaziuddin, and Radpour (1995) found that self-reports of general family dysfunction from psychiatric inpatients who had attempted suicide prospectively predicted self-harming behavior in the 6 months after they were discharged from hospital. The results from these two studies indicate that level of family support relates to whether or not an adolescent will make another suicide attempt, with higher levels of family dysfunction predicting further suicide attempts.

Family members' awareness of adolescents' problems

A study by Breton, Tousignant, and Bergeron (2003) was conducted to clarify whether there were any differences in the correlates of suicide ideation in young adolescents reported by both the adolescents and their parents. These researchers interviewed 825 adolescents and one of their parents (91% were mothers) simultaneously in different rooms. Their results indicated that 7% of the participants reported suicide ideation, although the parents of only 10% of these youngsters were aware of their adolescents' suicidal thinking. Four percent of the sample reported that they had made a suicide attempt, with parents of only 6% of these attempters reporting that they knew that their adolescent had attempted suicide. Sourander, Helstela, and Helenius (1999) and Ranta, Kaltiala-Heino, Rantanen and Marttunen (2009) also found evidence that parents were often unaware of the internalizing disorders (such as depression or suicidal behavior) in their adolescents. It is not clear, however, whether the adolescents have pushed their parents away and not allowed them to inquire about their well-being, or whether the adolescents are suicidal because their parents are not "in tune" with how they are feeling, which in turn could lead the adolescents to believe that they cannot negotiate with their parents or problem-solve with them.

We are aware of only one controlled study of family functioning that included all family members of adolescents who had committed suicide. In an American study, Kaplan and

Maldaver (1993) compared the responses of parents of 18 adolescent suicide completers with the responses of parents of 25 community adolescents on the measures of the Family Adaptability and Cohesion Evaluation Scales (Olson, Sprenkle, & Russell, 1979). The family measures were administered up to 6 months after the suicides, and responses may have reflected perceptions of the family influenced by the suicide of their child. The majority of the comparisons of subscale scores for the two groups were nonsignificant; however, compared to the control group, the fathers of suicide completers perceived their families as less structured and more flexible.

Kaplan and Maldaver (1993) suggested that this finding may indicate that either families of suicide completers are more chaotic, or fathers of suicide completers are more rigid and have a higher standard for structure compared to fathers in the community control group. These researchers also found that the mothers of suicide completers perceived their families as having a less active-recreational orientation. They suggested that these results indicated an enmeshed pattern for the suicide families in terms of a lack of engagement in pursuits outside the family. This situation may put an intolerable burden on the family itself, and block the emerging adolescent from outside activities essential to the development of a secure identity (Kaplan & Maldaver). Brent et al. (1993) found that parents of suicide completers reported higher levels of parent–adolescent conflict in the previous year than did the parents of community controls who were matched on demographic variables.

Attachment and Suicide

Results from a study of 990 adolescents by Maimon, Browning, and Brooks-Gunn (2010) indicated that family attachments reduced the probability that adolescents would attempt suicide. These results fit with those of Harvey and Byrd (2000) who found that secure attachment was clearly related to low levels of family conflict and control. Their results also indicated a number of trends that are relevant to our work outlined in this chapter. First, individuals with high levels of secure attachment perceived their families as cohesive, as valuing cultural and intellectual activities, and as engaging in more active problem-solving strategies to deal with problems. Conversely, these results could be interpreted to mean that anxious and avoidant individuals (insecure attachment) have families that are low in cohesion, do not value cultural and intellectual activities, and do not use active problem-solving strategies to deal with issues. Second, Harvey and Byrd's (2000) results indicated that individuals with high levels of anxious attachment reported high levels of conflict in their families, high levels of control by family members, and that their families discouraged independence. They did not find this pattern of results with the individuals with avoidant attachment and concluded that avoidant attachment leads to individuals having little interest in their families, and therefore is unrelated to these measures of family functioning.

In a recent study, we compared self-harming, depressed, and nonclinical adolescents on measures of attachment and family functioning. We expected that self-harming adolescents would have low levels of confidence in themselves and others (a dimension on the Attachment Style Questionnaire, Noller, Feeney, & Hanrahan, 1994) and would perceive their families as being low in cohesion, high in conflict, and high in control. Furthermore, we explore the relations among attachment security, family factors (e.g., perceptions of family environment, communication, conflict, and structure), and depression and self-harming behavior in adolescents.

Our Study of Attachment, Family Functioning, and Self-Harming Behavior

The study involved three groups of adolescents and their parents. The first group included adolescents who had self-harmed to the extent that they were admitted to a hospital; and the second group comprised adolescents who were assessed as clinically depressed but had not self-harmed. This group was categorized as the clinical control group and was included in response to Wagner's (1997) suggestion that researchers should control for psychiatric symptomatology, especially depression, when designing studies of suicidal adolescents. As noted earlier, because of the inclusion of this group, we could compare self-harming adolescents with those who were equally depressed but had not self-harmed. The third group comprised adolescents who were not clinically depressed and who had not self-harmed and were labeled the nonclinical control group. This design was similar to one used by de Wilde et al. (1992).

The participants were assessed using questionnaire measures including the Children's Depression Inventory (CDI; Kovacs, 1992), the Family Environment Scales (FES; Moos and Moos, 1981), the Attachment Style Questionnaire (ASQ; Noller et al., 1994), and the Parental Bonding Instrument (PBI; Parker, Tupling, & Brown, 1979). In addition, adolescents completed the Youth Self-Report Instrument (YSR: Achenbach, 1991a) and parents completed the Child Behavior Checklist (CBCL; Achenbach, 1991b) and the Bellvue Index of Depression-Modified (BID; Petti, 1978) so that we could see whether parents were aware of their child's depression and self-harming behavior. Qualitative data were obtained from content analysis of adolescents' audiotaped responses to an open-ended question about their relationships with their parents (Hurd, Wooding, & Noller, 1999). Our goal was to examine whether any of the family factors mentioned above were related significantly to self-harming behavior.

Our Findings

Questionnaire measures

Compared to the adolescents in the two control groups, self-harming adolescents were significantly more likely to self-report drug abuse, have a family history of psychiatric illness, and to be living with their single mothers rather than with both biological parents. Self-harming adolescents were also more likely to come from families where their parent or parents were receiving a government pension (e.g., supporting parent's pension, unemployment benefits, sickness benefit).

There were no sex differences in levels of depression. Self-harming adolescents also perceived their families as being less cohesive, less expressive, and having higher levels of conflict than adolescents in the clinical and nonclinical control groups. In contrast, adolescents in the nonclinical group perceived their families as being more cohesive and expressive, and having more of a focus on achievement, intellectual/cultural, and active/recreational pursuits than the adolescents in the two clinical groups. The finding that self-harmers are less likely than other adolescents to report having good communication with other family members or feeling understood by them fits with the findings of Shaffer et al. (1996). Adolescents who have harmed themselves are also less likely to seek help with their problems, even when they know they really need that help (Evans, Hawton, & Rodham, 2005).

In relation to attachment, adolescents in the clinical groups had lower confidence in self and others, higher discomfort with closeness, greater propensity to view relationships as secondary, and higher anxiety about relationships than adolescents in the nonclinical group. These results indicate that the clinical adolescents would be classified on the basis of Bartholomew and Horowitz (1991) as being insecure in attachment and the nonclinical adolescents would be classified as being secure in attachment. Interestingly, there was no indication that the self-harming adolescents were significantly more insecure in their attachment than the depressed adolescents. Nevertheless, the self-harming adolescents would generally be classified as fearful in terms of Bartholomew and Horowitz's typology, since their scores indicate that they have negative views of themselves and have difficulty trusting others.

One factor that differentiated adolescents in the clinical and nonclinical control groups was that self-harmers did not identify a sense of responsibility to the family as a reason for why they would not kill themselves. Linehan et al. (1987) also found that the importance of one's beliefs about one's responsibility to one's family was significantly related to whether one reported prior suicidal behavior or had recently attempted suicide. These researchers found that nonclinical individuals who reported that they had never considered suicidal behavior tended to attach more importance to family concerns.

Adolescents who reported that concerns for their family members would not be a reason for them to refrain from killing themselves were more likely to be uncomfortable with closeness and to consider relationships as secondary to achievement. In terms of Bartholomew and Horowitz's (1991) four-group model of attachment, these young people would be considered "Dismissing." Thus, if these young people were not close to others, including other family members, and they placed little importance on relationships, they were less likely to be concerned about the impact of their behavior on those close to them.

We also allocated adolescents to the four parenting styles identified by Parker et al. (1979) on the basis of levels of care and overprotection in the family: Self-harming adolescents were significantly more likely to experience parenting styles characterized by low care and high control (affectionless control) by both parents and both low care and overprotection (neglectful parenting) by their mothers. Clinical control adolescents were significantly less likely to experience optimal parenting (high care and low overprotection) from their fathers but otherwise their parenting was not characterized by any particular style. Seroczynski et al. (2003) have argued that for these young people, depression could be seen as an unsuccessful response to the many challenges that adolescents need to resolve, especially when they have not been aided by high-quality parenting to negotiate and resolve issues that arise for them.

Previous research has clearly shown that the quality of family relationships is crucial in determining the competence and confidence with which young people face the major transition from childhood to adulthood. Family relationships have been shown to significantly impact on the success with which adolescents negotiate major developmental tasks, avoid problem behaviors that are typically associated with this sometimes tumultuous time, and establish meaningful relationships. The aspects of family that are particularly relevant to this time of transformation are the encouragement of autonomy and independence, the degree of control desired by parents, the amount of conflict among family members, the closeness of family bonds, and the love and support available to the adolescents (Noller & Callan, 1991).

Parent–adolescent agreement

As expected, for all measures of psychopathology, the parents of nonclinical adolescents gave significantly lower ratings than did the parents of adolescents in the clinical groups. For the nonclinical group there was significant agreement between adolescent self-report measures and mothers' perceptions of their adolescents' low levels of depressive symptomatology. This level of agreement did not occur for nonclinical fathers and their adolescents.

For the two clinical groups, there was no significant agreement between the results for the adolescent self-report depression scales (CDI, Anxious/Depressed YSR problem scale) and the results for parent measures of their perceptions of their adolescent's depressive symptomatology (Anxious/Depressed CBCL problem scale). For internalizing behaviors (e.g., withdrawal, anxiety/depression, thought problems, and attention problems) adolescents gave higher ratings than their parents. Thus, parents of clinical adolescents did not assess their adolescents' depressive symptomatology in a similar way to their adolescents, both in terms of accurately assessing the internalizing psychopathology as depression, as well as not assessing depression at the same level of severity as their adolescents did. For the internalizing score on the CBCL, mothers gave significantly higher scores than fathers, indicating that they were more likely to make an accurate assessment of their child's depressive behaviors. Mothers and fathers assessed depressive behaviors in a similar way, but mothers' assessments were more consistent with adolescent perceptions. Thus, for both the clinical and nonclinical adolescents, mothers were more accurate in assessing their adolescent's psychological state.

Qualitative data

Another aim of this study was to use qualitative methodology to obtain insights into clinical and nonclinical adolescents' perceptions of their relationships with their parents (Hurd et al., 1999). In order to achieve this aim, variables were identified through content analysis and coding. The dependent variables derived to assess relationships with mothers and fathers were overall quality of the relationship and amount of communication and conflict.

Nonclinical controls reported better relationships with parents than the clinical controls or the self-harmers and these relationships seemed to be characterized by more communication and less conflict. Self-harmers experienced the least satisfactory relationships with their parents and more conflict with their mothers than either of the other groups. Contrary to what we expected, there were no effects for sex. There was, however, a trend for girls to report more frequent communication with mothers than boys which is consistent with the findings of Noller and Bagi (1985).

With regard to parent–adolescent relationships, there was only one dimension where responses by self-harming adolescents were perceived by the trained coders to be significantly different from the responses given by adolescents in the clinical control group. Self-harming adolescents were perceived as having more negative relationships with their mothers than were clinical and nonclinical control adolescents. In addition, adolescents in both clinical groups were perceived as having more negative relationships with their parents, characterized by more negative communication and greater conflict with their mothers and fathers than the nonclinical adolescents.

The findings for the nonclinical adolescents are supported by the research literature (for example, Joronen & Astedt-Kurki, 2005) which indicates that the features of the family environment that contribute to the well-being of family members include open communication, an emotionally warm atmosphere, parents being involved in young people's lives, and providing encouragement and supervision when needed. The Finnish adolescents in the Joronen and Astedt-Kurki study saw hostility in the family as a major contributor to their lack of well-being. Interestingly, many nonclinical adolescents in the present study acknowledged the validity of the role that parents have; for example "They're restrictive but that's because they care about me," "We argue but it's just part of being a teenager."

In the present study, there were no significant differences between adolescents in the two clinical groups for the number of stressful events adolescents had experienced (including loss and disruptions to major attachments) or how distressed they felt in relation to these events. The finding that adolescents in the self-harming group report higher levels of conflict in their families compared to depressed adolescents supports the findings of Conger, Conger, Elder, Lorenz, Simons, and Whitbeck (1993), although there is evidence that many depressed adolescents come from homes where there is a lot of conflict (Seroczynski et al., 2003) or from divorced or father-absent homes (Shiner & Marmorstein, 1998).

Conger et al. (1993) found that adolescents in lower socioeconomic groups experience greater family conflict, which in turn makes them more vulnerable to depression. Adolescents in the self-harming group in the present study were assessed as coming from families of lower socioeconomic status compared to the adolescents in the nonclinical group. Socioeconomic status is only one of many variables that would impact on the adolescents in the self-harming group perceiving higher levels of conflict in their families. In addition to conflict, these adolescents were more likely to perceive low levels of family cohesion than the depressed group. It is possible that perceiving less cohesion contributes to their being less likely to be concerned about the impact that killing themselves would have on their families.

In summary, results from the present study show that adolescents who self-harm are more likely than depressed adolescents to: abuse drugs, including alcohol; report problems with the law; perceive their families as low in cohesion and expressiveness, and high in conflict; have a family history of psychiatric illness; have less concern about the impact killing themselves would have on their families; perceive both of their parents to be low in care and high in overprotection and see their mothers as neglectful in terms of their parenting style (i.e., low in both care and overprotection); be perceived by independent raters as having negative relationships with their mothers; report higher suicide ideation and pessimism about the future; and avoid seeking help for their problems.

Parent Perceptions of Family Environment and Problem Behaviors

Unlike Kosky et al.'s (1990) study, the present study included both parent and adolescent perceptions of the family environment. The results show that mothers of self-harming adolescents, along with their adolescents, perceive their families as being lower in cohesion and higher in conflict compared to the depressed adolescents and their mothers. Adolescents who self-harm rate their families as higher in conflict compared to their parents, while depressed adolescents report higher levels of conflict compared to their fathers. The fathers of self-harming adolescents reported higher levels of cohesion in their families compared to their adolescents. This difference between adolescent and father perceptions did not occur for the depressed group. Finally, the mothers of the self-harming adolescents perceive that their families involve higher levels of control than do the mothers of depressed adolescents. Overall, these findings suggest a lack of awareness by parents of the problems in their families.

An interesting finding was that fathers' perceptions of the levels of cohesion and conflict in their family environments were similar for the three groups. Thus, irrespective of whether their adolescents were suicidal, depressed, or nonclinical, fathers' perceptions of levels of cohesion and conflict were similar, suggesting they were not aware of family problems or the unhappiness that their children experience.

Patterns of Attachment and Parental Bonding

Nonclinical adolescents were more likely than clinical adolescents to have higher levels of confidence in themselves and others (indicative of secure attachment). The clinical adolescents on the other hand, had higher scores than the nonclinical adolescents on the dimensions that reflect insecure attachment but there was no significant difference between the self-harming and depressed adolescents for their scores on dimensions of attachment.

The nonclinical adolescents were more likely to have received optimal parenting (high care and low overprotection). On the other hand, the majority of adolescents in the clinical groups perceived their parents to be low in care and high in overprotection in terms of their parenting style and there were no differences between the two clinical groups. The pattern of results for type of parenting style (identified by Parker et al., 1979) for the three groups showed, however, that the self-harming adolescents were significantly more likely than depressed adolescents to have parenting characterized by affectionless control (low care and high overprotection) from both parents and neglectful parenting from mothers.

The majority of nonclinical adolescents (85%) perceived their parenting to be characterized by a style that included high care (see also chapter 5 in this volume). For 68% of nonclinical adolescents this care was accompanied by low overprotection (optimal parenting), while for 17%, care was accompanied by high overprotection. On the other hand, only 22% of self-harming adolescents and 38% of depressed adolescents perceived their parenting to have included high care. This low level of care was accompanied by a high level of overprotection or control for the majority of the clinical adolescents (affectionless control). The lack of care could mean that these adolescents do not have the support, guidance, and appropriate limits to negotiate autonomy at an age-appropriate level. According to Sheeber, Hops, and Davis (2001), parenting behavior is a major way that parental psychopathology, marital problems, negative life events, and financial hardships come to be linked to depression in children and adults.

Neglectful parenting style (low care and low overprotection), especially from mothers, was the second most prevalent type (the first being affectionless control) of parenting perceived by the clinical adolescents. Because of the consequent lack of care or limits, this type of parenting is more likely to result in adolescents having to tackle developmental tasks with little guidance. This process increases the likelihood that these adolescents will rely on their peer group for guidance and support. If their peers also have similar dysfunctional families, they are likely to be participating in a culture that promotes risk taking and the challenging of boundaries, with limit setting left to external authorities.

The findings that the majority of the adolescents in the self-harming group perceive their parenting to be characterized by affectionless control fits with their self-harming and suicidal behavior. If adolescents (a) perceive that their parents do not care about them, (b) are not encouraged to develop autonomy and individuate, and (c) have not had the opportunities to take age-appropriate risks with the consequent development of coping skills and confidence (Evans et al., 2005; Seroczynski et al., 2003), then it is understandable that they may feel that temporary or permanent escape is a valid solution to their problems. Self-harming behavior may serve the purpose of providing a vehicle for these adolescents to mobilize help, to gain a sense of control, or to escape a situation because they do not have the problem-solving skills and support to deal with it.

Comparing Males and Females

The results from the analyses conducted with male and female adolescents separately showed, that for males only, the clinical and nonclinical groups were not significantly different on levels of optimal parenting from their fathers. Although in the predicted direction, that is, that nonclinical males would be more likely to have optimal parenting and self-harming males would be less likely to have optimal parenting, males in the three groups were less differentiated than females from the three groups. An interesting result is that the nonclinical males were more likely to receive neglectful parenting from their fathers compared to males in the self-harming group, and males in the nonclinical group were less likely to receive optimal parenting compared to females in this group. Explanations for these results may include (a) males may perceive their parents' behavior differently from females, (b) males may behave differently (including communicating less) compared to females, thus engendering different reactions or communication style from their parents, or (c) parents may treat sons and daughters differently.

Nonclinical females were significantly less likely than clinical females to report neglectful parenting; however, there was a trend for self-harming females to report more neglectful parenting. This pattern of results was not obtained for nonclinical adolescent males. Thus, the results show that self-harming females are more likely to have parenting characterized by affectionless control and neglectful parenting (both parenting styles that are low in care) when compared to depressed and nonclinical adolescent females. For self-harming males, their parenting style is more likely to be characterized by affectionless control when compared to depressed and nonclinical males.

Conclusion

As a consequence of their large longitudinal study of young people, Sroufe and colleagues (Sroufe, Egeland, Carlson, & Collins, 2005) argue that an important question concerning adolescents is "why some young people thrive and others seriously falter during this challenging period" (p. 175). These and other researchers (e.g. Bernburg, Thorlindsson, & Sigfusdottir, 2009; Martin, 2007) suggest that the answer lies in the extent to which young people are enabled by the family environments in which they live to develop a healthy self-esteem, have the kinds of close connections with others that are able to provide them with the support they need, and are available to give them necessary help. On the other hand, they found that adolescents with serious behavioral problems came from families where violence, chaos, and disruption were the norm. Our findings with regard to our three groups of adolescents fit nicely with these conclusions.

References

Achenbach, T. M. (1991a). *Manual for the Child Behavior Checklist/14–18 and 1991 profile.* Burlington, VT: University of Vermont, Department of Psychiatry.

Achenbach, T. M. (1991b). *Manual for the Youth Self Report and 1991 profile.* Burlington, VT: University of Vermont, Department of Psychiatry.

Asarnow, J. R. (1992). Suicidal ideation and attempts during middle childhood: Associations with perceived family stress and depression among child psychiatric inpatients. *Journal of Consulting and Clinical Psychology, 21*, 35–40.

Bartholomew, K., & Horowitz, L. M. (1991). Attachment styles among young adults: A test of a four-category model. *Journal of Personality and Social Psychology, 61*, 226–244.

Berman, A. L., & Schwartz, R. H. (1990). Suicide attempts among adolescent drug users. *American Journal of Diseases of Children, 144*, 310–314.

Bernburg, J. G., Thorlindsson, T., & Sigfusdottir, I. D. (2009). The spreading of suicidal behavior: The contextual effect of community household poverty on adolescent suicidal behavior and the mediating role of suicide suggestion, *Social Science and Medicine, 68*, 380–389.

Borowsky, I. W., Ireland, M., & Resnick, M. D. (2001). Adolescent suicide attempts: Risks and protectors. *Pediatrics, 107*, 485–493.

Brent, D. A., Kolko, D. J., Wartella, M. E. Boylan, M. B., Moritz, G., Baugher, M. et al. (1993). Adolescent psychiatric inpatients' risk of suicide attempt at 6-month follow-up. *Journal of the American Academy of Child and Adolescent Psychiatry, 32*, 95–105.

Brent, D. A., Perper, J. A., Moritz, G., Liotus, L., Schweers, J., Balach, L. et al. (1994). Familial risk factors for adolescent suicide: A case-control study. *Acta Psychiatrica Scandinavica, 89*, 52–58.

Breton, J. J., Tousignant, M., & Bergeron, L. (2003). Parents under-report children's suicide ideation and attempts. *Evidence-Based Mental Health, 6*, 12.

Bridge, J. A., Goldstein, T. R., & Brent, D. A. (2006). Adoelscent suicide and suicidal behavior. *Journal of Child Psychology and Psychiatry, 47*, 372–394.

Brinkman-Sull, D. C., Overholser, J. C., & Silverman, E. (2000). Risk of future suicide attempts in adolescent psychiatric inpatients at 18-month follow-up. *Suicide and Life-Threatening Behavior, 30*, 327–340.

Burless, C., & De Leo, D. (2001). Methodological issues in community surveys of suicide ideators and attempters. *Crisis, 22*, 108–123.

Conger, R. D., Conger, K. J., Elder, G. H., Lorenz, F. O., Simons, R. L., & Whitbeck, L. B. (1993). Family economic stress and adjustment of adolescent girls. *Developmental Psychology, 29*, 206–219.

De Wilde, E. J., Kienhorst, C. W. M., & Diekstra, R. F. (2001). Suicidal behavior in adolescents. In I. M. Goodyer (Ed.), *The depressed child and adolescent* (pp. 267–291). Cambridge, England: Cambridge University Press.

De Wilde, E. J., Keinhorst, I. C., Diekstra, R. F., & Wolters, W. H. (1993). The specificity of psychological characteristics of adolescent suicide attempters. *Journal of the American Child and Adolescent Psychiatry, 32*, 51–59.

Evans, E., Hawton, K., & Rodham, K. (2005). In what ways are adolescents who engage in self-harm or experience thoughts of self-harm different in terms of help-seeking, communication and coping strategies. *Journal of Adolescence, 28*, 573–587.

Gould, M. S., Fisher, P., Flory, M., & Shaffer, D. (1996). Psychosocial factors of child and adolescent completed suicide. *Archives of General Psychiatry, 53*, 1155–1162.

Gould, M. S., Greenberg, T., Velting, D. M., & Shaffer, D. (2003). Youth suicide risk and preventative interventions: A review of the past 10 years. *Journal of the American Academy of Child and Adolescent Psychiatry, 42*, 386–405.

Harvey, M., & Byrd, M. (2000). Relationships between adolescents' attachment styles and family functioning. *Adolescence, 35*, 345–356.

Hawton, K., Fagg, J., & Simkin, S. (1996). Deliberate self-poisoning and self-injury in children and adolescents under 16 years of age in Oxford, 1976–1993. *British Journal of Psychiatry, 169*, 202–208.

Hurd, K. P., Wooding, S., & Noller, P. (1999). Parent-adolescent relationships in families with depressed and self-harming adolescents. *Journal of Family Studies, 5*, 47–68.

Joronen, K., & Astedt-Kurki, P. (2005). Familial contributions to adolescent subjective well-being. *International Journal of Nursing Practice, 11*, 125–133.

Kaplan, K. J., & Maldaver, M. (1993). Parental marital style and completed adolescent suicide. *Omega: Journal of Death and Dying, 27*, 131–154.

King, C. A., Segal, H., Kaminski, K., Naylor, M. W., Ghaziuddin, N., & Radpour, L. (1995). A prospective study of adolescent suicidal behavior following hospitalization. *Suicide and Life-Threatening Behavior, 25*, 327–338.

King, C. A., Segal, H. G., Naylor, M., & Evans, T. (1993). Family functioning and suicidal behavior in adolescent inpatients with mood disorder. *Journal of the American Academy of Child and Adolescent Psychiatry, 32*, 1198–1206.

Kosky, R., Silburn, S., & Zubrick, S. R. (1986). Symptomatic depression and suicidal ideation: A comparative study with 628 children. *Journal of Nervous and Mental Diseases, 174*, 523–528.

Kosky, R., Silburn, S., & Zubrick, S. (1990). Are children and adolescents who have suicidal thoughts different from those who attempt suicide? *Journal of Nervous and Mental Disease, 178*, 38–43.

Kovacs, M. (1992). *Children's Depression Inventory manual.* North Tonawanda, New York: Multi-Health Systems.

Kuhlberg, J. A., Peria, J. B. & Zayas, L. H. (2010). Familism, parent–adolescent conflict, self-esteem, internalizing behaviors and suicidal attempts among adolescent latinos. *Child Psychiatry and Human Development, 4*, 425–440.

Lewinsohn, P., Roberts, R. E., Seeley, J. R., Rohde, P., Gotlib, I. & Hops, H. (1994). Adolescent psychopathology: II. Psychosocial risk factors for depression. *Journal of Abnormal Psychology, 103*, 302–315.

Lewinsohn, P. M., Rohde, P., & Seeley, J. R. (1996). Adolescent suicide ideation and attempts: Prevalence, risk factors, and clinical implications. *Clinical Psychology: Science and Practice, 3*, 25–46.

Linehan, M. M., Camper, P., Chiles, J. A., Strosahl, K. et al. (1987). Interpersonal problem-solving and parasuicide. *Cognitive Therapy and Research, 11*, 1–12.

Maimon, D., Browning, C. R., & Brooks-Gunn, J. (2010). Collective efficacy, family attachment, and urban adolescent suicide attempts. *Journal of Health and Social Behavior, 51*, 307–324.

Martin, G. (2007). Success! The Australian National Youth Suicide Prevention Strategy (1995–2000) worked. But what exactly made the difference? *Australian E-Journal for the Advancement of Mental Health, 6*, 1–5.

Moos, R. H., & Moos, B. S. (1981). *Family Environment Scale manual.* Palo Alto, CA: Consulting Psychologists Press.

Morano, C. D., Cisler, R. A., & Lemerond, J. (1993). Risk factors for adolescent suicidal behavior: Loss, insufficient familial support, and hopelessness. *Adolescence, 28*, 851–865.

Noller, P., & Bagi, S. (1985). Parent–adolescent communication. *Journal of Adolescence, 8*, 125–144.

Noller, P., & Callan, V. (1991). *The adolescent in the family.* London: Routledge.

Noller, P., Feeney, J. A., & Hanrahan, M. (1994). *Assessing adult attachment.* In M. Sperling & W. H. Berman (Eds.), *Attachment in adults: Clinical and developmental perspectives* (pp. 128–152). New York: Guilford Press.

Olson, D. H., Sprenkle, D. H., & Russell, C. (1979). Circumplex model of marital and family systems: Cohesion and adaptability dimensions, family types and clinical applications. *Family Process, 18*, 3–28.

Parker, G., Tupling, H., & Brown, L. B. (1979). A parental bonding instrument. *British Journal of Medical Psychology, 52*, 1–10.

Petti, T. A. (Ed.). (1978). *Childhood depression.* New York: Haworth Press.

Ranta, K., Kaltiala-Heino, R., Rantanen, P., & Marttunen, M. (2009). Social phobia in Finnish general adolescent population: Prevalence, comorbidity, individual and family correlates, and service use. *Depression and Anxiety, 26*, 528–536.

Rubenstein, J. L., Heeren, T., Housman, D., Rubin, C. et al. (1989). Suicidal behavior in "normal" adolescents: Risk and protective factors. *American Journal of Orthopsychiatry, 59*, 59–71.

Seroczynski, A. D., Jacquez, F. M., & Cole, D. A. (2003). Depression and suicide during adolescence. In G. R. Adams & M. D. Berzonsky (Eds.), *Blackwell handbook of adolescence* (pp. 550–572). Malden: Blackwell Publishing.

Shaffer, D. (1988). Developmental factors in child and adolescent suicide. In M. Rutter, C. E. Izard & P. B. Read (Eds.), *Depression in young people: Developmental and clinical perspectives* (pp. 383–396). New York: Guilford Press.

Shaffer, D., Gould, M. S., Fisher, P., Trautman, P. et al. (1996). Psychiatric diagnosis in child and adolescent suicide. *Archives of General Psychiatry, 53*, 339–348.

Sheeber, L., Hops, H., & Davis, B. (2001). Family processes in adolescent depression. *Clinical, Child and Family Psychology Review, 4*, 19–35.

Shiner, R. L., & Marmorstein, N. R. (1998). Family environments of adolescents with lifetime depression: Associations with maternal depression history. *Journal of Child and Adolescent Psychiatry, 37*, 1152–1160.

Sourander, A., Helstela, L., & Helenius, H. (1999). Parent–adolescent agreement on emotional and behavioral problems. *Social Psychiatry and Psychiatric Epidemiology, 34*, 657–663.

Sroufe, L. A., Egeland, B., Carlson, E. A., & Collins, W. A. (2005). *The development of the person.* New York: Guilford Press.

Wagner, B. M. (1997). Family risk factors for child and adolescent suicidal behavior. *Psychological Bulletin, 121*, 246–298.

26

Attachment and Depression Across the Transition to Parenthood

Social Policy Implications

Jeffry A. Simpson, W. Steven Rholes, and Sandra Shallcross

The transition to parenthood is one of the happiest, most stressful, and most life-altering events that most people ever experience (Cowan & Cowan, 2000; Heinicke, 1995). For many partners, having a child predicts eventual declines in marital quality (Belsky, Lang, & Rovine, 1985; Cowan, Cowan, Heming, Coysh, Curtis-Boles, & Boles, 1985) and personal well-being (Alexander, Feeney, Hohaus, & Noller, 2001; Feeney, Hohaus, Noller, & Alexander, 2001; Simpson, Rholes, Campbell, Tran, & Wilson, 2003). Some partners, however, report no declines or actual improvements (Cowan & Cowan, 2000; Tucker & Aron, 1993). Thus, individuals differ in how well they weather the trials and tribulations of having a first baby. Who are the more "vulnerable" individuals? What has happened or is happening in their personal lives and relationships that might explain these negative outcomes? And how can answers to these questions inform policy making to improve the health and well-being of new parents going through transition to parenthood?

For the past decade, we have studied how couples navigate the opening months of the transition to parenthood. Guided by attachment theory (Bowlby, 1969, 1973, 1980), we have adopted a diathesis-stress approach to understanding how and why certain people who encounter specific *stressors* experience increases in depressive symptoms across the transition. Our research has focused on the first 6 months of the transition when the stress of being a new parent is strong and chronic, the novelty of this new life role has begun to

The Wiley-Blackwell Handbook of Couples and Family Relationships, First Edition.
Edited by Patricia Noller and Gery C. Karantzas.

wane, and the permanent life changes are becoming apparent (Cowan & Cowan, 2000). Testing ideas put forth by Bowlby (1973, 1988), we have focused on whether certain *vulnerable* individuals—especially those who are more anxiously attached to their romantic partners—are especially susceptible to increases in depressive symptoms in the early stages of the transition to parenthood, particularly if they perceive low or declining partner support. Bowlby (1988) believed that this pattern should be especially true of highly anxious women, who not only must endure childbirth and then deal with all the challenges of being a "first-time/full-time" parent, but who might enter parenthood with worries about whether their partners will be sufficiently supportive.

In this chapter, we first introduce some empirical and theoretical foundations of the transition to parenthood. We then review the primary findings of our research on attachment and depressive symptoms, focusing on a sample of first-time parents going through the transition. We conclude by discussing some policy issues and implications that follow from our findings.

The Transition to Parenthood and Personal Well-Being

The birth of a first child launches a cascade of intense emotions and life-altering events. Prospective studies have documented modest declines in marital satisfaction and personal adjustment in the majority of new parents, especially women (Belsky et al., 1985; Belsky & Pensky, 1988; Belsky, Spanier, & Rovine, 1983; Cowan & Cowan, 2000; Cowan et al., 1985; Feldman & Nash, 1984; Levy-Shiff, 1994). These declines often co-occur with increases in marital conflict (Cowan & Cowan, 2000; Cowan et al., 1985; Crohan, 1996), reduced involvement by fathers and greater involvement by mothers in daily childcare activities (Levy-Schiff, 1994), lower pre-birth marital satisfaction (Cowan & Cowan, 1988; Wright, Henggeler, & Craig, 1986), more violated role expectations (Belsky, 1985; Cowan & Cowan, 1988; Gottlieb & Pancer, 1988), more sex-typed division of labor (Belsky, Lang & Huston, 1986), less affiliative and caregiving behaviors displayed by partners toward one another (Levy-Shiff, 1994), and less postpartum partner support (Cowan & Cowan, 2000). Women who perceive greater prenatal support from their partners, however, usually fare better. For example, they report easier labor and deliveries, their newborns are more alert and responsive upon delivery, and they experience less postpartum depression in the weeks following childbirth (Collins, Dunkel-Schetter, Lobel, & Scrimshaw, 1993).

The personality and psychological features of new parents and their babies also forecast changes in marital functioning and personal well-being. For example, men who claim to be more nurturing, caring, and protective of their partners experience smaller declines in marital satisfaction during the first few months of the transition. Women who have less impulse control, greater need for autonomy, view their jobs as a central to their lives, or have poorer organization and coping skills report poorer marital adjustment (Levy-Shiff, 1994). Declines in marital well-being are also associated with greater maternal anxiety and depression (Goldberg & Michaels, 1988), and with infants who have more difficult temperaments (Levy-Shiff, 1994).

Although most studies have documented declines in personal and marital well-being across the transition to parenthood, some have found no declines (e.g., Ryder, 1973) or slight improvements (e.g., Belsky & Rovine, 1990; Cowan & Cowan, 1988; Hobbs & Cole, 1976; Russell, 1974). Some couples report more sexual activity, more closeness, and better problem solving (e.g., Cowan & Cowan, 1988). Thus, not all new parents experience downturns in marital and personal well-being following the birth of a first child.

Attachment Theory

Attachment theory is relevant to understanding events that transpire during the transition to parenthood (Bowlby, 1988; see also chapters 13, 14 in this volume). The theory explains how ecological factors (e.g., the current environment) and dispositional factors (e.g., pre-existing tendencies) combine to influence the way in which individuals think, feel, and behave in certain social situations. Through his extensive observations Bowlby surmised that early caregiving experiences—especially in situations when individuals are distressed, vulnerable, and need comfort and support—exert powerful effects on how people view themselves and significant others over the lifespan (Bowlby, 1973). During social development, the quality and amount of care that individuals receive (or perceive they have received) shapes the content of their working models, which then guide how they think, feel, and behave in later relationships.

Working models have several components, such as relationship-relevant goals, attitudes, beliefs, and expectations, that affect how individuals perceive, interpret, and behave toward their attachment figures (Collins & Read, 1994), especially when attachment-relevant needs, concerns, or worries become salient (Simpson & Rholes, 1994). Current experiences as well as perceptions of partners/relationships are filtered through working models, which sometimes distort perceptions or memories of particular people, situations, or events (e.g., Simpson, Rholes, & Winterheld, 2010). Working models that lead people to question their self-worth in relationships should: (a) direct attention to cues that signal possible relationship loss or abandonment; (b) distort judgments or interpretations of recent events that might be harbingers of relationship loss or abandonment; and/or (c) bias memories of relationship events in model-consistent ways, all of which should fuel further worries about possible loss (Bowlby, 1973; Collins, Guichard, Ford, & Feeney, 2004). Indeed, one of the hallmarks of attachment insecurity is the tendency to process attachment-relevant information in biased, self-protective, and negative ways (Mikulincer & Florian, 1998). Instead of evaluating their partners based on what they say or do, insecurely attached people monitor, encode, interpret, and remember the actions of their partners in ways that verify and sustain their negative beliefs and expectations.

The transition to parenthood can be difficult for insecurely attached people, especially anxiously attached ones. Highly anxious individuals have received (or perceive they have received) inconsistent or unpredictable care in earlier relationships (Cassidy & Berlin, 1994). Given this history, they harbor doubts about their worth as relationship partners, worry that their partners do not really love them or might leave them, and are hypervigilant to signs that their partners could be pulling away (Cassidy & Berlin, 1994). One possible cue of abandonment is low or declining partner support, especially when one is distressed and may need support (Bowlby, 1973, 1988). Thus, when anxiously attached individuals encounter situations that tax them and their relationships, their perceptions, evaluations, and actions are likely to be impacted by concerns that they do not have—or will not receive—sufficient care and support from their partners when they need that the most.

Less anxious people, who are more likely to be securely attached, ought to fare better during the transition to parenthood. For most of their lives, these people have had their needs for proximity and support adequately met (Hazan & Shaver, 1994). This knowledge permits secure people to develop strong internal resources (e.g., positive beliefs and expectancies about themselves as being good relationship partners, which allows them be more benevolent and compassionate) as well as strong external resources (e.g., choosing and encouraging more supportive partners, developing larger and more supportive social networks). These internal and external resources are likely to lead secure individuals to rely more directly on their partners and close friends for comfort and support, particularly when they are upset (Mikulincer, Florian, & Weller, 1993). In fact, attachment security is likely to serve as an "inner resource" that allows securely attached people to appraise stressful life experiences more positively, to resolve them better, and to cope with them more effectively (Mikulincer & Florian, 1998). These capacities should *buffer* highly secure people from experiencing negative personal outcomes, including increases in depressive symptoms across stressful life transitions.

Attachment and the Transition to Parenthood

Attachment theory was developed in part to explain the origins of depression and other psychological disorders (Bowlby, 1980, 1988). Adopting a diathesis-stress perspective, Bowlby (1988) hypothesized that increases in depressive symptoms should occur when vulnerable people (e.g., highly anxious women) confront stressors that strain their relationships. Such experiences, if strong and persistent, should trigger depressive symptoms or even clinical depression by increasing negative beliefs about the self or confirming negative views of others (i.e., that partners are unloving or unsupportive). This negativity, in turn, may lead anxious individuals to behave less constructively toward their partners (cf., Anderson, Beach, & Kasl, 1999). Greater attachment security, on the other hand, should buffer individuals from depressive symptoms, especially during chronically stressful life transitions (Mikulincer & Florian, 1998).

Insecurely attached people are more prone to depression and depressive symptoms. Highly avoidant and highly anxious people, for example, tend to experience major depressive episodes more than secure people do (Mickelson, Kessler, & Shaver, 1997), with anxious persons typically reporting the most depressive symptoms, secure individuals reporting the least, and avoidant persons falling in between (Cooper, Shaver, & Collins, 1998). Similar effects are found in women making the transition from high school to adult life (Burge, Hammen, Davila, & Daley, 1997; Hammen et al., 1995). In these and other studies, highly anxious women are particularly susceptible to depressive symptoms (Carnelley, Pietromonaco, & Jaffe, 1994; Hammen et al., 1995).

Bowlby (1988) hypothesized that highly anxious women who enter parenthood perceiving that their partners are not sufficiently available and supportive should experience more postnatal depressive symptoms. As we have discussed, highly anxious individuals place great value on their relationships (Hazan & Shaver, 1987), and they anchor their self-concepts on the quality and well-being of their relationships (Campbell, Simpson, Boldry, & Kashy, 2005; Crocker & Wolfe, 2001). As a result, they should feel dejected if they perceive that their partners cannot or will not provide the amount of care and support they need, especially when in the throes of a chronic, stressful life transition. To complicate matters, the working models of anxious persons should lead them to expect and perceive less support from their partners than their partners may actually be providing. During the first few months of the transition, therefore, perceptions of low or declining partner support should be associated with more negative partner and relationship perceptions by highly anxious women, which should trigger increases in depressive symptoms. This process model is shown in Figure 26.1.

Prenatal perceptions of the partner should also predict the degree to which depressive symptoms remain stable (either high or low) across the transition to parenthood. For example, if highly anxious women experience depressive symptoms, their symptoms should remain constant across the transition or might increase if they perceive that their relationships are not functioning well. For highly anxious women, therefore, the connection between prenatal and postnatal depressive symptoms (i.e., the temporal stability of their depression scores) should be partially mediated by their prenatal perceptions of their spouse or their marriage. For less anxious women, other factors are likely to affect their depressive symptoms, such as work, leisure activities, or involvement in other events. Accordingly, the relation between prenatal and postnatal depressive symptoms should *not* be mediated by relationship perceptions in less anxious women.[1]

We tested these hypotheses in a large sample of married couples, all of whom were awaiting the birth of their first child (see Simpson et al., 2003). The sample consisted

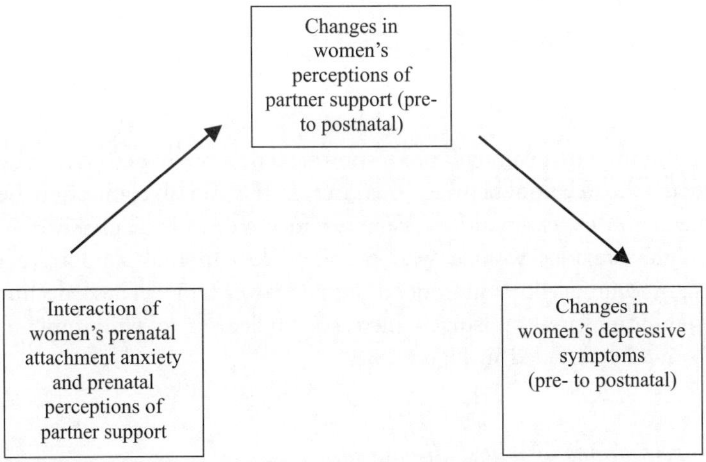

Figure 26.1 A model of how women's prenatal attachment anxiety interacts with their prenatal perceptions of spousal support to predict changes in their marital satisfaction and depressive symptoms, mediated through changes in their prenatal-to-postnatal perceptions of spousal support

of 106 couples (wives and their husbands) recruited from childbirth classes in Texas, United States. Both partners completed self-report questionnaires approximately 6 weeks before the birth of their first child (at Time 1) and approximately 6 months after delivery (at Time 2). The average age of women and men was 28.5 years, and the average length of marriage was 3.8 years. Seventy percent of the sample were European American, 20% were Hispanic American, and the rest were Asian American or African American.

At Time 1, women reported their romantic attachment orientations (on anxiety and avoidance scales), their perceptions of the amount of support available from their husbands, and their depressive symptoms. Husbands at Time 1 reported their romantic attachment orientations, their perceptions of how supportively they behave toward their wives, and their depressive symptoms. At Time 2 (6 months after the birth), both spouses completed the same scales a second time. We tested whether highly anxious women who entered the transition perceiving relatively less spousal support were more likely to experience pre-to-postpartum increases in depressive symptoms over the transition, along with the specific psychological variable(s) that could have generated these changes.

Anxiety and depressive symptoms

As predicted, we found that highly anxious women experienced significant increases in depressive symptoms during the transition, but that highly avoidant women did not. Also as anticipated, women who perceived more spousal support *before* childbirth did not report changes in depressive symptoms, even if they were highly anxious. However, highly anxious women who perceived less prenatal support became significantly more depressed across the transition, whereas less anxious women became slightly *less* depressed. The working models of highly anxious women probably explain at least part of this effect because highly anxious women perceived less support than would be expected based on their husbands' reports of support offered.

Mediation findings

We also hypothesized that women's pre-to-postnatal declines in perceived spousal support would mediate the relation between (i.e., act as the causal connection between) the prenatal interaction effects mentioned above and increases in depressive symptoms. As predicted, highly anxious women who perceived less spousal support prenatally also perceived significant declines in spousal support over time. These declines, in turn, predicted significant pre-to-postnatal increases in depressive symptoms. This finding supports the model depicted in Figure 26.1.

Husbands' perceptions of wives' dispositions

We found that highly anxious women perceived less support from their husbands than less anxious women did (see also chapter 28 in this volume). This finding most likely occurred for one of three reasons. First, the husbands of highly anxious women might have offered or provided less support. Second, highly anxious women may not have perceived the support that was actually available to them. Third, both processes could have transpired. Even though highly anxious women perceived less prenatal support than less anxious women did, women's prenatal levels of anxiety and men's prenatal reports of the support they provided were not correlated. Six months after childbirth, however, the husbands of highly anxious women reported that they were providing significantly *less* support than the husbands of less anxious women, even when husbands' attachment scores and other measures were statistically controlled. This finding suggests that some highly anxious women may have behaved in ways that undermined their husbands' willingness to provide support a few months into the transition (see Anderson et al., 1999).

To test this possibility, we examined whether husbands' postnatal ratings of their wives' dependency (emotional clinginess) and emotional instability mediated the relation between wives' attachment anxiety and their husbands' postnatal perceptions of support provided. As expected, the relation between women's attachment anxiety (assessed at 6 months postpartum) and their husbands' postnatal perceptions of support became nonsignificant once husbands' ratings of their wives' dependency and emotional instability were statistically controlled. This effect suggests that husbands' negative views of their highly anxious wives (as being dependent and emotionally unstable) could be one of the reasons why they withdrew support 6 months into the transition.

Depression maintenance

Bowlby (1980, 1988) also surmised that the association between prenatal and postnatal depressive symptoms should be mediated by perceptions of spousal support, especially among highly anxious women. As predicted, we found that highly anxious women who reported more depressive symptoms prenatally continued to be relatively more depressed at 6 months postpartum, but *only if* they held more negative prenatal perceptions of their husbands' support. Less anxious women who reported more prenatal depressive symptoms did not stay depressed if they held more negative prenatal relationship perceptions, but they did if other negative life events intervened. In sum, prenatal perceptions of the partner and relationship assume a stronger role in maintaining depressive symptoms among highly anxious women.

Policy Issues and Implications

According to these findings, only a subset of couples going through the first few months of the transition to parenthood experience personal or relational difficulties. Most couples weather the trials and tribulations of having a new baby reasonably well. New mothers who are more anxiously attached, however, are vulnerable to negative outcomes. We believe that our findings have important implications for intervention efforts for two reasons. First, our research identifies which *people* are most likely to benefit from interventions *before* they (and their partners) enter this challenging phase of life. Second, our research highlights the *psychological processes* that mediate the connection between being vulnerable to problems prenatally (i.e., being highly anxious *and* concerned about deficient partner support) and postnatal increases in depressive symptoms. Our findings, therefore, may help practitioners develop more effective interventions.

Causes for support perceptions

Perceptions of partner support harbored by new mothers may be one major source of problems encountered during the early stages of the transition to parenthood. Highly anxious women report increases in depressive symptoms, particularly when they enter parenthood perceiving lower levels of emotional support from their mates. However, if they perceive greater prenatal partner support, highly anxious women do *not* experience changes in depressive symptoms. Unfortunately, few highly anxious women view their husbands as highly supportive prenatally.

Several factors may contribute to decreases in perceptions of support in these women. First, highly anxious individuals have perceptual biases that may motivate them to "under-perceive" the emotional support that may actually be available from their partners (Collins et al., 2004). Greater attachment anxiety develops in response to prior attachment figures whose love and caregiving were unstable, variable in quality, or unpredictable (Ainsworth, Blehar, Waters, & Wall, 1978; Cassidy & Berlin, 1994). Based on these experiences, highly anxious people become wary of attachment figures and expect them to be unsupportive, uncaring, or not fully committed to the relationship, especially during times of need.

Second, some anxious women might unwittingly act in ways that discourage their partners from providing more support. Compounding matters, men who are married to highly anxious women tend to perceive their wives as more immature, emotionally weak, dependent, and clingy in the months following childbirth. These negative attributions may partially explain why the husbands of highly anxious women report significant declines in their supportiveness across the transition. The partners of highly anxious women may respond to their wives' passive, disorganized, or caustic attempts to elicit support by reducing the support that they provide, or by offering support that is not well suited to the needs of their anxious mates. This perceived lack of responsiveness may confirm the negative expectations of highly anxious women, resulting in increased distress and even *more* ineffectual attempts to garner support. This negative relational cycle highlights the need for interventions that address the cognitions and behaviors of *both* partners in support groups, couples therapy, and/or individual therapy.

Possible targets of intervention

One overarching goal of any intervention should be to help highly anxious people identify and understand how they might unknowingly minimize or discount support that might actually be available from their partners. In our research, for example, highly anxious women reported that their husbands provided significantly less support than their husbands claimed to give. This disparity is likely to generate further stress and strain on their relationships. In some relationships, therefore, recognition and acceptance of available support may be the first step toward reducing discrepancies between partners' perceptions of support provision.

Highly anxious people may also benefit from skills-based interventions that target the clear and direct expression of their needs for comfort and support while maintaining composure, particularly when they are upset. Highly anxious people crave support from their attachment figures, but they do not always seek it when they are distressed. Highly anxious women, for instance, seek less support from their mates during the transition to parenthood (Rholes, Simpson, Campbell, & Grich, 2001). They typically behave in a rather passive manner, perhaps because they may not know *how* to increase the support that could be available to them. Accordingly, highly anxious individuals may need to develop greater awareness of when they need support and then identify new ways of approaching their partners for support and communicating their needs. Learning how to seek support more assertively may also help highly anxious people develop stronger self-efficacy and greater self-worth in their relationships.

Of equal importance, the *partners* of highly anxious people may also need to be the targets of intervention. For example, the partners of highly anxious people might become more responsive if they recognize that, in certain stressful situations, some seemingly dysfunctional behaviors—especially persistent reassurance seeking—are difficult for their partners to control and may be *essential* to their partner's well-being. Skills-based interventions may help partners to structure and provide a more stable and supportive environment, especially during peak periods of stress (Feeney, Alexander, Noller, & Hohaus, 2003). Whereas less anxious women easily turn to their partners for support and reassurance when problems arise, highly anxious women may respond best to consistent reminders of their partners' love and support, even on days when there are no major difficulties and their anxious partners seem fine. The partners of highly anxious individuals may also need to learn how to tailor their support giving to better meet the needs of their insecure partners (cf. Simpson, Winterheld, Rholes, & Oriña, 2007). Postnatal outcomes are likely to be better if the partners of highly anxious people direct less anger at them when they (their anxious partners) feel frustrated and if they refrain from making negative attributions for their insecure partner's actions.

Possible intervention programs

Several different intervention programs could address the targets of intervention discussed above. Depending on the specific problem and goal, intervention programs could range from mass public education programs made available to all first-time parents to individualized psychological or psychiatric interventions designed to treat individuals or couples suffering from more severe problems or disorders. Different types of interventions could be developed and implemented, beginning with broadband prenatal transition to parenthood education programs that are then supplemented with postnatal support groups for new parents. For more difficult cases, individual or couple-based therapies may be necessary to revise dysfunctional working models or expectations about parenthood, using relationship-focused therapies (Heinicke, Fineman, Ruth, Recchia, Guthrie, & Rodning, 1999; Whiffen & Johnson, 1998), and/or behaviorally-oriented skills training (Schulz, Cowan, & Cowan, 2006) designed to buffer vulnerable individuals from depressive symptoms.

The specific type of intervention that works best is likely to depend on the severity of attachment insecurities of one or both partners, the nature and quality of their relationship, and the abilities, skills, and capacities that each partner brings to parenthood. For example, highly anxious individuals tend to be emotionally engaged yet less compliant in psychotherapy than highly secure individuals, and some have speculated that anxious people might benefit most from psychodynamic or interpersonal approaches to therapy (Daniel, 2006). Because the transition to parenthood should activate the attachment-related vulnerabilities of highly anxious people, the most effective interventions may be those that integrate past experiences and working models with present issues and concerns (Suess & Sroufe, 2005). Couples-based interventions such as emotion-focused couples therapy should be particularly effective at addressing attachment concerns, decreasing corrosive relational dynamics, and reducing the depressogenic effects of inadequate support (see chapter 23 in this volume; Whiffen & Johnson, 1998). These therapies might be even more effective in combination with comprehensive prevention programs that have educational components and group-level interventions (e.g., support groups consisting of new parents).

Recent experimental studies also imply that, regardless of their attachment orientations or specific life circumstances, individuals may benefit from interventions that enhance their felt security (chapter 14 in this volume; Mikulincer & Shaver, 2007). This research, which has used explicit (superliminal) and implicit (subliminal) security-based primes (i.e., information presented at or just below conscious awareness) to increase felt security and reduce negative affect toward disliked outgroups, reveals that people could be trained to view themselves, their partners, and outgroup members in a more caring, empathic, and benevolent way. Thus, interventions that induce feelings of greater attachment security might buffer new "expectant parents" from increases in depression across the transition, especially if interventions target both partners (see also chapter 14 in this volume regarding security priming). This novel intervention could augment more comprehensive treatment programs.

In addition, therapists could help highly insecure individuals and their partners find more effective ways to reduce different sources of stress associated with having a new baby, including stress that stems from the dysfunctional working models of one or both partners. Other sources of stress, however, may emanate from having to manage multiple and often competing life tasks, such as jobs, caring for extended family members, or other personal responsibilities. One way to reduce stress arising from these competing life tasks would be to establish standard maternity and paternity leave programs that allow new parents to reorganize their lives and adjust to the novel demands of parenthood.

We believe that *coordinated* education programs designed for new parents and delivered by professional personnel would best accomplish the goals outlined above. One principal way to reduce depression may be through good prenatal screening and early detection. Accordingly, professionals (e.g., pediatricians, obstetrics nurses, counselors) should routinely include screening questions for depression, marital conflict, and extreme levels of attachment insecurity as part of their regular examinations of expectant parents, both before *and* after delivery. Depressed and vulnerable individuals could then be identified early and referred for proper treatment immediately. One critical period for screening is likely to be when mothers are in the hospital immediately after childbirth. Unfortunately, most of these stays are too brief to detect the early signs of postpartum depressive symptoms. The most vulnerable new mothers, therefore, should remain hospitalized for slightly longer periods of time (e.g., 2–3 additional days) following childbirth. Another benefit of slightly longer post-delivery hospital stays is that vulnerable mothers would have more time to recover from delivery before having to deal with full-time child care.

Most couples cannot fathom the many new challenges and difficulties associated with becoming first-time parents. For this reason, basic education programs must be developed to identify, explain, and provide solutions to the most common and pressing problems that arise during the first few months of the transition. One salient issue for any education program would be to identify and explain why some people are sensitive to the perceived absence of actual or available partner support. A second issue would be to identify and explain why certain people have unrealistic, mistaken, or overly optimistic expectations about what parenthood will really be like (see Delmore-Ko, Pancer, Hunsberger, & Pratt, 2000; Pancer, Pratt, Hunsberger, & Gallant, 2000), including how dysfunctional expectations might exacerbate relationship difficulties. Practitioners should also educate new fathers about how the transition is likely to affect them and permanently alter their lives. Many new fathers struggle with the unexpected loss of free time and unexpected family–work conflicts (Cowan & Cowan, 2000). To prevent the onset of depressive symptoms, new parents should also be taught to recognize symptoms of depression in both themselves and their partners. For many couples, education programs could be delivered by hospital staff or as part of regular childbirth courses. For others, particularly impoverished or disadvantaged groups, other means of delivery may be necessary.

After teaching new mothers and fathers the telltale signs of depression and marital problems, new parents need to know whom they can turn to for guidance, assistance, and support. All new parents should be given information about the different forms of assistance available to them (e.g., medications, counseling services, new parent discussion groups), which they could receive from their physicians, nurses, or public mental health centers. As discussed above, information and emotional support from peers or new parents who have recently gone through the transition might also provide benefits that other sources of support do not or cannot provide.

Conclusions

These policy recommendations are targeted primarily to highly distressed and highly insecure women during the first few months of the transition to parenthood. At later stages of the transition, other types of programs, interventions, or therapies targeted to certain men (e.g., highly anxious men, who may eventually feel deprived of contact with their wives, or highly avoidant men, who may increasingly feel the need for greater independence and autonomy) or certain emergent relationship issues (e.g., how to maintain quality time and intimacy with one's partner, how to balance work, the relationship, and child care) may be required. As the permanence of changes in lifestyle associated with being new parents starts to restrict the autonomy and independence of highly avoidant people, we suspect that the burdens of parenthood may begin to adversely affect their personal and relational well-being as well.

In conclusion, the transition to parenthood is one of most challenging, joyful, stressful, and life-altering events that most people face. There is now a reasonably large body of research anchored in major theories and models that practitioners can use to identify which individuals and couples are most susceptible to personal or relational downturns in the first few months following childbirth. The prudent translation of this knowledge into effective intervention programs may help prevent the onset of depressive symptoms in some people and could stabilize "at-risk" relationships.

Note

1. Although highly avoidant persons also tend to be more depressed, prenatal perceptions of partner support and women's avoidance should not predict changes in depressive symptoms across the transition. Highly avoidant people want to be independent and emotionally self-sufficient, and they distance themselves from others when they are upset (Crittenden & Ainsworth, 1989; Simpson, Rholes, & Nelligan, 1992). During the transition to parenthood, therefore, highly avoidant women should *not* perceive low levels of spousal support; in fact, they may not even realize that support is low or deficient. If they do, perceptions of low partner support should not produce increases in depressive symptoms.

References

Ainsworth, M. D. S., Blehar, M. C., Waters, E., & Wall, S. (1978). *Patterns of attachment: A psychological study of the strange situation.* Hillsdale, NJ: Erlbaum.

Alexander, R., Feeney, J., Hohaus, L., & Noller, P. (2001). Attachment style and coping resources as predictors of coping strategies in the transition to parenthood. *Personal Relationships, 8,* 137–152.

Anderson, P., Beach, S. R. H., & Kaslow, N. J. (1999). Marital discord and depression: The potential of attachment theory to guide integrative clinical intervention. In T. Joiner & J. C. Coyne (Eds.), *The interactional nature of depression: Advances in interpersonal approaches* (pp. 271–297). Washington, DC: American Psychology Association.

Belsky, J. (1985). Exploring individual differences in marital change across the transition to parenthood: The role of violated expectations. *Journal of Marriage and the Family, 47,* 1037–1044.

Belsky, J., Lang, M. E., & Huston, T. L. (1986). Sex-typing and division of labor as determinants of marital change across the transition to parenthood. *Journal of Personality and Social Psychology, 50,* 517–522.

Belsky, J., Lang, M. E., & Rovine, M. (1985). Stability and change in marriage across the transition to parenthood: A second study. *Journal of Marriage and the Family, 47,* 855–865.

Belsky, J., & Pensky, E. (1988). Marital change across the transition to parenthood. *Marriage and Family Review, 13,* 133–156.

Belsky, J. & Rovine, M. (1990). Q-sort security and first-year nonmaternal care. *New Directions for Child Development, 49*, 7–22.

Belsky, J., Spanier, G. B., & Rovine, M. (1983). Stability and change in marriage across the transition to parenthood. *Journal of Marriage and the Family, 47*, 855–865.

Bowlby, J. (1969). *Attachment and loss: Vol. 1: Attachment.* New York: Basic Books.

Bowlby, J. (1973). *Attachment and loss: Vol. 2: Separation.* New York: Basic Books.

Bowlby, J. (1980). *Attachment and loss: Vol. 3: Loss.* New York: Basic Books.

Bowlby, J. (1988). *A secure base: Child–parent attachment and healthy human development.* New York: Basic Books.

Burge, D., Hammen, C., Davila, J., & Daley, S. E. (1997). The relationship between attachment cognitions and psychological adjustment in late adolescent women. *Development and Psychopathology, 9*, 151–167.

Campbell, L., Simpson, J. A., Boldry, J., & Kashy, D. A. (2005). Perceptions of conflict and support in romantic relationships: The role of attachment anxiety. *Journal of Personality and Social Psychology, 88*, 510–531.

Carnelley, K. B., Pietromonaco, P. R., & Jaffe, K. (1994). Depression, working models of others, and relationship functioning. *Journal of Personality and Social Psychology, 66*, 127–140.

Cassidy, J., & Berlin, L. (1994). The insecure/anxious pattern of attachment: Theory and research. *Child Development, 65*, 971–991.

Collins, N. L., Dunkel-Schetter, C., Lobel, M., & Scrimshaw, S. C. (1993). Social support during pregnancy: Psychosocial correlates of birth outcomes and postpartum depression. *Journal of Personality and Social Psychology, 65*, 1243–1258.

Collins, N. L., Guichard, A. C., Ford, M. B., & Feeney, B. C. (2004). Working models of attachment: New developments and emerging themes. In W. S. Rholes & J. A. Simpson (Eds.), *Adult attachment: Theory, research and clinical implications* (pp. 196–239). New York: Guilford Press.

Collins, N. L., & Read, S. J. (1994). Cognitive representations of attachment: The structure and function of working models. In K. Bartholomew & D. Perlman (Eds.), *Attachment processes in adulthood* (pp. 53–90). London: Kingsley.

Cooper, M. L., Shaver, P. R., & Collins, N. L. (1998). Attachment styles, emotion regulation, and adjustment in adolescence. *Journal of Personality and Social Psychology, 74*, 1380–1397.

Cowan, C. P., & Cowan, P. A. (2000). *When partners become parents: The big life change in couples.* Mahwah, NJ: Erlbaum.

Cowan, P. A., & Cowan, C. P. (1988). Changes in marriage during the transition to parenthood: Must we blame the baby? In G. Y. Michaels & W. A. Goldberg (Eds.), *The transition to parenthood: Current theory and research* (pp. 114–156). New York: Cambridge University Press.

Cowan, C. P., Cowan, P. A., Heming, G., Coysh, W. S., Curtis-Boles, H., & Boles, A. J. (1985). Transition to parenthood: His, hers, and theirs. *Journal of Family Issues, 6*, 451–481.

Crittenden, P. M., & Ainsworth, M. (1989). Child maltreatment and attachment theory. In D. Cicchetti & V. Carlson (Eds.), *Clinical maltreatment: Theory and research on the causes and consequences of child abuse and neglect* (pp. 432–463). Cambridge, England: Cambridge University Press.

Crocker, J., & Wolfe, C. T. (2001). Contingencies of self-worth. *Psychological Review, 108*, 593–623.

Crohan, S. (1996). Marital quality and conflict across the transition to parenthood in African American and White couples. *Journal of Marriage and the Family, 58*, 933–944.

Daniel, S. I. F. (2006). Adult attachment patterns and individual psychotherapy: A review. *Clinical Psychology Review, 26*, 968–984.

Delmore-Ko, P., Pancer, S. M., Hunsberger, B., & Pratt, M. (2000). Becoming a parent: The relation between prenatal expectations and postnatal experience. *Journal of Family Psychology, 14*, 625–640.

Feeney, J., Alexander, R., Noller, P., & Hohaus, L. (2003). Attachment insecurity, depression, and the transition to parenthood. *Personal Relationships, 10*, 475–493.

Feeney, J. A., Hohaus, L., Noller, P., & Alexander, R. P. (2001). *Becoming parents: Exploring the bonds between mothers, fathers, and their infants.* New York: Cambridge University Press.

Feldman, S. S., & Nash, S. C. (1984). The transition from expectancy to parenthood: Impact of the firstborn child on men and women. *Sex Roles, 11*, 84–95.

Goldberg, W. A., & Michaels G. Y. (1988). Conclusion: The transition to parenthood: Synthesis and future directions. In G. Y. Michaels & W. A. Goldberg (Eds.), *The transition to parenthood: Current theory and research* (pp. 342–360). New York: Cambridge University Press.

Gottlieb, B. H., & Pancer, S. M. (1988). Social networks and the transition to parenthood. In G. Y. Michaels & W. A. Goldberg (Eds.), *The transition to parenthood: Current theory and research* (pp. 235–269). New York: Cambridge University Press.

Hammen, C., Burge, D., Daley, S. E., Davila, J. et al. (1995). Interpersonal attachment cognitions and prediction of symptomatic responses to interpersonal stress. *Journal of Abnormal Psychology, 104*, 436–443.

Hazan, C., & Shaver, P. R. (1987). Romantic love conceptualized as an attachment process. *Journal of Personality and Social Psychology, 52*, 511–524.

Hazan, C., & Shaver, P. R. (1994). Attachment as an organizational framework for research on close relationships. *Psychological Inquiry, 5*, 1–22.

Heinicke, C. M. (1995). Determinants of the transition to parenthood. In M. H. Bornstein et al. (Eds.), *Handbook of parenting, Vol. 3: Status and social conditions of parenting* (pp. 277–303). Mahwah, NJ: Erlbaum.

Heinicke, C. M., Fineman, N. R., Ruth, G., Recchia, S. L., Guthrie, D., & Rodning, C. (1999). Relationship-based intervention with at-risk mothers: Outcome in the first year of life. *Infant Mental Health Journal, 20*, 349–374.

Hobbs, D. F., & Cole, S. O. (1976). Transition to parenthood: A decade of replication. *Journal of Marriage and the Family, 38*, 723–731.

Levy-Shiff, R. (1994). Individual and contextual correlates of marital change across the transition to parenthood. *Developmental Psychology, 30*, 591–601.

Mickelson, K. D., Kessler, R. C., & Shaver, P. R. (1997). Adult attachment in a nationally representative sample. *Journal of Personality and Social Psychology, 73*, 1092–1106.

Mikulincer, M., & Florian, V. (1998). The relationship between adult attachment styles and emotional and cognitive reactions to stressful events. In J. A. Simpson & W. S. Rholes (Eds.), *Attachment theory and close relationships* (pp. 143–165). New York: Guilford Press.

Mikulincer, M., Florian, V., & Weller, A. (1993). Attachment styles, coping strategies, and posttraumatic psychological distress: The impact of the Gulf War in Israel. *Journal of Personality and Social Psychology, 64*, 817–826.

Mikulincer, M., & Shaver, P. R. (2007). Boosting attachment security to promote mental health, prosocial values, and inter-group tolerance. *Psychological Inquiry, 18*, 139–156.

Pancer, S. M., Pratt, M., Hunsberger, B., & Gallant, M. (2000). Thinking ahead: Complexity of expectations and the transition to parenthood. *Journal of Personality, 68*, 253–280.

Rholes, S. W., Simpson, J. A., Campbell, L., & Grich, J. (2001). Adult attachment and the transition to parenthood. *Journal of Personality and Social Psychology, 81*, 421–435.

Russell, C. (1974). Transition to parenthood: Problems and gratifications. *Journal of Marriage and the Family, 36*, 294–301.

Ryder, R. G. (1973). Longitudinal data relating marriage satisfaction and having a child. *Journal of Marriage and the Family, 35*, 604–606.

Schulz, M. S., Cowan, C. P., & Cowan, P. A. (2006). Promoting healthy beginnings: A randomized controlled trial of a preventative intervention to preserve marital quality during the transition to parenthood. *Journal of Consulting and Clinical Psychology, 74*, 20–31.

Simpson, J. A., & Rholes, W. S. (1994). Stress and secure base relationships in adulthood. In K. Bartholomew & D. Perlman (Eds.), *Advances in personal relationships (Vol. 5): Attachment processes in adulthood* (pp. 181–204). London: Kingsley.

Simpson, J. A., Rholes, W. S., Campbell, L., Tran, S., & Wilson, C. L. (2003). Adult attachment, the transition to parenthood, and depressive symptoms. *Journal of Personality and Social Psychology, 84*, 1172–1187.

Simpson, J. A., Rholes, S. W., & Nelligan, J. S. (1992). Support seeking and support giving within couples in an anxiety-provoking situation. *Journal of Personality and Social Psychology, 62*, 434–446.

Simpson, J. A., Rholes, W. S., & Winterheld, H. A. (2010). Attachment working models twist memories of relationship events. *Psychological Science, 21*, 252–259.

Simpson, J. A., Winterheld, H. A., Rholes, W. S., & Oriña, M. M. (2007). Working models of attachment and reactions to different forms of caregiving from romantic partners. *Journal of Personality and Social Psychology, 93*, 466–477.

Suess, G. J., & Sroufe, J. (2005). Clinical implications of the development of the person. *Attachment and Human Development, 7*, 381–392.

Tucker, P., & Aron, A. (1993). Passionate love and marital satisfaction at key transition points in the family life cycle. *Journal of Social and Clinical Psychology, 12*, 135–147.

Whiffen, V. E., & Johnson, S. M. (1998). An attachment theory framework for the treatment of childbearing depression. *Clinical Psychology: Science and Practice, 5*(4), 478–493.

Wright, P. J., Henggeler, S. W., & Craig, L. (1986). Problems in paradise? A longitudinal examination of the transition to parenthood. *Journal of Applied Developmental Psychology, 7*, 277–291.

27

Recent Advances in Research on Social Support in Couples

Insights from Event-Sampling and Daily Diary Research

Carolyn E. Cutrona

Since its introduction in the public health literature as a protector against the ravages of stressful life events on health (e.g., Cassell, 1976), social support has lost its superhero status and is viewed more as a temperamental friend, who unpredictably bestows benefits, blows to morale, and indifference. Social support from others is not always helpful (Sarason & Sarason, 2009; Vangelisti, 2009); indeed, daily diary studies frequently show heightened distress following the receipt of social support from one's intimate partner (e.g., Bolger, Zuckerman, & Kessler, 2000; Gleason, Iida, & Shrout, 2008; Maisel & Gable, 2009).

In this chapter, I will review recent research on social support in couples. The past decade has brought a wealth of new insights into social support processes as they unfold in the context of intimate dyadic relationships. New theoretical advances have come from an integration of attachment theory into conceptualizations of social support. Observational techniques that analyze specific support transactions and event-sampling methods (daily diaries) that track the behaviors of intimate partners over time have provided rich new information. Studies using these techniques will be emphasized in this chapter.

First, theoretical advances in the conceptualization of social support will be discussed. Based primarily on attachment theory, newer social support models propose that social support plays an important role both in times of insecurity (see chapter 28 in this volume)

The Wiley-Blackwell Handbook of Couples and Family Relationships, First Edition.
Edited by Patricia Noller and Gery C. Karantzas.

and in times of confident goal pursuit. Newer models of social support also highlight the importance of responsiveness, a key construct from attachment theory. Second, a selective review of recent empirical research on social support in intimate dyads will be discussed. In particular, a provocative series of studies using daily diary techniques will be described, in which "visible" social support from one's intimate partner (support that the recipient is aware of receiving) has an unexpected negative effect on mood. Attempts to understand this surprising pattern will be described. Third, the role of perceived partner responsiveness in the success of social support interactions will be considered, including findings from both daily diary and observational studies. As noted above, new theoretical work has posited a role for social support in times of both high and low stress. Recent research that highlights the benefits of social support in response to a partner's positive experiences will be described, again based on a combination of daily diary and observational research.

Fourth, recent research on factors that influence the emotional tone of support transactions will be reviewed, including strategies for facilitating change in a partner's unhealthy behavior, the importance of nondefensiveness when trying to elicit social support from one's partner, and the role of accurate empathy in the success of supportive transactions. Fifth, a summary of new research that highlights the importance of in-depth cognitive processing of social-support communications will be discussed. In the final section, clinical and theoretical implications of the research findings will be considered.

Conceptualizing Social Support

A new framework for conceptualizing the construct of social support comes from the work of attachment theorists. Prior definitions of social support have viewed support primarily as a resource in times of adversity. A recent re-conceptualization of social support argues for the importance of support in both high- and low-stress situations (Collins & Feeney, 2000; Feeney, 2004; Feeney & Thrush, 2010). This re-conceptualization involves two types of support: safe haven and secure base. Safe haven support is defined as comfort and assistance to another in times of stress or adversity (traditional social support). Secure base support is defined as support for the individual's autonomy and exploration when not distressed. Feeney and Collins have contributed the insight that support has an important role in promoting goal attainment and autonomous functioning when the individual is not under stress. Some very interesting new research, to be summarized later in the chapter, demonstrates the psychological importance of support for competence and achievement (Gable, Gonzaga, & Strachman, 2006; Gable, Reis, Impett, & Asher, 2004; chapter 13 in this volume).

Also building on attachment theory, Cutrona (1996, p. 10) defined social support as "acts that reflect responsiveness to another's needs." Responsive caregiving is viewed by attachment theorists as the cornerstone of the bond that grows between infant and caregiver in the earliest months of life, and shapes the child's beliefs about the essential goodness of both the self and others (Ainsworth, Blehar, Waters, & Wall, 1978; Bowlby, 1969; chapter 14 in this volume). In adult relationships, intimacy grows when individuals disclose important aspects of themselves, and these self-disclosures are met with understanding, validation, and caring (Reis and Shaver, 1988). Expectations that form the core of trust are those that focus on the partner's responsiveness to one's needs in situations of stress (Holmes & Rempel, 1989). Social support, attachment, intimacy, and trust are closely related through the common element of responsiveness. Recent research that highlights the importance of perceived responsiveness in social support will be summarized later in this chapter (Maisel & Gable, 2009).

Negative Effects of Social Support

For many years, social support researchers grappled with the seemingly contradictory findings that although positive mental health outcomes were consistently associated with the *perception* that social support would be available if needed, reports of *received* social support were not, and were sometimes associated with worse outcomes (Dunkel Schetter & Bennett, 1990; Wethington & Kessler, 1986). More precise event-recording methods, such as daily diaries, were a welcome methodological advance in the context of trying to understand this contradictory literature. Most notably, Bolger and colleagues conducted a series of daily-diary studies of couples in which one member of the couple faced the stress of preparing for the bar examination (e.g., Bolger et al., 2000; Gleason et al., 2008; Shrout, Herman, & Bolger, 2006). Each day for several weeks before the exam, the examinee and his or her partner recorded whether or not they had provided and/or received support from the other. Daily ratings of mood were also collected. An unexpected but consistent finding across studies was that when examinees reported that they had received social support from their partner on a given day (termed "visible support" because the recipient was aware of having received it), their mood was worse the following day. By contrast, on days when partners reported that they had provided support to the examinee but the examinee did not notice this support (termed "invisible support"), the examinee's mood improved the following day (Bolger et al., 2000). The negative impact on mood of visible support was replicated, both by Bolger and associates (Gleason, Iida, Bolger, & Shrout, 2003; Gleason et al., 2008; Iida, Seidman, Shrout, Fujita, & Bolger, 2008) and by researchers outside of his group (Maisel & Gable, 2009).

A number of possible explanations for the negative impact of perceiving that one has been the recipient of a supportive act were proposed by Bolger and colleagues (2000). Receiving support may be interpreted as a threat to one's competence and may therefore damage self-esteem. In addition, receiving support may heighten awareness that others have noticed one's distress, which may lead to a loss of face. Interestingly, on days when both members of the couple provided support to the other, no negative effects of receiving support were observed (Gleason et al., 2003). It seems that receiving support places a person in a "one down" position that is not experienced if both individuals offer and receive support.

Support may also re-focus one's attention on the threatening situation and lead to increased rumination and heightened distress. By contrast, when support is provided but not encoded as such by the recipient, cognitions that question one's competence are probably not triggered and attention is not drawn to one's own distress.

To better understand the effects of visible support, Bolger and Amarel (2007) conducted an experimental study in which participants were randomly assigned to receive no support, visible support with negative implications for the recipient's efficacy, and visible support without negative implications for the recipient's efficacy. Results showed that changes in the support recipient's mood were a function of implied lack of efficacy. Visible support that had no negative message about the recipient's efficacy did not damage mood or self-esteem. Only visible support that called the recipient's competence into question led to negative changes in mood. One mechanism through which social support has negative effects on morale is clearly through implied challenges to competence.

Feeney and Collins theorize that social support has value as a "safe haven" in times of need and a "secure base" in times of self-confident goal pursuit (Collins & Feeney, 2000; Feeney, 2004; Feeney & Thrush, 2010). It may be that individuals preparing for the bar exam reacted negatively to the support they received because they perceived it to be the wrong type: instead of emphasizing their competence as they pursued a valued achievement goal (secure base support), the support they received may have addressed their fear of failure (safe haven support). Because both elements (confident goal striving and intimidation) were undoubtedly present, it may not have been possible for partners to satisfy the complex and even contradictory needs of the aspiring lawyers as they prepared for the most important examination of their careers.

Simultaneous negative and positive effects of support

People have complex sets of needs and preferences. It is possible that a single supportive act may satisfy one's need for safe haven support but violate one's need for secure base support. A pattern of results consistent with this potential outcome emerged in work by Gleason and colleagues (2008), who replicated the negative association between visible support and mood using the same methodology as Bolger and colleagues (2000). However, they also found a significant *positive* association between visible support and next-day ratings of closeness/intimacy with the spouse. The same behavior (visible support) showed a negative influence in one domain (mood) but a positive influence in another domain (relationship quality). Although the partner's attempts to provide support damaged the individual's mood, perhaps by suggesting weakness or incompetence, the same actions also reassured the individual that the partner was available and caring. The need for perceived autonomy was violated, but the need for comfort, or safe haven was met. Clearly, the mechanisms through which social support affects well-being are complex. Some complicated algorithm may determine the ultimate health consequences of "mixed" outcomes of social support, such as damaged pride plus enhanced relationship closeness. This area merits further research attention.

Responsiveness and Social Support

Responsiveness to another's needs is central to at least one definition of social support (Cutrona, 1996). Several studies have addressed the role of responsiveness in social support. Another replication of Bolger's daily-diary study was conducted to test the hypothesis that partner responsiveness determined the impact of visible and invisible support on mood (Maisel & Gable, 2009). Instead of a homogeneous sample of couples with one member preparing for the bar exam, a community sample of couples facing a range of individual stressors was recruited. The impact of support on mood and relationship quality was assessed. In addition, participants made daily ratings of their partner's responsiveness. Responsiveness was defined as the extent to which one's partner showed understanding, validation, and caring (Reis, Clark, & Holmes, 2004). The authors hypothesized that daily evaluations of the partner's responsiveness would moderate the impact of visible and invisible support on mood, such that when the partner was viewed as highly responsive, visible support would not have a negative effect. By contrast, when the partner was viewed as unresponsive, even invisible support would not be beneficial.

Results were highly consistent with the predictions. On days when the partner was viewed as responsive (above the sample median on responsiveness ratings), visible support was not associated with lower mood the next day. Furthermore, on high-responsive days visible support was associated with increased relationship quality (connectedness and security). On low-responsive days, invisible support had no beneficial effect on mood and was associated with diminished relationship quality. The greatest declines in mood and relationship quality were seen on days when both partners reported low responsiveness. Thus, even visible support, with its potential to damage self-esteem, was not harmful when the partner was viewed as responsive.

Of course, the findings do not provide insight into the determinants of perceiving one's partner as responsive. It is not clear whether the content of supportive acts was different on days viewed as responsive versus nonresponsive, or whether the same type of support was offered, but in a manner that differed in sensitivity of delivery. It is also possible that the receptivity or mood of the support recipient differed across days rated as high versus low on partner responsiveness, thus altering evaluations of partner responsiveness. Clearly, more research is needed on the components of perceived responsiveness. Observational studies that attempted to identify the behavioral correlates of perceived partner responsiveness are described below.

Behavioral correlates of perceived partner responsiveness

Collins and Feeney (2000) conducted an observational investigation to capture responsiveness in a study of support processes in married couples. The observational measures of responsiveness, applied by trained research assistants, included attentive listening, communication of understanding, and support effort (the extent to which the support provider was actively engaged in the interaction). At the end of the interaction, participants rated how supportive their partner had been during the interaction. Raters' scores on responsiveness significantly predicted perceived partner supportiveness during the interaction. In another observational study (Cutrona, Shaffer, Wesner, & Gardner, 2007), responsiveness was defined as interaction sequences in which the support seeker was provided with emotional support following the expression of emotions, or sequences in which he or she was provided with informational support following a request for advice. As expected, such "matching" sequences (where support seekers were actually provided with the type of support they were seeking) were experienced as responsive.

These observational studies of responsiveness suggest that both the content of support communications (e.g., understanding, providing the desired type of support) and the manner in which supportive communications are delivered (with attentiveness and apparent interest) contribute to perceptions of responsiveness. More research that examines the association between responsiveness and perceived support is needed.

Social Support in the Context of Positive Events

We do not expect our partners to respond to us only in times of stress, we also expect them to celebrate our pleasures, accomplishments, and triumphs. In an innovative program of research, Gable and colleagues have demonstrated the importance of supportive reactions to positive events (Gable et al., 2006; Gable et al., 2004). The process of informing another person about a positive personal event and deriving an additional emotional lift from the other's reaction is called *capitalization* (Langston, 1994). In a daily-diary study, results showed that on days when individuals shared a positive event with another person, they experienced more positive affect and life satisfaction than on days when a positive event occurred but they did not tell anyone (Gable et al., 2004). The effects of sharing exceeded those produced by the pleasant event alone. An enthusiastic response to a positive event by another person communicates important information: that is, that the responder understands the significance of the event, takes an interest in the discloser's experiences, and derives pleasure from the discloser's positive personal events (Langston, 1994).

In an observational study of dating couples, Gable and colleagues (2006) asked participants to take turns sharing a positive personal event and a negative personal event. After they shared their events, they rated their partner's responsiveness (how understood, validated, and cared for he or she made them feel). The more active and constructive the partner's reaction to their disclosure of a positive event, the more highly they rated the partner's responsiveness. Furthermore, in a later follow-up, the quality of their relationship was predicted by how responsive the partner had been following disclosure of the positive event, but not following disclosure of the negative event. The importance of an intimate partner's reaction to positive events is consistent with Feeney's (2004) belief that a valuable function of social support is to foster autonomous functioning and goal pursuit, which are exemplified by celebrating a partner's success.

The Potential for Conflict in Social Support Transactions

Social control as a component of social support

Models of social support include some components that do not necessarily foster perceptions of responsiveness or intimacy. One such component is *information support* or *guidance*, which refers to advice on how to think, feel, or behave with respect to a problem situation. Advice is not always welcome (Cutrona & Suhr, 1992). However, a common dilemma faced by couples is what to do when their partner is engaging in behaviors that endanger his or her health. Research on efforts to induce behavior change in an intimate partner ("social control") has yielded mixed results (Gallant, 2003; Lewis & Butterfield, 2007; Lewis & Rook, 1999; Tucker & Anders 2001; chapter 16 in this volume). Two important developments in this area are worthy of note. First, and not surprisingly, different methods of social control are differentially effective (Lewis & Butterfield, 2007; Lewis & Rook, 1999). Studies have shown that negative social-control tactics such as guilt induction are not associated with behavior change and tend to increase partner distress. Positive tactics, such as reinforcing behavior change are associated with positive change and are less likely to increase distress. Direct tactics (addressing the issue candidly) are more effective than indirect tactics (hinting) and bilateral tactics (bargaining and working together) are more successful than unilateral strategies (nagging or withdrawing affection; see chapter 16 in this volume).

Second, accurately gauging the partner's degree of readiness for change is important (Sullivan, Pasch, Bejanyan, & Hanson, in press). When individuals accurately assess the degree to which their partner is ready to change and tailor their approach accordingly, outcomes are more positive. When individuals ignore their partner's lack of readiness to change, less positive behavior change occurs. Once again, responsiveness seems to play a role in the effectiveness of social support, even support that is somewhat coercive in intent. Responsiveness to the partner's need for autonomy and to his or her readiness to change are both key factors in the ultimate success of attempts to change a partner's health-related behaviors.

Emotion regulation in support transactions

A very interesting innovation in social support research emphasizes factors that promote healthy emotion regulation in social-support transactions (Fruzzetti & Iverson, 2006; Fruzzetti, Shenk, & Hoffman, 2005). When emotional arousal becomes intense, people are not able to effectively solve problems, communicate, or complete complex tasks. According to Fruzzetti's transactional model, the support seeker is most successful in preventing emotion dysregulation (overly intense negative affect) if he or she can engage in *accurate expression* of his or her emotions, thoughts, and/or desires, without interpretation (extensive analysis) or judgment (assigning blame).

Furthermore, it is best if the support seeker expresses "primary emotions" rather than "secondary emotions." Primary emotions, such as sadness or fear, are defined as universal and adaptive emotional responses (Greenberg & Safran, 1989). By contrast, secondary emotions are learned, mediated by cognitions, and often defensive. When expressed, they have the effect of distancing and alienating the other person. An example is disappointment (e.g., over a forgotten birthday) that is expressed as anger or resentment. The expression of a primary emotion such as disappointment makes it easier for the support provider to respond with validation (communication of understanding and acceptance; Fruzzetti & Iverson, 2006). A validating or responsive communication keeps emotional arousal low, which helps individuals stay focused and process information.

By contrast, inaccurate expression of emotions and the expression of secondary emotions prevent the support provider from understanding the support seeker's real concerns, thus precluding a response that communicates genuine understanding and acceptance. Invalidating responses by the support provider (arguing, criticizing) are likely, and a cycle of mutual invalidation and escalating emotional intensity are the result (Fruzzetti & Iverson, 2006). Evidence for the validity of their approach comes from an intervention study with couples that focused on increasing accurate expression and validating responses (Fruzzetti & Mosco, 2009). The intervention was successful in decreasing both individual and relationship distress.

Negative behaviors in the context of seeking support from one's partner are not uncommon (Pasch & Bradbury, 1998). Furthermore, such behaviors are robust predictors of deterioration in marital satisfaction and stability (Pasch & Bradbury, 1998; Sullivan, Pasch, Johnson, & Bradbury, 2010). Sullivan and colleagues found that, among newlywed couples, negative behavior during laboratory social-support interactions predicted an increase 1 year later in negative affect displayed during conflict interactions, which in turn, predicted deterioration of marital satisfaction and relationship dissolution over a 10-year period. Thus, it appears especially important to contain the level of negative emotion displayed during social-support interactions.

Empathic accuracy in support interactions

A support provider's level of empathic accuracy, his or her capacity to correctly infer the support seeker's thoughts and feelings, should contribute to the probability of providing effective support to his or her partner (Verhofstadt, Buysse, Ickes, De Clercq, & Peene, 2005). The more complete and accurate the support provider's understanding of the partner's internal states, the more responsive his or her support should be. To test this prediction, an observational study was conducted in which married couples were asked to discuss a salient personal problem with their partner and then to individually review the videotaped interaction (Verhofstadt et al., 2005). The tape was periodically stopped and individuals were asked to report the content of their own and what they believed to be their spouse's unexpressed thoughts and feelings. Results showed that level of empathic accuracy (correspondence between the inferred and actual thoughts and feelings of the partner) correlated positively with the amount of instrumental social support and negatively with negative behavior displayed toward the partner. Surprisingly, empathic accuracy did not predict the level of emotional support provided to the partner. Emotional support provision was predicted only by the support giver's level of emotional matching with the support recipient (i.e., the degree to which the two spouses reported similar emotional experiences; Verhofstadt, Buysse, Ickes, Davis, & Devoldre, 2008). The provision of emotional support may depend more on the extent to which support providers react emotionally to their spouse's distress (empathic arousal) than on their ability to accurately infer the content of their partner's thoughts and feelings.

Responsive Interactions and Cognitive Processing of Support Messages

An innovative theoretical framework designed to explain the differential impact of social-support messages was proposed by Burleson (2009). Burleson argues for a dual-process model in which the benefits derived from supportive interactions vary as a function of the content of the supportive message and the degree of scrutiny or cognitive processing that people devote to the support message.

Burleson's earlier work (1994) identified characteristics of high-quality emotional-support messages. In brief, high-quality emotional-support messages (termed "high person-centered") are highly responsive, in that such messages acknowledge and legitimize the feelings and perspective of the recipient and encourage the recipient to explore and make sense of one's emotions.

The quality of the support communication alone does not guarantee that the recipient will benefit from it. The second requirement in Burleson's model is that the support message receives substantial cognitive processing if it is to have a lasting impact on adjustment (Burleson, 2009). A range of factors determine the extent to which such scrutiny occurs, including the recipient's ability and motivation to process the message (Petty, Rucker, Bizer, & Cacioppo, 2004). If the recipient is not able or motivated to systematically process the message, other less relevant elements of the situation will dominate his or her attention and the support communication will have little impact.

Burleson and his colleagues tested the predictions that responses to supportive messages vary as a joint function of cognitive-processing ability and motivation and that the way those messages are processed (thoughtfully vs. superficially) affects reactions to support communications. In a study of bereaved elderly individuals, participants were asked to answer a brief questionnaire about their loss and the degree of upset they experienced (Burleson, Bodie, Rack, Holmstrom, Hanasono, & Gill, 2007). The participants also completed a measure of cognitive complexity (the tendency to process information in depth). Participants were next asked to evaluate the helpfulness of a set of messages used by helpers to comfort the bereaved. These messages varied in their level of person-centeredness. Results showed that people who were most able (i.e., cognitively complex) and who were moderately distressed discriminated most accurately between good- and poor-quality support messages. Those who experienced extreme distress were not able to adequately focus their attention to discriminate accurately.

Severe consequences can occur when intimate partners do not facilitate opportunities to process stressors. Studies have demonstrated that when cancer patients perceive their close associates to be unreceptive or uncomfortable discussing their illness, the patients experience higher psychological distress (Lepore, Ragan, & Jones, 2000; Manne, Ostroff, & Winkel, 2007). Closing off communication increases the use of avoidant coping by the patient, which in turn, is associated with heightened distress (Manne, Pape, Taylor, & Dougherty, 1999). In an observational study of breast-cancer patients and their spouses, a particularly distressing sequence consisted of an emotional disclosure by the patient, followed by a nonresponsive reaction by the spouse. These sequences were found to predict both patient distress and deterioration in patient-rated marital satisfaction (Manne, Ostroff, Rini, Fox, Goldstein, & Grana, 2004).

Implications for Couple Interventions

Individuals who seek marital counseling may be disappointed with the social support they receive from their partner. It is possible that they have experienced the same drop in mood following their partner's support attempts as reported by Bolger and colleagues (Bolger et al., 2000). It is also possible that their partner has noticed that his or her support attempts have not been effective in alleviating distress, leading to frustration and feelings of inadequacy. Support providers face a significant challenge in gauging their partner's needs. Sometimes, facilitating autonomy is more important than providing nurturance. Accurate empathy, an important skill in assessing a partner's needs, develops as a function of open conversations about the types of support that partners find most helpful and trial-and-error attempts at providing support (Cutrona, 1996). Such conversations and experiments with different kinds of supportive responses can be facilitated by marital therapists.

Support that is delivered in a responsive manner is more likely to enhance the relationship and less likely to damage self-esteem. Conditions that increase the probability of a responsive exchange were identified by several researchers. These conditions can be discussed by marital therapists, and associated skills can be practiced during sessions. For example, a responsive exchange is more likely if emotion dysregulation can be prevented. Appropriate emotion regulation is more likely if disclosures of current difficulties can be made in a way that is not defensive or accusatory. Empathic accuracy on the part of the support provider also promotes affect regulation. Empathic accuracy is not something inborn, but grounded in attentiveness and effort. Individuals may not realize the importance of communicating understanding, validation, and caring, but may rush to problem-solve. Such tendencies can be identified by marital therapists, who may coach ongoing "rehearsals" of support transactions. Without a responsive reaction from the support provider, the support seeker may be unable to process his or her own feelings, thoughts, and behavioral options. The therapist can query individuals about their emotions in reaction to their partner's various support behaviors, to help individuals discover the kinds of communications that make them feel safe enough to engage in self-exploration. As noted by Burleson (2009), the support seeker may not be able to process even very high-quality support if circumstances are not conducive to safe personal exploration.

Couples may not realize the importance of celebrating each other's triumphs and successes. How an intimate partner responds to the revelation of "good news" conveys important information. Sharing positive events and enjoying them together is beneficial to both the discloser and the recipient of the good news. Marital therapists can emphasize the importance of communicating pleasure in their partner's positive experiences. Because such exchanges may be less emotionally charged than discussions of personal disappointments and fears, discussions of positive events may provide a good starting point for practicing effective social support. Of course, individuals may harbor jealousy about their partner's success, especially if their partner's success is in an area of endeavor that is important to the individual's own self-esteem (Tesser, Illar, & Moore, 1988). These issues can be dealt with in marital therapy, and perhaps rendered less problematic.

Furthermore, there are situations in which competing needs must be prioritized. The health needs of a partner who is experiencing the symptoms of a heart attack must be prioritized as more important than that partner's need for autonomy if she/he resists seeking medical care. However, the intimacy of the relationship may suffer as a result. Therapists can help couples understand the blows to autonomy that they sometimes must inflict upon each other and introduce the importance of discussing such occasions. Open discussions, in which individuals give voice to the reasons for their behavior, can build empathy and lead to forgiveness (Fincham, Paleari, & Regalia, 2002).

Implications for Future Research

The mystery of how to build the perception that one's intimate partner is a reliable source of social support has not been solved. Longitudinal studies of couples are needed in which observed support, support reported in daily diaries, and perceived support measures are obtained repeatedly over time to understand the developmental course of social support in couples. Support cannot be analyzed in isolation, however. As noted by Sullivan et al. (2010), social support disappointments can poison other aspects of a relationship. However, social support that persists through difficult times can build commitment and trust (Cutrona, Russell, & Gardner, 2005). Its ebb and flow must be considered in the context of the stressors faced by the couple, their problem-solving skills, the quality of their sexual relationship, their ability to enjoy each other's company, their relationships with other people, and their individual personalities, attachment styles, and relationship histories.

More research is needed on the mechanisms through which supportive acts foster positive outcomes. When social support has mixed consequences, such as bolstering intimacy but damaging efficacy, research is needed on their joint influences on health and whether the physiological mechanisms through which they influence health are the same or different. A better understanding is needed of the mechanisms through which systematic cognitive processing of support messages leads to positive outcomes. A significant body of work shows that perceived spousal support predicts adaptive coping behavior and multiplies the benefits of good coping (DeLongis & Holtzman, 2005; chapter 28 in this volume). It may be that emotion regulation enables people to engage in systematic processing that helps them distinguish between adaptive and maladaptive coping strategies and make rational choices about the strategies to adopt.

Many questions remain. However, insights gained from observing intimate partners and asking them to report on the ordinary events of their lives as they unfold hold boundless potential in the quest to understand the magic of perceiving another as responsive to our needs and supportive of our efforts to cope with good times and bad.

References

Ainsworth, M. D. S., Blehar, M. C., Waters, E., & Wall, S. (1978). *Patterns of attachment: A psychological study of the Strange Situation*. Hillsdale, NJ: Erlbaum.

Bolger, N., & Amarel, D. (2007). Effects of social support visibililty on adjustment to stress: Experimental evidence. *Journal of Personality and Social Psychology, 92*(3), 458–475.

Bolger, N., Zuckerman, A., & Kessler, R. C. (2000). Invisible support and adjustment to stress. *Journal of Personality and Social Psychology, 79*, 953–961.

Bowlby, J. (1969). *Attachment and loss* (Vol. 1) New York: Basic Books.

Burleson, B. R. (1994). Comforting messages: Significance, approaches, and effects. In B. R. Burleson, T. L. Albrecht, & I. G. Sarason (Eds.), *Communication and social support* (pp. 3–28). Thousand Oaks, CA: Sage.

Burleson, B. R. (2009). Understanding the outcomes of supportive communication: A dual-process approach. *Journal of Social and Personal Relationships 26*, 21–38.

Burleson, B. R., Bodie, G. D., Rack, J. J., Holmstrom, A. J., Hanasono, L., & Gill, J. N. (2007). *Good grief: Testing a dual-process model of responses to grief-management messages.* Paper presented at the annual meeting of the National Communication Association. Chicago.

Cassell, J. (1976). The contribution of the social environment to host resistance. *American Journal of Epidemiology, 104*, 107–123.

Collins, N. L., & Feeney, B. C. (2000). A safe haven: An attachment theory perspective on support seeking and caregiving in intimate relationships. *Journal of Personality and Social Psychology, 78*, 1053–1073.

Cutrona, C. E. (1996). *Social support in couples—Marriage as a resource in times of stress.* Thousand Oaks, CA: Sage.

Cutrona, C. E., Russell, D.W., & Gardner, K. A. (2005). The relationship enhancement model of social support. In K. Kayser, G. Bodenman, & T. Revenson (Eds.), *Couples coping with stress: Emerging perspectives on dyadic coping* (pp. 73–95). Washington, DC: American Psychological Association.

Cutrona, C. E., Shaffer, P. A., Wesner, K. A., & Gardner, K. A. (2007). Optimally matching support and perceived spousal sensitivity. *Journal of Family Psychology, 21*, 754–758.

Cutrona, C. E., & Suhr, J. A. (1992). Controllability of stressful events and satisfaction with spouse support behaviors. *Communication Research, 19*, 154–174.

DeLongis, A., & Holtzman, S. (2005). Coping in context: The role of stress, social support, and personality in coping. *Journal of Personality [Special issue: Advances in Personality and Daily Experience] 73*, 1633–1656.

Dunkel Schetter, C., & Bennett, T. L. (1990). Differentiating the cognitive and behavioral aspects of social support. In B. R. Sarason, I. G. Sarason, & G. R. Pierce (Eds.), *Social support: An interactional view* (pp. 267–296). New York: Wiley.

Feeney, B. C. (2004). A secure base: Responsive support of goal strivings and exploration in adult intimate relationships. *Journal of Personality and Social Psychology, 87*, 631–648.

Feeney, B. C., & Thrush, R. L. (2010). Relationship influences on exploration in adulthood: The characteristics and function of a secure base. *Journal of Personality and Social Psychology, 98*(1), 57–76.

Fincham, F. D., Paleari, F. G., & Regalia, C. (2002). Forgiveness in marriage: The role of relationship quality, attributions, and empathy. *Personal Relationships, 9*, 27–37.

Fruzzetti, A. E., & Iverson, K. M. (2006). Intervening with couples and families to treat emotion dysregulation and psychopathology. In D. K. Snyder, J. Simpson, & J. N. Hughes (Eds.), *Emotion regulation in couples and families: Pathways to dysfunction and health* (pp. 249–267). Washington, DC: American Psychological Association.

Fruzzetti, A. E., & Mosco, E. (2009). *Dialectical behavior therapy adapted for couples and families: A pilot group intervention for couples.* Reno: University of Nevada.

Fruzzetti, A. E., Shenk, C., & Hoffman, P. D. (2005). Family interaction and the development of borderline personality disorder: A transactional mode. *Development and Psychopathology, 17*(4), 1007–1030.

Gable, S. L., Gonzaga, G., & Strachman, A. (2006). Will you be there for me when things go right? Social support for positive events. *Journal of Personality and Social Psychology, 91*, 904–917.
Gable, S. L., Reis, H. T., Impett, E. A., & Asher, E. R. (2004). What do you do when things go right? The intrapersonal and interpersonal benefits of sharing positive events. *Journal of Personality and Social Psychology, 87*, 228–245.
Gallant, M. P. (2003). The influence of social support on chronic illness self-management: A review and directions for research. *Health Education and Behavior, 30*(2), 170–195.
Gleason, M. E. J., Iida, M., Bolger, N., & Shrout, P. E. (2003). Daily supportive equity in close relationships. *Personality and Social Psychology Bulletin, 29*, 1036–1045.
Gleason, M. E. J., Iida, M., & Shrout, P. E. (2008). Receiving support as a mixed blessing: Evidence for dual effects of support on psychological outcomes. *Journal of Personality and Social Psychology, 94*, 824–838.
Greenberg, L. S., & Safran, J. D. (1989). Emotion in psychotherapy. *American Psychologist, 44*, 19–29.
Holmes, J. G., & Rempel, J. K. (1989). Trust in close relationships. In C. Hendrick (Ed.), *Close relationships* (pp. 187–221). Newbury Park, CA: Sage.
Iida, M., Seidman, G., Shrout, P. E., Fujita, K., & Bolger, N. (2008). Modeling support provision in intimate relationships. *Journal of Personality and Social Psychology, 94*, 460–478.
Langston, C. A. (1994). Capitalizing on and coping with daily-life events: Expressive responses to positive events. *Journal of Personality and Social Psychology, 67*, 1112–1125.
Lepore, S. J., Ragan, J. D., & Jones, S. (2000). Talking facilitates cognitive-emotional processes of adaptation to an acute stressor. *Journal of Personality and Social Psychology, 78*, 499–508.
Lewis, M. A., & Butterfield, R. M. (2007). Social control in marital relationships: Effect of one's partner on health behaviors. *Journal of Applied Social Psychology, 37*, 298–318.
Lewis, M. A., & Rook, K. S. (1999). Social control in personal relationships: Impact on health behaviors and psychosocial distress. *Health Psychology, 18*, 63–71.
Maisel, N. C., & Gable, S. L. (2009). The paradox of received social support: The importance of responsiveness. *Psychological Science, 20*(8), 928–932.
Manne, S., Ostroff, J., Rini, C., Fox, K., Goldstein, L., & Grana, G. (2004). The interpersonal process model of intimacy: The role of self-disclosure, partner disclosure and partner responsiveness in interactions between breast cancer patients and their partners. *Journal of Family Psychology, 18*, 589–599.
Manne, S., Ostroff, J. S., & Winkel, G. (2007). Social-cognitive processes as moderators of a couple-focused group intervention for women with early stage breast cancer. *Health Psychology, 26*, 735–744.
Manne, S., Pape, S., Taylor, K., & Dougherty, J. (1999). Spouse support, coping and mood among individuals with cancer. *Annals of Behavorial Medicine, 21*, 111–121.
Pasch, L. A., & Bradbury, T. N. (1998). Social support, conflict, and the development of marital dysfunction. *Journal of Consulting and Clinical Psychology, 66*, 219–230.
Petty, R. E., Rucker, D. D., Bizer, G. Y., & Cacioppo, J. T. (2004). The elaboration likelihood model of persuasion. In J. S. Seiter & R. H. Gass (Eds.), *Perspectives on persuasion, social influence, and compliance gaining* (pp. 65–89). Boston: Allyn & Bacon.
Reis, H. T., Clark, M. S., & Holmes, J. G. (2004). Perceived partner responsiveness as an organizing construct. In D. J. Mashek & A. Aron (Eds.), *Handbook of closeness and intimacy* (pp. 201–225). Mahwah, NJ: Erlbaum.
Reis, H. T., & Shaver, P. (1988). Intimacy as an interpersonal process. In S. Duck (Ed.), *Handbook of personal relationships* (pp. 367–389). Chichester, England: Wiley.

Sarason, I. G., & Sarason, B. R. (2009). Social support: Mapping the construct. *Journal of Social and Personal Relationships, 26,* 113–120.

Shrout, P. E., Herman, C., & Bolger, N. (2006). The costs and benefits of practical and emotional support on adjustment: A daily diary study of couples experiencing acute stress. *Personal Relationships, 13,* 115–134.

Sullivan, K. T., Pasch, L. A., Bejanyan, K., & Hanson, K. (in press). Social support, social control, and health behavior change in spouses. In K. Sullivan & J. Davila (Eds.), *Support processes in intimate relationships*. New York: Oxford University Press.

Sullivan, K. T., Pasch, L. A., Johnson, M. D., & Bradbury, T. N. (2010). Social support, problem solving, and the longitudinal course of newlywed marriage. *Journal of Personality and Social Psychology, 98,* 631–644.

Tesser, A., Illar, M., & Moore, J. (1988). Some affective consequences of social comparison and reflection processes: The pain and pleasure of being close. *Journal of Personality and Social Psychology, 54,* 49–61.

Tucker, J. S., & Anders, S. L. (2001). Social control of health behaviors in marriage. *Journal of Applied Social Psychology, 31,* 467–485.

Vangelisti, A. L. (2009). Challenges in conceptualizing social support. *Journal of Social and Personal Relationships, 26,* 39–51.

Verhofstadt, L. L., Buysse, A., Ickes, W., Davis, M., & Devoldre, I. (2008). Social support in marriage: The role of emotional linkage and empathic accuracy. *Emotion, 8*(6), 792–802.

Verhofstadt, L. L., Buysse, A., Ickes, W., De Clercq, A., & Peene, O. (2005). Conflict and support interactions in marriage: An analysis of couples' interactive behavior and online cognition. *Personal Relationships, 12,* 23–42.

Wethington, E., & Kessler, R. C. (1986). Perceived support, received support, and adjustment to stressful life events. *Journal of Health and Social Behavior, 27,* 78–89.

28

Chronic Illness and Relationships

Mental Health Outcomes

Gery C. Karantzas, Marita P. McCabe, and Sian F. Cole

Chronic illness is a significant economic and social health problem across both developed and developing countries (World Health Organization, 2005). According to DeVol et al. (2007), over 50% of people living in the United States experience a chronic illness. Similarly, a recent Australian health survey found that well over half of the Australian population has at least one chronic health condition (Australian Institute of Health and Welfare [AIHW], 2005). Policy analysts estimate that chronic health conditions cost the United States in excess of $1 trillion a year (DeVol et al., 2007), while in Australia, 57% of the national health care budget is spent on supporting chronic illness sufferers (AIHW, 2010)—approximately 10% of gross domestic product—a trend reported across many developed countries (Organization for Economic Cooperation and Development, 2010).

In addition to the emphasis placed on the economic costs of chronic illness, research has investigated the physical health problems and the comorbidities associated with chronic illnesses as a means of tailoring the medical treatment of chronic illness sufferers (e.g., Fried, Ferrucci, Darer, Williamson, & Anderson, 2004; Starfield, Lemke, Bernhardt, Foldes, Forrest, & Weiner, 2003). However, while the economic and the physical impacts of illness are significant, chronic illness also influences the *mental health* of sufferers and their *relationships* with those around them. For instance, in Australia, nearly 50% of individuals experiencing a chronic illness also experience depression or anxiety—a rate that is double that of the general population (AIHW, 2005). In the United States between 25%

The Wiley-Blackwell Handbook of Couples and Family Relationships, First Edition.
Edited by Patricia Noller and Gery C. Karantzas.

and 40% of chronic illness sufferers report experiencing depression, let alone other forms of affective disorders (Davis & Gershtein, 2003).

Research suggests a reciprocal relationship between chronic illness and mental health. For instance, some studies have demonstrated that having a physical illness is one of the strongest risk factors for depression (e.g., Karantzas, McCabe, & Cole, 2010; Wilhelm et al., 2003) and other studies show that affective disorders such as depression are a risk factor for physical illness (Wulsin, Vaillant, & Wells, 1999; Zautra et al., 2004). Despite these associations, numerous studies highlight that chronic illness alone does not account for psychological well-being (e.g., Doeglas et al., 2004; Sherbourne, Meredith, Rogers, & Ware, 1992). The capacity for people with chronic illness to receive support in dealing with their illness has been argued as an important variable in shaping the mental health outcomes of chronic illness sufferers (e.g., Doeglas et al., 2004; Pennix, Van Tilburg, Deeg, Kreigsman, Boeke, & Van Eijk, 1997).

A number of studies have found that social support has direct, mediated, and moderated effects on the relationship between chronic illness and mental health outcomes (e.g., Pennix et al., 1997). Some studies have found that social support leads to positive mental health outcomes while other studies have found that social support increases negative outcomes such as depression, anxiety, poor mood, and low self-esteem (Newsom & Schultz, 1998; chapter 27 in this volume). While the type and manner in which support is provided is argued as a factor that may explain these inconsistent findings (for a review see chapter 27 in this volume), others argue that these mixed findings can be explained by assessing the quality of the relationship between the person experiencing the chronic illness and members of their familial and broader social network (Karantzas & Cole, in press; Maunder & Hunter, 2001; Newsom, 1999).

In this chapter, we discuss our research program which has examined the role of close relationships and social support in predicting the mental health and relationship outcomes for people experiencing chronic illness. Our research program has included people suffering a diverse array of chronic illnesses such as arthritis, motor neurone disease (MND), multiple sclerosis (MS), Huntington's disease (HD), and Parkinson's disease (PD). We begin by describing our research investigating the relationship experiences of sufferers of chronic illness. We then describe studies in which we have examined how the quality of close personal relationships influences the type and degree of social support sought by sufferers of chronic illness. We also report on our research investigating the effects of relationship quality and social support on the mental health outcomes of people experiencing chronic disease. Finally, we discuss the implications of our research for tailoring the support services and therapy provided to people experiencing chronic illness and their carers.

Relationship Experiences of Sufferers from Chronic Illness

Studies have repeatedly investigated how normative life transitions such as marriage, parenthood, even retirement impact on relationship outcomes (e.g., Huston, Caughlin, Houts, Smith, & George, 2001; Wang, 2007; chapters 7, 26 in this volume).

In comparison, however, fewer studies have examined the impact of chronic illness on the relationship experiences of sufferers from chronic illness.

To address this particular gap in the research, McCabe and McDonald (2007) conducted a dyadic study of relationship and sexual satisfaction comparing two groups of couples—one group consisted of a partner diagnosed with MS and the other group comprised healthy couples. Findings revealed that couples with a partner experiencing MS reported greater sexual dysfunction, but similar levels of sexual satisfaction to healthy couples. While MS sufferers and their partners experienced difficulties with the act of sex due to the physical aspects of the illness (e.g., twitching, slowing of movement), they were able to find means to compensate for these challenges and maintain sexually satisfying relationships. However, further analyses of the chronic illness group revealed that partners of MS sufferers reported significantly lower receipt of physical and emotional support than the MS sufferers themselves. While the difference in the receipt of physical support was expected, it is concerning that partners of MS sufferers, who usually are the primary carers, felt that they received less emotional support than their partners. These findings indicate that while chronic illness may not affect some aspects of relationship functioning for sufferers, there is no guarantee that partners won't experience negative relationship outcomes. McCabe and McDonald's findings highlight that chronic illness is very much a condition that can affect both partners.

In another study on relationship and sexual satisfaction, O'Connor, McCabe, and Firth (2008) found that both sexual and relationship satisfaction differed across various neurological illnesses. Specifically, people with HD and their carers experienced significantly lower relationship and sexual satisfaction compared to people diagnosed with MND, MS, and PD. The finding that HD sufferers and their carers fared worse compared to all other groups is not unexpected. The nature of HD is such that cognitive impairments and changes to personality often accompany the illness (Quarrell, 2004). In turn, these psychological changes can significantly affect the relationship dynamics between partners. In addition, relationships can be strained by relationship conflict, which can occur between partners resulting from the probability of existing or future children inheriting the illness (O'Connor et al.).

Furthermore, O'Connor et al. (2008) found that the psychological symptoms associated with MND such as anxiety significantly reduced the marital satisfaction of MND sufferers and their partners. We argue that the generalized anxiety associated with MND influences relationship satisfaction in two ways. Firstly, MND heightens sufferers' sensitivity to minor relationship issues resulting in the exacerbation of problems and secondly, the feelings of worry increase the attention given to the illness by MND sufferers and partners, and this focus reduces the couple's attention to engage in acts that maintain satisfaction in the relationship.

While McCabe and colleagues have attempted to address the gap in knowledge regarding the relationship experiences of middle-aged adults suffering from a chronic illness, even fewer studies have researched how young adults with a chronic illness experience relationships. We, like Packham and Hall (2002), argue that chronic illness presents many challenges (such as fatigue and reduced mobility) that add to the challenges that young adults experience in navigating the developmental task of forming romantic relationships. Druley, Stephens, and Coyne (1997) contend that young adults who experience a chronic illness may distance themselves from relationship partners, or give up pursuing relationships altogether, in order not to be a burden on others or to minimize a partner's worry about their illness. We argue that a chronic illness may interrupt young adults' normative development in forming adult romantic relationships. This situation in turn may mitigate the development of skills in managing relationships and the development of identity (Jacobson et al., 1997; Karantzas & Cole, in press; Kennedy, Sloman, Douglass, & Sawyer, 2007).

In response to this dearth of research on the close personal relationships of young adults with a chronic illness, Cole and Karantzas (2006) conducted a study comparing the romantic relationship experiences of young adults with arthritis with those of healthy young adults. Our research revealed that arthritic young adults reported significantly higher attachment insecurity and significantly lower relationship satisfaction than healthy young adults. Specifically, when examining attachment style differences between the two groups (from both a categorical and dimensional approach), we found that over 75% of young adults experiencing arthritis were categorized as either having a preoccupied or fearful attachment style. Consistent with this result, young adults with arthritis reported significantly higher attachment anxiety and avoidance compared to healthy young adults. Our findings were in accordance with previous research suggesting that adults with chronic illness are likely to report poorer relationship functioning than healthy adults (Packham & Hall, 2002).

However, we argue that it is not the illness per se that results in the poorer relationship outcomes. Rather, insecure attachment, particularly high levels of attachment anxiety, is likely to influence relationship experiences. However, Druley et al. (1997) argue that relationship issues such as those pertaining to attachment insecurity may be exacerbated by chronic illness. Certainly we commonly find this situation in our research. Across a number of our arthritis studies, we find that illness severity is significantly associated with attachment anxiety (Cole & Karantzas, 2006; Karantzas & Cole, in press; Karantzas et al., 2010). According to Doeglas et al. (2004) people experiencing arthritis tend to maintain a negative self-image due to their perceived inability to attain various professional and personal goals around work and relationships. Given that attachment anxiety is particularly associated with negative views of the self, an excessive need for approval, and a preoccupation with relationships, it is not surprising that attachment anxiety seems to be the critical dimension of attachment insecurity that influences young arthritic adults' relationship experiences. Therefore, while it is debatable whether chronic illness has a direct effect on relationship quality or satisfaction, at the very least, the effect of chronic illness on relationship experiences is likely to be partly mediated or moderated by relationship dynamics such as attachment insecurity.

Chronic Illness, Social Support, and the Role of Relationships

As part of our research investigating the role of relationships in the context of chronic illnesses, we have investigated the amount and type of care that chronic illness sufferers seek from family, friends, and other acquaintances, and their satisfaction with the support received. For example, O'Connor et al. (2008) found that satisfaction with social support was a significant predictor of marital satisfaction across four groups with neurological illnesses (MND, MS, HD, and PD). The findings from this study again question the interpretations made of past studies that length of illness and illness severity directly predict marital and sexual satisfaction (e.g., Bakke, Myhr, Gronning, & Nyland, 1996). O'Connor et al. contend that the marital satisfaction reported by people living with a neurological illness is strongly associated with their satisfaction with the social support received, rather than the severity of impairment.

The link between social support and chronic illness was also investigated by Karantzas et al. (2010). In this recent study, we found differences in arthritis sufferers' perceptions of the support provided by their social network based on illness severity. Individuals with high illness severity reported significantly less network social support than individuals with low severity across all six of Cutrona and Russell's (1990) forms of social provision (i.e., attachment, social integrations, reassurance of worth, reliable alliance, guidance, and opportunity for nurturance).

In another study comparing the support-seeking tendencies of young and middle-aged adults experiencing arthritis, Karantzas and Cole (in press) found that attachment style mediated the association between arthritis severity and the seeking of emotional and instrumental care. Furthermore, this effect was moderated by type of attachment figure (i.e., parent, romantic partner, or best friend). For young adults, anxious attachment towards a parent mediated the association between arthritis severity and both emotional and instrumental care; anxious attachment towards a romantic partner mediated the relationship between severity and instrumental care; while anxious attachment towards a best friend mediated the association between anxiety and emotional care. In contrast, for middle-aged adults, only anxious attachment towards a romantic partner was found to mediate the association between arthritis severity and emotional care.

Similar to the findings of Cole and Karantzas (2006), these findings highlight that attachment anxiety seems to be the critical form of attachment insecurity that influences the association between illness severity and relationship experiences—whether this be relationship satisfaction or perceptions of social support received from one's network of family and friends. This finding is not surprising given that anxious individuals' need for approval heightens their tendencies to seek comfort and emotional reassurance during periods of distress (Mikulincer & Florian, 1995; Mikulincer & Shaver, 2007; Ognibene & Collins, 1998).

Interestingly, the differing mediating roles of attachment anxiety across relationship types for young adults suggests that attachment insecurities with different attachment figures matter when seeking support. In contrast, for middle-aged adults, only attachment style with their romantic partner mediated the relationship between severity and emotional care seeking. This finding illustrates the significant role of romantic partners in providing emotional support. According to various attachment researchers, the significance of the relationship that develops between romantic partners results in romantic partners becoming the primary attachment figures that adults turn toward when experiencing threat or distress (Fraley & Davis, 1997; Zeifman & Hazan, 2008). However, for young adults, their social relationships are undergoing dynamic changes as they establish new friendships, relinquish old ones, and embark on romantic relationships. Thus, Karantzas and Cole (in press) suggest that the differing functions of relationships for young adults are typical of their life stage and can be explained via role theory and attachment perspectives.

From a role theory perspective, Bjorklund and Bee (2008) suggest that social networks contain people who serve different roles to meet the varied needs of young adults. Thus, friends are called upon for social affiliation, peer group inclusion, and to provide emotional comfort and support (Doherty & Feeney, 2004). In contrast, parents and romantic partners are called upon to offer emotional support but are also asked to provide instrumental help (Florian, Mikulincer, & Bucholtz, 1995; Larose & Bernier, 2001) that supports their daily activities.

From an attachment network perspective, it is argued that peers, parents, and romantic partners satisfy the attachment needs of young adults differently. The need to seek proximity is thought to be commonly fulfilled by friends (Fraley & Davis, 1997; Trinke & Bartholomew, 1997) while parents and romantic partners are required to meet young adults' attachment needs for safe haven and secure base (for a review see Trinke & Bartholomew, 1997). Accordingly, we argue that "highly anxious arthritis sufferers' calls for emotional support from friends, and instrumental support from parents and partners, may reflect social and developmental norms around the roles associated with distinctly different members of one's support network" (Karantzas & Cole, in press, p. 33).

To further understand the extent to which attachment figures meet arthritis sufferers' attachment needs, Karantzas and Cole (in press) also investigated how attachment figures fulfilled arthritis sufferers' needs for proximity maintenance, secure base, and safe haven (see chapter 14 in this volume). Examining how attachment figures fulfill these needs is in line with more recent conceptions of social support such as those outlined by Cutrona (chapter 27 in this volume). Cutrona describes safe haven support as the comfort and assistance provided to another in times of distress, whereas secure base support is conceptualized as support that promotes autonomy, independence, and exploration. Proximity maintenance, on the other hand, relates to the need to seek out the presence of another during positive and negative life events. Specifically, we found that romantic partners were most preferred for meeting all three attachment needs for middle-aged arthritis sufferers compared to parents and best friends. Furthermore, the extent to which romantic partners and parents fulfilled all three attachment functions was positively associated with the extent to which individuals with arthritis sought emotional and instrumental support from these relationships. Also, the extent to which a best friend fulfilled the attachment functions was associated with the degree to which arthritis sufferers sought emotional support from that best friend.

In another line of social support research conducted in a chronic illness context, Gallant (2003) found that social support had both positive and negative effects on self-management of a chronic illness. In her empirical review of 29 studies, Gallant identified that chronic illness sufferers' experiences of support as positive or negative was moderated by their perceptions of that support. Support perceived as either dismissive, which communicated a lack of regard for the ill person, or overcontrolling and highly intrusive, which challenged the sufferer's sense of competence, was reported as having a negative effect on the care recipient. In line with Canterberry and Gillath (chapter 14 in this volume) and Cutrona (chapter 27 in this volume), Gallant (2003) reported that overreactions to illness symptoms, the tendency to treat the ill person as an invalid, and a refusal to accept the seriousness of the illness were deemed as unsupportive behaviors.

Gallant's review also noted that highly visible support from friends that either singled out or restricted the lifestyle choices of the ill person was also deemed as unhelpful. These findings point to the distinct psychological outcomes associated with the receipt of visible and invisible social support by care recipients (see chapter 27 in this volume). Bolger, Zuckerman, and Kessler (2000) suggested that tacit help may heighten the care recipient's awareness about their illness and impact on their self-esteem, or, they may perceive a loss of face due to other people's explicit awareness of their need for help. Gallant also found that conflict with others regarding management of the illness was also deemed as unhelpful and associated with unresolved family conflicts. This finding again highlights the role that relationship dynamics play in the exchange of support between carers and care recipients.

Chronic Illness, Relationships, and Mental Health

Across a number of the studies, we have examined how the quality of the relationships experienced by people with chronic illness influences mental health outcomes, with a particular emphasis on depression, anxiety, and quality of life. As part of our research program, we have consistently examined the effects of relationship quality alongside the variables of social support and coping strategies due to their consistent theoretical and empirical links with chronic illness and relationship dynamics (e.g., Mikulincer & Shaver, 2007; chapters 26, 27 in this volume). In this section we outline the findings from some of these research studies.

A longitudinal study by McCabe, Stokes, and McDonald (2009) examined the effects of perceived social support and coping strategies on quality of life (QOL) in people dealing with MS. Over a 2-year period McCabe and colleagues examined the QOL, social support, and coping strategies used by people with MS and a comparison group of healthy adults. McCabe et al. found that MS sufferers experienced an increase in the use of social support and in QOL over the 2-year period. McCabe and colleagues suggested that in experiencing the illness, MS sufferers were able to call on the support of others in adjusting to their illness. A closer examination of the rate of change in QOL suggested that people with MS who reported their QOL as low at the beginning of the study reported the greatest increases in QOL over time. McCabe et al. argued that the low QOL experienced initially by MS sufferers may have led them to seek more social support than people who reported higher QOL at the initial stage of the study. Interestingly, social support was the most significant predictor of change in QOL across MS and healthy adult groups. These findings again suggest that chronic illness per se does not prescribe the psychological well-being of people with chronic conditions; rather the support they receive in relation to the illness is a critical factor in determining their QOL over time.

Similarly, the findings of McCabe and O'Connor (2010) regarding the QOL outcomes of people experiencing a neurological illness highlight the psychological benefits of satisfying relationships and the value of social support for the mental health of people living with a chronic illness. Specifically, McCabe and O'Connor found that both marital and social support satisfaction were significantly positively associated with QOL for those experiencing a neurological illness, especially PD and MS—a finding consistent with previous research (e.g., Boyce & Hickey, 2005; Rohrbaugh, Shoham, & Coyne, 2006; Zabalegui, Sanchez, Sanchez, & Juando, 2005).

In another longitudinal study, McCabe (2005) compared a group of adults with MS with a group of healthy adults on symptoms of depression and anxiety, as well as social support and coping over 18 months. She found that MS sufferers experienced significantly higher depressive and anxiety symptomatology over the 18 months compared to healthy adults. Furthermore, MS sufferers who experienced an exacerbation in their illness reported particularly high levels of anxiety. McCabe's findings were in line with past studies, in that people with MS often report greater psychological maladjustment than the general population. Further analyses revealed that people who did not experience an exacerbation in MS reported significantly less seeking of social support, less problem-focused coping, but significantly more behavioral and cognitive detachment from the illness than people with MS who experienced the exacerbation of their illness. These results underscore how situations that heighten the stress experienced by an individual, such as illness exacerbation, increase the tendency for people to seek the support of others alongside their use of constructive solution-focused strategies to deal with stressful events.

In another line of research, Cole & Karantzas (2006) examined how attachment style influences the psychological adjustment (i.e., depression and anxiety symptoms) of young adults experiencing arthritis, while controlling for illness severity and coping strategies. We found that attachment anxiety significantly increased depression and anxiety symptomatology above and beyond the effects of illness severity and coping strategies. Extending on this work, a recent study by Karantzas et al. (2010) tested both moderating and mediating effects of attachment style and social support on the mental health of arthritis sufferers. We found that the interaction between attachment style and perceptions of social support predicted arthritis sufferers' depression and anxiety symptoms, and that this effect was partly mediated by coping. Specifically, people high on attachment anxiety and avoidance (often termed fearful-avoidant, see Mikulincer & Shaver, 2007) who maintained perceptions of low support from their social network experienced greater depression and anxiety compared to fearful individuals who perceived high network support.

This moderated effect between attachment style and social support, which is similar to a finding described by Simpson et al. (chapter 26 in this volume), illustrates how attachment dynamics interact with people's perceptions of their social support to influence mental health. Our findings and those of Simpson et al. suggest that social support can buffer the effects of depression and anxiety, even for insecurely attached people. However, when support is perceived as inadequate by people experiencing insecure attachment (especially attachment anxiety), they are likely to be most at risk of mental health issues. Moreover, the fearfully-avoidant individuals in our study who perceived low network support, reported the use of emotion-focused coping strategies that intensified distress (i.e., wishful thinking, venting anger, rumination). In turn, the use of these coping strategies further exacerbated symptoms of depression and anxiety. This finding clearly highlights that the mental health outcomes of sufferers from chronic illness are complex, i.e., relationship experiences and perceptions of social support directly influence depression and anxiety, but also influence mental health through coping strategies.

Implications

In this section, we discuss ways in which the knowledge gained from our research program can be incorporated by health services and used by health professionals in supporting the psychological well-being of people with a chronic illness. In doing so, we hope that health providers, educators, and counselors see the opportunities for better supporting the needs of chronic illness sufferers and their carers.

The findings from our research program clearly point to the powerful role that relationships and social support play in shaping the mental health of people experiencing chronic illness. However, it is also true that the experience of an illness can shape the relationships of chronic illness sufferers, especially in young adulthood. For example, our research revealed that for young adults, the experience of a chronic illness may influence the relationship satisfaction and attachment orientation of the sufferer. Negotiating the path to a healthy and positive relationship is challenging enough as a young adult (see chapter 29 in this volume). Our research suggests that the added challenge of an illness further complicates the formation of positive and satisfying romantic relationships.

If in fact, the experience of a chronic illness interrupts the normative development of romantic relationships during young adulthood, then it seems prudent that organizations working in chronic illness provide relationship education to help young adults develop the skills to manage their illness while establishing meaningful and healthy relationships. Such psycho-educational programs could also include strategies for managing the need for social support. Relationship education programs such as those described by Halford and Hayes (chapter 19 in this volume) and Hawkins (chapter 29 in this volume) may be adapted and implemented for this group of young adults, thereby reducing the need to develop relationship education programs from the ground up.

Our longitudinal studies examining the quality of life of people with chronic illness suggest that sufferers from chronic illness who receive, and are satisfied with, the social support received in the earlier stages of their illness report and maintain high levels of QOL over time. Clearly, social support is required during the early phases of diagnosis of the illness as people attempt to come to terms with the diagnosis and adjust to their illness. Sensitive and responsive caregiving, as opposed to overly involved or controlling caregiving (see chapter 14 in this volume), is likely to validate the ill person's need for help, while encouraging them to confidently self-manage their illness as much as possible. This combination of social support is unlikely to undermine the ill person's sense of self-esteem or competence (see also chapter 27 in this volume). Gallant (2003) notes that caregiving that communicates a lack of regard for the ill person, challenges their sense of competence, or makes them feel like an invalid, is appraised as unsupportive by people with chronic illness. Consequently, we argue that social support should be put in place as soon as possible after a person receives a diagnosis of a chronic illness. However, the support provided should be such that it does not undermine the person and does not draw unnecessary attention to their illness. Support that focuses too much on the inabilities of people with illness is likely to heighten their distress and reduce their psychological well-being. To this end, it would be useful during the initial stages of diagnosis, for carers of people with a chronic illness to be given the opportunity to attend programs that provide education on how to give appropriate social support that promotes the physical and emotional well-being of people with chronic illness. Information about how best to help people with chronic illness could also be delivered as part of the various support group programs for carers that are provided by carer advocacy organizations. These programs should also provide emotional support to carers who have been found to report significantly lower satisfaction with the support they receive from their ill partner.

The need for the chronically ill to feel competent and valued as individuals, and for the carers of ill partners to feel supported, opens the door for the development of support programs that take a dyadic approach. For instance, programs can be designed where couples can discuss how to support each other's physical and emotional needs. In these programs, a skilled counselor can help the chronically ill partner become aware of the type of support that they are able to provide to their carer, and the degree to which this support is valued by the carer. In this way, people with an illness can maintain a sense of self-competence because they are actively "doing their part" in maintaining the relationship and in supporting their partner. Cutrona (chapter 27 in this volume) argues that providing people who require social support the opportunity to give assistance to others is important for their well-being. Piercy (chapter 7 in this volume) also highlights the importance of helping others as a means of maintaining a positive sense of self.

Our research into the role of attachment dynamics revealed a complex interaction between attachment insecurity and perceptions of social support in predicting the mental health outcomes of people experiencing chronic illness. In particular, fearful-avoidant individuals (i.e., high attachment anxiety and avoidance) who perceived low network support were most at risk of developing depression and anxiety. Furthermore, this effect was partly mediated through fearful-avoidant individuals' use of emotion-focused coping which tends to exacerbate distress.

Our findings point to the need for health professionals and counselors to consider the role of attachment dynamics in shaping people's perceptions of social support and the manner in which they cope with their illness. Specifically, understanding how to tailor social support for people experiencing attachment insecurity (especially fearful-avoidance) will improve the quality of care provided to sufferers from chronic illness and may augment the coping strategies used by these individuals. For instance, anxiously-attached individuals are highly dependent on others for support during periods of stress due to their lack of confidence in their own coping abilities and their excessive need for validation (Berant & Obegi, 2009). In working with these individuals and their carers, health professionals need to encourage anxious individuals to take more responsibility for managing their illness. In parallel, therapists need to ensure that carers provide support that validates anxious individuals' attempts at self-management, and encourages them to deal with some aspects of the illness in a more independent manner.

On the other hand, avoidant individuals place high value on independence and tend to mistrust others. Thus, the provision of help may be seen as highly threatening to these people, despite their actual need for assistance in dealing with their chronic illness.

For these individuals, explicit social support may be particularly harmful to their well-being as it challenges their need for self-reliance and independence. Avoidant individuals may experience enhanced emotional well-being when help is provided to them in a more implicit or invisible way that does not threaten their competence.

For a practitioner, understanding how attachment style shapes the appraisals by sufferers of chronic illness with regard to the care received, the type of care they seek, and the members of their social network from whom they receive such care, will provide critical and necessary information about how to best support these people. This information can then lead to interventions to improve the pathways of community and family-based care for this population.

Conclusion

In a recent special edition of the *Medical Journal of Australia* on chronic illness and mental health, Clarke and Currie (2009) contend that to provide the best help to people experiencing chronic illness, professionals need to better understand the complex association between the physical and mental health aspects of chronic illness. In addition, the American Medical Association (Council on Scientific Affairs, 1993) has for a long time recognized the importance of considering the roles of family and friends in enhancing the care of people with illness. In this chapter, we highlight that the quality of the relationships experienced by people with a chronic illness, and the support obtained from these relationships, can help explain the relationship between the physical and mental health outcomes of chronic illness. To this end, we encourage health providers and practitioners to take a relationships perspective in working with sufferers from chronic illness and their families, in order to support the emotional well-being of care recipients and their carers.

References

Australian Institute of Health and Welfare. (2005). *Arthritis and musculoskeletal conditions in Australia 2005.* AIHW Cat. No. PHE 67. Canberra: AIHW.

Australian Institute of Health and Welfare (2010). Health system expenditure on disease and injury in Australia, 2004–05. *Health and welfare expenditure series no. 36.* Cat. no. HSE 87. Canberra: AIHW.

Bakke, A., Myhr, K., Gronning, M., & Nyland, H. (1996). Bladder, bowel and sexual dysfunction in patients with multiple sclerosis—A cohort study. *Scandinavian Journal of Urology and Nephrology, 179S,* 61–66.

Berant, E., & Obegi, J. H. (2009). Attachment informed psychotherapy with adults. In J. H. Obegi & E. Berant (Eds.), *Attachment theory and research in clinical work with adults* (pp. 461–489). New York: Guilford Press.

Bjorklund, B. R., & Bee, H. L. (2008). *The journey of adulthood* (6th edn.) New Jersey: Pearson.

Bolger, N., Zuckerman, A., & Kessler, R. C. (2000). Invisible support and adjustment to stress. *Journal of Personality and Social Psychology, 79,* 953–961.

Boyce, P., & Hickey, A. (2005). Psychosocial risk factors to major depression after childbirth. *Social Psychiatry and Psychiatric Epidemiology, 40*, 605–612.

Cole, S., & Karantzas, G.C. (2006). The impact of chronic illness on relationships in early adulthood: A comparison study between healthy and arthritic young adults. *Proceedings of the 6th Australian Psychological Society Relationships Conference,* 33–41.

Council on Scientific Affairs, AMA (1993). Physicians and family caregivers: A model for partnership. *Journal of the American Medical Association, 269*, 1282–1284.

Cutrona, C. E., & Russell, D. (1990). Type of social support and specific stress: Toward a theory of optimal matching. In I. G. Sarason, B. R. Sarason, & G. R. Pierce (Eds.), *Social support: An interactional view* (pp. 319–366). New York: Wiley.

Davis, J. M., & Gershtein, C. M. (2003). Screening for depression in patients with chronic illness. *Why and how? Disease Management Health Outcomes, 11*, 375–378.

DeVol R., Bedroussian, A., Charuworn, A., Chatterjee, A., Kim, I., Kim, S., & Klowden, K. (2007). *An unhealthy America: The economic burden of chronic disease—Charting a new course to save lives and increase productivity and economic growth*. Santa Monica, CA: Maiken Institute.

Clarke, D. M., & Currie, K. C. (2009). Depression, anxiety and their relationship with chronic diseases: A review of the epidemiology, risk and treatment evidence. *Medical Journal of Australia, 190*, S54–S60.

Doeglas, D. M., Suurmeijer, T. P. B. M., van den Heuvel, W. J. A., Krol, B., van Rijswick, M. H., van Leeuwen, M. A., & Sanderman, R. (2004). Functional ability, social support, and depression in rheumatoid arthritis. *Quality of Life Research, 13*, 1053–1065.

Doherty, N. A., & Feeney, J. A. (2004). The composition of attachment networks throughout the adult years. *Personal Relationships, 11*, 469–488.

Druley, J. A., Stephens, M. A. P., & Coyne, J. C. (1997). Emotional and physical intimacy in coping with lupus: Women's dilemmas of disclosure and approach. *Health Psychology, 16*, 506–514.

Florian, V., Mikulincer, M., & Bucholtz, I. (1995). Effects of adult attachment style on the perception and search for social support. *Journal of Psychology: Interdisciplinary and Applied, 129*, 665–676.

Fraley, R. C., & Davis, K. E. (1997). Attachment formation and transfer in young adults' close friendships and romantic relationships. *Personal Relationships, 4*, 131–144.

Fried, L. P., Ferrucci, L., Darer, J., Williamson, J. D., & Anderson, G. (2004). Untangling the concepts of disability, frailty, and comorbidity: Implications for improved targeting and care. *Journals of Gerontology A: Biological Science/Medical Science, 59*, M255–M263.

Gallant, M. P. (2003). The influence of social support on chronic illness self-management: A review and directions for research. *Health Education and Behavior, 30*, 170–195.

Huston, T. L., Caughlin, J. P., Houts, R. M., Smith, S. E., & George, L. J. (2001). The connubial crucible: Newlywed years as predictors of marital delight, distress, and divorce. *Journal of Personality and Social Psychology, 80*, 237–252.

Jacobson, A. M., Hauser, S. T., Cole, C., Wolfsdorf, J. I., Dvorak, R., Wolpert, H. et al. (1997). Social relationships among young adults with insulin-dependent Diabetes Mellitus: Ten-year follow-up of an onset cohort. *Diabetic Medicine, 14*, 73–79.

Karantzas, G. C., & Cole, S. F.(in press). Arthritis and support seeking tendencies: The role of attachment. *Journal of Social and Clinical Psychology*.

Karantzas, G. C., McCabe, M. P., & Cole, S. F. (2010). *The impact of adult attachment on depression and anxiety for young and middle-aged adults dealing with arthritis*. beyondblue final report. Melbourne, Australia: Deakin University.

Kennedy, A., Sloman, F., Douglass, J. A., & Sawyer, S.M. (2007). Young people with chronic illness: The approach to transition. *Internal Medicine Journal, 37*, 555–560.

Larose, S., & Bernier, A. (2001). Social support processes: Mediators of attachment state of mind and adjustment in late adolescence. *Attachment and Human Development, 3,* 96–120.

Maunder, R. G., & Hunter, J. J. (2001). Attachment and psychosomatic medicine: Developmental contributions to stress and disease. *Psychosomatic Medicine, 63,* 556–567.

McCabe, M. P. (2005). Mood and self-esteem of persons with multiple sclerosis following an exacerbation. *Journal of Psychosomatic Research, 59,* 161–166.

McCabe, M. P., & McDonald E. (2007). Perceptions of relationship and sexual satisfaction among people with multiple sclerosis and their partners. *Sexuality and Disability, 25,* 179–188.

McCabe, M. P., & O'Connor, E. (2010). The economic impact of progressive neurological illness on quality of life in Australia. *Journal of Family and Economic Issues, 31,* 82–89.

McCabe, M. P., Stokes, M., & McDonald, E. (2009). Changes over a two-year period in quality of life and coping among people with multiple sclerosis. *Psychology, Health and Medicine, 14,* 86–96.

Mikulincer, M., & Florian, V. (1995). Appraisal of and coping with a real-life stressful situation: The contribution of attachment styles. *Personality and Social Psychology Bulletin, 21,* 406–414.

Mikulincer, M., & Shaver, P. R. (2007). *Attachment in adulthood: Structure, dynamics, and change.* New York: Guilford Press.

Newsom, J. T. (1999). Another side to caregiving: Negative reactions to being helped. *Current Directions in Psychological Science, 8,* 183–187.

Newsom, J. T., & Schultz, R. (1998). Caregiving from the recipient's perspective: Negative reactions to being helped. *Health Psychology, 17,* 172–181.

O'Connor, E., McCabe, M. P., & Firth, L. (2008). The impact of neurological illness on marital relationships. *Journal of Sex and Marital Therapy, 34,* 115–132.

Ognibene, T. C., & Collins, N. L. (1998). Adult attachment styles, perceived social support, and coping strategies. *Journal of Social and Personal Relationships, 15,* 323–345.

Organization for Economic Cooperation and Development (2010). *OECD health data 2010: Statistics and indicators.* Paris, France: OECD.

Packham, J. C., & Hall, M. A. (2002). Long-term follow-up of 246 adults with juvenile idiopathic arthritis: social function, relationships and sexual activity. *Rheumatology, 41,* 1440–1443.

Pennix, B. W., Van Tilburg, T., Deeg, D. J. H., Kreigsman, D. M. W., Boeke, A. J. P., & Van Eijk, J. T. M. (1997). Direct and buffer effects of social support and personal coping resources in individuals with arthritis. *Social Science Medicine, 44,* 393–407.

Quarrell, O. (2004). *Huntington's disease: The facts.* New York: Oxford University Press.

Rohrbaugh, M. J., Shoham, V., & Coyne, J. C. (2006). Effect of marital quality on eight-year survival of patients with heart failure. *American Journal of Cardiology, 98,* 1069–1072.

Sherbourne, D. C., Meredith, L. S., Rogers, W., & Ware, J. E. (1992). *Quality of Life Research, 1,* 235–246.

Starfield, B., Lemke, K. W., Bernhardt, T., Foldes, S. S., Forrest, C. B., & Weiner, J. P. (2003). Comorbidity: Implications for the importance of primary care in "case" management. *Annals of Family Medicine, 1,* 8–14.

Trinke, S. J., & Bartholomew, K. (1997). Hierarchies of attachment relationships in young adulthood. *Journal of Social and Personal Relationships, 14,* 603–625.

Wang, M. (2007). Profiling retirees in the retirement transition and adjustment process: Examining the longitudinal change patterns of retirees' psychological well-being. *Journal of Applied Psychology, 92,* 455–474.

Wilhelm, K., Mitchell, P., Slade, T. et al. (2003). Prevalence and correlates of DSM-IV major depression in an Australian survey. *Journal of Affective Disorder, 75,* 155–162.

World Health Organization (2005). *Preventing chronic diseases: A vital investment.* WHO global report. Geneva, Switzerland: World Health Organization.

Wulsin, L. R., Vaillant, G. E., & Wells, V. E. (1999). A systematic review of the mortality of depression. *Psychosomatic Medicine, 61*, 6–17.

Zabalegui, A., Sanchez, S., Sanchez, P. D., & Juando, C. (2005). Nursing and cancer support groups. *Journal of Advanced Nursing, 51*, 369–381.

Zautra, A. J., Yocum, D. C., Vilanueva, I., Smith, B., Davis, M. C., Attrep, J. et al. (2004). Immune activation and depression in women with rheumatoid arthritis. *Journal of Rheumatology, 31*, 457–463.

Zeifman, D., & Hazan, C. (2008). Pair-bonds as attachments: Revaluating the evidence. In J. Cassidy & P. R. Shaver (Eds.), *Handbook of attachment: Theory, research, and clinical applications* (2nd edn.) (pp. 436–355). New York: Guilford Press.

PART VIII

Implications for Policy

29

Promoting Positive Pathways for Youth and Young Adults to Healthy Relationships and Marriages

A Feasible Public Policy Agenda

Alan J. Hawkins

For youth and young adults, the pathways to a healthy, stable marriage are increasingly convoluted and challenging to traverse. The vast majority of youth and young adults participate in sexual activity before marriage (Finer, 2007) and most form cohabiting relationships before marriage (Wilcox, 2009). The timing of marriage now varies considerably but most wait until they are in their mid- to late 20s to marry (National Center for Family and Marriage Research, 2009). Divorce is common (Bramlett & Mosher, 2001) and family formation outside of marriage is widespread (Ventura, 2009; chapters 1, 3 in this volume).

Cherlin (2009) argues that these trends are manifestations of the deinstitutionalization of marriage. The institutional boundaries of marriage have shrunk; marriage no longer effectively governs intimate associations before or outside of marriage, or structures "proper" pathways to the desired goal of a healthy, stable marriage (chapter 2 in this volume). Personal development and individual emotions are at the core of modern marriage, rather than societal expectations and religious and civil norms (Cherlin, 2009; Coontz, 2005; chapter 2 in this volume). Moreover, increasing numbers of youth—especially disadvantaged youth—have had little exposure to models of healthy marriage

The Wiley-Blackwell Handbook of Couples and Family Relationships, First Edition.
Edited by Patricia Noller and Gery C. Karantzas.

(Malone-Colon & Roberts, 2006). All of this suggests that contemporary youth and young adults face a more complex pathway to marriage. Hymowitz (2006) argues that, especially for disadvantaged youth, marriage is no longer a core cultural institution that orders their lives; young adults have a thin "life script" that helps them achieve their family ideals.

From an empirical perspective, there are pathways more and less likely to lead to a healthy, stable marriage. That is, there are a number of known risk factors that impede forming and sustaining healthy marriages, such as many premarital sexual partners (Teachman, 2003), premarital parenthood (Amato and Booth, 2001), pre-engagement cohabitation (Rhoades, Stanley, & Markman, 2009), and premarital relationship violence (Jackson, 2009). Leaving youth and young adults on their own to try to figure out how they can achieve their hopes for a healthy, stable marriage seems a heartless and counterproductive strategy. Moreover, we all have a stake in the quality of intimate unions formed; there are substantial public costs to the private problems of family dissolution (Scafidi, 2008).

As a society, how can we help youth and young adults find more positive pathways to healthy relationships? In this chapter, I set forth a modest public policy agenda that I believe will help youth and young adults establish more positive trajectories to a healthy marriage. The agenda stresses the availability of a series of educational opportunities, including: (a) school-based relationship literacy for youth; (b) research-based positive relationship formation education for young adults to help them navigate the elongating period between adolescence and marriage; and (c) effective premarital education for engaged couples to help them learn the needed skills for a healthy marriage, as well as ongoing relationship-enrichment education in the early years of marriage. Within this agenda, I put a premium on feasible initiatives—policies that make voluntary, inexpensive educational services more available and build on service-delivery infrastructure already in place. Stressing the feasible accepts the inevitable difficulty of establishing new social policy, especially when it involves mandates and money. In addition, I place a significant emphasis on services for disadvantaged youth and young adults who are at greater risk for traversing problematic pathways to marriage (Ooms & Wilson, 2004). While outlining this policy agenda, I briefly highlight some ongoing social policy initiatives promoting relationship and marriage education that suggest the feasibility of this policy agenda.

Before proceeding, I provide three important caveats. First, it is important to acknowledge that there is ongoing debate in policy and academic circles about whether and how government should be involved in individuals' personal decisions about family formation (Amato, 2004; Cahn & Carbone, 2010; Haskins & Sawhill, 2009). While this debate must continue, most acknowledge two relevant, important points: (a) youth and young adults across class, race, and ethnicity still highly value marriage and desire a healthy, lifelong marriage for themselves (Wilcox, 2009); and (b) there are significant societal costs when healthy relationships fail to form or dissolve, especially when children are involved (Cherlin, 2009). Accordingly, while debate continues, it is legitimate to proceed with rigorous thinking about policy efforts that could help youth and young adults achieve their aspirations, especially when the public benefits of successful marriages are well documented (Wilcox et al., 2005).

Second, I acknowledge that this policy agenda does not directly address half of all marriages now that are remarriages for one or both spouses and that have a higher risk of divorce (Bramlett & Mosher, 2001). While this is an important population to serve (Adler-Baeder & Higginbotham, 2004), my emphasis will be on preventative efforts to help youth and young adults establish healthy first marriages.

Third, I acknowledge the need for this marriage-strengthening policy agenda to be attached to a broader agenda of coterminous social and economic policy. The goal of strengthening marriages is unlikely to be achieved without the ability to gain a good education, improve job skills, and, in general, a robust economy to support individuals' attempts to build healthy, stable marriages (Haskins & Sawhill, 2009). Similarly, social policy that effectively prevents unwanted pregnancies, reduces domestic violence and substance abuse, and supports responsible fatherhood will make it easier for couples to form and sustain healthy relationships (Fagan, Palkovitz, Roy, & Farrie, 2009; Ooms et al., 2006; Wilson, 2002). Advocating a policy agenda to enhance the economic and social ecologies that give individuals the best chance of marital success only reinforces efforts to help young adults form and sustain healthy relationships.

Relationship Literacy Education for Youth

The period of the life course between adolescence and first marriage has increased substantially in length (Arnett, 2000; chapters 1, 3 in this volume). For most young adults, there will be nearly a decade between high school graduation and serious consideration of marriage. Moreover, the age of reproductive capability and sexual exploration has been getting younger, leaving, on average, about 15 years between puberty and marriage, the institution that historically has been charged with channeling human sexuality. Thus, there is now a prolonged period of sexual and relationship exploration relatively unconnected to the ultimate goal of marriage shared by most youth (Carroll, Willoughby, Badger, Barry, & Madsen, 2007). Added to these trends is the reality that contemporary youth have experienced high divorce rates in their families of origin—and rates of nonmarital family formation and dissolution—suggesting that many cannot rely on proximate social modeling to find their pathway to their own healthy marriages. In addition, through the media, youth are exposed to a voluminous amount of information about, and a dizzying array of models of, sexuality and romantic relationships (Kunkel, Eyal, Finnerty, Biely, & Donnerstein, 2005; chapter 2 in this volume). Accordingly, I believe it is incumbent on a responsible society to help youth become "relationship literate" in order to handle better the choices that may impact their present lives, future relationships, and eventual marriages.

Relationship literacy, while it may encompass basic sex education, is broader because it pays significant attention to the relational and familial contexts of sexuality (Whitehead & Pearson, 2006). Furthermore, relationship literacy gives significant attention to basic communication and problem-solving skills that undergird the forming and sustaining of healthy romantic relationships. It also clarifies what a healthy relationship is and is not, including addressing the problem of relationship aggression and violence (Arias, Samios, & O'Leary, 1987; Lewis & Fremouw, 2001). And increasingly, youth relationship programs outline the research on how sexual partnering and cohabitation may impact the prospects for marital success.

Early marriage and relationship education efforts were focused on premarital and early marital couples (see chapters 19, 31 in this volume). Fortunately, marriage and relationship educators recently have given increased attention to developing youth relationship education, including programs targeted to at-risk, disadvantaged youth. (For a description of several current programs, see www.dibblefund.org.) Because increased efforts to promote relationship literacy for youth are recent, the body of evaluation research examining the efficacy of these programs is limited. The early, emerging research, however, provides some reason for optimism. For instance, Gardner, Giese, and Parrott (2004) evaluated the *Connections* curriculum in a quasi-experimental design with a mostly middle-class, California sample and found modest, short-term, positive effects on healthy relationship knowledge, decreased dating violence, decreased risk for teen pregnancy, and positive attitudes about marital success. In a 4-year follow-up of this study, however, most of the positive effects diminished, although there was still a significant effect for decreased dating and relationship violence (Gardner & Boellaard, 2007). In addition, in a quasi-experimental evaluation of the *Relationship Smarts Plus (RS+)* curriculum with a large, predominantly low-income and diverse group of Alabama youth, Kerpelman and colleagues (2010) found that, at 1-year post-intervention, *RS+* significantly reduced faulty beliefs about relationships and marriage (e.g., "In the end, our feelings of love should be enough to sustain a happy marriage") and increased positive relationship skills. Moreover, these effects generally were seen across socioeconomic and racial groups, although conflict-resolution skills were significantly more improved for disadvantaged over advantaged groups. Students in single-parent families benefited from the intervention but not as much as those in two-parent families. An earlier study with the same curriculum but a different sample also showed positive results (Kerpelman, Pittman, Adler-Baeder, Eryigit, & Paulk, 2009). However, more evaluation research is needed, especially longitudinal research that can ascertain whether relationship literacy programs actually help youth establish healthier romantic relationships in their young adult years and result in more positive marital outcomes. In addition, relationship literacy may be more effective if delivered in multiple, smaller, regular, doses across the adolescent years rather than at a single point in time.

An effective educational infrastructure to deliver relationship literacy programs to youth is already in place in secondary education. Teachers with backgrounds in the behavioral sciences, such as family and consumer sciences, psychology, sociology, or health sciences, are well situated to deliver this education. In the United States, Oklahoma has used public funds to train public school educators in a scientifically based relationship-literacy program, significantly increasing the numbers of students taking the course. From 2004–2010, 100,000 high school students have received the course. With a federal grant for support, Alabama has also made youth relationship education widely available.

One barrier to promoting youth relationship literacy is the increased emphasis on traditional academic subjects embodied in the U.S. legislation, *No Child Left Behind.* This emphasis can limit the number of opportunities for students to take nontraditional subjects. In Utah, a course on relationship literacy was merged with a state-mandated course on financial literacy to create a popular year-long course option and increased the number of students receiving relationship-literacy education. These kinds of initiatives can be supported within regular funding channels making their implementation more feasible.

Positive Relationship Formation Education for Young Adults

Even though youth relationship education may achieve its objective of helping more youth begin a positive trajectory toward a healthy marriage, it still may be unrealistic to think that it can sustain that positive effect for nearly a decade between high school and the average age of marriage. Moreover, young adults will be in more serious romantic and cohabiting relationships that provide more proximate issues and challenges associated with positive trajectories toward marriage. Many serial sexual partnerships appear to be a risk factor for maintaining stable marriages (Teachman, 2003). Cohabitation in the United States before engagement also appears to be a risk factor for eventual divorce (Jose, O'Leary, & Moyer, 2010; Rhoades et al., 2009). Premarital parenthood and especially multiple-partner fertility, common in disadvantaged populations (McLanahan, 2009; Meyer, Cancian, & Cook, 2005), reduce the chances of future relationship and marriage success (Jackson, 2009). And relationship violence in dating and cohabiting relationships continues to be a problem in young adults (Wood, McConnell, Moore, Clarkwest, & Hsueh, 2010) and can impact later marital success (Jackson, 2009).

Cohabiting young-adult couples may be an especially important target for preventative intervention. Rhoades and colleagues (Rhoades et al., 2009) have begun to explore the issues facing cohabiting couples and their implications for relationship education. Perhaps the most prominent issue explored is commitment. Cohabiting couples can have different levels of commitment and different notions of where the relationship is headed and what the timetable is. Moreover, these scholars note how many couples slide into a decision to marry rather than decide to marry with a firm commitment to the long-term future of the relationship. These issues have important consequences for the health and stability of a potential marriage. In the absence of a decision to marry, the quality and stability of the cohabiting relationship is also important, especially if children are a part of the union. Young adults need to be aware of these issues and may benefit from interventions designed to help them make careful decisions.

Hence, I believe youth's early exposure to relationship literacy will need to be supplemented with relationship education targeted to the unique issues and concerns of young adults, with special attention to at-risk, disadvantaged young adults. Relationship education for young adults who are dating, in serious relationships, or living together is probably the newest category of relationship education. Contemporary young adulthood, or emerging adulthood, has been viewed as a period of "marital latency" (Carroll et al., 2007). But we know that relationship behaviors in young adulthood impact future marital options and some young adults will cohabit long term and rear children together.

In response to these issues, marriage and relationship educators are developing and implementing programs for young adults who are single, dating, or cohabiting. Programs such as the PREP-based *Within My Reach* (singles)/*Within Our Reach* (couples),

Love Notes, and *Caring for My Family* have been developed with a particular target audience of lower income individuals and couples.

Research is only beginning to emerge on the effectiveness of positive relationship-formation education for young adults, with a good deal of research now in the pipeline. Interestingly, in contrast to most marriage and relationship education programs, these emerging educational efforts appear to be targeted primarily toward lower income couples and individuals. And it should be noted that many of these program participants already have significant risk factors for their relationships, such as premarital pregnancy and multiple-partner fertility. Getting positive relationship-formation education to at-risk individuals sooner may help some avoid these risk factors. The emerging research suggests some reason for early optimism (Hawkins & Fackrell, 2010). Cox and Shirer (2009), in a quasi-experimental study of *Caring for My Family* with low-income parents of young children, found significant post-intervention effects for self-reported communication and problem-solving skills, increased intentionality and goal planning for family behavior, and greater positive co-parenting attitudes and behaviors. Antle and her colleagues (in press) followed 200 unmarried, disadvantaged individuals for 6 months after they attended the *Within My Reach* program. Comparisons of follow-up scores to pre-test scores indicated significant increases in healthy relationship knowledge, relationship quality, self-reported communication skills, and a trend for reduction in relationship violence. Cowan, Cowan, Pruett, Pruett, and Wong (2009), in a randomized-control trial with a large, diverse sample of low-income cohabiting and married parents, evaluated the effectiveness of the *Supporting Father Involvement* program in a couple-oriented group with couple relationship education. More than a year after the intervention, the researchers found increases in relationship quality, regardless of relationship status, as well as increases in father involvement.

Finally, the strongest evidence to date on the effectiveness of couple education for low-income cohabiting couples comes from the *Building Strong Families* (BSF) study, a rigorous, 8-site, U.S. federally funded evaluation study of 5,000 low-income, romantically involved couples randomly assigned either to a relationship-education intervention (and support services) or a control group (Wood et al., 2010). At about 1 year after the intervention, the results were mixed. An examination of the rigorous intent-to-treat effects (i.e., comparing all treatment-group couples, regardless of treatment dosage, to all control-group couples, regardless of self-delivered relationship education) found little overall evidence to support the efficacy of the intervention on the couple relationship. However, further analyses revealed a pattern of significant positive effects across sites on couple relationships and father involvement for African American couples. In addition, one site (Oklahoma City) revealed an overall pattern of positive relationship and father-involvement effects. This site delivered a smaller dosage (30 hours) in a more condensed format (6–10 weeks) compared to the other sites. This site also had by far the highest level of full participation in the intervention with nearly half of couples receiving 24 hours or more of the intervention compared to an average of 10% in the other sites. While the results of this BSF study indicate that we still have much to learn about effective relationship education for romantically involved, low-income unmarried couples, the potential for positive impact exists.

One of the challenges of delivering relationship education to young adults will be finding the right infrastructures to deliver these services. Social service agencies that work regularly with disadvantaged young adults could be a good source for delivering relationship education, although it will take some time and effort to help them see that this kind of service is appropriate to their organizations, which have traditionally been focused on working with single mothers (Palm & Fagan, 2008). Current U.S. federal Healthy Marriage Initiative grants have been used to stimulate more outreach to disadvantaged young adult couples. Community colleges and universities also may be effective settings for reaching young adults. Anecdotally, I have observed an increasing number of course offerings at U.S. colleges and universities focused not just on the institutional aspects of marital and family formation but on the personal aspects of dating, cohabitation, marriage, sexual relationships, and relationship skills. Some formative evaluation research on these kinds of course offerings is beginning to emerge (Nielsen, Pinsof, Rampage, Solomon, & Goldstein, 2004). Limited public funds could be made available for grants to develop and test effective programs in community college and university settings and to expand interest in such offerings. One such grant to researchers at Florida State University is testing the effectiveness of a PREP-based curriculum for college students (Olmstead, Pasley, Meyer, Stanford, Fincham, & Delevi, 2010).

Oklahoma has taken seriously the need to reach young adults with tailored programs delivered in many different settings, including traditional social-service organizations that work regularly with single parents. No doubt creative web-based delivery of services will play an important role in delivering relationship education to young adults given the omnipresence of the Internet in the lives of most of them (chapter 19 in this volume; see also www.twoofus.org, developed under a U.S. federal grant to the National Healthy Marriage Resource Center, for an example of a website targeting young adults with healthy marriage and relationship information.) The early evidence on web-based delivery of relationship education is encouraging (Duncan, Steed, & Needham, 2008).

Premarital Education for Engaged Couples

When couples make the decision to marry, they may be more open to receiving programmatic help to build a stronger foundation for their marriage. Individuals who have experienced the divorce of their parents may be especially interested in formal preparation as they are 2–3 times more at risk of experiencing divorce (Wolfinger, 2005). Formal premarital education emphasizes building better communication and problem-solving skills to deal with the challenges of married life. It also usually addresses a wide range of issues that influence marital quality, from money management to the division of household labor to in-law issues. A meta-analysis by Fawcett, Hawkins, Blanchard, and Carroll (2010) demonstrated that premarital education for engaged couples is effective at increasing couples' communication skills. And there is some limited evidence that couples who invest in formal premarital education are less likely to divorce in the early, high-risk years of marriage (Nock, Sanchez, & Wright, 2008; Stanley, Amato, Johnson, & Markman, 2006). Also, researchers have observed that 10–15% of couples taking premarital education decide to call off the wedding because they come to believe that the relationship will not succeed (Stanley, 2001). Research has not yet confirmed that premarital education for lower income, more disadvantaged engaged couples is effective.

In the United States, a large majority of weddings take place in religious rather than civil settings. Many clergy offer or even require couples they marry to attend a formal premarital education program. Research suggests that premarital education delivered by clergy or their designates in religious settings is as effective as those programs delivered by trained family-life educators or clinicians in secular settings (Stanley et al., 2001). Thus, there is a ready-made infrastructure for delivery of premarital education to engaged couples that requires no public support. However, public funds could be used to promote greater use of these services, which several U.S. states are doing, including Oklahoma, Texas, and Utah. In addition, six states (Florida, Maryland, Minnesota, Oklahoma, Tennessee, and Texas) have provided an incentive for participation in premarital education by discounting the cost of a marriage license for those couples who invest in educational services that meet legislated standards. (Services from religious organizations that meet the standards are acceptable.) No state yet mandates premarital education. Legislation to do so would be difficult, even though one analysis concluded that lost revenues from such incentives would quickly be recovered by even minimal reductions (1–2%) in divorce and the public assistance costs associated with marital breakup (Hawkins, 2007). But given its potential for reducing divorce, governments could do more to promote the use of premarital education services.

Some couples, however, will marry civilly or prefer secular options. Lower income couples may be least likely to marry within religious settings. These couples could be reached efficiently in the United States, however, through various means. Social and family service agencies that serve more disadvantaged young adults with other kinds of support services may be a prime venue for reaching lower income couples with premarital education. As mentioned previously, however, the challenge here will be to get service providers in these organizations to shift their mindset from providing services only to single individuals and parents to helping couples achieve their aspirations for a healthy, stable marriage. In addition, the Cooperative Extension Service (CES) of the U.S. land-grant universities is another existing infrastructure that could be used. Every county in every state has a CES that delivers research-based educational services to its population. Virtually all have extension agents trained to deliver family-life education. Historically, extension agents have focused primarily on positive youth-development programs and parenting education, and greater attention has been given to rural populations than to urban communities. But recently more attention has been devoted to marriage and relationship education (Futris, 2007) and greater emphasis is being given to urban outreach. Because programs often are widely shared across extension services in the various counties and states, programs developed and tested in one place can be used in many places helping to stretch limited funding.

In Australia, the federal government recently funded Family Relationship Centers in all areas of the country with the mission to strengthen marriage and family relationships. The centers are staffed by well-qualified family professionals. Many services are free or offered on a sliding scale of charges. The recent changes to the Family Law Act in Australia mandated these centers provide 8 hours of mediation to divorcing couples to help families navigate family break-up in less conflictual ways. The current focus on divorce mediation services makes it difficult for these centers to provide educational programs for couples forming families. But with a modest increase in funding, this currently existing infrastructure could provide helpful educational services to engaged couples.

Marriage enrichment education for early-married couples

Unfortunately, even if couples invest in formal premarital education, there is still no guarantee that smooth marital sailing is ahead. Accordingly, I think it is wise to extend the conceptualization of premarital education to encompass early-marital enrichment education, as well. There is a need for continuing efforts to help early-married couples strengthen their relationship skills.

A large body of evaluation research on marriage enrichment programs has been directed largely at couples in the early years of marriage. Meta-analytic studies suggest that these programs can improve communication skills and enhance relationship quality, sustaining these effects over the first year of marriage (Blanchard, Hawkins, Baldwin, & Fawcett, 2009; Hawkins, Blanchard, Baldwin, & Fawcett, 2008). A recent study documented an 11-year follow-up of a sample of couples who were randomly assigned to a marriage enrichment program or a control group (Hahlweg & Richter, 2010). These researchers found a significantly lower divorce rate in the treatment group. The few evaluation studies of marriage enrichment programs for more disadvantaged married couples suggest positive results as well (Cowan et al., 2009; Hawkins & Fackrell, 2010; Stanley, 2010), although more research is needed. A rigorous, large-scale, randomized control trial study of lower income married couples—*Supporting Healthy Marriages*—is in the pipeline (Knox & Fein, 2009).

Again, religious organizations may provide a natural educational infrastructure to deliver early-marriage enrichment programs to couples, especially if the couples also took a premarital education class in a religious setting. But nonreligious, community-based services should be strengthened as well. Several U.S. states have statewide initiatives to develop marriage enrichment services. Oklahoma has gone the farthest to date. Public funds have trained more than 2,500 instructors. Free classes based in the well-researched PREP curriculum (Markman, Stanley & Blumberg, 2010) are widely advertised and run in community settings all over the state. These classes are widely available in Spanish as well as in English. In states that have not invested so thoroughly in a statewide healthy-marriage initiative, the presence of CES family-life educators in virtually every county of U.S. states provides a ready infrastructure for the delivery of marriage enrichment programs. Also, recent U.S. federal grants to Head Start programs that help disadvantaged preschool children and their parents have facilitated implementation of healthy marriage and relationship programs for the parents. These venues have a history of providing parenting-support services and may provide an effective way to reach many young, lower income couples with enrichment education.

Summary and Conclusion

The social policy agenda I have proposed to increase the proportion of youth and young adults who establish positive pathways towards healthy and stable marriage is hardly dramatic. I have emphasized feasible policies to promote delivery of educational services using existing educational infrastructures. Admittedly, this agenda, portrayed in Figure 29.1,

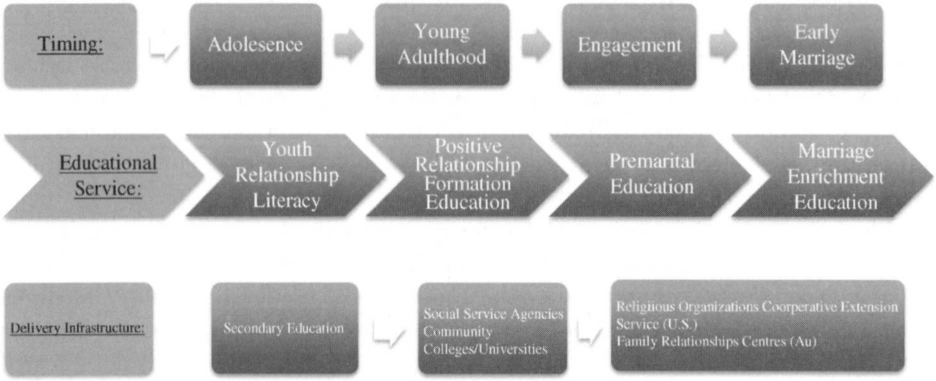

Figure 29.1 A policy agenda of a series of relationship and marriage education services to help youth and young adults form and sustain healthy relationships and marriages.

puts much faith in the power of education. Emerging research points to the positive potential of youth relationship literacy, relationship education for single, dating, and cohabiting young adults, premarital education, and early-marital enrichment, although further evaluation research is needed. Voluntary educational interventions may seem weak in the face of powerful historical and cultural forces working against individual hopes for lifelong marriage (Coontz, 2005). Certainly, there are scholars who doubt the ability of government efforts to change how we form and sustain marriage in our societies. Wilson (2002) argues that broad cultural change is needed, but this must be done privately by individuals, families, churches, neighborhoods, and the media. He does not consider the possibility, however, that extensive educational efforts over time encouraged by modest public funding could help to shift the cultural current and bring youth and young adults along in its wake.

I believe this possibility is a reasonable one. I am not alone in thinking about the merits of publicly funded efforts to increase the availability of relationship and marriage education services. For instance, Amato (2004), one of the most prominent scholars of marriage and divorce, generally supports the concept of government efforts to provide more relationship education services, especially to lower income couples (Amato, 2004; Amato, Booth, Johnson, & Rogers, 2007). Amato, however, does not outline as specific an agenda as I have done here. In addition, Cherlin (2009), another prominent family sociologist, implies the need for better education for young adults, especially around the issue of cohabitation and family formation. "We don't want a cohabitation tax or a marriage police" (p. 194), he says, but he does imply the need for educational efforts to send stronger messages to young adults to "slow down" (p. 194) and think carefully before rushing into relationships, especially when children's lives are at stake. His recommendations for how to get this message out, however, are vague. Legal scholars Cahn and Carbone (2010) intellectually tackle the culture wars around marriage and family formation and conclude that marriage and relationship education should be a part of the solution: "While those who prize autonomy may be wary of celebrating traditional marriage, most do not begrudge efforts to encourage commitment, educate young people in the qualities that effectively promote relationship stability, or establish voluntary marriage [education] promotion programs" (p. 168). The fuller agenda they embrace, however, includes more controversial elements around fertility and abortion that I have not addressed here. But again, these scholars have not been as specific as I have been about what effective education for young people should look like. U.S. President Barack Obama also has publicly acknowledged the value of this approach to strengthening marriage: "Expanding access to such services [marriage and relationship education] to low-income couples, perhaps in concert with . . . other services already available, should be something everybody can agree on" (2006, p. 334).

I believe the merit in my policy agenda to promote educational programs to help youth and young adults find a safer path to achieving their marital aspirations—and avoid the detours that put those aspirations at more risk—derives from its specifics, its political and financial feasibility, and the emerging evidence that relationship and marriage education can improve relationships. Research to date has examined the effectiveness of specific programs. What remains unexamined, however, is the value of a string of educational opportunities beginning in adolescence and stretching through the young-adult years, engagement, and the early years of marriage. The accumulation of modest educational effects at each time point in the early life course may provide significant help for young people; repeated, timely exposure to research-based, helpful information and relationship skills may be able to guide many more youth from adolescence to quality relationships, healthy marriages, and stable family life.

References

Adler-Baeder, F., & Higginbotham, B. (2004). Implications for remarriage and stepfamily formation for marriage education. *Family Relations, 53*, 448–458.

Amato, P. R. (2004). Tension between institutional and individual views of marriage. *Journal of Marriage and the Family, 66*, 959–965.

Amato, P. R., & Booth, A. (2001). The legacy of parent's marital discord: Consequences for children's marital quality. *Journal of Personality and Social Psychology, 81*, 627–638.

Amato, P. R., Booth, A., Johnson, D. R., & Rogers, S. J. (2007). *Alone together: How marriage in America is changing.* Cambridge, MA: Harvard University Press.

Antle, B. F., Sar, B. K., Christensen, D. N., Ellers, F. S., Karam, E. A., Barbee, A. P., & van Zyl, M. A. (in press). The impact of the *Within My Reach* relationship training on relationship skills and outcomes for low-income individuals. *Journal of Marital and Family Therapy.*

Arias, I., Samios, M., & O'Leary, K. D. (1987). Prevalence and correlates of physical aggression during courtship. *Journal of Interpersonal Violence, 2*(1), 82–90.

Arnett, J. (2000). Emerging adulthood: A theory of development from the late teens through the twenties. *American Psychologist, 55*, 469–480.

Blanchard, V. L., Hawkins, A. J., Baldwin, S. A., & Fawcett, E. B. (2009). Investigating the effects of marriage and relationship education on couples' communication skills: A meta-analytic study. *Journal of Family Psychology, 23*, 203–214.

Bramlett, M. D., & Mosher, W. D. (2001). First marriage dissolution, divorce, and remarriage: United States. *Advanced Data from Vital & Health Statistics, no. 323.* Hyattsville, MD: National Center for Health Statistics.

Cahn, N., & Carbone, J. (2010). *Red families v. blue families.* New York: Oxford University Press.

Carroll, J. A., Willoughby, B., Badger, S., Barry, C. M., & Madsen, S. D. (2007). The impact of varying marital horizons on emerging adulthood. *Journal of Adolescent Research, 22*, 219–247.

Cherlin, A. J. (2009). *The marriage-go-round*. New York: Knopf.

Coontz, S. (2005). *Marriage, a history: How love conquered marriage*. New York: Penguin.

Cowan, P. A., Cowan, C. P., Pruett, M. A., Pruett, K. D., & Wong, J. J. (2009). Promoting fathers' engagement with children: Preventive interventions for low-income families. *Journal of Marriage and the Family, 71*, 663–679.

Cox, R. B., Jr., & Shirer, K. A. (2009). Caring For My Family: A pilot study of a relationship and marriage education program for low-income unmarried parents. *Journal of Couple and Relationship Therapy, 8*, 343–364.

Duncan, S. F., Steed, A., & Needham, C. M. (2009). A comparison evaluation study of web-based and traditional marriage and relationship education. *Journal of Couple and Relationship Therapy, 8*, 162–180.

Fagan, J., Palkovitz, R., Roy, K., & Farrie, D. (2009). Pathways to paternal engagement: Longitudinal effects of risk and resilience on nonresident fathers. *Developmental Psychology, 45*, 1389–1405.

Fawcett, E. B., Hawkins, A. J., Blanchard, V. L., & Carroll, J. S. (2010). Do premarital education programs really work? A meta-analytic study. *Family Relations, 59*, 232–239.

Finer, L. B. (2007). Trends in premarital sex in the United States, 1954-2003. *Public Health Reports, 122*, 73–78.

Futris, T. (2007). *Cultivating healthy couple and marital relationships*. Athens, GA: National Extension Relationship and Marriage Education Network.

Gardner, S. P., & Boellaard, R. (2007). Does youth relationship education continue to work after a high school class? A longitudinal study. *Family Relations, 56*, 490–500.

Gardner, S. P., Giese, K., & Parrott, S. (2004). Evaluation of the connections: Relationships and marriage curriculum. *Family Relations, 53*, 521–527.

Hahlweg, K., & Richter, D. (2010). Prevention and marital instability and distress: Results of an 11-year longitudinal follow-up study. *Behaviour Research and Therapy, 48*, 377–383.

Haskins, R., & Sawhill, I. (2009). *Creating an opportunity society*. Washington, DC: The Brookings Institution.

Hawkins, A. J. (2007). Will legislation to encourage premarital education strengthen marriage and reduce divorce? *Journal of Law and Family Studies, 9*, 79–99.

Hawkins, A. J., Blanchard, V. L., Baldwin, S. A., & Fawcett, E. B. (2008). Does marriage and relationship education work? A meta-analytic study. *Journal of Consulting and Clinical Psychology, 76*, 723–734.

Hawkins, A. J., & Fackrell, T. A. (2010). Does relationship and marriage education for lower-income couples work? A meta-analysis of emerging research. *Journal of Couple and Relationship Therapy, 9*, 181–191.

Hymowitz, K. S. (2006). *Marriage and caste in America*. Chicago: Ivan R. Dee.

Jackson, J. B. (2009). *Premarital predictors of marital relationship quality and stability: A meta-analytic study of couple factors*. Unpublished Ph.D. dissertation. Provo, UT: Brigham Young University.

Jose, A., O'Leary, K. D., & Moyer, A. (2010). Does premarital cohabitation predict subsequent marital stability and marital quality? A meta-analysis. *Journal of Marriage and the Family, 72*, 105–116.

Kerpelman, J. L., Pittman, J. F., Adler-Baeder, F., Eryigit, S., & Paulk, A. (2009). Evaluation of a statewide youth-focused relationships education curriculum. *Journal of Adolescence, 32*, 1359–1370.

Kerpelman, J. L., Pittman, J. F., Adler-Baeder, F., Stringer, K. J., Eryigit, S., Cadely, H. S., & Harrell-Levy, M. K. (2010). What adolescents bring to and learn from relationship education classes: Does social address matter? *Journal of Couple and Relationship Education, 9*, 95–112.

Knox, V., & Fein, D. (2009). Supporting healthy marriage: Designing a marriage education demonstration and evaluation for low-income married couples. In E. Peters & C. M. Kamp Dush (Eds.), *Marriage and family: Complexities and perspectives* (pp. 247–280). New York: Columbia University.

Kunkel, D., Eyal, K., Finnerty, K., Biely, E., & Donnerstein, E. (2005). *Sex on TV, 2005*. Menlo Park, CA: Henry J. Kaiser Family Foundation.

Lewis, S. F., & Fremouw, W. J. (2001). Dating violence: A critical review of the literature. *Clinical Psychology Review, 21*, 105–127.

Malone-Colon, L., & Roberts, A. (2006). Marriage and the well-being of African American boys. *Research Brief No. 2*. Institute for American Values Center for Marriage and Families.

Markman, H. J., Stanley, S. M., & Blumberg, S. L. (2010). *Fighting for your marriage*. San Francisco: Jossey-Bass.

McLanahan, S. (2009). Fragile families and the reproduction of poverty. *Annals of the American Academy of Political and Social Science, 621*, 111–131.

Meyer, D. R., Cancian, M., & Cook, S. T. (2005). Multiple-partner fertility: Incidence and implications for child support policy. *Social Science Review, 79*, 577–601.

National Center for Family and Marriage Research (2009). *Median age at first marriage in the U.S., 2008*. Retrieved May 13, 2010 from http://ncfmr.bgsu.edu/pdf/family_profiles/file78895.pdf.

Nielsen, A., Pinsof, W., Rampage, C., Solomon, A. H., & Goldstein, S. (2004). Marriage 101: An integrated academic and experiential undergraduate marriage education course. *Family Relations, 53*, 485–494.

Nock, S. L., Sanchez, L. A., & Wright, J. D. (2008). *Covenant marriage: The movement to reclaim tradition in America*. New Brunswick, NJ: Rutgers University.

Obama, B. (2006). *The audacity of hope*. New York: Crown.

Olmstead, S., Pasley, K., Meyer, A. S., Stanford, P. S., Fincham, F. D., & Delevi, R. (2010). *Implementing relationship education for emerging adults: Insights from the field*. Manuscript submitted for publication.

Ooms, T., Boggess, J., Menard, A., Myrick, M., Roberts, P., Tweedie, J., & Wilson, P. (2006). *Building bridges between healthy marriage, responsible fatherhood, and domestic violence programs: A preliminary guide*. Washington, DC and Denver, CO: Center for Law and Social Policy and the National Conference on State Legislators.

Ooms, T., & Wilson, P. (2004). The challenges of offering relationship and marriage education to low-income populations. *Family Relations, 53*, 440–447.

Palm, G., & Fagan, J. (2008). Father involvement in early childhood programs: Review of the literature. *Early Child Development and Care, 178*, 745–759.

Rhoades, G. K., Stanley, S. M., & Markman, H. J. (2009). Working with cohabitation in relationship education and therapy. *Journal of Couple and Relationship Therapy, 8*, 95–112.

Scafidi, B. (2008). *The taxpayer costs of divorce and unwed childbearing: First-ever estimates for the nation and all fifty states*. New York: Institute for American Values.

Stanley, S. M. (2001). Making a case for premarital education. *Family Relations, 50*, 272–280.

Stanley, S. M. (2010). Decreasing divorce in U. S. Army couples: Results from a randomized controlled trial using PREP for Strong Bonds. *Journal of Couple and Relationship Therapy, 9*, 149–160.

Stanley, S. M., Amato, P. R., Johnson, C. A., & Markman, H. J. (2006). Premarital education, marital quality, and marital stability: Findings from a large, random household survey. *Journal of Family Psychology, 20*, 117–126.

Stanley, S. M., Markman, H. J., Prado, L. M., Olmos-Gallo, P. A., Tonelli, L., St. Peters, M., Leber, B. D., Bobulinski, M., Cordova, A., & Whitton, S.W. (2001). Community-based premarital prevention: Clergy and lay leaders on the front lines. *Family Relations, 50*, 67–76.

Teachman, J. (2003). Premarital sex, premarital cohabitation, and the risk of subsequent marital dissolution among women. *Journal of Marriage and the Family, 65*, 444–455.

Ventura, S. J. (2009). *Changing patterns of nonmarital childbearing in the United States*. NCHS Data Brief, No. 18. Hyattsville, MD: National Center for Health Statistics.

Whitehead, B. D., & Pearson, M. (2006). *Making a love connection: Teen relationships, pregnancy, and marriage*. Washington, DC: The National Campaign to Prevent Teen Pregnancy.

Wilcox, W. B. (2009). *The state of our unions: Marriage in America 2009. Charlottesville*, VA & New York: The National Marriage Project and the Institute for American Values.

Wilcox, W. B., Doherty, W. J., Fisher, H., Galston, W. A., Glenn, N. D., Gottman, J., Lerman, R., Mahoney, A., Markey, B., Markman, H. J., Nock, S. L., Popenoe, D., Rodriguez, G. G., Stanley, S. M., Waite, L. J., & Wallerstein, J. (2005). *Why marriage matters: Twenty-six conclusions from the social sciences*. New York: Institute for American Values.

Wilson, J. Q. (2002). *The marriage problem*. New York: HarperCollins.

Wolfinger, N. (2005). *Understanding the divorce cycle*. New York: Cambridge University Press.

Wood, R. G., McConnell, S., Moore, Q., Clarkwest, A., & Hsueh, A. (2010). *The Building Strong Families project: Strengthening unmarried parents' relationships: The early impacts of Building Strong Families*. Princeton, NJ: Mathematica Policy Research.

30

Improving Child and Family Outcomes through a Collaborative Service Model

Challenges and Opportunities

Michael White and Gail Winkworth

The multiple and interlinked problems faced by many families who access family relationship services are not addressed effectively by the siloed, single-disciplinary approaches that have traditionally dominated human services agencies. This problem of professional silos, which is experienced internationally (Kaspiew et al., 2009), is made more complex in Australia by the policy and organizational divisions created by the diversity of Australian service systems. Responsibility for service delivery and service funding to support vulnerable families in Australia is divided between various levels of government and between the government and nongovernment sectors.

As the National Framework for Protecting Australia's Children 2009–2020 recognizes, despite significant public investment in family support and child protection across federal and state jurisdictions, the separate efforts of these services still fail many children and young people (Council of Australian Governments [COAG], 2009a, 2009b). The Framework highlights that individual services, and indeed service-delivery systems, operate separately from each other, sometimes in ways that compromise children's safety and well-being.

This chapter focuses on improving the collaborative relationships between the professionals and service-delivery systems that interact with families before, during and after separation, particularly where there are concerns about the safety and well-being of children.

The Wiley-Blackwell Handbook of Couples and Family Relationships, First Edition.
Edited by Patricia Noller and Gery C. Karantzas.

Collaboration to achieve a shared vision broadly refers to actions right across the spectrum, from highly integrated joint initiatives to simple measures to exchange information (Huxham & Vangen, 2005). At its best, collaborative practice inspires all involved and opens up opportunities not possible with professionals or agencies working alone. At its worst, it can be inefficient and ineffective. However, the increasing level of theoretical knowledge about collaboration and its enduring place in rhetoric about policy has not been well translated into practice knowledge. In this chapter we draw on recent Australian research on how collaboration is built between agencies and service-delivery systems concerned with supporting families, particularly where children and parents are vulnerable.

Policy makers and practitioners over decades have consistently pointed to the reasons for collaboration—including the moral imperative to work together to solve the complex issues facing society. Such issues include poverty, crime, economic development, social inclusion, climate change, and child abuse and neglect. Trist, in a seminal article (1983), argued that these difficult issues fundamentally belong in the "inter-organizational domain" (see Huxham & Vangen, 2005). In the context of recent changes to the Australian family law system we examine the case for increased collaboration between family relationship, family support and child protection agencies to support separating families. We discuss the need for particular strategies to align with the level of vulnerability of children and families. Using Moore's public-value model (Moore, 1995, 2000) as a conceptual framework, we analyze existing barriers and enablers of collaborative practice. Finally, we propose a model for increased collaboration that we argue has universal relevance across systems that work to support families and keep children "safe and well" (COAG, 2009a).

The Policy Context

Collaboration to increase children's safety and well-being

Policy frameworks across Australia identify the key social, political, and moral imperatives for improving the level of support to vulnerable children and their families. Common themes are the belief that children need to grow up in a society where their safety, health, development, and learning are paramount, they are nourished and supported to thrive, learn and grow, and are valued in their own right as children (COAG, 2009a, 2009b; Victorian Department of Human Services, 2006; White & Wookey, 2009).

However, over recent years reported numbers of substantiated child abuse and neglect cases have steadily increased (Australian Institute of Health and Welfare [AIHW], 2009). In response to rising community concern, government reform agendas have been initiated across the country that focus on more coordinated efforts at a systemic level to prevent harm to children.

There are many good reasons to focus on more collaborative efforts between services working with families affected by separation and divorce. Firstly, children exposed to violence and high-conflict situations in families form the largest group reported to state child protection agencies (AIHW, 2009). Recognition of the relationship between child abuse and separation and divorce has been slow due to the dominant view that abuse is incidental to separation. More recently research has shown that child abuse occurs not only at the point of separation but is often the reason for separation and may continue for years afterwards (Brown & Alexander, 2007; McIntosh, 2002; McIntosh & Long, 2005).

Secondly, the recent changes to the Australian family law system have shifted the initial stages of family dispute resolution away from the courts and into the realm of practitioners specializing in family dispute resolution based at Family Relationship Centres around Australia. Furthermore, the Shared Parental Responsibility Act was amended in 2006 so that the assumption that parents will equally share parental responsibility after separation could be challenged on the grounds that violence and/or other child abuse exists in the family. This decision means that dispute-resolution practitioners ascertain risks to children and share this information with the courts, creating a clear imperative for information sharing (Winkworth & White, 2010). Other practitioners in these services also need information about risks to children to assist parents to make safe parenting plans where there are concerns about child abuse and neglect.

Collaboration to support families in need

Information sharing about risks to children, while important, is only one of many reasons for greater collaboration between state and commonwealth systems of family service delivery. If children are indeed to grow up in a society in which their safety, health, development, and learning are paramount, parents (by far the most powerful influence on children's development; Heckman, 2008; Shonkoff & Phillips, 2000) need to be supported in their roles. This support is not found in one place. It crosses the boundaries of many services and service systems.

For example, Australian studies show that families need, first, enough money to live on and somewhere safe to live (Bartholomew, 1998; Bray, 2003; Butterworth, 2003; Freiberg & Homel, 2007; Vinson, 2007). They also need access to health care for themselves and their children, as well as information and advice about parenting. At times they will need practical help in the home and relief from parenting, especially when children are young (Slee, 2006; Winkworth, Layton, McArthur, Thomson, & Wilson, 2009). If parents separate, they may need assistance with their child support payments and with the development of safe parenting plans. If there are concerns that children are at risk of harm and their interests are not best served in the care of one or either parent, protective measures will need to be taken to keep them safe (Attorney-General's Department, 2004; Murphy, Campbell, & Pike, 2005).

Federal government services in Australia such as Family Relationship Services and Centres, the Family Support Program, the Child Support Agency, and Centrelink are examples of settings where families are encountered when they may be particularly vulnerable, as are family support, family violence, mental health, and drug and alcohol services in state and territory jurisdictions. Though not directly practicing at the "hard end" of statutory child protection, these diverse settings are critical to supporting many families as they face parenting challenges. After decades of attention to increasing collaboration between service-delivery agencies, coordinated and integrated service systems are only beginning to emerge in some jurisdictions. Collaboration is even less visible across federal and state service systems. Families needing assistance with family relationships and parenting their children must still navigate multiple systems which are often not in communication with each other.

Within the child and family service-delivery context there is a critical need to build knowledge for professionals who work across the many agencies designed to assist families and their troubled relationships, especially where there are risks to children.

Building Knowledge of Collaboration

A project to build knowledge about service-system collaboration

In 2009 the authors were commissioned by the Commonwealth Department of Families, Housing, Community Services and Indigenous Affairs (FaHCSIA) to propose a model that could advance the level of "collaboration and integration" between state Child Protection Services, state-funded family-support agencies, and federally funded Family Relationship Services. The project is described comprehensively in other publications (White & Wookey, 2009; Winkworth & Healy, 2009; Winkworth & White, 2010), however, in summary our approach included interviews and focus groups with 59 people from 39 federal and state, government and nongovernment agencies working across these systems. We applied the collaboration and public-policy literature to the data and developed several theoretical perspectives that can be applied generally to the child and family policy area. These perspectives, or "collaboration constructs," and a model for building collaboration across sectors, form the basis of the remainder of this chapter.

Getting the right level of collaboration

A theme in the collaboration literature is that collaboration strategies should be aligned with specific purposes. Because partnerships are often slow and costly to establish, it is necessary to ensure that scarce resources are used responsibly. Our findings from consultations with service providers increased knowledge about the purpose of particular strategies and reinforced the message that collaboration strategies should align with the vulnerability of children and their families. In practice this meant that to keep children safe, increasing levels of risks to children would need to be met by greater collaboration within and between state and commonwealth systems. Furthermore, collaboration would need to be more complex and sophisticated for the more complicated cases of vulnerable high-risk children.

Most families can keep children safe if they are provided with informal support from their extended families, friends, and local communities and formal support from the service-delivery system should such a need arise. However, at the other end of the spectrum, where these "protective factors" are not present, increasingly formalized and complex collaborations are required to protect vulnerable children who may be exposed to violence and other forms of abuse such as sexual abuse.

Our consultations with service providers confirmed that collaboration increases along a continuum of complexity and commitment (Himmelman, 1992). We identified three increasingly complex levels in the family relationships context that aligned with increasing vulnerability and risks to children and families: Networking (Level 1); Coordinating (Level 2); and Integrating (Level 3).

Table 30.1 summarizes collaborative levels identified through a synthesis of the literature and supported by the project. It considers these by purpose and structure. Examples at each level in the family services context are also identified.

However, the research also indicated that while good examples at all three levels existed within either state or commonwealth service systems, effective collaborative strategies between federal and state systems were not identified. To better inform a model to enhance collaboration between all the various services that are important to families, especially vulnerable families, we asked specific questions of participants about the enablers and barriers to building collaboration.

Enablers and barriers

The enablers and barriers to collaborative practice are best understood in the context of a theory of action such as that proposed by Moore (1995, 2000). In short, Moore postulates that effective action in a complex hierarchical system needs to be a product of three intersecting dynamics. The absence of any one of these will mean that even the best intentions will fail to deliver effective change.

At their highest level these dynamics can be described by the concepts of authority, public value, and capability.

1. Authority (what the system "may do"): Without an appropriate authorizing environment, the momentum for multidisciplinary and multiservice collaboration will be quickly lost and more traditional ways of doing things will emerge and re-establish themselves.
2. Public value (what the system "should do"): Effective collaboration will only take place if it is seen to produce desirable outcomes for the public. These outcomes need to be agreed between participants and, at best, are able to be described and measured.
3. Capability (what the system "can do"): Collaborative efforts between agencies and individuals need to be appropriately resourced. Many efforts in this area have failed due to the lack of resources or lack of skill on the part of those who are seeking to collaborate.

The intersection between these three dynamics underlies effective action. Thus, the capacity for effective action is restricted to the point of intersection between the three dynamics—should one of these be lost the desired outcome will not occur.

The operation of these dynamics in federal and state systems has been discussed in detail elsewhere (Winkworth & White, 2010). However, in summary, it is clear from the consultations with service providers that these three dynamics provide a powerful way of

Table 30.1 Levels of Collaboration

Level of collaboration	*Purpose and target groups*	*Structure and form*	*Examples*
Level 1 Networking	To gain a better understanding of the service systems involved and issues confronting all children and their families To develop trust between services and build the foundation for more complex partnerships	Individual relationships and small-scale cooperative activities that will benefit all families. No or limited formal agreements. Agencies may work towards different goals, affiliations primarily towards own agency or discipline	Family Services Partners Network (services come together regularly to increase knowledge of issues confronting families) Family Relationship Centre and Community Legal Service present joint information sessions to parents. Maternal and child health nurses provide information to single fathers at Family Relationship Centre
Level 2 Coordinating	To make information and services more accessible for vulnerable children and families including those whom formal services find "hard to reach"	More complex and formal levels of organizational involvement and planning. May involve changes to intake, assessment, and referral processes. Collocation or agencies and outposting of staff to form a bridge between services. Simple protocols and Memorandums of Understanding	A family violence worker from a Family Relationship Service is collocated at a Community Health Service Child protection workers are based in community settings to consult with agencies about best level of intervention to assist vulnerable families Portfolio positions (health, housing, police) in state child protection services facilitate better problem solving between services with concerns about vulnerable children

Level 3 Integrating	High level of collaboration to address concerns about children and parents right across the spectrum including at high risk of harm	Formal agreements between services, clearly identified shared goals and targets, legislation which requires partnerships, some unified management systems, pooled funds, shared practice frameworks, common governance arrangements, shared training, shared data systems	Victoria's Integrated Family Support system (IFS) provides readily accessible entry point at a sub-regional catchment area level for parents, professionals, and members of the public who are worried about children As part of the IFS a cross-sectoral Consultancy Panel meets bimonthly to consider system responses to specific high-risk situations

understanding the enablers and barriers to collaboration between commonwealth- and state-funded services. Services struggled to balance what they "may do" (authority), "should do" (public value), and "can do" (capability) to achieve the level of collaborative practice necessary to improve their work with children and families. In turn, this information on enablers and barriers enabled us to form a platform on which a model of collaborative practice could be developed.

Results of consultations—the enablers and barriers

Authority

Mandate and legitimacy. Consultations with federal and state service providers emphasized that new legislation and state government policies provide the mandate and legitimacy for cooperative and collaborative practice. These service providers pointed out that they had made informal attempts at collaboration in the past, and to some extent these had been successful, forming a background for effective collaboration later on. However, they also emphasized that it was the "top-down" approach created by new legislation and policy that provided the mandate for "true" collaboration.

While for the state-based services it was particularly legislative change that drove changes in practice, federal and state agencies pointed out that the signing of the National Framework for Protecting Australia's Children by commonwealth, state, and territory governments signaled a strengthening environment for collaborative practice.

This environment was further strengthened when professional and stakeholder bodies similarly endorsed the new policy and legislative directions. In this way formal legislation, policy directions, and professional endorsement provide a platform from which collaborative practice can emerge. However, in the absence of such an "imprimatur" for collaboration, services tend to maintain their separation and attempts to provide a holistic response to clients fail.

Tendering processes. In addition, a number of agencies drew our attention to the fact that the competitive tendering practices that underlie government funding have acted as a disincentive to agencies working together. It is apparent that there is an inherent conflict between governments' expressed desire to see better-integrated services collaborating for the well-being of families and children, and, on the other hand, tendering practices which pit agencies against each other as competitors. In this context a number of agencies pointed to the positive changes that occurred when the tendering requirements demanded that services show evidence of collaborative arrangements with other service providers.

Identifying public value. Our consultations demonstrated the importance of agencies developing a shared vision that clearly defined common goals and principles to give meaning to terms such as family-centered or child-centered practice. A clear focus on family and child outcomes rather than on the professional activities of staff was what brought agencies together and gave strength to collaborative practice.

While it is important to clearly define what services are trying to achieve together, it is equally important that this goal be measured and described. Without such measures services are unable to clearly articulate what they have achieved and are unable to cooperate in joint-planning processes. From this perspective, the lack of effective data-collection procedures emerges as a barrier to building collaborative enterprises in the human services.

At its simplest level this data collection can take the form of attempts to elicit client feedback and measure client satisfaction with services. We noted that some mechanisms for effective feedback exist in agencies, with feedback being sought by telephone, mail, and community-reference group. However, this area needs to be extended or it can become a barrier to, rather than an enabler of, further collaborative practice.

Capacity to implement. Services that were successful in collaborating developed an authorizing framework for collaboration and were able to describe the outcomes that collaboration might achieve. We also found that successful services were those which put in place specific mechanisms to implement collaboration in a practical way.

These collaborative mechanisms reflected the complexity and continuity of collaboration which we have identified earlier in this chapter—from simple networking to coordination and attempts to create integrated services. The mechanisms that we observed included: the creation of organizational cultures supporting inter-service relationships and interactions; the creation of staff positions with bridging roles to assist services to navigate the divide between services; shared practice frameworks and joint training to provide staff with common understandings of each other's practice; and the provision of resources to support these collaborative practices.

In addition, we found services would second staff to other services in situations where this secondment would enhance the outcomes for children and families. We also observed the impact of shared planning and, to some extent, resource sharing which allows agencies to have a greater impact on the outcomes for children and families.

A Model for Collaboration Across Sectors

The proposed model

Australia has made extensive use of a differentiated network of nongovernment agencies to deliver human services. While this process has leveraged important social, economic, and community resources in support of broad family and child well-being, it has also led to a fragmented sector that will require active intervention and leadership by governments to move towards a desired goal of collaborative and, where necessary, integrated practice. This complex mix of services funded and authorized by different levels of government and delivered by a mix of nongovernment and government agencies provides a good basis for an effective service system.

The combination of Moore's theory of action (1995, 2000) with our own observations and interviews with practitioners has led us to develop a simple statement of the key features of a collaborative and integrated service system for children and families. Further, we have identified five key areas where action needs to be taken to create such a service system. An effective service system for children and families is one in which services: share a common vision focused on commonly agreed priority outcomes; plan together on a local basis; collect and share information to ensure that service users' needs are met; share high-quality evidence-based practices; and engage in the flexible management of their resources to improve client outcomes. To this end, we argue that our five areas of action are likely to deliver effective reform.

The current reality of Australia's service systems reflects a vastly different approach. Separate, sometimes competing, commonwealth and state priorities drive service systems to quite different definitions of desirable outcomes, even though there are times when these are described in the same language. For example, in our consultations we found that the term "best interests of the child" was defined quite differently through the commonwealth family law system and the state child protection system. In this situation it is unreasonable to expect effective collaborative practices to develop since the service systems are progressing to different endpoints. As well as differences in policy, services face quite substantial differences in practice approaches, in perceptions of each other's roles, and understanding of each other's resources, even in a confined local area.

Our observations and work with community agencies and governments through this project has led us to conclude that there are five areas in which governments and service providers have the opportunity to build an effective system. These five critical areas of reform are: (i) authorization; (ii) governance; (iii) performance measurement; (iv) joint professional practice; and (v) practice reform mechanisms. The ways in which these critical success factors combine to support the development of a collaborative and integrated service system are presented schematically in Figure 30.1.

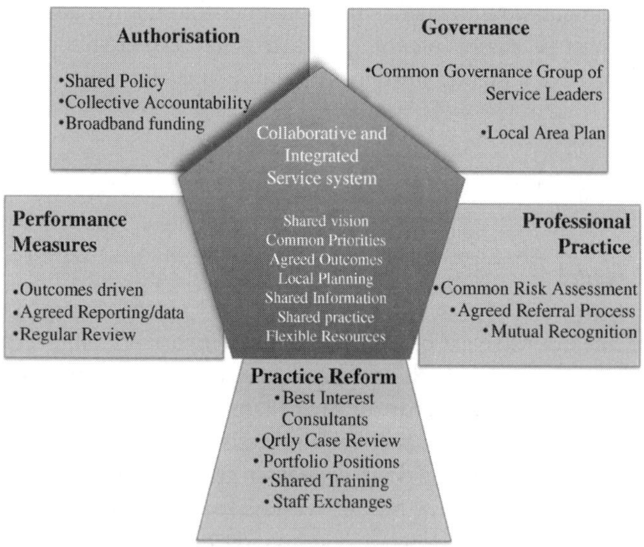

Figure 30.1 Model for a collaborative service system
Source: Adapted from White, M., & Wookey, J. (2009). *Victorian Community Linkages Project: A model for increased collaboration between federal and state service systems to improve the safety and well-being of vulnerable children.* Melbourne: MW Consulting Group

Building a system—whose responsibility?

In order to describe how such a system might be built, it is necessary to identify three levels of action: (i) action by governments; (ii) action by providers (nongovernment agencies and government providers); and (iii) action by professionals.

Action by governments

Shared policy frameworks. If the child and family service systems are to genuinely develop collaborative approaches it is essential that federal and state government departments provide leadership through shared legislative and policy frameworks that include agreements on shared outcomes and funding processes to implement change. For example, regular commonwealth/state intergovernmental mechanisms should facilitate the development of shared policy frameworks based on the principles of children's best interests remaining paramount. While each system separately would maintain that this is their approach now, in practical terms differences in the definition of the phrase "best interests" have resulted in a lack of congruence in approaches. Governments can, however, provide leadership in this area by jointly agreeing to a consistent statement of outcomes for children and families. This statement can build on existing outcomes frameworks which already link outcome statements to particular measures.

Collective accountability at the local level. In the past decade all child and family service agencies have found themselves accountable for government funding according to a range of measures. Unfortunately many of these measures have been reduced to the level of outputs or "targets" which too often describe the activity of the agency rather than its achievement with families. White (2006) argues that one of the most powerful actions government can take is to focus services on broader outcomes rather than on specific outputs of the program of activity. It is difficult to ask individual services to be accountable for the broad outcomes of children's well-being. However, when we consider the service system as a whole, governments and agencies can jointly focus on broader outcomes that become the basis of collaboration. On this basis governments have an opportunity to articulate an expectation that all services within the local area are accountable for agreed outcomes. New funding documents and procurement policies can articulate the expectation that services will be responsible for coordinating their programs to meet the broader good of children and their families. In this way, government can begin the process of creating collaborative service systems to meet these broad community needs rather than focusing on the specific program activities of individual services. Procurement policies regarding competitive tendering where agencies are funded on the basis of their collaboration with other service providers is a very practical means of articulating expectations around collaboration.

Action by service providers. The framework in which collaborative service systems can develop must be set by governments; however, the implementation is the responsibility of the agencies delivering the services. Given the breadth and complexity of the child and family service systems in Australia, individual agencies will need to establish active partnerships through which they can collaborate to achieve broad goals without losing their identities or compromising their legal responsibilities.

Local alliance of services. If governments are able to move to higher levels of collective accountability, based on outcomes for children and families, local agencies will need to respond with new ways of organizing their services and in linking with other agencies. Due to the complexity and diversity of dysfunction in families, it is rare for a single organization to be funded to provide a full range of services to address broad family and child well-being outcomes. More often, federal and state agencies operate in overlapping ways along a broad continuum of family needs which range from widely available universal services to more targeted, and sometimes intrusive, services, where the needs of children are most dire and the opportunities for families to choose to participate is reduced.

In this environment it would be necessary to develop local networks (alliances) of services where the full continuum of child and family needs are met by a number of different agencies working together. These alliances would be responsible for: ensuring strong leadership; actively driving planning and integration of services; promoting and encouraging a shared responsibility for all children within a local area; and developing a strong commitment and responsibility to improve outcomes for children.

The details of the operations of these alliances have been described elsewhere (White & Wookey, 2009), however, key aspects of these alliances would include: (i) the identification of a single fund-holder and facilitating partner who will enable the partnership and manage the funds allocated specifically for alliance projects; (ii) the development of a partnership agreement endorsed by senior regional representatives of key funding agencies and the CEOs of funded organizations describing the mutual accountabilities of the agencies and business rules of day-to-day operations; (iii) agreed practice frameworks for assessment, prioritization, case allocation, and inter-agency referral; and (iv) agreed reporting frameworks for data collection and analysis.

Local area catchment planning. One of the functions of the proposed alliances would be to develop a local area plan to guide the strategic development of the service system. Key performance and outcome measures would be chosen by the alliance from the set agreed between federal and state governments and a commitment would be made between government and the alliance to share responsibility for performance. Models for these processes often exist in place-based planning and community-building activities already embedded in some federal and state programs. These existing models provide a platform upon which a broader local area catchment process can be built and integrated into federal and state program and policy frameworks.

Action by professionals. The third level of action required in order to establish a genuinely collaborative system is action at the level of individual professionals. One of the outcomes of the establishment of effective partnership such as alliances is that they provide an authorizing environment for shared practice between professionals and improved service-delivery coordination.

Our consultations with service providers revealed that significant duplication of service activities could be reduced significantly through the development of common screening, assessment, referral, practice, and reporting frameworks carried out by the professionals in each agency. In response to this finding, the National Framework for Protecting Australia's Children proposed the development of a common approach to assessment, referral, and support (CARRS). This approach is to be used by professionals in universal and targeted services as a common way of identifying and addressing family needs (Department of Families, 2010).

Similar mechanisms are required to enable better communication between the targeted family support intervention services and the statutory services in the commonwealth (family court) and state (child protection) systems. In this regard the Framework for Screening, Assessment and Referrals in Family Relationship Centres and the Family Relationship Advice Line (Attorney General's Department, 2008) provides a useful basis for developing a shared assessment and referral approach for professionals. In particular, this document provides a risk assessment and referral framework, including a range of practice guides reflecting the different levels of direction and support required by families depending on their family functioning and the vulnerability of children. In developing these systems, it is important that professionals learn to value each other's work and give formal recognition to processes that exist in each other's systems.

Best interests consultant. In addition to developing joint professional recognition and improved referral processes our consultations revealed that service coordination and collaboration could be substantially improved through the use of shared staff between organizations. Perhaps the best example of this coordination was the use of a community-based child protection worker whose role it was to bridge the gap between the statutory child protection system in the state of Victoria and other state-funded family-support services systems.

Similar positions could be created in those programs that require the navigation of uncoordinated federal and state services to achieve the best outcomes for vulnerable families and children. The role of these consultants could include: the facilitation of referrals between service systems; the provision of information, advice, and consultation on specific cases in the catchment area; the facilitation of joint approaches to reducing risk and to promoting child safety and well-being; the facilitation of case coordination mechanisms where there are identified issues relating to vulnerable children and their families; and the purchase of case management services to children and families across service systems. These approaches would maximize children's and families' access to appropriate community supports regardless of the service system in which they operate.

Information sharing. Perhaps one of the most challenging areas of collaborative practice between professionals within service systems is the capacity and willingness to share information about children and families, even where consent is given or when high-risk situations ethically and legally override consent (FaHCSIA, 2009; Frost, Robinson, & Anning, 2005) It is clear that a collaborative approach depends on the development of flexible information-sharing arrangements between professionals. Some of these arrangements may need to be supported by legislative change, but at the very least, staff in parallel systems should have access to guidelines regarding when and how information can be shared, by whom, and when, and situations where safety considerations require information to be shared without consent.

While such information sharing is desperately required, our consultation revealed that effective information sharing did occur between services. Across some services, senior professionals would facilitate joint planning and decision making in relation to individual families through a common case review process. This mechanism was deemed highly effective not only in dealing with situations which separately challenged both federal and state services, but also in providing an opportunity to develop shared approaches to complex scenarios that could be used as the basis for future decision making. It modeled excellence in collaboration at a senior level, and became a platform from which best-practice models, the need for staff training, and gaps in service delivery or policy could be identified.

Conclusion

At the most basic level a lack of working together across agencies and jurisdictions means that parents have greater difficulties accessing services specifically set up to assist them. At a more serious level, failure to coordinate information and service responses leaves some children at high risk of harm.

The provision of child and family services in Australia is characterized by substantial fragmentation and division. The service system is divided "horizontally" between two and sometimes three levels of government with the federal, state, and local governments all playing a role in policy, program design, funding, and service delivery.

The system is also split "vertically" between program types with family law, family support, family intervention, child protection, family income, employment, housing programs, and early childhood education and care being provided by a multitude of federal and state departments. Furthermore, the service-delivery system is divided between the federal and state governments as providers and the not-for-profit nongovernment sector which is characterized by extraordinary diversity.

The Australian research reported in this chapter provided a number of insights into the status of collaboration in child and family service-delivery systems and identified some key features of the way forward in the development of further collaboration. In this chapter we essentially identify four key points. Firstly, the continuum of collaboration can form the basis of an effective service system when linked to concepts such as child and family vulnerability. In short, the more vulnerable the child the greater the level of service integration required.

Secondly, if governments and service providers wish to enhance collaboration in their service systems to improve outcomes for children, this collaboration needs to be considered within a theory of action such as that provided by Moore (1995). From this perspective, change will only occur where the authorizing environment is strong, the public value of collaboration is clear, the activities necessary are properly resourced, and staff are appropriately trained. Thirdly, an effectively collaborating service system can be defined as one in which services share common goals leading to shared priorities. These collaborative service systems are best delivered through locally based partnerships of services, using evidence-based practices which are transdisciplinary and are regularly reviewed. Finally, models of good practice exist and platforms for reform are available within existing service and professional mechanisms. However, a genuine reform movement towards a collaborating and, where necessary, integrated service system will require joint action by governments, service providers, and professionals.

References

Attorney-General's Department (2004). *Child support scheme facts and figures 2003–2004*. Canberra: Attorney-General's Department.

Attorney-General's Department (2008). *Framework for screening, assessment and referrals in family relationship centres and the Family Relationship Advice Line*. Canberra: Commonwealth of Australia.

Australian Institute of Health and Welfare (2009). *Child protection Australia 2007–08*. Canberra.

Bartholomew, T. (1998). Family poverty, family homelessness and the systems abuse cycle. *Family Matters, 51*, 37–40.

Bray, J. (2003). *Hardship experiences of Australian families*. Paper presented at the 8th Australian Institute of Family Studies Conference, February 12–14.

Brown, T., & Alexander, R. (2007). *Child abuse and family law: Understanding the issues facing the human service and legal professions*. Crows Nest, NSW: Allen & Unwin.

Butterworth, P. (2003). Multiple and severe disadvantage among lone mothers receiving income support. *Family Matters, 64*, 22–29.

Council of Australian Governments (2009a). *Protecting Children is Everyone's Business—National Framework for Protecting Australia's Children: Implementing the First Three Year Action Plan. 2009–2012*. Canberra: Commonwealth of Australia.

Council of Australian Governments. (2009b). *Protecting Children is Everyone's Business—National Framework for Protecting Australia's Children. 2009–2020*. Canberra: Commonwealth of Australia.

Department of Families, Housing, Community Services and Indigenous Affairs (2009). Information sharing to assist families and children in the child protection system. Canberra.

Department of Families, Housing, Community Services and Indigenous Affairs (2010). *Common approach to assessment, referral and support*. Retrieved July 9, 2010, from http://www.aracy.org.au/index.cfm?pageName=the_CAARS_taskforce.

Freiberg, K., & Homel, K. (2007). The pervasive impact of poverty on children: Tackling family adversity and promoting child development through the Pathways to Prevention Project. In A. France & R. Homel (Eds.), *Pathways and crime prevention: Theory, policy and practice*. Devon, England: Willan.

Frost, N., Robinson, M., & Anning, A. (2005). Social workers in multidisciplinary teams: Issues and dilemmas for professional practice. *Child and Family Social Work, 10*(3), 187–196.

Heckman, J. (2008). The case for investing in disadvantaged young children. In *Big ideas for children: Investing in our nation's future* (pp. 49–58). Washington, DC: First Focus.

Himmelman, A. T. (1992). *Communities working collaboratively for a change*. Minneapolis, MN: The Himmelman Consulting Group.

Huxham, C., & Vangen, S. (2005). *Managing to collaborate: The theory and practice of collaborative advantage*. New York: Routledge.

Kaspiew, R., Gray, M., Weston, R., Moloney, L., Hand, K., Qu, L. et al. (2009). *Evaluation of the 2006 family law reforms*. Melbourne: Australian Institute of Family Studies.

McIntosh, J. (2002). Thought in the face of violence: A child's need. *Child Abuse and Neglect, 26*, 229–241.

McIntosh, J., & Long, C. (2005). Current findings on Australian children in postseparation disputes: Outer conflict, inner discord. *Journal of Family Studies, 11*(1), 99–109.

Moore, M. H. (1995). Creating public value: Strategic management in government. Cambridge, MA: Harvard University Press.

Moore, M. H. (2000). Managing for value: Organisational strategy in for profit, nonprofit governmental organisations. *Non Profit and Voluntary Sector Quarterly, 29*, 183–208.

Murphy, P., Campbell, A., & Pike, L. (2005). Our children's health and safety needs: Progress report on a parenting plan template. Paper presented at the 9th Australian Institute of Family Studies Conference, Melbourne, February 9–11.

Shonkoff, J. P., & Phillips, D. A. (2000). *From neurons to neighbourhoods: The science of early childhood development*. Washington DC: National Academy Press.

Slee, P. (2006). *Families at risk: The effects of chronic and multiple disadvantage*. Adelaide: Shannon Research Press.

Trist, E. (1983). Referent organizations and the development of inter-organizational domains. *Human Relations, 36*, 269–284.

Victorian Department of Human Services (2006). *The state of Victoria's children*. Melbourne: Victoria.

Vinson, T. (2007). *Dropping off the edge: The distribution of disadvantage in Australia*. Melbourne: Jesuit Social Services and Catholic Social Services Australia.

White, M. (2006). Victoria's approach to putting children first. *Public Administration Today, 8*.

White, M., & Wookey, J. (2009). *Victorian Community Linkages Project: A model for increased collaboration between federal and state service systems to improve the safety and well-being of vulnerable children*. Melbourne: MW Consulting Group.

Winkworth, G., & Healy, C. (2009). *The Victorian Community Linkages Project: Increasing collaboration between state and commonwealth service systems to improve the safety and well-being of vulnerable children*. Canberra: Institute of Child Protection Studies.

Winkworth, G., Layton, M., McArthur, M., Thomson, L., & Wilson, F.(2009). *Working in the grey: Increasing collaboration between services in inner North Canberra*. A Communities for Children Project. Canberra: Institute of Child Protection Studies, Australian Catholic University.

Winkworth, G., & White, M. (2010). May do, should do, can do: Collaboration between federal and state service systems for vulnerable children. *Communities, Children and Families Australia, 5*(1).

31

Are Governments and Marriage Strange Bedfellows?

Social Policy and Couple Relationship Education

W. Kim Halford and Elizabeth van Acker

An interesting development since the 1950s has been that some national governments introduced social policies that promote and fund couple relationship education (CRE). This situation represents a new focus for governments in attempting to promote certain characteristics of intimate couple relationships. In this chapter we describe the changing nature of couple relationships, which provides the context within which such policies developed; and we analyze the social policies on CRE of the national governments in Australia, the United States (U.S.) and the United Kingdom (U.K.). The chapter also includes recommendations on how the available evidence should influence social policy.

Social Policy and Marriage

National governments have attempted to influence marriage through social policy for centuries. For example, laws on who can marry have existed for hundreds of years in the U.S., Australia, and the U.K. Divorce laws date back to the 1800s (Coontz, 2005).

The Wiley-Blackwell Handbook of Couples and Family Relationships, First Edition.
Edited by Patricia Noller and Gery C. Karantzas.

The focus of social policy on marriage in most Western countries reflects a consistent goal to encourage the stable, married heterosexual family units as the essential basis of society (Cott, 2000). This policy focus is based on the assumption that such marriages promote broad social benefits (e.g., Waite & Gallagher, 2000).

The notion that promoting stable marriage is a broad social good is somewhat problematic. It is true that divorce and family breakdown have substantial personal, social, and economic costs (Huang, 2005; Ooms, 2005; van Acker, 2003). The annual economic costs of divorce and family breakdown were estimated for 2005 to be AUS $6 billion (U.S. $4.8 billion) in Australia (Halford & Simons, 2005), U.S. $33.3 billion in the U.S. (Schramm, 2006), and U.K. £22 billion (U.S. $53 million) in the U.K. (Social Justice Policy Group, 2006). However, it does not follow from these costs that promoting marital stability is necessarily a desirable social policy.

People living in distressed marriages have high rates of problems like anxiety disorders, depression, alcohol and other drug problems (Whisman, 2007), the individual and couple relationship problems seem to exacerbate each other (Whisman, Uebelacker & Bruce, 2006; Whisman & Uebelacker, 2005), and people leaving relationships with severe marital conflict or violence show improved mental health (Aseltine & Kessler, 1993). Family violence is a major social problem, and almost 50% of distressed couples have significant episodes of violence between the partners (Heyman & Slep, 2009). Children exposed to chronic parental conflict show a range of ongoing adjustment problems (Knickerbocker, Heyman, Slep, Jouriles, & McDonald, 2007; chapter 9 in this volume). Yet, there have been some moves in the early 21st century, particularly within the U.S., to enact social policy designed to provide financial incentives to marry (e.g. lowering tax rates for married couples), and to make divorce harder to attain, in the name of strengthening marriage (Hawkins, Wilson, Ooms, Nock, Malone-Colon, & Cohen, 2009). Such moves are highly problematic as financially and legally restricting the capacity to leave a distressed marriage is associated with ongoing exposure for spouses and children to that distressed marriage. Moreover, barriers to leave distressed marriages could increase exposure to the risk of inter-partner violence, particularly toward women.

In contrast to the debatable evidence on the value of promoting marriage per se, there is significant evidence that mutually satisfing, stable marriages accrue significant benefits for the spouses and their children (e.g., Amato, 2005; Halford, in press; Horn, 2004; Nock, 2005; Whitehead, 2005). This evidence has generated interest from national governments who have attempted to promote quality couple relationships. One notable example is the U.S. government which seeks to promote relationship programs, and commends the use of couple relationship education (CRE) as a key means to promote "healthy marriage" (Hawkins et al., 2009; chapter 29 in this volume). Government funding of the wide dissemination of CRE has not been without controversy. In particular, questions have been raised about whether governments should seek to influence intimate relationships (van Acker, 2008), and whether there is sufficient evidence of the efficacy of CRE in achieving its stated goals to warrant government-supported dissemination (e.g., Bradbury & Karney, 2004). In the next section we review the changing nature of couple relationships, which provides the context that is associated with the current social policies on promoting CRE.

The Changing Nature of Couple Relationships as Context for Social Policy

The decline in marriage and the rise in divorce rates

Across most nations of the world with reliable data, marriage rates have declined and divorce rates have increased since the 1970s (United Nations Economic and Social Affairs Population Division, 2003; chapters 1, 3 in this volume). People are delaying marriage and marrying at older ages. Divorce rates increased in most countries between the 1950s and 1990s, and are substantially higher in developed than developing countries. The median divorce rate in developed countries increased from 13 to about 25 per 1,000 population between the early 1970s and 2000, and in developing countries from 6 to 14 per 1,000 (United Nations Economic and Social Affairs Population Division, 2000).

The decline in marriage rates and increase in divorce rates reflect, in part, the side effects of some positive socioeconomic changes. In the last half of the 20th century, declining marriage rates and increasing divorce rates correlate with women gaining more access to education, greater control over their fertility (i.e., more access to reliable contraception), and greater participation in the paid workforce (United Nations Economic and Social Affairs Population Division, 2003; chapter 3 in this volume). In the 1950s almost all women in developed countries needed to marry to attain economic security. Women found it very difficult to leave a marriage—no matter how dysfunctional the marriage might have been—because they typically had many dependent children, and lacked the economic means to support themselves (Coontz, 2005). In North America, Western Europe, and Australasia, increasing divorce rates correlate across time with increasing education and participation of women in the workforce (United Nations Economic and Social Affairs Population Division, 2003).

In parallel with these social changes, the social meaning of marriage also has evolved. Marriages negotiated by family members were the normal process for arranging marriage for much of recorded history, and concepts of economic security, capacity to raise a family, and benefit to the extended family were strong in the rhetoric around marriage (Coontz, 2005). However, in the last 100 years in Western societies the notion of marriage as a romantic attraction between the partners has become predominant (Coontz, 2005).

Changing laws about divorce have both reflected and shaped the concepts of couple relationships. In developed countries, divorce laws typically date from the 19th century (Gonzalez & Viitanen, 2006). When first introduced, most divorce laws required establishing a partner's blameworthy act, such as perpetrating violence or adultery (Gonzalez & Viitanen, 2006). Implicit in such laws was the assumption that divorce was an act of last resort in response to an untenable situation. Since the 1960s most Western countries have introduced "no-fault" divorce laws where the only required grounds for divorce are that the couple has separated, and the process of divorce has been made less expensive (Gonzalez & Viitanen, 2006). Thus, in Western countries marriage has evolved from an economic and social union between extended families, often enforced by strong social disapproval of divorce and difficult divorce processes, to a private voluntary union between partners that can be dissolved by unilateral action by either partner.

The rise of cohabitation

Another major social change in most Western countries is that cohabiting heterosexual couples are a substantial and increasing minority of all households. For example, cohabiting couples as a percentage of all couple households has increased from 2% in 1970 to 16% in 2006 in Australia (Australian Bureau of Statistics, 2008) while in the U.S. approximately 8% of all couple households are cohabiting (United States Census Bureau, 2003). Furthermore, a large and increasing number of cohabiting couples have children together. For example, in Australia one third of all births in 2009 were to cohabiting couples, rising from 18% in 1987 (Australian Bureau of Statistics, 2008a), with similar trends for increasing rates of nonmarital births evident in the U.K. and the U.S.

Since the 1980s changes in laws across many developed countries have granted similar status and rights to cohabiting couples as married couples. For example, the Australian Labor government under Prime Minister Rudd (2007–2010) passed laws to ensure that those in cohabiting relationships were not discriminated against relative to married couples, providing equality in areas such as tax, social security, employment, health, and aged care.

The trend for more couples to cohabit, to have children together, and to gain similar legal entitlement as married couples, has been a significant source of concern to some prominent religious leaders, social scientists, and social policy analysts (e.g., Abbott, 2009; Australian National Marriage Coalition, 2004; Bradford, et al., 2005; Wilson, 2002). A key issue for many of these commentators is that marriage is an important social institution involving a firm commitment to the partner, that commitment is often based on strongly held social and religious values, and that there are broad social supports for marriage from extended family and community. In contrast, cohabitation lacks the social and religious underpinnings of marriage, the level of long-term commitment to the relationship is frequently unclear, and often extended family and the broader community are less supportive of the relationship than is true for a marriage. Commentators have expressed concern that cohabitation is (wrongly) seen as equivalent or even superior to marriage (e.g., Australian National Marriage Coalition, 2004; Institute for American Values, 2007).

There is substantial social science research showing that cohabitation is different from marriage. While marriage is universally accepted as a commitment intended to be lifelong (even if that intention is not always realized), cohabiting couples vary substantially in their long-term commitment. In Australia about half of cohabiting couples report that they are likely to marry their partner, 25% state they are not sure, and 25% think they probably will not marry their partner (Qu, 2003). Most often cohabitation is a transitional arrangement for couples that either leads to marriage or separation. Across a range of Western countries, more than 80% of cohabiting couples either marry or separate within 5 years (Qu & Weston, 2001). Cohabitation is now the most common means for couples in Western countries to begin a committed relationship. The vast majority of couples cohabit before marrying, with recent research showing that 85% of marrying couples in Australia cohabited premaritally, and 74% cohabited premaritally in the U.S. (Australian Bureau of Statistics, 2008; United States Census Bureau, 2003).

Declining thresholds for initiating separation and divorce

The high threshold to initiate divorce in earlier eras reflected particular social attitudes. In the 1960s, most adults in the U.S. and Australia believed that divorce should only occur when the marriage had severe problems (Australian Institute of Family Studies, 1997; Thornton & Young-DeMarco, 2001). However, by the late 1990s the majority of adults in the U.S. (Thornton & Young-DeMarco, 2001), most countries of Western Europe (de Graaf & Kalmijn, 2006), and Australia (Australian Institute of Family Studies, 1997), endorsed the view that divorce is acceptable if the partners no longer wish to remain together. Relative to the 1960s, in the early 2000s more people describe psychological motives (e.g., "I felt we had grown apart," "We were not communicating") as the reasons for their divorce (de Graaf & Kalmijn, 2006), rather than severe conflict, violence, or adultery. Both cross-sectional (Kalmijn & Poortman, 2006) and longitudinal studies (Amato & Rogers, 1997) show that severe marital problems like violence or adultery now predict the occurrence of only a minority of divorces. Separation is often the outcome for relationships that initially have only mild problems (Amato & Rogers, 1997), and relationships that were once highly satisfying (Johnson & Booth, 1998). In other words, the threshold for marital dissolution has declined. This trend is accelerated even further by increasing rates of cohabitating couples. The absence of any legal requirements to initiate separation from cohabiting relationships, and the high rate of break up from cohabiting, further underscores how the threshold to end relationships has declined.

In summary, relationship satisfaction has become central to the fate of couple relationships. Given the social and economic consequences of relationship dissolution, it is not surprising that the social policy of some governments has started to address ways to promote mutually satisfying couple relationships.

Social Policy and Couple Interventions

Australia

Since the 1960s, the Australian government has intervened specifically in couple relationships by promoting psychological interventions that seek to promote stable, satisfying relationships. The *1960 Matrimonial Causes Act* established a program of Family and Relationship Counselling to support stable marriage and family life by providing psychological counseling. The focus of this policy was on couples seeking divorce, and the aspiration was to promote reconciliation. The *1975 Family Law Act* replaced the *Matrimonial Causes Act,* introduced no-fault divorce laws nationally, and substantially broadened the focus of promoting psychological interventions. It provided funding for organizations to offer CRE which was seen as desirable for all couples and should be made universally available to marrying couples. These psychological interventions sought to promote stable, mutually satisfying marriages by helping couples develop key relationship knowledge and skills, e.g., shared realistic expectations, and effective communication

(Halford & Simons, 2005). These programs were seen as enhancing the health of the relationship, the satisfaction of the spouses, and the stability of the marriage.

While the Australian government was one of the first to fund couple counseling and CRE, funding for CRE has always been quite modest in scope. In the early 1990s just AUS $500,000 (U.S. $400,000) per year was provided nationally to support CRE. In the late 1990s, the Howard Coalition (Conservative) government expanded funding to approximately AUS $4 million (U.S. $3.2 million) per annum via the Family Relationship Services Program (FRSP). One key aim was to increase the rate of participation in CRE because only 20% of couples took CRE at that time. There was some modest increase in the rate of CRE participation by marrying couples by 2005, but disadvantaged groups (Indigenous and ethnic minority groups, people living in rural and remote communities, stepfamilies, and people with a mental illness or disability) remain under-represented in accessing CRE (Catholic Welfare Australia and the Department of Families, Community Services And Indigenous Affairs, 2006; Simons & Parker, 2002).

In 2005, the national government under Prime Minister Howard implemented major reforms to family law, and provided funds of AUS $397 million (U.S. $320 million) to establish a large number of Family Relationship Centres (FRCs). While FRCs were described as promoting CRE, almost all of the funding was allocated to the FRC's main goal of providing mediation, counseling, and dispute resolution for separating couples. After his election in 2007 Prime Minister Kevin Rudd and his Labor government increased FRSP funding by a further AUS $277 million (U.S. $222 million) over 3 years from 2008 to 2011, with no attention to expanding CRE. Funding CRE is not on the political agenda in Australia in 2010, and there is little social policy debate about marriage. Instead the former Prime Minister Rudd targeted supporting "working families." It is likely that current Prime Minister Julia Gillard will develop social policies that focus more on work–family conflict, with couple relationships forming a rather invisible subset of these matters.

United States

Supporting marriage and relationship education has been firmly on the policy agenda in the U.S., at least since the mid-1990s. In 1996 under President Clinton, the *Personal Responsibility and Work Opportunity Reconciliation Act* connected the values of self-reliance and hard work. The Act initiated the *Temporary Assistance for Needy Families* (TANF) program, a welfare-reform package aiming to reduce welfare dependency, encourage two-parent families, and strengthen marriage. It asserted that "marriage is the foundation of a successful society" and "an essential institution of a successful society which promotes the interests of children." In 2002, the Administration for Children and Families (ACF) within the Department of Health and Human Services launched the *Healthy Marriage Initiative*. The 2006 TANF reauthorization provided $500 million of funding (over 5 years) for advertising campaigns on the value of marriage, marriage education, and skills training.

In his book *The Audacity of Hope* (2006) President Obama specifically refers to marriage education, acknowledging that research shows it can help "married couples stay together" and can encourage "unmarried couples who are living together to form a more lasting bond" (Obama, 2006, p. 334). He advocates expanding access to these services along with job training and placement and medical coverage. Current funding continues until 2011 and if bipartisan support continues, it is likely that some form of the healthy marriage initiative will also continue. However, this initiative will be subsumed underneath the umbrella of fatherhood programs and with smaller amounts of funding.

United Kingdom

Supporting couple relationships was championed for the first few years of the U.K.'s Labour government from 1997, with the introduction of support for CRE during the late 1990s and early 2000s (Advisory Group on Marriage and Relationship Support, 2002; Hart, 1999; Home Office, 1998). However, levels of funding for CRE declined markedly between then and 2010. The U.K. Labour government became less concerned about strengthening marriage as the best way to enhance the well-being of children. Stable families—including cohabiting heterosexuals or same-sex couples—rather than stable marriages were perceived as the key drivers of more policy objectives. Social policy was framed by a concentration on children and parenting and the couple dimension of family life has been ignored (van Acker, 2008).

The issue of strengthening couple relationships, and specifically marriage, has been resuscitated by the U.K. Conservative Party. Prime Minister David Cameron laments the demise of marriage, arguing that this demise should be reversed, stopped, or at least slowed, by government policy. The Conservative Party argues that by supporting marriage and the family, people have better opportunities and the best possible start in life. Its goal is to "make Britain the most family-friendly country in the world." When in Opposition, the Conservative Party commissioned the Social Justice Policy Group (SJPG) to investigate family problems and poverty. In its *State of the Nation Report—Fractured Families* (2006) it is argued that marriage lies at the heart of stable families and safe communities. The SJPG's final report (2007) proposes a raft of recommendations such as creating "a positive policy bias in support of marriage" through tax incentives and reforms to the welfare system, childcare, and housing. It also advocates an expansion of preventative relationship and parenting education by the voluntary sector through government-supported schemes (2007, pp. 44–50). *Breakthrough Britain* acknowledges that a transferable tax allowance for married couples—U.K. £20 per week—is a modest amount, but that it is important in providing a "symbolic recognition of the institution of marriage." Given the budgetary problems that the Coalition government is facing, these tax breaks may not be implemented.

Related policy developments

Many policies are relevant to CRE, including the idea of supporting relationships via further strategies to alleviate poverty, reforming family law, and recognizing gay marriage. In the U.S., the Center for Law and Social Policy (CLASP), a progressive think tank, has devised *Marriage Plus* as a way to assist groups at high risk of couple-relationship breakdown such as low-income families. While CLASP endorses programs that attempt to strengthen relationships, it proposes a wider set of goals for the U.S. government's Healthy Marriage Initiative. First, public policies and programs should aim to help more children grow up with their two biological parents in a healthy, stable relationship. However, marriage may not be a feasible or desirable option for all parents. Therefore, the second goal is to help parents who are not married, or who are separated, divorced, or remarried to be financially responsible and to cooperate in raising their children. Accordingly, one of CLASP's former researchers, Theodora Ooms (2002, pp. 4–7), argues for *Marriage Plus*, advocating a combination of "soft" and "hard" services. "Soft" services include relationship skills and marriage education workshops, financial management classes, and peer support groups, while "hard" services include job training and placement, housing, medical coverage, and substance-abuse treatment if necessary. Not just governments, but the legal, education, health, business, faith, and media sectors should work to pursue these goals. Programs should also be designed to meet the needs of disadvantaged and culturally diverse groups (Ooms, 2007). Clearly, this approach encompasses an ambitious wish list, but it is worth consideration.

There is deliberation concerning other social policy reforms that target couple relationships. For example, there are demands from some politicians, policy makers, and religious and community groups to reform family law to give economic incentives for couples to marry rather than cohabit (Abbot, 2009; Centre for Social Justice, 2009). In the U.S., several states, including Arizona, Florida and Oklahoma, spend TANF funds on programs that attempt to lower the divorce rate or to encourage couples to marry. Louisiana passed the *Covenant Marriage Act* in 1996, meaning that couples intending to marry must first undertake marriage education and must wait for 2 years after separation before a no-fault divorce can be granted. Other state initiatives include fatherhood programs, attempts to reduce teen pregnancies (mainly via abstinence education), community-based and faith-based initiatives.

There are a number of contentious social policy issues surrounding marriage versus cohabiting that have different interpretations in the U.K., U.S., and Australia. In the U.K., gays and lesbians have similar rights and obligations to those of married couples after the passing of the *Civil Partnership Act* in 2004. Nevertheless, civil partnerships and marriage are not recognized as the same thing: marriage in Britain remains exclusively the preserve of heterosexual couples. Federal governments in the U.S. and Australia strongly oppose same-sex marriages: marriage is defined as a union between a man and a woman. While U.S. states such as Vermont recognize gay marriages, this is not the case in Australia. In Australia, Prime Minister Howard (1996–2007) introduced the *Marriage Act Amendment Act 2004*, supported by the then Labor Opposition, which not only asserts that gay marriage is illegal, but prevents same-sex couples who marry overseas from having their marriages recognized in Australia. Gay groups argued that the legislation enshrines discrimination in law, and sends the message that same-sex couples and parents are second-class citizens. At the same time, retirement benefits were extended to same-sex couples through the creation of a new relationship category entitled "interdependency." This act removed death taxes on retirement benefits left to same-sex partners.

While the U.S., U.K., and Australian governments seem to share social policy objectives of reducing the costs of the breakdown of couple relationships, the investment in the family is occurring with different goals and agendas. Policies that promote couple relationship education have developed primarily in the U.S., with a strong focus on marriage, which has been linked to combating poverty and lessening dependency on welfare. The Australian government has espoused the value of couple relationship education but provided very limited funding to match the rhetoric, and instead focused funding on reducing conflict during separation and divorce. In the U.K. the focus has been on parenting and the needs of children in different couple arrangements including cohabitation, marriage and parental separation without preferentially supporting any particular form of couple arrangement (van Acker, 2008).

Effective Couple Relationship Education

As the psychological research reviewed in other chapters of this book demonstrates, there are crucial skills, attitudes, and knowledge that give partners a better chance of developing and sustaining a healthy, mutually satisfying couple relationship (see parts III–VII in this volume). Some people acquire these attitudes, skills, and knowledge through life experiences, but many people do not. CRE is the provision of structured education to couples about relationship knowledge, attitudes, and skills (Halford, Markman, & Stanley, 2008; chapter 19 in this volume). CRE works with couples who are currently satisfied in their relationship, and are committed to that relationship. The goals of CRE are to assist couples to sustain healthy, mutually satisfying relationships, and to reduce the prevalence of relationship distress and separation (Halford et al., 2008).

Approaches to couple relationship education and their effectiveness

There are two broad approaches to CRE that are often used by practitioners and are sufficiently structured to be amenable to evaluation: (i) structured, inventory-based assessment and feedback; and (ii) curricula-based teaching of specific relationship skills and knowledge. Inventory-based assessments are often used to give couples detailed feedback about relationship strengths and weaknesses (Larson, Newell, Topham, & Nichols, 2002), based on the assumption that such feedback can guide couples to strengthen their relationships. Sometimes inventory assessments constitute the entire process of CRE, sometimes inventories are used as part of curricula-based CRE (Larson et al., 2002). While inventories are widely used and have an empirical basis to their development, there are very few published studies evaluating their effects on couple relationships (Halford, in press). Assessment and feedback, and curriculum-based skill-training approaches are the approaches that have been shown to be effective. Furthermore, the benefits of CRE seem predominantly to be for high-risk couples (see chapter 19 in this volume), though CRE can be of benefit to couples with already positive relationships by teaching them how to deal with relationship issues that may arise in the future.

CRE as offered in practice is often brief (Halford et al., 2008; Halford & Simons, 2005; Stanley, Amato, Johnson, & Markman, 2006), and typically has little or no focus on active training of relationship skills (Halford & Simons, 2005) even though this is the only approach to CRE with clear evidence for its efficacy. Evaluation of government-funded CRE is required as a condition of funding, but is restricted to assessing rates of attendance and consumer satisfaction, and it is likely that much currently provided CRE is ineffective (Halford & Simons, 2005). There is no requirement to utilize evidence-based approaches to CRE, nor is funding available for rigorous evaluation.

Ultimately for CRE to have a population level impact, evaluation of CRE with disadvantaged couples, and knowledge of how to promote access to services for those couples, is very important. Significant current work in the U.S. is testing the proposition that widespread delivery of CRE can be achieved by embedding CRE in services already accessed and trusted by couples (see Halford et al., 2008 for a review of these efforts). For example, current demonstration projects are assessing the effectiveness of working through agencies, such as adult education, employment services, and even jails, to provide CRE (often in combination with other services) to disadvantaged groups (Hawkins & Fackrell, 2010). The institutional contact also enables educators in relevant organizations and communities to contextualize the curriculum to fit the needs of the couples. For example, chaplains in the U.S. Army have been successfully trained to serve military couples before and after deployment (Stanley et al., 2005).

There have been some examples of sustained initiatives in which government, religious organizations, and community groups have collaborated to promote the value of evidence-based CRE. The Oklahoma Marriage Initiative (see www.Okmarriage.org) began in the late 1990s with the goal of reducing the state's high divorce rate and nonmarital births. Under the leadership of the Governor and the Department of Health and Human Services, the state sought to promote high levels of support for marriage via a public–private, multi-sector collaboration. It is too early to evaluate the impact on relationship satisfaction or separations from this initiative, but an estimated 100,000 people have completed at least 12 hours of CRE over a 4-year period, showing such efforts can lead to widespread uptake.

Implications and Conclusions

Governments face many challenges in developing acceptable and effective policies. Supporting couple relationships is an unusual policy development that does not sit easily with other aspects of government programs. However, as Hawkins et al. (2009) note, there were recent points in history when government policy to regulate drink driving or smoking in public places was questioned as appropriate targets of social policy. Now these areas of social policy are widely accepted as appropriate, and have achieved many positive benefits.

Promotion of CRE has waxed and waned as a social policy issue in the U.S., the U.K., and Australia since the 1970s, receiving different degrees of priority and funding at different times (van Acker, 2008). The U.S. government seeks to enhance self-reliance and personal responsibility via marriage, and has led the push to make CRE more widely available. A somewhat different focus by some U.S. state governments has been to restructure the pathways into and out of marriage via legislation promoting covenant marriages or making divorce more difficult to attain. In our view, the focus should be more on enhancing the quality of couple relationships so people will be more likely to choose to remain in the relationship, rather that attempting to place barriers to entering or exiting relationships.

Relative to the U.S., in the U.K. and Australia, there is more implicit acceptance of different forms of parenting and partnering that exist outside marriage as modern lifestyle choices. The U.K. has tended to avoid any focus on couple relationships, except where it is relevant to effective parenting. Australia has espoused the importance of the couple relationship and access to CRE, but not placed the emphasis upon marriage evident in U.S. initiatives. However, Australian governments have not matched the rhetoric of the value of CRE with substantial funding.

Focusing on couple relationships in isolation is unlikely to be the best approach to strengthen families. Alleviating poverty, reducing unemployment, and improving work–-family balance are important measures that impact on the well-being of couples and families. At the same time, policy makers can help build the capacity to provide CRE, which can strengthen relationships of those who are interested in participating in the various programs. However, current policy pays insufficient attention to promoting evidence-based types of CRE, or to focusing outreach on the groups of couples most likely to benefit. High-quality evaluations of CRE programs are sparse in Australia and the U.K., although progress in this area is encouraging in the U.S.

References

Abbott, T. (2009). *Battlelines*. Melbourne: Melbourne University Press.

Advisory Group on Marriage and Relationship Support (2002). *Moving Forward Together: A proposed strategy for marriage and relationship support for 2002 and beyond. London*: Lord Chancellor's Department.

Amato, P. (2005). The impact of family formation change on the cognitive, social, and emotional well-being of the next generation. *The Future of Children, 15*, 75–96.

Amato, P. R., & Rogers, S. J. (1997). A longitudinal study of marital problems and subsequent divorce. *Journal of Marriage and the Family, 59*, 612–624.

Aseltine, R. H., & Kessler, R. C. (1993). Marital disruption and depression in a community sample. *Journal of Health and Social Behaviour, 34*, 237–251.

Australian Bureau of Statistics. (2008). *Australian social trends 2007*. Canberra: Australian Government.

Australian Bureau of Statistics. (2008a). *Australian social trends 2009*. Canberra: Australian Government.

Australian Institute of Family Studies (1997, April 3). Beliefs about marriage. *The Brisbane Courier Mail*, p. 4.

Australian National Marriage Coalition. (2004). *Why marriage matters*. Wollongong, Australia: National Marriage Coalition.

Bradbury, T. N., & Karney, B. R. (2004). Understanding and altering the longitudinal course of marriage. *Journal of Marriage and the Family, 66*, 862–879.

Bradford, W. W., Doherty, W. J., Fisher, H., Galston, W. A., Glenn, N. D., Gottman, J., et al. (2005). *Why marriage matters: Twenty-six conclusions from the social sciences* (2nd edn.). New York: Institute for American Values.

Catholic Welfare Australia and the Australian Department of Families, Community Services and Indigenous Affairs (2006). *Lessons from the field: Family relationships services in rural and remote Australia—Challenges and good practice.* Canberra, Australia: Department of Families, Community Services and Indigenous Affairs.

Centre for Social Justice (2009). *Every Family Matters: An in-depth review of family law in Britain.* London: Centre for Social Justice.

Conservative Party (2008). *Policy: Where We Stand: Family.* http://www.conservatives.com/Policy/Where_we_stand/Family.aspx, retrieved February 16, 2010.

Coontz, S. (2005). *Marriage, a history: From obedience to intimacy, or how love conquered marriage.* New York: Viking Press.

Cott, N. (2000). *Public vows: A history of marriage and the nation.* Cambridge, MA: Harvard University Press.

de Graaf, P. M., & Kalmijn, M. (2006). Divorce motives in a period of rising divorce: Evidence from a Dutch life-history survey. *Journal of Family Issues, 27,* 483–505.

Gonzalez, L., & Viitanen, T. K. (2006). *The effect of divorce laws on divorce rates in Europe.* Bonn, Germany: Institute for the Study of Labour.

Halford, W. K.(in press). *Marriage and relationship education: What works and how to provide it.* New York: Guilford Press.

Halford, W. K., Markman, H. J., & Stanley, S. M. (2008). Strengthening couple relationships with education: Social policy and public health perspectives. *Journal of Family Psychology, 22,* 497–505.

Halford, W. K., & Simons, M. (2005). Couple relationship education in Australia. *Family Process, 44,* 147–259.

Hart, G. (1999). *The funding of marriage support: A review.* London: Lord Chancellor's Department.

Hawkins, A. J., & Fackrell, T. A. (2010) Does marriage and relationship education for lower-income couples work? A meta-analytic study of emerging research. *Journal of Couple and Relationship Therapy, 9,* 181–191.

Hawkins, A. J., Wilson, R. F., Ooms, T., Nock, S. L., Malone-Colon, L., & Cohen, L. (2009). Recent government reforms related to marital formation, maintenance and dissolution in the United States: A primer. *Journal of Couple and Relationship Therapy, 8,* 264–281.

Heyman, R. E., & Slep, A. M. S. (2009). A translational research orientation to family violence. *Violence and Victims, 24,* 283–301.

Home Office (1998). *Supporting families, a consultation document.* London: The Home Office.

Horn, W. (2004). Marriage, family, and the welfare of children: A call for action. In D. Moynihan, T. Smeeding, & L. Rainwater (Eds.), *The Future of the Family.* New York: Russell Sage.

Huang, W. J. (2005). An Asian perspective on relationship and marriage education. *Family Process, 44,* 161–173.

Institute for American Values, (2007). *Why marriage matters: Twenty-six conclusions from the social sciences,* retrieved at http://www.americanvalues.org.

Johnson, D. R., & Booth, A. (1998). Marital quality: A product of the dyadic environment or individual factors? *Social Forces, 76,* 883–904.

Kalmijn, M., & Poortman, A. (2006). His or her divorce? The gendered nature of divorce and its determinants. *European Sociological Review, 22,* 201–214.

Knickerbocker, R., Heyman, R. E., Slep, A. M. S., Jouriles, E. N., & McDonald, R. (2007). Co-occurrence of child and partner maltreatment: Definitions, prevalence, theory, and implications for assessment, treatment, and policy. *European Psychologist: A Journal of the American Psychological Association, 12,* 36–44.

Larson, J. H., Newell, K., Topham, G., & Nichols, S. (2002). A review of three comprehensive premarital assessment questionnaires. *Journal of Marital and Family Therapy, 28,* 233–239.

Nock, S. (2005). Marriage as a public issue. *The Future of Children, 15*, 13–32.

Obama, B. (2006). *The audacity of hope: Thoughts on reclaiming the American dream*. New York: Crown.

Ooms, T. (2002). *Marriage-Plus*. Washington, DC: Center for Law and Social Policy.

Ooms, T. (2005). *The new kid on the block: What is marriage education and does it work?* Washington, DC: Center for Law and Social Policy.

Ooms, T. (2007). *Adapting healthy marriage programs for disadvantaged and culturally diverse populations: What are the issues?* Washington, DC: Center for Law and Social Policy.

Qu, L. (2003). Expectations of marriage among cohabiting couples. *Family Matters, 64*, 36–39.

Qu, L., & Weston, R. (2001). Starting out together through cohabitation or marriage. *Family Matters, 60*, 76–79.

Schramm, D. (2006). Individual and social costs of divorce in Utah, *Journal of Family and Economic Issues, 27*, 133–151.

Simons M., & Parker R. (2002). *A Study of Australian Relationship Education Service Activities*. Canberra, Australia: Australian Government, Department of Family and Community Services.

Social Justice Policy Group (2006). *Breakdown Britain: State of the Nation Report – Fractured Families*. London: Centre for Social Justice.

Social Justice Policy Group (2007). *Breakthrough Britain: Ending the costs of social breakdown, Volume 1: Family breakdown*. London: Centre for Social Justice.

Stanley, S. M., Allen, E. S., Markman, H. J., Saiz, C., Bloomstrom, G., Thomas, R. et al. (2005). Dissemination and evaluation of marriage education in the Army. *Family Process, 44*, 187–201.

Stanley, S., Amato, P., Johnson, C., & Markman, H. (2006). Premarital education, marital quality, and marital stability: Findings from a large, random, household survey. *Journal of Family Psychology, 20*, 117–126.

Thornton, A., & Young-DeMarco, L. (2001). Four decades of trends in attitudes toward family issues in the United States: The 1960s through the 1990s. *Journal of Marriage and the Family, 63*, 1009–1037.

United Nations Economic and Social Affairs Population Division (2003). *World fertility report*. New York: United Nations.

United States Census Bureau. (2003). *Census 2000 special report: Married couples and unmarried partner households 2000*. Washington DC: U.S. Government.

van Acker, E. (2003). Administering romance: Government policies concerning pre- marriage education programs. *Australian Journal of Public Administration, 62*, 15–23.

van Acker E. (2008). *Governments and marriage education policy: Perspectives from the UK, Australia and the US*. Basingstoke, England: Palgrave Macmillan.

Waite, L. J., & Gallagher, M. (2000). *The case for marriage: Why married people are happier, healthier, and better off financially*. New York: Doubleday.

Whisman, M. A. (2007). Marital distress and DSM-IV psychiatric disorders in a population-based national survey. *Journal of Abnormal Psychology, 116*, 638–643.

Whisman, M. A., & Uebelacker, L. A. (2009). Prospective associations between marital discord and depressive symptoms in middle-aged and older adults. *Psychology and Aging, 24*, 184–189.

Whisman, M. A., Uebelacker, L. A., & Bruce, M. L. (2006). Longitudinal association between marital dissatisfaction and alcohol use disorders in a community sample. *Journal of Family Psychology, 20*, 164–167.

Whitehead, B. D. (2004). *Testimony before the Committee on Health, Education, Labor and Pensions Subcommittee on Children and Families*. U.S. Senate, 28 April.

Wilson, J. Q. (2002). *The marriage problem: How our culture has weakened families*. New York: Harper Collins.

PART IX

Integration and Conclusion

32

Common Themes in Couple and Family Relationship Research and Practice

Gery C. Karantzas and Patricia Noller

In this book we have sought to cover many areas involving families and relationships. In this closing chapter we seek to integrate discussion across the major themes that have been dealt with by the authors from various disciplines and subdisciplines in the social sciences including sociology, public policy, communication, developmental psychology, social and personality psychology, clinical and counseling psychology, and child protection. We have identified eight major themes that were discussed across a number of chapters. These eight themes were: family structure versus functioning; attachment theory; divorce and family breakdown; conflict and communication; self-regulation, partner regulation, and behavior change; caregiving and parenting; relationship education and therapy; and finally policy implications. We deal with each of these themes in the following sections of this chapter.

Family Structure versus Functioning

A number of contributors focus on the changing social context of the family in the 21st century with the evolution of a wider range of family forms including cohabiting couples and families as well as gay and lesbian couples. Weston et al. (chapter 1) note that irrespective of family form or structure, all children need to have their basic needs met. They also note that the meeting of these needs can be affected not just by what happens in

The Wiley-Blackwell Handbook of Couples and Family Relationships, First Edition.
Edited by Patricia Noller and Gery C. Karantzas.

the family, but also by external factors such as economic circumstances (e.g., the global financial crisis), government policies around health and education, and advancements in technology (e.g., the Internet and mobile phones). Weston et al. argue that "family functioning is an important mediator of the association between family structure and the well-being of the family" and that irrespective of family structure, government policy needs to focus on how the family functions across the lifespan and tailor interventions to meet changing requirements (see also Antonucci et al., chapter 4).

De Vaus (chapter 2) focuses on the erosion of guidelines that have traditionally regulated relationship behavior such as sexual activity, marriage, and parenthood. He argues that this change has led to people having to make many more choices and to take responsibility for those choices. In addition, people need to deal with the consequences—both positive and negative—of those choices. The erosion of these guidelines has led to much diversity in form and function and a blurring of the distinctions about what is considered appropriate and what is not. As a result of the choices available, people can be paralyzed into doing nothing rather than making careful plans.

Hawkins (chapter 29) acknowledges similar trends in relationship formation and functioning as de Vaus, and also claims that shifts in social timing such as delayed marriage and high divorce rates in the parent generation mean that many young people do not have models that correspond to the new ways of forming and maintaining relationships, especially outside of marriage. Wilkinson (chapter 5) argues that adolescent problems are frequently associated with either poor relationships with parents or a poor relationship between their parents, and notes, as does Hawkins (chapter 29), that many adolescents develop problems because of the poor role models to which they are exposed of how to manage relationships.

Bianchi et al. (chapter 3) argue that these changes in family form have detrimental effects on children because of increasing economic inequality and family instability. While there are different opinions on this issue, there is general agreement that changes in family structure have increased poverty and the risks of negative outcomes for children. While some, especially in the United States, see supporting marriage as the answer, Bianchi et al. argue that marriage in and of itself is unlikely to increase the economic well-being of families in areas where unemployment, crime, and substance abuse are at high levels.

Antonucci et al. (chapter 4) acknowledge the importance of family in the lives of individuals and for the stability of society. They note, however, that families, whatever their form, can have both negative and positive impacts on the developing person and that these positive and negative effects depend on the broader social context of the family across the lifespan. Karantzas (chapter 6) also notes that changes in family structure related to these shifts in social trends have resulted in families needing to negotiate the care of older parents to a greater extent than was true for previous generations. Competing life responsibilities and reduced family size have made it more difficult for adult children to attend adequately to parents' needs for emotional and instrumental support.

Hurd and Noller (chapter 25) report on the effects of form and function in self-harming adolescents. Specifically, self-harming adolescents were more likely to be living with their single mothers than both their biological parents and also more likely to come from families lower in socioeconomic status compared to nonclinical and depressed adolescents. These young people also saw their families as more conflicted, less cohesive, and less expressive than did the adolescents in the other groups. They were also less likely to report good communication with other family members or feeling understood by them, and were less likely to seek help with problems. They also saw their parents as being low in care and high in overprotection and their mothers as neglectful.

Attachment Theory

Many of the chapters highlight the importance of relationship partners and family members experiencing love, comfort, and security in their family relationships. Thus it is not surprising that attachment theory is often cited throughout this volume to explain relationships with parents (Karantzas, chapter 6; Wilkinson, chapter 5), caregiving (Canterberry and Gillath, chapter 14; Karantzas, chapter 6), social support (Cutrona, chapter 27; Karantzas, McCabe, & Cole, chapter 28; Simpson et al., chapter 26), love and sex (Shaver & Mikulincer, chapter 11), communication and conflict (Noller, chapter 9), attributions and self-regulation (Hazelwood, chapter 15), and couple and family therapy (Canterberry and Gillath, chapter 14; Feeney & Fitzgerald, chapter 20; Johnson & Rheem, chapter 23; Shaver & Mikulincer, chapter 11).

Attachment theory was developed by Bowlby as a broad theory of relationships essential to understanding the family. According to attachment theory, the primary relationship between the parents and their infant is crucial to their children's ongoing relationships throughout life. Stemming from this primary relationship, the individual develops mental representations of themselves and others in relationship contexts, which influence their cognitive, affective, and behavioral responses in relationships.

Wilkinson (chapter 5) reports a series of studies showing the links between attachment insecurity and adolescent mental health. These studies demonstrate that attachment insecurity is negatively associated with adolescents' self-esteem and positively associated with depression. Wilkinson also found age and gender differences in the impact of parental attachment relationships on adolescent psychological health. These studies indicate the importance of parent–adolescent relationships and particularly the security of this relationship bond. The work of Wilkinson ties in with research reported by Hurd and Noller (chapter 25) that specifically examines the links between attachment, parenting style, and self-harming and suicidal behavior in depressed adolescents. Hurd and Noller highlight that the toxic combination of low parental care, high parental overprotection, and insecure attachment increases the risk of adolescents becoming depressed or even engaging in self-harming behavior and suicide attempts.

The importance of attachment relationships between parents and children is also emphasized by Karantzas (chapter 6) at the other end of the lifecycle. His work focuses on the nexus between attachment and caregiving in the context of adult children and their elderly parents. In studying the provision and receipt of care, Karantzas found that attachment insecurity decreased adult children's caregiving of older parents and increased perceptions of carer burden. Furthermore, older parents' attachment insecurity affected their perceptions of the care they were receiving currently and their willingness to receive care in the future. Canterberry and Gillath (chapter 14), drawing on Bowlby's argument regarding the link between the attachment and caregiving systems, propose a model of caregiving that aligns with the behavioral sequelae associated with attachment system dynamics. Drawing on previous literature, Canterberry and Gillath argue that attachment styles seem to predict the emotional well-being of an individual caring for another person, with insecure spousal carers tending to report higher levels of depression.

Cutrona (chapter 27) discusses a re-conceptualization of social support based on attachment theory. Specifically she discusses two types of social support: safe haven and secure base. Safe haven involves providing comfort and assistance to another person who is stressed or facing adversity and is more clearly aligned with the traditional conceptualization of social support. Secure base, on the other hand, involves providing support for a person's autonomy and exploration, in much the same way that having a parent as a secure base allows a young child to explore his/her world. Where these two types of support are provided in response to another's expressed needs, then the individual is likely to develop a sense of felt security. Simpson et al. (chapter 26) further highlight the associations between attachment and social support. In their longitudinal study of couples transitioning into parenthood these researchers revealed that highly anxious women who perceived their husbands as providing little support prenatally and perceived declines in spousal support after the birth were most likely to experience increases in depression. Simpson and colleagues suggest screening women in particular for depression, marital conflict, and extreme levels of attachment insecurity as part of their regular prenatal assessments, and again after the birth. Similarly, Karantzas et al. (chapter 28) found that sufferers of chronic illness (in this case arthritis) who were high on both attachment anxiety and avoidance and who perceived low support from members of their social networks reported higher depressive and anxiety symptomatology than secure arthritis sufferers. Karantzas et al. also argue that taking account of the interaction between arthritis sufferers' attachment style and perceptions of social support could be important in tailoring the psychosocial treatment of chronic diseases such as arthritis.

Shaver and Mikulincer (chapter 11) theorize about how individual differences in attachment security are likely to affect sexual functioning in close relationships. They argue that avoidant individuals' preferences for distance and emotional detachment limit them engaging in sex for emotional closeness and in the context of long-term commitment. Rather they prefer impersonal and uncommitted sex, or may even use sex for their own personal gains (status, etc.) without any concern for a partner's feelings. On the other hand, anxious individuals tend to have positive attitudes to sex and to use it to gain closeness, protection, security, and validation. It seems likely that neither avoidant nor anxious individuals are likely to be able to relax and let go and really enjoy sex with a partner. Research tends to support these hypotheses.

In her studies of communication, Noller (chapter 9) has shown that at least some conflict styles in marriage are driven by attachment insecurities, particularly for those who are anxious about the relationship and concerned about how much the partner cares for them. Partners' attachment style was related to coercion and demand/withdraw during conflict. Hazelwood (chapter 15) discusses the association between attachment insecurity and self-regulation with a person's negative attributions about partner behavior as the mediating variable. She contends that this association may strengthen the argument that insecurely attached individuals have biases in what they attend to and how they process relational information.

A number of contributors have focused on attachment as an important aspect of couple and family therapy. These approaches will be discussed in a later section in this chapter devoted to therapeutic interventions.

Divorce and Family Breakdown

De Vaus (chapter 2) points out that divorce has become more common over the last half century because changes in family law have made it easier to dissolve marriages. In addition, divorce has become more acceptable and is considered better than an unsatisfactory marriage. Bianchi et al. (chapter 3) note that the fallout of marital breakdown is an increase in economic inequality and family instability, both of which involve negative outcomes for children.

Although it is often argued that divorce has the positive effect of ending children's exposure to conflict between their parents, Noller (chapter 9) points out that this conclusion does not reflect reality. She reports a study comparing levels of conflict in separating/divorcing families that included adolescents, with conflict in stable married families that included both the adolescents and their biological parents. The divorced or separated families tended to be involved in more conflict than the stable married families across three relationships: marital, parent–child, and siblings. She also found that in families who were both high in conflict and separated or divorced the children had more adjustment problems than those in the stable married families.

Sweeper (chapter 24) acknowledges the problems created for children by parental conflict following separation or divorce, but suggests that the focus should move away from relying on both parents engaging in cooperative parenting and focus instead on enhancing the parent–child relationship as the critical relationship for the children following separation and divorce. Caughlin et al. (chapter 8) discuss conflict avoidance, and argue that where there is a great deal of conflict, the ideal of the open discussion of issues should be abandoned. In such instances Caughlin et al. maintain that the emphasis on openness and resolving conflicts frequently promoted by counselors and social workers may make it difficult for family members to set appropriate boundaries about what should be discussed. It is better, they claim, for ex-partners seeking to co-parent, to avoid rather than engage in conflict with the ex-partner, especially when safety is an issue.

Conflict and Communication

Caughlin et al. (chapter 8) contend that avoiding conflict is functional in situations of couple violence and in co-parenting following separation or divorce (see the previous section). In situations involving violence, it may be important to help abused women avoid conflict in order to minimize the risk of possible violent consequences. These researchers argue that proscriptions against conflict avoidance often promoted by marriage counselors and educators are overly simplistic because conflict avoidance can also have benefits by saving children from being exposed to severe conflict between their parents. They also acknowledge that there may be costs associated with conflict avoidance because of the link to poor adjustment in family relationships, although they see avoidance as having benefits that may outweigh the costs in some situations.

Noller (chapter 9) reports a number of studies of marital and family conflict, focusing first on different conflict styles (including withdrawal) and showing how these styles are learned in the family. When discussing another of her studies, she shows how misunderstandings of partners' messages or intentions can lead to conflict in couples. The results of another series of studies of communication and conflict in violent couples indicate that couple conflict tends to be characterized by husbands' withdrawal from discussion of issues raised by their wives, and the communication of both husbands and wives tends to be driven by anxiety.

Eldridge and Baucom (chapter 10) focus on the demand–withdraw pattern in conflict across the lifespan. They suggest that to understand the links between emotional arousal and demand–withdraw behavior it is important to focus on the emotions associated with demanding (anger and frustration), and withdrawing (anxiety). These authors also note that demand–withdraw behavior can be affected by whose issue is being discussed, gender, and cultural norms such as individualism–collectivism and patriarchal tendencies.

Goldhammer and McCabe (chapter 12) review research investigating the psychological and interpersonal factors (such as problems with communication and resolving conflict) that contribute to the development and maintenance of sexual dysfunction. They point out that sexual dysfunction has a negative impact on relationship functioning that affects both men and women. Of course, it is also possible that sexual dysfunction may cause relationship difficulties because of the dissatisfaction created by the sexual dysfunction.

Overall (chapter 16) focuses on the difficulties that many couples have in persuading partners to change their behavior in the desired direction because even asking for change can be detrimental to the relationship. She argues that seeking change may not be detrimental if couples are taught to communicate the need for change in a way that assures the partner of positive regard, expresses one's own willingness to change, and acknowledges the partner's attempts to resolve issues. Such an approach would provide motivation for change and would also avoid problems such as hurt feelings, defensiveness, and reactance associated with direct requests for change.

Fitness (chapter 18) discusses ways to deal with the strong emotional pain that is often the consequence of conflict and betrayal in close relationships. She also considers the role of punishment in dealing with betrayal and considers whether punishment and forgiveness are incompatible with one another. Fitness points out that emotional intelligence is likely to be an important factor in the extent to which couples are able to forgive each other and repair the relationship. She argues that even very serious betrayals do not need to destroy relationships especially if couples are highly in tune with their own and their partner's emotional states. Feeney and Fitzgerald (chapter 20) also focus on the consequences of different types of hurtful events and their differing consequences in couple relationships. They comment on the extent to which destructive conflict cycles intensify the distress of dealing with betrayal and make relationship repair more difficult.

Self-Regulation, Partner Regulation, and Behavior Change

Hazelwood (chapter 15) discusses the way in which attachment insecurity and attributions for negative partner behavior are associated with individuals' perceptions of how much effort their partners are investing in regulating their own behavior. As noted in the section on conflict and communication, Overall (chapter 16) focuses on both self- and partner regulation efforts. She also discusses the extent to which successful changes in one's own behavior can indicate to the partner that one is committed and responsive, and hence increase the satisfaction of the partner who wants the change. Of course, as we noted earlier, the way in which change is requested is critical to the whole process. In the Couple CARE program described by Halford and Hayes (chapter 19), there is a strong focus on self-regulation, with partners encouraged to identify and implement plans for changing their own behavior in line with relationship goals.

Gable (chapter 13) proposes an approach–avoidance model of social motivation associated with close-relationship processes in which she argues that a critical dimension of motivation and behavior regulation is the focus of goals. Specifically, she contends that individuals are motivated either by approach goals (a focus on relationship rewards) or avoidance goals (a focus on avoiding threats in the relationship). Gable maintains that models of relationship functioning are inadequate unless they include both motivations, which she sees as having important implications for attention, cognitions, emotions, and behaviors in close relationships. Cutrona (chapter 27) focuses on the expression of social support and suggests that support that is appreciated by the care recipient needs to be expressed by the support provider in ways that do not undermine their autonomy. A central aspect of sensitive and responsive support giving involves the appropriate emotion regulation with regard to how support is expressed. In other words, support providers should control their own emotional needs to try and solve the problem, and be sensitive to the needs of the support receiver to work through the issue and find their own solution.

Caregiving and Parenting

Weston et al. (chapter 1) point out that despite the many changes in society, families remain the basic unit of society and involve much caring and sharing. They also play a central role in the health and well-being of family members and parents are expected to raise their children to become productive members of the larger society. As noted earlier, Bianchi et al. (chapter 3) see extensive changes in family form as being detrimental to children because of the increased family instability and economic inequality that result from these changes.

Antonucci et al. (chapter 4) explicitly discuss the role of the parent in the family and draw attention to ways in which parents shape children's socioemotional development for good or ill. Wilkinson (chapter 5) also acknowledges that families can be problematic and argues that when relationships begin to fail, adolescents are at risk of problems, whether the issue is the relationship between their parents or their own relationship with their parents. He argues that our children's best interests are served by the older generation maintaining their own close relationships and modeling positive relationship behavior to their adolescents. Hurd and Noller (chapter 25) focus explicitly on parenting behavior and show the importance of parenting behavior in the development of depression, suicidal ideation, and self-harming behavior in young people. For example, the self-harming behavior of adolescents of both genders was associated with parenting characterized by low levels of care and high overprotection.

Sweeper (chapter 24) focuses on separated families where co-parenting is needed. She claims that the most effective option in terms of childhood outcomes is to focus on strengthening parent–child relationships rather than trying to improve the conflictual relationship between the parents. Sweeper contends that programs that focus on teaching parents skills for effective parenting, encourage the scheduling of quality time with children, and engagement in positive family activities are important to children's adjustment post-separation, especially when children are exposed to high levels of conflict between the parents.

Canterberry and Gillath (chapter 14) propose a lifespan and life-course model of caregiving that details the functioning of the caregiving behavioral system—a system geared towards attending to the needs of individuals experiencing emotional and physical suffering—and examine the links between the caregiving and attachment systems. They show that increasing the attachment security of caregivers can lead to an increase in sensitive and responsive caregiving behaviors. They also draw on evidence linking this proposed model with caregiver outcomes. Karantzas (chapter 6) also reviews research regarding the factors that influence caregiving and the outcomes of care for caregiver and care recipients. He also expands the view of family caregiving to include current and future care arrangements, viewing care from a task-based perspective and as a negotiated commitment between family members.

Simpson et al. (chapter 26) emphasize that the care provided to a relationship partner, and the perceptions regarding the adequacy of that care, is particularly important to the mental well-being of couples experiencing the transition to parenthood. Simpson and colleagues point out that both parents are likely to have overly optimistic and unrealistic expectations about what parenting will be like and how the couple will work together. However, new mothers struggle with the responsibilities of caring for a newborn and fathers have problems with the unexpected loss of free time and family–work conflicts. Simpson et al.'s findings illustrate the importance of providing good support to one another to ensure the ongoing mental health of both partners.

Cutrona (chapter 27) reviews research highlighting the finding that the timing and manner in which care is provided can influence the emotional well-being and mood of the support recipient. She notes that empathic accuracy plays an important role in sensitive and responsive caregiving. Cutrona highlights the mutual benefit of relationship partners supporting each other, not only in times of difficulty but also in times of success and happiness.

Relationship Education and Therapy

Numerous chapters include discussion of the therapeutic implications of their authors' research. However, in this section we focus on only those chapters where the primary focus is on relationship education or couple and family therapy. Halford and Hayes (chapter 19) review the research regarding the effectiveness and efficacy of couple relationship education that focuses on the active training of key relationship skills and on building knowledge about relationships. They emphasize the barriers to attending relationship education for many couples and propose the use of modern technologies (i.e., Internet and phone) to increase the availability and accessibility of couple relationship education to those who are constrained by time or distance from attending face-to-face workshops. Halford and Hayes provide research evidence for the effectiveness of programs delivered via distance methods. Feeney and Fitzgerald (chapter 20) describe a relationship education program that focuses on repairing relationships following relationship transgressions. Although the program does not require a dyadic approach, involving both members of the couple seems most effective. Their program encourages the promotion of respect and support for the hurt partner and their emotional distress, as well as supporting the offending spouse's efforts to acknowledge the hurt, manage the shame and guilt, and apologize.

Sturmey et al. (chapter 21) argue that evidence-based therapies combined with a common factors approach to couple and family intervention is most effective in bringing about relationship change. Common factors include therapist characteristics (e.g., friendliness and nondefensiveness), client characteristics (e.g., gender, degree of therapy engagement), the therapeutic alliance, motivation to change, and expectancy effects. Sturmey et al. contend that this interactionist perspective to therapy is necessary given the complex dynamic nonlinear process involved in helping couples to change.

Howell (chapter 22) reviews two of the most widely used and empirically supported couple therapies. The chapter focuses on cognitive behavioral couple therapy and integrative behavior couple therapy and reviews studies documenting the efficacy of these therapies. He argues that there is much to be gained from further research into these interventions to uncover the essential elements that yield change in couple relationships.

Johnson and Rheem (chapter 23) describe emotion focused therapy (EFT), another of the empirically validated interventions, which is based on attachment theory. In this therapy negative interactional patterns are seen as resulting from the deprivation of attachment needs, loss of a secure emotional connection with a partner, and unhelpful ways of dealing with separation distress. The goal of EFT is for the therapeutic relationship to provide a safe haven and a secure base for couples to explore relationship difficulties and trauma. Couples in EFT shape each other's behavior as they learn to be safe havens and secure bases for one another. Establishing a safe haven and secure base provides a foundation on which to build a more open and trusting relationship.

Sweeper (chapter 24) argues that therapists dealing with families following separation and/or divorce need to focus their efforts at improving the parent–child relationship rather than trying to reduce parental conflict. She also reviews the efficacy of parenting programs aimed at reducing parental conflict. Based on her review of this literature, she contends that trying to change the level of parental conflict is very difficult and resource intensive, and not as effective for the child as working to improve the parent–child relationship. Relationships with each parent can be improved without the need for interaction between former partners who may use this time as an opportunity to further their conflict.

Policy Implications

Weston et al. (chapter 1) argue that policy needs to take a lifespan development approach whatever the form or structure of families. They also contend that governments need to work toward policies around health, education, and technology that support the stability of families and the healthy development of children. Meeting these needs will require an economic climate that ensures low unemployment and reasonable remuneration for working parents to meet the needs of their families, along with government services for more vulnerable families. Bianchi et al. (chapter 3) echo these sentiments with regard to the United States noting that the U.S. government invests significantly less than other Western countries in education, health care, employment, and welfare. Bianchi et al. point out that when families are not strong, stable, or financially secure enough to ensure children's well-being, the government does little to meet the needs of those families.

White and Winkworth (chapter 30) discuss government services but are concerned about the difficulties that agencies in various jurisdictions have in working together. They argue that because services tend not to share common goals and priorities regarding the needs of families, there is a serious lack of coordination and communication. Hence already fragile families become even more vulnerable, with the possibility of real harm coming to children. As well as focusing on the lack of coordination, White and Winkworth note that services are frequently underresourced and staff are not always appropriately trained in service delivery.

Hawkins (chapter 29) outlines a public policy agenda stressing the value of providing opportunities for relationship education for young people. He suggests three phases to this educational program. Phase one would involve a school-based relationship education program that would include basic sex education but also attention to the relational context of sexuality and would also include basic communication and problem-solving skills. Phase two would encompass an education program in positive relationship formation for young adults to assist them in mapping out positive pathways toward healthy marriage. Such a program seems particularly important given the long period between adolescence and marriage in the current context. Phase three involves delivering premarital education for engaged couples and marriage enrichment to those in the early years of marriage using programs similar to those described by Halford and Hayes (see chapter 19) and Halford and van Acker (see chapter 31) to help them learn the skills necessary for a healthy marriage. Obviously, government resources would be needed to establish and maintain such a policy agenda and governments would need to be convinced of the importance of this type of education.

Halford and van Acker note that relationship education has received different levels of priority and funding at different times in the United States, the United Kingdom, and Australia. They argue that couples will be more likely to remain in quality relationships and therefore the focus should be on improving the quality of those relationships, especially given that the threshold for relationship dissolution has decreased with couples breaking up not necessarily because of severe marital problems but because they have grown apart or just don't want to live together anymore.

In conclusion, the contributors to this volume have provided much food for thought for all those researchers and professionals involved in helping families struggling to survive in the current social context. There is a great deal of information about relationships across the lifespan, "from the cradle to the grave" as John Bowlby (1979) put it. In addition, a wide range of relationship processes relevant to couples and families are covered, including communication and conflict, love, sex and intimacy, parenting, caregiving and care receiving, and social support. In addition, a number of authors focus on specific interventions that can be used by counselors and therapists seeking to help their clients have more fulfilling relationships. We trust that this volume will provide helpful resources for those counselors and therapists.

Reference

Bowlby, J. (1979). *The making and breaking of affectional bonds.* London: Tavistock.

Index

ABS *see* Australian Bureau of Statistics
abusive couples 338–9
acceptance 328–30
accountability 447
accuracy
  empathic 399, 476
  expressed emotions 398–9
  judgments 251–5
  tracking 252–5
  see also biased judgments
accusation 293
active disassociation 290, 297
active withdrawal 118, 121, 131–3
Actor-Partner Interdependence Model (APIM) 227–9
AD *see* Alzheimer's disease
adjustment *see* post-separation adjustment
admissions of guilt 266
adolescence 3, 66–81
  adult attachment 163–4, 171
  attachment theory 69–70, 73–4, 366–72
  challenges 74–6
  child–parent relationship 69–74
  common themes in research and practice 470–1, 473
  conflict avoidance 116–18
  conflict processes 4, 134, 137–9
  continuity–discontinuity dialectic 69–70
  demand–withdraw pattern of conflict 154–5
  depression 363–76
  family dissolution 75–6
  family form and functioning 364–72
  family members' awareness of problems 365–6, 371
  gender factors 372–3
  interpersonal processes 6
  intimacy and isolation 68
  lifespan development 57, 68
  parent–adolescent agreement 369
  patterns of attachment and parental bonding 371–2
  policy 423–9, 432
  positive pathways to healthy relationships 423–9
  positive relationship formation 427–9, 432
  prospective studies 365
  psychological adjustment 139
  qualitative data 369–71
  questionnaire measures 367–9
  relationship education 424–33
  relationship evaluation and assessment 70–2
  relationship literacy 425–7, 432
  self-harming 366–73
  social change 38–9
  storm and stress view 68–9
  suicidality 363–7
  two predominant views 67–70
  unbalanced media representation 66–7, 76–7
adult attachment
  anxiety and avoidance 164, 165–71
  attachment security 162–3, 165–9
  behavioral systems 161–4, 165–8
  caregiving 216
  effects on couple relationships 165–6

The Wiley-Blackwell Handbook of Couples and Family Relationships, First Edition.
Edited by Patricia Noller and Gery C. Karantzas.

adult attachment (*cont'd*)
  interplay with sexual system 166–8, 169
  proximity to attachment figures 162–3
  sexuality 161–74
  therapeutic implications 170–1
adult children
  current context 1, 3
  family caregiving 82–96
  late-life transitions 106
advice-giving 119, 120–1, 398
affect-intense sibling relationships 136–7
affective processes 4–5
  forecasting error 253
  incentives and threats 201
  therapeutic interventions 6
affective-reconstructive therapy 322
aggressive blaming 334, 339
aging populations
  caregiving 82
  late-life transitions 97–111
  lifespan development 53
  social change 37
Alzheimer's disease (AD) 101–4
ambiguous information 200–1
American families
  children 41–2
  delayed marriage 39–40
  division of labor 37, 39, 43–5
  fertility 37–8, 40–2
  single parenting 42–3
  social change 36–47
  trends and transitions 36–8
  union dissolution 42
  young emerging adulthood 38–9
anger
  anger–shame spirals 266
  relationship education 300–1
  withdrawal 118
anticipatory caregiving 91
anxiety
  betrayal 261
  chronic illness 406–7, 412–14
  common themes in research and practice 472
  conflict processes 132–3
  parenthood transition 378–88
  post-separation adjustment 349
  social change 33–4
anxious attachment
  adult attachment and sexuality 164, 165–71
  bias and accuracy of judgments 256
  caregiving 90–2, 209, 211, 213, 215
  chronic illness 409–11, 415–16
  conflict processes 131
  parenthood transition 379–83, 384–8
  self-regulation 224–5, 228–30
apartheid 59
APIM *see* Actor-Partner Interdependence Model
apologies 266
approach and avoidance goals 195–203
  common themes in research and practice 475
  future directions 202–3
  hierarchical model 195–7
  mediating processes linking goals and outcomes 199–202
  relationship outcomes 197–9
arousal dysfunctions 176–7
arthritis 407, 409, 410
Asian families 59–60
ASQ *see* Attachment Style Questionnaire
assertion 135
assessment with feedback CRE 275
attachment bonding 5, 6
attachment figures
  chronic illness 410–11
  parenthood transition 384
  suicidality 364
  violation by 340
attachment injuries 291, 295
attachment security 90, 93
  attribution theory 224–5
  bias and accuracy of judgments 256
  caregiving 213–16
  chronic illness 409, 415–16
  common themes in research and practice 471–3, 476
  conflict processes 131, 140
  interpretation of findings 229–31
  mediation hypothesis 227–32
  negative partner behavior 223–33
  parenthood transition 379–80, 386
  relationship education 293, 296
  self-regulation 225–32
  sexuality 162–3, 165–9
  suicidality 366–7
  testing the hypothesis 227–9
  therapeutic implications 231–2
  trauma survival 333–4, 340–2
Attachment Style Questionnaire (ASQ) 367

attachment theory
  adolescence 69–70, 73–4, 366–72
  caregiving 89–92, 93–4, 207–19
  child–parent relationship 73–4, 76
  chronic illness 409–11
  common themes in research and practice 471–3, 476
  emotion-focused couples therapy 334–6, 340–2
  individual differences 208–9, 211–12
  interpersonal processes 6–7
  interplay with caregiving system 212–14
  parental bonding 371–2
  parenthood transition 377–8, 379–88
  perceived partner responsiveness 396–7
  post-separation adjustment 350–1
  relationship education 291–3, 296–7
  responsiveness 393–7
  security 213–14
  self-harming 366–72
  self-regulation 5
  sexual relationships 4
  social support 392–7
  suicidality 366–7
  therapeutic implications and directions 214–17
  trauma survival 334–6, 340–2
  see also adult attachment; anxious attachment; attachment security; avoidant attachment
attention-without-intervention condition 307
attribution theory
  attachment security 224–5
  context and processes 223–4
  interpretation of findings 229–31
  mediation hypothesis 227–32
  negative partner behavior 223–33
  self-regulation 226–7
  testing the hypothesis 227–9
  therapeutic implications 231–2
Australian Bureau of Statistics (ABS) 13–14
Australian Institute of Family Studies 19
Australian social policy 457–8, 462–3, 478
authority figures 68–9
authority to implement 441, 444
autocracy 238
autonomy 393, 402
availability of caregivers 85–9
avoidance 4
  emotion-focused couples therapy 334, 340
  incentives and threats 193–4, 195–202
  relationship education 290
  trauma survival 334, 340
  see also conflict avoidance
avoidant attachment
  adult attachment and sexuality 164, 165–71
  caregiving 90–2, 209, 211, 213, 215
  chronic illness 409, 415–16
  parenthood transition 380, 382, 387–8
  self-regulation 224–5, 228–30

baby boomers 37
barriers to resolution 294–5
BAS *see* behavioral activation system
behavior change *see* partner regulation; self-regulation
behavioral activation system (BAS) 198, 200
behavioral inhibition system (BIS) 198, 200
Behavioral Marital Therapy 309
Behavioral Self-Regulation for Effective Relationships Scale 227
behavioral systems 161–8, 207–19
Bellvue Index of Depression-Modified (BID) 367
best interests consultants 449
betrayal 5, 259–70
  admissions of guilt 266
  common themes in research and practice 474
  context 259–60
  couple relationships 194–7
  definitions and characteristics 260
  emotional processes 260–1, 265–6
  forgiveness 260, 261–8
  punishment 261–5
  relational breakdown and repair 259, 261–5
  relationship education 297
  therapeutic implications 265–8
biased judgments
  integration of findings 255–6
  intimate relationships 248–58
  love is blind hypothesis 248–9
  prior beliefs and theory-guided judgments 250–1
  projection 251
  as rational process 249–51
  reality tracking 251–5
  welcome and acknowledged bias 253–5
BID *see* Bellvue Index of Depression-Modified
BIS *see* behavioral inhibition system

blame 334, 339
blended families
  adolescence 72, 75
  family form and functioning 15
  social change 42
breadwinning
  family form and functioning 20–1
  social change 27, 38, 39, 41

capability to implement 441, 445
capitalization 397
care-time arrangements 16–17
caregiving 4, 82–96
  attachment theory 4, 89–92, 93–4, 207–19
  availability 85–9
  common themes in research and practice 475–6
  current context 2, 3, 82–3
  definitions 83–4
  family caregiving 82–96
  family form and functioning 82–3, 84
  filial obligation 89–90, 91–2, 93
  frailty, illness and disability 84, 89
  gender factors 85–9, 93
  implications and future directions 214–17
  individual differences 211–12
  interplay with attachment system 212–14
  late-life transitions 97, 101–4
  life transitions 3
  obligatory and discretionary motives 89–92
  optimal care management strategies 103–4
  roles and responsibilities 85–9, 93
  sandwich generation 2, 3
  social change 44, 82
  task-based approach 84–5, 92–3
  task specialization 85–9, 93
  therapeutic interventions 103–4
  value placed on caregiving tasks 84–5, 92
causal attributions 223
CBCL *see* Child Behavior Checklist
CBCT *see* cognitive-behavioral couple therapy
CBT *see* cognitive-behavioral therapy
CCET *see* Couples Coping Enhancement Training
CCP *see* Couples Communication Program
CDI *see* Children's Depression Inventory
Center for Law and Social Policy (CLASP) 459–60
CES *see* Cooperative Extension Service
changing intimate partners *see* partner regulation
child abuse 339
Child Behavior Checklist (CBCL) 367, 369
child–parent relationships
  adjustment, conflict and relationships 350–2
  adolescence 69–74
  adult attachment 171
  attachment theory 73–4, 76, 350–1
  caregiving 89, 90
  child outcomes and conflict 349–50
  clinical interventions 353–5
  common themes in research and practice 471, 473, 475–7
  conflict avoidance 116–18, 121–2
  conflict processes 129, 133–4, 138, 140
  demand–withdraw pattern of conflict 154–5
  gender factors 351–2
  nature of parental conflict 346–7
  post-separation adjustment 345–59
  reducing parental conflict 347–52
  treatment efficacy 348–9
child safety and well-being 438–9
childcare 28, 44
childlessness 27–8, 41
children
  collaborative service model 437–52
  common themes in research and practice 471–2, 473, 478
  conflict avoidance 122–4
  conflict processes 4, 6, 137–8
  current context 1
  family form and functioning 16–20, 53
  lifespan development 53, 56–7
  social change 27–8, 41–2, 44–5
  see also adult children
Children's Depression Inventory (CDI) 367, 369
choice 3, 25–6, 29–34
Christianity 60
chronic family discord 364
chronic illness 7, 406–19
  attachment and caregiving 215–16
  attachment theory 409–11, 415–16
  caregiving 84
  common themes in research and practice 472
  context 406–7
  late-life transitions 99, 101

mental health 406–9, 412–14
relationship counseling 309
relationship experiences of sufferers 407–9
social support 407, 409–12, 414–16
therapeutic implications 414–16
civic engagement 107
civil partnerships 459–60
CLASP *see* Center for Law and Social Policy
closeness
adult attachment 166–7, 169
caregiving 211–12
parenthood transition 379
partner regulation 235–6
coercion
adult attachment 166, 168–9
conflict processes 130, 133–4, 135, 140
evidence-based couple therapy 328
partner regulation 237, 238
cognitive processes 4–5, 400
cognitive-behavioral couple therapy (CBCT) 6
causes of dysfunction and change 326–7
evidence-based practice 320, 322, 324–5, 326–8
therapeutic approach and strategies 327–8
cognitive-behavioral therapy (CBT) 307
cohabitation
adolescence 74
couple relationship education 278
current context 1–2
late-life transitions 98
policy 456
positive pathways to healthy relationships 423–4, 432
social change 29, 32–3, 36, 39–40, 456
collaborative service model 437–52
best interests consultants 449
building knowledge 440–5
child safety and well-being 438–9
context 437–40
enablers and barriers 441, 444–5
government actions 447
information sharing 449–50
level of collaboration 440–3
local alliance of services 448
local area catchment planning 448
professional actions 448–9
proposed model 445–6
responsibilities and actions 447–50
service provider actions 447–8
service-system collaboration 440
support for families in need 439–40
collective accountability 447
college educations 39
Communication Patterns Questionnaire (CPQ) 131, 133
communication processes 3–4
adolescence 74
attribution theory 225
common themes in research and practice 472, 473–4
conflict avoidance 115–28
couple relationship education 274
desire for change 5
late-life transitions 98–9
partner regulation 236–44
relationship education 294–5
sexual dysfunction 179, 182–5
social support 392–405
see also conflict processes
community
family form and functioning 22
late-life transitions 107
commuting marriages 16
companionship
caregiving 85
couple relationships 194–7
complex PTSD 340
compulsive caregiving 211–12
conflict avoidance 115–28
case against and harmful effects 115–16, 118–19, 125
case for and potential benefits 116–17, 119, 121, 125
common themes in research and practice 474
context 120–2
demand–withdraw pattern of conflict 118–19, 121
forms of avoidance 117–19
influencing factors 117–19
meaning of avoidance behaviors 119–20
practical implications 122–5
relationship protection 119–20
strategies 135, 139
unresolved conflicts 116–17
conflict processes 3–4, 129–43
adjustment, conflict and relationships 350–2
adolescence 68–71, 76, 366–7
attachment theory 350–1
child outcomes 349–50

conflict processes (*cont'd*)
  child–parent relationships 129, 133–4, 138, 140
  clinical interventions 353–5
  common themes in research and practice 472–4, 476–7
  competition for family resources 129
  couple relationship education 274
  differential parenting 139
  divorce and separation 135–8
  evidence-based couple therapy 321
  family form and functioning 19
  family members' perceptions of one another 133–4
  gender factors 351–2
  implications 139–40
  late-life transitions 98
  learning family conflict patterns 133
  marital violence 132–3, 140
  marriage and marital relationships 129–35, 137–8
  mediation and counseling 6
  misunderstandings 130, 139–40
  nature of parental conflict 346–7
  partner regulation 234–8
  post-separation adjustment 345–59
  psychological adjustment 139
  reducing parental conflict 347–52
  relationship counseling 312
  relationship satisfaction 130–1, 134–5
  sexual dysfunction 183
  sibling relationships 129, 134, 136–7, 139–40
  social support 397–9
  strategies 134–5
  styles of conflict 130–3, 140
  treatment efficacy 348–9
  withdrawal 131–3
  see also demand–withdraw pattern of conflict
conflict structure 145–6
Confucianism 60
congruence hypothesis 136
Connections curriculum 426
consumerism 30–1
containment strategies 328
contingent choices 32–3, 34
continuity–discontinuity dialectic 69–70
control mechanisms 397–8
Cooperative Extension Service (CES) 430
coordinating level of collaboration 442
coordination, policy 7
co-parental relationships 4
  common themes in research and practice 476
  conflict avoidance 123–4
co-residency 54
counseling *see* relationship counseling
counselor-guided dyadic interventions 104
Couple Commitment and Relationship Enhancement (Couple CARE) 275, 276, 281–2, 283, 475
couple relationship education (CRE) 273–88
  adolescence 77
  approaches 274–6
  assessment with feedback 275
  common themes in research and practice 477
  curriculum-based 275–7, 279
  definitions and characteristics 274
  efficacy 276–7, 279–80, 461–2
  impacts 277–80
  implications 462–3
  information technology advances 280–3
  limited reach 278–9
  policy 453–4, 458–9, 461–3
  services expansion 282–3
couple relationships
  adult attachment 161–74
  affective experience 201
  approach and avoidance goals 195–203
  betrayal 259–70
  chronic illness 408–11, 414
  common themes in research and practice 473–4, 476, 478
  dyadic nature 197
  future research directions 202–3
  incentives and threats 193–206
  mediating processes linking goals and outcomes 199–202
  memory bias and ambiguous information 200–1
  partner regulation 234–47
  policy 455–7, 462–3
  relationship outcomes 197–9
  social support 392–405
  temporal nature 197
  weight of social information 201–2
  see also intimate relationships; marriage and marital relationships
couple therapy
  client factors 309–10
  common factors perspective 305–19

common themes in research and practice 477
expectancy effects 305, 307, 310
implications for practice and service delivery 312–13
match between therapist and client 310
parenthood transition 385–6
research findings and directions 310–12
therapeutic alliance 306–7, 313–14
therapist factors 307–9
treatment outcomes 307–10
see also evidence-based couple therapy
Couples Communication Program (CCP) 275, 282
Couples Coping Enhancement Training (CCET) 275
covert avoidance 118
CPQ *see* Communication Patterns Questionnaire
CRE *see* couple relationship education
criminality 72
criticism
couple relationships 194–7
emotion-focused couples therapy 335
partner regulation 236–7
relationship education 290, 297, 302
cultural factors
conflict processes 4
demand–withdraw pattern of conflict 148–9, 155
lifespan development 53–5, 59–61
curriculum-based CRE 275–7, 279

daily diary research 392, 395–7
Darwinian natural selection 249
de facto relationships
current context 1
family form and functioning 13
deactivation of attachment systems 163, 165, 210
deception 290
decoding errors 130
de-differentiation of affect 337
defensiveness
emotion-focused couples therapy 339
partner regulation 244
relationship education 293
social support 393
deinstitutionalization of marriage/family 27, 32
delayed childbearing 41, 45
delayed marriage 39–40, 470
demand–withdraw pattern of conflict 4, 130–1, 133–4, 140, 144–58
common themes in research and practice 474
conflict avoidance 118–19, 121
conflict structure 145–6
context 144–5
cultural/social factors 145–6, 148–9, 155
distal context 147–9, 151–2
future research directions 154–5
gender factors 145–6, 149–50, 151
immediate consequences 152
immediate goals 151
individual differences 145–6, 147
interaction of proximal and distal variables 151–2
long-term consequences 153
mood variables 150–1
multiple goals 145–7
partner regulation 236–7
proximal context 149–52
relational differences 147–8
relationship counseling 312
relationship satisfaction 145, 148, 150–1, 153
replicated findings 145
theories 145–7
topic variables 145, 149–50
treatment responsiveness 153
demanding behavior 236–7
dementia 101–4, 106
depression 6
adolescence 73, 75, 363–76
attachment theory 366–72
chronic illness 406–7, 412–14
common factors perspective 307
common themes in research and practice 470–2, 476
family form and functioning 364–72
family members' awareness of problems 365–6, 371
gender factors 372–3
late-life transitions 99, 106
parent–adolescent agreement 369
parenthood transition 377–8, 380–3, 386–8
patterns of attachment and parental bonding 371–2
post-separation adjustment 349
prospective studies 365

depression (*cont'd*)
  qualitative data 369–71
  questionnaire measures 367–9
  self-harming 366–73
  social change 33–4
  suicidality 363–7
desire
  for change 5, 6
  dysfunctions 176–7
  incentives and threats 198
developmental science 311–12
Diagnostic and Statistical Manual of Mental Disorders (DSM-IV) 176–7
diathesis-stress approach 377–8
differential parenting 139
direct communication strategies 238–43
disability 84
discretionary motives 89–92
dissatisfaction *see* relationship satisfaction
distal context of demand–withdraw pattern 147–9, 151–2
diversity
  family form and functioning 52–3
  social change 28–9
division of labor 27, 37, 39, 43–5
divorce 3–4
  adolescence 75–6
  betrayal 263, 266
  common themes in research and practice 470, 473
  conflict avoidance 122–4
  conflict processes 135–8
  late-life transitions 98
  mediation and counseling 6
  policy 455, 460
  positive pathways to healthy relationships 423–5, 429
  social change 26, 29, 32–3, 455, 457
domestic violence
  conflict avoidance 123–4
  conflict processes 132–3, 140
domestic work
  partner regulation 234
  social change 27, 38, 39, 44
DSM-IV *see Diagnostic and Statistical Manual of Mental Disorders*
dual-process model 400
dyadic cognitive-remediation interventions 104
dyspareunia 177
Eastern European families 37
economic factors
  late-life transitions 100
  policy 425
  social change 30, 38–9
ECR *see* Experiences in Close Relationships
ED *see* erectile dysfunction
emotion-focused couples therapy (EFT) 6
  adult attachment 170–1
  background 335–6
  betrayal 268
  case example 340–2
  common factors perspective 309, 311
  common themes in research and practice 477
  evidence-based practice 322, 324–5
  interventions 336–7
  model of intervention 334–5
  parenthood transition 386
  post-traumatic stress disorder 337–42
  relationship education 291
  self-regulation 231–2
  trauma survival 333–44
  traumatized couples 338–42
emotional intelligence 267–8, 474
emotional numbing 335–6, 340–2
emotional processes 4–5
  accurate expression 398–9
  adolescence 69, 72
  adult attachment 168
  attachment theory 90
  betrayal 260–1, 265–8
  caregiving 85, 92
  common themes in research and practice 472, 476
  evidence-based couple therapy 328
  parenthood transition 383
  relationship counseling 308
  relationship education 291–2, 301–2
  sexual dysfunction 183
  social support 393, 398–402
  trauma survival 334–6, 337–8
empathic accuracy 399, 476
empathic reflection 336
empirically-validated therapies 308–9
enactments 336–7
erectile dysfunction (ED) 176, 177, 178–81
escape-conditioning model 146, 154
ethnicity *see* race/ethnicity
event-sampling 392, 395–7

evidence-based couple therapy 320–32
  causes of dysfunction and change 326–7, 328–9
  common factor perspective 323–4
  common themes in research and practice 477
  definitions and characteristics 321–3
  efficacy 324–6
  importance of evidence-based practice 321–3
  relationship functions and outcomes 320–1
  therapeutic approach and strategies 327–8, 329–30
evocative questioning 336
expectancy effects 305, 307, 310
Experiences in Close Relationships (ECR) Scale 165, 227
explicit avoidance 118
extended household families 15

Facilitating Open Couple Communication Understanding and Study (FOCCUS) 275
family caregiving 82–96
  attachment theory 89–92, 93–4
  availability 85–9
  current context 82–3
  definitions 83–4
  filial obligation 89–90, 91–2, 93
  gender factors 85–9, 93
  obligatory and discretionary motives 89–92
  roles and responsibilities 85–9, 93
  task-based approach 84–5, 92–3
  task specialization 85–9, 93
  value placed on caregiving tasks 84–5, 92
family dissolution 75–6
Family Environment Scales (FES) 367
family form and functioning 2–3, 11–24
  adolescence 364–7
  caregiving 82–3, 84
  challenges 20–1
  common themes in research and practice 469–71
  definitions of family forms 12–17
  family functioning 18–21
  less common family forms 15–17
  life transitions 3
  lifespan development 52–5
  pitfalls and prospects 21–2
  policy 19, 20–1
  self-harming 366–72
  social change 469–71
  statistical definitions 13–14
  suicidality 364–6
  traditional family forms 13–14, 52–3
  trends and transitions 11–12
Family Functioning Scales 138
Family Relationship Centres (FRC) 430, 439, 458
family systems theory 129
family therapy
  client factors 309–10
  common factors perspective 305–19
  expectancy effects 305, 307, 310
  implications for practice and service delivery 312–13
  life transitions 104
  match between therapist and client 310
  research findings and directions 310–12
  therapeutic alliance 306–7, 313–14
  therapist factors 307–9
  treatment outcomes 307–10
female orgasmic disorder (FOD) 177
female sexual arousal disorder (FSAD) 177
female sexual dysfunction (FSD) 181–4
feminism 31
fertility 28, 34, 37–8, 40–2
FES *see* Family Environment Scales
filial obligation 89–90, 91–2, 93
FOCCUS *see* Facilitating Open Couple Communication Understanding and Study
FOD *see* female orgasmic disorder
forecasting error 253
forgiveness 5
  betrayal 260, 261–8
  relationship education 291
fragile families 40–1
frailty 84, 89
freedom-based insecurities 32, 34
Freud, Sigmund 68, 161
friendships 195–6, 198
FSAD *see* female sexual arousal disorder
FSD *see* female sexual dysfunction

gay marriages 459–60
gender factors
  adolescence 73–4, 372–3
  caregiving 85–9, 93
  conflict processes 4, 130, 132

gender factors (*cont'd*)
  demand–withdraw pattern of conflict 145–6, 149–50, 151
  depression 372–3
  family form and functioning 20–1
  late-life transitions 100, 104–6
  lifespan development 59–60
  post-separation adjustment 351–2
  relationship education 298–301
  self-regulation 228–9
  sexual dysfunction 175–6, 178–84
  social change 27, 37–9, 43–5
gender role socialization 146
ghettoization 59
global negative emotions 326
globalization
  lifespan development 61
  social change 38–9
Godparents 60
government actions 447
grandparents 15, 58
guided discovery 328
guilt
  betrayal 265
  induction 237, 398

harmonious sibling relationships 136–7
HD *see* Huntington's disease
health problems *see* chronic illness; physical health
Healthy Marriage Initiatives 429, 431
helpful behaviors 294
HER *see* Hurtful Event Records
higher education 39
homecare providers 97
homemaking
  family form and functioning 20–1
  social change 27, 38, 39, 44
homosexual relationships *see* same-sex couples
hostility
  conflict avoidance 117, 118, 121
  partner regulation 236–7, 241
  sibling relationships 136–7
household families 13–14
HSDD *see* hypoactive sexual desire disorder
Huntington's disease (HD) 407–8, 410
hurt feelings
  betrayal 260–1
  partner regulation 244
  relationship education 5–6, 289–302
Hurtful Event Records (HER) 296–8, 300–1
hyperactivation of attachment systems 163, 165, 210
hypoactive sexual desire disorder (HSDD) 176, 177, 181–2

IBCT *see* integrative behavioral couple therapy
identity
  chronic illness 409
  sexual dysfunction 178
  social change 31, 41
illness *see* chronic illness; physical health
immediate goals 151
immigration 55, 148
implicit avoidance 118
implicit rejection 297
incentives
  affective experience 201
  approach and avoidance goals 195–203
  couple relationships 193–206
  future research directions 202–3
  mediating processes linking goals and outcomes 199–202
  memory bias and ambiguous information 200–1
  relationship outcomes 197–9
  weight of social information 201–2
indigenous families 13
indirect avoidance 118
indirect communication strategies 238–43
individual differences
  attachment theory 208–9, 211–12
  caregiving 211–12
  demand–withdraw pattern of conflict 145–6, 147
individualization 32–3, 38–9, 40
infidelity
  forgiveness 266–7
  relationship education 290, 297
information sharing 449–50
information support/guidance 397–8
information technology
  couple relationship education 280–3
  family form and functioning 21
  positive pathways to healthy relationships 429
inheritence 106
Insight-oriented Couple Therapy 309
institutionalized care 97
integrating level of collaboration 443

integrative behavioral couple therapy (IBCT) 6
causes of dysfunction and change 328–9
common factors perspective 311
demand–withdraw pattern of conflict 153
evidence-based practice 320, 322, 325
therapeutic approach and strategies 329–30
interpersonal factors 6–7, 176–85
interpersonal therapy 307
intimate partner violence 3–4
family form and functioning 19
self-regulation 226
intimate relationships
adolescence 68, 77
adult attachment 166–7
attachment theory 90
bias and accuracy of judgments 248–58
incentives and threats 194–7
integration of findings 255–6
late-life transitions 98–9
love is blind hypothesis 248–9
prior beliefs and theory-guided judgments 250–1
projection 251
rational bias 249–51
reality tracking 251–5
sexual dysfunction 175–92
welcome and acknowledged bias 253–5
see also couple relationships; sexual relationships
isolation 68

Japanese families 37
jealousy
betrayal 265
couple relationships 194–7
partner regulation 234
self-regulation 226
Judaism 60

kinship terminology 13

labor markets
lifespan development 59
social change 27, 37, 39, 42, 43–5
laissez-faire economics 30
LAT *see* living apart together
late-life transitions 97–111
health problems 99, 101
implications for practitioners 106–7
marital quality and satisfaction 98–9
marriage 97–9
mild cognitive impairment and dementia 101–4, 106
optimal care management strategies 103–4
remarriage 97–8, 103, 105–6
retirement 100–1
therapeutic interventions 103–4
volunteerism and civic engagement 107
widowhood 97, 99, 104–5, 106
legislative factors
collaborative service model 444
social change 26–7
life-course theory 51–2, 58–61, 476
life-threatening illness 99, 101
life transitions
attachment theory 377–8, 379–88
caregiving 3
common themes in research and practice 476
demand–withdraw pattern of conflict 154
depression 377–8, 380–3, 386–8
family form and functioning 3
intervention programs 385–6
mediation outcomes 382
parenthood transition 377–91
personal well-being 378–9, 388
social policy issues and implications 383–8
spousal perceptions of well-being/support 382–3, 384–5
targets of intervention 384–5
see also late-life transitions
lifespan development 51–65
adolescence 68
caregiving 89–90
changing family dynamics 57–8
children 56–7
co-residency 54
common themes in research and practice 474, 476, 478
cultural factors 53–5, 59–61
family form and functioning 52–5
future directions 60–1
grandparent roles 58
immigration 55
lifespan and life-course 51–2, 58–61
parental roles 56
policy and societal influences 58–60
roles across the lifespan 55–8
sandwich generation 53, 57–8
spousal roles 56

living apart together (LAT) 16, 18
local alliance of services 448
local area catchment planning 448
loneliness
  incentives and threats 195–6, 198
  late-life transitions 105–6
love 4
  adult attachment 167, 168
  bias and accuracy in intimate relationships 248–58
love is blind hypothesis 248–9

male sexual dysfunction 178–81
managed-care models 322
mandates 444
manipulation 135, 238
manufactured insecurity 32, 34
marital therapy *see* couple therapy
marriage enrichment education 431, 432
marriage and marital relationships
  adolescence 74
  betrayal 263–4, 266–7
  common themes in research and practice 473, 478
  conflict avoidance 115–16, 117, 120–3
  conflict processes 129–35, 137–8
  couple relationship education 278
  deinstitutionalization 27
  demand–withdraw pattern of conflict 145–6, 148–9
  evidence-based couple therapy 321
  incentives and threats 198
  late-life transitions 97–9
  life transitions 3
  parenthood transition 378–9
  policy 453–65
  positive pathways to healthy relationships 423–5, 431–2
  social change 26–7, 29, 32–4, 36–40, 45–6, 455–7
masculinity 178
materialism 2
MCI *see* mild cognitive impairment
mean-level bias 251–5
media representations 66–7, 76–7
mediation hypothesis 6, 227–32
  interpretation of findings 229–31
  testing the hypothesis 227–9
  therapeutic implications 231–2
medical technologies 28
memory bias 200–1
mental health 6–7
  adolescence 72–3, 75, 363–76
  attachment theory 215–16
  caregiving 91–2, 93–4, 215–16
  chronic illness 406–9, 412–14
  common themes in research and practice 470–2
  demand–withdraw pattern of conflict 154–5
  family form and functioning 19
  late-life transitions 99, 101–4, 106
  parenthood transition 377–8, 379–83, 386–8
  post-separation adjustment 349, 354–5
  social change 33–4
mental representations 162, 170–1, 214
Mexican American families 59
mild cognitive impairment (MCI) 101–4
misunderstandings
  conflict processes 130, 139–40
  demand–withdraw pattern of conflict 152
  incentives and threats 196
MND *see* motor neurone disease
mood variables 150–1
motivation theory 161
motor neurone disease (MND) 407–8, 410
MS *see* multiple sclerosis
multiple goals 145–7
multiple sclerosis (MS) 407–8, 410, 412–13
mutual avoidance 130, 133–4
mutual discussion 130

nagging 119, 237
narrative therapy 215–16
National Survey of Family Growth (NSFG) 42
natural selection 249
NBP *see* New Beginnings Program
negative communication strategies 236–42
negotiation behaviors 351
networking level of collaboration 442
New Beginnings Program (NBP) 353–5
No Child Left Behind legislation 426
non-adapting caregivers 103
nonconflict activities 116
nondefensiveness 6
nonmarital childbearing 41–2
nonverbal behavior 130, 132
NSFG *see* National Survey of Family Growth
nursing homes *see* institutionalized care
nurturing caregivers 103

obesity 72
object relations theory 161
obligatory motives 89–92
older parents 3, 82–96
openness
  conflict avoidance 118, 125
  conflict processes 132
  illusion of 118
orgasm dysfunctions 176–7
overt avoidance 118

pain dysfunctions 176–7
Pakistani couples 148
paradox of choice 33–4
parent–adolescent agreement 369
parent–child relationship *see* child–parent relationship
Parental Bonding Instrument (PBI) 367
parenthood transition
  attachment theory 377–8, 379–88
  common themes in research and practice 476
  depression 377–8, 380–3, 386–8
  intervention programs 385–6
  mediation outcomes 382
  mental health and well-being 377–8, 379–83
  personal well-being 378–9, 388
  social policy issues and implications 383–8
  spousal perceptions of well-being/support 382–3, 384–5
  targets of intervention 384–5
Parenting Through Change Program (PTCP) 353–5
Parkinson's disease (PD) 407, 410
partner-caused offences 263–5
partner regulation
  alternatives 242–4
  common themes in research and practice 474, 475
  communication strategies and successes 236–44
  costs and benefits 234–47
  perceived regard 235–7
  practical and therapeutic implications 240–4
  self-change and self-regulation 243–4
  social support 398
  strategies 236–40
partner support 135
passion 194–7
passive avoidance 118
passive disassociation 290
PBI *see* Parental Bonding Instrument
PD *see* Parkinson's disease
PE *see* premature ejaculation
perceived partner responsiveness 396–7
perceived regard 235–7
personal growth 105
personal injury 292
personal well-being 378–9, 388
pharmaceutical interventions 307
physical health
  adolescence 72–3
  attachment and caregiving 215–16
  demand–withdraw pattern of conflict 154
  late-life transitions 99, 101
  see also chronic illness; sexual dysfunction
policy 7
  adolescence 423–9, 432
  Australia 457–8, 462–3
  best interests consultants 449
  building knowledge of collaboration 440–5
  child safety and well-being 438–9
  cohabitation 456
  collaborative service model 437–52
  common themes in research and practice 478
  coordination 7
  couple interventions 457–61
  couple relationship education 453–4, 458–9, 461–3
  current context 1–2
  divorce 455, 460
  enablers and barriers 441, 444–5
  family form and functioning 19, 20–1
  government actions 447
  implications 462–3
  improving child and family outcomes 437–52
  information sharing 449–50
  level of collaboration 440–3
  lifespan development 58–60
  local alliance of services 448
  local area catchment planning 448
  marriage enrichment education for early-marrieds 431, 432
  marriage and marital relationships 453–65
  parenthood transition 383–8
  positive pathways to healthy relationships 423–36
  positive relationship formation 427–9, 432

policy *(cont'd)*
premarital education for engaged couples 429–31, 432
professional actions 448–9
proposed collaborative model 445–6
relationship education 424–33
relationship literacy 425–7, 432
responsibilities and actions 447–50
same-sex relationships 459–60
separation 457
service provider actions 447–8
service-system collaboration 440
social change 38, 45–6, 455–7
support for families in need 439–40
United Kingdom 459, 462–3
United States 458–60, 462–3
polite avoidance 118
pop culture 1–2
positive communication strategies 238–43
positive relationship formation education 427–9, 432
positive sentiment override 307
positivity bias 5
postmodernity 29, 32
post-separation adjustment 345–9
adjustment, conflict and relationships 350–2
attachment theory 350–1
child outcomes and conflict 349–50
clinical interventions 353–5
gender factors 351–2
nature of parental conflict 346–7
reducing parental conflict 347–52
treatment efficacy 348–9
post-separation stressors 352
post-traumatic stress disorder (PTSD) 337–42
power struggles 131–2
premarital CRE 278
premarital education for engaged couples 429–31, 432
Premarital Relationship Enhancement Program (PREP) 275
premature ejaculation (PE) 177
prenuptial agreements 106
PREP *see* Premarital Relationship Enhancement Program
PREPARE 275, 276
primary emotions 398–9
primary goals 146
prior beliefs 250–1
professional actions 448–9
projection 251
protective behavior 90
proximal context of demand–withdraw pattern 149–52
proximity maintenance 411
proximity to attachment figures 162–3, 214
psychoanalytical approaches 68
psycho-education 216
psychological adjustment 139
psychological disorders
adolescence 72–3, 75
couple relationship education 279
sexual dysfunction 176–85
psychotherapy
couple relationships 194
evidence-based couple therapy 323
parenthood transition 386
PTCP *see* Parenting Through Change Program
PTSD *see* post-traumatic stress disorder
public value 438, 441, 444–6
punishment 5
betrayal 261–5
relationship education 293

quality of life (QOL) 412–13

race/ethnicity
late-life transitions 97
lifespan development 59
social change 41, 42
RAM *see* Relationship Attribution Measure
rational bias 249–51
rational reasoning 238, 241–2
RE *see* Relationship Enhancement
reality tracking 5, 251–5
reason 135
rejection of adult values 68–9
RELATE *see* Relationship Evaluation
relational breakdown and repair 259, 261–5
relational devaluation 292
relational transgression 292, 301
Relationship Attribution Measure (RAM) 227
relationship counseling
client factors 309–10
common factors perspective 305–19
expectancy effects 305, 307, 310
implications for practice and service delivery 312–13
match between therapist and client 310

research findings and directions 310–12
therapeutic alliance 306–7, 313–14
therapist factors 307–9
treatment outcomes 307–10
relationship dissolution
common themes in research and practice 473
evidence-based couple therapy 321
social support 399
relationship education 5–6, 289–304
adolescence 77
barriers to resolution 294–5
broader context 291
clinical implications 301–2
common themes in research and practice 476–7, 478
current context 2, 3
emotional processes 291–2, 301–2
general measures of relational functioning 298–9
hurt feelings 289–302
impacts of workshops 298–301
marriage enrichment education for early-marrieds 431, 432
newly committed couples 295–302
perceptual and responsive differences 292–3
policy 7
positive pathways to healthy relationships 424–33
positive relationship formation 427–9, 432
premarital education for engaged couples 429–31, 432
prevention of hurtful events 295–302
program evaluation 297–8
relationship literacy 425–7, 432
resolution of hurtful events 293–302
responses to Hurtful Event Records 300–1
signification of hurtful events 292
types of hurtful event 290–1, 302
workshop content and process 296–8
see also couple relationship education
Relationship Enhancement (RE) 275
Relationship Evaluation (RELATE) 275, 276, 281–2, 283
relationship literacy education 425–7, 432
relationship satisfaction
attribution theory 224
bias and accuracy of judgments 255–6
chronic illness 408
conflict avoidance 117, 118, 120–2
conflict processes 130–1, 134–5
couple relationship education 274
demand–withdraw pattern of conflict 145, 148, 150–1, 153
incentives and threats 193–4, 196–9
parenthood transition 381
partner regulation 234–6, 238, 240–1
relationship education 294
social change 457
social support 399
Relationship Smarts Plus curriculum 426
relationship-threatening issues 119–20
religion
couple relationship education 278
lifespan development 60
positive pathways to healthy relationships 431
remarriage 97–8, 103, 105–6
remorse 300–1
reproductive technologies 28
responsibility attributions 223
responsiveness 393–7
retirement 100–1
revenge
betrayal 262–3
relationship education 289–90
rewards 4
risk 3
conflict avoidance 120–1, 125
social change 25–6, 32, 33–4
risky freedoms 32, 34
romantic relationships *see* couple relationships; intimate relationships
rule violations 260, 264–5

sacrificing behavior 199
same-sex relationships
current context 1
demand–withdraw pattern of conflict 149, 154
family form and functioning 15–16
policy 459–60
social change 26, 36
sandwich generation 2, 3
family caregiving 82, 93
lifespan development 53, 57–8
schooling disruptions 352
scientist-practitioner model 313, 322
SCRT *see* self-regulatory couples therapy
secondary attachment strategies 163–4, 165, 210

secondary emotions 398–9
secondary goals 146–7
secularization 30, 40
security primes 214
self-attributes 236, 243–4
self-caused offences 263
self-esteem 73, 75
self-harming 6, 366–73
  common themes in research and practice 470–1, 476
  family members' awareness of problems 371
  gender factors 372–3
  parent–adolescent agreement 369
  patterns of attachment and parental bonding 371–2
  qualitative data 369–71
  questionnaire measures 367–9
self-regulation 5, 243–4
  attachment security 225–32
  attribution theory 226–7
  common themes in research and practice 472–3, 475
  context and processes 225–6
  interpretation of findings 229–31
  mediation hypothesis 227–32
  testing the hypothesis 227–9
  therapeutic implications 231–2
self-regulatory couples therapy (SRCT) 231–2
self-verification theory 253–4
separation 3–4
  adjustment, conflict and relationships 350–2
  attachment theory 350–1
  betrayal 266
  child outcomes and conflict 349–50
  clinical interventions 353–5
  common themes in research and practice 473
  conflict processes 135–8
  family form and functioning 16–17, 18–19
  gender factors 351–2
  nature of parental conflict 346–7
  policy 457
  post-separation adjustment 345–59
  reducing parental conflict 347–52
  social change 457
  treatment efficacy 348–9
serial arguing 119
service providers 2, 447–8
service-system collaboration 440
sexual aversion disorder 177
Sexual Behavioral System Scale (SBSS) 165–6
sexual dysfunction 175–92
  classification 176–7
  common themes in research and practice 474
  female sexual dysfunction 181–4
  male sexual dysfunction 178–81
  recommendations for clinical practice 184–5
  treatment implications 180–1, 183–4
sexual relationships 4
  adolescence 72
  adult attachment 161–74
  anxiety and avoidance 164, 165–71
  attachment security 162–3, 165–9
  behavioral systems 161–2, 164–8
  chronic illness 408
  common themes in research and practice 472
  effects on couple relationships 165–6
  emotion-focused couples therapy 339
  incentives and threats 198
  interplay with attachment system 166–8, 169
  parenthood transition 379
  partner regulation 234
  social change 27, 28
  therapeutic implications 170–1
sexual selection 249
shared activities 234
Shared Parental Responsibility Act 439
shared policy frameworks 447
Sibling Relationship Questionnaire (SRQ) 136–7, 138
sibling relationships
  attachment and caregiving 212–13
  common themes in research and practice 473
  conflict processes 4, 129, 134, 136–7, 139–40
sildenafil 180, 183
single-parent families
  adolescence 74, 75–6
  family form and functioning 16–17, 18
  social change 42–3
SJPG *see* Social Justice Policy Group
skills-based interventions 385
social change 3, 25–35
  American families 36–47

caregiving 82
children 27–8, 41–2, 44–5
choice 25–6, 29–34
cohabitation 29, 32–3, 36, 39–40, 456
common themes in research and practice 469–71
consumerism 30–1
context of family changes 29–31
delayed marriage 39–40
diversity 28–9
division of labor 27, 37, 39, 43–5
divorce 455, 457
family form and functioning 469–71
family and relationship trends 26–9
feminism 31
fertility 28, 34, 37–8, 40–2
individualization 32–3, 38–9, 40
laissez-faire economics 30
marriage and marital relationships 26–7, 29, 32–4, 36–40, 45–6, 455–7
paradox of choice 33–4
policy 455–7
relationship satisfaction 457
risk 25–6, 32, 33–4
secularization 30, 40
separation 457
single parenting 42–3
union dissolution 42
young emerging adulthood 38–9
social information 201–2
Social Justice Policy Group (SJPG) 459
social motives 4, 195–6, 198, 200
social neuroscience 311–12
social policy *see* policy
social psychological research 311–12
social structure 145–6, 148–9
social support 6–7, 392–405
attachment theory 392–7
chronic illness 407, 409–12, 414–16
collaborative service model 439–40
common themes in research and practice 472, 475, 478
conceptualization 393–4
conflict processes 397–9
control mechanisms 397–8
emotion regulation 398–9
empathic accuracy 399
event-sampling/daily diary research 392, 395–7
negative effects 394–5
perceived partner responsiveness 396–7
positive effects 395
positive event contexts 397
research directions 402
responsive interactions and cognitive processing 400
responsiveness 393–7
theoretical advances 392–3
therapeutic implications 401–2
visible support 394–5
societal factors
adolescence 77
lifespan development 58–60
socio-demographics
diversity 28–9
family form and functioning 21–2
post-separation adjustment 352
relationship counseling 308
social change 36–7
socioemotional selectivity theory 106–7
Socratic questioning 328
soft approach 238, 241–3
South African families 59
Southern European families 37
spousal caregivers 97, 101–4
spousal perceptions of well-being/support 382–3, 384–5
SRQ *see* Sibling Relationship Questionnaire
standoffs 116
step-families 15
adolescence 72, 75
conflict avoidance 116, 119–20
late-life transitions 106
social change 42
storm and stress view of adolescence 68–9
subjective vitality 164
substance abuse
adolescence 72, 75
family form and functioning 19
post-separation adjustment 354
suicidality 364
suicidality
adolescence 72, 75, 363–7
attachment theory 366–7
common themes in research and practice 471, 476
family form and functioning 364–6
family members' awareness of problems 365–6, 371
prospective studies 365
supplication 238

supporting caregivers 103
surrogacy 22n

tailored activity program 104
task-based caregiving 84–5, 92–3
task specialization 85–9, 93
TBCT *see* traditional behavioral couple therapy
teenagers *see* adolescence
tendering processes 444
theory-guided judgments 250–1
therapeutic alliance 306–7, 313–14
threats 4
  affective experience 201
  approach and avoidance goals 195–203
  couple relationships 193–206
  future research directions 202–3
  mediating processes linking goals and outcomes 199–202
  memory bias and ambiguous information 200–1
  relationship outcomes 197–9
  weight of social information 201–2
tolerance-building strategies 329–30
topic variables 145, 149–50
tracking accuracy 252–5
traditional behavioral couple therapy (TBCT)
  common factors perspective 311
  demand–withdraw pattern of conflict 153
  evidence-based practice 325
trauma survival
  case example 340–2
  EFT interventions 336–7
  EFT model of intervention 334–5
  emotion-focused couples therapy 333–44
  post-traumatic stress disorder 337–42
treatment responsiveness 153

unhelpful behaviors 294
uninvolved sibling relationships 136–7
union dissolution 42
United Kingdom social policy 459, 462–3, 478
United States social policy 458–60, 462–3, 478
  see also American families
unpacking emotional responses 337

vaginismus 177
violation by attachment figures 340
violence 3–4, 132–3, 140
  common themes in research and practice 473–4
  conflict avoidance 123–4
  family form and functioning 19
  self-regulation 226
visible support 394–5
volunteerism 107
VSA *see* Vulnerability Stress Adaptation
vulnerability
  emotion-focused couples therapy 334–6
  parenthood transition 377–8, 383, 387
Vulnerability Stress Adaptation (VSA) 311

weight of social information 201–2
widowhood 97, 99, 104–5, 106
withdrawal
  active 118, 121, 131–3
  chronic illness 409
  common themes in research and practice 474
  emotion-focused couples therapy 334–6, 340–2
  partner regulation 235–6
  relationship counseling 309
  see also demand–withdraw pattern of conflict

young emerging adulthood 38–9, 429–31, 432
Youth Self-Report Instrument (YSR) 367